U0636217

国家社科基金
GUOJIA SHEKE JIJIN HOUQI ZIZHU XIANGMU
后期资助项目

袁同礼年谱长编

Yuan Tongli: A Chronicle

五

雷 强 撰

中华书局
ZHONGHUA BOOK COMPANY

一九六一年　六十七岁

一月三日

徐炳麟覆函先生,告中国大陆出口图书至香港、日本略有差异的原因。

3/1/61

守和先生：

一日惠示暨支票 U.S. $31.39 均收到,谢谢!

敝处业务蒙殷殷指示,具见关注,盛情至感,谨致万分敬意。

关于大陆新书能出口而在国会圃购书规定范围内者已尽量寄发,至于能出口而港澳发现有货时,亦设法在 U. S. $25 限额内购寄。日本同业经销大陆书亦系在港购,如大安、极东等。曾与港总经销之新民主出版社谈及,据云日本经销书不会比香港多,目录所列较多者,恐系将国际书店预订书目列上,实际许多不能出口,若真有日本有而港无,恐系走私货,而私自影印者。

今后大陆书无论能出口不能出口,当尽力搜罗,不负厚望。《中国历代书画家篆刻家字号索引》九月间已寄出,想已收到,并闻。敬请时祉。

晚徐炳麟上

〔University of Chicago Library, Yuan T'ung-li Papers, Box 8〕

按:徐炳麟(1909—1991),字梦云,湖南桂阳人,军人,早年毕业于广州培正中学、黄埔军校,抗战期间曾参加三次长沙战役、长衡会战,1949 年后赴澳门,曾在蔚林图书公司、港门华兴行任练习生、办事员、秘书、副经理,1955 年受李济深委托于香港创办万有图书公司(Universal Book Company)。《中国历代书画家篆刻家字号索引》,商承祚、黄华编,1960 年人民美术出版社初版。

一月十一日

罗家伦覆函先生,续聘先生为"国史馆"名誉采访,并告购买邮寄《故宫名画三百种》细节,另请先生与布莱克威尔书店核对寄书一种。

守和吾兄道鉴：

奉读十二月一日手教，敬悉种切。兹寄奉本馆本年聘书，续聘吾兄为名誉采访，务乞惠允，至深感纫！附上征集费空白收据六张，并希加章寄下。尊编《国父文献目录》，英文部份共有若干页？如在美以极廉价之方法印少数册，以备国内外与有关国父事迹者之参考，所费几何？尚乞见示，以便于国内印刷费用作一比较，因此间外汇亦甚不易也。弟必就力所能及为之。承费神代为影印之史料二种，至感贤劳。《故宫名画三百种》已向此间华国出版社购来，计新台币五千四百元正收条附上，除吾兄去年所存征集费四千五百元外，由弟垫付九百元，当在今年征集费内计算，请不必寄来。惟此书邮寄前，尚须办理免结汇手续，故日内尚不克付邮也。去年承吾兄为本馆搜集及代购之史料书籍多种，有劳清神，曷胜感谢！兹将寄下之收据八张，另附一清单，敬希核对。其中代向英国 B. H. Blackwell 订购之 Jones etc.: *The Far East 1942-1946* 一书，至今尚未寄到，不知是否因未写明本馆地址 "2 Peiping Road" 所致，曾向此间邮局查询，因不知寄件挂号号码，无法查到。可否请吾兄费神致函该书店一查，兹将发票及收据抄奉附副本一份，为托。崀此，敬颂道绥！

弟罗家伦敬启

一，十一

〔University of Chicago Library, Yuan T'ung-li Papers, Box 1〕

按：B. H. Blackwell 即 Benjamin Harris Blackwell（布莱克威尔书店），英国著名的学术出版社、书店。Jones etc.应指 F. C. Jones, Hugh Borton and B. R. Pearn 三人合著之书，1955 年牛津大学出版社初版。该函为文书代笔，落款处则为其签名。先生收到后，于 2 月 9 日致信布莱克威尔书店询问能否补寄。

一月十五日

美国学术团体理事会给予先生 650 美金资助，用以扩编 *Russian Works on China in American Libraries* 。〔Library of Congress, *Information Bulletin*, Vol. 20, No. 3, 1961, p. 37〕

按：*Information Bulletin* 中标记资助方为美国大学与研究图书馆协会（Association of College and Research Libraries），但根据 5 月

25 日先生致 Heinrich Busch 信可知,似应为美国学术团体理事会资助,此处暂依先生自己的表述。

先生致信 Heinrich Busch,为因故未能及早寄回校样表示歉意,并请增补一条注释,另请在文章刊发后寄赠抽印本给某些日本图书馆。

January 15, 1961

Dear Father Busch:

I am slow in thanking you for your recent letter and in making corrections on the proofs sent to me from the printer. Owing to my absence from Washington, I regret that I was not able to return the proofs earlier.

The appearance of a good bibliography on Japan necessitated a few minor changes. A note should be printed at the end of the article, and I shall rely on your help in final proof-reading.

Dr. Loewenthal and I have read the proofs and both of us wish to congratulate you for having chosen such a good printer. His work is most satisfactory.

As soon as the reprints are ready, will you send a few copies to libraries in Japan for me in addition to those I mentioned in my previous letter. There is no need to send copies to Communist China at this time.

With many thanks,

Yours sincerely,

Yuan Tung-li

〔University of Chicago Library, Yuan T'ung-li Papers, Box 7〕

按: A note 即 In the course of printing of this bibliography, a standard bibliographical work on Japan has appeared. Sponsored by the Institut narodov Azii, Akademiia nauk SSSR, it is entitled: *Bibliografiia Iaponii; literatura, izdannaia v Sovetskom Soiuze na russkom iazyke s 1917 po 1958 g.* Moskva, Izd-vo Vostochnoi lit-ry, 1960. 327 p. 此件为录副。

一月十六日

晚,林语堂赴国会图书馆并作有关中国现代文学之演讲,叶公超、恒慕义、先生等人受邀出席。〔Library of Congress, *Information Bulletin*, Vol. 20, No. 4, 1961, p. 46〕

　　　　按:演讲前,众人曾聚餐,席间林语堂就其对中美两国图书馆之体会略作描述。

一月十八日

先生致信吴大猷,谈梅贻琦病情及在美友人捐款事。

　　大猷吾兄惠鉴:

　　　　前奉手教,至以为谢。近来友人自台北来此者,均谓月涵患癌疾,已传遍骨中,前途极难乐观。关于清华原子研究所事,颇盼吾兄惠允担任,最为理想,不识尊处之事能摆脱否? 台北友人现为月涵募集捐款,名义上虽为祝寿,但实际上拟用之付其欠款(闻欠台大医院已八千美金),想尊处亦接到此项通知。此间同学会捐款事由任之恭兄负责办理,如有愿加入者,盼将支票径寄任君是盼。C. K. Jen, 10203 Lariston, Silver Spring, Md. 匆匆,顺候教祺。

　　　　　　　　　　　　　　　　　　　　弟袁同礼顿首

　　　　　　　　　　　　　　　　　　　　　　一,十八

　　　　　　　　　　　　　　　　　　　　〔袁同礼家人提供〕

　　按:1960 年 5 月,梅贻琦患病,后入台湾大学医院疗养。任之恭(1906—1995),山西沁源人,1926 年毕业于清华学校,同年赴美留学。1928 年获麻省理工学院电机学士学位,1929 年获宾夕法尼亚大学无线电硕士学位,1931 年获哈佛大学物理博士学位。

一月十九日

莫余敏卿致函先生,称赞《西文汉学书目》具有极高的学术价值,并询问先生是否会编辑汉学期刊文章目录。

　　　　　　　　　　　　　　　　　　　　　January 19, 1961

Dear Dr. Yuan,

　　Thank you and Mrs. Yuan for the box of delicious cookies you sent us. We are enjoying them every day. It was very thoughtful of you to remember us.

　　Our Library is getting along. Prof. Rudolph has been back. He bought some books for us from Formosa, Hong Kong and Japan.

The copy of your excellent bibliography, the *China in Western Literature*, in the Reference Room here is in great demand and many scholars find it most valuable.

Many people who are doing research work on China have asked me many times whether you are working on the periodical articles in Western languages. Since it involves such a tremendous amount of work, maybe you could ask some assistants, say 10 or 12 to work on different subjects under your direction. This way this monumental work may be finished in a comparatively short time. I am sure many people would be interested in seeing it done.

Are you going to attend the AAS annual meeting in Chicago this year? I understand S. Y. Chen is going but we are not going.

Again, with many thanks & best regards.

Yours sincerely,

M. Mok

〔University of Chicago Library, Yuan T'ung-li Papers, Box 7〕

按：此函为其亲笔。

一月二十五日

刘国蓁覆函先生，告代转信函及购书、订刊等事。

守和博士先生尊鉴：

敬启者，未修书敬候，又将两月，引领慈云，倍深瞻仰。恭维著述丰宏，履躬清胜，至以为颂。拜奉先后两手教，敬悉种切。嘱转寄令岳丈大人信即为付邮，想已到达，如有回信，定当代为转呈。欣悉付上莲子经已收到，甚慰。关于冯馆职位事，久已弃如散屣，更兼俗语有云"好马不食回头草"，诚哉是言。晚现在虽然工作辛苦，但入息好过在港大时，故从不作此想，盛意拳拳，殊深感铭。嘱查各人名之中文姓名，幸不辱命，惟已几经搜集，辗转垂询，方得结果。兹抄录如后，敬希亮察为幸。一九五九之北京图书馆善本书目经已询各书店，皆云缺货，倘将来有售，定当代购一册奉上。《新闻天地》周刊至本月底期满，已代续订半年，交妥报费廿三元，前存五十元〇三角半，比对尚存廿七元三角半也。日前港中天气严寒，颇难抵受，惟近来已回暖矣。美国新总统就职大典,想有一番高庆也。专此奉覆,敬请撰安。

愚晚国蓁顿首
一九六一年一月廿五日

〔University of Chicago Library, Yuan T'ung-li Papers, Box 6〕

按:该函后附七人姓名,分别为陈继平(Chan, Kai-ping)、陆佑(Loke Yew)、刘桂焯(Lau, Kwai-cheuk)、张耀轩(Cheung Iu-hin)、张弼士(Cheung, Pat-sze)、苏开文(Soo Hoy-mun)、曹善允(Ts'o Sean-wan)。

一月二十六日

郭廷以致函先生,谈其与福特基金会接洽,抄呈华盛顿会议文电四份,并告董作宾等人在韩国获得名誉博士时间。

守和先生道席:

客夏西城、加州、华府数度晤教,快慰良深。归来之后,琐事丛集,未克早日问候,罪甚!月初接诵大笺,欣悉尊况佳胜,而于敝所关注之切,尤为感荷。福特基金会代表去秋来台,数次恳谈,颇为具体。最近两月,继续函商,大致良好,看来可望有成。敝所修正计划已于周前邮去矣。谨以奉陈,以慰廑系。承询华会有关文电,已着人检查档卷,获得有关资料四件,另纸抄呈,用备参考。其中十二月卅一日电与大作所引,或系一事,惟字句稍有出入耳。彦堂先生接受韩国学位,事在一九五五年五月廿日,为文学博士,同时朱骝先、溥心畬(儒)二先生亦分别被授为法学博士,以是年四月,三先生应邀偕往讲学也。纽约之行,想甚愉快,润章、淬廉诸公曾否见到?日前淬廉兄来信,谓月内即去夏威夷大学,为期半年。檀岛风光宜人,于淬廉兄健康当大有裨益。华府师友,得便希代问好,光清先生处尤祈多为致意。专此敬复,并颂俪福,不一。

弟郭廷以拜上
元,廿六

〔University of Chicago Library, Yuan T'ung-li Papers, Box 6;《郭量宇先生日记残稿》,页 241〕

按:"西城"即西雅图。

一月三十一日

先生收顾维钧来函,并附捐款百元。〔University of Chicago Library, Yuan T'ung-li Papers, Box 1〕

二月一日

先生致信赵元任、杨步伟夫妇,谈为梅贻琦捐款治病事。

> 元任先生、夫人:
>
> 　　连奉赐书,至为感谢。为月涵捐助事,各方虽在进行,但距离尚远。昨接"顾大使"来函,除捐百元外,并谓已与廷黻兄商议,将来或须请"教部"建议于中基会在清华息金项下,提出若干作为月涵养老及医药费等项之用,惟须到本年九月间方能提出,如此则兄、嫂亦不必捐助太多也。兹在 *Proceedings of Symposia in Applied Mathematics* 十二卷内拜读大著,至为钦佩,如有单行本并盼检寄壹份是盼。进行中之大著两种均系不朽之作,贤劳可想,尚希两位格外节劳。草此,敬颂俪祺。
>
> 弟同礼、慧熙仝拜
> 二月一日
>
> 〔University of California, Berkeley, The Bancroft Library, Yuen Ren Chao papers, carton 10, folder 39, Yuan, Tongli and Yuan, Huixi〕

按:中基会代理清华基金,年度会议均在每年 9 月,所以由清华息金项下补助梅贻琦养老和医疗费用之议只能到此时提出。1962 年 5 月 19 日,梅贻琦病逝,享年 73 岁。赵元任在 *Proceedings of Symposia in Applied Mathematics*(《应用数学研讨会论文集》)发表题为 Graphic and Phonetic Aspects of Linguistics and Mathematical Symbols 的文章,为其 1960 年 4 月 14 日至 15 日在纽约举行的应用数学研讨会上的发言。"进行中之大著两种",其中一种应为正在撰写的 *A Grammar of Spoken Chinese*(《中国话的文法》),1965 年初版;一种似为 *Language and Symbolic Systems*(《语言与符号系统》),1968 年初版。

二月六日

先生致信傅泾波,请代向司徒雷登询问燕京大学是否向王正廷等人授予过名誉学位。

February 6, 1961

Dear Mr. Fugh:

In the long history of Yenching, some honorary degrees were conferred upon Chinese scholars. As Dr. Stuart has a wonderful memory, I wonder if you could ask him the names of those who have been thus honored.

I seem to remember that Dr. C. T. Wang was one of those receiving an honorary degree from Yenching, but I may be wrong. Dr. Edwards in his history of Yenching, did not mention any honorary degrees.

I trust that Dr. Stuart is keeping well despite this cold weather. Kindly give him my best wishes for his health.

Yours sincerely,

T. L. Yuan

〔北京大学图书馆特藏部〕

按:Dr. C. T. Wang 即王正廷(1882—1961),原名正庭,字儒堂,号子白,浙江奉化人,中国近现代政治家、外交官、体育活动家,基督教人士,欧美同学会、中华全国体育协进会的创始人之一。Dr. Edwards 即 Dwight W. Edwards, history of Yenching 即 *Yenching University* ,1959 年亚洲基督教高等教育联合董事会出版,该书另外一位作者是梅贻宝,负责撰写成都时期的燕京大学。此件为打字稿,落款处为先生签名。

二月八日

叶良才覆函先生,请代为留意《中国社会及政治学报》,如有该学会员名单(地址)请影照一份。

Feb. 8, 1961

Dear Dr. Yuan:

Referring to your letter of January 13, 1961 regarding the list of members of the Chinese Social and Political Science Association, we have inquired at the Public Library and was told that they do not have the *Review* . We shall appreciate it if you can make a photostat copy of the list of members, which you said in your letter " can be found in the last issue of the *Review*". Please also let us know the cost of the photostat. Thank you.

Sincerely,

L. T. Yip

〔University of Chicago Library, Yuan T'ung-li Papers, Box 1〕

按:此件为打字稿,落款处为其签名。

二月十五日

杨联陞致片先生,告知两位留学生中文姓名及胡适来美日期。

守和先生:

新年附近惠示,因收贺年片遗失,未及奉覆,深觉惶恐。徐怀启、周世逑二君汉字,请于震寰兄代为查出,谨此奉闻。报载胡适之三月下旬将来美参加麻省理工百年纪念,想已见及矣。敬请双安,并拜贺旧年新禧。

晚杨联陞顿

一九六一年二月十五日

〔University of Chicago Library, Yuan T'ung-li Papers, Box 5〕

按:胡适受邀赴美参加麻省理工学院百年校庆之事,可参见其本年 1 月 23、24、27 日日记。①

二月十六日

先生致信顾维钧(荷兰海牙),并附印照的各种资料。

February 16, 1961

Dear Dr. Koo:

Thank you so much for your letter of December 28th. To the list of honorary degrees conferred upon you, I have added another one—D. G. L. from the University of Miami.

Enclosed herewith please find photostat material relating to your work in China. I hope you would find these documents useful. They cost less than ＄10.00.

I shall continue to search material of this kind, but the Photoduplication Service at the Library of Congress is very slow in filling

---

① 《胡适日记全集》第 9 册,页 728。

orders owing to the amount of work on hand.

　　　　With cordial regards,

　　　　　　　　　　　　　　　　　　Yours sincerely,

　　　　　　　　　　　　　　　　　　T. L. Yuan

〔University of Chicago Library, Yuan T'ung-li Papers, Box 1〕

　　按:此件为录副。

二月二十日

罗家伦致函先生,告知《故宫名画三百种》最近将交邮寄出,并请在美拨付期刊费用。

　　守和吾兄道鉴:

　　　　去年十二月廿六日奉上一函,并检奉聘书一件及空白收据六张,计邀惠察。《故宫名画三百种》一部,因申请办理免结汇手续关系,日内方能交邮海运寄上。兹有恳者,本馆前订之*Facts on File*期刊一种,自一九六一年一月起至十二月底止续订一年,订价美金七六.〇〇元,敬将单据二张随函附奉,拟请吾兄劳神在本馆所存尊处购书款项下代为拨付,并请将收据费心寄还,以便报销。专此,敬颂道祺!

　　　　　　　　　　　　　　　弟罗家伦敬启

　　　　　　　　　　　　　　　二,二〇

〔University of Chicago Library, Yuan T'ung-li Papers, Box 1〕

　　按:*Facts on File*似指纽约 Facts on File Inc.出版的历史期刊,待考。此函为文书代笔,落款处为罗家伦签名。

二月二十二日

罗家伦致函先生,请与美国国家档案局再度接洽询问摄印文献的价格等信息,并请留意国会图书馆所藏民国初年及北洋时期的文献资料。

　　守和吾兄道鉴:

　　　　前上一函,报告《故宫名画三百种》已买就事,想已收到。因春节关系,所谓前函中所提到的《故宫名画三百种》于今晨才寄出,系海运,恐需一个多月方能收到。装一木箱,挂号寄出。本馆为编纂《开国实录》,对于上次我们一同到美国国家档案局所看见他们正在摄影的清末民初(大约至一九二六年)有关我国政情的报告,说是今年三四月间可以完成,其中必有我们可以参考的资料,当时我们谈到要买,他们也表示愿意。现在可否请兄从速与彼方再度接洽,问其(一)何时摄印完成,(二)全套定价若干,以便对此有所准备,拜托拜托! 又洪宪时代与军阀时代(民五至民十七),关于中国政情军事的文献,国会图书馆必多,亦请为一查,择其重要者惠告,多谢多谢! 匆匆,即颂春祺!

弟家伦敬启

二月二十二日,台北

〔University of Chicago Library, Yuan T'ung-li Papers, Box 1〕

二月二十三日

金问泗致函先生,告知先生所辑文献材料已转寄顾维钧,并请代查日本驻华公使小幡酉吉的英文名拼写。

守和吾兄惠鉴:

日昨电话领教为快,吾兄所集材料摄影件已遵嘱寄呈少公,邮局单送乞尊存。其中关于华府会议讨论关税事件各纸最后两叶,弟以拙稿本拟引用,故为剪留,想蒙惠许,同时弟亦通知少公矣。又,华府会议时日本驻华公使小幡酉吉英文姓 Obata,而其英文名或写 yukichi,或写 tarikichi,未知孰是,拟请吉便一查,见告为感。气候渐暖,颇拟往图书馆走访我兄,当再电话奉闻。匆布,敬候俪祺,并颂潭福。

弟泗谨启

2-23-61

〔University of Chicago Library, Yuan T'ung-li Papers, Box 7〕

按:小幡酉吉(Obata Yūkichi,1873-1947),日本外交官,1918 年 10 月至 1923 年任驻中国公使,曾负责山东问题的对华谈判,并处理"二十一条"悬案。

徐家璧覆函先生,谈李书华跌伤一事,并告知查得博士人名信息。

守和先生尊鉴:

敬肃者,二月十六日来示奉悉。前昨两日,业已分别见过唐德刚兄暨李润章先生。承李先生告与王太太相识,故得伊名。Ta 在通常情形,应读"达",但在伊实"德",盖将音读别所致。二月十八日李先生在唐人街口外践冰块上跌断左臂,现住医院,接骨经过甚佳,乞毋远虑。另土木工程张君,无人认识。此外 David Lu,据唐兄告,或为韩国学生,或为留日中国学生,在此并未与各同学来往,故不识其姓氏,甚为歉仄。谨将原单奉还,至乞亮察是幸! 匆此,敬颂福安!

晚徐家璧鞠躬

二月廿三日

〔University of Chicago Library, Yuan T'ung-li Papers, Box ?〕

二月二十八日

先生致信李书华,问安。

润章先生惠鉴:

　　顷接嫂夫人来函,知旬日前行路滑倒,左臂上骨折断,闻之无任悬念,至盼遵医生之嘱,安心静养,无任企盼。下月如能来纽,当趋附问安。先此,敬颂痊安。

嫂夫人同此。

弟同礼顿首

内人附笔问候

二月廿八日

〔Columbia University Libraries Archival Collections, Shuhua Li Papers, 1926-1972, Volume II: Modern Eminent Chinese Leaders〕

劳榦致函先生,告知李济、胡适等人近况。

守和先生:

　　久未通讯为念,近想起居安适为慰。前寄茶叶等,如已用完,仍祈赐示代购。此间一切均安,济之先生目疾稍愈,已出医院,惟不能多用目力耳。适之先生上星期六(二十六日)因太劳累(原有感冒),在钱校长宴会前发心脏病。幸当时正在市内,即到台大医院,经医悉心诊视,已就平复。惟尚有小部阻塞,仍须充分休养。现在正住台大医院,最近期间可能不到美国也。专此,敬颂道祺,并叩俪安。

后学劳榦敬上

二月二十八日

李霖灿兄来美参加故宫展览附信乞代转。

〔University of Chicago Library, Yuan T'ung-li Papers, Box 2〕

按:2 月 25 日(周六),胡适赴钱思亮夫妇宴会,非信中所写"二十六日"。会前胡适突感不适,但得及时送医,后在台湾大学医院休

养 56 天方得出院。① "故宫展览"即"中国古艺术品展览会"，
1961 年 5 月至 1962 年 6 月，先后在美国华盛顿、纽约、波士顿、芝
加哥、旧金山五大城市举办。

二三月间

先生患眼疾。

三月四日

樊际昌覆函先生，寄赠"中国农村复兴联合委员会"出版物，并告胡适病情
已稳定。

> 守和先生惠鉴：
>
> 　二月廿四日大函奉悉。吾兄致力于我国留美学生之博士论文之
> 编辑工作，至有意义。国内想尚无此种材料。出版后分送国内各有关
> 机关，想必在兄计划中矣。Minnesota 同学之中文姓名，已请彦士兄注
> 明。兹选择本会近几年内刊物十一种另邮寄呈，请查收。另附上本会
> 《职员录》乙份，有红圈为记者，均有博士学位，亦请察收。台湾农工
> 业近年来确有不少改观处，吾兄亦拟来一游否？教育界中尚有许多熟
> 人，想必一致欢迎也。匆此奉复，敬颂时绥。
>
> 　　　　　　　　　　　　　　　　　　弟樊际昌顿首
> 　　　　　　　　　　　　　　　　　　三，四，1961
>
> 　昨日到台大医院去看适之先生，情况已恢复正常，惟医嘱须多休
> 养，顺以附闻。
>
> 〔University of Chicago Library, Yuan T'ung-li Papers, Box 3〕

> 按："彦士兄"应指蒋彦士（1915—1998），浙江杭州人，金陵大学
> 农学院毕业，后赴美留学，获明尼苏达大学博士学位，归国后在金
> 陵大学任教。"本会"应指"中国农村复兴联合委员会"，其通讯
> 处在台北市南海路二十五号。

三月十二日

顾维钧覆函先生，感谢寄赠二三十年代史料影照件。

　　　　　　　　　　　　　　　　　　　　　March 12, 1961

---

① 《胡适日记全集》第 9 册，页 732-733。

Dear Dr. Yuan:

I am glad to receive your letter of February 16, 1961 together with the photostat material enclosed therein. I find it most interesting to refresh my memory after more than 30 years. You must have spent much time looking it up.

In the past few months, I have been looking over some source material relating to my part in the work of the League of Nations. It is time consuming but serves to recall many things which I have entirely forgotten.

You are very kind in continuing your effort to search material of the kind you have just sent me. I can understand the slowness of the Photoduplication Service of the Library of Congress in filling orders, as I think the amount of work demanded of it must be tremendous.

With warm personal regards and best wishes,

Yours sincerely,

V. K. Wellington Koo

〔University of Chicago Library, Yuan T'ung-li Papers, Box 1〕

按：此件为打字稿,落款处为顾维钧签名。

三月十五日

李霖灿和那志良至国会图书馆,先生告知此前所托寻找寓所之事已有合适结果,遂带李霖灿前往办理入住手续。〔李霖灿著《国宝赴美展览日记》,台北:台湾商务印书馆,1972年,页43〕

> 按：那志良(1908—1998),字心如,北京宛平人,满族,家道衰落,因陈垣资助,完成学业并进入故宫博物院,1933年随古物南迁,1949年去台。李霖灿和那志良有"白日办公,夜间读书"的计划,故想在国会图书馆附近觅一住处,此前来函请先生代为物色住所。

三月二十日

陈受颐覆函先生,告知钟荣光、李应林个人信息,并谈《中国文学史略》书稿进展。

> 守和尊兄著席:
>
> 顷奉手教,欣感莫名,钟荣光先生生卒年月为公元一八六六九月

七日至一九四二—月九日,李应林业已于八九年前大陆变色后在港逝世,其接受欧柏林学院名誉博士 LL. D 则一九三八年夏间事也。拙作草样已于前月匆匆校毕,页样则仍未寄到。AAS 闭会后,颇思续飞纽约与出版家一谈,并拟取道华京,藉聆教益。月初传闻适之月底飞美,今读钱思亮致叶良才电报,知其不易如期就道矣。专此,敬颂撰祺。

弟受颐顿首

三月二十日

〔University of Chicago Library, Yuan T'ung-li Papers, Box ?〕

按:钟荣光(1866—1942),字惺可,广东香山人,教育家、岭南大学首任华人校长。"欧柏林学院"即 Oberlin College,1833 年建校,位于俄亥俄州克利夫兰西南。

三月二十一日

先生寄一批英文文献资料给顾维钧。〔University of Chicago Library, Yuan T'ung-li Papers, Box 1〕

加斯基尔致函先生,告知可长期持有馆际互借图书,并告图书馆新馆开馆时间再次被推迟。

March 21, 1961

Dear Mr. Yuan:

I trust that you were able to keep the book you had on Interlibrary Loan as long as you needed it. I spoke to the Interlibrary Loan people about it.

The formal dedication of the library has been postponed to the fall of 1962, when the old library will have been made over into the undergraduate library. It will be for the two libraries as a unit. I hope you can come up then if not before.

Sincerely yours,

Gussie E. Gaskill

Curator of the Wason Collection on China and the Chinese

〔Cornell University Library, Wason Collection Records, 1918–1988, Box 1, Folder Koo, T. K. Letters〕

三月二十七日

叶良才覆函先生,告知蒋廷黻所获名誉博士信息,并请寄送中国政治学会图书委员会早期名单。

March 27, 1961

Dear Dr. Yuan:

Referring to the footnote in your letter of March 8, 1961, Dr. T. F. Tsiang, in addition to the Honorary Degree from Oberlin, received an Honorary LLD from Park College in 1955.

Your letter of February 28 referred to the creation of the Board of Management of the Library of CSPSA on June 17, 1918. We shall be grateful if you will kindly secure for us a copy of that resolution.

Sincerely

L. T. Yip

〔台北"中央研究院"近代史研究所档案馆,〈中华教育文化基金董事会〉,馆藏号 502-01-08-031,页 125〕

三月二十九日　哈佛

晚七点半,廖家艾、曾宪七、杨联陞和缪钤夫妇、王守竞夫妇、先生、袁澄等在大中园聚餐。〔《杨联陞日记》(稿本)〕

四月初

陈受颐抵华盛顿,拜访先生。

四月一日

普实克致函先生,告知已为先生购得一册《中国书目》并寄出。

April 1st, 1961

Dear Professor Yuan,

Referring to my letter of February 24, 1960, we were now able to secure one copy of the publication: P. J. Skachkov, *Bibliografiya Kitaya*, which I instructed our Library to mail to your address.

Wishing you a further success in your work, I remain, Dear Professor Yuan,

Very truly yours,

J. Průšek

〔University of Chicago Library, Yuan T'ung-li Papers, Box 8〕

四月二日

顾维钧致函先生，请协助查找有关其早年在北洋政府出任外交事务的相关文献记录。

April 2, 1961

Dr. Yuan:

Recently reminiscing about my first years of public service in the President's Office and the Ministry of Foreign Affairs in Peking, I tried to make some notes about the several important negotiations in which I was specially instructed to take a part. But I am unable to find some relevant documents or data here.

I. In 1912 or 1913, the Russian minister suddenly one day presented Mr. M. T. Liang, Foreign Minister, with a document outlining three demands concerning Mongolia. The minister was so indignant not only at the nature of the demands but also at the high-handed manner and the threatening language of the minister that as a protest he resigned his post. Could you find the date of this interview and the text of the demands? The memorandum was kept secret at the time but was published later.

II. In 1921-4 Great Britain kept pressing China to settle the Tibetan question. Sir John Jordan, considering himself a personal friend of President Yuan Shih-kai, preferred to negotiate directly with him. As Secretary to the President as well as of the Foreign Ministry, I was designated by him to interpret and take notes of their interviews and frequently sent by him to interview Sir John at his Legation. As an outcome, Mr. Chen Yi, a veteran diplomat versed in the Tibetan question, was sent to Shimla to conclude a definitive agreement defining the boundaries between China and Tibet. He spent several months there. He referred back and forth to certain difficult points of delimitation, but one day he suddenly initialed a draft agreement without authorization. President Yuan was so displeased and angry that he dismissed Chen to the protest of the British Government. Could you find out the date of this incident and the text of the initialed document? Recently the Indian

Government again referred to this alleged agreement as one of the grounds in support of India's case in the negotiations with Communist China concerning her claims in the dispute over the boundary with Tibet.

　　III. The notorious 21 demands were presented by Japan in January, 1915. I was designated as one of the members of the Chinese delegation headed by the Foreign Minister, but on objection by the Japanese Minister I was not appointed to it actually. Instead, I was directed to work on the question closely with our delegation and to take charge of keeping in contact with the friendly Legations in Peking and with publicity abroad. Consequently, I had numerous interviews particularly with Dr. Paul S. Reinsch, U. S. Minister, both for informing Washington and getting its views. The most pernicious 5th Group was in due course published abroad, and this publicity aroused a wave of protest from Tokyo and indignation from the friendly Powers in our favor. On May 4, 1915 Japan presented to China the now well-known ultimatum for acceptance of the negotiated terms within 48 hours. I was asked to study its contents and draft a reply. This I did in the German Hospital where I had been confined for influenza with a high temperature. The draft was readily approved by the Government, though the paragraph relating to the Fifth Group was softened on the suggestion of the Japanese educated secretary of our Delegation after seeing the Japanese Minister. I was convinced of the need of an official statement by the Government to explain the course of the negotiations and its reasons for accepting the ultimatum to the people of China and to the world at large. This I did by dictating all night a text to William H. Donald and it was typed by his assistant Mr. Pratt, both representing at the time *The Times* of London. Could you find a copy of the ultimatum and China's reply for me? I think they were both inserted in the Memorandum on the Twenty-One Demands submitted to the Versailles Peace Conference in 1919 as one of China's Desiderata.

　　IV. During the period of May, 1912–August, 1915 when I was first Secretary and then Counsellor of the Foreign Ministry, the Foreign

Minister was changed four or five times either as result of Cabinet reshuffle or due to resignation. Could you find the names of these Foreign Ministers and the dates of their respective appointment? I would also appreciate a list of the Cabinet changes with their composition and the dates of such changes.

I am afraid I have raised too many questions. There is, however, no hurry to get the material. If you would be good enough to make some research in your spare moments, I would greatly appreciate it.

Thanking you in advance and with cordial personal regards,

Yours sincerely,

V. K. Wellington Koo

〔University of Chicago Library, Yuan T'ung-li Papers, Box 1〕

按：M. T. Liang 即梁如浩（1863—1941），原名滔昭，字如浩，号孟亭、梦亭，广东香山人，清末民初外交官。1912 年 11 月 8 日，俄国驻华公使库平斯基（Крупенский В.Н.）偕翻译将与库伦当局签署的《俄蒙协约》及其附约《俄蒙商务专条》告知梁如浩，后者坚决反对并辞职。Sir John Jordan 即朱迩典爵士（1852-1925），英国外交家，曾任英国驻华公使。Mr. Chen Yi 应指陈贻范（1870-1919），字安生，江苏苏州人，清末民初外交官，顾维钧此处似有笔误；Shimla 即西姆拉，印度喜马偕尔邦的首府。one day he suddenly initialed a draft agreement 应指 1914 年 4 月 27 日，this alleged agreement 即所谓的"西姆拉条约"。Dr. Paul S. Reinsch 即芮恩施（1869-1923），美国外交官；William H. Donald 即端纳（1875-1946），澳大利亚人，英国《泰晤士报》记者，先后担任孙中山、张学良、宋美龄等人的私人顾问，如顾维钧所言，在 1915 年他首先揭露日本"二十一条"，引起世界范围的强烈反响，并引发倒袁运动。

四月六日

先生致信钱存训，询问留学生相关信息，并告知《中国留美同学博士论文目录》行将付印。

公垂吾兄：

上周年会因事未能前来参加，想定有一番盛况也。兹有下列二人

不识已结婚否？如已成婚,其先生之姓名能见示否？弟所编之《留美
同学博士论文目录》业已完成,共收 4200 余人,恐尚有遗漏也。大著
已由芝大出版部允为印行否,为念。顺颂大安。

弟同礼顿首

四,六日

〔钱孝文藏札〕

　　按:"上周年会"即 3 月 27 日至 29 日在芝加哥 Palmer House 举行
的美国亚洲学会年会,约有 640 人到场出席。[1]

四月九日

钱存训覆函先生,告知在亚洲学会年会中的见闻,并谈其博士论文已获匿
名审查通过,将由芝加哥大学出版社出版。

守和先生:

　　奉到四月六日手教,敬悉一一。周前亚洲学会年会未见大驾到此
参加,甚觉怅怅。中国同仁与会者虽亦不少,然东西两岸来者似并不
太多,图书馆之会参加者亦有限,裘开明因病未来,会中闻 Frankel 将
去 Yale,李田意亦回耶鲁,柳无忌将去 Indiana,Hucker 去 Michigan
(Oakland),Nunn 应夏威夷之聘任 assoc. prof. of Japanese & Director
of Asian History,此事为去年夏大曾来相聘者(正教授名义),Nunn 君
颇喜连络推广工作,想甚合宜也。闻英国 Pearson 所编之《西文论华什
志索引》*Index Sinicus* 即将出版,如谭君之作迟不问世,恐将全功尽弃矣。
闻大著《留美博士论文目录》即将出版,搜罗宏富,不胜钦佩,此间正
编一芝大有关远东论文目录与哥大所编者相仿,有关中国者计 180 种,约
有博士二十四种,硕士 55 种为中国人所作,想前者均已收入大作矣。
所询章珍馨女士已与一美国人结婚(亦系芝大 Ph. D 化学系),名
Sheldon Kaufman(全名可在 LC 目录一查),现在 Princeton 教书,章则
在 Brookhaven (?) National Lab.研究也。黄仁华(黄嘉音之妹)似未结
婚,现在一 Ohio 某大学教书也。梁远则并未写博士论文,伊现任某广
告公司副经理,大约无意于学位矣。又,训之论文前交此间 Press 审

---

① "News of the Profession." *The Journal of Asian Studies*, vol. 20, no. 4, 1961, p. 567.

查,该处曾请二人先后审阅,评语均甚好(其中之一似系中国人或系杨联陞,惟出版部未将姓名相告),故允予出版,但须津贴,现正由图书馆学校商洽津贴数额之中。大约可无问题,因学校已通过列入 Univ. of Chicago Studies of Library Science 丛书之内,并允加资助也。匆匆不赘,即请大安。

后学存训拜上
四月九日

〔University of Chicago Library, Yuan T'ung-li Papers, Box 2〕

按: Hucker 即 Charles O. Hucker(1919-1994),时任密歇根州立大学中国语言和历史教授。Pearson 即 James D. Pearson(1911-1997),英国图书馆学家、目录学家, *Index Sinicus* 全称为 *Index Sinicus: a catalogue of articles relating to China in periodicals and other collective publications, 1920-1955*,1964 年初版,实际编纂者为 John Lust、Werner Eichhorn,非 Pearson。

四月十二日

陈可忠覆函先生,告知无法追忆某学生中文姓名,并谈梅贻琦病情及清华大学(新竹)近况。

守和先生赐鉴:

前奉手示,敬悉一是。关于何君中文名,虽经忠尽力记忆及查询,仍无法记起。何君系檀香山土生,平时总是以 Ellert Ho 相称呼,彼从未以中文名见示(第一次见面时,可能曾问过,现在已无法记起),此君为人颇怪,不喜与吾人交谈,闻回檀香山后任教职,已去世多年矣。辱承垂询,无以报命,至歉。

月涵师病体日渐康复,现在精神甚好,惟两足软弱,故遵医嘱仍在台大附属医院疗养中。清华原子科学研究所自创办至今,将近五年,毕业生第一、二、三届达五十人,多数出国续求深造,其中回国返校服务者五人。清华目前最困难问题仍为缺乏良好之师资。月涵师出国三次,孙观汉先生回国两次,仍无法解决此问题。幸校内同仁颇能通力合作,故学校各方面建设及施为,尚能按照计划进行,而来校参观之外国专家,亦均寄以莫大之同情与希望。原子炉之安装及炉房之建造已全部竣工，日内(三五日内)即可开始运转。此为中国科学界一大事，想先生亦必乐于预知此一消息也。兹另邮寄上《清华概况》二册，以供参考。

一九四八年，忠奉命赴粤接长中山大学校长，继忠接任编译馆馆长之赵士卿君，胆小而无识，致编译馆全部人员及资料均沦散，真为可惜。后"国立编译馆"在台重新办起，其中编订名词工作，仍系由忠继续主持，数年来已有相当成就。素知先生对此一项工作，甚为关怀，谨此附闻。顺颂时祺。

后学陈可忠敬上

四月十二日

〔University of Chicago Library, Yuan T'ung-li Papers〕

按：孙观汉(1914—2005)，浙江绍兴人，浙江大学毕业后赴美留学，获匹兹堡大学物理学博士学位，时应任台湾清华大学原子研究所首任所长。赵士卿(1891—1974)，字吉云，江苏常熟人，法兰克福大学医学博士，曾任同济大学校长。

罗家伦覆函先生，告"国史馆"所欲购买美国国家档案所摄日本外务省及陆海军档案编号，请就近接洽，并请联系布莱克威尔书店查询所购书籍寄送情况。

守和吾兄道鉴：

两接二月二十二日及三月三日手教，均敬奉悉。吾兄偶患眼疾，谅已全愈，甚为系念！关于购备档案局有关中国史料事，已决定购备1910-29第N329、N339、N341三项复本各一全份，请费神先行代向该局接洽，寄款当于彼方印就寄出以前汇到，因我方办理结汇手续，亦需时间，但一定可以汇到，则可保证也。承兄寄下《俄人研究中国文献总目》及《国父伦敦蒙难记》两书，均已收到，谢谢。去年二月十五日代向牛津 Blackwell 书店订购之 Jones: *The Far East 1942-1946* 一书，已向此间"中央研究院"查询，该院亦未收到，此书可否烦请吾兄致函该店请其查询究竟，为感。承代付 *Facts on File* 期刊订费七十六元，收据请便中寄下，琐事奉扰，不安之至。《故宫名画三百种》装一木箱，于二月二十一日交邮寄奉，未知收到否？邮费及包装等共计台币三百零六元五角，在尊款内代付矣。专复，敬颂撰祺！

弟罗家伦敬启

四，十二

〔University of Chicago Library, Yuan T'ung-li Papers, Box 1〕

按：N329、N339、N341 据以后各信可以推知应属笔误，实际应为 M329、M339、M341。3 月 2 日，布莱克威尔书店出口部负责人 G. H. Barnett 致信先生，告知由于去年该书在寄送途中丢失，应 2 月 9 日先生来信要求，该店免费补寄一册与"国史馆"。该函为文书代笔，落款处为其签名。

四月十三日

先生致信马克尔，询问英国大学中国委员会或其他机构有无可能资助编纂《中国留英同学博士论文目录》。

April 13, 1961

Dear Mr. Morkill:

From your last letter I am delighted to know that you have been serving as Chairman of the Kensington Borough Council Public Libraries Committee and you have been building a new Central Library in a traditional style. Hearty congratulations!

It happened that I used to live very near your present address when I attended University College almost forty years ago. I should like so much to revisit London and meet so many of my old friends there. As to the building of the Peking National Library, it was built in 1931. Now it has been enlarged considerably under the Communists, but my old staff have all remained and still active.

For some time, I have been collecting data for a Guide to doctoral dissertations by Chinese students in Great Britain. Over 400 dissertations have been cited and the Guide could be published in the autumn. As I am in need of support, I wonder if you think it to ask for a small grant from the Universities' China Committee, or the China Institute in London as you see fit. I shall be grateful to have your advice and suggestions, so that it could be published as soon as the editorial work is completed. I now enclose a brief statement.

　　With cordial regards,

　　　　　　　　　　　　　　　　　　Yours sincerely,

　　　　　　　　　　　　　　　　　　T. L. Yuan

P. S. I have never received the annual report 1955－56 and the ensuing issues which you were kind enough to send to me. Could you send me another set?

　　　　　　　　　〔University of Chicago Library, Yuan T'ung-li Papers, Box 5〕

　　按:该信应由西门华德转交,此件为录副。

四月十四日

罗家伦致函先生,告知收到布莱克威尔书店补寄的书籍。

　　守和吾兄道鉴:

　　　　日昨甫寄一函,敬托吾兄代向档案局订购有关中国史料一全份事,计邀惠察矣。今日收到牛津 Blackwell 书店寄出之 Jones: *The Far East* 一册,除径函复谢外,知关锦注,特此奉闻,并颂道祺!

　　　　　　　　　　　　　　　　　　弟罗家伦敬启

　　　　　　　　　　　　　　　　　　　　四,十四

　　　　　　　　　〔University of Chicago Library, Yuan T'ung-li Papers, Box 1〕

　　按:该函为文书代笔,落款处为其签名。

四月二十日

刘国蓁覆函先生,告知寄送粮包至大陆接济亲友的渠道,另告嘱查信息并无所获。

　　守和博士先生尊鉴:

　　　　敬启者,日昨拜奉华翰,敬聆种切。关于寄粮包至大陆接济亲友,已成惯例。晚现在每月付出粮包款项要七八十元,是救济在广州之堂嫂与堂弟等,皆可得收无误,亦有三四个月之久。最近两三月则可寄连关税及运费在内之粮包,系由在港各大陆食品公司办理,如寄生油一公斤(每种数量之最低限度),在港交八元七角(时价不同多种或数量类推)则由代运公司发回领取证一张,将该证用挂号邮寄至收件人,收到后隔十二天(前时只七天而已,是广州计),持该证到指定地点领取(广州在华侨旅运社收),则无须再付其他费用。但广东省以外加收运费,如江苏省则每公斤加一元六角,各省不同,并时日需多几天。粮食包可代运者只普通食品,如油、糖、豆、粉、麦片、花生肉等,罐头食物则有勒吐精奶粉、炼奶、阿华田、鸡肉、猪牛肉、火腿等,至维他命丸是属于药品,公司不能代运。如交邮局寄去,未知可能准入口否?如能收到,亦必须纳税,因凡由邮局寄发各物等,皆要收件人纳税,不是完税者,但寄付人则可不必多付款项也。闻由邮局寄收到之时间比代运公司较为迟滞也。此乃大概情形,谨以奉闻。普仁斯顿大学代表MOTE 教授尚未见其来接洽,晚有到美领馆询问,亦不得要领,因渠如不到馆登记报到,则无法知其住址,惟有听其自然而已。嘱查张弼士等生卒年月一事,颇为困难,因该五人皆非本港人,甚至港大亦无记录,惟晚所知张弼士、张耀轩、陆佑(俱是前清南洋富商)皆已去世许久,至苏开文尚年幼,则不知也。云南白药已购得一小瓶,价银二元,但原装玻璃圆瓶投寄不方便,故将其倒出用蜡纸包好,由航空邮奉上。如得收后,敬希示知为幸。尊账前存二十七.三五元,上次与今次航邮费共四元,白药二元,共六元,比对尚存二十一.三五元在晚处也。匆匆,拜俟续陈。专此,敬请撰安。

愚晚刘国蓁顿首

一九六一年四月二十晚灯下

〔University of Chicago Library, Yuan T'ung-li Papers, Box 7〕

按:张振勋(1841—1916),字弼士,号肇燮,广东梅县人;张鸿南(1861—1921),字耀轩,广东梅县人;陆佑(? —1917),字弼臣,号衍良,广东鹤山人;苏开文,待考。

四月二十五日

先生致信罗家伦,告已与美国档案局初步接洽购买该局影照史料,但须提前付费到其上级机构方能开始复制档案资料。

志希馆长吾兄惠鉴:

奉到四月十二日手教,欣悉尊处决定购备美国档案局影照有关中国之史料,当即前往该局接洽,据云该馆隶属于总务署,必须该署收到汇款后方能开始影照,支票抬头应写总务署云云。尊处汇款由台发出时,望即函告,以便催其速办,并嘱在最短时期内予以完成。又前嘱拨付*Facts on File* 期刊订费 76 元,当即照付,兹将各项收据随函奉上,并附清单备查。存款尚有十余元,拟购《在二次大战中美空军小史》,全书共出七册,关于中日战争部分在第四、五两册,故拟专购此二册,谅荷同意也。又弟近在台湾银行开一甲种活期存款户头,嗣后征集费即请开送该行,以免屡次麻烦贵馆会计也。

《故宫名画三百种》,承费神代购,感谢感谢。顷接邮局通知,日内即能提取。

〔University of Chicago Library, Yuan T'ung-li Papers, Box 1〕

按:此件为底稿。

四月二十六日

罗家伦致函先生,告知前请在美复制国家档案馆所藏日本外务省及陆海军档案费用已请叶公超转拨。

守和吾兄道鉴:

本月十三日及十四日寄上两函,计邀惠察矣。请吾兄费神代向美国国家档案局复制有关我国史料一九一〇至一九二九年第 M329、M339、M341 三项各一全份,计需美金壹千三百七十四元三角,已于本月二十五日由"总统府"电请"叶大使"拨交吾兄转付。专此奉托,敬祈惠洽费神代为办理,并希能早日寄下,无任感盼! 前请代付 *Facts on File* 期刊订费七十六元,收据已由该社径行寄来矣。顺此奉闻,有渎清神,至为感谢! 敬颂撰祺!

弟罗家伦敬启

四,二六

〔University of Chicago Library, Yuan T'ung-li Papers, Box 1〕

按:"本月十三日"似指 12 日函。此函为文书代笔,落款处为其签名。

四月二十九日

陈受颐致函先生,告知书稿校改进展等事。

守和尊兄有道:

月初侍教,厚承渥待,至今铭感。别后在纽约小住三日,拙稿初样又复多所改动,出版家以照例不负改批费用,故无异议。弟亦只好作苦工七八小时,盖弟眼虽不高而手乃特别之低,自然有此结果也。久邀垂注,敬以奉闻。敝校教席人选仍无着落,虽非急需,亦不得不早为之计,望兄以时教督,甚悬悬也。专此申谢,并颂撰祺。敬祝嫂夫人俪福。

弟受颐顿首

四月廿九日

〔University of Chicago Library, Yuan T'ung-li Papers, Box ?〕

按:"拙稿"应指 *Chinese Literature: a historical introduction*(《中国文学史略》)。

Dorothea Scott 致函先生,告其将至华盛顿并前往国会图书馆,期待与先生晤面。

90 Morningside Drive,

New York 27, N. Y.

29th April, 1961

Dear Dr. Yuan:

My husband and I will be paying a very brief private visit to our friends in Washington and hope to visit the Library of Congress on Friday, 5th May, and would very much like to drop in to your office for a few minutes if this will be possible. I have written to Miss Morsch that she will call at about 10.30 a. m. and to Dr. Beal that we will be in the Orientalia section about 11 a. m. I believe you are in another division now but we will find out where you are when we arrive.

I think I wrote to you last year that we were leaving Hong Kong and planning to spend a year or two in the States. We are both at Columbia for the time being. We will give you our news when we meet, we hope next Friday.

Yours sincerely,

Dorothea Scott

〔袁同礼家人提供〕

按:该函为其亲笔。Dorothea Scott 及其丈夫应如约访问国会图书馆并面会先生。

四月三十日

晚,先生设宴款待李霖灿等人。〔《国宝赴美展览日记》,页73〕

五月三日

罗家伦覆函先生,答覆诸事。

守和吾兄道鉴:

顷接四月廿五日复示暨单据,均敬奉悉。兹分别敬复于后:

一、四月廿六日寄上一函,奉告复制史料款项已由"总统府"电请"叶大使"转拨,计邀惠察,即请吾兄转托美国档案局开始影照,早日寄下。

二、党史会前托唐心一先生带奉美金外汇二百元,"国史馆"亦于去岁汇上美金二百元,共计四百元,托吾兄在国外代为征购史料图书之用。先后承代购之图书等十二批,均已收到,连同代付 *Facts on File* 订费,合计二百八十元六角,附奉清单一份,不知其中有无遗漏之处?因与来函提到之数有相当出入,尚乞核对见示。

三、承示拟购《二次大战中美空军小史》有关中日战争部份两册一节,极为赞同。

四、吾兄之征集办公费至本月份计存一千三百四十八元八角五分,今日本馆出纳在邮局取出送存台湾银行吾兄之存款户内,无如台湾银行总行查不到吾兄户头号码,一时未能存入。请兄示知存户号码,是总行抑系分行? 以便照办。

五、兹又有恳者,本馆所订之西文杂志五种,原系委由此间正中书局经办,无如该局本年停办西书业务,以致本馆本年应续订之杂志尚未付款,续订一年共计订价为美金三十六元五角,为此备就续订函五件附上,烦请吾兄代为垫付订费,分别开具支票五张附入函中加封转寄各社,至所感托。

六、此项续订书刊之款及代付之邮费,本馆正在办理申请结汇,最近谅可汇奉。

屡渎清神,无任感谢,专此奉复,顺颂撰祺!

弟罗家伦敬启

五,三

〔University of Chicago Library, Yuan T'ung-li Papers, Box 1〕

按:此函为文书代笔,落款处为其签名。

马克尔覆函先生,告知已将申请转交英国大学中国委员会,并期待先生再次访英。

3 May, 1961

Dear Dr. Yuan:

I was delighted to have your letter of April 13th and to hear of your proposal to visit this country.

I have mentioned your application to the Executive Council who have referred it to the special Committee of the Council which has been appointed to deal with these things.

I sincerely hope that they will agree and that I shall have the pleasure of meeting you again later this year. I certainly consider that it is most desirable to have a record such as you suggest. I am posting you the old U. C. C. reports.

With best wishes.

Yours sincerely

A. G. Morkill

〔University of Chicago Library, Yuan T'ung-li Papers, Box 5〕

五月十二日

陈受颐致函先生,寄还嘱查留美同学人员名单,并谈托吴相湘在台购书事。

守和尊兄有道:

前月侍教,厚承宠侍,至今辄感。顷检书桌,获一名单,谨随函缴上。第三人中国名字曾遍询此间粤东朋友,均云不知,故无法填上也。弟近年在台采买书籍均托吴君相湘代办,最后一批去年年杪专函寄去书目,迄今消息渺然,此种琐事又不好意思再函催促,不知转托台北联合出版中心手续简捷否?我兄有无更好之办法,便乞赐教为感。专此,敬颂著祺,并祝嫂夫人俪福。

弟受颐顿首

五月十二日

〔University of Chicago Library, Yuan T'ung-li Papers, Box 2〕

五月十四日

Dorothea Scott 致函先生,感谢在华盛顿的款待,并已致信香港大学图书馆索取馆藏目录,另建议先生联系刘若愚以获取香港中英俱乐部名录。

14 May 1961

Dear Dr. Yuan:

It was a great pleasure to meet you again last week. My husband and I both wish to thank you for your hospitality. We enjoyed our brief visit to Washington immensely, I am so glad that the city was looking beautiful for my husband's first glimpse of it.

Your kind letter and Dr. Wu's were both here when we returned. I should have given you a little more notice.

I have written to Hong Kong to ask the Registrar to send you a catalogue of the University, unfortunately I omitted to bring even one with me.

For the directory of the Sino-British Club in Hong Kong, as my husband suggested, it would be a good idea to write to Mr. James Liu. He is leaving for Honolulu in late July or August, but you could suggest he passes your letter on to the Secretary, who it is this year I don't know. His name, by the way, is 刘若愚(君智).

I hope it won't be thirteen years before you and my husband meet again!

With best wishes from us both,

Yours sincerely,

Dorothea Scott

〔University of Chicago Library, Yuan T'ung-li Papers, Box 3〕

按:刘若愚(1926—1986),1948 年毕业于辅仁大学,后赴英留学,专攻中西比较文学。该函为其亲笔。

五月十五日

杨云竹致函先生,邀请国会图书馆同仁参加"中国古艺术品展览会"在美国国家美术馆的预展。

守和乡长兄:

我艺展定五月二十八日正式开幕,事前我"叶大使"定于五月廿六日(星五)下午四时半至六时,在国家美术馆举行预展,并以茶会招待中外来宾。国会图书馆内我国工作各位同人,甚盼惠临参观并指

导,因地址未确悉,恕不克一一柬邀,敢乞代为通知为感。峕此,并候
研祺。

弟杨云竹拜启

五月十五日

〔袁同礼家人提供〕

按:先生应按时出席预展,但未见相关记录。

五月十八日

罗家伦致函先生,谈续订期刊、在美国档案局复制史料、国会图书馆所藏日
文档案复制费用等事。

守和吾兄道鉴:

(一)五月三日寄上一函,已邀惠察,承代付续订期刊之款,The
University of Chicago Press 三项及 *Foreign Affairs* 之收据,均已寄到,
费神至感!

(二)编纂开国及抗战实录,为本馆中心工作,年前复奉中枢之
命,会同中国国民党中央党部编辑中华民国开国五十年文献,预定本
年双十节陆续出版,除在国内征集有关资料外,仍感不足,承兄转托美
国档案局复制一批史料,即为此项之用,款项谅已拨到,不知何时可以
制成寄下,甚以为念! 尚乞见示,为盼!

(三)美国国会图书馆所藏自一八六八年至一九四五年期间,日
本外务省、陆军省、海军省以及其他机关等,与我国有关军事外交文件
档案之原始资料,实为本馆所急需。兹拟择其与我国最有关系者复制
胶片一千七百余卷,不知每卷价格若干? (1)文件号码单,打好后即行寄上;
(2)如有折扣可打,尚祈费心接洽。是否 35mm 宽、一百呎长者? 拟恳吾兄即
行代为作初步商洽,见示为盼。本馆为选购此项史料胶片,现正在筹
措经费,希望该馆能有优待价格代为复制,并乞吾兄商之,拜托拜托。
专此,敬颂道祺!

弟罗家伦敬启

五,十八

〔University of Chicago Library, Yuan T'ung-li Papers, Box 1〕

按:该信凡两页,第二页右侧有两段打印文字,内容如下:1.
Checklist of Archives in the Japanese Ministry of Foreign Affairs,

Japan, 1868−1945, Microfilmed for the Library of Congress 1949−1951, Compiled by Cecil H. Uyehara under the Direction of Edwin G. Beal, Photoduplication Service, Library of Congress, Washington, 1954. 2.Checklist of Microfilm Reproductions of Selected Archives of the Japanese Army, Navy, and other Government Agencies, 1868−1945, Compiled by John Young, Georgetown University Press, Washington, D. C. 1959. "This publication is distributed by the Photoduplication Service, Library of Congress, Washington 25, D. C……"此函为文书代笔,落款处为其签名。

西门华德致函先生,告知前此申请最好以旅费的方式申领资助,并告其将赴多伦多讲学,另谈巴黎友人近况。

18th May, 1961

My dear Dr. Yuan:

Your letter of 13th April, addressed to Mr. Morkill, was passed on to "the Experts Committee" of the UCC, whose chairman I am. When considering your application at its meeting of yesterday's date, the Committee was not clear whether you wanted a travel grant or a subsidy towards publication, and I undertook to write to you to clear up this matter. As you will realize it would not be possible to make a decision concerning the publication without the manuscript.

May I take this opportunity to thank you also on my part for the most charming way you received Harry when he called on you and for devoting so much time to him. I myself hope to "look in" sometime during the session 1961/62 as I shall be in Toronto as from 1st October for a session as a visiting professor. I was in Paris for a fortnight in April, and though I was unable to see Madame Mozère I understood that she is now divorced. She had to undergo an operation some time ago, but everything seems to have gone well. One of her children is at the École des Langues Vivantes Orientales.

With very kind regards also for Mrs. Yuan, in which my wife joins me,

Yours very sincerely,

W. Simon

〔University of Chicago Library, Yuan T'ung-li Papers, Box 5〕

五月二十四日

罗家伦致函先生,请在前信所列目录外就近搜集国会图书馆所藏有关中华民国重要史料,并谈胶片阅读机、各款项收讫等事。

守和吾兄道鉴:

(一)五月三日及十七日寄上两函,谅均邀惠察矣。请吾兄代向美国国会图书馆接洽订购史料胶片事,除前函所列之目录两册以外,如尚有其他重要史料足为本馆编纂开国及抗战实录等参考之用者,务请吾兄惠示高见,并恳费心搜集,无任感盼!(如荷速示尤感,因在预算年度终了及开始时期也。)

(二)胶片阅读机(Microfilm Reader)如柯达出品之 Kodagraph Film Reader, Model C 固属优良,惟售价高且不易搬动,如有价格低廉、使用简便、适合 35mm 一百呎长胶片之用者,倍数须较大,阅读时不费目力,本馆需购备两架,以便应用,亦请吾兄就近调查介绍,为托。(弟意以为如能安置在桌上,使阅览或翻译者能顺利使用为适宜,请以尊见惠告。)

(三)兹附奉台湾银行汇票一张(No. C44885)计美金一百十二元五角,为归还吾兄代本馆垫付 *Facts on File* 七十六元,及续订杂志五种三十六元五角之款,请查收。又承代垫之邮费若干,务请开示。

(四)五月三日函中附奉之代购图书款项清单一张,不知其中有无遗漏,请核对见示。如数额相符,除单中第十二项为伦敦蒙难史料一本计四元九角一分,书及单据交党史会,在托唐心一先生带上之二百元中报销外,第一至十一项由本馆报销,共计一九九.六九元,拟请兄补开邮资三角一分收据一纸寄下,则本馆去年汇上之二百元收支两讫矣。

专此,敬颂撰祺!

弟罗家伦敬启

五,廿四,台北

附汇票一张,日本军部档案胶片目录号码一纸。

一、日本局部档案目录,全部共有胶片一百六十三卷,经选其重要者有九十八卷,号码如上。

二、请兄费心与贵馆商洽,如全部(一六三卷)复制一份,共需费用若干? 选制九十八卷,需费几何? 胶片是否均为 35mm 宽、一百呎长者? 均请询明示知,无任感盼。

三、日本外务省目录,俟号码选定后,再行抄奉。请兄询问该目录中每卷复制费用(是否同样价钱)见示,为托。

此种麻烦事劳兄不断费心,不安之至! 好在为学术的热忱,是兄胸中不断燃烧的光焰也!

弟伦附启

五,二四

请速询覆,以便办理汇款等手续,至感!

〔University of Chicago Library, Yuan T'ung-li Papers, Box 1〕

按:起始处"十七日"应指 18 日的函件,特此说明。该函为文书代笔,两处落款和多处插入语、补语则为罗家伦亲笔。附有 1 页选目,内含 98 个胶卷号。

五月二十五日

先生致信 Heinrich Busch,因受美国学术团体理事会和社会科学研究委员会联合资助,拟将此前发表在《华裔学志》的 Russian Works on China, 1918-1958: a selected bibliography 扩充,并以专著的形式出版,询问该刊对此意见,并请其联系印厂催问前文的抽印本是否寄出。

May 25, 1961

Dear Father Busch:

The Joint Committee on Contemporary China of the American Council of Learned Societies and the Social Science Research Council has asked me to publish a larger bibliography of Russian Works on China. To enable me to publish it at the earliest moment, the Committee has given me a publication subsidy.

In this work, I hope I may have your permission to incorporate the items already published in the *Monumenta Serica* last year. If so, I shall put it in a foot-note at an appropriate place.

As soon as it is published, I shall present a copy to your Editorial Board. It is possible that Dr. Loewenthal may like to write up a book-review for your valued journal.

As to the reprints of my article on Russian Works on Japan, I only received three copies by air two months ago. The copies to be mailed by ordinary mail have not yet been received. I shall be grateful if you could check with your printer, as several scholars have asked for them.

Thanking you again for your courtesy,

Yours sincerely,

T. L. Yuan

〔University of Chicago Library, Yuan T'ung-li Papers, Box 7〕

五月三十一日

先生覆信罗家伦,告知已与国会图书馆相关负责人初步洽商复制日本军部档案,但整个过程需要相当时间。

志希馆长吾兄惠鉴:

连奉本月十八及廿四日赐书,欣悉馆中正在赶编开国五十年文献,实为艺林盛事。关于复制日本军部档案已与馆中负责人商洽。兹将开来清单奉上,尊处如何决定,望即赐覆,以便遵办。至于运费,须俟全部装箱起运后,方知确数。目前各方托照之件为数甚多,而馆中办事又慢,恐非一月以内所能完成。其情形与档案局略有不同,至于阅览机,近有 Model MPE 价格低廉,使用简便,可放在桌上阅览,不费目力,已向厂中函询价目,一俟得复,当再奉闻。寄下汇票美金 112.50,业已拜收,随函奉上收据 31 ¢ ,凑足贰百元,收支两抵。另交邮寄上 Feis 教授近著 *Japan Subdued* ,其末页列有引用书目,如有所需,望即示知。

五,卅一日

〔University of Chicago Library, Yuan T'ung-li Papers, Box 1〕

按:"Feis 教授"即 Herbert Feis(1893-1972),美国历史学家、经济学家,曾任胡佛、罗斯福国务院顾问。*Japan Subdued* 全称 *Japan Subdued: the atomic bomb and the end of the war in the Pacific* ,1961 年普林斯顿大学出版社初版。此件为底稿。

方闻覆函先生,感谢为其获取"中国古艺术品展览会"预展邀请函,并附上近著文章目录,另告郑德坤正在普林斯顿大学访学。

May 31, 1961

Dear Dr. Yuan:

Thank you for your kind note of the 24th, and also for your thoughtfulness in securing an invitation for me for the preview of the Chinese Art exhibition. I managed to spend two hours at the opening of Friday afternoon, and was happy to renew my acquaintances with some of the masterpieces as well as my T'ai-chung friends, Messrs. Li, T'an and Na. I was sorry not to have found you there.

I have enclosed a list of my publications along with a reprint of one of my recent articles. I am afraid that this is the best I can do now, as I am all out of other reprints. I am going to be away from Princeton for a year on a Guggenheim fellowship, but Dr. Cheng Te-k'un of Cambridge University will be here as a visiting professor to take care of the special Chinese Art and Archaeology Program for me. I am sure that you are acquainted with his three recent volumes on Chinese archaeology (*Archaeological Studies in Szechwan*, Cambridge 1957; *Prehistoric China*, Cambridge 1959; *Shang China*, Cambridge 1960). You can reach him through this department after the first of September.

As I have to finish a manuscript before leaving for Japan and Hong Kong sometime in late September, we are going to be in Princeton all summer. My wife and I would be delighted if you and Mrs. Yuan could arrange to visit Princeton for a weekend and stay with us. It would give me great pleasure to show you our museum collection and teaching facilities in the Chinese art field.

With best wishes for an early meeting.

Cordially yours,

Wen Fong

〔University of Chicago Yuan T'ung-li Papers, Box 3〕

按：方闻（Wen C. Fong，1930—2018），美术史家、艺术文物鉴赏专家，时在普林斯顿大学任教。"中国古艺术品展览会"预展在 5 月 26 日（周五）、27 日举行，首日为招待"驻美使馆"邀请的嘉宾，次日则为招待美国国家艺术馆邀请的宾客。① Li. T'an and Na 应分别指李霖灿、谭旦冏、那志良三人。落款处为其签名,附 1 页系其 20 世纪 50 年代以后的著作、文章、书评、手稿目录。

六月五日

Heinrich Busch 致函先生,告知其并不反对将刊登《华裔学志》的书目扩充并出版发行,并告将寄出剩余抽印本。

June 5, 1961

Dear Mr. Yuan:

We are glad to hear that you are composing a comprehensive bibliography of Russian Works on China, and have, of course, no objection to your making use of the bibliography which you published.

Months ago, we have conducted our printer to make the offprints of your article on Russian Works on Japan. I am glad that you received at least the three air-mail copies for which you had asked. We are asking the printer once more to make the rest of the offprints as soon as possible. In any case it would not be very long any more since the whole issue will—at last—be out in the near future.

With best wishes and kind regards,

Sincerely yours,

H. Busch, S. V. D.

〔University of Chicago Library, Yuan T'ung-li Papers, Box 7〕

按:该函写于信封展平后的内面,但已断裂,因此录文可能有些许错误。

六月七日

先生致信顾维钧,寄上所需民国早期内阁名单并告知所询外交往事细节,另请教首位获得哥伦比亚大学博士学位的中国学生的中文姓名。

June 7, 1961

Dear Dr. Koo:

I must apologize for the delay in answering your recent letter. There

① 《国宝赴美展览日记》,1972 年,页 87-94。

is only one complete set of the Chinese Government Gazette in the Library of Congress which was sent to the bindery and detained there for several months. Last week when it was bound, I looked for the information about the cabinet changes taking place between 1912 and 1915. The enclosed list indicates only a few members of each cabinet. If you wish to have a full list, please let me know.

It was Krupenskii who presented to Mr. M. T. Liang with a document outlining three demands: 　　　　　　There is a full account of these negotiations in a Russian document I wanted someone to translate it for you, but everyone seemed to have been fully occupied these days, so I am enclosing an excerpt from Peter. S. H. Tang's book which is well documented.

Other documents you wanted are being reproduced and I shall mail them to you as soon as ready. (Such as the Tibetan question and the 21 demands)

In this connection, I may add that the National Archives in Washington has reproduced on microfilms the Department of State relating to China, 1910 - 1929. I have already ordered a set for the Academia Historica at Taipei 　　　　　and if you need them, you may suggest to the Librarian of the Peace Palace at the Hague to buy a complete set.

The first Chinese who received the Ph.D. degree from Columbia was the late Dr. Yen Chin-yung whose dissertation was entitled: Rights of citizens and persons under the Fourteenth Amendment submitted in 1905. If you happen to know his Chinese name, will you let me know?

　　　　　　　　　　　　　　　　　　　　　Yours sincerely,

　　　　　　　　　　　　　　　　　　　　　　T. L. Yuan

〔University of Chicago Library, Yuan T'ung-li Papers, Box 1〕

按：Peter. S. H. Tang 即唐盛镐（1919—?），信中提到的著作应为 *Russian and Soviet Policy in Manchuria and outer Mongolia, 1911-1931*，1959 年杜克大学出版社初版。该件为录副，空格处付诸阙如。

西门华德(特威克纳姆)覆函先生,告知英国大学中国委员会给予先生一百八十英镑,用以支付编纂《中国留英同学博士论文目录》的差旅费用。

13, Lisbon Avenue, Twickenham,

7th June, 1961

Dear Dr. Yuan:

Thank you for your letter of 31st May. I am happy to inform you that the Experts Committee of the U. C. C. now, under action of their chairman, recommended the award of a travel grant of one hundred and eighty pounds to you, and I would suggest that you get in touch with Mr. Morkill, to whom I am sending a carbon copy of this letter, about the payment of this grant.

Thank you also for all personal news and for your invitation to call on you in Washington. I shall certainly do so but hope to see you before in Toronto.

All good wishes and kindest regards to you and Mrs. Yuan in which my wife joins me,

Yours very sincerely,

W. Simon

〔University of Chicago Library, Yuan T'ung-li Papers, Box 2〕

按:此件为打字稿,落款处为其签名。

六月十一日

先生致信马克尔,请其将英国大学中国委员会的资助汇入巴克莱银行账户下,并感谢寄来所撰文章。

June 11, 1961

Dear Mr. Morkill:

I have been informed by Dr. W. Simon that the Experts Committee of the U. C. C. has recommended the award of a grant of £180.0.0. to enable me to compile a Guide of Doctoral Dissertations by Chinese Students in Britain. It is a great honour indeed to have received such a grant and I shall be most grateful if you could convey my heart-felt thanks to members of the U. C. C.

It is my hope that the Guide will not only serve as a permanent record of the scholastic achievements of Chinese students in British universities, but it would also reflect the excellent training which the learned faculties in these universities have given to them.

As soon as payment for this grant can be arranged, please send your cheque to the Barclay's Bank, Marylebone Branch, London, W. 1. for the credit of my account there. A letter to this Bank is enclosed for your convenience.

It was very sweet of you to send me a copy of your article published on the occasion of the opening of your new Public Library in Kensington. Your remark about the Peking Library was especially appreciated.

Yours sincerely,

T. L. Yuan

〔University of Chicago Library, Yuan T'ung-li Papers, Box 5〕

按：此件为录副。

马克尔致函先生，转告英国大学中国委员会已批准先生的资助申请，并告其联系方式。

11 June 1961

Dear Dr. Yuan:

I was very delighted to hear that the Committee had approved the travel grant and much look forward to the pleasure of seeing you again.

Would you let me know at your convenience how you would like it paid? I could pay it into a bank here to your credit if you wish.

My telephone No. is Fremantle 1588, and address Flat 5. 53 Drayton Gardens, S. W. 10. (Nearest underground station Gloucester Road or South Kensington).

My wife and I shall be leaving London for a few weeks on July 27th.

Yours sincerely,

A. G. Morkill

〔University of Chicago Library, Yuan T'ung-li Papers, Box 5〕

六月十二日

Enid Bishop 拜访先生,请教如何扩充澳大利亚(堪培拉)东方馆藏文献。

> 按:Enid Bishop(1925-?),生于墨尔本,1958 年起担任澳大利亚国立图书馆亚洲馆藏的负责人,1960 年受富布赖特项目资助前往美国进修,在哥伦比亚大学学习,并于 1961 年获得硕士学位。

先生致信张君劢,推荐王人麟向《世界日报》(旧金山)定期投稿。

> 君劢先生尊鉴:
>
> 违教以来,时深企念。大著想正在校对之中,未识今冬能否出版,为念。《世界日报》自大明先生去世后,不识由何人主持? 兹有王人麟先生,现正赋闲,惟文笔甚佳,如能按期投稿略得报酬,似亦不无小补。如承便中向负责人接洽,尤所感盼。附上王君致同礼之函,足征所言不虚也。华京天气今日到达九十余度,引领西望,金山实一胜地也。专此,敬候时祉。
>
> 同礼拜上
> 六月十二日
>
> 内人附笔问安。

〔国家图书馆善本组手稿特藏〕

> 按:"大明先生"即李大明(1904—1961),广东台山人,华侨,自 20 世纪 30 年代后期担任《世界日报》社长,与张君劢往来密切。张君劢新址为 Dr. Carsun Chang, 826 Baker Street, San Francisco, Calif.

先生致信西门华德,感谢其协助申请英国大学中国委员会资助,已联系马克尔告知偏好的支付方式,另将寄赠"中国古艺术品展览会"展览图册。

June 12, 1961

Dear Professor Simon:

I am deeply grateful to you for your letter of 7th June and for your recommendation for a grant from U. C. C. Will you convey my hearty thanks to other members of the Experts Committee? I feel sure that without the recommendations of your Committee, no favorable action could have been taken.

In accordance with your suggestion, I have written to Mr. Morkill, suggesting that when the amount of the grant is available, a cheque should be sent to the Barclay's Bank for the credit of my account there.

I wrote to you about the Exhibition of Chinese Art Treasures held in Washington. An illustrated catalogue has just been issued, a copy of which I take pleasure in presenting to you. It is being mailed by surface mail, and I hope you and Mrs. Simon would enjoy it.

I presume that Harry has left for Melbourne and will enjoy the work of organizing a new department there. To-day I had a visit from Miss Bishop, Librarian of the Oriental Collection at Canberra which is to be one of the important centers for Asiatic studies in that part of the world. She is making the necessary contact here and will reap a good harvest out of this trip. She is keenly interested in enlarging the Oriental Collection at Canberra and her efforts will be successful, I am sure.

With renewed thanks,

Yours sincerely,

〔University of Chicago Library, Yuan T'ung-li Papers, Box 2〕

按:此件为底稿,Harry 待考。

六月十三日

李济覆函先生,告知已收到代转之款,并欢迎来台一游。

守和吾兄如握:

前奉吾兄及嫂夫人手书,知代嫂夫人裁制之衣着,谭旦冏兄已代为送达,欣慰无似。李幹兄代转之三十七元八角亦已收到,请释念。弟目疾虽尚未愈,可已不若往日之严重,知关锦注,特以奉闻。此次艺展能顺利依计划进行,全赖护持古物诸公辛勤擘划,所致为国宣势,至堪钦敬。闻嫂夫人云吾兄公务繁忙,短期内无法分身,他日能忙里抽闲,望能来台一游,是时弟当充东道主,以示欢迎之意。匆覆,并颂俪安。

弟济敬启

六,十三

内子附笔问候。

〔University of Chicago Library, Yuan T'ung-li Papers, Box 2〕

按:谭旦冏(1906—1996),江西九江人,1930 年赴法国学习绘画,归国后曾任国立北平艺术专科学校、四川省立成都艺术专科学校教员,后任中央博物院筹备处专门设计委员及编纂委员,1949年赴台,任台北故宫博物院古物处处长、副院长。

六月十四日

队克勋覆函先生,就所询问博士的中文姓名提供线索。

> 4421-4th Rd., N
>
> Arlington 3, Va
>
> June 14, 1961

Dear Dr. Yuan,

Your letter was forwarded to me just at the time when my wife was being hospitalized for an operation and when I was soon going up into N. Y. State for my 50th Reunion (Class of 1911) at Hamilton College. So, I failed to reply and beg your pardon for this long delay.

Even now I can find no trace of Dr. Wu Tse-kao. The only possible suggestions I can think of would be to write to Ohio State where the Chinese characters <u>might</u> be inscribed on his Ph. D. thesis 1941. The former secretary of our Hangchow Alumni in New York City is Dr. Sailung Pan, 620 W. 149th St., New York 31, N. Y. He might have a clue to follow. Here is the name and <u>old</u> address (as of 1951) of one of our Hangchow Alumni in Hong Kong:

> Chow T'ien-Chen
>
> China Photo Supplies Co.
>
> 5 Wellington St., Hong Kong

who might put you in touch with Wu Tse-kao.

I think T. J. Ku never submitted a <u>final</u> draft of his thesis and never actually got his Columbia Ph. D. degree.

Sorry my information is so meager.

My book won't be off press until fall.

> Very sincerely,
>
> Clarence B. Day

〔袁同礼家人提供〕

按：Wu Tse-kao 应指吴志高（1910—2002），浙江杭州人，化学工程专家，1934 年之江大学化学系毕业，后赴美留学，1941 年获俄亥俄州立大学化学博士，其博士论文题目为 Relation between softening agents and drying，1944 年归国，时应在华东化工学院任教。Sai-lung Pan 即潘赛龙，1951 年获伊利诺伊大学工程学学位；Chow T'ien-chen 和 T. J. Ku 待考。

六月十六日

罗家伦覆函先生，拟复制美藏日本军部及外务省档案胶片并获批外汇，请先生在美多多协助，并谈代购、寄赠书刊等事。

守和吾兄道鉴：

接奉五月十九日及三十一日复教，敬悉种切。兹将各事分复如下：

一、关于复制日本军部及外务省档案，承费心代洽，甚以为感！本馆因限于经费，拟择其与我方有关而最重要者，先行选制四百一十卷，除军部九十八卷号码目录于前函寄上外，兹寄奉外交三百十二卷号码目录单全份，请先行代洽，本馆现正在办理申请外汇手续中，月内可将款项汇上（正拟发函时知外汇四千余美元已经核准，不成问题，故可放手做去，兄必乐闻也）。并望代请其早日将复制各卷即行动手选出，早日制就，以便争取时间。

二、胶片阅览机日本制造者亦颇合用，每架合美金二百余元，拟即向日本订购。

三、承代购 Feis 教授近著 *Japan Subdued*，甚感！ R. Butow：*Japan's Decision to Surrender* (1954) 一书，即请代购。

四、承费心抄示贵馆所藏史料清单，甚以为感！俟有需要之件，再当奉托。另附一单，有五项史料，请吾兄代为征购。

五、附致台湾银行一函，派员送往，并将吾兄之款新台币壹千八百五十元存入，兹将送款簿存根及账目清单附上。

六、《革命文献》已编印二十四辑，《国父年谱》上下两篇，奉赠吾兄全份，另邮寄上。

七、考试委员黄麟书先生，广东龙州人，民前十九年生。嘱代索之职员录，俟要到寄奉。

八、附上本年七月至十二月史料征集费空白收据六张,请加盖章后寄下。

专此奉复,敬颂道祺!

弟罗家伦敬启

六,十六,台北

〔University of Chicago Library, Yuan T'ung-li Papers, Box 1〕

按:《国父年谱》应指《国父年谱初编》,"国史馆史料编辑委员会"、中国国民党党史史料编辑委员会编辑,罗家伦主编,1958 年10 月初版。

六月十八日

大维德爵士(Sir Percival Victor David)夫人致函先生,告知大维德爵士正在翻译《格古要论》,请教该书增订版编纂者王佐的卒年。

June 18, 1961

Dear Dr. Yuan,

My husband & I regret so much that the short duration of our stay in Washington did not permit us to meet. We have the happiest recollections of our visit to the Library of Congress last year, and of seeing you. My husband is now engaged in writing a book on the *Ko Ku Yao Lun*, which may well sum to perhaps three octavo or two great volumes. For such an undertaking he will naturally have to have all the information on the subject that may be available.

Your world-wide & almost fabulous knowledge of Chinese bibliography, prompts him to ask you what may be a very simple question. He wishes to know the year in which Wang Tso, the compiler of the augmented version of the Chinese work in question, died.

We will be most grateful to you for this piece of information, which will of course be duly acknowledged.

With our kind regards and best wishes,

Yours sincerely,

Sheila David

〔University of Chicago Library, Yuan T'ung-li Papers, Box 8〕

按:Sheila David 为大维德爵士第二任妻子,1953 年 10 月结婚。
大维德爵士对《格古要论》及《新增格古要论》的翻译,最终题名
为 *Chinese Connoisseurship: The Ko Ku Yao Lun, the essential
criteria of antiquities* ,1971 年初版。该函为其亲笔,6 月 20 日
送达。

六月二十四日

罗家伦致函先生,告申请外汇手续须与"中央信托局"接洽,并请搜购书籍
数种。

　　守和吾兄道鉴:

　　　　本月十六日寄复一函,计邀惠察矣。关于复制档案胶片申请外汇
事,业经核定,但因有几道手续,须于月底月初方能汇出,照规定须经
"中央信托局"转汇,该局在美设有代表,弟当告该局主管友人转告其
与兄接头如何付给国会图书馆。兹有下列各书,拟请费心代购:

　　　　一、加利福尼亚大学出版 *Metaphor, Myth, Ritual and the People's
Commune* 请购两部,收据分开两张,原通知附奉。

　　　　二、据六月十八日《香港时报》载,美国国务院新近出版有第二次
大战最高层会议秘密文件及纪录之第四卷 *The Conferences at Cairo
and Teheran 1943* ,尚有以前所发表关于波茨坦会议之文件二卷,及雅
尔达会议之文件一卷,均请设法代购。至于以后还要继续出版者,亦
请注意。

　　　　三、又美国国务院以前出版文件《年刊》Far East China 部份,此间
尚缺一九三五年一册(从 1933 到 1942 十年中,只 1935 一册),亦请代为补购。

　　　　专此奉托,敬颂道祺!

　　　　　　　　　　　　　　　　　　弟罗家伦敬启

　　　　　　　　　　　　　　　　　　　六,二四

　　　　再者,《革命文献》已检一套精装者寄出,此后陆续寄上。弟
又及。

　　　　　　　〔University of Chicago Library, Yuan T'ung-li Papers, Box 1〕

按: *Metaphor, Myth, Ritual and the People's Commune* 为夏济安所
著,通译为《隐喻、神话、仪式和人民公社》。该函为文书代笔,落
款及补语则为罗家伦亲笔。

六月二十五日

顾维钧覆函先生,感谢寄来有关外蒙问题的文件影照本,并告所询之人的中文名应为严锦荣。

June 25, 1961

Dear Dr. Yuan:

I wish to acknowledge receipt of your letter of June 7, 1961 with enclosures and more recently a roll of photostats relating to the question of Outer Mongolia. They are most useful and just what I needed.

As regards the State Department microfilm records relating to China, I shall keep your suggestion in mind and try to approach the Peace Palace Librarian with it, though I know the funds for new documents and books are also rather limited.

I recall that Dr. Yen Chin-yung's Chinese name is 严锦荣, though I am not sure. I believe his Chinese name may be found along with his English name in his dissertation. In any case the 美洲日报 of New York must have carried a report of his receiving the Ph. D. in June 1905.

Enclosed please find a check for ＄100 to meet the incidental expenses of typing and making photostats, as I am certain that a similar sum sent some time ago must have been exhausted long ago.

With many thanks for your help and hoping I can continue to reply on your valuable assistance,

Yours sincerely,

V. K. Wellington Koo

〔University of Chicago Library, Yuan T'ung-li Papers, Box 1〕

六月二十六日

先生覆函 Sheila David,告知虽多方查找《格古要论》增补者王佐的卒年,但仍未获得确切时间,另谈正在编纂"中国艺术目录",并请寄来大维德爵士有关中国艺术的著述目录。

June 26, 1961

Dear Lady David:

Since receiving your recent letter, I have done some research concerning the year of death of Wang Tso who Sir Percival is especially interested. The first reference book I consulted is the Index to 89 Ming dynasty biographies   . As he was not listed there, it indicates that his biography was not recorded in any of the 89 biographies. I then looked up the Gazetteer of Chi-an   of Kiangsi province which is his native city. Failing to find him there, I searched him in the Index to the biographies of the Twenty-Five Histories   which as you know is also a useful tool. Although there are many references of persons of the same name, this particular person was not listed. All we do know is that he was also known by his courtesy name K'ung-ts'ai   as noted in the preface to the *Ko Ku Yao-lun*.

I am particularly delighted to know that Sir Percival's monumental work on his treatise is nearing completion. Hearty congratulations! It is an important piece of research which the scholarly world has been waiting. You can well imagine how anxious I look forward to its publication.

You may be interested to know that I have been engaged in a comprehensive bibliography of Chinese art. The first part contains entirely Western literature with special emphasis on periodical articles. Hidden in unexpected places and fugitive in character, they are more important than monographs. It will take another year before the whole work is completed.

In view of the high cost of printing in America and in view of its limited interest, I shall arrange to publish the bibliography in several arts, such as Pottery and Porcelain, Painting, Bronzes, Sculpture, Architecture and Landscape Gardening, Minor Arts, etc. etc.

When you return to London, I hope you would be so kind as to send me a complete list of articles which you and Sir Percival have written on Chinese art. I have already included a number of these articles, but I should like to have a complete listing of articles as well as monographs.

Please convey our best wishes to Sir Percival for his health and scholarly achievements.

Sincerely,

T. L. Yuan

〔University of Chicago Library, Yuan T'ung-li Papers, Box 8〕

按:该件为录副,空格付诸阙如,应填写的汉字依次为《八十九种明代传记综合引得》、吉安、《二十五史》、功载。

七月四日

吴大猷覆函先生,告知一位留学加拿大的中国学生信息。

July 4, 1961

守和先生大鉴:

承询数中国同学出处,只知刘易英名为 I. Liu,系 Laval University (在 Québec)博士,伊论文题未悉,但知系关于 molecular spectrum (infrared)方面,可能系在化学系得学位。

大驾如来加京,请示知,当来迎接。匆匆,即颂著祺。

弟吴大猷顿首

尊号如误书,乞原谅!

〔University of Chicago Library, Yuan T'ung-li Papers, Box 2〕

七月六日

邓嗣禹覆函先生,表示愿意协助获取所需信息,并将为研究计划赴华盛顿、纽约等地查询资料,另告印第安纳大学图书馆拟聘副馆长负责非西方馆藏的扩充。

6 July 1961

Dear Dr. Yuan:

Your letter has been forwarded to me by my wife. I have immediately written two letters to assist you in securing the information you are seeking. I hope you will get results from them. If not, will you please let me know so that I can try some other means through the president or other higher officers.

I am writing a book on the Taiping Rebellion within three months. At first, I thought that I might be able to get to make a quick trip to Washington, New York, and elsewhere to round up source materials about the Taiping Rebellion. Now I think that I will not have time to do this. If you happen to know of any Russian material apart from what is listed in your catalogue, I should be most grateful to receive this information.

Respectfully yours,

邓嗣禹拜复

S. Y. Teng

Professor of History

Indiana University

P. S. Indiana University Library is looking for an assistant Director of the University Library in charge of non-Western Civilization collections: Far Eastern, Near Eastern, Russian and Africa and India. The rank could go up to full professorship depending upon the applicant's qualification and expansions. Do you have any suggestion?

S. Y.

〔University of Chicago Library, Yuan T'ung-li Papers, Box 7〕

按：a book on the Taiping Rebellion 应指 *Historiography of the Taiping Rebellion*（《太平天国历史学》），1962 年哈佛大学出版社初版。此件为打字稿，落款签名和补语为邓嗣禹亲笔。

七月十一日

萧一山致函先生，告知所请于右任题字，已付邮寄上。

守和吾兄尊右：

去岁华府会晤，欣慰奚如，辱承照拂，尤深感激。属请于院长书字，早经写好，因贵址遗忘，迟未奉寄，歉歉。原拟裱好带来，现以无便人，特先由邮寄呈也。即颂暑祺。

弟萧一山敬上

七月十一日

〔University of Chicago Library, Yuan T'ung-li Papers, Box 2〕

按：该函存信封，萧一山地址为台北板桥新埔一号。

七月十九日

先生致信"中央信托局"驻美代表孔士谔，告知该所与国会图书馆接洽时须准备的目录和注意事项。

径启者：

奉到七月十七日公函种切，"国史馆"委托贵局向美国国会图书馆采购日本档案内与我国有关文件之胶片,共分两批:(一)日本陆海军及其他机关文件之胶片共九十八卷,(二)日本外务省文件之胶片共三百十二卷,以上两批共四百〇十卷。贵局与该馆洽办时,应附目录五纸以利进行,兹随函奉上,即希查照办理为荷。又该馆办事甚慢,而"国史馆"需要孔殷,望将贵局致该馆公函复本惠寄一份,以便随时催促早日运台,实为公便。此致

"中央信托局"驻美代表办事处

十九日

附应照胶片目录五纸,支票抬头应写 Library of Congress。

〔University of Chicago Library, Yuan T'ung-li Papers, Box 1〕

按:此件为底稿。

七月二十五日

罗家伦覆函先生,感谢协助获取调查报告、复制胶片、购书。

守和吾兄道鉴:

六月十六日及廿四日寄奉两函,计邀惠察矣。

一、请吾兄费心代为搜集一九五二年美国国会国内安全小组调查报告(调查美国共党及其同路人——如太平洋学会——之活动)一份,以备参考之用。

二、关于复制档案胶片,已由"中央信托局"通知驻美采购团与吾兄洽办,谅蒙惠察,有渎清神,无任感谢!

三、前承代为洽制美国档案局有关中国史料胶片,共二六三卷,计一七,一七八呎,日前收到由 John S. Connor, Inc.寄来清单及提单,已于本月五日运出,下月谅可运到矣。此皆大力所促成也!铭感铭感!

四、今日收到 Capitol Hill Bookshop 寄来 Herbert Feis 所著 *The China Tangle* 及 *Churchill Roosevelt Stalin* 二书,谅系吾兄代购,便中请将付款收据附下,为感!

专此,敬颂道祺!

弟罗家伦敬启

七,廿五

〔University of Chicago Library, Yuan T'ung-li Papers, Box 1〕

按:John S. Connor, Inc.为美国物流运输公司, Capitol Hill

　　　　Bookshop 为华府旧书店。信中两中书的全称为 *The China Tangle: the American effort in China from Pearl Harbor to the Marshall Mission*（1953）;*Churchill, Roosevelt, Stalin: the war they waged and the peace they sought*（1957）。此函为文书代笔,落款处为其签名。

七月二十八日

徐家璧覆函先生,告知暂不能查实所询论文信息,并谈大陆近况。

　　守和先生尊鉴:

　　　　敬肃者,顷奉七月念五日手示,诵悉一是。嘱查杨、苏二人论文,经已分别去总馆暨□圕查过,但均无结果。私意以为倘二人系本年毕业,则论文卡片,或尚未编就,是以目录中,尚未有也。姑将人名存此,以待稍缓再查,或可望能查明,亦未可知。邓君衍林初回国时,尚有信来,近则久已不得其音讯矣,亦不详其近况何似。至于大陆灾荒,或系实情,观于香港寄往大陆之粮包激增,当非虚构。璧休假尚未开始,将来亦不拟他往,以免溽暑旅行之苦也,承询极感! 耑此,敬颂暑安!

　　　　　　　　　　　　　　　　　　　晚徐家璧鞠躬

　　　　　　　　　　　　　　　　　　　七月二十八日

　　阖府统此问候!

　　　　　　　　　〔University of Chicago Library, Yuan T'ung-li Papers, Box 7〕

七月二十九日

先生致信罗家伦,谈协助催办影照日本军部及外务省档案的进展情况及其他各事。

　　志希馆长吾兄:

　　　　前奉六月十六日及廿四日惠示,敬悉一一。承示影照日本军部及外务省档案需用之外汇业经核准,即与馆中交涉,请其从速进行。馆中以数目较大,必须汇款寄到方肯从事□□,七月十八日始接"中央信托局"驻美代表处来信,询及应办各项手续,当即函复并将尊处寄来四百一十卷号码目录径寄该处,请其速将支票一并寄馆,并请其以公函复本寄弟一份,以凭从旁催促。截止本日为止,尚未接到复音。该局办事之迟缓,实不可解,除再函催外,兹将其他各事分陈于后:

　　　　(一)美国档案局影照有关我国史料 1910-1929 年,经从旁催促,已于七月三日装箱□□馆,轮船于七月五号左右离开 Baltimore,八月中旬必可收到,运费想可免收。

（二）嘱代购之书已分数批寄上,兹将单据奉上备查,均在唐先生交下之二百元拨付。

（三）关于中日战史之资料,以□□□大陆军武官之记载较有系统,原系分期登载,但该杂志早已绝版,屡次嘱旧书店搜集,迄未获得,不得已影照一全份,想不日可以寄到。

（四）参议院太平学会文件早已绝版,迄未获到。

（五）白皮书已绝版,购到纸面□,需在台北□□。

承赐寄《革命文献》、《国父年谱》。

其余需要之资料,正在搜集,容再函达。

七,廿九

〔University of Chicago Library, Yuan T'ung-li Papers, Box 1〕

按:此件为底稿,正反两面字迹彼此浸渍,极难辨识。

七月

叶良才致函先生,告知胡适病已渐愈,计划八月底来美参加中基会年会。

〔台北胡适纪念馆,档案编号 HS-NK05-090-003〕

八月七日

先生致信钱存训,询问博士论文出版情况,并请代查所附名单的中文姓名。

公垂吾兄:

暑假中想正在休假,前谈印行之论文已决定由芝大出版部印刷否?如已有校样,望将全书页数示知,以便在《博士论文》中予以注明。兹因出版费无着而预购之人极少,未敢付印,因之延期,将来出版后能否托 Chinese Students and Alumni Association 代为销售,亦望代为决定。附上名单一纸,如能在以往印行芝城同学录中代查其中文姓名,尤所企盼1960年通讯录望代索一份。弟今夏不拟旅行,以天气凉爽,尚能工作,较去夏远胜也。顺颂俪安。

弟袁同礼顿首
八月七日

〔钱孝文藏札〕

按:Chinese Students and Alumni Association 应为 Midwest Chinese

Students and Alumni Association,1959 年钱存训与友人改组原"教育部"资助的"美中西部中国留学同学服务协会"。

八月十日

钱存训覆函先生,告知除马某外名单各人均已查明中文名,并谈其著作已改名《书之竹帛》即将出版付印。

守和先生:

接奉手教,藉悉尊况佳胜,为慰。附下名单已就所知注明,马君无人相识,无法查出其中文姓名也,其他想无大误。闻大著《博士论文目录》延期出版,此间亦拟购订,但未预约,如印就出售,想买者必不致太少也。将来美中同学会自可代售,上期通讯中曾印有简讯一则也。拙著现已交芝大出版部印行,由图书馆学校补助印费三分之一,并列入 University of Chicago Studies in Library Science 之一。合约已经签订,全稿亦已修改完毕交卷,将在英国排版,寄回后用 Offset 付印,可较在美排版省三分之一以上也,大约明春可以出版。又修改时曾见张秀民书中述及敦煌卷子内有帛书四卷,但未注明何处,遍查 Giles 目录不见,曾去函大英博物馆询问,亦谓并无帛书,只有帛画一卷。先生所闻必多,如有所知,请告知出处为幸。又,此书现已改以"书之竹帛"为名:*Written on Bamboo and Silk: the beginnings of Chinese books and inscriptions*,虽内容不限竹帛,但用竹帛作为中国书史中之一代表时期,想尚不致太谬。因此名较原名为通俗,与销售或有关,未知尊见以为何如? 专此,敬请著安。

后学存训拜上

八月十日

〔University of Chicago Library, Yuan T'ung-li Papers, Box 2〕

按:Offset 应指胶印。"张秀民书"应指《中国印刷术的发明及其影响》,1958 年 2 月人民出版社初版。"Giles 目录"即翟林奈所编《大英博物馆藏敦煌汉文写本注记目录》。钱存训博士论文题名原为 The Pre-printing Records of China: a study of the development of early Chinese inscriptions and books.

八月十五日

李田意覆函先生,对先生大著改由他所出版,表示遗憾。

同礼先生道鉴：

大札由新港转抵此间，得悉尊著已决由他人出版，至怅。远东印刷所以设备及人手不齐，按 Kono 夫妇估计，由印刷至订装需时二三月，乃无可如何之事，极为遗憾。今后当力加整顿，务使效率增加，以副先生之期望也。专此，并颂著安。

晚学李田意敬上
一九六一，八，十五

〔University of Chicago Library, Yuan T'ung-li Papers, Box 2〕

八月二十三日

何廉覆函先生，告知其已返回纽约，并谈此前曾介绍郭颖颐赴夏威夷大学任教。

守和尊兄道席：

八月十五日手示，已由夏威夷大学转弟，拜悉种切。弟六月底由夏威夷返抵 N. Y.，月来以贱体欠适，鲜有机会外出。弟在夏威夷大学时，曾悉其历史系正在物色中国历史教授，当即以 Danny Kwok 介绍，已由该系聘为助理教授；顷闻 Kowk 已赴夏威夷就任矣。Kowk 君为耶鲁之 Ph. D，曾在 Knox College 任教两年，附闻。夏威夷大学聘任 Kowk 君后，是否尚需中国文化史之教授，据弟观察，恐成问题。倘兄有便，似可函询 Professor John A. White, Dept. of History, University of Hawaii, Honolulu 14, Hawaii。弟在檀岛五月，因责任无多，该处风景宜人，甚为快乐。专此奉覆，祗颂道安。

弟何廉拜启
八月廿三

〔University of Chicago Library, Yuan T'ung-li Papers, Box 2〕

按：Danny Kwok 即郭颖颐（Kwok, Danny Wynn-ye），1961 年赴夏威夷大学任教。

八月二十四日

先生致信钱存训，告张秀民著作暂时无法借到。

公垂兄：

前奉到环云，欣悉大著将在英排版，明春可以出版，闻之至慰。书名改用“书之竹帛”自可引人注意，于销路不无小补。张秀民之书，此间仅有一部，为他人借去，无从翻检。关于帛书仅知有长沙出土为

Cox 所得的,此外尚未见,大英博物院似无帛书,只好暂缺,于大体无妨也。又周玉良君并未嫁查良钊君_{其夫人仍在大陆},想系另一查君,只要姓氏不错,即将其论文列入查周玉良名下。内中尚有女士多人,因不知其出嫁以后之姓名,只得照旧排列,将来出版自当奉赠,就正于有道也。顺颂暑祺。

弟袁同礼顿首

八,廿四

〔钱孝文藏札〕

　　按:周玉良(1923—?),女,1952 年毕业于芝加哥大学,其毕业论文为 Floral morphology of three species of Gaultheria.

八月二十六日

李霖灿致函先生,告台北故宫博物院古物已运抵纽约。

　　守和长者赐鉴:

　　　　在华府时多蒙诲示,获益无量。临行匆促,未能驱府向夫人辞行,谨于此遥致谢意及歉意,垂鉴是幸。

　　　　古物安稳抵纽约,已开箱布置,颇忙迫,不似在华府时之逍遥自在,且便宜而好之 Apt.不可再得,令人感怀不置也。余容再报。敬叩道安。

　　夫人前叩安。

晚李霖灿鞠躬

八月二十六日

　　那心如兄嘱问候不另。

〔University of Chicago Library, Yuan T'ung-li Papers, Box 2〕

八月三十日

罗家伦覆函先生,请从旁协助询问国会图书馆可否更换拍摄胶片。

　　守和吾兄道鉴:

　　　　一、七月廿九日复示及单据等,均敬奉悉。承费心为本馆多方搜集之绝版图书及资料,已陆续寄到,无任感谢!

　　　　二、请贵馆复制日本军部及外务省档案胶片四百十卷,承吾兄代为催促与联系,谅已开始复制矣。顷向党史会借来一批胶片资料,其中有日本军部档案一部份,经查与本馆此次复制之目录清单中有十五卷相同,为节省经费增多资料使用起见,万一本馆所订制之日本军部档案尚未复制,可否减去军部十五卷,增加外务省十五卷(军部每卷九元,外务省每卷十元,增加费用自应照算),附上拟更换胶片目录清单一份,先请吾兄代向贵馆商洽,如属可能,请即见示,再由"中央信托局"办理更换手续;倘因已制就而不可能更换,则作罢论可也。

三、美国档案局复制之胶片史料二六三卷,承我兄就近从旁催促,得于七月初装船运来台,提单已寄到,该轮将于九月四日到达基隆,此事多蒙费心,感谢之至!

四、七八两月份征集费新台币壹千元,已代为送存台湾银行,兹将送金簿存根一纸附奉。

专此,敬颂道祺!

弟罗家伦敬启

八,卅

〔University of Chicago Library, Yuan T'ung-li Papers, Box 1〕

按:此函为文书代笔,落款处为其签名。

八月三十一日

顾维钧致函先生,表示有意撰写中文回忆录,请先生代为汇集史料,并建议请刘麟生作为助手一同搜集。

The Alcott,

27 West 72nd Street

New York, N.Y.

August 31, 1961

Dear Dr. Yuan:

For some time I have been considering the idea of publishing a Chinese edition of my memoirs and I am glad to know that you recommend it, too. One difficulty, I am afraid, is the fact that the documentary material for it is so scattered that the task of gathering it in a fairly comprehensive manner may take much time and work. But no one is more competent and experienced than yourself. It would be an excellent idea if you could start to collect the essential material. Only the other day in connection with the Columbia University Chinese oral history project I came across many documents in the *China Year Book* of 1923 – 24 regarding the Lin Cheng incident, the Weihaiwei case, the Gold Franc question and the Sino-Soviet negotiations for an agreement. They are of course all in English and some of the translations done by the editors are rather poor. But they give a hint as to where the original texts might be found.

I have often heard from mutual friends of Mr. L. S. Liu as a scholar good in both English and Chinese, and he will certainly be competent and undertake the task as you have suggested. Since I am coming to Washington in mid-September to attend the annual meeting of the China Foundation, I hope to have an opportunity of seeing you and discussing the idea together and the possible arrangement for the execution. I should like very much to be guided by what you consider necessary or advisable, before I reach any decision about it.

Looking forward to seeing you soon and with warm personal regards,

Yours sincerely,

V. K. Wellington Koo

〔University of Chicago Library, Yuan T'ung-li Papers, Box 1〕

按:Lin Cheng incident 即临城劫车案(1923),Weihaiwei case 即英国归还威海卫案(1924),Gold Franc question 即金佛朗案(1923–1924),Sino-Soviet negotiations for an agreement 应指中苏谈判(《中俄解决悬案大纲协定及声明书》,1924);the annual meeting of the China Foundation 应指中基会第 32 次年会。[1] 此函为其亲笔。

九月四日

张贵永致函先生,告嘱购之物将托谢觉民带美面交,并感谢协助其夫人谋职。

---

① 《胡适中文书信集》第 5 册,2018 年,页 453。

守和先生道席：

　　前奉手示,敬悉一一。嘱办之事,弟已购就,将请谢觉民兄携往华府,惟谢兄因应"教育部"聘请,在台讲学,故稍缓返美,但九月底当可抵达华府,绝无问题。内人屡以职业问题求教,深感不安,谨此道谢。阳明山会谈过份热闹,花费尤大,谋国耶、宣传耶。不知有何效果,诚无法推察。此间学人清苦,难以形容,而国外学人到此整日忙于应酬与听报告,大有脑昏肚胀、说不出之苦衷矣。此覆,并颂著祺。

后学张贵永顿首
九月四日

〔University of Chicago Library, Yuan T'ung-li Papers, Box 2〕

　　按:谢觉民(1918—2015),浙江绍兴人,地理学家,浙江大学毕业,曾任职于台湾师范大学,后赴美并在匹兹堡大学执教。

九月十一日

罗家伦致函先生,附上新目请协助更新摄制胶片卷号。

守和吾兄道鉴：

　　八月三十日寄上航函,及附更换胶片目录一份,请吾兄代向贵馆洽商,减去军部十五卷,改制外务省十五卷,谅邀惠察。昨接"中央信托局"通知,得悉胶片价款改用光票支付,想贵馆在价款尚未收到之前,胶片不致着手复制,故未得吾兄复示,即已将修订之目录函送"中央信托局"航函驻美采购服务团办理更换手续矣。前寄上之目录中尚漏列WT89号。又油印目录第五页Treaty Series部份,系reels: TR7-13,误为TR8-14,一并更正。兹特检奉修订之目录清单一份,即请察收,并请吾兄费心从旁催促,早日制就运来,以利参用,无任感盼。专此,敬颂道祺!

弟罗家伦敬启
九,十一

〔University of Chicago Library, Yuan T'ung-li Papers, Box 1〕

　　按:此函为文书代笔,落款处为其签名。

九月十二日

刘麟生覆函先生,感谢代为谋事。

守和尊兄馆长勋右：

　　承赐八日芳翰，乃知重劳车骑，远适普大，为弟接洽工作，诚惶诚感，匪言可宣。明代研究文献目录，自当遵旨办理，日内当往哥大观书，自不为外人道也。蒙赐"顾大使"函印本，尤征推爱之深，一切纂述均以资料收集与应用为依归，他日追随从者，所获必多也。敬谢，并颂节禧。

小弟麟生谨上

内子叩安

九月十二日

〔University of Chicago Library, Yuan T'ung-li Papers, Box 2〕

马大任覆函先生，感谢寄赠《华裔学志》文章抽印本，告前信所询三个人名未能查出，另寄送最近所编期刊，并告知其将前往康乃尔大学图书馆负责中文编目工作。

September 12, 1961

Dear Dr. Yuan:

　　Many thanks for your letter of Sept. 6 and your book RUSSIAN WORKS ON JAPAN. It is certainly very useful to us and we shall have it properly catalogued and made available to all researchers.

　　I am very sorry to tell you that I have not been able to find the Chinese names of the three ministers mentioned in your letter. There is no directory for Chinese ministers anywhere. If we know their denominations, we may ask the headquarters of these denominations for information. Without denomination, it is almost impossible to find their names unless they are very prominent.

　　Under separate cover, I am sending you a copy of the CURRENT PERIODICALS IN THE MISSIONARY RESEARCH LIBRARY which I compiled not long ago. I hope it will be of some interest to you.

　　By the way I wish to tell you that I am leaving for Ithaca in two weeks. I shall be working as Chinese Bibliographer-Cataloguer at Cornell University Library with the responsibility to build up its Chinese collections. My new address after Sept. 24 will be: –

John T. Ma

Cornell University Library

Ithaca, N. Y.

Since you are the leader in this field of Chinese librarianship, I would certainly appreciate your advice and support in my new job.

With my best regards,

Sincerely,

John. T. Ma

Associate Librarian

〔University of Chicago Library, Yuan T'ung-li Papers, Box 7〕

按：马大任（John. T. Ma，1920—2021），浙江温州人，1944 年毕业于国立中央大学，获文学士学位，1947 年赴美深造，次年获威斯康星大学新闻学硕士学位，1958 年获哥伦比亚大学图书馆学硕士学位，时应在纽约 Missionary Research Library 工作。

九月十三日

先生寄一批中英文文献资料给顾维钧。〔University of Chicago Library, Yuan T'ung-li Papers, Box 1〕

先生致信罗家伦，告知"中央信托局"并未及时付款，导致国会图书馆尚未开始复制所需胶片。

志希馆长吾兄著席：

关于复制日本军部及外务省档案胶片事，馆□已准备就绪，一俟款到，即行开始。馆方于八月十日致函"中央信托局"时，说明按照政府规定，必须先行付款。该局九月十二日始行复函，仍谓 we shall issue our check …… to you in the near future。此中原因，实不可解。弟于昨日复致办事处孔处长士谔一函，请其速办生效。兹将来往信件复本奉上，即希备查。

九月十三日

附购书收据十一元三角。

〔University of Chicago Library, Yuan T'ung-li Papers, Box 1〕

按：此为底稿。

九月十七日

汪敬熙致函先生,谈其对本年"中央研究院"院士候选人的看法,并表示不愿投票。

守和吾兄大鉴:

　　日前接到"中央研究院"来信,通知已选定之院士候选人。由此通知单,弟想到陈省身兄今年只列候选人一名。过去两次他均列四人,□□每年只有一人被选。钟□□先生被列入之机会似乎须再等一二年也。院士选举似在台人物影响至大,似尤以钱思亮先生为有力量。今年台大人员列入他的名字,他极力请求评议会取销。名单中有梅月涵先生之名,不知系何人所为。在教育界梅先生自有其地位,何必与穷酸科学工作人员争一日之短长!院士中有汪厥明,至不成熟。"中央院"研究化学所所长魏嵒寿亦至不高明。骝先生不知听何人的话将魏拉入!今年弟想不投票。票不关重要。在台自教育界至政界均不高明,大可不必混入也。黄季陆做"教长",不成话。弟只知其曾为戴季陶(请按广东音读,而以北平音解!)之喽啰而已。其人既无见解,又无魄力,比张晓峰还差!留学生学位名单何时可以印出?弟曾见 *CHINA INSTITUTE* 广告,以为早已印出。匆此,顺颂俪安。

弟汪敬熙拜上

六一,九,一七。

〔University of Chicago Library, Yuan T'ung-li Papers, Box 2〕

　　按:汪厥明(1897—1978),字叙伦,浙江金华人,农学家、生物统计学家,早年赴日本留学,入东京帝国大学并获农学硕士学位,1959年被选为"中央研究院"院士。魏嵒寿(1900—1973),浙江鄞县人,微生物学家、应用化学家,早年赴日留学。黄季陆(1899—1985),原名陆,字季陆,以字行,四川叙永人,1918年赴日留学,入庆应义塾大学,后转美,获俄亥俄州立大学硕士学位,1922年北上加拿大,又入多伦多大学旁听,1943年任四川大学校长,1961年2月至1965年1月任"教育部部长"。

九月十八日

徐家璧覆函先生,告并未查到有关"曾珹益"信息,并谈观看"中国古艺术品展览会"之印象。

守和先生尊鉴：

敬肃者，十三日手示到时，璧尚在假中，因他事所阻，未能即时去总馆查明"曾瑊益"其人，至以为歉！今日业已恢复工作，乃得机尚往总馆检查，全馆总目录暨博士论文专目（系按年序列），均已查过，不幸未能查得曾君其人。璧所查者，系 under Tseng 及 Cheng 二字，以及一九五〇至一九六一年，各组中均未见有与"曾瑊益"三字相近者。未识曾君如何拼个人姓名，并其毕业年份何年，倘能将此二点明了，则查找较为简易耳。

中华文物在纽约展览，业经往观一次，觉字画至为精美，其他实物未免过少而已。但闻李霖灿兄见示，始知运送困难，实物未能多选，此亦不得已之事耳。得便欢迎先生来纽，俾亲训诲。余言不尽，敬颂崇安！

尊夫人暨阖府并此问候！

晚徐家璧鞠躬

九月十八日晚

〔袁同礼家人提供〕

按："曾瑊益"即曾昭安（1892—1978），字瑊益，江西吉水人，数学家，1917 年毕业于武昌高等师范学校，后赴日留学，1918 年又入哥伦比亚大学学习，《中国留美同学博士论文目录》未收录。9 月 15 日至 11 月 1 日，"中国古艺术品展览会"在纽约巡展。

九月二十一日

金问泗致片先生，告知将赴国会图书馆查阅报纸。

守和吾兄大鉴：

兹因日内拟往纽城一行，特将此册挂号寄还，乞为察收。关于梁燕老与小幡会晤事，伦敦及纽约《泰晤士报》以及《字林西报》等等，必有记载。弟拟于回华府后仍欲往贵处图书馆一查，好在只须查 1921 年年底几天，以及次年一月间半个月的报，约费一天工夫即可查明。届时尚须兄为指导协助，当再电话先洽也。少公仍在港埠，闻须年底方来纽约。专候著祺，并颂嫂夫人坤福。

弟泗谨启

9-21-61

〔University of Chicago Library, Yuan T'ung-li Papers, Box 2〕

> 按:"梁燕老"即梁士诒(1869—1933),字翼夫,号燕荪,广东三水人,清末民初政坛人物,1921 年 12 月在奉系军阀张作霖的支持下,出任中华民国国务总理。

九月二十二日

陈源覆函先生,寄上在英获得博士学位的九名中国学生名单,并谈其赴台探望梅贻琦经过。

> 守和兄:
>
> 　　弟于八月十八日去台北一行,前日始回。尊函未能早覆为罪。询及单中同学中文姓名,鲠生之女及婿与鲍必荣君为弟所知。尧圣兄又知三人,但胡光熹君是否单中之名,则不确定。另三位则不知。名字列另一页。
>
> 　　俞忽(字子慎)亦在武大任教。彼母校为格拉斯科之工科专校,非大学,恐不能授博士学位。武大一览及职员录,弟久已无存。
>
> 　　中英文化协会现仅有其名,并无活动,附设于"自由中国"新闻社,出版时如用此名义,似无不可,惟恐不能为贵刊生色也。在台北曾往医院访月涵兄。彼背部痛苦,夜不能睡,常于晨间熟睡,故第三次于下午五时往,方得晤谈。彼平睡床上,不能起坐,惟言谈风度,仍如往昔。梅夫人每日往侍。病状恐难乐观。专此,顺颂大安。

弟源顿首

六一,九,廿二

叔华附候

〔University of Chicago Library, Yuan T'ung-li Papers, Box 5〕

> 按:"鲠生之女"应指周如松,其夫婿为陈华葵。该函背面附有 9 人中英文姓名对照单。

九月二十四日

大维德爵士致函先生,请为其论文集撰写稿件,并告知范围和交稿时间。

24/9/61

My Dear Dr. Yüan,

　　I wish to ask a favor of you and hope that your reply to my inquiry will be in the affirmative.

As you will know, I have been engaged in the production of a History of Chinese Art and Letters for some time past. In addition to my own work (which will not be inconsiderable, since it will be my own book) this will include a good many special articles on special subjects by a number of specialists, who will total more than a score. Amongst them you will find many familiar names, I am sure.

In the U.S. there will be at least I hope Mr. George Yeh, Li Ling-tsan, Archibald Wenley, and Aschwin Lippe. I would like very much to include you. The subject may be of your own choosing (biographical I would prefer), the book on which the great part of the work will hang being the *Ko ku yao lun* . I have done the translation and the interpretation of the difficult technical jargon of both the 1388 3 chapters edition & the 1462 (not 1459, as originally believed) editions, a number of special articles by me (done) an appreciation of a number of topics, mostly done, a title "A discussion of the Essential Criteria of Chinese Antiquities)," a Dedication (done), a Preface (done), Introduction (done) □□□□ (very, very difficult I have found this) done. Your subject may be as I have said of your own choice. It may be things or subjects Chinese, Mongol, □□□□□□□ or et cetera. The only limitations are

1.The subjects touched may not be later in date than 1485.

2. The article should be in my hands by the first week in February 1962.

I sincerely hope I may have the pleasure & privilege of welcoming you within our charmed □□□□ circle.

With our warmest greetings and with every good wish, I am

Yours very sincerely,

Percival David

P. S. I should have added the name of Dr. Wen Fong who has done an admirable article on "Copies & fakes in Chinese painting" to have said that of course every such article will appear over the contributor's name. P. D.

〔University of Chicago Library, Yuan T'ung-li Papers, Box 8〕

按:该函中所提论文集本拟作为《格古要论》译本的组成部分,但并未落实。Mr. George Yeh, Li Ling-tsan, Archibald Wenley, and Aschwin Lippe 依次为叶公超、李霖灿、文礼(佛利尔艺术馆馆长)、Prince Aschwin of Lippe-Biesterfeld(大都会艺术博物馆策展人)。函中所指论文 Copies & fakes in Chinese painting,待考。该函为其亲笔。

九月二十八日

郭有守(巴黎)覆函先生,告知其子郭成吉博士论文题目。

守和学长兄:

大示稽覆,至怅。兹奉告小儿成吉论文题目,十一月四日授学位典礼,弟拟去格城参加也。何研奎著子师文收到否?顾季皋同学在华府地址便祈见告为感。敬叩俪安。

弟有守上

九,廿八

何时再来欧?

Chengi Kuo Glasgow University Ph. D. 1961

"Vertical Ship Vibration Investigation with an 11ft. Xylonite Model."

〔University of Chicago Library, Yuan T'ung-li Papers, Box 2〕

按:Chengi Kuo 即郭成吉,郭有守之子,英国格拉斯哥大学毕业,后任该校教授兼船舶及航海技术系系主任。[1]

十月五日

大维德爵士覆函先生,感谢代为向吴讷孙、方闻、李铸晋等人邀稿,并坚请先生为论文集撰稿。

5/10/61

My dear Yuan,

Thank you very much for your letter of September 30.

---

[1] 郑会欣编注《董浩云日记》上册,香港:中文大学出版社,2004 年,页 163。

I am glad and grateful to know that you have written to Professors Wu and Li on my behalf and anything from their pen that does not run absolutely counter to my views (which I think would be <u>most</u> unlikely) will be very welcome. But they and their contributions will not excuse you. You <u>must</u> contribute something of your own choice. But it be anything. The book I am doing is <u>by no means</u> limited in its scope to Chinese Art. It includes literature and subjects as diverse as music and architecture, paintings and calligraphy, silk and jades, ceramics and bronzes, lacquer and horn. So, I am not going to let you off-you say you are at present tied up with a bibliography of Chinese Art? Nothing, but nothing, could possibly be more welcome than that for my book. So, I shall be counting on you to be one of 36 other collaborators. You ask Lady David for a list of my publications. I have never done a book but what I have published are listed in Pope's *Chinese Porcelains from the Ardebil Shrine*, p. 165. Counting on your collaboration. With every good wish for us both.

Yours very sincerely

Percival David

〔University of Chicago Library, Yuan T'ung-li Papers, Box 8〕

按：Professors Wu and Li, 前者应指吴讷孙, 后者应指李铸晋（1920—2014）, 广东从化人, 中国艺术史家, 1943 年毕业于金陵大学外语系并留校任教, 1947 年赴美, 1949 年获爱荷华大学英文硕士学位, 1955 年获艺术史博士学位, 时在爱荷华大学执教。Pope 即 John A. Pope, *Chinese Porcelains from the Ardebil Shrine* 通常译作《阿德比耳神殿收藏的中国瓷器》, 1956 年由史密斯森协会和佛利尔艺术馆联合出版, 此书第 165 页确实记录了大维德爵士的五篇文章。该函为其亲笔。

十月六日

大维德爵士致函先生, 请先生不必担心汉字印刷问题, 并补充了自己两篇文章的信息。

6/10/61

My dear Yüan,

I sent you a cable this morning telling you that your work on the Bibliography of Chinese artists would be ideal for my book. May I beg you then to complete it-send it on to me, as soon as you possibly can.

I am not afraid of Chinese characters, the more the merrier. They will all be reproduced in one form or another in a Glossary. In case I have not told you this already, ☐☐☐☐when you send in your contribution, you will be in distinguished company. Here are two additions you may make to Pope's list of my publications in Far Eastern art and culture:

1. "The Shōsō-in" Reprinted for the *Japan Society*, New York City with revisions by the Author, 1932, The Eastern Press Limited, London and Reading.

2. The Shōsō-in-Pottery, paper read by Sir Percival David on Dec. 9 1931 reprinted in *T.O.C.S.* vol. 10, pp. 21−43.

Awaiting your favorable reply, my dear Yüan

Yours hopefully

Percival David

〔University of Chicago Library, Yuan T'ung-li Papers, Box 8〕

按: The Shoso-In 即日本正仓院, *T.O.C.S.* 应指 *Transactions of the Oriental Ceramic Society* (《东方陶瓷学会会刊》)。该信为其亲笔。

大维德爵士致电先生,欢迎先生的书目类文章作为论文集的一部分。

NOTHING COULD BE BETTER FOR MY BOOK THAN YOUR BIBLIOGRAPHY OF WORKS ON CHINESE ART. WILL YOU PLEASE BE GOOD ENOUGH TO CONTRIBUTE THIS.

〔University of Chicago Library, Yuan T'ung-li Papers, Box 8〕

十月八日

大维德爵士夫人致函先生,补充其夫的一篇论文信息。

October 8th, 1961

Dear Dr. Yuan,

Further my husband's letter to you of yesterday, I write to say that he omitted to mention the first of his publications, entitled, "Some Notes on Pi-se Yao", which appeared in *Eastern Art* for January 1929 (Vol. I, no. 3, pp. 137-143).

　　With kind regards,

　　　　　　　　　　　　　　Yours sincerely,

　　　　　　　　　　　　　　Sheila David

　　　　〔University of Chicago Library, Yuan T'ung-li Papers, Box 8〕

　　按:Some Notes on Pi-se Yao 即《论秘色窑》。该函为其亲笔。

十月九日

童世纲覆函先生,告知无法代为影照"胡先生之法文著作"。

　　守公尊鉴:

　　　手教奉悉。前次我公驾临此间参观,招待多疏;反荷齿及,益增汗颜! 关于"胡先生之法文著作",上次系自严文郁先生处借来者,该书已于展览闭幕后寄还。承以影照此书见嘱,深以无法代办为歉! 兹将原支票叁元奉还,乞查入! 尊著《俄人研究日本文献目录》一俟收到,当为转交负责人不误也。内子日渐康复,承念极感! 敬叩双福。

　　　　　　　　　　　　　　晚世纲拜上

　　　　　　　　　　　　　　十月九日

　　　　〔University of Chicago Library, Yuan T'ung-li Papers, Box 2〕

　　按:《俄人研究日本文献目录》即《华裔学志》所刊先生文章 Russian works on Japan: a selected bibliography。

十月十一日

先生覆信大维德爵士,表示愿意为论文集递交明代瓷器的书目尤其是明早期者。

　　　　　　　　　　　　　　October 11, 1961

Dear Sir David:

　　Thank you so much for your cable and your recent letters. I should like so much to comply with your request, but as I am so much tied up with other work, I do not have much energy left especially when I have to work eight hours daily for the Library of Congress.

However, in view of your significant service to the history of art, I shall compile a bibliography of Ming ceramics which you may like to include it at the end of the volume. If the entries are too many for your purpose, we could limit it to early Ming-up to 1485. Since it will be limited to books and articles in western languages, the number of Chinese characters would not be very large.

My larger work-the Bibliography of Chinese art and archaeology would not be ready until 1963. When the times for its publication, I shall, of course, seek your advice again. Perhaps your Foundation may like to sponsor it as one of your monograph series.

With all good wishes and cordial regards,

Yours sincerely,

〔University of Chicago Library, Yuan T'ung-li Papers, Box 8〕

按：此件为底稿。

十月十四日

先生致信李铸晋，请其为大维德爵士组稿的论文集撰写文章。

October 14, 1961

Dear Professor Li:

Sir Percival David, 53 Gordon Square, London, W. C. 1, has repeatedly asked me to contribute an essay on Chinese art to be included in his latest work on Chinese Art and Letters. As I am now tied up with a bibliography on Chinese art and archaeology, I suggested that you should be asked to contribute a scholarly essay. I recommended you to him in the highest terms and I think he may have written to you already.

As he is to publish his translation of the   on which he has worked for many years, he is anxious that the subject of the essay may not be later in date than 1483. Also, the essay should be in his hands in February, 1962. It is my hope that you will comply with his request if you hear from him.

My bibliography on Chinese art and archaeology will not be

published until the end of next year. If you could send me a list of your papers and available reprints, I shall be grateful.

　　With cordial regards,

Yours sincerely,

T. L. Yuan

〔University of Chicago Library, Yuan T'ung-li Papers, Box 8〕

　　按：此件为底稿，空格处付诸阙如，但应指《格古要论》。

十月十六日

大维德爵士致函先生，表示有关中国艺术和文字的论文集不会早于 1963 年出版，仍望先生作为撰稿人之一。

16/10/61

My dear Yüan,

　　My name is "Percy" in case you want to know! And may I call you "Tung-li"?

　　I was delighted to get your air-mail letter of Oct. 11th. The work will never be ready before 1963, if in that year. So, may I have your *"Bibliography of Chinese Art and Archæology"*? Nothing from your distinguished pen can be too long for my book; if you can include two or three or four or more illustrations all the better. So, I look forward to it. I think the King of Sweden may contribute a brief "foreword." All the best & again many thanks,

Percy

〔University of Chicago Library, Yuan T'ung-li Papers, Box 8〕

　　按：该函为其亲笔。

十月十八日

严文郁覆函先生，告所托影照胡适讲稿费用。

守和先生大鉴：

　　敬覆者，来美十余年，聆教一次，迄未谋面，但常以尊况为念。近接手示，欣悉一一。所需适之先生联大讲稿，兹摄制英法文本各一份奉上，乞查收后将费用（原估计为六元七角伍分，本组织同仁可享折扣）二元五角正赐下，以便代为交付散影印部为祷。专此，敬请撰安。

弟严文郁谨上

十，十八

〔University of Chicago Library, Yuan T'ung-li Papers, Box 2〕

按："本组织"应指联合国下属图书馆。

十月二十三日

李铸晋覆函先生，表示大维德爵士并未来信邀稿而自己亦无暇再写它文，并告两篇中国艺术史研究论文的篇目信息。

October 23, 1961

Dear Dr. Yuan:

　　Thanks for your letter of October 14. I am very much honored by your suggesting my name to Sir Percival David as a possible contributor to his work on Chinese Art and Letters. However, I have not yet heard from him and I doubt that he will write me, since we have never met and since he has probably never heard of me. On the other hand, I have been very much tied up by the preparation of a lengthy article on Chao Meng-fu for the *Artibus Asiae* which I hope to finish by Christmas. That actually does not leave very much time to do another one. As a matter of fact, I have just been asked to do a short article on a painting by P'u-ming for the Oberlin Museum bulletin. All these mean that there is not much time to do anything else before February 1962.

　　I am very much interested in your bibliography on Chinese art and archaeology and hope that it will be completed soon. I am now offering a course called "seminar on Sung and Yuan Painting." Right from the start, I found that I needed a good bibliography. Your book will certainly fill the need.

　　As far as my own publications are concerned, the list is very short. I was a student of Western art, and moved into Chinese art only in recent years. The list includes:

　　　"Recent History of the Palace Collection," *Archives of the Chinese Art Society of America*, XII, 1958, pp. 61-75.

"Rocks and Trees and the art of Ts'ao Chih-po," *Artibus Asiae*, XXIII, 3/4, 1960, pp. 153 – 208. (This is also issued as a monograph, a prospectus of which I include herewith for your use)

I am sorry that no more reprints are available. Those for the monograph have been in such great demand from my friends and scholars that I have to disappoint many of them.

Glad to hear from you, reminding me of the pleasure of meeting you in Maryland last May. My best regards to you.

Sincerely,

Chu-tsing Li

〔University of Chicago Library, Yuan T'ung-li Papers, Box 8〕

十月二十六日

吴讷孙覆函先生,表示其对是否为大维德爵士的论文集撰稿仍感犹豫,并告最近著述及即将出版的书籍,另谈《未央歌》在美出版的种种问题以及盗版困扰。

October 26, 1961

Dear Dr. Yuan:

Thank you very much indeed for your letter of October 1st. I thought that I was going to see Professor Fong of Princeton during my scheduled visit to New York last week and discuss Sir Percival David's book, but at the last moment he could not come to New York and told me over the phone that he was not certain about his contribution to it either. I am afraid I would have to hear directly from Sir Percival before I could decide whether a contribution from me would be appropriate. On the other hand, I am most interested in your bibliography on Chinese art and indeed look forward most eagerly to seeing it.

An article by me on Tung Ch'i-ch'ang will appear in Arthur Wright's fifth volume on Confucianism. My book, *Tung Ch'i-ch'ang: the Man, his Times and his Landscape Painting*, is scheduled to be submitted to press, I hope, sometime next summer. My other writings, all not very important but some of which have become rather well-liked, I hope to send by separate mail in a few days. Depending on the cutting off date of your bibliography, I may have a few items slightly more important to add.

On the subject of publication, I had a strange experience with the American copyright law in 1958－59 when I published my novel *Wei-yang Ko (未央歌)* under my pen name Lu Ch'iao (鹿桥). It was impossible to get the book printed in this country as it was 600 pages long even using the new No. 5 type, and involves perhaps the largest vocabulary since the new literary movement of 1919. The fact that I published it in Hong Kong deprived me of copyright protection in this country. Within a few months of its publication, one pirated edition appeared in Taiwan, and recently in a newspaper announcement there I read an apology from a publisher known as I-ming Book Store (一鸣书局) to my distributor the Asian Press (亚洲出版社) for this illegal act. Here I learned that actually two pirated editions had been put on the market, each under a different name (*未央曲 ,及星月悠扬*). I have been able to purchase two copies of one of these editions and shall begin to look for the other soon. Let me first present you with a copy of the authentic first edition. The mutilation of the book by the Taiwan publishers and the corners they cut can be easily discovered by comparison. However, until I can get hold of more copies, I rather treasure the souvenir copies I have been able to acquire. This anecdote, of course, has nothing to do with your compilation of bibliography, but I think it might amuse you.

Now that my second edition is about to be printed, a translation of it into English is quite likely. I wonder whether I can have at least the translation rights protected. Do we respect the copyright of books published in Hong Kong? I shall appreciate any advice from your experience.

With all best wishes,

Sincerely yours

Nelson I. Wu

Assistant Professor History of Art

〔University of Chicago Library, Yuan T'ung-li Papers, Box 8〕

按：函内中文及落款签名均为吴讷孙亲笔。

十月二十九日

先生寄送一批中英文文献资料给顾维钧。〔University of Chicago Library, Yuan T'ung-li Papers, Box 1〕

十一月三日

先生致信大维德爵士，请其为申请美国学术团体理事会资助出具推荐信。

3rd November, 1961

Dear Percy:

I am most grateful for your recent letter and for the catalogues which Lady David so kindly sent to me. Please convey to her my hearty thanks.

I wish it were possible for me to complete my *Bibliography on Chinese Art and Archæology* in the time for inclusion in your monumental work. But as I am doing this work in my spare hours, I cannot complete it until the spring of 1963. Under these circumstances, may I say that my proposal to compile a bibliography on Ming ceramics is a practical one, and that it would be rather appropriate for your purpose. So, I shall get it started next month and have it ready before February 1, 1962.

The American Council of Learned Societies (345 East 46th Street, New York 17, N. Y.) has limited funds which its Committee on Grants can use in support of scholarly research (Each grant not exceeding ＄3,000). Last November I applied for such a grant, but my request was turned down. Now, I am going to try again, but I have to be supported by strong recommendations from art historians and leading scholars. Since your recommendation would carry considerable weight, may I ask you to be good enough to write such a letter on my behalf? In this letter you might mention the urgent need for such a bibliography felt by all art historians as well as my competence in undertaking such a task. This letter should be mailed directly to the American Council of Learned Societies on the form herewith enclosed.

　　The letter of recommendation should reach the Council in November, while the grant will be announced in February or March. If I could get it, I could have clerical assistance and could travel to centers to gain access to necessary material, and the work will be greatly expedited.

　　Thanking you once again for your support and with warm regards to Lady David,

Sincerely yours,

Tung-li

〔University of Chicago Library, Yuan T'ung-li Papers, Box 8〕

十一月九日

西门华德覆函先生,为其个人因故推迟前往华盛顿而表示谦意,建议先生联系 Sidney H. Hansford 询问《中国留英同学博士论文目录》作为 China Society 或英国大学中国委员会出版物的可能性。

9th November 1961

Dear Dr. Yuan: -

　　Thank you for your letter of November 3, 1961. We are, of course, all very sorry that you should have to postpone your visit. I find I am spending a useful and enjoyable time here and I am very much looking forward to going to Washington. But maybe this will have to wait until the end of this session (end of May).

　　I am delighted to hear that the travel grants the UCC awarded you has been useful. I have given some thought to the other question you raised in your letter. I don't think that UCC would be an institution that could acquire and distribute copies of your bibliography, but the China Society might be interested in it. I suggest that you write about this to Professor Hansford who is both on the Council of the UCC and the China Society. You will have seen from the last report of the UCC that the publication committee worked out detailed rules for application for a subsidy and I have no doubt in my mind that a publication like yours would be eminently eligible for a subsidy. But since you have apparently the intention to pay for the printing, it is difficult to see how the subsidy should come in. I am sure that Professor Hansford would be willing to take up this matter with the chairman of the publication committee. (I do not know who he is, since I resigned my chairmanship before my departure to Toronto. It is likely however, that it is Professor Pulleyblank).

If you write to Professor Hansford, he will either give advice himself or induce the chairman of the publication committee to do so, I can only repeat that my impression is that the UCC will be most glad to be of help in whatever way they can.

Hoping that you and Mrs. Yuan are well I remain,

With very kind regards,

Yours sincerely

W. Simon

〔University of Chicago Library, Yuan T'ung-li Papers, Box 5〕

按：此时，西门华德已从伦敦大学退休，前往多伦多大学担任访问教授。如该函建议，先生于 12 月 1 日致信 Sidney H. Hansford，询问有无可能出版该名录。

大维德爵士覆函先生，告已按前信所请为先生向美国学术团体理事会申请资助背书，并希望先生将自己的艺术和考古书目可以列入其论文集中。

9/11/61

Dear Tung-li,

Thank you very much for your letter of the 3rd & the enclosures.

Of course, I shall be glad to do all I can to help you in your project.

Meanwhile, I wish to say that our work has been deferred until the spring of 1963 to enable us to include *Bibliography of Chinese Art and Archaeology*. There has long been an impression that is wholly fake that I am interested only in Ceramics. Nothing could be further from the truth! Looking forward to a reply in the affirmative to this request of mine.

With our warmest greetings, regards, yours sincerely.

Percy

〔University of Chicago Library, Yuan T'ung-li Papers, Box 8〕

按：该函为其亲笔。

十一月十日

大维德爵士致函先生，介绍论文集的主题并谈有可能提供论文的作者。

10/11/61

Dear Tung-li,

May I here enumerate the subjects dealt with in our work: 1. Religious philosophies, China's contacts with India, Scythia Siberia, Persia, Korea, Japan and Indo-China, in addition to the arts & the applied arts, amongst the former being included literature & calligraphy. You will be amongst quite distinguished colleagues and collaborators, e.g., Arthur Waley, Basil Gray, Bernhard Karlgren, Archibald Wenley, and I very much hope Prof. Chu Chia-hua, Dr. Hu Shih, I have not approached. Could you tell me what his particular subject is?

As ever yours,

Percy

〔University of Chicago Library, Yuan T'ung-li Papers, Box 8〕

按：Basil Gray（1904-1989），英国艺术史学家，1946 年起担任大英博物馆东方部负责人。该函为其亲笔。

十一月中旬

先生前往波士顿。〔University of Chicago Library, Yuan T'ung-li Papers, Box 8〕

十一月二十一日

洪业覆函先生，婉拒为《戡定新疆记》撰写跋文之请，并建议联系杜联喆。

守和馆长先生史席：

大札到时，弟正在赶完一篇小文，直至今日才到图书馆借魏光焘之《戡定新疆记》，稍稍读之，弟于此段史实素未研究，不敢妄写跋文，贻笑后来，尚乞原谅为幸。朋友中之于此题曾下工夫者，今记得有杜连喆房兆楹夫人，惜今远在澳洲矣。我兄为旧籍续命，弟至所佩服，但觉排印不如影印，其抬头避讳等等陋习，识者自能一笑置之，不必为改易也。大驾何时再降，能得一谈，快甚。专此，顺请道安。

弟 业 顿首

十一月廿一日

〔University of Chicago Library, Yuan T'ung-li Papers, Box 2〕

按：魏光焘（1837—1916），字午庄，湖南邵阳人，曾任新疆布政使、新疆巡抚、两江总督等要职。后，先生联系房兆楹请其撰写跋文。

十一月二十二日

先生致信孟治，因"教育部"大幅缩减了订购《中国留美同学博士论文目录》册数，询问可否由华美协进社订购相当册数或代为销售。

November 22, 1961

Dear Dr. Meng:

I am writing to ask for a favor.

The Guide to Doctoral Dissertations by Chinese Students in America, 1905-1960 will be published at the end of this month. I shall send a copy to you and to Dr. Cheng with my compliments.

Although it is a labor of love, I did not foresee the financial risks involved. When Minister Huang Chi-lu was here in August, Dr. P. W. Kuo told him that we would not be able to print it unless "the Ministry of Education" could subscribe a number of copies. He readily assured Dr. Kuo and myself that "the Ministry of Education" will subscribe three hundred copies (at a pre-publication price of $ 3.50) for distribution to individual scholars and institutions. With this assurance, 1,200 copies were printed. It was only last week that he wrote that "the Ministry" would subscribe only one hundred copies, but would subscribe three hundred copies if an abstract of each dissertation is inserted.

If we knew he would not keep his promise, we could have less number of copies printed. Since it has put us in an embarrassed situation, I wonder whether the China Institute could subscribe a number of copies for presentation to your Trustees and friends. Knowing your financial troubles, we shall leave the matter to your discretion. At any rate, please inform me how many copies are needed, so that they will be mailed to you direct from the printers.

　　Since your Institute is the center of intellectual activities, perhaps you could help by selling a number of copies at a special pre-publication price. Will you also let me know how many copies are needed?

　　Thanking you for an early reply.

Yours ever,

T. L. Yuan

The guide consists of xxii, 248 p.

〔University of Chicago Library, Yuan T'ung-li Papers, Box 2〕

　　按:Dr. Cheng 应指程其保。此件为录副。

徐家璧致函先生,拟申请马来亚大学图书馆副馆长一职,请先生担任保证人。

　　守和先生尊鉴:

　　　　敬肃者,暌违道范,倏忽多日,比维福躬康强,潭第清泰,为祝为颂。兹接新嘉坡友人函告,谓马来亚大学(英人经办)圕现有副馆长一职出缺,劝璧备书申请,如将来事成,则不难将滞留大陆之家属设法迁移至新,如此多年离散之家庭,庶可藉此重聚耳。璧觉其言有理,又因马大圕似属意一国人接充,于是略经考虑,已于日昨将申请书填就寄新,以资审查。此事结果如何,尚难逆料,惟关于保证人一项,拟请先生担任一名(共需三人)。素承提携爱护,谅必蒙俯允也。倘不久马大来函咨询,总乞善语圆成为祷。缘璧漂泊海外业逾十四载,个人既不愿于此时回国,家人亦无法前来,长此僵持终非善策,且目前国际世局对于我国似有庞大之逆流不断冲击,其目的无非形成两个中国。倘不幸一旦成功,则美国亦非吾人安居之所,何况若干友人早已谓璧独自留美为无理,家人亦屡经催促矣。综此各项情形,璧觉实有把握时机从速离美之必要,于是对于马大缺额乃行毅然申请焉。想先生卓见或亦同情而谓然乎。不过此事甫经开始进行,一切毫无端倪,暂乞勿向他人道及而免贻日后笑柄。专此奉达,预献谢忱。敬颂崇安。不一。

晚徐家璧鞠躬谨上

十一月二十二日

尊夫人暨阖府前统乞代为候安为感。

〔University of Chicago Library, Yuan T'ung-li Papers, Box 7〕

十一月二十五日

徐家璧覆函先生,告知申请马来西亚大学图书馆职务的前期准备和相关推荐人情况。

> 守和先生尊鉴:
>
> 敬肃者,顷奉月之二十四日手示,诵悉一是。对于申请马大馆职,渥蒙慨然赞助,曷胜感幸。至于托人预为吹嘘以利促成事,尊见极是。贺光中先生名字业经得闻,其夫人现主管马大圕中文书籍,谅早洞悉。先生既与渠暨 Blofeld 教授熟谂,倘蒙去函关照推荐,于事当大有助益,乞即烦便中惠书二公致意为感。又,现任馆长 Ernest Clark 于渠年前访美时,曾得机晤谈一次,不知渠尚能忆及否?此次璧未另致渠个人私函,盖避运动之嫌也,再者璧所请保证人除先生外,尚有马大医学院药理系主任教授林春猷先生暨英国 Somerset 县立圕分馆主任 Pickles 女士,林太太系贱内护士学校时代之老同学,后又同在北平协和医学院共事。璧与林先生即于一九三三年在平结识,此番所得内线消息即由林家供给也。Pickles 女士前系 Derbyshire 县立圕副馆长,十余年来与璧未断联络,故对璧颇为数谂,今既向一英人大学圕申请职务,故请伊人分任保荐亦属允当。刻下只静候星洲消息耳,若有些许幸运,似尚不无希望。
>
> 嘱查四人名,现仅知 Chen Chih-wen 中文姓名为"陈志文",其他尚待探询,如有所获当再修书奉陈不误。专此申谢,敬颂崇安。
>
> 晚徐家璧鞠躬谨呈
> 十一月二十五日夜
>
> 尊夫人暨阖府前乞代候安为感。

〔University of Chicago Library, Yuan T'ung-li Papers, Box 7〕

> 按:贺光中(Ho Kuang-chung),又名贺德新,北京大学法文教授贺之才(1887—1958)之子[1],1950 年至 1951 年任香港大学中文系主任,后赴澳大利亚,时任马来西亚大学中文系首任主任。林春猷,广东揭阳人,燕京大学化学系毕业,后赴英国剑桥大学留学,时在马来西亚大学任教。

---

[1] 胡颂平编著《胡适之先生年谱长编初稿补编》,台北:联经出版事业公司,2015 年,页 133。

十一月二十七日

先生覆信大维德爵士,建议其不要因自己的艺术和考古书目推迟论文集出版至 1963 年,并谈艺术和考古书目编纂亟需支持的现状。

November 27, 1961

Dear Percy:

Your letter of 9th November arrived while I was in Boston in connection with the Exhibition of Chinese Art Treasures there. Please excuse the unavoidable delay in answering your very charming letter.

If I understand from your letter correctly, your forthcoming publication will be in the nature of a symposium consisting of essays by noted scholars on Chinese art and letters. Since you will have all essays ready for printing by first of February next, it seems advisable that you go ahead with your original plans. At any rate, please do not defer its publication until 1963 simply for the sake of my bibliography on Chinese art and archaeology.

Whether my bibliography would be ready in 1963 would depend in a large measure on financial support from the American Council of Learned Societies. The Committee on Awards usually consists of men who know nothing about the history of art. I shall have a good chance of obtaining the grant, if my application is supported by such outstanding scholar like yourself.

If I am lucky to get the grant, I shall come to London in the summer and shall make my headquarters at your Foundation, if I may. My European travel would enable me to gain access to materials not available in this country.

In view of the size of the bibliography, it will be published as monograph under the auspices of your Foundation. I shall reserve the copyright for myself. I trust this arrangement will meet your approval.

Both Dr. Hu Shih and Dr. Chu Chia-Hua are not enjoying good health and I would suggest that you write to each of them, but I doubt if they could contribute an essay unless their health is fully restored. (Chu suffers from high-blood pressure, while Hu had a severe heart attack) I give their addresses below:

> Dr. Hu Shih, President
>
> "Academia Sinica"
>
> Nan Kang, Taiwan
>
> Dr. Chu Chia-Hua
>
> c/o "Academia Sinica"
>
> Nan Kang, Taiwan

Dr. Li Chi who could write on any subject in the field of Chinese art also had an attack of diabetes, so it is too tragic that he could not do much research at the present time,

Yours sincerely,

〔University of Chicago Library, Yuan T'ung-li Papers, Box 8〕

按：此件为底稿。

陈祚龙覆函先生，告巴黎出售中文书籍的书店情况及两位留法学生中文姓名，此外谈其申请资助以编纂工具书的计划。

　　守和先生有道：

　　拜读复示（廿三），藉悉各节。关于龙代巴大中院选购大陆、台湾与香港出版之重要汉文典籍，一向均系在香港或日本函托书商办理，缘以此间唯一销售大陆出版品之 Lib. du Globe, 21 Rue des Carmes, Paris 5e 事实尚不如伦敦之 Collet's Chinese BookShop, 40 Great Russell St. London, W. C. 1，如请代购任何汉籍，既费时日，尤少成果！旅巴中国同学，照例各自操作，少有往还，台北虽已派有专人在此连络，然其景象，仍难乐观。"同学会"至今根本无人筹组，"同学录"事实一直犹付阙如。就龙所知，孙参事处可能有一寄送"文教通讯"之名单，而该名单是否全系现在旅法之"学人"或"同学"，则龙仍觉难于忆测也。好在先生所问之三位同学，其中两位已经龙向中院常见之友好探明，即 Ma Min-yuan 为"马民元"、Shih Wei-shu 为"时为述"，至于彼等之住址以及 Chen Che-pen 之汉名，且容以后查得，再予报命。承允赐寄大著，委实感谢不尽。将来拜读之后，定当试在此间学界，为文介绍。至于在此商恰销售大著之代理书店，当以 A. Maisonneuve, 11 St.

Sulpice, Paris 6e 较有希望。唯以该店代销一书,每本往往高索折扣(如原书一本在此售价一千法郎,实际由彼归还书主犹不足其售价之40%,换言之,该店代售某书一本,至少其售价之60%,常为该店之进益与净利也)。先生如仍愿意请其作为代理,则盼来示告知,俾便由龙在此进行商洽。如说先生不必定在巴黎觅定代售书店,愚意先生似可径函莱登之 Brill 当局,商谈此事为宜,盖以该店本身即有英文书籍出版,而且亦如纽约之 Paragon、伦敦之 Kegan、牛津之 Blackwell、剑桥之 Heffer,并为经售汉学著述之中心也。兹有恳者:龙现在欲在美觅一公私基金资助纂制(主用英文,附印汉字):(一) A Glossary of the Technical Terms of Chinese Book(主要对象为西方中文图书馆之工作人员及一般从事汉学教学者);(二) Bibliography of the Study of Tun-huang Art(主要对象为中外从事研究敦煌艺术者);(三) Anthology of T'ang Poems on Wang Chao-chün(旨在作为西方一般读者与中国文学专家之参考)。如说目前或将来有此机缘,还祈先生惠予荐介,鼎力玉成,实为感祷。肃此,敬颂潭安!

愚陈祚龙拜上

六一,十一,廿七,于巴黎

〔袁同礼家人提供〕

按:"商恰"当作"商洽"。A. Maisonneuve 即 Adrien Maisonneuve,1936 年搬入 11 St. Sulpice,以经销东方和美洲出版物为特色。

十一月

叶楷致函先生,询问《中国留美同学博士论文目录》是否收录其论文,并告其论文相关信息。

同礼先生:

月前偕友人参观 Library of Congress,顺便在 Catalogue Sector 查看在场各人之博士论文,发现竟无弟之卡片,经管员之指导,又到另一处参看,亦未查到。失望之余,当即修书该馆,请为查察,迄尚未得覆音。今尊著《留美学生博士论文目录》亦已出版,是否亦无弟之纪录,如蒙抽暇查问,无任感祷。按弟系 1936 年 Harvard University 之 Doctor of Science,论文题目为" The properties of low-pressure gas discharge in a thermionic tube at high frequencies",西文名 Chai Yeh。

专此,即颂秋安。

弟叶楷谨上
〔袁同礼家人提供〕

按:叶楷(1911—1997),浙江杭州人,应用物理学家,1931 年毕业于浙江大学电机工程系,即赴美留学,归国后曾在北洋大学、清华大学、西南联合大学任教,1947 年赴美。《中国留美同学博士论文目录》收录其博士论文,编号为 2649。此函无落款时间,寄送地址恐误写,后被退回。12 月 1 日,叶楷又在其下补写"昨接 Library of Congress 之回信,嘱函 Chief, Exchange and Gift Division 接洽,想必无纪录也。又尊址是否已迁居? 上书为何退回? 楷又及,十二月一日。"

十二月一日

先生致信 Sidney H. Hansford,申请将《中国留英同学博士论文目录》作为 China Society 名下的特刊出版。

December 1, 1961

Prof. S. Howard Hansford

David Foundation of Chinese Art

53 Gordon Square

London, W. C. 1

Dear Professor Hansford:

Professor Simon recently suggested that I should ask your advice about the publication of *A GUIDE TO DOCTORAL DISSERTATIONS BY CHINESE STUDENTS IN GREAT BRITAIN, 1916-1961*, which I am compiling at present. He thought that if the Council approves, it could be published under the auspices of the China Society as one of its occasional papers.

The Guide will consist of 350 dissertations and will take about forty pages when printed. I shall be responsible for the printing cost, and it does not involve any expenditure to the China Society. If it could be published as an occasional paper, I shall use the same format and same color of the cover.

I shall appreciate it very much if you could advise how many copies would likely be needed for distribution in England at 15/-per copy. Do you send out advance notice to members, or leave it to a book dealer? Any advice from you will be much appreciated.

Needless to say, I am looking forward to the early publication of the second edition of your Glossary of Chinese Art and Archaeology.

With kindest regards,

Yours sincerely,

T. L. Yuan

P. S. I enclose my preface to this publication.

〔University of Chicago Library, Yuan T'ung-li Papers, Box 2〕

十二月三日

先生致信许绍昌,请"外交部"将职员中获取欧洲博士学位者开列清单并寄下。

绍昌"次长"尊鉴:

违教以来,时深企念。近年以来,吾兄主持"部务"得展长才,引企贤劳,至为佩仰。弟前以我国对外宣传,关于文化方面之资料为数无多,不无遗憾,爰将我国留学欧美之博士论文编一总目,以供政府各机关作宣传之用,亦为我国学者科学研究之忠实记录。兹《留美同学博士论文》(共二千八百人,250页)业已出版,特奉赠壹部 平邮寄上,即希指正。不识大部能否订购若干部,分发各"使领馆",即希尊酌示复是感。留欧部分正在编辑,已收壹千余人。查大部同事颇多在欧洲获到博士学位者,可否嘱人事室开列一单,注明学位名称及授与之年与学校,以资汇编。我兄对于文化事业素极提倡,想必乐为赞助,早观厥成也。专此,敬候道祺。

弟袁同礼顿首

十二月三日

又驻外"使领馆"人员名单及贵部职员录,亦盼惠寄一份是感。

〔台北"国史馆",〈"外交部"兼任职员调查表等〉,典藏号020-162300-0016〕

按:许绍昌(1913—?),字持平,浙江杭州人,时应任"外交部政务次长"。

十二月六日

先生致信钱存训,赠《中国留美同学博士论文目录》并请代为介绍、销售。

公垂吾兄:

　　弟前编之《博士论文目录》以印刷人耽误,延至最近始行出版。原拟为中国学者之成就做些宣传,只以经费困难未能多印,及普遍赠送亦实无法也。兹奉赠壹部,即乞指正,如发现有错误之处并盼示知,以便更正是盼。另寄贰拾部由印刷人径寄府上,即暂存尊处,便中望代为介绍。凡机关购买每部五元,友人愿购者则按三元五角计算可也。留美同学服务协会能代售否? 亦盼代为接洽为感。此上,顺候俪祺。

　　　　　　　　　　　　　　　　弟袁同礼顿首
　　　　　　　　　　　　　　　　十二月六日晚

　　　　　　　　　　　　　　　　　〔钱孝文藏札〕

十二月七日

莫余敏卿覆函先生,感谢告知李宗侗出售藏书的消息,已致信劳榦请其离台前获取一份书目清单,并已联系在洛杉矶分校的林同骅、胡世桢,请他们提供相应名单,另谈《西文汉学书目》等书订购事。

December 7, 1961

Dear Dr. Yuan:

Thank you very much for your letter of Nov. 3 and for your kindness to inform me about Prof. Li Tsung-tung's personal collection of Chinese books. I have written to Prof. Lao Kan and asked him to get a list for us. We are not giving up hope of Prof. Lao's coming.

Dr. Ting's address is 401 De la Fuente Street, Monterey Park, Calif.

I also have forwarded your letter to him, as soon as I received it from you.

The Chinese faculty and staff at UCLA are not very active now. As soon as I received your letter, I called Prof. Lin Tung-hua who is unofficially in charge of the group. He asked me to get in touch with Prof. S. T. Hu of the Mathematics Dept. and I did. Prof. Hu promised to give me the list of names in a week or so and several times he said he forgot about it because he has been very busy. I was waiting for the list, that is why I did not answer your letter earlier. I just called him again today and he said he will give it to me next week. I will forward it to you immediately when I receive it.

We have a copy of your bibliography: the *China in Western Literature* and our Main Library has a copy also. I suggested to Dr. Rudolph to order one for his Dept. I also recommended our Library to buy 2 copies of your *Russian Works on China in American Libraries*.

I hope everything is fine with you and your family. Season's greetings,

Yours sincerely,

Man-Hing Mok

〔University of Chicago Library, Yuan T'ung-li Papers, Box 5〕

按:1962 年,劳榦赴美在加州大学任教。Dr. Ting 应指丁骕（1913—2000）,云南曲靖人,地理学家,1927 年考入辅仁大学,次年转入燕京大学地学系,1934 年在苏格兰格拉斯哥大学（University of Glasgow）地理系学习,1937 年获博士学位,回国后长期在中央大学和中山大学任教;Prof. Lin Tung-hua 即林同骅（1911—2007）,祖籍福州,生于重庆,结构工程师、工程力学家,1928 年毕业于北京汇文中学,后考入燕京大学,不久转入交通大学唐山工学院,1935 年入密歇根大学,翌年毕业于麻省理工学院,1937 年归国,抗战期间坚持研究,并与其他工程师一同设计、制造了中运 1 号并成功试飞,1955 年在加州大学洛杉矶分校执教;Prof. S. T. Hu 即胡世桢（Sze-Tsen Hu,1914—1999）,生于浙江湖州,数学家,1938 年毕业于中央大学,1947 年获曼彻斯特大学博士学位,后在美国杜兰大学（Tulane University）、佐治亚大学（University of Georgia）执教。

房兆楹覆函先生,感谢寄赠著述并就《新疆研究丛刊》选目提出建议,如刊印西人旧绘中俄地图。

守和先生:

航笺及《勘定新疆记》均收到,惟大著一包尚未到（书款附上,日内当照寄无误）。承允赐一册，至感。

《新疆研究丛刊》应甚有用。草目十种之外，似尚可加，如《金轺筹笔》等，联喆当另有建议。依弟愚见，不妨寻出若干 1850 前出版亚洲、俄属亚洲及中国地图，以西洋人所绘制者为主，予以复制，以见当日俄国、中国界线，以与 1870 以后之地图相较。所谓事实胜于雄辩也。若用俄国出版古地图尤佳。其实即此即可作一篇文也。我案头即有伦敦出版 John C. Cary 1806 绘印之中国 Tartary 图一帧，即可作参考（L. C.舆图部可参考）。专覆，敬颂撰安。

弟兆楹
十二月七日

夫人安好，不另。

跋文或由联喆，或由我写。

〔University of Chicago Library, Yuan T'ung-li Papers, Box 2〕

按："大著"似指 *Russian Works on China 1918-1960 in American Libraries*，待考。《金轺筹笔》《勘定新疆记》，后分别作为《新疆研究丛刊》第八种、第十种刊行。

十二月九日

王方宇覆函先生，愿意将《中国留美同学博士论文目录》编入其宣传书目中。

同礼先生大鉴：

奉大函，敬悉一是。大作《留美同学博士论文目录》，方宇极愿列入所出书目之内，收到书后当即设法编辑。惟方宇近来校中业务纷繁，同时又参加 IBM 研究翻译机器中之汉语问题，时间有限，下次书目何时出版，尚不敢定。谨先函报，顺颂年喜。附拙作短文，敬请指正。

王方宇拜上
十二，九

〔University of Chicago Library, Yuan T'ung-li Papers, Box 3〕

按：王方宇（Fred Fangyu Wang, 1913—1997），生于北京，辅仁大学毕业后，赴美留学，入哥伦比亚大学，时在耶鲁大学任教。函中所谈"书目"应属同人性质，具体名称待考。

十二月十一日

陈祚龙致片先生,告知三位留法学生中文姓名及联系地址。

> 守和先生有道:
>
> 　　前次复函(客月廿七日)谅承青及。关于 Shih Wei-shu 之相当汉字,实为"施维枢"(据说渠现已经不在法国矣)。至于"马民元"之地址为"21 Rue de Stalingrad, Grenoble"。而 Chen Che-pen 之相当汉字为"沈士本",且其住址为"61 Bd. St. Marcel, Paris 13e"。肃此补复,敬颂潭安!
>
> 　　　　　　　　　　　　　　　　　　愚陈祚龙拜上。
>
> 　　　　　　　　　　　　　　六一,十二,十一,于巴黎。
>
> 　　　　　　　　　　　　　　　　　　〔袁同礼家人提供〕

十二月十二日

Sidney H. Hansford 覆函先生,告知 China Society 不便作为《中国留英同学博士论文目录》的出版方。

12th December, 1961

Dear Dr. Yuan:

I was glad to receive your letter, and I have been considering your suggestions. I think it unlikely that the China Society would be a suitable publisher for your *Guide to Doctoral Dissertations by Chinese Students in Great Britain, 1916–1961*. In the first place, the Society only accepts for publications writings which the Council considers are primarily of interest to its members, most of whom are British. Each member is entitled to a free copy of all the Society's publications. Other copies are sold to the public, but the highest price charged for an Occasional Paper is 6/-. The Society has no sales organization and most of its publications are sold through its agents, Luzac & Co., 46 Great Russell St., London, W. C. 1.

Luzacs' would probably be a suitable publisher for your Guide. In the case of China Society publications which Luzacs' sell, they receive a commission of 50% of the published price, from which they have to give a commission to retail booksellers. To advertise your guide, I should suggest that you prepare, when the book is printed, a short prospectus, which Luzacs' would circulate with their quarterly book-list. You might write to Luzacs' and ask for their suggestions.

Please let me know if I can be of further help.

Yours sincerely,

S. Howard Hansford

〔University of Chicago Library, Yuan T'ung-li Papers, Box 2〕

按：此件为打字稿，落款处为其签名。

十二月十四日　波士顿

下午三时，先生赴波士顿美术馆（Museum of Fine Arts, Boston）参观"中国古艺术品展览"在该地之巡展，遇李霖灿。〔《国宝赴美展览日记》，页242〕

按：此次先生来波士顿是参加哈佛的某学会会议。

徐家璧覆函先生，告知钱兆麒姓名的准确信息。

守和先生尊鉴：

敬肃者，本月六日来示，业已早经诵悉。尊著《留美同学博士论文目录》编竣出版，至感兴奋。此项工作繁琐艰钜，深为洞悉，大抵编纂工作，无有如此之难者。先生始终其事，不折不懈，精神至堪敬佩！渥蒙赐赠壹册，拜感无既！俟各书寄到，当细读其内容。所嘱办理各节，一切自当遵照不误，乞勿远念！前报关于钱兆骐女士姓名，"骐"字实应作"鹿"旁，此系据其本人告知也。至于 David Lu，尚未查得结果，歉甚！将来果能查悉，自必另行奉报。余不多渎，尚此敬请崇安！并贺年节，阖府百福！

晚徐家璧谨叩

十二月十四日

再者，今日并得机晤见 Walter Simon 教授，渠云日内当来华府拜访。

〔袁同礼家人提供〕

按：钱兆麒即钱泰之女。[①] David Lu 即卢焜熙（1928—2022），生于基隆，二战结束后赴美留学，获哥伦比亚大学政治学博士学位，自1960年起长期在巴克内尔大学（Bucknell University）执教。

十二月十九日

许绍昌覆函先生，遵嘱开列"'外交部'暨驻外'使领馆'职员在欧洲各大学获得博士学位人名名单"。

[①] 钱兆麒等辑《阶平老人重游泮水纪念册》（《近代中国史料丛刊》第九十七辑），台北：文海出版社，1966年，页81。

同礼先生大鉴：

　　接奉十二月三日惠书，藉悉吾兄从事编印我国留学欧美学生之《博士论文总目》，曷胜钦佩。承惠赠业已出版之《我国留美同学博士论文总目》尚未收到，谨先申谢。至本部同事在欧洲获得博士学位者，业经遵嘱编列名单一份，兹连同《驻外"使领馆"团处首长名录》暨第 199 号本部《职员名录》各一册，随函附奉，即请察收参考为荷。岢复，并颂撰祺。

　　　　　　　　　　　　　　　　　弟许○○拜启

　　　　〔台北"国史馆"，〈"外交部"兼任职员调查表等〉，典藏号 020-
　　　　162300-0016〕

　　按：该件原有询问《中国留美同学博士论文目录》定价等语，后被划掉，又此件无落款日期，但其"'外交部'稿"上标注了发函时间。"'外交部'暨驻外'使领馆'职员在欧洲各大学获得博士学位人名单"，共收录 24 人。

十二月二十日

先生致信罗家伦，商洽《国父文献目录》印行成本、印数等细节问题。

志希馆长学兄惠鉴：

　　关于影照日本外务省档案，以支票久未寄到，未能进行。两次函催"中央信托局"驻美办事处，延至　　月　　日该款始行拨出，正值馆方影照部工作最繁之时，屡次从旁催促，始分两批寄出十一月十六日及十二月十二日。最近又收到续照之件十卷，该局仍不寄款，又来信嘱先估价，手续繁多，所有□面恐非短期内方能寄上印摄。拙编《国父文献目录》大致告成，拟请吾兄写一序文中英文各一，以光篇幅，如能代恳于院长题一书签，尤所盼祷。如因目力关系不能写小字，即请吾兄大笔。此目包括英、德、法、意、俄、荷、西班牙、捷克、凶牙利各国文字，以校对关系必须在此付印，如印一千部每部成本约美金一元八角，必须预知台北方面能订购若干部，方敢付印。又该书是否可用贵馆赞助名义，抑用两馆赞助名义（党史会），敬希尊酌，俾有遵循。日前奉赠（一）拙编《苏联研究中国文献目录》由耶鲁大学出版寄上；（二）《留美同学博士论文目录》由"大使馆"转寄，即乞教正。《国父文献目录》之格式拟照第一书办理，谅荷同意。专此，即颂并贺年禧。

十二月廿日

弟之序文一俟写好再行寄上,届时当请指正也。另寄 *From Marco Polo Bridge to Pearl Harbor.*

〔University of Chicago Library, Yuan T'ung-li Papers, Box 1〕

按:《国父文献目录》(Dr. Sun Yat-sen: father of the Chinese Republic, a bibliography)先生生前、身后均未刊行。*From Macro Polo Bridge to Pearl Harbor* 即卢焜熙的博士论文,1961 年在华盛顿出版。此件为底稿,空格处付诸阙如,先生修改甚多且为正反面书写,字迹前后浸渍,不易辨识。

十二月二十一日

先生致片李书华,告知《中国留美同学博士论文目录》即将出版,请其写介绍文章。

润章先生:

前闻尊体逐渐恢复,近来当已霍然。屈指忽又一年,极愿聚谈。《博士论文目录》不日装订成帙,自当奉赠壹部,请予指正。所印无多,未能寄往台北,如承写一中文介绍刊载于台湾任何期刊,尤所感盼。虽系小品,但查明中文姓名及年岁却费去不少的时间,希望对于我国学人之科学研究有一忠实的记载也。英庚款会多赖吾兄主持,派遣优秀青年赴英研究,成绩斐然。弟近又编成《留英同学博士论文目录》,共三百五十人,已函骝先询明台北方面能订购若干部,方敢付印,一俟出版自当奉赠,请求教正也。敬候俪祺,并贺年喜。

弟同礼

十二,廿一

〔Columbia University Libraries Archival Collections, Shuhua Li Papers, 1926-1972, Volume II: Modern Eminent Chinese Leaders〕

按:该信写于先生及夫人所印贺卡上。

先生致信普实克,告耶鲁大学出版社将寄赠《苏联研究中国文献目录》,并请其在捷克文献中留意中国艺术与考古书籍、孙中山相关文献。

December 21, 1961

Dear Professor Prusek:

I have recently asked my publisher to send you a copy of my

compilation entitled: *Russian Works on China in American Libraries, 1918–1960*. Please accept it with my compliments.

I am at present compiling two bibliographies: (1) on Chinese Art and Archaeology; and (2) on Sun Yat-sen, 1866–1925. I am sure that there is a great deal of literature in Czech language which is not found in the United States. I would therefore appreciate your help if you could solicit the assistance of your experts to send me a list of Czech literature on these two subjects.

Your help in sending me the literature on Marco Polo is especially appreciated. When the ms. is published, I shall certainly send you a copy. If you need any American book, please let me know. I shall be glad to send it to you.

With Season's greetings,

Yours sincerely,

T. L. Yuan

按：此件为录副。

十二月二十二日

郑天锡覆函先生，愿为《中国留英同学博士论文目录》撰写序言，但须稍待至明年一月。

670 E. Lincoln Ave., 1, 1A

Mount Vernon, New York

22nd Dec., 1961

Dear Dr. Yuan:

Thanks for your letter dated 11th Dec. enclosing a draft Preface for your coming work. I have been extremely busy lately. That is why I have been rather late in my reply. I was also a little confused when I received your letter, because just two days before I met at the China Institute a man, named Albert Lu, who spoke to me more or less about the same or rather same sort of thing. Now, I have found out that what he wants is my biographic notes, and so the matter is clear.

As you do me the honor of asking me to write the Foreword of your work, I shall be glad to do so. But I have some urgent work to do at present and, therefore, hope that you won't mind if I send you my draft by the end of January.

We had the pleasure of seeing your daughter in London at our house last year. We hope she is quite well.

With best wishes for a Happy New Year.

Yours sincerely,

F. T. Cheng

〔University of Chicago Library, Yuan T'ung-li Papers, Box 2〕

按：此件为打字稿，落款处为其签名。

十二月二十八日

罗家伦覆函先生，感谢代为复制日本军部及外务省档案胶片，并告汇美金及续订杂志等事。

守和吾兄道鉴：

（一）九月十三日惠书及附件，均敬奉悉。

（二）关于复制日本军部及外务省档案胶片事，承吾兄费神代为联络办理，无任感纫！顷接 John S. Connor, Inc.通知，该项胶片已于本月十二日交"Pioneer Mart"轮运台，下月当可到达矣。

（三）本馆为编写《开国》及《抗战实录》，须在国外搜购有关史料图书，兹再由本馆寄奉美金外汇壹仟元之汇票壹张（系台湾银行美金汇票，号码为 C49567），票面写明吾兄抬头，请收到后见复为感！

（四）兹附奉承本馆续订之杂志通知单三份，每种均续订一年，请费神代开支票分别寄往，拜托拜托！

（五）吾兄之征集办公费，均已代为送存台湾银行，兹将九月至十二月份送款单两张附奉，请查收。又附上一九六二年一月至六月份空白收据六张，请加盖名章寄下。

专此奉复，敬颂道祺！

弟罗家伦敬启

十二，二八

此信正将发出时，接奉十二月二十日手书，容另复。惟尊函中提及代印 mirco 系于十一月十六与十二月十二两批寄出，本馆所接到通知只十二月十二日的一批。容查明稍后再闻。

〔University of Chicago Library, Yuan T'ung-li Papers, Box 1〕

按：此件为文书代笔，落款、补语为罗家伦亲笔。

十二月三十一日

先生致信钱存训，请其协助台北故宫在美巡展人员觅一合适住所。

公垂吾兄大鉴：

弟近到波士顿参观故宫文物展览，该项文物将于一月二十日运往芝城，将来到芝城后，尚希予以协助。弟已告杨云竹"公使"，渠与令兄在"外部"同事多年，想必来请教。又工作人员李霖灿、那志良、庄尚严三人将随古物乘大汽车或火车来芝城，愿在 Art Institute 左近觅一小旅馆或能做饭之 apt.，不识能代觅否？该处在市中心恐不易也。《论文目录》已转寄贵馆，日内即可寄出（共二十一部），一切偏劳，谢谢！顺候教祺。

弟同礼

十二月卅一日

〔钱孝文藏札〕

按：1961 年 12 月 1 日至 1962 年 1 月 1 日，"中国古艺术品展览会"在波士顿美术馆巡展，2 月 16 日至 4 月 1 日，在芝加哥美术馆（The Art Institute of Chicago）巡展。27 日，李霖灿、那志良等人赴芝加哥大学图书馆拜访钱存训，后者驾车陪他们寻找合适的住处，最后在黑石公寓觅得一间。[1]

庄尚严致函先生，述病况并谈其拟辞去台北故宫博物院职务。

守和先生道席：

严于上月廿一到纽约，廿二日即来 Boston。长途飞行，来此之后应酬频繁，更以展览诸事忙乱，遂致病倒入院。在院之时欣闻先生因事来波，因不能外出，缘悭一面，怅惘何如。严来美之先曾作种种计划，华盛顿之行原在计拟之中，此番病后是否能于波士顿城展览完毕之前赶往，此刻仍不敢定也。小儿庄申庆生于北平，长于抗战逃亡之中，大学卒业曾在南港"中央研究院"史语所从事研究工作，于今秋来

---

① 《国宝赴美展览日记》，页 277。

美,刻在 Princeton 研究院专攻东方美术与考古,后生晚辈谨报告先生知之。严明夏归国,拟辞去故宫主任名义,能得退休更好,否则今后亦只能从事研究工作。行年六五,体力日衰,此种打算,先生以为何如?玄老在台甚好,惟血压仍高耳。寂居旅舍,拉杂书此。敬候年安,并请夫人懿安!

后学庄严顿首

一九六一、十二、卅一

　　故宫近刊《汝窑》一本,刻印卅六幅,由严主持,由吴玉璋写作,已出书(香港开发公司印行)。闻值美金卅五元。

　　又《王羲之墨迹》一册,将现存右军法帖均皆收入,编写考证诸文,由严一人包办,由日本大塚承印,闻不久亦可出书。近来工作如何而已。严又及。

〔University of Chicago Library, Yuan T'ung-li Papers, Box 8〕

按:"玄老",应指李宗侗。《故宫藏瓷:汝窑》版权页标注的时间为 1961 年 6 月。"《王羲之墨迹》一册"即《晋王羲之墨迹》(《故宫法书》第一辑),"国立故宫"、"中央博物院"联合管理处发行,日本大塚巧艺社印刷,1962 年 3 月初版。

十二月

先生所编 *A Guide to Doctoral Dissertations by Chinese Students in America, 1905-1960*(《中国留美同学博士论文目录》)出版。

按:先生编辑留美、留英、留欧各国博士论文目录之设想,可追溯到北京图书馆时期,1928 年夏,该馆曾致函留学各国学子征求博士论文。[1] 本书由蒋梦麟题中文书名,郭秉文撰英文序言,"中美文化协会"("Sino-American Cultural Society", Inc.)赞助发行。

是年冬

先生联系石田幹之助(Mikinosuke Ishida)教授,请其协助搜集有关新疆的外文史料,后者为先生介绍其学生渡边宏(Hiroshi Watanabe)。〔《新疆研究文献目录:1886-1962》(日文本)序〕

先生所编 *Russian Works on China, 1918-1960 in American libraries*(《苏联

---

① 《北京图书馆月刊》第 1 卷第 2 号,1928 年 6 月,页 126。

研究中国文献目录》①)以单行本刊行,出版方为耶鲁大学。

　　按:本书共分八大类,书目词条 1348 个,此前《华裔学志》登载之 Russian Works on China, 1918–1958 a selected bibliography 则只收录书目词条 318 个。

是年

先生曾赴耶鲁大学查阅文献资料,时任该校图书馆中文编目工作的胡应元对先生印象非常深刻,且就实际问题多多请益,先生不厌其详、一一解答,并嘱今后如有问题可以随时来函讨论。〔《思忆录》,中文部分页 25〕

　　按:此后,胡应元曾多次写信求教先生,其接受圣路易斯华盛顿大学图书馆东方部负责人之聘亦是听取先生的意见。

---

① 该书译名参照本年 12 月 20 日先生与罗家伦信中的表述,徐家璧与先生信函中则称作"俄文中国论著"。

一九六二年　六十八岁

一月三日

先生致信罗家伦,告知美金汇票已收并已按要求续订期刊三种。

> 志希:
>
> 　　奉到十二月廿八日手书并台湾银行美金壹仟元汇票壹张,均已拜收。应购何种书报,望开单示知,以便遵办。敝意 German Pol. Docum 应购全份,尊处续订杂志三种,均已续订,支票亦已寄出,俟收据寄到再行寄奉。关于日本档案胶片,尊处第一批通知书一事,正在查办中,容再□。
>
> 一月三日
>
> 〔University of Chicago Library, Yuan T'ung-li Papers, Box 1〕
>
> 　　按: German Pol. Docum 应指 Documents on German Foreign Policy,参见本年 8 月 23 日先生覆罗家伦信。此件为底稿,本信应于 1 月 9 日送达。①

一月八日

李济覆函先生,告其将为大维德爵士撰写论文。

> 守和吾兄大鉴:
>
> 　　奉新年惠函,敬悉种切。晓梅兄处已转达尊意。弟一切如恒,惟眼力日衰,工作更受限制耳。大维爵士亦有函向弟征文,并限一九六三年底缴卷,弟已允其所请。希望贱体尚能维持两年。知关锦注,特以奉闻。匆覆,并颂年禧。
>
> 　　内人附笔致候。
>
> 弟李济谨启
>
> 一,八
>
> 〔University of Chicago Library, Yuan T'ung-li Papers, Box 8〕

---

① 《罗家伦先生文存补遗》,页 670。

按:"晓梅兄"即高去寻(1909—1991),河北新安人,考古学家。

此件为打字稿,落款处为其签名。

莫余敏卿覆函先生,告预售《中国留美同学博士论文目录》情况,并寄上先生所需加州大学教职员名录,另谈劳榦尚未到校及李宗侗旧藏出售等事。

January 8, 1962

Dear Dr. Yuan:

　　Thank you for your letter of Dec. 11th and for your beautiful Christmas present. It was very kind of you and Mrs. Yuan.

　　I have sold 4 copies of your *Guide to Doctoral Dissertations*, 2 to institutions and 2 to individual persons. I am sorry to say that I have not yet received the books so I can not do anything for you now. Did you send them to my home address or to UCLA Library?

　　If it is convenient for you, will you please send me 2 invoices (3 copies each) addressed to Oriental Library UCLA Library, Los Angeles 24, Calif., and to Dept. of Oriental Languages, University of California, Los Angeles 24, Calif.

　　I am enclosing herewith a copy of UCLA Faculty and Staff, which you requested sometime ago.

　　Prof. Lao Kan has not arrived yet. After you told me about Prof. Li Tsung-tung's collection, I have written to Prof. Lao. He did not answer my letter but he wrote to Dr. Rudolph saying that Prof. Li will send me a list direct but up to the time of writing, I have not received it yet. Anything I should do now?

　　Our kindest regards to you and your family,

Yours sincerely,

Man-Hing Mok

〔University of Chicago Library, Yuan T'ung-li Papers, Box 6〕

一月十一日

先生致信杨光祖,请其寄下个人所撰理论、应用数学论文篇目。

January 11, 1962

Prof. Kwang-Tzu Yang

University of Notre Dame

Notre Dame, Ind.

Dear Prof. Yang:

As my bibliography on Chinese mathematics will soon be published by the American Mathematical Society, I take the liberty of writing to you for a favor.

Although I have included a number of your articles selected from various journals, I am afraid that I might have overlooked your other papers of mathematical interest. I shall therefore be much obliged if you could send me a list of your papers in the field of pure and applied mathematics which in your opinion should be included in this bibliography. As I shall submit my manuscript to the AMS at the end of this month, I hope you could send me your list at your convenience.

I shall be glad to send you a copy of this work, if desired. With sincere thanks for your help,

Yours sincerely,

T. L. Yuan

〔University of Chicago Library, Yuan T'ung-li Papers, Box 7〕

按:杨光祖(1926—2020),苏州人,1948 年赴美留学,入伊利诺伊理工学院(Illinois Institute of Technology),1955 年获博士学位,随后受聘于圣母大学(University of Notre Dame)航空和机械工程系。此件为打字稿,落款处为先生签名。该信底部有杨光祖的标注"I would love to have a copy, Thank you. K. T. Yang 1/13/62"。

一月十五日

郑天锡致函先生,寄上《中国留英同学博士论文目录》序言,并指出先生自序中的细节问题。

15th January, 1962

Dear Dr. Yuan:

I hope you received my letter dated 22nd Dec. last. Though I said I would send you the Foreword by the end of this month, I am glad that I am able to do so now.

In your Preface you said: "The present listing begins with the year of 1916 when Dr. Fatting T. Cheng and Dr. M. T. Z. Tyau received the LL. D., etc."

In the interest of historical accuracy, it may be advisable to have this verified by the academic Registrar of the London University. For when the degree was formally conferred on me in 1916 by Lord Rosebery, then Chancellor of the University, I was the only one (with my wife present) to receive the LL. D. And as degrees (apart from Hon. ones) are conferred only once a year, there could not be another person to receive the same degree in the same year, if he did not receive it at the same time as I did. It is possible that Dr. Tyau's thesis was approved in 1916; for I do remember that, after my thesis had been approved, Sir John Macdonell, in congratulating me, told me in advance that Dr. Tyau's thesis would be approved too.

As to the spelling of my first name, I would suggest to have it spelt as "Futting", which is that I use now.

Lastly, I hope that my Foreword will, in your opinion, serve the purpose.

With best regards,

Yours Sincerely,

F. T. Cheng

〔University of Chicago Library, Yuan T'ung-li Papers, Box 2〕

按:该目刊行时,先生自序中就郑天锡英文名表述仍为 Fatting T. Cheng,并未修改为 Futting T. Cheng,但根据郑天锡意见,未将刁敏谦(M. T. Z. Tyau)与其并列为最早在英国获得博士学位的中国留学生。

一月十八日

先生致信郭廷以,对福特基金会批准资助近代史所颇加赞赏,并请代询所查庚款留英学生姓名及博士论文题目一事的进展。

量予吾兄著席:

年前 Ford 基金会发表补助贵所研究工作,弟等闻之无任欣慰,此皆吾兄年来努力之结果,敬贺敬贺。只要政局安定,大家可以安心工作,以后美国补助之机会尚多,此仅为开始之举动也。日前与廷黻兄谈及此事,渠亦以为然。关于补助同人生活一事,如必须在此款内挪用,似可用研究补助费名义(Research assistance),报账时当无问题。惟其他各所人员不能分润者,或须另设他法,亦一头痛之事也。鎦先先生处常见面否?弟现编一《留英同学博士论文目录》,十一月杪时曾函请写一封面,并询留英庚款学生九批,每批若干人,请查覆,迄今月余未奉只字,想渠身体健康均无恙也。如不进城,能电询否?至盼至盼。拙编《留美同学论文目录》已由"教育部"转送,约月后方能寄到。另寄《苏联研究中国文献目录》,即乞教正是幸。顺候教祺。

弟袁同礼顿首
一月十八日

　　弟近编《俄人研究新疆论文目录》,以杂志论文为最多,贵所新印关于新疆之书并盼赐寄一份是感。

〔台北"中央研究院"近代史研究所档案馆,〈郭廷以〉,馆藏号069-01-02-089;《郭量宇先生日记残稿》,页303〕

按:时,朱家骅身体违和。此信于23日送达南港,25日送达郭廷以处。

一月十九日

伍藻池覆函先生,遵嘱在纽约代售《中国留美同学博士论文目录》。

同礼先生大鉴:

　　大札拜读,大著亦同时拜收。遵命每册价五元,如是中国学生或学者则减为三元五角。吾辈远寄异国,公还能纵笔著作,感佩非常。池为个人生活与兴趣,乃以此小小商店,遣其余生,诚非得已,为之奈何!生逢离乱,亦只此而已。如驾临纽约,还请过我,得聆教益,感幸多矣。匆匆寄言,不尽一一。专此,即请文绥。

弟伍藻池顿首
一月十九

〔University of Chicago Library, Yuan T'ung-li Papers, Box 3〕

按:"小小商店"即友方图书公司(Hansan Trading Company),位于纽约拜也街(Bayard Street)65号。

一月二十九日

陈省身覆函先生,寄上其发表论文清单并告数学所研究人员杰出者姓名。

　　守和先生惠鉴:

　　　　前奉手示,稽覆为歉,以索拙作论文单,兹附上一份(候印此论文单系稽覆主要原因)。数学所大约系 1947 成立,研究人员之杰出者有:李华宗,陈建功,王宪钟,胡世桢,吴文俊,杨忠道,廖山涛,陈杰等。经弟手聘请者先后约十五人。附单中文姓名,只知道一人,可见孤陋,大作出版后希见赐一份为感。

　　　　专覆,即请大安。

　　　　　　　　　　　　　　　　　　　　　　　弟陈省身上

　　　　　　　　　　　　　　　　　　　　　　　一月二十九日

　　　　　　　〔University of Chicago Library, Yuan T'ung-li Papers, Box 7〕

　　按:李华宗(1911—1949),广东新会人,英国爱丁堡大学博士;陈建功(1893—1971),浙江绍兴人,三次赴日留学;王宪钟(1918—1978),祖籍山东,生于北京,英国曼彻斯特大学博士;吴文俊(1919—2017),祖籍浙江嘉兴,生于上海,法国斯特拉斯堡大学博士;杨忠道(1923—2005),浙江平阳人,美国杜伦大学博士;廖山涛(1920—1997),湖南衡山人,美国芝加哥大学博士;陈杰(1924—2005),四川大学数学系毕业。

郭廷以覆函先生,谈近代史研究所人事、研究近况。

　　守和先生道席:

　　　　去春病后,体力迄未复元,益以俗务丛集,遂使问候有缺。日昨获诵手教,多承关垂,感愉难宣。福特补助计划,商谈两年,卒底于成,实有赖于长者及诸友好之大力协助,公私均感。此事接洽伊始,弟即预料一旦实现,定有不少麻烦。台湾人事既极端复杂,鸡虫得失争夺尤烈。适之先生为敷衍应付(实同自找烦恼),力主将补助费分润于近史所以外人士若干名,并特置一咨询委员会处理之。及消息正式发表,吴相湘首先发难,无理取闹,其师姚从吾(咨询委员)起而和之。吴尚可不论(此君近五六年来,对罗志希、李玄伯、刘寿民等不断攻击,去冬尤烈。即先时与之合作之李定一、全汉昇、王德昭亦一一闹翻,恶言丑诋,对弟比较还算客气),而从吾举动,则不可解。因之弟决心请去，半月未到所办公，适之先生坚留不放，所内同事且以一同进退相胁，而客居此间之韦伯先生 Martin Wilbur 亦以大义相责，情意至为殷切。适在此时，公权兄以在美看到吴某攻诋近史所文章，大为愤慨，专函劝勉，更给予不少勇气，遂暂打消辞意。惟今后问题仍多，正如长者所言，仍一头痛事也。照规定，近史所同人可有十二名（所外四名）接受补助，但今春实仅七名，研究计划有"民六—十一之中俄交涉"、"民六—九年白俄在华活动"、"恭亲王传"、"淮军志"等，张贵永、杨绍震、胡秋原另有专题（"淮军志"、"恭亲王传"由弟协助）。廷黻先生于近史所之爱护一如长者，便中请代达一切。

骝先生去年健康欠佳，近月大为好转，不时晤及。关于《留英同学博士目录》一书封面题签，弟可负责办到。关于留英庚款学生名单及每次人数，前天已与前庚款会总干事徐可熛兄谈及，须检阅庚款会档案，稍需时日，以开箱既费手续，又值旧历新年也。按此项档案三年前已决定移交近史所，以人力不足，且无空余房间放置，迄未接收。无论如何，弟必有以报命也。

尊著《苏俄研究中国文献目录》已收到，谨谢。此类工作，造福士林实钜。近史所新刊《中俄关系——新疆边防》月前曾邮呈一部，如未邀鉴，当续寄，希示知。

适之先生卧病两月，刻仍在静养中。渠准备于三月初去华府主持中华基金会，惟亲友均不赞同其作长途旅行。鸿声校长想常晤及，恳为致意。拉杂写来，不成章法，至希谅宥。祗此，敬问双福！

　　　　　　　　　　　　　　　　弟郭廷以拜启

　　　　　　　　　　　　　　　　元、廿九

〔University of Chicago Library, Yuan T'ung-li Papers, Box 2〕

按：徐可熛（K. P. Hsu，1903—？），字公起，浙江鄞县人，上海圣约翰大学学士，后任私立光华大学史地教员，20 世纪 30 年代在管理中英庚款董事会服务，后赴英，1946 年 11 月接替朱家骅出任该会总干事。[1]

李济致函先生，请协助史语所拍摄平馆暂藏国会图书馆红格本《明实录》

---

① 《中央日报》，1946 年 11 月 15 日，第 5 版。

钞本。

守和吾兄：

本所校勘《明实录》工作，前后已逾三十年，此兄所素知。最近为付印事，曾前后奉达，并蒙惠允将贵馆所藏之红格本，由本所校勘付印。去年暑假已将《太祖实录》全部校勘完毕，并用国会图书馆之显微照相摄制翻印，经过困难甚多，但已陆续克服。现可奉告者太祖部份可望于本年暑假出版。惟续印问题，困难仍多，一切详黄彰健君函中。

今所求于吾兄者，为下列二事：

一、请惠允开箱将红格钞本《太宗实录》至《熹宗实录》重摄一次，并将其 negative microfilm master 直接径寄本所。

或二、由国会图书馆将原装之 negative microfilm master 惠借本所。

此二事以何种较为适宜，应请吾兄代为决定。其一切费用，自当由本所担任。惟有一事需请吾兄特别惠予注意，此次所筹之印刷经费系由长期发展科学委员会拨付，但有年度限制，如逾期不用，此款即需缴还。

此项印刷费用限今年十月底以前用完，故弟希望最迟于三月底以前能将此项底片航空邮寄本所。此事关键在国会图书馆，敬祈转达本所此项申请。便中并祈告以台北学术界对于国会图书馆之合作与协助，极感欣佩。

此间学术界亦愿尽力促进此项合作。最近台湾大学将其所藏之世界孤本《琉球宝案》，交本院摄制，并由东亚学术研究计划委员会出资摄制一份，专送国会图书馆，大约暑假前可以寄奉。

由此一例，即可表示此间学术界同仁合作之诚。

不尽一一，专此奉恳，敬颂春安。

弟济敬启

一九六二年元月廿九日

〔University of Chicago Library, Yuan T'ung-li Papers, Box 3〕

按：《琉球宝案》后定名为《历代宝案》，是 15—18 世纪琉球国首里王府的外交文件，全书包括三集 262 卷、目录 4 卷及别集 4 卷，现存三集 242 卷、目录 4 卷及别集 4 卷，由汉文写成。黄彰健

（1919—2009），湖南浏阳人，历史语言学家，后当选台北"中央研究院"院士。此件为打字稿，落款处为其签名。

黄彰健致函先生，谈"中研院"史语所影印平馆所藏红格本《明实录》（缩微胶卷）校勘问题，拟请先生在国会图书馆将该书找出并摄成负片寄台或将其母片寄台。

守和先生道鉴：

贵馆所藏红格钞本《明实录》，本所据美国国会图书馆摄赠之positive microfilm copy 放大影印，前承先生惠允，无任感谢。该书中之《太祖实录》，于去夏付印，今年夏季可以印成。现为继续影印太宗以下各朝，须解决影印技术困难，谨奉命向先生提出一请求。

红格本原书及显微影卷之中缝，均无书名、卷数及全书总页数。而微卷所摄，系原书不同一页之两面，印行时势须剪开，并剔出其所摄重复处。为免印刷厂商将卷页次序弄乱，本所所定影印程序如下：

（1）据红格本微卷，以洗像纸放大成黑底白字照片。

（2）清理照片次序，剔出其重复处。于照片旁添注书名、每卷卷数、每卷页数及全书总页数。

（3）取红格本之晒蓝本再核对一次，以免次序有误。并补钞红格本缺页，附入影印。

（4）仿阮刻《十三经注疏》例，于照片正文右旁，各本有异文处，作一圆圈，以便读者检对校勘记。

（5）以整理毕黑底白字照片，交印刷厂商照相制版。

此一影印程序唯一不满人意之处，厥为所放大之黑底白字照片，有些字的笔划不甚明晰，须用白粉描。否则照相制版后，师字可以变成帅，天字可以变成大，有些字笔划不全，失去本所校刊之意义。

既需用白粉描，未免描错，遂嘱印刷厂商描时须比对红格本之晒蓝本。但事实上印刷厂商并不遵守此一规定，因此描错不少。彰健及三助手遂只好取晒蓝本与印刷厂商所描过之照片一一比对，经四校，始将其描错处一一改正。《太祖实录》正文计三千七百二十面，比对需时，结果去夏付印，要本年夏才能印成。

本年度长期发展科学委员会拟拨款新台币 69 万元，以为影印《明实录》之一部份费用，本所为免除上述之缺陷，遂与此间印刷厂研究，据 positive microfilm copy 直接照相上板,不修版中之字。结果所印出之样张,字体不走样,亦不错,但其缺点则为:

(1)某些字的笔划不够明晰。

(2)添注书名、卷数、每页页数及全书总页数,需在印刷厂中为之,技术上较困难。彰健因无法取与晒蓝本核对,不能保证卷页一定不错。

(3)无法在照片正文右侧作一圆圈,与即将印成之《太祖实录》,格式不一样。

(4)据 positive microfilm copy 直接上版,需高度技术,费用贵约一倍多。

因此考虑再三,认为只有据红格本之 negative microfilm master 放大制版,最经济,不需描,字体不走样,不会错,印行格式可与《明太祖实录》一样,方便学者利用。

在去年年初,彰健即曾请敝所图书室主任蓝乾章先生,函请美国国会图书馆据其所藏 negative microfilm master 覆制 negative microfilm master。惟据函覆,覆制所得,字迹不清楚,而原书已装箱,遂只好作罢。

现在印行结果既不理想。因此只好提出一新的请求,请先生惠允开箱,将太宗、仁宗、宣宗、英宗、宪宗、孝宗、武宗、世宗、穆宗、神宗、光宗、熹宗《实录》取出,交美国国会图书馆直接根据原书,摄成 negative microfilm master。由《太宗实录》至《熹宗实录》,约 26000 叶(每页两面)。摄影时一次可摄不同一页之两面。每一次摄影所需费用为美金 0.035 元,总计约需美金 910 元。其开箱、照相及航空邮寄等费用,均由本所负担。

红格本《明实录》藏于京师图书馆时,缺卷缺页甚多。及贵馆成立,陆续访求搜购,并据北京大学所藏本钞配缺卷缺页。其后经本所商借晒蓝,据各本校雠,遂成善本。此书得成善本,此实贵馆及本所两机构之功劳。

此书如能影印完成,此自为先生所渴愿。适之先生、济之先生虽已康复,但尚在调养。此函由彰健执笔。想先生一定愿意协助完成此一计划。

已另函美国国会图书馆 Dr. Beal.

专此,敬颂道安。

后学黄彰健顿首敬上

壹月廿九日

又有一策,即请美国国会图书馆惠借所藏《明实录》红格钞本之 negative microfilm master 用航空邮寄本所。本所收到后,立即用晒像纸放大,再将母片用航空邮寄奉还,航空寄此费用由本所负担,如此似更省事。书成后,当奉赠美国国会图书馆若干部。此事不知是否可行,亦敬请先生惠允代为洽办酌订,无任感祷。彰健谨又及。

〔University of Chicago Yuan T'ung-li Papers, Box 3〕

按:此件为打字稿,落款处为其签名。

二月十二日

古根涵基金会主席 Henry A. Moe 致函先生,请审察陈受颐申请资助的研究计划。

February 12, 1962

Dear Dr. Yuan:

May I have your careful judgment of Dr. Shou-yi Ch'en's quality as a scholar, of his proposal for research, and of him with reference to that proposal? A statement of the project is attached hereto.

As always, anything you say will be held in the strictest confidence.

Sincerely yours,

Henry Allen Moe

President

〔University of Chicago Library, Yuan T'ung-li Papers, Box 3〕

按:该函所附研究计划未存,但应为中西文化关系史研究。

二月十三日

先生致信黄彰健,告已与毕尔商洽暂借平馆寄存国会图书馆《明实录》缩微胶片母片与史语所。

彰健先生:

奉到一月廿九日惠书,欣悉《明实录》太祖部份可望本年暑假出版,此项伟大工作经过若干困难,竟底于成,首赖执事热心、毅力,始终其事,学术界同深感佩。今后续印自应克服以往困难,俾能早观厥成。惟敝馆所藏之红格本现由 Dr. Beal 保管,以种种关系不便开箱,已将第二办法向其提出,惟渠尚须以书面与有关方面商谭,方能作复。弟自当从旁催促,请馆中以原装之底片暂借贵所,其空邮寄费弟可预为垫付。恐劳远念,先此奉复。敬候时祉。

弟袁同礼顿首
二月十三日

〔University of Chicago Library, Yuan T'ung-li Papers, Box 3〕

按:此件为底稿,有相当程度的修改。

二月十九日

李济覆函先生,告已与胡适、钱思亮沟通,由中基会购买二百部《中国留美同学博士论文目录》。

守和吾兄:

今晨曾于黄彰健兄函中附呈数语,谅荷鉴察。今日下午已分别与适之先生及思亮兄在电话中交换关于购买尊著《留美中国学生博士论文集目录》之意见,他们均主张向 China Foundation 作此申请。适之先生并嘱弟函达左右此意,请兄即向中华教育基金会纽约办公处正式请求。胡公赴美开会之愿望,照近日情形看来,大约可以实现。胡公并拟在此间之预备会先提出此一小数(两百部的购买费),胡、钱二位都认为不成问题也。专此奉达,并颂著安。

弟济拜覆
二,十九

〔University of Chicago Library, Yuan T'ung-li Papers, Box 1〕

按:先生在右下标注"三,五日复"。此函应以航空信方式寄出,但似因邮资不够被退回。

黄彰健覆函先生,请协助获取平馆暂存国会图书馆《明实录》红格钞本的缩微胶片。

守和先生道鉴:

今晨济之先生转来先生赐书,知蒙惠允为敝所洽借美国国会图书馆图书馆所藏贵馆《明实录》红格钞本之 negative microfilm master,无任感谢。上月底,敝所图书室主任蓝乾章先生曾有信与 Dr. Beal 商洽此事,惟尚未得覆。仍敬请先生鼎力洽催,玉成此事,无任感祷,临颖神驰。耑此,敬请道安。

后学黄彰健顿首敬上

一九六二年二月十九日

守和兄:

购买大著事已与思亮兄洽商,俟有确信再奉覆,《明实录》事一切拜托。

济,附笔。

〔袁同礼家人提供〕

Heinrich Busch 致函先生,告知因刊物内容和成本因素,《华裔学志》《华裔学志丛书》均不适宜刊行先生 Russian Studies on Sinkiang 书目,并告知可能的刊印成本。

February 19, 1962

Dear Mr. Yuan:

We have repeatedly discussed your inquiry concerning the publication of your Russian Studies on Sinkiang and have come to the conclusion that your bibliography is too lengthy for inclusion in *Monumenta Serica*-it should take up rather more than 150 printed pages. We also feel that the bibliography would not well fit in our monograph series. This however should be immaterial to you since in any case we are unable to publish the bibliography as a separate volume unless somebody bears the printing expenses. If this is the case, we are willing to cooperate in the publication in any capacity you wish, whether as publishers, or co-publishers, or agents. A note to this effect, for which you ask in your letter of January 16, is enclosed in this letter.

It may help you to form a rough estimate of what the printing expenses will be when you know that the production of 500 copies of a 500 page volume of *Monumenta Serica* costs about one million Yen (360 Yen=1 USA $). The costs could probably be somewhat lowered if the printing were done in another press (by linotype) and on less good paper.

We have just received the copy of your *Guide to Doctoral*

Dissertations by Chinese Students in America, which you kindly sent us. We are glad to have this useful reference work and thank you very much for it.

Sincerely yours,

H. Busch S. V. D.

〔袁同礼家人提供〕

　　按:此件为打字稿,落款处为其签名。

二月二十日

陈源致函先生,告中英文化协会现状,建议先生可向 China Society 申请出版资助。

　　守和吾兄:

　　　　手教未早覆为罪。所询名单中九人,除周慧敏女士(闽人,海军武官之妹)外,均无知者。

　　　　中英文化协会现在仅存名义,会长为 Sir Alwyne Ogden(前上海总领事),执行委员会残缺未补,已多年未开会,会员名单亦不存,经费久无来源,现仅为“自由中国”新闻社之附庸。主持新闻社者为陈尧圣兄,每年借用文协会及“自由中国”之友社名义,聚餐三四次,如是而已。尊刊出版,恐不能有何资助。曾商之尧圣兄,彼辞以爱莫能助也。此外有 China Society 对此毫无兴趣。又有 Universities China alumni,即为管理从前庚款学生者,与此有关,且有基金,惟与中国庚款委员会已断关系,执行委员多左派学者,不知有无兴趣也。专此,顺颂著祺。

弟源顿首

二月廿日

〔University of Chicago Library, Yuan T'ung-li Papers, Box 5〕

　　按:Sir Alwyne George Neville Ogden(1888–1981),剑桥大学毕业,1912 年 12 月来华,先后在北京、河南、山东、汉口等使领馆服务,1937 年任上海总领事。

二月二十一日

徐家璧致函先生,告收到《中国留美同学博士论文目录》册数及推销进展。

　　守和先生尊鉴:

　　　　敬肃者,十九日下午,McGregor & Werner, Inc.(Washington 12, D.

C.)寄下之尊编《中国留美同学博士论文目录》十一册,经已收到,欣慰无似! 拜检内容,深觉搜罗完备,编排翔实,足征工作浩繁,煞费苦心,苟非具有卓绝毅力如先生者,曷克臻此! 行见风行海内外,其造福于学术界,裨益于中美文化沟通者,诚匪浅鲜,敬谨为先生成功贺! 两日来除本馆已购二册,璧自购一册外,其余尚在设法推销中,一俟集有成数,或全部售罄时,当将书款汇上不误。本馆所购,书款拾元,即由总馆会计组直接寄上。谨此奉报,并颂崇安!

晚徐家璧鞠躬

二月廿一日

尊夫人前,并乞叱名候安为感!

〔袁同礼家人提供〕

二月二十二日

先生致函朱家骅,感谢其撰写《中国留英同学博士论文目录》题签,并询两位留德同学中文姓名。

骝先先生尊鉴:

顷奉赐书,并承惠寄题字,至以为谢。《留英同学论文目录》虽已编就,以此间筹款不易,只得暂缓付印,颇愿能于一年之内将留德、奥、瑞、法、比、意、荷兰部份分别完成。如能改在台北付印较为经济,届时再请援助。此类工作原系"教育部"应办之件,只以年来国家忧患频仍、文献无征。及今不图,以后更难着手。故愿勉力为之,谅荷赞许。又民元以前,留德学生获到博士学位者有:(一)马德润(1907 Berlin),(二)Li, Fo-ki(1907 Bonn)研究物理,(三)周泽春(1909 Berlin),(四)Tsur, Nyok-ching 政治(1909 Leipzig),(五)周慕西(Berlin 1911)。颇愿知第二及第四人之中文姓名,如承指示,尤所欣感。敬候道祺。

晚同礼顿首

二月廿二日

〔University of Chicago Library, Yuan T'ung-li Papers, Box 6〕

按:Li, Fo-ki 即李复几(李福基),1907 年在波恩大学获物理学博士学位,先生在《中国留欧大陆各国博士论文目录》中误作"李赋基"。Tsur, Nyok-ching 即周毅卿,经济学家,1909 年获得莱比锡大学经济学博士学位。题签虽经朱家骅撰写,但《中国留英同学博士论文目录》似未使用。此件为底稿。

二月二十三日

钱思亮致函先生,告已与李济、胡适商妥《中国留美同学博士论文目录》印刷费补助事宜。

　　守和先生惠鉴:

　　　　济之先生转示二月十三日手教,敬悉尊编《留美同学博士论文目录》印刷费之申请补助事宜,弟意似以向中基会提出为宜,经与适之先生商谈,亦表同意。届时弟自当从旁力促其成也,济之先生另有函奉复,想已察及。弟定于三月八日离台飞美参加中基会年会,良晤匪遥,诸容面罄。耑此,敬颂时绥。

　　　　　　　　　　　　　　　　　　弟钱思亮敬上
　　　　　　　　　　　　　　　　　　二月二十三日

　　　　　〔University of Chicago Library, Yuan T'ung-li Papers, Box 1〕

　　按:此件为打字稿,落款处为钱思亮签名。

二月二十四日

叶公超致函先生,感谢寄赠《中国留美同学博士论文目录》。

　　守和吾兄左右:

　　　　顷承惠赠《留美同学博士论文目录》一册,搜集达十年之久,煞费苦心,置诸案头,可资稽考。特复布谢,顺颂时绥。

　　　　　　　　　　　　　　　　　　弟叶公超敬启
　　　　　　　　　　　　　　　　　　二,廿四

　　　　　　　　　　　　　　〔袁同礼家人提供〕

二月二十六日

下午,先生和夫人致电江冬秀,吊唁胡适去世。

GREATLY SHOCKED PASSING OF BELOVED DOCTOR HU. WISH CONVEY YOU OUR SORROW AND DEEPEST SYMPATHY.

　　　　　　　　　　　YUNG TUNGLI AND HUIHSI

　　　　〔台北胡适纪念馆,档案编号 HS-NK01-283-035〕

　　按:2月24日下午6时半,胡适因心脏病猝发离世。

宋晞覆函先生,告知"国防研究院"无力补助《新疆研究文献目录》中文本出版。

守和先生道鉴:

一月卅一日,手书祗悉。承赐《目录》两种,至以为感。俟收到后,当珍藏参阅。本院图书馆出版之期刊论文索引,已洽请林馆长子勋奉赠一套。关于《新疆目录》之补助经费事,业经面报晓峰师,渠以本院经费困难,不如"中央党部"或"教育部"时之活动,无能为力为歉,嘱转请鉴谅为幸。后学所编《宋史研究文录目录》,已成初稿,拟于年内出版,印行后当呈奉指正。专此布复,祗颂道安。

后学宋晞敬上

二月廿六日

〔University of Chicago Library, Yuan T'ung-li Papers, Box 5〕

按:《宋史研究文录目录》应指《宋史研究论文与书籍目录》,后由"中华学术院""中国文学学院"史学研究所列为"史学研究目录"第一种,1966 年 11 月初版。先生在此函右下注"五月四日复"。

二月二十七日

袁同礼覆函 Henry A. Moe,建议该基金会给予陈受颐资助以进行相关研究。

February 27, 1962

John Simon Guggenheim Memorial Foundation

551 Fifth Avenue

New York 17, N. Y.

Dear President Moe:

Thank you for your letter of February 12 with regard to Dr. Shou-yi Ch'en's application for a Fellowship.

Having done considerable research in this special field, Dr. Ch'en is undoubtedly the most suitable person for undertaking this important task. I earnestly hope that it will be possible for your Foundation to give him the necessary support.

Owing to my absence from Washington, I much regret that I have not been able to write to you earlier.

Sincerely yours,

Tung-li Yuan

〔University of Chicago Library, Yuan T'ung-li Papers, Box 5〕

　　　　　按：该件为录副。

二月二十八日

钱泰致函先生,感谢赠书并允诺撰写《留欧博士论文目录》序言。

　　　守和先生左右：

　　　　奉手教并惠赠《留美同学博士论文目录》,捧读一过,觉其搜罗完
备、体裁精细,尤以注明中文姓名难能可贵。此编非常困难,在他人恐
早半途中止,而我兄毅力精进卒底于成,嘉惠后进,洵为必传之作,佩
谢佩谢。承示拟续编留欧部分,并谓"忧患频仍,文献无征,以后益难
着手",语重心长,更佩高瞩。委作弁序,容当勉力为之,附去小品,聊
供一粲。专此布谢,敬颂著安,并祝潭福。

　　　　　　　　　　　　　　　　　　　　　　　　弟钱泰上言
　　　　　　　　　　　　　　　　　　　　　　　　二月二十八日

　　　　再,大著何处可以购得,便中示及以备友人询问。

　　　　再,留法同学第一人得博士者为陈继善,一九一二年毕业,并及。

　　　　　　　　　　　　　　　　　　　　　　　　〔袁同礼家人提供〕

叶良才覆函先生,告收到悼念胡适函件并《中国留美同学博士论文目录》三册。

　　　　　　　　　　　　　　　　　　　　　　　　Feb. 28, 1962

Dear Dr. Yuan:

　　　Thank you for your letter of February 25.

　　　We were deeply grieved by Dr. Hu's death. It was a great loss!

　　　The foundation meeting has been postponed. We have received 3
copies of your Doctoral Dissertations.

　　　　　　　　　　　　　　　　　　　　　　　　Sincerely,

　　　　　　　　　　　　　　　　　　　　　　　　L. T. Yip

　　　　　〔University of Chicago Library, Yuan T'ung-li Papers, Box 1〕

　　　按：此件为打字稿,落款处为叶良才签名。

三月五日

先生覆信李济,请史语所同人代写致胡适挽联,并告与国会图书馆商洽借
用《明实录》胶片进展。

　　　济之先生：

　　　　上周奉到手教,承示各节,至以为感。廷黻兄于旬日前接到适之

先生电报,谓已决定三月八日搭机来美,弟等正拟在此欢迎,不意突然作古,实为国家无法衡量的损失,悲从中来,不能自已。曾函请劳贞一兄代拟挽联,于公祭前送到。近闻贞一兄业已来美,将来如再举行追悼会,可否请兄委托院中同事代拟代写一挽联 代垫款容再补呈,至为感荷。今后院务谅当局必请吾兄主持,以资熟手,想亦无法摆脱,惟贵体尚未完全恢复,仍盼遵医生之嘱格外节劳。院中人事方面较为复杂,适之先生久不痛快,今后可请总干事代为应付,可省却不少的麻烦也。关于借用《明实录》胶片事,馆中已同意照办,惟有一条件即请特别注意,勿将底片予以损坏,请转告照像人格外小心是盼。馆中公事须经过五部门之核准,恐非短时期内所能办到。弟已再四催询,请其速办,但迄至本日为止,该公文尚未由 Dr. Beal 处发出也。除每日催办外,恐劳远念,特以奉闻。专此,敬候俪安。

弟袁同礼顿首
三月五日

〔"中央研究院"历史语言研究所档案〕

先生致信 Eugene L. Delafield,邀请其一同增补胡适西文著述目录,并寄赠《中国留美同学博士论文目录》。

March 5, 1962

Dear Mr. Delafield:

All of us are shocked by the sudden passing away of our beloved Dr. Hu. As you probably know, he was scheduled to fly to Washington on the 8th of March, and I have been expecting to see him here. You can well imagine what a severe blow to all of us.

When we compiled the selected bibliography of his writings in 1957, there were a number of papers which Dr. Hu did not think it worthwhile to have them included. Since then, I have recorded other papers which he contributed to various journals, but which did not remain in his memory. If you are not too busy in the next month or so, perhaps we might compile a fuller bibliography and have it published in Taipei.

I wonder if you have a copy of his paper read before "the Sino-American Conference on Intellectual Cooperation" at Seattle, July 10,

1960. If you do not happen to have it, I shall be glad to make a copy for you.

Under separate cover, I am sending you a copy of my recent work. On pages 225 – 226, you will find a record of the honorary degrees conferred upon him by various institutions of higher learning.

With cordial regards,

Yours sincerely,

T. L. Yuan

〔袁同礼家人提供〕

陈祚龙覆函先生,告知龙章个人信息及工作情况,并谈先生寄来书籍之分配。

> 守和先生有道:
>
> 前接大示(二,廿),敬悉各节。龙君担任此间"使馆"专员之职务,其别号为"平甫",其贤内助系来自台北,现已有一千金。彼与龙相互亦有过从多年。兹以陈雄飞业经任命为"驻比大使",龙君是否会被调动,一时尚难定言也。
>
> 关于前承寄下之大著:《留美博士论文录》原收六份,除龙留一份,给戴一份,给 Gernet 一份,尚余三份。《新疆书目》原收五份,除龙留一份,给亚洲学会一份,尚余三份。
>
> 两种所余共六份,现已悉数售予此间之书商,合计凑得 100(壹佰)新法郎,今特附此奉上,尚请查收。
>
> 另由海路邮奉拙纂《汉官七种通检》一份,将来先生收到后,当请勿吝教正是幸。耑此,恭颂潭安!
>
> 愚陈祚龙拜上
>
> 六二,三,五于巴黎。

〔University of Chicago Library, Yuan T'ung-li Papers, Box 2〕

按:"戴"指戴密微;Gernet 即 Jacques Gernet(1921-2018),法国汉学家,通译作"谢和耐"。《汉官七种通检》,1962 年由巴黎大学汉学研究所出版。

三月六日

孟治致函先生,告华美协进社将在下月举行胡适悼念活动,请先生协助收集胡适本人著作和相关文献。

March 6, 1962

Dear Dr. Yuan:

Our mutual friend, Dr. Hu Shih, died in Taiwan on February 24, 1962.

A memorial meeting will be held here at four o'clock the afternoon of Monday, April 16, 1962, at which time addresses will be given by a few of his intimate friends including "Ambassador T. F. Tsiang" and President Grayson Kirk of Columbia.

Dr. Hu Shih had many friends in the United States who may not be able to attend this meeting. We are asking some of his friends to send tributes in Chinese or English, anecdotes, and other historical or biographical material such as letters and other writings by him, either on loan or for permanent preservation. We aim to have a permanent repository of Hu Shih papers by and concerning him. This material would be made available to researchers and others. Part of the collection may be published in a memorial volume.

Anything you may send, any suggestions you may make toward this project would be greatly appreciated. We would also appreciate your sending us a list of persons whom you think knew Hu Shih well and are in a position to contribute to the collection.

Sincerely yours,

弟治

Director

〔University of Chicago Library, Yuan T'ung-li Papers, Box 9〕

按：3 月 1 日，孟治致信蒋廷黻，询问出席悼念活动的人选，后者于 2 日覆信，建议华美协进社邀请华盛顿地区的洪培克、恒慕义、先生，此外刘锴作为胡适任驻美大使时的顾问也应受邀出席。此件为打字稿，落款处为其签名。

三月八日

先生致信陈之迈，询问有无可能订购《中国留美同学博士论文目录》。

之迈"大使"仁兄著席：

　　上年年底大驾来京，适弟赴波士顿，未及倒屣，至以为歉。返澳洲后，贤劳如何？闻该处对于中国文化之研究日见进展，吾兄宣扬文化，为国增光，引企新猷，至为佩仰。兹交邮奉上《留美同学博士论文目录》，即乞教正。主旨侧重文化宣传，如贵馆经费稍裕，可否订购一二十部_{每部美金三元五角}，赠送澳洲各学术机关。即希卓裁，示复为感。专此，敬候俪祺。

弟袁同礼顿首
三月八日

〔台北"中央研究院"近代史研究所档案馆，〈陈之迈〉，馆藏号062-01-07-110〕

　　按：1959 年 7 月 11 日，陈之迈被任命为驻澳大利亚"特命全权大使"，"赴波士顿"即先生前往波士顿参观故宫文物展览。

刘麟生致函先生，请在国会图书馆代查《昭代明良录》《国朝分郡人物考》二书中关于张弼之生平史料，并抄录相关文字。

守和先生博士赐鉴：

　　弟已缮清《张凤翼小传》，现正从事于张弼之资料。惟馆中无童时明《昭代明良录》及过廷训《国朝分郡人物考》。童书第 18 卷 40a 叶，及过书 25 卷 31a 叶，皆载有张弼之事迹。如原文不长，可否烦明公托人抄录。抄录费用，由弟酌偿。如原文太长，尚烦望代印，印费亦请示知。渎神，无任惶汗之至，敬请著安。

小弟麟生谨上
三，八

　　此二书皆见尊处《善本书目录》。

〔University of Chicago Library, Yuan T'ung-li Papers, Box 2〕

西门华德覆函先生，告知前往华盛顿的行期安排，对伦敦大学注册课未能积极配合查找博士论文题名和中文姓名表示歉意并提出建议，另询问国会图书馆是否藏有西夏文《华严经》。

8th March 1962

Dear Dr. Yuan: -

　　Your letter of 5th March reached me this morning. It is awfully good of you to think of us in making your plans as far as Boston is concerned but I do not propose to go to Washington before the latter half of April. So please do not let our trip in any way interfere with your plans though I gratefully appreciate that you had been thinking on those lines.

I am not expecting my wife in Toronto before the end of the month; however, she will be in New York as early as Saturday. So, there would be no possibility of complying with your wishes. She will stay in New York with my brother and I shall be sending to my wife your letter and a carbon of the first part of my reply to find out whether there are any alternative ways to meet with your wishes. Let me in any case kindly have your measurements.

I am afraid I have not thanked you yet for your letter of 11th February. When writing to you about Forke's work-a bibliographical delicacy, I would say in view of the wrong first name put in by no less a person than the editor of the series! -I did not realize that you are not aiming at completeness when compiling your bibliography.

I was also sorry to hear that you found Miss □□□□ the registrar of our school non-cooperative. The registrations for Ph. D. thesis, and yours probably go back a very long time and are in any case not kept by the registrar of any of the many colleges of the University but by the University itself, since the University is responsible for conferring a degree. So, my advice would be to write to both the Internal and External Registrars about any Chinese name you still wish to find out about, giving the approximate time of registration. I am quite sure that Dr. Whitaker would oblige to let you have the Chinese characters once the registration forms in question have been dug out and forwarded to her on the understanding that she will return them immediately.

I do not know who Dr. Ma Yi-Yi is. I don't recall her as an internal student who would have worked in the field of Chinese Language and Literature and thus came within the purview of the Far Eastern Department.

There is one further matter. This concerns the Hsi-Hsia language.

When at Columbia I came across the Japanese made replica of part of the *Avatamsaka Sutra* (*Hua-yen ching*). I wrote about this to Mr. Grinstedt of the British Museum who writes as follows: "Your letter of October did not reach the Museum. I am intrigued by the modern *Avatamsaka*. I suppose it is a copy made by the sons of Lo Chen-yu with their specially designed movable Hsi-hsia type. Oddly enough, the Library of Congress and Tenri library both have *Avatamsakas*. I hope they are not both chapter 41. Sorry I do not know more about the subject, but my reference is Nevsky, Tangutskaya filologiya, Vol. 1, p. 28, footnote. I suppose the best person to ask would be Nishida Tatsuo, who worked on the Tenri fragments." I am fairly sure in my mind you would be able to let me know what the Congress Library has. I have not so far written to Mr. Nishida.

　　With many thanks and all good wishes.

Yours sincerely.

W. Simon

〔袁同礼家人提供〕

按：When at Columbia 应指 University of British Columbia，非纽约之哥伦比亚大学；Mr. Grinstedt 即 Eric Grinstead（1921—2008），新西兰汉学家、西夏文学家，20 世纪 40 年代赴英国并在伦敦大学进修，曾任大英博物馆东方印本及写本部（Department of Oriental Printed Books and Manuscripts）助理；Tenri library 指日本天理大学图书馆；*Avatamsaka Sutra* 即《华严经》；Nevsky 即聂斯克；Nishida Tatsuo 即西田龙雄（1928—2012），日本语言学家，专攻西夏文、藏语。

谢寿康覆函先生，告其博士论文题名。

守和吾兄赐鉴：

　　顷得手示，藉悉起居安泰为慰。令爱来此观光，至欢迎，达到时当有照拂，请释锦注。弟在比京大学所提论文名称为 Les Emprunts de guerre français (1914—1918)，弟并未接受名誉博士学位，惟比国王家文学院 Académie Royal de Langue et de Littérature Françaises de Belgique 曾于 1946 十月十二日选举弟为该院院士。专此奉覆，敬请双安。

弟谢寿康拜上

内人附候

三月八日

〔University of Chicago Library, Yuan T'ung-li Papers, Box 5〕

按：Les Emprunts de guerre français (1914–1918)，直译作"一战时期法国的战争公债"。

三月九日

先生覆信孟治，表示将出席纪念胡适活动，并愿意协助华美协进社收集胡适的著述，询问其能否寄来美金 30 元用于复制相关文献。

March 9, 1962

Dear Dr. Meng:

Thank you for your letter of March 6 in regard to a memorial meeting to be held April 16 at the China House. I shall certainly arrange to be present on this occasion.

It is most fitting that the China Institute will pay tribute to him by setting up a permanent repository of his papers and writings about him.

As it may take sometime for you to gather together printed materials, I am enclosing herewith a number of printed cards which would serve as a bibliographical guide. I shall also send you a copy of my bibliography of his writings from which you could select items of interest.

There are a number of Dr. Hu's earlier writings buried in a number of journals. The only way to make them accessible to the public is to reproduce them either by photostat, or by zerox. If you could send me a small check for $ 30, I shall be glad to do this for your Institute. Receipts from the Library of Congress will be sent to you when I send you the reproductions.

If there is anything else you wish me to do, please do not hesitate to let me know.

Yours sincerely,

T. L. Yuan

Kindly inform me the present address of Mr. Frank M. H. Shu.

〔Wesleyan University, Meng Archive〕

按:孟治在该信 30 美元部分标注 OK; Frank M. H. Shu 似指徐铭信(Frank M. H. Hsu),此处拼写或有误,且影响了孟治 3 月 14 日的覆信。

钱泰致函先生,寄赠其新著《中国不平等条约之缘起及其废除之经过》。

　　守和先生左右:

　　　　日昔张府喜事,得亲雅教,丰采依然,不减当年,甚以为慰,近惟著祺顺适为颂。拙作《中国不平等条约之缘起及其废除之经过》寄奉教正,另一本可否乞兄代送国会图书馆,费神至感。此外,美国何处对于中文著作有兴趣之图书馆或大学可以致送者,拟请指示一二,琐渎殊不安也。专布,敬颂著安,并颂潭福。

弟钱泰上言
三月九日

〔University of Chicago Library, Yuan T'ung-li Papers, Box 2〕

　　按:《中国不平等条约之缘起及其废除之经过》,1961 年 6 月台北"国防研究院"初版。

三月十二日

先生致信李书华,告知将赴纽约参加胡适追悼会并请协助查明留法博士中文姓名。

　　润章先生著席:

　　　　前奉手教,诸承指示,至以为谢。此次适之突然作古,虽因心脏关系,但年来院中人事复杂,心中实感不快,如不担任院长,必可多活数年则无疑问,实国家之大损失也。下月之纪念会弟拟前来参加,并愿于前一日到府拜访,藉可畅谈。近见北平电话簿1958,下列诸人尚有电话,其他友人均已撤去矣。弟鉴于我国留欧博士论文迄无记载,究有若干人得学位者亦无人知之,颇愿于一年之内予以完成。此中困难重重,尤以查明中文姓名为甚。兹奉上一单,多系中法学生,想有熟识之人,即希赐予注明。如承转询其他同学,尤所感荷。余容面谈。顺候俪安。

弟同礼顿首
三月十二日

　　又 Institut d'urbanisme 之论文是否博士论文? 法国硕士之论文亦

称 thesis，故须详细查明。

〔Columbia University Libraries Archival Collections, Shuhua Li

Papers, 1926–1972, Volume II: Modern Eminent Chinese Leaders〕

按："下列诸人"未存名单，Institut d'urbanisme 似指巴黎城市规划

学院（Institut d'urbanisme de Paris），其可授予的最高学位应为

硕士。

先生致信叶良才，告知将出席在纽约举行的悼念胡适活动，并向中基会申

请由该会购买 200 部《中国留美同学博士论文目录》。

March 12, 1962

Dear Mr. Yip:

　　Dr. Chih Meng has written to say that a Memorial Meeting in honor of Dr. Hu will be held at the China House on April 16. It is most fitting that such a meeting is to be in New York. I shall certainly arrange to be present and shall assist in gathering material about Dr. Hu's writings.

　　From the enclosed letter of Dr. Li Chi, you will note that Dr. Hu and Dr. Chien suggested that I should submit a request to the Foundation with regard to the subscription to the 200 copies of the *Guide to Doctoral Dissertations*. I am therefore enclosing herewith my request. I shall be grateful to you if you could bring it to the attention of the Trustees at their next meeting.

　　With sincere greetings.

Yours sincerely,

T. L. Yuan

〔University of Chicago Library, Yuan T'ung-li Papers, Box 1〕

　　按：Dr. Chien 应指钱思亮。

刘麟生致先生两函，代郑天锡、钱泰订购《中国留美同学博士论文目录》。

其一，

　　守和尊兄勋右：

　　　　顷郑莼老交下支票一纸，计 12.50 元，敬烦惠寄《留美博士论文目录》二册至华昌公司"郑大使"Dr. F. T. Cheng，又三册请寄"钱大使"Dr. T. Tsien, 99–31 64th Avenue Forest Hills, Apt. D17, Long Island, N.

Y. 至为感荷。再颂俪绥。

弟麟生敬启
12/3/62

其二，

守和博士：

顷奉上支票一纸，应为 17.50 元，误作 12.50 元，故再补奉一纸，计五元，即祈莞存。敬颂著绥。

弟麟生再上
三，十二

〔袁同礼家人提供〕

徐家璧覆函先生，已遵嘱将《中国留美同学博士论文目录》赠予赵曾珏并请其登载广告，另告知自己将赴耶鲁大学图书馆工作。

守和先生尊鉴：

敬肃者，昨接月之七日手示，敬悉一是。嘱送赵曾珏先生之函件暨《博士论文目录》一册，业于今午遵示送到，乞毋远念！赵先生允于将出版消息登载中国工程师学会 *Newsletter*，以广周知，并立即通话该刊主编知照，想将来订购者或甚踊跃也。另致哥大图发票三份，亦已照转，但近日林顿卧病，付款事恐又将稍缓数日。耶鲁方面，因需人孔亟，于璧面洽，嗣将申请表格填就寄去后，不出五日，即行收到耶鲁图正式聘函，名义为 Chinese Bibliographer and Research Assistant，负责中文图书事宜，年薪定为柒仟伍佰元，较之哥大强胜甚多，故当即回覆允就，于是此一大转变，竟于短期内洽定。刻下璧尚未与林顿谈及此事，但于本月十五日呈辞时，谅无过大困难。现时计划拟在哥大工作至四月底为止，五月间前来华府、康桥学习两周，再行清检杂物，觅房搬迁，于六月一日即在耶鲁上班。俟来华府后，尚拟详请训示，以备遵循，不胜翘企之至！匆匆，敬颂崇安！

晚徐家璧鞠躬
三月十二日

尊夫人前候安！

〔袁同礼家人提供〕

按：赵曾珏（1901—2001），字真觉，上海人，1924 年毕业于南洋大学,后由交通部委派赴英、德两国学习,1928 年转美国哈佛大学学习电机工程,翌年获得硕士学位,归国后曾任浙江大学教授,时应在哥伦比亚大学电子研究所从事研究工作。

三月十四日

先生致信钱存训,告所寄《中国留美同学博士论文目录》延迟之缘由并请转赠图书。

公垂吾兄:

此次艺展想多帮忙,本拟来芝观光。兹以琐事相缠,未能如愿。《论文目录》经印刷人一误再误,延至二月中旬方始寄上,共 21 部,想已收到。内中以校对不精,尚有错字。兹奉上一单,请便中代予更正,再行出售。又中美学人服务社 Studley 女士来信,谓迄未收到,亦盼提出壹部代赠该女士是荷。代售事是否委托该社办理,诸希尊照。一切费神,统俟面谢。顺候俪安。

弟袁同礼顿首

三,十四

〔钱孝文藏札〕

按:“此次艺展”即中国古艺术品展览。Studley 即 Ellen M. Studley,应为 1963 年 3 月 12 日钱存训致先生函中的“桑女士”,1924 年来华,曾担任北平 Woman's Union Bible Training School 校长。[1]

孟治覆函先生,寄上支票用以支付复制胡适相关文献的初步费用,并表示十分高兴先生愿意担任此项工作。

March 14, 1962

Dear Dr. Yuan:

Many thanks for your prompt response. Referring to your kind suggestion, I am enclosing a check for the amount you mentioned. It is very kind of you to volunteer to undertake this important work.

We also need your help in making a plan to collect other materials by

---

[1] Xiaoxin Wu, *Christianity in China: a scholars' guide to resources in the libraries and archives of the United States*, Taylor and Francis, 2008, p. 153.

or concerning Hu Shih, such as his letters or anecdotes from specific individuals, particularly his intimate American friends.

It has been some time since I heard from Frank Shu. The only address we have for him is c/o Mrs. Frank M. Shu, Hartford Theological Seminary, Hartford, Conn., which we received in 1959. I believe he is in Brazil.

Sincerely yours,

Chih Meng

〔University of Chicago Library, Yuan T'ung-li Papers, Box 9〕

按：Frank Shu 似有误，或指徐铭信（Frank Hsu），待考。此件为打字稿，落款处为其签名。

三月十五日

先生为 *Bibliography of Chinese Mathematics, 1918-1960*（《现代中国数学研究目录》）撰写前言。〔*Bibliography of Chinese Mathematics, 1918-1960*, 1963〕

按：除自序外，本书前冠有陈省身本年 11 月 30 日所写引言。

先生致信西门华德，告知国会图书馆藏西夏文《华严经》所存章节，并愿意协助影照，并追忆一九三四年聂斯克出示苏联所藏西夏文献。

March 15th, 1962

Dear Professor Simon:

Thank you so much for your letter of 8th March. I am glad to hear that Mrs. Simon is expected to be in New York soon. I presume that this is her first visit and hope she enjoys the life there.

About the Hsi-Hsia sutra, I checked it with the Curator and we found it is chapter 41. If Grinstedt wishes to have a photostat copy for the British, it can be easily arranged. Just ask him to write a letter to the Chief, Chinese Section, Library of Congress, Washington, D. C.

As to Nevsky's book, it was only published in 1962, although he passed away in 1938. I had the privilege of meeting him several times in Leningrad and he showed me all the Hsi Hsia MSS. (in 1934). But I never thought that he would be liquidated so soon. Prof. Ivanov   , who was also an expert in the Hsi Hsia language also suffered the same fate about that time.

We are looking forward to your forthcoming visit as we have so much to talk about the old Peking days.

Yours sincerely,

T. L. Yuan

〔袁同礼家人提供〕

按：As to Nevsky's book, it was only published in 1962 应指 *Тангутская филология*（*Tangut Philology*），1960 年出版，1962 年 获列宁奖（Ленинская премия）。1937 年，聂斯克被捕并遭杀害，先生误记作 1938 年。该件为录副，空白处付诸阙如。

崔道录覆函先生，略述学历经过并附上留学意大利中国学生名单之部分中文姓名。

同礼先生尊鉴：

曩在国内，素仰高风，三十八年罗马识荆，益增向往。犹忆当时蒙赐通信地址，时光易逝，忽忽十有二年矣。日前奉读三月九日赐书，欣闻先生近编《留欧同学博士论文目录》，对于中西文化交流贡献必巨，曷胜钦庆。承询晚所提论文题目及留义经过，用敢陈述如下：晚系西南联大法律学系毕业，三十五年侥幸考取教育部第二届公费留学生，翌年受派罗马大学（并非传信大学）攻习法律，一九五一年获法学博士（Dottore di Giurisprudenza）学位。论文指导教授 Fulvio Maroi 先生以典权系中国独特之物权制度，希望晚作一介绍，遂决定论文题目为：《论典权》（Il Diritto di Tien）。晚除根据我国法典及学说将典权制度作一分析研究，并与义大利民法中类似典权之各种物权加以比较外，似无多大新义。就晚所知，中国留义学生无论战前战后大多学习政治、艺术、音乐，在义大利国立大学中正式获得法律学位者似尚以晚为第一人。义大利法律传统宏富深厚，刑法实证学派（positive school）自 Lombroso 以降，尤开现代刑法及犯罪学之先河。晚原思不揣浅陋，聊尽介绍之责，不幸生逢乱世，连年奔波，求生不遑，所志百无一成，每念及此，未尝不怅恨而长叹息也。大函诸多奖饰，感愧交并，爰略陈衷曲，倘蒙长者不以琐渎见责则幸甚矣。附下同学名单，其英文姓名谨就晚所知者附注奉上，尚祈检收，为祷。他日来华府自当趋前拜谒，敬聆教益。崀此奉覆，敬请大安。

晚崔道录谨启

三月十五日

〔University of Chicago Library, Yuan T'ung-li Papers, Box 5〕

按：时，崔道录应在克拉夫林大学（Claflin University）任教。

三月十六日

先生致信莫余敏卿，询问劳榦是否已经到美，感谢代售书籍，并告已请陈受颐为胡适撰写讣告。

March 16, 1962

Dear Mrs. Mok:

In my letter yesterday, I forgot to ask whether Professor Lao Kan has by any chance arrived. Has Professor Li sent to you his list?

Thank you for your letter of March 12 with the check for $24.50. I hope I have not given you too much trouble, as it is not easy to sell books of this kind. I only hope that the users of this volume may find it useful to their work.

I have sent a copy to Prof. Chen and have asked him to write an obituary for Dr. Hu Shih to be published in the *Journal of American Oriental Society*.

The Royal Society in London published obituaries of all scientists of Great Britain. So with men of letters. But we Chinese do not have the inclination to write obituary notice, and there is no way of finding out the year of death, except going through the daily papers.

The death of Dr. Hu is a great loss to China. Men like Professor Chen who knows him well should write such notices as a record.

With many thanks,

Yours sincerely,

T. L. Yuan

〔University of Chicago Library, Yuan T'ung-li Papers, Box 2〕

按：该件为录副。

三月十七日

黄彰健覆函先生，请竭尽可能从旁催促国会图书馆早日借出《明实录》缩微胶片之母片。

守和先生道鉴：

得赐书，承惠允代敝所接洽，感何如之。日前济之先生出示尊函，知国会图书馆 Dr. Beal 已有允意，为之欣喜无已。旋敝所图书室主任蓝乾章先生亦得 Dr. Beal 来书，谓已将敝所请求层转该馆行政最高当局请其决定，惟需时数月始可分晓。敝所蓝君昔曾受业于 Dr. Beal，当即函覆告以此间印书款，拨款机构有时间限制，希国会图书馆能早日决定。此事以健愚计，既需层转决定，苟非先生及 Dr. Beal 惠允层层洽催，则公文旅行势将担搁时日，此则健不得不百拜敬请者也。

Dr. Beal 去年来台，健曾于适之先生处见之。未敢作函以请，亦敬祈先生转达健意，为感。先生年尊德劭，饮誉学林，健夙所钦仰。屡以事奉渎清听，无任惶恐。余不一一。专此，敬颂道安。

后学黄彰健顿首敬上

一九六二年三月十七日

济之先生言"所借 negative master，如有损坏，史语所当负责赔偿。"今日阅蓝先生覆 Dr. Beal 书底稿，漏言此事。后日星期一，当请蓝先生补致 Dr. Beal 一书。彰健谨又及。

〔袁同礼家人提供〕

三月二十一日

徐家璧覆函先生，前请在哥伦比亚大学馆藏《中国社会及政治学报》影照胡适文章业已办妥。

守和先生尊鉴：

敬肃者，三月十日函后，复又连奉十二日暨十六日两示，均已知悉。前胡先生在联合国大会演讲辞，经已遵嘱托请严文郁兄影照，但迄今尚未寄下。如尚未照，当请其停止，以免与"蒋大使"所影者重复也。此间所有《中国社会政治学报》，并非庋藏本馆，故查找借影，手续较繁，因之迟误若干时日，至感歉仄，伏乞宽恕为祷！兹于日昨，业将该志所载胡先生一文照妥二份，用特交邮寄上，以便应用。影照费每张壹角，计共壹元贰角，似可由售出之《博士论文目录》款中支付（现又售出一册），未识可否？另本馆藏有少数《留美学生季刊》，惟因迁移，各书凌乱，尚未能查得，可否再缓数日，以备检查。倘发现有胡先生作品,自当代影不误。谨此奉报,敬颂崇安!

晚徐家璧鞠躬

三月二十一日

尊夫人前,并乞代为候安!

〔袁同礼家人提供〕

按:"《中国社会政治学报》所载胡先生论文"即 Intellectual China in 1919,刊《中国社会及政治学报》(*The Chinese Social and Political Science Review*)第4卷第4期。

保君建(安曼)覆函先生,寄上三册《中国留美博士论文目录》书款。

守和吾兄大鉴:

前奉手教,当已函覆。顷接到寄下《中国留美博士论文目录》,共参册,除壹册交馆,另由馆购贰册外,特遵嘱随函奉上美金捌圆,敬请查收。耑此敬谢,并祝大安。

弟保君建谨上

三月廿一

附美金支票一纸。

〔University of Chicago Library, Yuan T'ung-li Papers, Box 1〕

按:1959年8月至1967年2月,保君建担任"驻约旦哈希姆王国大使"。

三月二十二日

先生致信 Robert B. Ekvall,告知自己无法参加美国亚洲学会年会,但希望其在会后可以途经华盛顿面谈。

March 22, 1962

Dear Mr. Ekvall:

It is a pleasure to learn that you plan to attend the meeting of the Association for Asian Studies to read a paper on Tibet. I should like so much to be present, but owing to pressure of work, I have to give up the trip.

I hope that after the meeting you could arrange to pay us a visit here. Among other things, I should like to show you my bibliography (on cards) on Sinkiang. Sometime ago I asked Dr. Wilhelm to come to

Washington, but I have not had a reply.

Looking forward with much pleasure to seeing you,

Yours sincerely,

T. L. Yuan

〔University of Chicago Library, Yuan T'ung-li Papers, Box 1〕

按:该年美国亚洲学会年会在波士顿举办。此件为录副。

三月二十六日

卫德明覆函先生,赞同先生将书稿在香港或日本印刷的想法,并建议先生直接联系戴德华等人。

March 26, 1962

Dear Mr. Yuan:

Thank you very much for your good letter of March 7th. Your idea of having your manuscript published in Hong Kong or Japan is excellent as in this case the insertion of Chinese characters would not provide any problem. I do hope that your appeal to the National Science Foundation for a subsidy will be successful. If not, you should not hesitate to ask the Far East and Russian Institute of the University of Washington for publication help. I have been out of Seattle for some time now so that I am not familiar with current details but I would expect that some money for your project could be found there. I am also confident that either George Taylor or somebody from the Inner Asia Seminar will be only too happy to support your application to the National Science Foundation.

I have sent your letter on to Seattle. Both George Taylor and Franz Michael are, however, currently out of the country so that it might take some time until you get any response from them. I advised George to get in touch with you directly so that you can furnish him with the necessary material for his supporting letter.

Sincerely yours,

Hellmut Wilhelm

〔University of Chicago Library, Yuan T'ung-li Papers, Box 1〕

按:此时,卫德明赴普林斯顿大学执职。

三月二十九日

马大任覆函先生，告知胡适旧作 A Defense of Browning's Optimism 撰写时间，但暂时无法查到另一篇文章《非留学议》刊登卷期。

March 29, 1962

Dear Dr. Yuan:

Many thanks for your letter of March 28.

I wish to tell you that the year that Dr. Hu submitted his essay on Browning for contest was 1914. Dr. Hu used a pseudonym, Bernard W. Savage. And the title of the essay is "A defense of Browning's optimism."

I am sorry to say that I was unable to locate Dr. Hu's article 非留学议. The magazine in which this article appeared is, as you said, *Chinese Students Monthly*. And you gave the Chinese title of the magazine as 留美学生季刊. We have a complete run of the *Chinese Students Monthly* from the vol. 2 on. It is an English magazine and Dr. Hu wrote a number of articles in it. But there is no accumulative index and I do not know when the article was published. I looked through the tables of contents of almost all volumes and found no title similar to the Chinese title of the article you mentioned. I wonder if you could give me a more definitive clue so that I might have a better luck in finding it.

Miss Gaskill is still the curator of the Wason Collection. I have shown your letter to her. And she is glad to hear from you.

If you are coming to the annual meeting of the Association for Asian Studies at Boston, I shall see you next week.

Best wishes.

Sincerely
John T. Ma
〔袁同礼家人提供〕

按：1914 年，《非留学议》刊登于《留美学生年报》（第三年）"建言"一栏，非 *The Chinese Students Monthly*（《中国留美学生月报》），亦非《留美学生季刊》。

劳榦覆函先生,告知在美情形及胡适先生挽辞事。

守和先生赐鉴:

奉到惠书,敬悉壹是。附寄挽适之先生辞,大致可用,惟有数处稍有问题,谨予酌改,附上祈斟酌为幸。榦现住在距学校约十个 blocks 之处,幸附近尚有公共汽车,可乘公共汽车到校。惟此间公共汽车次数较少,每十五分钟方有一次耳,每次汽车二十分钟可以到校。内子初到略有不习惯处,大致尚能适应也。专此,敬颂时安,并问阖府均安。

后学劳榦敬上
三月二十九日

附寄榦之挽胡先生辞,此挽辞已寄台北,因纽约方面亦应寄一份,以致敬意。因榦不悉华美协进会地址,敬恳先生寄挽辞时附寄此挽辞至纽约,至为拜托。

后学榦再上

〔University of Chicago Library, Yuan T'ung-li Papers, Box 2〕

按:时,劳榦应该在加州大学访学。

三月三十日

徐家璧覆函先生,询问拍摄胡适所撰文章的原则并附清单。

守和先生尊鉴:

敬肃者,前于本月二十一日寄上一九一九年《中国政治社会学报》所载胡先生论文一篇,嗣又于二十七日转上童世纲兄代摄(按即严文郁兄委托)胡先生在联大演说词,想两者均已寄达矣。童君影照之费,现正在探询中,一俟得覆,当即禀告。

此外则关于《留美学生季刊》各文事,只因该志为一研究生借去,昨始索还,璧检其内容,仅一九一七年第四卷中载有若干胡先生文字。而此等文字,多已见胡先生成册专著之中,究竟是否应一律影照,颇费踌躇。兹特将各文细目抄奉,用备选择,敬请于便中将应照各文圈示,掷还原单,以资遵办,无任企荷之至! 谨此奉呈,敬颂崇安!

晚徐家璧鞠躬
三月三十日

尊夫人前,敬乞叱名候安为祷!

〔University of Chicago Library, Yuan T'ung-li Papers, Box 10〕

按:该函附"《留美学生季报》(*The Chinese Students' Quarterly*)中
所载胡适之先生论文暨诗词"单一纸。

王赓武覆函先生,就所询之事略作答复。

　同礼先生台鉴:

　　本月十六日来函所问,不能详答,只知(一)*Straits Chinese Magazine*
新加坡国立图书馆有全份,大英博物馆则缺三五号,弟早已向新洲图书
馆定购 Microfilms,但至今尚未摄成。(二)Ma Yi Yi 为弟伦大同学,缅
甸 Arakan 回教徒,今执教于仰光大学历史系。新洲马大已改名为新加
坡大学,本校则仍为马大。弟《南洋学报》一篇为学生时代作品,取笑前
辈学者,今得先生鼓励,诚以为荣幸。西门先生抵华京,请代问候。

　　　　　　　　　　　　　　　　　　　　弟王赓武上
　　　　　　　　　　　　　　　　　　　　三月三十日

〔University of Chicago Library, Yuan T'ung-li Papers, Box 5〕

按:王赓武(1930—),华裔历史学家,生于荷属东印度(印度尼西
亚),1947 年曾入中央大学学习,1949 年后转入马来西亚大学新加
坡分校,1957 年获伦敦大学亚非学院博士学位,时在马来西亚大学
(University of Malaya in Kuala Lumpur)历史系任教,后曾任香港大
学校长。*The Straits Chinese Magazine* 是马来西亚出版的第一份英
文杂志,由峇峇娘惹(Peranakan)①中的精英人士,如宋旺相(Song
Ong Siang)、林文庆(Lim Boon Keng)等人于 1897 年创刊,1907
年终刊。Arakan 应指若开邦,位于缅甸西南部,与孟加拉国毗邻。

三月

《中国文化季刊》刊登先生文章,题为 American Cultural Influence on China
in the Field of Libraries。〔*Chinese Culture: a quarterly review,* Vol. 4, No. 1, pp. 144-
146〕

　　按:该文失收于《袁同礼文集》。

四月三日

杨云竹致函先生、夫人,告"中国古艺术品展览会"在芝加哥已顺利举办,
将赴旧金山继续巡展。

────────────────

① 峇峇娘惹,指中国移民和东南亚原住民通婚的混血后裔。

守和兄、嫂惠鉴：

久未函候为怅。芝加哥展览业于一日顺利结束。当初对此一关，各方颇多悬系，今得此结果，如释重负矣。弟于上月底曾偕那先生赴金山安排一切，留三日返此。兹定本月十日由此装火车运旧金山，金山展期为五月一日至六月十五日，未识兄等有机会来西岸一游否？金山预展定本月卅日晚举行，如有友好，望示知，当照发预展请柬。弟以杂务羁身，原拟赴西岸前访华府一行，现只得作罢，料展览全部结束后将赴华府洽办结束各事宜。芝城已届春暖，金山则百花盛开，颇呈初夏之观。在金住所尚未觅定，容另函叙。匆候俪福。

弟杨云竹拜启

内子附候

四月三日

袁清弟好。

钱教授时相晤，并承其招宴，芝大东方部有关人士曾为同人举一宴会，来宾多为熟悉中国情形之人士。

〔University of Chicago Library, Yuan T'ung-li Papers, Box 2〕

叶良才覆函先生，补寄购书费支票，并约本月十六日聚餐。

April 3, 1962

Dear Dr. Yuan:

Thank you for your card of March 29 and letter of April 2, 1962. The Book "*Foreign Relations of the United States 1943: China*" has been received. It was very kind of you to get it for us. Enclosed is our check.

I hope you will be able to have lunch with me on Monday, April 16 at about 12 o'clock. Please let me know.

Sincerely,

L. T. Yip

〔University of Chicago Library, Yuan T'ung-li Papers, Box 1〕

按：此件为打字稿，落款处为叶良才签名。

Eugene L. Delafield 覆函先生，感谢寄赠《中国留美同学博士论文目录》，并表示愿意协助增补胡适西文著述目录，但须等到夏季才能开始。

April 3, 1962

Dear Mr. Yuan

Thank you for your kind letter and for the volumes you compiled with Dr Hu's honorary degrees listed. "A Guide" certainly must have taken you many months of writing and hard work. We can use it as one more tool. Meaning that — Yes, I will be pleased to work with you in a bibliography Dr. Hu Shih's works. There is still a great deal of work to do to prepare it, and many months of work.

The passing of Dr. Hu somehow still does not seem real to me yet. I somehow expect to see him appear and say, "How are you, Eugene." I can even hear the tone of his voice as he says it. For me Dr. Hu will never die. I have had the honor of meeting many important men and women. He is the greatest that I have ever had the honor to know. We first met in 1943, that seems in some way a long time ago. Time moves on, especially as one grows older.

To come back to the bibliography, I shall not be able at present to give the time to it, I should like to. I can do a little work on it off and on this summer. When fall comes I can do much more. I hope I can come down to Washington this spring or early summer. When you and I can sit down together and do some planning of it. For there are so many details to discuss with you. How complete we would attempt to make it, etc.

Thank you again so much for your volume and your kind thought.

I remain, most sincerely,

Eugene L. Delafield

P. S. Have been out of town, so have lately returned.

〔袁同礼家人提供〕

按:该函为其亲笔。

四月五日

先生致信叶良才,告收到支票并愿于十六日与其聚餐,另告发现胡适佚文。

April 5, 1962

Dear Mr. Yip:

Thank you for your letter of April 3 and a check for $4.00. It is very kind of you to ask me for lunch on Monday, April 16, which I accept with much pleasure.

Recently I have made a considerable number of photostats of Dr. Hu's writings to be exhibited on April 16. Among them there is an article entitled: China Foundation regains its independence, which he did not remember the last time I saw him. I shall send it to you as soon as it is ready.

Yours sincerely,

T. L. Yuan

〔University of Chicago Library, Yuan T'ung-li Papers, Box 1〕

按:1929 年 1 月,China Foundation regains its independence 刊于《密勒氏评论报》第 47 卷第 9 期。该件为录副。

先生致信马大任,对因故未能前往波士顿表示歉意,并请继续查找胡适中文文章。

April 5, 1962

Dear Mr. Ma:

Thank you for your letter of March 29. I had hoped to meet you at Boston, but at the last minute, I had to give up the trip owing to the pressure of other duties.

Dr. Hu's article was published either in the *Chinese Students Quarterly* or the *Chinese Students Annual* for 1914. If you could check your Chinese collection, you might be able to find it. Both publications were issued in Chinese.

I understand that the Chinese Students Club in Ithaca has issued a directory. Could you be good enough to secure a copy and send it to me?

Please also check if the following are in your collection:

Yuan: *Russian Works on Japan*, *Russian Works on China in American Libraries*.

Yours sincerely,

T. L. Yuan

〔袁同礼家人提供〕

按:此件为录副。

四月六日

先生致信孟治,附上胡适著述影本的清单,并告已请童世纲径寄部分文献,此外建议其向 Eugene L. Delafield 发送纪念胡适活动邀请函。

April 6, 1962

Dear Dr. Meng:

Under separate cover, I am sending the photostats of some of Dr. Hu Shih's writings. Kindly check with the list herewith enclosed. Additional material from Harvard and Princeton will be sent to you as soon as received.

I have asked Mr. S. K. Tung of the Gest Oriental Library to send you some reprints of Dr. Hu's writing which I loaned to Mr. Tung and which I wish to present to your Institute.

Mr. Eugene Delafield who has made a collection of Dr. Hu's writings may wish to loan some of his material. If you have not yet sent him an invitation to the Memorial Meeting on April 16, please do so. His address: 104 East 81st Street, New York 28, N. Y.

The cost of reproducing these materials amounts to $ 50.00. I shall send all the vouchers to you as soon as the bills from Harvard and Princeton are received.

Yours sincerely,

T. L. Yuan

〔Wesleyan University, Meng Archive〕

按:此件为打字稿,落款处为先生签名。所附清单共计 20 件,包括胡适的照片、文章,时间跨度为 1914 年至 1960 年。

四月七日

先生致信 Eugene L. Delafield,代邀其参加华美协进社举办的纪念胡适活动,并询问有无兴趣向该会借展或捐赠其收藏的胡适文章册件。

April 7, 1962

Dear Mr. Delafield:

Thank you so much for your letter. I wonder if you have received an invitation for a memorial meeting in honor of Dr. Hu Shih at the China Institute on Monday, April 16, at 4 p. m. At any rate, I shall ask the

Institute to send a card to you, if it has not been mailed to you before.

I have made photostats of some of Dr. Hu's earlier writings and sent to the Institute for an exhibition. If you wish to send some of your papers, for loan or donation to the Institute, you might like to get in touch with Dr. Chih Meng, the Director of the Institute.

I expect to be in New York that day and certainly hope to see you there. Herewith I am sending you a portrait of Dr. Hu which I made from the class of 1914 year book of Cornell University.

With cordial regards,

Yours sincerely,

T. L. Yuan

按：此件为录副。

四月十日

萧孟能(台北)致函先生,告知即将推销《中国留美同学博士论文目录》,并请赐寄美国购买中文图书的各公私图书馆、学校、书店的联络方式。

同礼先生：

《留美博士论文目录》捌部已收到。鄙人已向有关学术机构联络,完成销售之准备工作,祈释念。

美国各公私立图书馆,对我国新出图书,想必按时搜购。又各学校图书馆(包括华侨学校)及各书店,需要中文书籍者,想已不少。因而鄙人急需此类资料,以便取得联系,特恳先生于便中供给上项资料。如有所成,皆先生之赐也。尚此,即颂旅安。

萧孟能

一九六二,四,十,于台北

〔University of Chicago Library, Yuan T'ung-li Papers, Box 2〕

按：萧孟能(1920—2004),湖南常宁人,萧同兹之子,毕业于南京金陵大学经济系,1952年与妻朱婉坚在台北创办文星书店,1957年创办《文星》杂志。先生在该函左下角注有"四,廿九复"。

戴德华覆函先生,表示愿意支持先生的研究计划,但请先寄送相关的材料用以撰写推荐信。

April 10, 1962

Dear Dr. Yuan:

Hellmut Wilhelm has passed on to me your letter to him of March 7 to which I am replying at time because I have been away for the last month. Please excuse the delay. We shall be most happy to support your request for a subsidy, and if you will send me the necessary materials on which a supporting letter can be written I shall write it as soon as you suggest. We are glad to hear that the work has progressed so favorably and will assure you of giving you every possible help we can in bringing about its publication. I shall look forward to hearing from you.

Sincerely yours,

George E. Taylor

Director

〔University of Chicago Library, Yuan T'ung-li Papers, Box 1〕

按:此件为打字稿,落款处为其签名。

四月十一日

Eugene L. Delafield 覆函先生,感谢寄赠胡适在康乃尔大学学习时的照片复印件,并请再寄胡适在西雅图"中美文化合作会议"上的发言。

164 East 81St, New York City

Dear Mr. Yuan:

Thank you for your letter, and especially for your kindness in sending me a copy you made of Dr. Hu in the 1914 Year Book.

Now, I have not received an invitation to the memorial meeting, and will certainly go to it, and will see you there.

I have been looking to see if I had a copy of Dr. Hu's preface read at "the Sino-American Conference on Intellectual Cooperation" at Seattle, July 10,1960, I don't find out, so would be honored to receive a copy from you.

With kindest regards,

Eugene L. Delafield

April 11, 1962

〔University of Chicago Library, Yuan T'ung-li Papers, Box 7〕

按：该函为其亲笔。

四月十四日

上午十时半，华盛顿学术界、文化界人士假乔治敦大学（Georgetown University）国际堂举行胡适追悼大会，郭秉文、Stanley K. Hornbeck、先生、恒慕义等人出席，郭秉文致开幕词，先生等作简要的演讲，胡祖望致答词。

〔台北胡适纪念馆，档案编号 HS-NK01-281-018〕

> 按：Stanley K. Hornbeck（1883-1966），美国政界人士，中文名"洪培克"，胡适的好友，早年曾赴中国生活多年，任浙江高等学堂教员，归国后担任罗斯福总统的远东司司长，国务院高级政治顾问。

四月中旬

先生赴纽约，出席胡适哀悼纪念活动。

> 按：具体时间应为 4 月 16 日，地点应该在华美协进社。

四月十七日

先生致信中基会理事会，申请资助壹千贰百美金用以编纂《中国留欧大陆各国博士论文目录》。

April 17, 1962

Dear Sirs:

After the publication of the *Guide to Doctoral Dissertations by Chinese Students in America* which I published early this year, I was asked by a number of friends in Taiwan to make a similar survey of the dissertations by Chinese students in Europe. I welcome this suggestion partly because of the lack of any authoritative record and partly because the publication of this work has been assured by the Editorial Board of *Chinese Culture* which will issue it as a special supplement.

According to a preliminary survey, over 400 Chinese students obtained the Ph. D. degree in Great Britain, 500 in Germany, 500 in France, and 100 in Austria, Italy, Belgium, and Switzerland from 1907 to 1961. A record of the academic accomplishment of these scholars would be an invaluable document for the history of higher education in China. It would also serve to prevent unnecessary duplication of scientific research by Chinese students in American universities.

This record would be of particular interest to the Trustees of the China Foundation, as most of the research fellows sent to Europe with the support of the Foundation earned the doctorates in European universities especially in the field of pure science.

In compiling such a record, I shall need a full year of painstaking work, particularly in identifying the Chinese name of each author, in verifying the kind and date of each degree, and in furnishing full bibliographical information of each dissertation. Since a great deal of research is involved and access to foreign sources is necessary, I beg to request for a grant-in-aid of $ 1,200.00 in order to bring the research to completion. In view of its significance to Chinese education, I hope the Trustees will give favorable consideration to this request.

Yours sincerely,

〔University of Chicago Library, Yuan T'ung-li Papers, Box 1〕

按:此件为底稿。

张伯谨(东京)覆函先生,遵嘱购入五册《中国留美同学博士论文目录》。

守和吾兄台鉴:

北平一别,忽将廿年。顷奉大札,真似天外飞来,喜何可言。大著嘉惠士林,为国宣传,尚其余事。敝馆经常费极为拮据,兹遵嘱购买五部作馆内同人参考,支票附呈,即祈台收,并赐收据以便报销为荷。风便望教言时赐。特覆,即颂时祺。

弟张伯谨顿首
四月十七日

〔University of Chicago Library, Yuan T'ung-li Papers, Box 2〕

按:张伯谨时任"中华民国驻日公使"。

四月十八日

先生致信孟治,寄上此前影照胡适文章的费用凭单,并表示在华美协进社未授权前不会采取进一步措施。

April 18, 1962

Dear Dr. Meng:

Referring to the photostats of Dr. Hu's writings, I enclose vouchers with a total expenditure of ＄55. 51. With your advance payment of ＄30. 00, there leaves a balance of ＄25. 51.

There are many more of Dr. Hu's writings, but I did not proceed any further until I have authorization from you. Perhaps you prefer to wait until you have better financial situation.

Yours sincerely,

T. L. Yuan

〔University of Chicago Library, Yuan T'ung-li Papers, Box 9〕

按：此件为录副。

西门华德致函先生，告知行期并请代订酒店。

18/4, 1962

Dear Dr. Yuan,

Our timetable, as far as Washington is concerned, has now been fixed. We are departing here on Wednesday 9th May and should arrive at Washington sometime in the late afternoon. I wonder if you would most kindly book accommodation for us at the Plaza Hotel, which you recommended, until Sunday, 13th when we shall be leaving for Berkelcy (San Francisco), unless I shall be meeting my brother and his wife then, when we may delay our departure until Monday 14th.

Needless to say, that my wife and I are very much looking forward to seeing you and Mrs. Yuan.

With an □□□ □□ and many thanks.

Yours very sincerely,

W. Simon

〔袁同礼家人提供〕

按：该函为其亲笔。

四月二十一日

先生致信蒋梦麟，谈对中基会董事补选的想法及建议。

梦麟先生尊鉴：

前闻大驾或能于三月中旬来美，正拟在此欢迎，面聆训诲，后因适之先生突然作古，年会延期，大约须俟秋间方能晤教。适之先生去世后,此间学术界极为震悼,本月十三、十四、十六在康桥、华府及纽约分别举行追悼会,兹将秩序单随函奉上,即乞尊览。中基会李、胡两董事遗缺,本年俟须另补他人,敝意赵元任、何廉、汪敬熙三人均可予以考虑。至于美国董事Brodie等,闻将退休,查Henry Luce、Pearl Buck二人三十年来对于中国热诚赞助,如能递补为董事,颇有号召之能力,想已在钧座考虑之中。近年以来美国对于印度资助甚多,兹奉上关于印度工学院消息一则,可见一班。如台大能先此在台北之□□□□□作一初步接洽,思亮兄来美时再继续谈商,此类合作之计划或能实现。盼便中与之一谈是盼。

四,廿一日

〔University of Chicago Library, Yuan T'ung-li Papers, Box 1〕

按:"李"指李国钦,1957年起担任中基会董事,1961年3月去世。Brodie即Donald M. Brodie,1944年至1966年担任董事。另,1962年补选的董事为吴大猷、叶良才、Everett F. Drumright(庄莱德)。此件为底稿,有大量修改。

四月二十三日

罗家伦覆函先生,商《国父文献目录》印行细节,请再从国会图书馆查日本外务省档案及补拍胶片清单,并请代为核对寄台胶片数量、垫付复制胶片费用、代购书刊等。

守和吾兄道鉴:

(一)一月三日及三十日手教,均敬奉悉。

(二)尊编《国父文献目录》即将完成,闻之至佩。嘱写序文及转请于院长写书签,俟吾兄序文寄来,均当遵办。该书可用"国史馆"赞助名义,台湾方面预计约可订购二三十部(此间实因图书馆及研究机关太少;日本方面或有若干销路)。承寄赠《苏联研究中国文献目录》一册,收到谢谢。

(三)美国国会图书馆东方部主任Mr. Edwin G. Beal上月来台,据其告称:日本外务省档案胶片,除于一九四九至五一年在日本摄制之二一一六卷(即本馆已在其中选制三二二卷者另有军部九十八卷)外,曾在美国摄制有七十二卷,未曾列入在日本摄制之目录中。拟请吾兄设法索取或出资抄录此项胶片目录一份寄下,为托。

（四）本馆委托复制日本档案胶片，由 Pioneer Mart 轮运来两大箱及交邮寄来包裹两件，均已收到。共计四百〇五卷，尚缺少五卷。因发票及装箱单迄未由"中信局"转到，不知是否复制寄出此数？兹将与原订清单核对，附奉缺少五卷之号码单一份，请费神代向贵馆经办人员查询见示，无任感盼！

（五）又本馆增制之胶片十卷，接"中信局"通知，共计价款为美金一百十四元零一分，除已汇出之一百元外，须再补请外汇十四元零一分。为节省手续起见，如第一批四百十卷汇去美金四千一百廿五元中，尚有剩余，即可在剩余部份匀支，否则请吾兄就近代付（但须另取此尾款收据一份寄下）。已函复"中信局"转知采购团。

（六）本馆请吾兄代购书籍及代付书款，如下：

1、国务院发表《一九四三年中美外交关系白皮书》两册；加州大学出版"*Survey of the Chinese Language Reform and the Anti-Illiteracy Movement in Communist China*"一册，附原通知。

2、美国最近出版之德国外交部文件，其中如有涉及中国部份，请代购一册。

3、本馆向伦敦 Arthur Probsthain 订购书籍一批，请其检寄并由尊处代付书款（因本馆伦敦方面无存款）。接其发票，共寄出书籍二十种，今已全部收到，计书价及邮费二十四镑六先令，折合美金六十八元七角五分，请吾兄代为汇去，兹将本馆去信及其发票抄奉。

4、本馆向美国直接订购之西文杂志，其中有缺少数期，附奉清单一份，拟恳吾兄设法代为补购。

5、兹再附奉本馆续订 *Current History* 及 *The Journal of Near Eastern Studies* 两种杂志通知单各一份，请费神代开支票分别寄往续订各二年，为托。

（七）兹寄上吾兄本年聘函一件，及本年一至四月份征集费台湾银行缴款单两张，请察收，为荷。

专此，敬颂撰祺！

弟罗家伦敬启

四，二三

再者,如兄要于髯公写挂幅,弟可代请。

〔University of Chicago Library, Yuan T'ung-li Papers, Box 1〕

按:*Survey of the Chinese Language Reform and the Anti-Illiteracy Movement in Communist China*, 1962 年初版,作者为 Paul Leo-Mary Serruys(1912-1999),圣母圣心会来华传教士,比利时籍,中文名司礼义。Arthur Probsthain 为伦敦独立书店,1903 年创立,以经营有关亚非两洲书籍著称。*Current History* 和 *The Journal of Near Eastern Studies* 分别由加州大学出版社、芝加哥大学出版社发行。此件为文书代笔,落款和补语为罗家伦亲笔。

四月二十五日

孟治覆函先生,表示华美协进社暂无资金支持编纂胡适(西文)著述目录。

April 25, 1962

Dear Dr. Yuan:

Many thanks for your kind letter of April 18th and for all you have done for us in regard to Dr. Hu Shih's writings.

So far we have not yet been able to raise any funds for this purpose. However, as you know, this is a long-term project. I am quite sure that eventually we shall be able to do more and I hope that you will continue to advise and help us in this matter.

Sincerely yours,

Chih Meng

〔University of Chicago Library, Yuan T'ung-li Papers, Box 9〕

四月二十六日

先生致信戴德华,告知待《新疆书目》得到承印方估价后再寄上申请资助的相关文件。

April 26, 1962

Dear Professor Taylor:

I am most grateful for your letter of April 10 with regard to the possibility of requesting some support for the publication of my bibliography on Sinkiang. Owing to my absence from Washington, I regret that I was not able to write to thank you earlier.

Before requesting for a publication subsidy, I thought it would be helpful if the application could be more specific. Although I have written to ascertain the approximate cost, I have not yet had a reply. I shall be writing you again as soon as replies are received.

With sincere appreciation for your interest and assistance,

Yours sincerely,

T. L. Yuan

〔University of Chicago Library, Yuan T'ung-li Papers, Box 1〕

按:此件为录副。

先生覆信西门华德,告已代订旅馆并附备案,并拟五月十二日设家宴款待。

April 26, 1962

Dear Professor Simon:

As soon as I received your letter, I made inquiries about accommodation in various hotels in walking distance from the Library of Congress. As May is in the tourist season, Hotel Plaza and all nearby hotels are booked in advance. The rates are $ 14.00 for a double room with bath.

Next to Hotel Plaza and facing opposite to the Union Station, there is a tourist house known as "Lee's Tourist". Since a double room costs only $ 7.00, I have paid it for you for May 9th. The room is No. 4, facing the street; but if you find it too noisy, you can ask for a change to an inner room, if it is available on the day of your arrival. I enclose two cards on which you will find its address and telephone number.

The other possibility is Hotel Bellevue, 15 E Street, N. W. (ME 8-0900) which charges only $ 10.00 for a double room, though the size of the room is very small. After one night's stay in the Lee Tourist, you may like to transfer to this hotel which have plenty of rooms.

You did not indicate whether you come by train or by plane. If you come by plane, you can take the bus from the airport to Hotel Statler Hilton, 16th & K Streets, N. W. and get a taxi to the Lee's Tourist. If by train, you can walk to the place within two or three minutes.

Mrs. Yuan and I would like very much to have you and Mrs. Simon to come to our house for an informal dinner on Saturday evening, May 12th. Please reserve that evening for us.

Looking forward with much pleasure to seeing you both.

Yours sincerely,

T. L. Yuan

〔袁同礼家人提供〕

按：此件为录副。

四月二十七日

程其保致函先生，请在国会图书馆代查早年中英文版《清华学报》。

> 守和先生道右：

> 上周尊驾莅纽约，以各务丛集，未遑招待，罪甚罪甚，尚乞见谅为幸。兹有托者，查民六及民七年间，清华出有英文及中文《清华学报》（英文名为 *Tsing Hua Journal*）。在民七，弟同时为两种刊物主编，英文顾问为王文显先生，中文则为孟宪承先生。不识国会图书馆是否藏有此种刊物，弟亟需参考一用，如荷费神代查，感激万分。五月十一日当可在华府见面，余恕不尽。敬颂道安。

弟程其保拜

四，廿七

夫人前均此问安。

〔袁同礼家人提供〕

陈源覆函先生，略述竺可桢夫妇来英时晤谈经过。

> 守和吾兄：

> 奉手教，敬悉——。叔永作古，初不知悉。适之兄去年八九月在台北曾有数度畅叙，虽谈话稍喘，但精神仍好，不意突然而去，至可痛也。

> 藕舫夫妇去年来英，弟初无所知，偶闻人言，设法探听，在其离去前会谈一小时。据云彼等到英时，曾与该方使馆说明，有亲戚在英，希望一晤。虽已获准，尚未排得时间也。匆匆一见，未能详谈。皮皓白是否健在，未曾问及。惟皮母及杨（端六）母均长寿，按诸遗传之例，应尚在人间也。

> 仲揆之婿，似名邹承鲁，无锡人。在剑桥与熙泳同学。邹君极左

倾。专此,敬颂俪祺。

弟陈源顿首

27.4.62

〔University of Chicago Library, Yuan T'ung-li Papers, Box 5〕

按:1961 年 11 月 13 日,任鸿隽去世。"藕舫夫妇"即竺可桢和夫人陈汲,后者即陈源之妹。此时,皮宗石尚健在,后于 1967 年去世。邹承鲁确为李四光女婿,其夫人为李林。

四月二十九日

先生致信 College of William and Mary 图书馆馆长 James A. Servies,请其继续聘用纪凝娴。

April 29, 1962

Mr. James A. Servies, Librarian

College of William and Mary

Williamsburg, Va.

Dear Mr. Servies:

　　As old friends of Mrs. Lucy G. Chang and her family, we are always happy to bear witness to her fine character and professional competence. We take the liberty of writing to you in the hope that you will keep her on your staff on the basis of her work.

　　Since she joined your staff last year, she has rendered useful services to your Library. Conscientious and faithful in the discharge of her duties, she has made a creditable record. She herself considers it a great privilege to be able to associate herself with the important work in the development of your Library.

　　Recently we are distressed to learn that you have received a mimeographed circular, the contents of which must be unfavorable to her. Since it must have been engineered from certain quarters, we hope you would see fit to disregard it. If you find her services satisfactory, you would not be influenced by gossips and anonymous letters.

　　Her husband Professor Kuei-yung Chang of the Taiwan University is a well-known scholar whom we have known for many years. Her son is a most promising student in history and is coming to the University of Chicago on a partial fellowship. Since Mrs. Chang has to support her son to complete his graduate studies, we hope she will continue to work under your able direction.

Yours sincerely,

〔University of Chicago Library, Yuan T'ung-li Papers, Box 1〕

按：James A. Servies(1925-2014)，1957 年至 1966 年担任该校图书馆馆长。

五月四日

西门华德覆函先生，询问与先生在华府见面的时间可否改期，并感谢为其预定宾馆。

4th May 1962

Dear Dr. Yuan: -

Thank you so much for your letter of 26th April, which reached me only this morning because I was away in Bloomington and Chicago, where I saw Professors Teng and Creel and Dr. Tsien who all asked me to send you their kind regards,

Thank you so much for booking the room at "Lee's Tourist". My brother is flying in from New York on Friday and so I am afraid it will not be possible for us to accept your most kind invitation for Saturday. Would there be a possibility of shifting it to Thursday? Saturday night will be the parting night for us since both my brother and his wife and we shall be leaving on Sunday. I shall attempt to ring you after we have got to the "Lee's Tourist".

Thank you also for giving us the alternative address of the Hotel Bellevue which I shall pass on to my brother who also in vain attempted to get into the Hotel Plaza.

With very much looking forward to seeing you and Mrs. Yuan soon.

Yours very sincerely,

W. Simon

〔袁同礼家人提供〕

按：此件为打字稿，落款处为其签名。

渡边宏覆函先生，告知即将完成《新疆研究文献目录》（日文本）部分书稿，并将自认为最合适的分类方式寄来请先生审阅，此外提议用成本更低的活版印刷方式刊印。

May 4, 62

Dear Prof. Yuan

Thank you very much for your letter dated the 15 Avril.

By talking over the date of completion of the Bibliography with Prof. Ishida, I decided only to collect the titles from several published bibliographies, as far as the books and treatises which had not yet been examined. Then I will be able to send you complete one earlier than the schedule.

Soon I have to begin finishing up the manuscript, but I have some questions on the form of compilation, on which you gave some indications in your last letter. To make clear these points I should like to send you one sample of the list that I myself concluded to be the best one.

I understand that you have an intention of printing it by the offset printer, and that you want to have the fair copy written in Indian ink, but here, it will take rather much time and cost much to do so.

However, the printing with typography 活版印刷 may be less expensive and may take less time in Japan than in your U. S. A.

Later on I would send you an estimate of both cases, so would you please study it and write me your decision.

Your truly,

H. Watanabe

P. S. typography-about 1,500 yen-one page. Printer yet no contact, because almost printer already forget the classical Chinese letter.

I like Française. (no lesson anglaise)

〔University of Chicago Library, Yuan T'ung-li Papers, Box 8〕

按：此件为打字稿，补语为其亲笔。

五月中上旬

先生在家中设宴,程其保应邀前往。〔University of Chicago Library, Yuan T'ung-li Papers, Box 8〕

五月十二日

谭旦冏覆函先生,告《故宫藏瓷》两册售价并将寄赠《故宫瓷器录》两分册,另告留法博士中文姓名已联系友人查询。

> 守和先生有道:
>
> 五月一日手教谨悉。冏返国后,公私猬集,加以慕陵兄等出国,此间职责均被集中一身,致疏函候,良以为歉。
>
> 外双溪新馆已于上周决标,规模自较此间原有之陈列室为大,设备亦力求现代化,但以困难尚多,致后年完成,是否能符理想,尚待努力。
>
> 承嘱代订《汝窑》、《钧窑》两辑,《汝窑》已出版,定价美金三十元,为香港开发公司承印总销。先生如需,冏当专函介绍,可打折扣,至在此间售台币,则无折扣。《钧窑》尚在印刷中,二个月后始能出版。《瓷器录》已出版第一辑(宋元)、第二辑(明甲,包括洪武、永乐、宣德、成化)两本,此系此间出版,容冏日内寄上各一册,呈请指教,均系冏经手者。此间尚出版有《故宫法书》,第一辑为《王羲之墨迹》已问世,二辑《孙过庭书谱序》在印刷中。先生如需,乞示知。
>
> 另承嘱注明留法得博士中文姓名,已重打字数张,分寄在台同学,及法国有关友人,代为填注,俟收齐,即汇呈。因冏在法所学为绘画,事属隔行,知者仅一二人,余多系冏返国后之得博士者。
>
> 余容续陈,尚乞勿以在远,时锡教言,以匡不逮,毋任铭感。嵩此,敬请道安。
>
> 夫人公子均此候安。
>
> 后学谭旦冏拜上
> 五月十二日

〔University of Chicago Library, Yuan T'ung-li Papers, Box 6〕

按:"中国古艺术品展览会"在纽约巡展结束后,1961年11月8日谭旦冏由纽约乘飞机离开美国,途径日本返台。[①] 1950年4月

---

① 《国宝赴美展览日记》,页213。

起,迁台故宫文物全部藏于台中县雾峰乡的北沟库房,1965 年 11 月 12 日,台北士林外双溪新馆落成,文物随之迁移。

五月十三日

渡边宏致函先生,寄上修改后的书籍分类,请先生过目。

13, Mai 62

Monsieur le Professeur

J'ai envie de modifier à votre classification, rédigé un projet, comme

1······General works.

2······ Religion.

Buddhism general, history, scripture, temple.

Mohammedanism——

Manichaeism——

Other

3······ History.

General, archaeology (non including Tun-Huang 燉煌), periodic, regional, biography, genealogy

4······ Geography.

Geography (non historical), travel, exploration.

5······ Social science.

Condition, political, law, economy, society, ethnology, defence, foreign.

6······ Natural science.

Geology, biology, medical, metallurgy.

7······ Productive arts.

Agriculture, commerce, transportation.

8······ Fine arts.

Collected, sculpture, painting, material, calligraphy, engraving, decorative, music.

9······ Language & Literature.

Sankrit, uigur, tokharian, tibetan, etc.

Le prix d'écrire est 1 yen à une lettre.

Une page est 1,500 lettres.

Le prix d'imprimer est 1,500 yen à une page.

c-a-d, ils sont égals.

Veuillez agréer, mon cher Monsieur, mes salutations très respectueuses.

Hiroshi Watanabe

c/o Otani-kata, 30, Oiwake-cho

Bunkyo-ku, Tokyo, Japon

〔University of Chicago Library, Yuan T'ung-li Papers, Box 8〕

五月十四日

先生致信芝加哥大学出版社,代"国史馆"续订杂志另告部分杂志的卷期并未寄到,请补寄。

May 14, 1962

Subscription Dept.

University of Chicago Press

Chicago 37, Ill.

Dear Sirs:

　　On April 27, I sent you a check for ＄13.50 for two-years' renewal subscription to the *Journal of Near Eastern Studies* . (For the Library of the Academia Historica, 2 Peiping Road, Taipei, Taiwan).

　　In that letter I also indicated that the issues of the following journals failed to reach the Academia Historica, and requested that you send replacement copies:

　　1. *Journal of Near Eastern Studies* for January 1960.

　　2. *Journal of Modern History* Dec. 1959 and March 1960.

　　3. *Library Quarterly* Jan. 1960

If there is any charge, please send me the bill. I shall look forward to your reply.

Yours sincerely,

T. L. Yuan

〔University of Chicago Library, Yuan T'ung-li Papers, Box1〕

宋晞覆函先生,告《中国文化季刊》社愿意承印《中国留欧大陆各国博士论文目录》。

守和先生道鉴：

五月四日手示祗悉。关于《中国留欧学生博士论文目录》之印行，《中国文化季刊》社愿与合作，即分期刊布，列为附录。加印二百份，装成专册，亦可照办。该社则不负担任何编辑费。末校由先生担任，当遵办云。专此布闻，祗颂道安。

后学宋晞敬上

五月十四日

〔University of Chicago Library, Yuan T'ung-li Papers, Box 5〕

李迪俊覆函先生，感谢寄赠《中国留美同学博士论文目录》等书，并告徐铭信暂离巴西，所托函件尚需时日才能转寄。

守和吾兄惠鉴：

昨辱手翰，敬悉种切。承惠赠《留美同学博士论文目录》及美政府《白皮书》各一册，无任感谢。我兄年来在美以在野之身致力文化，功在士林。《留美同学博士论文目录》一书，搜罗赡富，纲举目张，尤为不刊之作，引企鸿猷，曷胜钦佩。徐铭信君寓圣保罗，弟与之已久未谋面，近闻赴欧，尚未返巴，尊函及附书当设法转交，结果如何，容当奉告。弟最近将有西印度之行，约六月上旬返馆。知念并闻。专此奉复，顺颂文祺。

弟李迪俊谨启

五月十四

〔University of Chicago Library, Yuan T'ung-li Papers, Box 2〕

按：此件应为文书代笔，落款处为其签名。徐铭信（Frank Hsu），祖籍天津，生于烟台，时应在华美协进社设立奖学金[1]，"尊函及附书"或为先生向其申请资助编辑留英、留欧《博士论文目录》。

五月十五日

先生致信罗家伦，前函所缺及增补之胶片均已办理，惟毕尔所言日本外务省档案并非由国会图书馆拍摄，故暂无目录可循。

---

[1] 台北胡适纪念馆，档案编号 HS-US01-086-026。

志希馆长:

前奉四月廿三日手教,嘱办之件均已前后办妥,分述如左:

(一)国会图书馆复制日本档案胶片尚缺少五卷,已由"中央信托局"孔处长于四月廿四日径函馆中办理,当可补照。

(二)增制胶片十卷,共计美金114.01,除已由尊处汇来百元外,接孔处长来信嘱寄支票14.01业已照办(来往信件附上)。

(三)Beal所言外务省档案七十二卷,系美国务院所摄,故未列入馆中所编之目录内,此七十二卷并无目录,为免遗漏起见,似须影照全份云云。一时亦难另觅他人编此目录,现正在进行中,容再奉告。

五月十五日

〔University of Chicago Library, Yuan T'ung-li Papers, Box 1〕

按:此件为底稿。

五月十六日

先生致信鲁桂珍,询问数位留英、欧博士的中文姓名及执教院校信息。

May 16, 1962

Dear Dr. Lu:

It seems to be a long time since I had the pleasure of seeing you in Paris. As you may recall, you treated us with Chiao-tze in your apartment which every one of us very much enjoyed.

Since then, I have made several trips to Paris, but you had left for Cambridge where you have been assisting Dr. Needham in his monumental work on *Science and Civilization in China*.

Dr. C. P. Cheng was in my house for lunch the other day. Dr. Ging Hsi Wang, as you know, is now with the University of Wisconsin. Both wish to be remembered to you.

There are two scientists who studied at the University College in the thirties and whose Chinese names I am anxious to know. I hope you could help me in checking the files of Dr. Needham. They are:

Chiong Yen-shou (Physics)

Hsu, Shing-kong (Chemistry)

In Dr. Needham's "Science Outpost", p. 111, Chiang's name was given as Chiang Rjeng-shou. I presume he must have Chiang's Chinese name recorded.

On the same page, Dr. Needham mentions also Dr. Yeh Chiao. If possible, please inform me his Chinese name and the university he attended.

I hope to visit London next spring, and it goes without saying I shall call on you and Dr. Needham when I come to Cambridge.

With warmest regards,

Yours sincerely,

T. L. Yuan 袁同礼

按：Chiong Yen-shou 即江仁寿（1906—1988），安徽歙县人，物理学家，1930 年赴伦敦大学理学院学习，1936 年获得博士学位后归国，历任武汉大学物理系主任、中山大学教授等职；Hsu, Shing-kong 即徐贤恭（1902—1994），安徽怀宁人，化学家，1936 年获伦敦大学化学博士学位，翌年归国，任武汉大学化学系教授，抗战期间长期担任该校总务长；Yeh Chiao 即叶峤，浙江永嘉人，化学家，1926 年赴德国留学，1931 年获柏林大学博士学位，旋即归国，在中央大学等校任教，1935 年任武汉大学化学系教授，后曾担任武汉大学理学院院长、化学系主任、有机化学教研室主任等职。鲁桂珍收到该信后，在其下方写了亲笔回函，因无落款日期，暂系此处，函文如下：

Dear Dr. Yuan,

Joseph & I had not time to go to the University Press basement where our old files are kept until yesterday. He has found all the information and we have to go to London in 10 minutes time. As I have delayed it long enough, so I now hurry to send it back in this form with enough regret for the delay. Both Dr. Needham and I will be glad and are looking forward to seeing you in Cambridge when you come.

Lu Gwei-Djen

〔University of Chicago Library, Yuan T'ung-li Papers, Box 8〕

五月二十日

沈亦云致函先生、夫人,告访问张公权并转袁澄语,另述行踪。

> 守和先生、夫人惠鉴:
>
> 　　此次道经华府饱扰,至深感谢。承教尤为快乐,得晤公子及未婚令媳更为兴奋。公子嘱达公权先生语,已经面述,答言:聪明极了,仍记得当时英俊情况,请作家报时提及是祷。云到此兼旬,在小芳家做客,伊夫妇招待亲切。七月间拟偕往西雅图参观博览会,此间气候温和,宜于老年,故暂时不作东归之计。倘蒙赐教,请寄下列地址:Mrs. Yi yun Huang, 1035 Ashbury St. San Francisco, Calif.小芳嘱笔问好。旅中栗碌,早欲修笺,羁迟乞恕为幸。匆布,顺候双安。
>
> 沈亦云拜启
五月廿日

〔University of Chicago Library, Yuan T'ung-li Papers, Box 8〕

　　按:本年 6 月 9 日,袁澄结婚,新娘为陈藏珠(Christina Chen)。"西雅图参观博览会"即世界博览会,本年 4 月 21 日至 10 月 21 日举行,以"太空时代的人类"为主题。

五月二十一日

先生致信查良钊,请代为悼念梅贻琦,并致挽联"戚友情亲卅载京华萦旧梦,大师教远万千士子泣春风"。[1]〔University of Chicago Library, Yuan T'ung-li Papers, Box 8〕

五月二十二日

先生致信戴德华,请其为申请《新疆研究文献目录》出版资助向美国国家科学基金会(National Science Foundation)撰写推荐信。

May 22, 1962

Dear Dr. Taylor:

　　Referring to our recent correspondence in regard to the proposed request for a publication subsidy for *the Bibliography of Sinkiang*, I have had preliminary discussions with Mr. K. Kitagawa of the National Science Foundation. He has promised to give me his full support, but he feels that

---

[1]《梅贻琦传稿》,页 459。

a supporting letter from you would carry considerable weight.

I enclose herewith the draft of a memo which I shall submit to the National Science Foundation at the end of this week. If you approve it, perhaps you will be good enough to write a letter to the following gentleman whose office handles requests of this kind:

Dr. Burton W. Adkinson

Office of Scientific Information Services

National Science Foundation

1951 Constitutional Ave., N. W.

Washington 25, D. C.

As you know, Dr. Adkinson was the Director of the Reference Department in the Library of Congress before he joined the National Science Foundation. Being a geographer himself, he would be interested in this project. But in view of the many requests for support, he has to give some priority to more significant projects.

May I assure you my sincere appreciation for your interest in the completion of this work. If your letter and mine could reach him at the same time next Monday, it may be more convenient for the officers of the Foundation to evaluate the merits of this request.

Sincerely yours,

T. L. Yuan

〔University of Chicago Library, Yuan T'ung-li Papers, Box 1〕

按：K. Kitagawa 即 Kay I. Kitagawa，时应为美国国家科学基金会下属外国科学信息办公室职员。[1] 该件为副本。

五月二十八日

先生致信渡边宏，建议其将"宗教"归类在"社会科学"门类下，对其在日本出版书目的想法表示赞同，并询问其是否编纂过关于伊斯兰学的书目。

May 28, 1962

―――――――――――

[1] Godfrey Raymond Nunn, *Publishing in Mainland China*, M. I. T. Press, 1966, p. 83.

Dear Mr. Watanabe:

I wish to congratulate you for your excellent French. You may write to me in French, if you prefer.

I am particularly delighted to hear that Dr. Ishida has almost recovered from his illness. I wish to send him my very best wishes for his speedy recovery. When you see him next time, I hope you will convey to him my concern and all good wishes.

I fully agree with you in your classification scheme. It is very well thought of. I wish only to suggest that "religion" should be grouped near "Social science". For instance, "Islam" in Sinkiang is closely related to social conditions, ethnology, and political conditions. I hope you will agree to this change.

As the cost of printing in Japan is much cheaper than in the United States, and as you have good publishers who would likely to be interested in publishing it, I quite agree with you that your bibliography be published in Japan (type-setting is, of course, much better than photolithography), provided you could help in reading the final proof.

When your manuscript is about to be completed, will you show it to a prospective publisher and ascertain from him whether he is interested in publishing it, and on what terms? If you could have a good publisher in publishing and distributing this work, it will be a permanent contribution.

Professor Ishida wrote me some time ago that you have published a bibliography on Islam. If copies are still available, could you send me two copies. One copy of which is intended for Dr. Rudolf Loewenthal who has compiled a bibliography of Russian sources on Islam. He would like to send you a copy if you are interested.

Through the Riggs Bank in Washington, I am sending you a draft of another US $ 100.00. Please acknowledge its receipt.

Mr. Hayashi (Hayasi?) Kenzo 林谦三 wrote a book entitled: 西域音乐东渐史. If it has been published, will you include it in your bibliography? Possibly he has written other books and articles relating to

Sinkiang. Do you think you could write to him and ask for a bibliography of his writings?

In your letter of May 4, you promised to send me a form of compilation, but so far, I have not yet received it. In addition to Chinese characters, there will be an English translation of very title which will facilitate the use of the bibliography by western readers.

〔University of Chicago Library, Yuan T'ung-li Papers, Box 8〕

按：林谦三（Kenzō Hayashi，1899－1976），日本音乐学家，1924 年毕业于东京艺术学院，其著作中并无《西域音乐东渐史》，或指《东亚乐器考》，1962 年音乐出版社初版。此件为底稿。

先生致信 Douglas G. Haring，寄上有关琉球群岛的书目卡片，并询问其有无兴趣购入《历代宝案》缩微胶片，另推荐图书馆员协助雪城大学扩充东亚馆藏。

May 28, 1962

Professor Douglas G. Haring

117 Euclid Terrace

Syracuse 10, N. Y.

Dear Professor Haring:

I was very much delighted to meet you in Mr. Kitagawa's office the other day. As promised, I am enclosing a few cards on Ryukyu Islands which you may find useful. Some of the material are very fugitive in character and should be acquired right away before they become out of print.

The Chinese work on the history of Ryukyu Islands which I mentioned to you is in manuscript and is in the process of being microfilmed. Consisting of 249 volumes, it covers the period from 1424 to 1867. Since it is the only copy in existence, I would suggest that you get a copy of the microfilms for your collection.

At present, no price has been fixed, as the microfilming work is still in progress. I shall be glad to make further inquiries for you, If you are interested.

I enclose also two cards for the bibliographies by Birkenstein and Kerr which you know already.

With the increasing interest in East Asiatic studies at Syracuse, I wonder if you and Professor Cressey would like to have a trained librarian to help building up your collections in this field. I have seen your collection in the past, and I think it could be further developed by obtaining material in other languages.

I know of a Chinese trained librarian who would be available after July 1st. if your Library is interested, perhaps you may like to explore the possibilities.

Sincerely yours,

T. L. Yuan

〔袁同礼家人提供〕

按:Douglas G. Haring(1894-1970),美国人类学家,专攻日本文化。先生关于《历代宝案》之提议应被接受,参见本年9月1日钱思亮覆先生函。该件为录副。

查良钊覆函先生,略述梅贻琦病逝、出殡经过。

守和先生:

五月廿一日大函奉到,敬悉一切。

致梅师母唁函暨挽月涵先生联已转送,嘱谢谢。

挽联未请人另书写,即用尊笔所书原件,加木框镜送悬新竹清华校园中梅校长灵堂中,用志哀思。

月涵先生去的太快了! 五月十八夜我守到夜一时半,见他安息始离医院。十九晨五时三刻再到台大医院,知见好转。九时三刻情况并不如过去几次危险,没想到十时余突变紧张,至十一时竟仙逝。

丧事由政府人士及生前友好合组治丧委员会,廿三日举行追思礼拜,各界公祭,一时大殓,一时半发引。到新竹送殡者约五百人,最动人场面是新竹约八千中学生及市民男女老幼数万人夹道欢迎梅先生灵柩。治丧一切隆重肃穆,至为感人。月涵先生精神不死,常活世人心中。

匆复，不尽顾言，即颂时绥。嫂夫人仝敬候。

弟查良钊谨启

五，廿八

〔University of Chicago Library, Yuan T'ung-li Papers, Box 8〕

是年春夏

先生赠《中国留美同学博士论文目录》与日本国际基督教大学（International Christian University）图书馆馆长高桥たね。〔《裘开明年谱》，页802〕

> 按：高桥たね（Tane Takahashi，1918−2018），女，日本图书馆学家，早年赴美国留学，1954年担任日本国际基督教大学图书馆馆长。
>
> 5月28日，她致信裘开明，表示收到赠书，请其代向先生致谢。

六月一日

戴德华覆函先生，告知已应前请向国家科学基金会发电推荐。

June 1, 1962

Dear Dr. Yuan:

Thank you for your letter of May 22. I am afraid that I was at the Conference in Canada and therefore did not get it in time to have a letter in Washington, D. C., by last Monday. I am therefore sending them a telegram supporting the project and hope that this is not too late.

Sincerely yours,

George E. Taylor

Director

〔University of Chicago Library, Yuan T'ung-li Papers, Box 1〕

> 按：此件为打字稿，落款处为其签名。

六月十日

谢寿康覆函先生，告此前寄来留意博士人员名单存疑不少，并告意大利博士学位质量不高，核对之事须等暑假结束方能开始。

> 守和吾兄惠鉴：
>
> 前得手示，藉悉起居安泰为慰。掷下名单不知来自何处，其中不无错误，如林某不但未作论文且从未卒业任何学校，而意国（国立、省立大学一样）博士学位无甚价值，大学毕业后提出二三十页之油印论文即可获得，因之德国人讥之曰"意国博士等于德国驴子"。惟教会

大学自庇护十一世整顿大学后,给予学位异常认真,其手续与德法相同。现各大学正在结束学年,不能查抄,嘱件暑假后当饬办也。先此奉覆,敬颂道安。

弟谢寿康拜上

六月十日

〔University of Chicago Library, Yuan T'ung-li Papers, Box 5〕

按:庇护十一世(Pope Pius XI, 1857-1939),第 257 任教皇,1922 年至 1939 年在位。

六月十一日

渡边宏覆函先生,告知收到第二张支票,拟去掉文章的英文译名,并谈印刷问题,另告自己研究伊拉克巴士拉地区的历史地理学,先生如有兴趣阅读可以寄上相关文章。

11 Juin

Monsieur le Professeur Yuan,

J'acceptais aujourd'hui (11, juin) votre second chèque de la Banque Industriel au Japon. Après 3 jours, il échangera.

En ce qui concerne l'ouvrage de m. Hayashi, comme on ne le trouve dans aucune bibliographie et que son nom ne figure pas sur la liste des membres de la "Toho-gakkai 东方学会" et "Shigak-kai 史学会"; je suis bien heureux si vous vouliez m'en indiquer l'année de la parution, etc.

D'autre part, pour ce qui est de la Bibliographie, je vous ai déjà envoyé des documents et informations nécessaires; je crois que vous avez déjà la peine de les examiner, je vous prie donc d'arrêter votre attitude à ce sujet et de m'en répondre dans un proche avenir.

L'imprimerie que je vous ai dit l'autre jour, imprime la "Shigaku 史学" de l'université Keio; comme elle est manié des caractères chinois peu en usage, donc je pense que l'on pourrait s'y fixer. (Je va sans dire que je m'occuperai moi-même de corriger des errata.)

Pour peu de temps dont je dispose, j'abroge d'une version anglaise de chaque article, mais je classiferai d'article que j'accompagnerai d'ailleurs des commentaires nécessaires pour qu'on puisse savoir de quoi il s'agit, et annxerai une carte historique et geographique.

(Nous aurons fallu recherche en méthode de la transportation et le droit de douane).

Grâce à l'article continuée dans *"Monumenta Serica"*, je suis au courant des exploits de Monsieur le Professeur Rudolf Loewenthal. Je ne puis faire autre chose que m'incliner devant les efforts qu'il a déployés.

Pour parler de moi-même, j'étudie la geographie historique de al-Basrah. Cependant occupé par le travail quotidien (maître d'école supérieure), je ne puis pas affecter beaucoup de temps à mon étude préférée. (Si votre ami veut, je présenterais mon article d'al-khashabat : le Phare dans le Golfe persique.)

Prof. Ishida n'est pas encore guéri de l'échaudure aux pieds, le docteur m'interdit de le voir.

Je vous souhaite une bonne santé et veuillez agréer, Monsieur le Professeur l'expression des mes sentiments les plus distingués.

Hiroshi Watanabe

c/o Otani-kata, 30, Oiwake-cho, Bunkyo-ku, Tokyo, Japon

〔University of Chicago Library, Yuan T'ung-li Papers, Box 8〕

六月十五日

先生致信亚利桑那大学图书馆，有意推荐华裔图书馆员前往该校图书馆编目。

June 15, 1962

Director

University Library

University of Arizona

Tucson, Ariz.

Dear Sir:

It is a pleasure to learn that Professor Earl H. Pritchard has joined your University as Chairman of the Department of East Asiatic studies. I have great admiration for Professor Pritchard's scholarship and I am confident that under his direction and leadership the University of Arizona will expand rapidly its program in the Far Eastern field.

To facilitate instruction and research your Library will no doubt collect Far Eastern materials will be needed in the years to come. During my last visit to your University, no one seemed to have charge of your Far Eastern collection.

I have now in mind a Chinese lady who is an expert in cataloging western and Oriental materials. If you should need the services of a trained librarian, perhaps you would let me know.

With all good wishes,

Yours sincerely,

Tung-li Yuan

〔University of Chicago Library, Yuan T'ung-li Papers, Box 1〕

按:Earl H. Pritchard(1907-1995),美国汉学家、亚洲学会创始人之一,曾任芝加哥大学副教授,时任亚利桑那大学东亚系主任。a Chinese lady 应指张贵永夫人。

六月二十五日

萧瑜覆函先生,感谢寄赠《中国留美同学博士论文目录》,并就所知填写留法博士中文姓名。

守和先生文几:

久疏笺候,昨奉五月二日惠书并大著《留美学生博士论文目录》,知大驾仍在华盛顿,诸凡迪吉,至为忻慰。大著精祥,为研究国际文化交流不可少之参考书,敬佩敬谢。另附留法博士论文名单,遵命填写中文,十分确错者只得四人,因与弟有直接关系或供给材料或代筹论文印刷费,故记忆确切,余有模糊影响者不敢妄填。小女婿黄益号仰昇,住 Apt. 7J, 790 Riverside Drive, New York City 32, N. Y.,并以覆闻。耑此,顺颂时祺。

弟萧瑜顿首

一九六二年六月廿五

又近几年来,此间人士从弟习中国书画者先后已逾两千人,颇有成绩优良者,其兼能作四体书法者竟多誉之为赛郎世宁者。我"教育部"亦颁发奖辞、奖品以褒扬之。前曾举行展览会,最优者四十余人,展出作品百二十幅，南美最大日报曾出特刊，另封寄上。弟在此间为沙漠上一园丁，但尚不寂寞也。又及。

附寄还名单两纸。

〔University of Chicago Library, Yuan T'ung-li Papers, Box 8〕

按："十分确错"似应为"十分确鑿"，"模糊影响者"似应为"模糊影像者"。

六月二十八日

先生覆信渡边宏，感谢寄来有关伊斯兰参考书目，建议《新疆研究文献目录》（日文本）每个词条都有英文翻译及主题索引，并将分批支付 400 美金作为酬谢，另提议与其联名出版该书。

June 28, 1962

Dear Mr. Watanabe:

Thank you so much for your letter and for sending me the sample cards and sample pages of your work. Owing to my absence from this city, I regret very much that I have not been able to write to you earlier.

It was very kind of you to have sent me and Dr. Lowenthal a copy each of your scholarly bibliography on Islam. I have passed a copy on to Dr. Loewenthal who will no doubt send to you his bibliography of Islam in Russian literature. At present he is on vacation, but you will receive a copy of his work when he returns.

The sample cards are most satisfactory. Since you will need them in preparing for the final manuscript, I shall return them to you by surface mail. As you may recall, each title should be followed by an English translation which will facilitate the use of the bibliography by western scholars.

I am glad to note that you will give a number to each entry. This numbering system will be extremely useful when you compile the index at the end of the volume. There should be an English subject index, as it will also help western readers to locate the desired title very quickly.

As to its printing, I prefer type-setting rather than offset printing. The sample pages which you so kindly sent to me show the good work of Japanese printers. So I shall follow your advice to have it printed in Japan.

But if you could write to Isseido, a large publisher in Tokyo, it may be possible to have it published without a subsidy. Would you like to try?

When I was in Boston, I asked the Riggs National Bank in Washington to send you a draft for US $ 100.00, being my third payment. In the middle of July, I shall send another remittance of US $ 100.00, making a total of US $ 400.00 which I wish to offer you as a token of my appreciation of your scholarly help. I know that the work has taken much of your time and I thank you most sincerely for your valuable collaboration. I hope that the bibliography will be published under our joint name. I shall write a preface and acknowledge your expert assistance.

As to Mr. Hayashi's work on music in Sinkiang, I read it somewhere in a Chinese book, but now I forgot its title and its publisher. So let us forget him.

I earnestly hope that the health of Professor Ishida has already improved. Is he still confined in a hospital? Please convey my best wishes for his health when you see him.

Yours sincerely,

T. L. Yuan

〔University of Chicago Library, Yuan T'ung-li Papers, Box 8〕

六月三十日

渡边宏覆函先生,告收到第三张支票,并已完成书目分类,另请先生支付美金五元用以弥补误工。

le 30, Juin

Monsieur Yuan,

Hier, le 29 juin, je reçus votre 3em cheque. Je déjà finis la classification, et etant inspecter par MM. Ishida.

Je me permettrais ici de vous demander 5 dollers, aux termes de l'horaire que je vous ai achevé auparavant : parce que pour donner plus de précision, je dois m'absenter de mon travail pour aller a la bibliothèque, ce qui ne me permettra pas naturellement de gagner mon salaire journalier 5 $.

L'etat de santé de Prof. Ishida s'ameliore de jour en jour.

Veuillez agréer, monsieur, l'assurance de mes sentiments respectueux.

Hiroshi Watanabe

〔University of Chicago Library, Yuan T'ung-li Papers, Box 8〕

七月九日

亚利桑那大学图书馆 Patricia Paylore 致函先生,表示暂时无意聘请专业图书馆员对东亚文献进行编目整理。

July 9, 1962

Dear Mr. Yuan:

As yet no attempt has been made to integrate most of the oriental language materials we have been purchasing into our general catalog, nor do we feel even yet that the volume of these acquisitions justifies the expert assistance that your friend could give us. These particular materials, as you may know, are now housed separately and do not actually constitute part of our collection. We realize, however, that the time may come when we shall be seeking a person with the specialized knowledge of the librarian you mention, and for that reason we are grateful to you for your interest in our situation.

We hope that when you are next in Tucson you will visit us. We are distressed that your past trip here evidently resulted in some frustration. Undoubtedly the new director of the Oriental Studies Program will help to minimize our present shortcomings.

Yours sincerely,

Patricia Paylore

Assistant Librarian

〔University of Chicago Library, Yuan T'ung-li Papers, Box 1〕

按:此件为打字稿,落款处为其签名。

渡边宏覆函先生,告知《新疆研究文献目录》(日文本)书稿已经完成,开始印刷,并建议在日本销售。

9 juillet

Monsieur Yuan

The work of the manuscript has been finished. It is in printing now.

Will you sell the Bibliography in Japan also? Many librarians and specialists will want it, because there is not any other editions except "*新疆文献综览*" was published in 1934, at the 满铁大连图书馆.

There is a prospect that about two hundred copies will be sold.

(no attach a map, for high cost)

Hiroshi Watanabe

〔University of Chicago Library, Yuan T'ung-li Papers, Box 8〕

七月十一日

王云五覆函先生,依前请汇上美金七百元用以补助《中国留美同学博士论文目录》印刷。

同礼吾兄勋鉴:

接奉六月二十八日大函,敬悉华府"中美文化协会"编辑之《中国留美博士论文目录》即由本院补助印刷费美金七百元,作为购买该书二百部,分赠欧美各大学及学术团体,以宣扬中美学术合作。该款业已汇奉,即希察收,并烦为分赠欧美各大学及学术团体,得便并将各该大学、团体名单见示为荷。耑此布复,顺颂勋祺。

王云五敬启

七月十一日

〔University of Chicago Library, Yuan T'ung-li Papers, Box 9〕

按:此件为打字稿,落款处为其签名。

七月十五日

顾毓琇覆函先生,谈为袁清谋取宾夕法尼亚大学图书馆奖学金事。

守和先生道鉴:

昨奉赐函,敬悉——。今日午后得郑绳武先生来舍面谈论文已面交,据云德文组 Library Scholarship 须俟候补人 alternate 放弃方可正式由令郎递补,但亦未始无望。中日文组之 Scholarship 至多半年后,可补。因朝鲜人预定半年后读完。又此朝鲜人正在 apply 别的 Fellowship。如得到,则随时可提前放弃现有之 Library Scholarship。此事图书馆有一委员会共四人,内三人本已赞成将定额由令郎递补。但第四人提出 Technical Point,须先通知原有候补人。如此人已得其他 Fellowship 则仍有望。专复,即请道安。

晚顾毓琇顿首

七月十五日

今晚飞伦敦，匆复不恭。

梅校长贺仪已提出三十万台币改送梅太太，并此附闻。

〔University of Chicago Library, Yuan T'ung-li Papers, Box 8〕

按：此函笔者请教袁清前辈，得知是年他申请宾夕法尼亚大学历史系博士较迟，未能获得奖学金，故此在该校图书馆中文部勤工俭学，时郑绳武为图书馆中文部主任。"梅校长贺仪"或应为"梅校长奠仪"，待考。

七月十七日

张贵永覆函先生，告知今年无法访美并祝袁澄新婚快乐。

守和先生道席：

顷奉手教，敬悉一是，附致量宇兄书已转交。王院长到职不久，即嘱今年暂不出国，只得遵命。内人已离华府，一切承先生照顾，衷心感激。□□仍在港，不□□□。世兄新婚，谨此道贺，并颂暑祺。

后学张贵永顿首

七月十七日

夫人均此函候。

美国外交文件1943，郭兄说已收到。

〔University of Chicago Library, Yuan T'ung-li Papers, Box 2〕

按："王院长"即王世杰，本年5月出任"中研院"院长。"美国外交文件1943"应指本年4月23日罗家伦覆函中所欲购买的《一九四三年中美外交关系白皮书》(*Foreign Relations of the United States: diplomatic papers, 1943, China*)，William M. Franklin 和 E. R. Perkins 编纂，1957年美国政府出版局刊印。

加斯基尔致函先生，将为先生谋得康乃尔大学奥林研究图书馆（Olin Research Library）、本科生图书馆开幕典礼的邀请函，并告知华生特藏已进一步扩充。

July 17, 1962

Dear Dr. Yuan:

Plans are now being made for the formal dedication of the Olin

Research Library and the Undergraduate Library on October 10, and I have told Dr. McCarthy of your interest in coming. Partly because of limited housing accommodations in Ithaca, especially while the university is in session, the number invited has to be severely limited, but I trust you will receive an invitation when they go out in September.

Sincerely yours

Gussie Gaskill

The Wason Collection has been so greatly expanded recently you won't recognize it. I am looking forward to retiring next June.

〔University of Chicago Library, Yuan T'ung-li Papers, Box 2〕

按:Olin 指 John M. Olin(1892-1982),美国工商业人士,1913 年毕业于康乃尔大学。Dr. McCarthy 即 Stephen A. McCathy(1908-1990),美国图书馆学家,1946 年出任康乃尔大学第五任图书馆馆长。此件为打字稿,落款及补语均为其亲笔。

郭廷以覆函先生。〔《郭量宇先生日记残稿》,页 338〕

按:此前,先生应致信郭廷以,商议译书事。

七月十八日

先生致信叶良才,请其忽略此前向中基会提交的协助推销《中国留美同学博士论文目录》的请求。

July 18, 1962

Dear Mr. Yip:

In my letter of March 12, I requested the assistance of the Foundation in a wider distribution of the *Guide to Doctoral Dissertations by Chinese Students in America*.

Since a number of copies have been sold in the meantime, it is no longer necessary to seek the help of the Foundation. May I therefore be allowed to withdraw my application?

In my previous letter, I also enclosed a letter from Dr. Li Chi in regard to this matter. Please return it to me if you can locate it.

With best wishes for a pleasant summer,

Yours sincerely,

T. L. Yuan

〔University of Chicago Library, Yuan T'ung-li Papers, Box 1〕

七月二十日

叶良才覆函先生,告知中基会已按其要求停止协助推销《中国留美同学博士论文目录》。

July 20, 1962

Dear Dr. Yuan:

Your letter of July 18, 1962 received. We are glad to hear that a number of copies of the *Guide to Doctoral Dissertations by Chinese Students in America* have been sold and you are withdrawing your application to the Foundation for help as that is no longer required.

The letter from Dr. Li Chi you sent us on March 12, 1962 is herewith returned.

With best regards,

Sincerely,

L. T. Yip

〔University of Chicago Library, Yuan T'ung-li Papers, Box 1〕

按:此件为打字稿,落款处为其签名。

七月二十一日

先生致信王云五,感谢资助并按约定将收据及图书分赠名单汇呈。

岫庐院长勋鉴:

奉到七月十一日赐书,荷承钧院补助《留美博士论文目录》印刷费美金七百元,厚意援助,本会同人感谢良深,除收据已寄纽约中国银行转呈外,兹将分赠欧美各大学及学术团体名单七纸随函奉上,即希鉴核备案为感。专此申谢,敬候道祺。

七月二十一日

〔University of Chicago Library, Yuan T'ung-li Papers, Box 9〕

按:此件为底稿。

七月二十二日

刘麟生致函先生,请为其在美大学图书馆中谋事。

守和尊兄勋右：

华昌闻年来营业不振，续行裁减员司，弟亦在其列，正拟驰书左右，恳祈留意工作。承筱峰兄奔走，始知大贤不弃，允为设法，感谢可言。弟流离暮齿，觅事似不易，然体力尚健，并无其他病症，亦似可以有为。闻美方大学中有中文书籍者颇多，近方添置，必需华人编目。弟虽非习图书馆学，而对于版本及内容亦曾涉猎，如需校订、编译，亦可供奔走之劳。贤者为典籍权威，一言重于九鼎，或可为之推毂，而令司其事者不斤斤较量其资历也。弟已托若干友朋留意，尚无成熟之期，故敢再烦神思，曷胜向往之至。专此，敬请俪安。

教弟刘麟生谨上
七，廿二

弟之永久居住系于 59 年四月中核准。

〔University of Chicago Library, Yuan T'ung-li Papers, Box 2〕

七月二十三日

渡边宏覆函先生，告知《新疆研究文献目录》（日文本）所收录篇目之最新数量，并建议出版后每本定价 500 至 600 日元。

23 juillet

Prof. T. L. Yuan

Cher professeur,

Je reçois votre 3eme lettre.

Prof. Ishida entre encore dans l'Hopital Toranomon 虎门病院 (no. 406, Aoi-cho, Minato-ku, Tokyo).

La Bibliographie collectionnais 1118 articles,

de Nishi, Tokujiro 西德二郎: 中亚细亚纪事 (voyage) 1886.

a Kameyama, Shuki 龟山修幸: 龟兹国における秘密佛教 (religion) 1962.

La vente de la Biblio. demandera au Isseido, mais la demande de la publication n'est point necessaire.

L'imprimerie et le papetier acceptait des facilites de paiement de mon charge.

Une copie se vendra 500−600 Yen.

La nom de la publication demandera au Tohogakkai 东方学会.

L'indexe des personnes (romanization) est environ 450.

Seulement je suis necessaire la lettre de M. Fujieda, L'autres ne retrouvent pas.

Toutes ouvrages de Prof. Hayashi sont chinoise.

L'index des per. sera achevé aujourd'hui.

La reste est seulement l'index des subjectives.

Veuillez agréer, Monsieur le Professeur,

avec mes regrets, l'assurance de ma consideration distanguée.

Hiroshi Watanabe

〔University of Chicago Library, Yuan T'ung-li Papers, Box 8〕

按:西德二郎(1847—1912),日本明治维新时期的外交官,曾任驻巴黎公使馆秘书,1880 年归国时曾游历伊犁并经西伯利亚等地,后出版《中亚细亚纪事》。龟山修幸,日本僧人。

七月二十四日

先生致信钱思亮,请其与蒋梦麟等人商讨由中基会资助《中国留欧大陆各国博士论文目录》出版的可能性。

思亮校长仁兄尊鉴:

前奉二月廿三日赐书,敬悉种切。关于《留美博士论文目录》之印刷费,前承吾兄提议可向中基会申请补助,惟近月以来已另筹办法,无须资助,故弟已函请会中予以撤销矣。承吾兄盛意援助,感何可言。兹有一事须请吾兄考虑及赞助,查我国留欧博士约在二千人以上,其论文题目前此向无记录载在留学史上,不无遗憾,内中有多人系由中基会资助者。弟去年已收集若干资料,亟愿早日完成。兹随函奉上说明一纸,至盼得便时先与梦麟先生一商,如能在预备会中先行审议,弟再正式提出。倘今年经费无着,则俟明年再行补助亦无不可。如何之处,统希尊酌,并盼赞助,不胜感荷。专此敬候。

七月廿三日

又 Li Fo-ki 于光绪三十二年在德 Bonn 获得物理博士南洋公学毕业,返国以后迄未发表专门论文,故不易知其中文姓名,不识台大物理系同人有知之者否,亦盼便中一询。

〔University of Chicago Library, Yuan T'ung-li Papers, Box 1〕

按:此件为底稿,另附编印《中国留欧博士论文目录》说明一纸,两者修改均甚多,最终写就似在 24 日,可参照 9 月 1 日钱思亮覆函。

七月三十一日

先生致信郭廷以,商讨《巴布阔福回忆录》翻译事宜,并告将编印《新疆研究文献目录》三册。

量予吾兄著席:

近奉七、十七日手教,藉悉起居清豫,至以为慰。关于《巴布阔福回忆录》共五百七十五页,曾托纽约市立图书馆及国会图书馆将影照费分别估价,以国会馆估价较廉三十七元余,纽约照费为四十三元一角,乃决定交该馆影照,日内照就当即寄上付款收据在该书包裹内。如台北有精通英俄两国文字之人,则以译英为宜,因出版后可在国外流通,亦可为贵所增加一种英文刊物也。如译者英文不佳,则改译中文,将中文本先行出版,亦是一种圆满办法。弟近遍阅时贤,关于西北边疆之文献,对于新疆所失之土地竟无任何有系统之记载,故愿此书早日译成中文及英文也。弟近编《新疆书目》共三册中日文及俄英等文,拟在港付印,将来出版后应委托台北何家书店代为推销,亦盼便中代为一询是荷。前信述及黄膺白夫人来谈,询□吴相湘索资料事,并无重要也。至于巴布阔福所订条约均载于《同治条约》及"外交部"印《光绪条约》之内,想贵所均已入藏。此外,《夷务始末》、《光绪外交史料》亦有记载,其俄文原著早已绝板,并未译成英德文也。承寄刊物三种,至以为谢,尚未收到,先此申谢,顺候时祉。

弟袁同礼顿首

七月卅一日

所照复本九月初旬必可寄到。

〔台北"中央研究院"近代史研究所档案馆,〈郭廷以〉,馆藏号 069-01-02-089〕

按:□处破损,或有一字。该信于 8 月 5 日送达南港。

吴权覆函先生,告嘱查留法学生中文姓名一事进展,并告其姐在美国获博士学位但未能收录在先生所编博士名录中,另谈愿意将其父母行述影本寄赠国会图书馆供学者利用。

守公左右赐鉴:

前奉手示,敬稔起居佳胜为慰。承嘱将留法历年同学论文著者法文姓名译华一节,奉命之余细察各拼法,确实无误者。权仅能译九人(钢笔所写),实不足以符厚望,因思候权便中赴巴黎亲到"大使馆"领事事务处,按历年名册一一查出,岂不甚妙! 但两三月来迟迟未能成行,因而裁复稽迟为憾。

昨日到巴黎乃与领事处负责人史秘书克定及职员梁宗恒兄分别出示大函及名单,请予协助,不料遍查卷宗,姓名有据者仅得其七(铅笔所书)。据梁兄云,领馆全部卷宗于德军占领时,由我方全加以销毁,故目前在馆无任何卷宗可查云云。

尚有多名仍在开示单内,无法确知。如有疑问,仍以宁缺为原则,以候将来之补充可也。(如 Woo Soo,权认识他,但不确实其名之写法"素"或"书"?)

在英图书馆拜读大作关于留美同学论文名单,细查内无家姊吴叔班 Shu-Pan Wu 之纪录,甚以为憾。姊系毕业上海大同大学 B. A.,于1926 年? 入司丹福大学 Stanford University 再得 B. A.后,改入欧海欧之 Columbus State University 得 Ph. D(论文:教育学),学业列最优等。姊返国后任职东北大学教授廿余年。

关于先严一生政治经过,除已有记录其口述之历史,原稿仍在大陆一时不得出版外,权手中存有先母及先严之行述各一册,前者系先严手稿,后者系家姊叔班及权上次在津举行公葬时刊印,内容对于其一生之事迹真确多为外间所不知或有传闻之误者,此项史实必有助于研究中国近代史之学者。权闻美国会图书馆存藏此项材料,广为收集。如能将此项亦登入目录编入收藏,则拟将此二册孤本照像印之奉呈转赠。如何之处,便中示知以便去交印也。

大维爵士在医院病似见轻,伊前见面与权晤谈时曾云在伊将出版之《中国艺术史》中将证明宋徽宗之画与字(瘦金体)皆系他人代笔,权当云在中国史籍曾载有其画有时系画院中人代笔,但未闻其字亦系代笔者! 伊云有确实证据云云,未谙尊见以为可否? 大维爵士收藏中国古物近分二次拍卖,权购到一清初御题诗缂丝《耕织图》一巨幅,另一仇英扇,及一大端砚等,以为"收回"古物中之二件。权藏各品上自史前新石器时代以迄现代各时期精品甚少,将来拟设一"小型中国历史文物博物馆"在海外为国宣传文化,以启外人对我国文化有系统之了解,以时代顺序展览而不以类分(如铜,瓷……)。但以兹事重大,所收者太少,有不能确知其年代物品,故未敢率尔。何时来欧,当倒履以迎,尚望前辈不吝教言,时赐以为南针。崇此奉复,敬颂著安。

晚吴权再拜上

一九六二,七,卅一,于巴黎旅次

Wou Kiuan

69 Highland Rd

Northwood

Middlesex, Eng.

〔University of Chicago Library, Yuan T'ung-li Papers, Box 2〕

按:"先严"即吴景濂(1873—1944),辽宁宁远人,清末出任奉天咨议局议长,中华民国时期政治家,国民党创始人之一,曾四次出任国会议长。吴权为其次子,二战后曾在海牙国际法庭任法官。吴叔班为其三女,美国斯坦福大学教育学硕士、俄亥俄大学教育学博士。

渡边宏致函先生,告将于 8 月 3 日寄上《新疆研究文献目录》(日文本)精装封面和书名页的印刷样本,供先生选择,另告日本可代售此书的书店。

31 juillet.

Tokyo

Professeur T. L. Yuan

L'épreuve en première sera livrée de 3 août.

En reliure, j'emploierai le vinyle, pour que la cartonné aie hors de prix (un volume est de plus de 200 Yen).

En style de title, j'ai envie de votre indication exacte.

Ci-joint, vous trouverez des échantillons de la reliure et de la page du title. Je vous prie de me faire parvenir au plus vite votre decision.

Aujourd'hui, Isseido est un bouquiniste, cependant Issemdo,

Yamamoto-shoten 山本书店, Komiyama-shoten 小官山书店 et Ibundo 汇文堂 (Kyoto) sont dans l'attente de vendre notre Biblio.

En prix, 500 – 600 Yen est raisonnable, (Macro: Biblio, of the Arabian Peninsula est 1100 Yen par 80 pages, Nihon Orient Gakkai: A Biblio. of Islamic Studies in Japan-300 Yen 47 pages 1959, Jimbunkagaku Kenkyusho: Biblio. of Mongalia–150 Yen 1953, –note Biblio. est environ 100 pages avec l'indexe utile et bel reliure vinyle).

La commission de la librairie est environ 20 – 30%. Le total de l'article se multiphie en 1129.

Veuillez agréer, professeur, nos salutations distinguées.

Hiroshi Watanabe

c/o Otani-kata, 30, Oiwake-cho

Bunkyo-ku, Tokyo, JAPON

〔University of Chicago Library, Yuan T'ung-li Papers, Box 8〕

八月三日

Eugene L. Delafield 覆函先生,感谢寄赠胡适早期文章及胡适先生西文著作目录草稿副本。

Dear Mr. Yuan,

I am so very sorry that I have been out of town working for some weeks, and on my return found your most kind enclose of the extra copies of the bibliography and the photostat of Dr. Hu's article in the *Columbia Spectator* for January 1916. Also, your letter concerning a book of tributes to Dr. Hu, in Taiwan, on which they want a bibliography of the Doctor. All I can supply now would be that check list I sent you originally of two hundred and thirty or forty titles which Dr. Hu cut down to 84 titles. As they say, it would not contain details of books, etc. But if they are satisfied with that, it is alright with me. You have a few more you can add. As it is more than two and half times longer, it is worth that much more.

I work often out of town in the summers on □□□ libraries. So do not come in for weeks. So, regret so much to have had you wait to hear from me.

With kindest regards and best wishes.

Eugene L. Delafield

Aug 3, 1962

〔University of Chicago Library, Yuan T'ung-li Papers, Box 9〕

按：Dr. Hu's article in the *Columbia Spectator* 即 Analysis of the Monarchical Restoration in China，此件为其亲笔。

八月十一日

台北"中央研究院"函聘先生为胡适遗著整理委员会顾问。〔University of Chicago Library, Yuan T'ung-li Papers, Box 9〕

按：该委员会于 8 月 8 日举行第一次会议。

八月十四日

富路德致片先生，感谢寄赠贺片并告知其将在日本盘桓两周多。

14 August, 1962

Dear Mr. Yuan:

How very thoughtful of you to write a note of congratulation on the award of the degree. It was totally undeserved; I still don't understand it.

We have enjoyed our visit in this country, and are due to leave in 2 ½ weeks.

Sincerely,

Carrington Goodrich

(We occupy a modern house next door to this.)

〔University of Chicago Library, Yuan T'ung-li Papers, Box 2〕

按：a modern house next door to this，因该片正面是东京某古建筑物的风景照片。该片由海运寄送。

八月十五日

罗家伦覆函先生，请向纽约 Paragon Book Gallery 购入两种书刊。

守和吾兄道鉴：

五月十五日手教暨帐单等均敬奉悉。承代购之书籍，亦已陆续寄到，俟帐目查对清楚后，再行奉告。兹拟请吾兄即为本馆向纽约 Paragon Book Gallery 代购下列两书：

1. *The China Yearbook*, a complete set of 20 volumes,

2. *The National Review China*, Vol. IX and X

书价及邮费付出后,请即将收据寄下,以便报销。专此奉托,敬颂
著祺!

弟罗家伦敬启

八,一五

〔University of Chicago Library, Yuan T'ung-li Papers, Box 1〕

按:1942 年,Paragon Book Gallery 在上海创立,以出售有关东方艺术的书籍著称,后在纽约和芝加哥设立店面,今通译作"佳作书局"。*The China Yearbook* 应指《中华年书参考书》(《中华年鉴参考书》),由 H. T. Montague Bell、H. G. W. Woodhead 主编;*The National Review China* 应指《中国公论西报》。该函为文书代笔,落款处为其签名。

渡边宏覆函先生,告知《新疆研究文献目录》(日文本)印刷因故迟缓,其刚收到第一次试印书目的第 413 至 641 页的部分。

15 aout

Tokyo

Prof. T. L. Yuan

Cher Monsieur,

Je reçus votre 4 ème lettre et la carte.

L'impression de la Biblio. est en retard. Aujourd'hui, je reçois de no. 413 à 641 (pp. 27−41), des premières épreuves.

Je ne sais pas M. Sato, mais je collectionnais l'ouvrage des MM. Saguchi, Kuroda et Hino.

Toutes les 检 corrigent aux 险, mais des titles cité par la critique abrégent, parce que il n'y a pas des marges.

Le paiement est apres l'achevement (vers fin de aout).

La épreuve vous sera envoyé de 2ème, parce que la première est beaucoup erreur, comme je vous déjà envoyai. Mais toutes les manuscripts envoient, je corrige les épreuves par la carte.

Votre prix est très raisonnable.

Je reçus des extraits de M. Loewenthal, vous seriez bien aimable de luis presenter mes respectueux hommages.

Veuillez agréer, mon cher Monsieur, mes salutations très respectueuses.

Hiroshi Watanabe

c/o Otani-kata, 30, Oiwake-cho

Bunkyo-ku, Tokyo, Japon

〔University of Chicago Library, Yuan T'ung-li Papers, Box 8〕

八月十八日

先生致信钱存训,感谢寄赠*Written on Bamboo and Silk*,并建议寄送各学术期刊以利书评宣传,此外请在芝加哥大学图书馆代查所需期刊。

公垂吾兄著席:

日前承赐尊著,体大思精,允称不朽之作,今能如期出版,受益者当不少也。已与子明兄商定,由渠起稿写一书评,写就后再行寄上请正。因插图精美,成本不轻,不能出版部愿寄若干部于各东方学期刊否(如《通报》等)?至于台北出版之*Chinese Culture*,学术地位不高,登载与否无大关系也。小儿成婚承寄贺电,至感。次儿途经芝城荷承款待,尤以为谢。渠下年将到 Penna 大学研究,并盼明年能转芝大或耶鲁,须看能否获到奖学金耳。承代售《博士论文》数册,至感。支票已拜收,谢谢。此书极难推销,如有中国学生夏令会,可按特价三元出售,不识易办否?兹需用下列各种期刊,皆是 L. C.未入藏者,尊处如有存本,盼托馆际借书处暂借一用,当由 L. C.寄还。暑假尚希多加休息是盼。专此,顺候俪安。

弟同礼顿首

八月十八日

尊夫人同此致意。

American Historical Review 常请 Hummel 写书评,能寄该刊一部否?

〔钱孝文藏札〕

按:"不能出版部"似应为"不知出版部"。"书评"应指吴光清撰写 *Written on Bamboo and Silk: the beginnings of Chinese books and inscriptions* 之书评,刊登于 *The Library Quarterly* 第 33 卷第 1

期(1963 年 1 月)。1969 年,袁清获得宾夕法尼亚大学博士学位。"博士论文"即《中国留美同学博士论文目录》。此信右下角标注"8/21 覆"。

八月二十日

渡边宏覆函先生,寄上《新疆研究文献目录》(日文本)第二次试印的部分页面,并讨论书中个别字词上的谬误。

20 août

Tokyo

Prof. T. L. Yuan

Je vous informe par la présente, je vous avoir envoyé par courrier séparé une partie de la 2ème épreuve qu'on avait imprimée. Je même épreuve a été expédié aussi à prof. Ishida.

Quant aux études sur Sinkiang contemporain, il est insuffisant, j'ai cependant réussi à m'en collectionner les documents de MM. Nohara 野原, Kue 久重 et Kasahara 笠原.

Ainsi que le mot "险", il me semble qu'il est mieux d'améliorer le mot "回" en "回" et le mot "砂" en "沙". (回鹘、沙漠).

Par la carte de "Library of Congress", vous avez corrigé le mot "书" en "查", alors que c'est le premier qui est correct. L'auteur en est secretaire du Ministère des Affaires Etrangères, Takahashi 高桥.

Comme vous voyez, il est très difficile de faire les épreuves, mais nous faisons notre mieux pour qu'elles soient exactes et authentiques.

Enfin, nous pensons à attaquer aussi "Marzen", une des plus fortes sociétés d'édition et de vente des livres japonaises, afin qu'elle accepte à mettre en vente le dit livre, votre Bibliographie.

Veuillez agréer, Monsieur le Professeur, nos salutations distinguées.

Hiroshi Watanabe

c/o Otani-kata, 30, Oiwake-cho

Bunkyo-ku, Tokyo, JAPON

〔University of Chicago Library, Yuan T'ung-li Papers, Box 8〕

八月二十三日

先生覆信罗家伦,告知配购各期刊、文件进展,并询问"国史馆"购买《政府公报》、日本外交部档案全套的可能性。

　　志希馆长吾兄著席:

　　　　日前奉到八月十五日手教,嘱购英文本《中国年鉴》及 *National Review* 九及十两卷,当即函请 Paragon 书店予以配购,顷得复函谓该二书早已售罄,只得再候机会另行设法。Nat. Rev. 已托馆中照像。兹有三事奉陈:

　　　　(一)国会图书馆正拟以胶片翻印《政府公报》全份,Beal 先生正在估价,不识贵馆愿购一份否?

　　　　(二)*Documents on German For. Policy* 由英美两处分别印行,因美方所印者多已绝版,乃向英国配购。据 Heffer 书店来信,除已购到各册,已由英国径寄贵馆外,其余已绝版者只得陆续搜求,来信奉上备查。

　　　　(三)Beal 影照关于日本外交部档案七十二卷一案,据 Beal 先生言,因馆中并无目录可资选择,不如购一全份,并由馆中负责人估价,共需四九〇元,原单奉上候酌。

　　　　　　　　　　　　　　　　　　　　八,廿三日

　　　　　　〔University of Chicago Library, Yuan T'ung-li Papers, Box 1〕

　　按:此件为底稿。

八月二十四日

谭旦冏覆函先生,告《故宫藏瓷》等书代购已相机办理,并告古物在台展览已结束。

　　守和先生有道:

　　　　十三日手教拜悉。

　　　　《汝窑》已函托香港开发公司径寄,并请其折扣优待,《钧窑》尚未出版,出版后即寄。《瓷器录》弟处有存书,且价亦不高,当于日内寄呈奉赠。尊款俟代付后,少多再行奉闻。

　　　　留法博士名称,曾分函各友转托,并无一回音。当即函催,总希最近有所结果。

　　　　弟返国后,诸务集于一身,繁忙异常。现古物已返国,展览今日闭幕,此后当可清闲。

余容续陈。耑此,敬颂撰安。

后学谭旦冏拜上

八月廿四日

〔University of Chicago Library, Yuan T'ung-li Papers, Box 6〕

按:"现古物已返国"指"中国古艺术品展览会"在美巡展结束,于1962年7月28日乘美国军舰回抵基隆。[①] 为示文物完好无损,特在台举办小型展览。《故宫藏瓷:钧窑》版权页标注的出版时间为1961年12月,与信文中"现古物已返国"一节不能自洽,故不拟采用。《瓷器录》指《故宫瓷器录:宋元》,为其丛书的第一辑,1961年4月"国立故宫"、"中央博物院"联合管理处印行。

八月二十五日

罗家伦致函先生,请代为查询美国国家档案局所存有关苏联军队入侵绥芬河事件档案,并谈购书、续订期刊等事。

守和吾兄道鉴:

日前寄上一函,请代订购《中国年鉴》等书,计邀惠察矣。兹将烦请吾兄为本馆搜购图书史料各事,分陈如下:

一、关于一九二九年俄军侵入绥芬河满洲里之役及交涉报道,经查美国国家档案局胶片中有国务院档案三种(档号893.00计二二七卷,711.93计二卷及793.00计三四卷)之目录共八卷,其中仅约略提及关于中东路之中俄冲突,美国劝告中俄双方遵守《凯洛格非战公约》(Kellog Pact),俄国反诬美国另有企图等简单语句,但并无关于此事之正式报道文件;且凡关此案处,均注有参见861.77号档案字样,惟本馆现无861.77号档案胶卷可查。拟恳吾兄费神设法一查此一号码档案,是否均系有关中国史料卷? 如全部是的,添购价若干? 如局部是的,选购价若干? 请惠示,以便预备外汇。

二、兹请吾兄代本馆订购书籍及杂志如下,定单三份附奉:

1、*The World of Learning 1962-63* 一本,定价七镑。

---

① 《国宝赴美展览日记》,页399-400。

2、*The China Quarterly* 自一九六○年第一期起订三年,每年美金三元,共九元。

3、*Foreign Affairs* 续订两年,共计美金十一元。(前承补购 *Foreign Affairs* 缺期四本,甚感。惟本馆仅收到一九五九年者三本,尚有 October 1957 一本未寄来,便中请一询)。

三、本馆委托"驻日本大使馆"张伯谨"公使"代购参考书籍,上年度汇去外汇中,尚缺少美金五十三元六角一分,拟请吾兄费神就本馆余款中代为汇还。(请兄费此转汇手续,甚为不安,系因外汇预算,有按年度报销之规定,尚祈见谅。加兄以许多麻烦,罪甚!)

四、本馆前向伦敦 Arthur Probsthain, 41, Great Russell Street, London, W. C. 1.选购书籍二十余种,其中有两书售缺,现已补寄到馆,计美金五元一角五分,请吾兄费神代为汇还,为托。

五、承代购德国外交文件 *Documents on German Foreign Policy*,已收到 Series C Vol. 1-3 三册,Series D Vol. 1-5 & Vol. 10 六册。近又承寄到书籍多种,请费神付款后即将收据寄下,以便报销。

六、去年五月间请兄代本馆续订杂志六种,共计美金一百一十二元五角,其中 *Current History* 收据未寄来,虽去信催寄,亦未见复。杂志均按期寄到,兹附上一经办单,请兄加章后寄还,以便办理结帐手续。

七、吾兄为本馆代购图书史料所用之汇费及邮费,共计若干?请开一总数收条,在购书款内列支。又去年吾兄为本馆所购书籍一批,共计一百○一元五角四分,其中有书籍二本计二元及邮费三元,缺少收条,及本年代向加州大学所购一书亦无收据,兹分别备就证明单三张寄奉,请加章附下。

八、承代向美国军史编辑部函索出版书籍 *Guide to the Japanese Monographs on Manchuria* 已收到,当径函致谢,并请其继续寄赠。

九、附奉本年七月至十二月征集费空白收据六张,请加章后寄下。附上六月份台湾银行送金簿存根一张,请查收。

专此,敬颂道绥!

弟罗家伦敬启

八,二五,台北

嫂夫人前叩安。

〔University of Chicago Library, Yuan T'ung-li Papers, Box 1〕

按：*The World of Learning 1962-63* 由伦敦 Europa Publications 出版；*The China Quarterly*，1960 年由伦敦大学亚非学院创办。此件为文书代笔，落款、补语为罗家伦亲笔。

八月三十日

先生致信中基会，申请补助《中国留欧大陆各国博士论文目录》编纂工作。

August 30, 1962

Dear Sirs:

After the publication of the *Guide to Doctoral Dissertations by Chinese Students in America*, I was asked by a number of friends both in Taiwan and in this country to make a similar survey of the dissertations by Chinese students in Europe.

According to a preliminary survey, over 2,000 Chinese students were awarded the doctorate by European universities. A record of the academic accomplishment of these scholars would be an invaluable document for the history of higher education in China. It would also serve to prevent unnecessary duplication of scientific research by Chinese students in American universities.

This record would be of particular interest to the Trustees of the China Foundation, as most of the research fellows sent to Europe with the support of the Foundation earned the doctorate from European universities especially in the field of natural science.

In compiling such a record, I shall need a full year of painstaking work, particularly in identifying the Chinese name of each author, in verifying the kind and date of each degree, and in furnishing full bibliographical information of each dissertation. Since a great deal of research is involved and since a trip to Europe is necessary, I beg to request for a grant of $1,200.00 in order to bring the research to completion. In view of its significance to the cause of Chinese education, I hope the Trustees will give favorable consideration to this request.

Yours sincerely,

T. L. Yuan

〔University of Chicago Library, Yuan T'ung-li Papers, Box 1〕

按：同日，先生致信叶良才，请其协助申请。此件为录副。

八月

先生为《新疆研究文献目录》撰写序言。〔《新疆研究文献目录：1886~1962》（日文本），1962 年初版〕

九月一日

钱思亮覆函先生，告中基会在台董事对《中国留欧大陆各国博士论文目录》的资助申请表示支持，请先生径向中基会提交书面申请。

> 守和先生道鉴：
>
> 　　接奉七月廿四日手教，敬聆一一。尊编《中国留欧博士论文目录》所拟申请之补助，于日前（八月廿四日）蒋梦麟先生约集中基会在台同仁餐叙时面陈，孟麟先生及李芑均先生、霍亚民先生均表赞成，愿予支持。请先生径向中基会申请，此案提出时，弟自当支持。
>
> 　　承询之 Li, Fo-Ki 先生，本校物理系同仁亦不知其人，至 Syracuse 大学拟购本校所藏历代《琉球宝案》影本一节，此书前经本校委托"中央研究院"摄照，仅有拷贝五份，已分配完毕。现已另函商"中研院"再为冲洗，费用若干，俟准复后再行奉告。专此，敬颂时绥。

弟钱思亮敬启

九，一

〔University of Chicago Library, Yuan T'ung-li Papers, Box 1〕

按：此件为打字稿，落款处为其签名。

九月四日

先生赴美国国家档案局为"国史馆"查询卷宗目录，后致信罗家伦。

　　一、关于一九二九年俄军侵入绥芬河一案，今日到档案局查明，另纸报告。

　　二、嘱购 *World of Learning* 及 *China Quarterly* 并预订 *F. Q.* 两年均已照办，所缺 *F. Q.* Oct 1957 之一份，亦告其配补。

　　三、嘱寄张伯谨"公使"美金 53.61 一节，业在馆中购书费余款内如数提出代为汇还。

四、订购 *Current Hist.* 七元五角,该处不寄收条,并寄弟之支票后面盖章作为收据,兹检出奉上,可作报账之用,其缺少收据之三笔小款,兹在证明单上加章奉上。

九月四日

〔University of Chicago Library, Yuan T'ung-li Papers, Box 1〕

按:此件为摘要性质的底稿。

九月十日

徐炳麟覆函先生,告所托购买书籍已托大陆友人相机进行。

守和先生:

七月十四日惠书早已奉悉,以嘱购各书尚无着落,致稽裁复。

嘱购书四种,未到港,已托国内友好代为购寄,能否出口,尚难预料。

尊著《博士论文目录》拾部已收到,正积极推销。《西人研究中国文献目录》未收到,请通知先寄三本。

关于大陆书刊,近来纸张、数量较为好转,至旧书除佛经、碑帖外,久无货来,有供不应求之势。夏道泰先生前月过港,一般情形,已为陈述。

港中如恒,上周飓风损失甚大。弟处托适,杨宗翰先生旅港亦好。此颂时绥。

弟徐炳麟上
九月十日

〔University of Chicago Library, Yuan T'ung-li Papers, Box 2〕

九月十一日

郭廷以覆函先生,谈《巴布阔福回忆录》翻译、《新疆研究文献目录》代售,以及近代史研究所近况。

守和先生道席:

上月拜奉大示,祗悉一是。《巴布阔福回忆录》复印本日昨亦已收到,价款支票随函呈上,敬祈查收。关于该书今后翻译问题,日内当再切实接洽,一俟确定,即行函告。此间俄英两种语文俱精者,恐不易得,如不得已,只好先转为中文,但译者之外交历史及西北地理知识如何,亦须考虑。

尊编《新疆书目》，将来不妨交由台北商务书馆或正中书局代销，手续费约为百分之十五上下。此外近史所亦可经办，但不及书店之方便。又巴布阔福书无论译英或译汉，均须本所研究人员从旁协助。年来同人工作十分紧张，各有单独研究计划，并须如期完成，一时尚未想到妥人。福特计划，现在参加专题研究者十五人，其中国内史（政治、经济、军事、制度、思想）八人，中俄关系四人，中美二人，中日一人。所有工作，几均须弟照顾协助，能力、时间俱感不足。另出国者三人，分赴哈佛、哥伦比亚、东京，正在办理手续。弟内外肆应，极以为苦，而外间压力尤大，一切可想而知。有便务希多多赐教为幸。匆此，祗颂撰安！

弟廷以拜启

九、十一

〔University of Chicago Library, Yuan T'ung-li Papers, Box 2〕

九月十二日

徐家璧覆函先生，告知耶鲁大学图书馆东亚馆藏、人事情况。

守和先生尊鉴：

敬肃者，昨奉月之九日手示，诵悉一是。藉谂福躬康泰，阖府清吉，颂以慰并。六月初澄兄嘉礼，欣能出席申贺，莫名快慰！至于所献微敬，实不足道，而反蒙挂齿，尤感愧歉之至！澄兄嫂蜜月旅行在德，曾赐谢卡，异常周至，想现下或已回美矣。

璧抵新港后，倏忽已逾三月，工作重点，全在采购，惜较好较重要之图书期刊，无从购求，事实使然，暂亦无可如何。耶鲁远东部中文方面现有 professional 职员四人，而 clerical 仅半人，不匀现象，无有甚于此者；此亦可见近年习文法者每转业图书馆，遂使 professional 人员过剩，而较 clerical 员工更易于聘请也。先生嘱查各期刊暨《新疆论丛》，此间均一无所有，深为惶歉！耶鲁过去采购，毫未注意期刊，是以抗战前后期刊，均付阙如。刻虽立意搜购，毋乃为时已晚，许多珍贵资料，均不易获得，奈何奈何！草此奉闻，敬颂崇安！

晚徐家璧鞠躬

九月十二日夜

尊夫人前并乞叱名叩安为感！

〔University of Chicago Library, Yuan T'ung-li Papers, Box 2〕

九月十三日

蒋复璁致函先生,请寄赠个人著述以便"国立中央图书馆"典藏。

> 守和先生大鉴:

> 久疏音候,至以为歉。年来先生著述宏富,甚佩甚佩。王云老及黄"部长"皆曾提及,政府亦有补助,惟敝馆迄未蒙颁赐,敢乞赐寄全套,藉光典藏。《文物精华》又出一册,另印《研究计画指南》一册,谨以邮奉,祈察存为荷。即请著安。

> 弟蒋复璁顿首

> 九月十三日

> 〔University of Chicago Library, Yuan T'ung-li Papers, Box 2〕

> 按:"王云老及黄'部长'"即王云五和黄季陆,《文物精华》应指台北中国文化研究所出版品,该套丛书自1960年起陆续出版,根据历史朝代分册发行。

九月十五日

伍藻池覆函先生,告知《中国留美同学博士论文目录》售出情况,并表示愿意代售《新疆研究文献目录》(日文本)。

> 同礼前辈先生惠鉴:

> 日前拜读大教,久未裁答,深以为歉。叶恭绰先生之书,小店尚无此书,一时未能如命奉上。大作已售出三四部,每部都是学生购去,顷先奉上 $15.00,到时记账。此种两种价目办法,在商业言商,十分不便。因购者多是学生,此事一经传播,凡购者都以学生身份来购,通得每部三元。如是五元之价,形同伪设价目了。公以为然否? 新著面世,欢迎代售。匆匆奉覆,□颂著安。

> 伍藻池顿首

> 九月十五日

> 〔University of Chicago Library, Yuan T'ung-li Papers, Box 3〕

> 按:"叶恭绰先生之书"应指《遐庵谈艺录》。先生在该函第1页右上角标有"十二月廿三日函寄日文三十部@3.50,七折收账"。

九月十六日

谢寿康覆函先生,告知曾委托梵蒂冈教廷查找档案,但以档案浩繁且中文不易识别而无所获。

守和吾兄惠鉴：

　　日前得六日华翰，拜悉种切。旋嘱敝馆施森道蒙席往各大学查询，奈以档案太多且远东人名又大同小异、不易分晓，均无结果。其实此间不重视博士，故有 Doctor Romanus ＝ Asinus Germanicus 之谬也。其他垂询各件亦无从作答，有负雅命，至为抱歉。专此，敬颂日安。

弟谢寿康拜上

九月十六日

〔University of Chicago Library, Yuan T'ung-li Papers, Box 5〕

九月十七日

先生致信王云五，奉上"行政院"资助《中国留美同学博士论文目录》印刷费收据，并告《新疆研究丛书》编纂进展。

岫庐院长尊鉴：

　　七月间奉到赐书，并承贵院补助《留美博士论文目录》印刷费美金柒百元，当即函谢并寄上赠与国外文化机关名单壹份，请予备案，谅荷垂察。顷闻前寄中国银行之收据须由该行保管，用特另缮正式收据随函奉上，即希转交贵院会计处是感。日前寄上著作两种，即乞教正。近又编就《新疆文献目录》两种一、中文，二、日文，一俟出版当再奉呈。专此，敬候道祺。

弟袁同礼顿首

九月十七日

书内并附张菊翁宋版杜诗跋文。

〔《岫庐巳故知交百家手札》，台北：台湾商务印书馆，1976 年〕

　　按："张菊翁宋版杜诗跋文"即 1957 年 8 月 1 日张元济为《宋本杜工部集》撰写的跋文，是书于 1957 年 12 月出版。

九月十八日

先生致信郭廷以，希望近代史研究所尽快翻译、出版《巴布阔福回忆录》，并询问郑宪毕业后的去向。

量予先生著席：

　　奉到九、十一日赐书，欣悉翻译《巴布阔福回忆录》正在计划之中。查新疆失地数十万里多由此人主持，而国人著作鲜少注意，故盼贵所能早日予以出版也。又悉贵所同人专题研究积极进行，便中尚希赐一名单,注明研究题目,如此间有史料为国内所无者,当设法影照,以供参考。又郑君 Sally 闻已在华大完成学业,不识在美何处工作,抑已返所研究,便中并希函告是盼。《回忆录》影照费前已由弟代为付清,此次寄下之支票 $ 37.43,曾请馆中照像部予以副署,该部不肯照办,并嘱寄还。尊处另写弟名抬头,只得仍行寄还,即乞另写一纸,寄下为祷。匆匆,顺候道祺。

弟袁同礼顿首
九,十八

〔台北"中央研究院"近代史研究所档案馆,〈郭廷以〉,馆藏号 069-01-02-089〕

　　按:"郑君 Sally",先生拼写有误,当即郑宪(Shelley Hsien Cheng,? —1966),福建闽县人,南京政治大学外交系毕业,后留学美国入西雅图华盛顿大学并获博士学位;其父郑烈(1888—1958)为同盟会早期会员,南京国民政府成立后,长期担任最高法院检察署检察长。该信于 9 月 24 日送达南港,郭廷以在信封正面标记"9,25 复"。

庄泽宣致函先生,寄上书稿请转托恒慕义校阅。

2945 Sixth St.
Riverside, Calf.
Sept. 18, 1962

守和兄:

　　一个月前承寄《年鉴》并指示一切,至感。兹将《年鉴》奉还,谢谢。关于拙著请人校阅一节,因性质通俗(备仅受中等教育者阅读),原拟少数章烦专家过目,免有错漏。其中"佛教"一章已请 Princeton 陈观胜(Kenneth Chen)兄核阅得复,拟加一二小节大致可用,至以为慰;"绘画"一章拟请蒋重哑兄(Chiang Yee);"文学"一章拟请陈受颐兄分别一校。蒋游西印各岛,陈往欧渡假,尚待接洽,惟各人开课后均忙。因念 Hummel 先生已退休,或有兴一阅(全稿或若干章),恨未识荆,可否请兄先容后示复,再行寄他府上,尊意以为如何? 屡渎清神,不胜泥首,即颂近祺。

弟泽宣

九月十八

〔University of Chicago Library, Yuan T'ung-li Papers, Box 2〕

按："拙著"所拟题名似为 *Chinese Heritage*，该书稿最终似并未出版。收到该信及书稿后，先生将书稿转交牟复礼审读。

九月二十日

何炳棣致函先生，告知袁清所撰论文尚未细读，并告近期行程安排。

守和先生赐鉴：

令郎论文及抽印本八月中即收到。随即先匆匆一读；甫拟再读试做简评。北美三个数学团体在敝校举行联合年会，旧日同学如林家翘兄等五六位皆携眷来温，迎送酬酢几无虚日。本月初又忙于赶撰赴台开会所用论文一篇，以致清君文章迄未得机细读，至歉至歉。现晚与内子景洛将于本月廿三日赴日转台、港，十月三十日归。十月初一定细读奉覆。匆此，敬请道安。

晚何炳棣再拜

一九六二九月二十日

〔University of Chicago Library, Yuan T'ung-li Papers, Box 2〕

按：林家翘（1916—2013），生于北京，原籍福建福州，力学和数学家，1937 年清华大学物理系毕业后留校任教，1939 年考取庚子赔款公费留学生资格赴英国留学，翌年改派加拿大，1941 年获得加拿大多伦多大学硕士学位后进入美国加州理工学院学习，1944年获得博士学位。

九月二十二日

先生致信渡边宏，对石田幹之助无意担任《新疆研究文献目录》（日文本）合编者表示遗憾，请渡边宏决定该书售价，并表示该书出版后将在 200 册外再给予其 50 册，以示感谢。

September 22, 1962

Dear Mr. Watanabe:

Thank you for your two recent letters. I am sorry that Mr. Ishida declines to be our collaborator. I wish to thank him for his interest and encouragement. Please convey my hearty thanks for his help.

If the price of the bibliography is too high, it will affect the sale. So,

I shall leave it to your own judgement.

In order to compensate your labors, I wish to offer you two hundred copies of this bibliography. The proceeds from the sale of these two hundred copies will go to you. In addition, you should have fifty extra copies for presentation to your friends, review copies, and the like.

I shall write you in a day or two about other matters.

Yours sincerely,

T. L. Yuan

〔University of Chicago Library, Yuan T'ung-li Papers, Box 2〕

按:该件为录副。

九月二十五日 波士顿

先生赴哈佛大学汉和图书馆。〔University of Chicago Library, Yuan T'ung-li Papers, Box 2〕

程其保致函先生,请先生指示参考书获取途径,并询国会图书馆是否藏有其著述。

守和先生道鉴:

弟刻从事一项写作,需要一种中国近百年大事记作参考,拟请费神指示,如何可以谋得此种资料(中英文均可,但最好有中文的)。如荷惠助,感激之至。

再,弟一生曾写有关教育专著近十余种,多系由商务出版,现查各处均无存本。弟之私藏留在大陆,未及带出,此类著述大都无经世价值,但不知国会图书馆曾否收藏一二,敬乞便中一查,实所感祷。此事不急,有空为之可也。专恳,即颂道祺。

弟程其保拜上

九,廿五

〔University of Chicago Library, Yuan T'ung-li Papers, Box 2〕

郭廷以覆函先生,再议《巴布阔福回忆录》翻译,并告知郑宪通讯地址。

守和先生道席:

十八日手示祗悉,诸承关注,谨再谢。支票已遵嘱另开附呈,请查收。巴布阔福书译英恐不易,不得已将拟先转为中文,人选尚待进一步接洽。关于近史所专题研究情况,另表附陈,尚希予以指导,并恳将

美方所藏有关资料,随时示知,以便制为复本,无任感祷。郑宪
(Shelley Cheng)现在 Iowa State College 任教,其通信处为 2303
Franklin St. Cedar Falls, Iowa。此君确为一有希望之青年学者,其《同
盟会史》不失为精审之作。匆覆,顺颂时福。

　　　　　　　　　　　　　　　　　　　　　　弟廷以谨启

　　　　　　　　　　　　　　　　　　　　　　　九,廿五

尊编《博士论文目录》可否见赐一册? 何处代售? 又及。

　　　　〔University of Chicago Library, Yuan T'ung-li Papers, Box 2〕

按:《同盟会史》应指郑宪专著《同盟会:其领导、组织及财务》
(*The Tung-meng Hui: its organization, Leadership and Finances,*
1905-1912),西雅图华盛顿大学 1962 年出版。该函另附近史所
专题研究情况 5 页,分为已完成之专题、正在进行中之专题研究、
集体编纂工作正在进行者,前者 16 项,次者 4 项,后者 22 项,每
项均注明负责人。

九月二十六日

于震寰致函先生,答复所询各节。

　　守和先生尊鉴:

　　　昨日台驾贲临,未获瞻谒为憾。聂崇岐之别号为筱珊,史语所之
子范为谁,曾以询全君汉昇,全不能答,无碍光及。《西北问题论丛》
哈佛均未入藏,陈力著《伊宁事变记略》当在一九四六前后,未见著
录,以后随时留意,如有所得再行奉陈。敬颂道安,不备。

　　　　　　　　　　　　　　　　　　　　　　震寰拜上

　　　　　　　　　　　　　　　　　　一九六二年九月廿六日

夫人前乞叱名请安。

　　　　〔University of Chicago Library, Yuan T'ung-li Papers, Box 2〕

按:子范即周法高(1915—1994),字子范,号汉堂,江苏东台人,现
代语言文字学家。1939 年毕业于中央大学文学系,1941 年获北
京大学中国语言学硕士学位,曾任“中央研究院”历史语言研究
所研究员。

九月二十七日

先生打电话与杨联陞,后者约午饭,先生因故未应。〔《杨联陞日记》(稿本)〕

九月二十八日

庄泽宣致片先生,请代询恒慕义是否愿意协助校阅书稿。

守和我兄:

旬前寄回《中国年鉴》,内附一信,谅邀鉴及,未识兄有机会询及 Arthur W. Hummel 先生,愿校阅拙著否(*Chinese Heritage*)? 全稿共约打字纸一百页,如承他老人家惠允,先将一半寄去,他是否仍到国会图书馆工作,应寄该馆中文部,抑寄他府上(示址)。一俟得复,即行照办。阅后如认为可印,或将请他写一短序,此是后话。即颂近祺。

弟庄泽宣

9/28/62

〔University of Chicago Library, Yuan T'ung-li Papers, Box 2〕

九月二十九日

先生致信毕乃德,寄上有关同文馆的材料,并告已建议毕尔拍摄缩微胶片,如获批准,康乃尔大学亦可获得副本。

September 29, 1962

Dear Professor Biggerstaff:

I have recently gone over the volumes of *Chiao hui kung-pao* and the *Wan Kuo kung-pao* edited by the late Young John Allen.

Knowing your interest in the history of T'ung Wen Kuan, I am enclosing some material which may be of possible interest to you.

I am suggesting to Dr. Beal that these volumes be microfilmed before I return them to the Emory University Theological Library. If the plan can be carried out, Cornell University may like to get a copy.

I have accepted Cornell's invitation to attend the Library Conference and Dedication on October 9 – 10. I shall certainly look forward to the pleasure of seeing you.

Yours sincerely,

T. L. Yuan

〔University of Chicago Library, Yuan T'ung-li Papers, Box 2〕

按:*Chiao-hui kung-pao* 应指《教会新报》,此处拼写略有错误。Young John Allen 即林乐知(1836-1907),基督教美南监理会来

华传教士,以办报、办学、译书著称,《万国公报》确由其创办,其
初名即《教会新报》(*Church News*)。Emory University 通译作埃
默里大学,主校区位于乔治亚州亚特兰大市,该校神学图书馆确
存有较为齐全的《教会新报》《万国公报》。此件为录副。

十月一日

罗家伦覆函先生,请代向美国国家档案局查实有关中东路事件卷宗号并复
制一份,另请先生向国会图书馆询问补拍胶片是否制作完成。

守和吾兄道鉴:

两奉手教暨单据等,均敬收悉。承吾兄费神代向美国国家档案局
查询国务院档案 866.77 号胶片,关于俄国内部情况档案内中东路问题
之件,其号码为 No. 316-Rolls142-164 共二十三卷,全部复制壹份需
美金一百三十六元,外加邮费,三星期可以竣事。经本馆征校处检查
有关一九二九年至三〇年中东路争执事件档案之编号为 861.77 号,吾
兄查示者为 866.77 号,不知该两号档案系同属一事,抑为联续纪载?
拟请吾兄再费神复查一番,如属一事之首尾联续纪载,则请吾兄即在
本馆购书款内拨付,代为定制一全份,并请于付款后先将收据寄下。
牛津出版 R. Maxwell:*Information U. S. S. R.* 请代购一帙。又本馆前向
国会图书馆添制之胶片十卷,未知已否制竣寄出,便中亦请一询,为
托。兹将吾兄七月至十月份征集费新台币贰千元转存台湾银行,送金
簿存根二纸附奉,并希察收。专复,敬颂道祺!

　　　　　　　　　　　　　　　　　　　　　　　弟罗家伦敬启

　　　　　　　　　　　　　　　　　　　　　　　　　　十,一

〔University of Chicago Library, Yuan T'ung-li Papers, Box 1〕

　　按:*Information U. S. S. R.* 由 Robert Maxwell 编,1962 年牛津大学
　　初版。此件为文书代笔,落款处为罗家伦亲笔。

刘国蓁致函先生,转袁道冲致袁慧熙信并略谈香港经济现状。

守和先生尊鉴:

敬启者,上月前后曾奉上令岳致尊夫人信两封,量邀尊览。今日
又再接到渠手教,嘱代转尊夫人函一封,故特奉上,敬希察收为幸。港
中各样如常,惟新楼屋租则陆续加增,各物亦因此涨价,影响社会经济
甚大,尤以一般受薪阶级难于应付者也。匆匆,专此,敬请撰安。

愚晚国鏊顿首

一九六二年十月一日

〔University of Chicago Library, Yuan T'ung-li Papers, Box 2〕

毕乃德覆函先生，感谢帮助录副《教会新报》、《万国公报》，并请国会图书馆考虑将此报刊缩微胶片化，另告知自己因课无法参加图书馆落成典礼。

October 1, 1962

Dear Dr. Yuan:

Thank you very much for the prints from the *Chiao-hui kung-pao* and the *Wan kuo kung-pao* . I hope that you have persuaded Dr. Beal to microfilm the volumes of these two journals edited by Young J. Allen; certainly, Cornell would wish to secure a copy.

I shall not be able to attend the Library Dedication Luncheon on October 10 because I have a class at that hour, but I hope to see you at some of the ceremonies at other times of the day.

Sincerely yours,

Knight Biggerstaff

〔University of Chicago Library, Yuan T'ung-li Papers, Box 2〕

按：此件为打字稿，落款处为其签名。

十月二日

叶良才覆函先生，告先生的出版资助申请将在中基会下年度执委会上予以讨论并作出决定。

Oct. 2, 1962

Dear Dr. Yuan:

Your letter of August 30, 1962 requesting a grant of $ 1,200 for the compilation of a *guide to doctoral dissertations by Chinese students in Europe* was considered by our Trustees at the 32nd Annual Meeting held on September 14, 1962. It was decided that the application be referred to the Executive Committee of the Foundation for consideration after the accounts of 1962 are closed.

We will write you next year after our Executive Committee has made a decision.

Yours sincerely,

L. T. Yip

Financial Secretary & Assistant Treasurer

〔University of Chicago Library, Yuan T'ung-li Papers, Box 1〕

渡边宏覆函先生,告知《新疆研究文献目录》(日文本)印刷的总成本,并将寄送该书修改后的封面。

le 2 oct. Tokyo

Prof. T. L. Yuan

Je recevais votre lettre de 22.

Toute dépence est décidé 245000 Yen (680 u.s. $).

Parce que les couts d'anglais et d'offset sont très hauts.

Une refonte de votre preface achevait.

La préparation de notre imprimerie acheverai le 8 oct.

Après-demain je vous enverrai l'offset de la couverture.

Aujourd'hui envoyais des épreuves.

Je vous remercie de votre cadeau.

Votre tout dévoué.

H. W

(University of Chicago Library, Yuan T'ung-li Papers, Box 8)

十月四日

Wolfgang Seuberlich 致函先生,询问某位中国学者的姓名。

October 4, 1962

Dear Dr. Yuan:

It is already long time since I had for the last time the pleasure to communicate with you by correspondence. May I venture today to bother you again with a question?

We could not find here the Chinese equivalent of the following author's name: Maurice H. Tseng. He compiled the bibliography listed below:

Recent Chinese Publications on the Chinese Language: an

annotated bibliography. New Haven, Conn., Institute of Far Eastern Languages, Yale University, 1961.

Would it be possible to you to give me the correct Chinese form of the above author's name (with characters)? I would be very much obliged to you for this favour.

If I can reciprocate in some way or other, please, let me know.

I hope that you personally and Mrs. Yuan are both well and had nice summer vacations. With my very best wishes and kind regards, I remain,

Yours sincerely,

Wolfgang Seuberlich,

Keeper of the Far Eastern Collection

（University of Chicago Library, Yuan T'ung-li Papers, Box 2）

按：Maurice H. Tseng 即曾宪斌（1927—?），1945 年入金陵大学学习，后赴美，1961 年起执教于旧金山州立学院（San Francisco State College），主要负责中文教学。

十月六日

赵赓飏致函先生，请协助在国会图书馆查找《清华周刊》文章，并告月涵堂筹建情况。

守和先生：

顷有一事相求：《清华校友通讯》刊载"忆旧"文字，极有益于爱校精神之发扬与校友学谊之敦睦，记得弟在校时（1930–1935）《清华周刊》（学生会出版者）刊有春夏秋冬四篇，仿《儒林外史》、《水浒传》等手笔，渲染清华园景物与生活情趣。虽属游戏文章，但内容文字均属上乘，如能找到，通讯极愿转载。惟在台湾找《清华学报》尚有（胡适之先生在"中研院"找到一全份），而《清华周刊》则绝无。闻月涵先生生前谈及美国国会图书馆存有全帙，敬恳先生拨冗代为检查，或借出寄下，用毕奉还，或请人抄掷。倘有花费，均由校友通讯社负担。刊载年月，似在 1931–1932 春季，为投稿清华之学生介绍清华，当时似名为"向导专号"。刻台湾与美国航寄甚便，极少拖延或意外（《学报》及《通讯》航空挂号，刊物照片从未遗失损坏），最好能借出寄下也。不悉贵圕有无禁例？先生肯赐助否？

　　　　梅师母(月涵先生夫人)九月十九日离台飞英,到祖彤小姐处,十二月初来美,Xmas 到祖彬小姐处,谅已有函奉告。"月涵堂"筹建会正努力募捐,清华代教务长朱树恭兄在 Ill.,可忠代校长十月内亦将由欧来美,届时当来华府拜访。专此奉渎,敬祈裁夺示复,不胜感激! 即颂时安。

晚学 1934 赵赓飏敬上

十月六日

　　　　　〔University of Chicago Library, Yuan T'ung-li Papers, Box 2〕

　　按:1962 年 4 月 29 日,《清华校友通讯》在台复刊,赵赓飏担任主编职务。梅贻琦逝世后,陈可忠被任命为代理校长,9 月赴维尔纳参加国际原子能总署召开的第六次会议。[1] 1967 年 5 月 19日,校友捐建于台北市之月涵堂落成,后又在 1985 年扩建。

十月十日　伊萨卡

康乃尔大学奥林研究图书馆、本科生图书馆举行开幕典礼,先生受邀参加。
〔University of Chicago Library, Yuan T'ung-li Papers, Box 10〕

　　按:此次受邀人数众多,先生外套遗落,后曾与该校图书馆中文编目马大任联系寻找。

牟复礼覆函先生,就庄泽宣书稿的审查意见询问先生,并略谈普林斯顿大学中文善本书编目计划的进展。

October 10, 1962

Dear Dr. Yuan:

　　In reply to your note of October 2, I should be happy to read the manuscript of Dr. Chuang's *Chinese Heritage* . Please advise me frankly what kind of comment he expects from me. I want to do whatever you think appropriate, I do not know how thoroughly you would want me to go into the comment on it.

　　On the matter of a catalogue for our rare books, it gets more complicated all the time. I have gotten the Librarian to re-open the issue, and he is actively seeking funds. But also, it turns out that our earlier

---

① 清华大学校友服务中心编著《人物清华》,新竹:清华大学出版社,2011 年,页 11。

attempts to find a cataloger (going back three or four years) leave us committed in principle to one or two other persons whom we contacted in this regard at that time. Of course, we shall review the whole matter if it seems we shall get the funds and I shall write you again before we come to any decision.

Again, with thanks for your kind interest,

Sincerely,

Fritz Mote

〔University of Chicago Library, Yuan T'ung-li Papers, Box 2〕

按：该函为牟复礼亲笔。

徐家璧覆函先生，感谢寄赠《新疆研究文献目录》（日文本），并告耶鲁大学图书馆订购《中国留美同学博士论文目录》及《苏联研究中国文献目录》。

守和先生尊鉴：

敬肃者，昨奉月之六日手示，诵悉一是。欣闻尊著《新疆文献目录》又告杀青，曷胜敬佩！蒙允于出版后，赐赠此间中日文本各一部，备极感戴！兹将日文本序文遵嘱奉还。又已出之英文本尊著两种，经与常石先生商妥，将博士论文指南再购壹册，俄文中国论著则购二册，以资参考应用。随函附上订购片二份，至乞于便中将各书交邮寄下为祷！此间为报销需要，发票请开具叁份，抬头用 Order Department, Yale University Library, New Haven, Com.，可由此间转致，再行汇款也。最后散部采购中文书籍，以交流、岭南二家较多，其他书店，另单列奉，以备稽考。耑此奉覆，敬颂崇安！

晚徐家璧鞠躬

十月十日

尊夫人前并乞代为候安！

〔University of Chicago Library, Yuan T'ung-li Papers, Box 2〕

按："常石先生"及以下各信中的"常石公"皆为常石道雄。该函另附耶鲁大学图书馆采购中文书各书店名单，涉及东京、香港、台北11家书店或个人。

十月十二日

渡边宏致函先生，告《新疆研究文献目录》（日文本）的封面和序言均已更换,石田幹之助教授对凡例略作修改。

> le 12 oct
> Tokyo

Professeur,

J'ai bien reçu votre lettre par l'avion.

Des échanges de la couverture et des additions de la réclame, ils sont fait assurément.

Vous envoyez votre chèque, à moi.

Cette nuit, je vous envoyerai l'offset de votre préface et couverture dernier, mon anglais.

Votre note (凡例) est amendé quelque chose par prof. Ishida, comme particule.

Votre tout dévoué,

> H. Watanabe

N. B. l'épreuve d'index presse

〔University of Chicago Library, Yuan T'ung-li Papers, Box 8〕

十月十三日

蒋复璁覆函先生,告所托查询、影钞各节均需等待,另请转告印刷所补寄先生著述数种。

守和吾兄大鉴:

九月三十日大函敬悉,嘱查留德博士二人之中文姓名及陈力所著《伊宁事变纪略》一书,暂时无从查询,俟后获有结果当随时奉告。至影钞《哈密事迹》事,容当觅工影钞寄上。

承盛意允将近年出版大著寄赠本馆,至深感纫。惟据尊示所列书目查对,只收到一九六一年出版之 *Russian Works on China in American Libraries* 一种,其余皆未收到,恳再关照印刷人赐予补寄为祷。又本馆《善本书目索引》虽已编成,顷以书有增加,拟另重编,故尚未付印,将来出版后定寄请教正也。耑复,顺颂撰安。

> 弟蒋复璁顿首
> 十月十三日

〔University of Chicago Library, Yuan T'ung-li Papers, Box 2〕

按：此件为文书代笔，落款处为其签名。

杨云竹致函先生，告知行踪及返台后的近况。

守和乡长兄大鉴：

离金山前记曾奉上一函，尔后弟曾为检查身体（体重激减十余磅）略作延缓。于上月廿日自金山搭机，在东京留一夜，廿二日换机安抵台北。为慎重起见，曾入近郊设备较完备之荣民医院检查体格，日前已退院，幸未获见任何疴疾，知注谨闻。在美京各友好，有询及此，敢祈代为致意。离美前原拟折回华府分访友好辞行，竟未能如愿，不无歉仄。

艺展成果，国内甚为满意，王云老、王雪公均赞为年来罕睹之盛举。艺展会业于九月底结束，弟仍被"送回""外交部"，一俟内子自金山返来，再作住所之布置。现台北天气仍残暑未消，"国庆"前海外侨界返台祝贺者甚多，"国庆"之日有盛大花车游行，诸多彩节目，市面繁荣气象到处可见。国内如有嘱办之件，务乞随时示及。敬候□福，袁清弟好。

弟杨云竹敬启
十月十三日

惠函请寄台北"外交部"即可。弟近租得一公寓式住屋，在市郊市民住宅之旁，附近有同事数家，可得望助之便，惜太隘小，仍系过渡性质耳。弟又及。

〔University of Chicago Library, Yuan T'ung-li Papers, Box 2〕

按：该函左上角破损。

十月十四日

先生拟一信与郭廷以，告欲印《新疆条约集》，请其在近代史研究所接收"外交部"档案中代为查询有无遗漏，并请该所代售《新疆研究文献目录》（日文本）。

量予先生道席：

奉到九月廿五日手教，并承寄下支票，谢谢。《巴布阔福回忆录》如能印成中文，已是一种贡献。弟鉴于时贤著述对于西北边界语言不详，拟先印一小册名曰《新疆条约集》。兹奉上目录二纸，拟请贵所在接收"外交部"档案中代为一查，如有遗漏并盼录副寄下，以便一并付印,至为感荷。又拙编《新疆研究文献目录》日文本本月杪可以出版,已告印刷人径由东京先寄上五十部,请贵所代为推销,另寄二百部于商务印书馆托其代售,附上致文星书局一函,即请代为付邮。该书局经理萧孟能往往不复信,所购之书亦无下文,如吾兄与之熟识,能否便中一托,弟尚有他书拟托其代售也。顺候教祺。

弟袁同礼顿首

十,十四

专题研究目录洋洋大观,如有新资料,当再奉闻。

〔University of Chicago Library, Yuan T'ung-li Papers, Box 2〕

按:该信应未寄出,参见 10 月 21 日先生致郭廷以信。《新疆条约集》最终定名为《中俄西北条约集》。

先生致信牟复礼,感谢校阅庄泽宣书稿,请其坦诚给予评价及意见,并推荐刘麟生到普林斯顿大学图书馆协助编纂中文善本书目。

October 14, 1962

Dear Professor Mote:

Thank you so much for your letter of October 10th and for your readiness to help Dr. C. H. Chuang at my request. I am quite sure Dr. Chuang would welcome heartily the criticism and suggestions from such an outstanding scholar such as your good self. Please go into it as thoroughly as you can. I am writing to him to-day to convey to him this good news.

As to the selection of a good cataloger for your rare Chinese books, I must say that I am rather distressed to learn that the matter seems to get rather complicated. After having had a talk with you last month, I ventured to inform Mr. L. S. Liu the possibilities of his employment if and when funds are available. As he is very much interested in this kind of bibliographical research, he has already declined two other offers since then.

As far as my knowledge of the qualifications of Chinese personnel goes, Mr. Liu is the most suitable person to undertake this work, especially when the catalogue of the collection is to appear in print. It was very gracious of you to say that you will write me again before you come to any decision. Meanwhile, I shall be glad to send you a confidential report on other applicants, if you would let me know their names.

Hearty congratulations on your new book which has just come to my desk after my several days' absence to attend the Conference and dedication of the new library at Cornell.

Sincerely yours,

T. L. Yuan

〔University of Chicago Library, Yuan T'ung-li Papers, Box 2〕

按:该件为录副。

十月中下旬

先生赴纽约,在纽约摩根图书馆观 John M. Crawford, Jr.收藏国画展览,并与李书华晤谈。〔Columbia University Libraries Archival Collections, Shuhua Li Papers, 1926-1972, Volume II: Modern Eminent Chinese Leaders〕

> 按:John M. Crawford, Jr.(1913-1988),中文名顾洛阜,美国中国书画收藏家,斋号"汉光阁"。1962 年,顾洛阜先后在纽约摩根图书馆(Pierpont Morgan Library)、哈佛大学弗格艺术博物馆(Fogg Art Museum)、堪萨斯城纳尔逊艺术博物馆(The William Rockhill Nelson Gallery of Art)举办个人展览,展品多为 14 世纪以前的作品,并由史克门为其编撰展览图录——*Catalogue of the Exhibition of Chinese Calligraphy and Painting in the Collection of John M. Crawford, Jr.*

十月十八日

先生致信富路德,推荐刘麟生任参与《明代名人传》编纂计划。

October 18, 1962

Dear Professor Goodrich:

I was most happy to have had a brief visit with you on my way to Ithaca. I hope you have seen the Crawford collection of Chinese calligraphy and paintings in Morgan Library. I am sure both you and Mrs. Goodrich could enjoy seeing these specimens of Chinese art. I was simply thrilled by them.

I am delighted to know the Ming biographical dictionary project is a going concern. At the initial stage, you may need a part-time assistant whom can be depended upon to carry on the editorial work under your direction.

If you need such a person, may I venture to recommend Mr. Liu Lin-sheng who is very much interested in the history of the Ming dynasty and who knows the literature very well. As his knowledge of Chinese is ten times better than mine, I am sure you will find him most helpful to your important work.

Mr. Liu is a graduate from St. John's University, Shanghai, and served as the Chairman of the Chinese Department in Ginling College. He has had considerable experience in editorial work and has published several important works in the field of history and literature.

During recent years he was the Secretary to Dr. Hollington K. Tong and the late Mr. K. C. Li. I can recommend him to you in highest terms. His address: 415 East 82nd Street, New York 28, N. Y. (Apt. 3A)

Sincerely,

T. L. Yuan

〔University of Chicago Library, Yuan T'ung-li Papers, Box 2〕

十月十九日

罗文达致函先生,就《新疆研究文献目录》(西文本)的编纂范畴提出意见。

9607 Culver Street

Kensington, Md.

19 October 1962

Dear Dr. Yuan:

After looking over your Sinkiang titles, I feel that it is necessary for you to decide what you want to include in your bibliography without drowning the items of general interest in highly technical and rather inaccessible items of specialized geography and natural science (resources, etc.). Also, many of the titles refer to Russian territory rather than to Chinese. To clarify that, it would be necessary to look at each individual article.

The following comments and suggestions may help you to make your decisions:

1.<u>Kalmucks</u>: all the titles refer to the Volga Kalmucks, not to Sinkiang.

2.<u>Irtysh</u>: most of the items probably refer to Russian territory.

3.<u>Kazakh</u>: though some of the items refer obviously to Russian territory, their inclusion could be justified in the preface, because the Kazakhs used to cross the border all the time nomadizing.

4.<u>Travellers</u>: there must be a vast literature in Russian, but you could justify the small number of items by expressing in the preface that you made a selection in order not to balloon the bibliography unnecessarily. Many of the explorers went mainly to Tibet and Mongolia and merely passed on their way through Sinkiang without making it their primary objective.

5.<u>Pamirs</u> and <u>Altai</u>: it is impossible to say which items might refer to Sinkiang without consulting the literature in each individual case. That is obviously an impossibility. Moreover, many of the articles are highly specialized. This also applies to the <u>Ili</u> region, as well as to the <u>T'ien-shan</u> and <u>Dzungarian Ala-Tau</u> ranges. You could eliminate all of them and say that marginal materials like specialized items on geography, resources, natural science, many of which transcend the Sinkiang border, will be included in a special supplement.

Hoping that this may be of help to you and that we might talk over some of the problems directly, I am,

With kindest regards,

Yours sincerely,

Rudolf Löewenthal

〔University of Chicago Library, Yuan T'ung-li Papers, Box 2〕

按:此件为打字稿,有些许改动,落款处为其签名。

十月二十一日

先生致信李书华,略谈顾洛阜书画展所涉及文献。

润章先生著席:

上周晤教,见贵体完全复元,气色尤佳,深以为慰,并为吾兄道贺也。Crawford 书画展览想已参观,据弟观察,大部分为长春伪宫溥仪之旧藏,惜手边无故宫所编《赏溥杰之书画目录》可以核对也。承惠借适之夫人寄来剪报,兹一并奉还。日内祖望由台北返此,想可明了,总以"以大化小,以小化无"为上计,想兄亦赞成也。专此,顺候俪安。

弟同礼顿首

十,廿一

〔Columbia University Libraries Archival Collections, Shuhua Li Papers, 1926-1972, Volume II: Modern Eminent Chinese Leaders〕

先生致信郭廷以,希望可以将《巴布阔福回忆录》译成中文,并托推销《新疆研究文献目录》(日文本)。

量予先生道席:

前奉九月廿五日惠书,并承寄还垫款,谢谢。近代贵所购到 Skachkov 所编《俄人研究中国文献目录》,日内当交邮寄上。《巴布阔福回忆录》如能先译成中文,亦一极大之贡献(同治三年《勘分西北界约》、同治八年《科布多界约》、光绪九年《中俄科塔界约》均由渠主持)。承惠寄专题研究目录,洋洋大观,想见贤劳一班情形,尚希格外珍摄。教书事如能摆脱,更可节劳,谅荷同意。弟近在东京印行之《新疆研究文献目录》日文本,诸承赞助,允为销售,至为感荷。已告印刷人寄上五十部,另寄商务、正中各壹百部,收到后并盼示复价目尚未确定。嘱寄《博士论文目录》,自当遵办。兹附上致文星书局萧经理一函,请代为付邮是盼。专此,顺候教祺。

弟袁同礼顿首

十月廿一日

〔台北"中央研究院"近代史研究所档案馆,〈郭廷以〉,馆藏号 069-01-02-089〕

按:该信后有一页纸,标注"《巴布喀夫回忆录》影印本:1——二页(封面)重复,2 四七二——四七三页缺",似非郭廷以字迹,更不是先生所书,应为近代史研究所负责人员的记录。该信于 10 月 27 日送达南港,郭廷以在信封处标记"11,17 复"。

十月二十二日

先生致信刘国蓁，请在香港代为物色印刷公司承印《中俄西北条约集》。

> 国蓁先生惠鉴：
>
> 　　前上一函，拜托调查港九印刷厂，拟请推荐一家肯负责校对并能从速付印者末校寄弟，无须寄原稿，谅荷鉴及。兹奉上《中国西北条约集》全部稿件，拟请查照港大罗香林教授所印下列两书之格式、纸张每半叶十五行，行四十三或四十四字，交印刷公司付印。如须先付定金，并盼示知。此书拟印八百部，装订用布面或硬纸，标点，or 。印在字之下面，较印在字之旁边可省钱也。吾兄对于印刷事业久具宏富之经验，定能贡献宝贵之意见也。可交二三家估价，立一合同以期便利。专此奉托，敬候时祉。
>
> 　　　　　　　　　　　　　　　　　　　弟袁同礼顿首
> 　　　　　　　　　　　　　　　　　　　　十月廿二日
>
> 罗香林 （一）《蒲寿庚研究》十五行，行四十三字，大约五号字
> 　　　　（二）《一八四二前以前之香港对外交通》十五行，行四十四字，小注十七行
>
> 　　　　　　〔University of Chicago Library, Yuan T'ung-li Papers, Box 2〕

按："一八四二前"当作"一八四二年"。《中俄西北条约集》后作为《新疆研究丛刊》第四种，1963 年 2 月初版。此件为底稿，先生在左上角标注"十一月七日又函催"。

余又荪致函先生，告知台北商务印书馆愿代售《新疆研究文献目录》，并告寄书地址及海关入口问题，另请在美为其谋教职或进修机会。

> 守和先生道席：
>
> 　　违教多年，虽由朋友处时闻尊况，而未奉书问候，深为歉仄！顷奉十二日大示，如晤尊颜，快慰之至！
>
> 　　新疆研究文献目录一书，已与商务商定，愿为在台代销。
>
> 　　1. 如该书订价为台币六十元，照例七折缴款。（商务虽收三成，但同业八折发出，商务只得一成也）。广告费等由商务自负。
>
> 　　2. 请即日通知寄书，寄交：
>
> 　　a)台北市和平东路一段金山街 40 号赵叔诚
>
> 　　b)台北市许昌街 36 号叶友梅

c)台北市哈密街 59 巷 56 弄 52 号张学训

d)台北市云和街 120 号余又荪

e)台北市罗斯福路台湾大学历史学系研究室

（大函谓寄 250 部，请即照上开地址各寄 50 部。赵、叶二人为商务正副经理，张为其职员。）

（大约寄书过多，则须向政府申请入口手续。此机关审查内容，彼机关审核出入口外汇。费时，费力，往往难通过。弟去年在港出版大学丛书中国通史一书，某书局代申请入口五百部，半年未成！）

适之先生已于十五日安葬。丧事已毕，哀思永留人间！

弟于 1949 与孟真先生同来台大后，不觉十余年矣。1958 年休假，本拟来美进修，因内子在港府任医生，故到港，任珠海大学文史系主任三年。去年又返台大。历年均授"中国通史"，"魏晋南北朝史"，"日本史"，"中日关系史"等科。昔年适之、叔永先生主持中基会编辑委员会期间，参加"日本史"编译。明年拟来美进修。近年美国各大学对东方学研究盛行，或增设科系，或开办图书馆、研究室。中国文史暨日本语文历史尚有基础（昔年受中基会之资助在东京帝国大学大学院研究五年），谅可任 Oriental Studies 之工作。

先生在美多年，情形甚熟，在美学术界声誉尤隆。尚恳就近代为注意，俾明年能来美一行。弟为天主教徒，倘天主教大学有此种机会，更为适宜。倘一校创办一图书馆或系，当能为之设计并采购图书而兼教学，谅能达成任务也。

叨在爱末，肃此奉恳。敬颂研安。

弟余又荪敬上

十月廿二日夜

〔University of Chicago Library, Yuan T'ung-li Papers, Box 8〕

按：余又荪（1908—1965），原名锡嘏，字又荪，以字行，四川涪陵人，北京大学哲学系毕业，旋赴东京帝国大学学习哲学，师从桑木严翼（1874-1946），时任台湾大学历史系教授，后因车祸离世。

十月二十三日

刘麟生覆函先生，告哥伦比亚大学人事招聘、明史计划等事。

守和尊兄勋右：

（一）本月廿日手示，敬悉一是。（二）弟今日持尊柬往访淬廉兄。渠对于函内所提二点，答复如次："（A）哥大惯例，某部门需打字员，须向人事科接洽。尊夫人可向此科申请。应征者，须有若干速记知识。（B）明史计划，尚无固定经费。目前仅凑数千元。有一周君，系助手。待遇不高。将来请经费，必不困难。缓当与 Prof. Goodrich 一谈，以便阁下往谒"云云。（三）《历代名人年谱目录》及《新疆国界图志》（无图），已收到。（四）《图志》当遵命圈点。圈点毕，再拟跋语呈教。（五）《图志》共有乙百余叶，圈点少需时日，故本周中未克奉上也。（六）兹附奉题签二纸，乞正。鄙意《条约集》上，应有"中俄"二字也。（七）J. P. Morgan Library 所陈我国字画，已往观。希世奇珍，洵堪宝玩。敬请俪安，书不尽意。

弟麟生敬上

内子附候

十月廿三夜

〔University of Chicago Library, Yuan T'ung-li Papers, Box 2〕

按：题签即刘麟生用大篆所书"中俄西北条约集"，后确被先生采纳。J. P. Morgan Library 即以金融家 J. P. Morgan 藏书为基础营建的图书馆，位于纽约曼哈顿岛东。

富路德覆函先生，告知刚聘任了一位助教，如其未通过试用期再考虑刘麟生。

23 October 1962

Dear Mr. Yuan:

I wish you had written or spoken to me earlier about Mr. Liu. Only just this last week I offered the job of assistant to another Chinese. He is coming on a trial basis for the next 2 months. If he proves unsatisfactory, of course I may talk to your candidate.

I asked Professor de Bary about the copies of the bibliography by Professor Yamane. His response was that you deserved a complimentary copy, but that he should charge for the second copy ($ 5.00).

Yours sincerely

L. C. Goodrich

Professor Emeritus of Chinese

〔University of Chicago Library, Yuan T'ung-li Papers, Box 2〕

按：Professor de Bary 即 William Theodore de Bary（1919-2017），美国汉学家，中文名狄培理，1953 年在哥伦比亚大学获得博士学位，旋留校任教。Professor Yamane 应指山根幸夫（Yukio Yamane, 1921-2005），日本历史学家，专攻明史。本函中提到的目录应指《明史研究文献目录》，约于 1960 年 12 月印行，主要收录 1900 年以来中日两国学者的明史研究论著。此件为打字稿，落款处为其签名。

渡边宏覆函先生，就《新疆研究文献目录》（日文本）凡例是否附英译一节询问了石田幹之助教授，后者认为从时间和经费上考虑此举意义不大，并告收到支票。

Tokyo le 23 oct.

Professeur T. L.Yuan

J'ai bien reçu votre aimable lettre et le chèque ($ 680).

Sur réapparition de la "note anglaise", je consultais à Prof. Ishida va mieux, il doute qu'il soit effectif, ne que perdre le temps et la dépense.

Le papetier mettait autre papier à couverture, ci-inclus. Je lui demande des réductions avec ce changement.

Au imprimerie je presse très vite.

Votre bonte pour moi, Prof. Ishida il dit, est vraiment sans bonnes, et il regrette de ne pouvoir trouver de mots suffisants pour vous exprimer sa vive gratitude.

Votre tout dévoué,

H. W.

〔University of Chicago Library, Yuan T'ung-li Papers, Box 8〕

十月二十四日

先生致信渡边宏，请其删除《新疆研究文献目录》"补遗"部分的一个重复条目，并告对"件名索引"略作订正，且再次确认了给予其和石田幹之助教授的赠本数量。

October 24, 1962

Dear Mr. Watanabe:

I hope you have duly received my check for US $ 680.00 mailed to you on October 19th.

In checking over the titles in the Addenda, I find that No. 1150 is already duplicated with No. 1129 written by Mr.　　. Please cancel the latter.

Congratulations for the subject index you have made. I made only a few minor changes. For instance, when we refer to the Ming period, we use　　in Chinese; but when we refer to the Ming-Ching period, we use 　　. This is merely a customary usage.

As I wrote to you before, no price of this bibliography should be printed on the last page. It will be sold at a lower price in Japan and Taiwan, and a higher price in U. S. A.

Please let me know, however, the price you have fixed in Japan. In my last letter, I offered 250 copies to you and 50 copies to Professor Ishida. You are welcome to sell them or to send complimentary copies to your friends.

Your sincerely,

T. L. Yuan

〔University of Chicago Library, Yuan T'ung-li Papers, Box 1〕

按:《新疆研究文献目录》(日文本)第 1129 号属于补遗类,其信息为——眞田有美,西域出土梵本法華經の一寫本に就いて 〔Khashgar 出土 Petrovsky 將來〕。该件为录副,空格处付诸阙如。刘麟生致函先生,告圈点《新疆国界图志》需费时三周。

守和尊兄勋右:

(一)昨书谅蒙鉴及。(二)《图志》八卷,共 250 叶,昨函所言一百余叶,系笔误。弟圈点恐需三星期左右也。(三)明史卡片事,拟俟前途聘书及薪水(支薪日期)发表后,再追随左右执笔。无米难为巧妇,想为大贤所深亮也。勿罪勿罪。即颂著绥。

弟麟生顿首

　　　　　　　　　　　　　　　　　　　　　十,廿四,夜

〔University of Chicago Library, Yuan T'ung-li Papers, Box 2〕

十月二十五日

先生覆信富路德,再次推荐刘麟生。

October 25, 1962

Dear Professor Goodrich:

　　Thank you for your letter of October 23.

　　After glancing over the bibliography by Professor Yamane, I found that there were many serious omissions. It should have been checked by an expert before it was printed.

　　After leaving your office the other day, I mailed the second copy of the bibliography to a library in Taipei. I now enclose my check for $5.00. Please pass it on to Professor de Bary.

　　Mr. L. S. Liu has been compiling a bibliography of Ming history with special emphasis on periodical literature representative of modern Chinese scholarship. Although it is a labor of love on his part, I hope you could find support for him in order to enable him to bring the work to early completion. He is such a good scholar that whatever collaboration you could obtain from him would greatly enhance the usefulness of the Project.

　　As Mr. Liu often comes to the East Asiatic Library, I trust that you may like to make his acquaintance. I shall give him a card of introduction.

　　　　　　　　　　　　　　　　　　　　Yours sincerely,

　　　　　　　　　　　　　　　　　　　　T. L. Yuan

〔University of Chicago Library, Yuan T'ung-li Papers, Box 2〕

　　按:该信应由刘麟生转交,此件为录副。

十月二十八日

刘麟生覆函先生,略谈诸事。

　　守和尊兄勋鉴:

　　(一)廿五日台简,指示周详,感佩无既。(二)淬廉兄来电话,谓"哥大打字员,需速记,且无任期,可不必登记。Prof. Goodrich 已晤过,今岁无款,不增聘人员,明年再说。"云云。(三)明公致 Prof.
Goodrich 措辞粹美,已照发。缓当造访。容续陈。敬请著安。

弟麟生谨上
十月廿八日夜

〔University of Chicago Library, Yuan T'ung-li Papers, Box 2〕

十月三十一日

先生为《中俄西北条约集》撰写英文导言(Prefatory Note)。〔《中俄西北条约集》,1963 年 2 月初版〕

王伊同覆函先生,谈交易古瓷情况,并告个人行程。

老伯大人尊前:

敬禀者,昨承宠召,拜感拜感。今晨与 Pole 君电约一面,十时半往晤,出宋磁两件,渠谓均属真品。就价格论,与拍卖门市即卢芹斋目录渠所标价相若。建窑一件,渠意品质视青白尤佳,与尊意相合。今日或到馆,恐电相左,因亟禀闻。今晚五时,飞返匹城。何日命驾,渴盼小驻是祷。承惠日文本《文献目录》,特再谢。敬请金安。

侄伊同倚装
卅一日

〔University of Chicago Library, Yuan T'ung-li Papers, Box 2〕

刘麟生致函先生,略述会见富路德经过。

守和尊兄道长勋鉴:

昨复一笺,并缴还大序,谅邀台览。今日上午十时卅分,谒 Prof.
L. C. Goodrich。因渠事冗,谈六七分钟,便告辞。渠甚和蔼,谓"新聘一位,即日莅此,用二月再说。今年无款增聘人士。"云云。敬请双安。

弟麟生顿首
十,卅一

〔University of Chicago Library, Yuan T'ung-li Papers, Box 2〕

十月底

先生与渡边宏合编《新疆研究文献目录:1886－1962》(日文本)在东京出版,《新疆研究丛刊》第二种,发行人为先生,承印方为 Shoei-Insatsu Co. Ltd
(昌荣印刷株式会社)。

十月

先生撰写《〈中俄西北条约集〉序》。〔《中俄西北条约集》,1963 年 2 月初版〕

先生草拟《重印〈西疆交涉志要〉序》。〔University of Chicago Library, Yuan T'ung-li Papers, Box 9〕

> 按:《西疆交涉志要》,清末钟镛编撰,清宣统三年(1911)由金梁刊行,《新疆研究丛刊》第六种。

先生撰写《重印〈新疆国界图志〉序》。〔《新疆国界图志》,1963 年 7 月初版〕

先生向美国学术团体理事会申请资助,用以编纂《中国艺术和考古目录》(Bibliography of Chinese Art and Archaeology)。〔University of Chicago Library, Yuan T'ung-li Papers, Box 3〕

> 按:翌年,此项申请未获得批准。

十一月一日

先生致信钱存训,请协助影照书籍并询问芝加哥大学在香港购书途径。

> 公垂吾兄:
>
> 　　闻尊处有余绍宋《书法要录》十七卷二编十一卷,请将该书之序跋用 Xerox 各照一份,连同校中发票一并寄下,如须先行付款,望暂垫付。又贵馆在港购书除刘君外,尚有其他书店否? 望将地址示知,以便通讯。弟近编《新疆书目》,已告东京印刷人径寄壹部,请指正是荷。
>
> 　　　　　　　　　　　　　　　　　　弟同礼
> 　　　　　　　　　　　　　　　　　　十一,一日
> 　　　　　　　　　　　　　　　　〔钱孝文藏札〕

> 按:"刘君"应指刘国蓁。

罗家伦致函先生,请代向美英三处分购西文书刊。

> 守和吾兄道鉴:
>
> 　　十月一日奉上航函,谅邀察及。前托吾兄费神代向美国国家档案局查询国务院档案 861.77 号胶片,有关中东路问题事件二十三卷全部复制一份,及牛津出版 R. Maxwell: *Information U. S. S. R.* 请代购一帙,谅蒙分别洽办。为年度报销起见,如已订购,付款后请先将收据寄下,为盼为托。兹又有恳者,本馆拟向纽约巴拉贡书店、美国康奈尔大学、伦敦克干保罗公司等三处分购西文书籍一批,共计四十三种,附上书单(二份),请费神在本馆购书款内分别代为洽购,付款后亦请将单据

寄下,为托。本馆前向国会图书馆添置之胶片十卷,承协助催办,已于上月底运抵台北,劳神谢谢。兹将吾兄十一月份征集费新台币五百元,转存台湾银行,附上送金簿存根一纸,并希察收。专此,敬颂道祺!

弟罗家伦敬启
十一,一

〔University of Chicago Library, Yuan T'ung-li Papers, Box 1〕

按:该函为文书代笔,落款处为其签名。

十一月七日

先生致信钱存训,询问有无刘国蓁消息,并告知行程有变。

公垂吾兄:

手教拜悉,《书法要录》序文已由贵校影印部寄来,其款 $1.80 已直接寄还矣。香港刘国蓁君久未来信,不识是否卧病。弟之《新疆书目》中文本拟托其在港付印,迄无回音,颇为悬系。前拟感谢节左右来芝城观书,近又改赴康桥,只好候至明春再来晤教矣。顺候时祉。

弟袁同礼顿首
十一,七

影印《大典》想已购到,近中华又影印《天一阁蓝格写本录鬼簿》,望尊处订购一部。

〔钱孝文藏札〕

按:"影印《大典》"应指 1960 年 9 月中华书局影印《永乐大典》,共计 202 册;《录鬼簿》即 1960 年 2 月中华书局影印《天一阁蓝格写本正续录鬼簿》,分上下两册,书名由徐森玉题写。此两种书皆以平馆旧藏为底本。本年感恩节为 11 月 22 日。

十一月九日

谭旦冏覆函先生,告知代购书籍已经寄出,并谢赠书,但嘱查留法博士姓名则尚无结果。

守和先生有道:

十月十五日手教,早经拜读,因候开□回信,稽覆为歉。《汝窑》及《钧窑》,已经该公司于本月六日寄出,《汝》一部(前已寄出一部)、《钧》二部,想不久当能寄到。兹将发票附呈,乞察阅。

《故宫瓷器录》宋元及明甲各一册,早经包就,嘱内人上街买菜时寄出,讵料近日收拾书架,始知仍在原处,实属荒谬,现已于十月二十日平邮挂号寄上矣。

承赐寄 Watson 所著《铜器》一书,已亦拜收,其中多新出土及大英博物馆所藏之件,颇为难得,感谢不尽。

关于留法论文作者,经多方设法托人,尚无结果。留台同学不多,且多脱节,即有熟悉如同乡陈宗经者,亦竟拒绝,其理由谓其中作者多在大陆,且有未得博士者。弟亦莫可奈何,乃函留法友人,亦有几函,仍未得覆,愧对之至。附最近返国潘君来函,藉知梗概。

余容续陈。耑此,恭叩道安,并候潭福。

后学谭旦冏拜上
十一月九日夜

〔University of Chicago Library, Yuan T'ung-li Papers, Box 6〕

按:"Watson 所著《铜器》一书"应指 *Ancient Chinese Bronzes*,1962 年出版;"潘君"待考。

刘麟生致函先生,感谢暂借《宋代研究文献目录》,并告傅冠雄去世。

守和尊兄博士赐鉴:

顷奉到《宋代研究文献目录》,极为心感。他日用毕,自当归赵。编订本项目录,未知抑有时限否?顷闻筱峰兄仙逝,甚为哀悼。一周前在此聚叙,尚觉其无恙也。即请俪安。

弟麟生敬上
9/11/62

今晨从哥大,已知其两项索引所在。

〔University of Chicago Library, Yuan T'ung-li Papers, Box 2〕

十一月十四日

牟复礼覆函先生,告知葛斯德图书馆善本书目编纂计划并未有实质进展,并祝贺刘麟生受聘哥伦比亚大学,参与《明代名人传》编纂工作。

November 14, 1962

Dear Dr. Yuan:

Some time has passed since your kind letter offering to help us evaluate any candidates that the University Library might have in mind for the task of preparing a rare books catalog of the Princeton Gest collection. The matter has been in a state of flux, and I have not really had anything further to report to you on it. Now I must bring you up to date with the present state of the idea. I am sad to have to report that it is still just an "idea."

The Institute for Advanced Study apparently will assume a major role in the matter, since the Gest collection technically belongs to them. Hence, they will assume the major financial responsibility, and they will do it according to their methods and standards. They also will take their time about coming to final conclusions. Apparently, they hope to invite a distinguished scholar from China or Japan. In any event, the initiative now lies with them, and they are unwilling to be pressured by us on how to proceed. Since this effectively takes the matter out of our hands, I don't really know what we should do next.

Fortunately, Mr. L. S. Liu has taken employment at Columbia. Professor de Bary told me last week that Mr. Liu had joined their staff, and that they are delighted to get him. I am very glad that he has not been injured by Princeton's inability to conclude this matter more rapidly. Our loss is Columbia's gain.

Mr. Chuang's ms. has arrived, and I am reading it. I shall finish within a week. I find it quite interesting.

With all good wishes to you, and again thanks for your very generous offers of help to us, I remain,

Sincerely yours,

F. W. Mote

〔University of Chicago Library, Yuan T'ung-li Papers, Box 3〕

按:Mr. Chuang's ms 即庄泽宣的书稿。此件为打字稿,落款处为其签名。

十一月十六日

先生致信香港集古斋,告知已嘱东京印所径寄《新疆研究文献目录》(日文本)五十部,其中四十六部委托代售。

集古斋经理先生大鉴:

前奉十月十一日大函,嘱寄《新疆文献目录》五十部,自当照办,已告东京印刷人照数寄上，收到后望示知。每部售价港币十五元，七折收款。将来售完后，其书价可付港币，直接送交香港东亚银行，收入弟之账内（第 11057-4, T. L. Yuan）为荷。此书为研究史地人士之所必需，大陆方面各机关均愿购买，不识贵处能设法否？顺候时祉。

袁同礼手启
十一月十六日

贵处目录如一时不能付印，可印一种通告，将此书列入。尊处收到后望交刘国蓁先生四部，系弟赠送友人者，计收四十六部。

〔University of Chicago Library, Yuan T'ung-li Papers, Box 2〕

按：1958 年集古斋创立于香港，以经营金石书画、古籍善本、文房四宝等为主要业务。此件为底稿。

先生致信香港新华印刷公司，告知已收到该公司报价单，并告《中俄西北条约集》印数，所需定金明日汇出。

新华印刷公司大鉴：

昨由刘国蓁先生转来十一月一日贵处报价单，并悉对于校对一事，贵处绝对负责。兹决定先印壹千部，已请刘先生将稿送上，即乞从速排印，另有序文及附录等下星期即行寄上。序文页数用 I、II、III、IV、V、VI，正文用一、二、三、四、五、六等数字，故不必等候也。所需之定金半数明日汇上。见贵处罗香林先生所印各书，极为精美，即照其格式排印是盼。末校请以航邮寄下。顺候时祺。

袁同礼谨启
十一月十六日

〔University of Chicago Library, Yuan T'ung-li Papers, Box 1〕

按：此件为底稿，该信应由刘国蓁转投。

先生致信拉铁摩尔，不建议购入《中国经济社会发展史目录》，并请其撰写推荐信用以申请美国科学基金会资助《新疆研究文献目录》出版。

November 16, 1962

Dear Mr. Lattimore:

Your letter of 13 November to the Office of the Cultural Councilor of "the Chinese Embassy" has been referred to me.

This bibliography, compiled in 1956 for the Human Relations Area

Files, New Haven, was on sale at that organization. Recently, I learnt that it turned all its publications to a commercial agent in New York.

Since it is not worth anything, I would not advise you to procure a copy. You may ask the University Library to buy a copy if it has not had it in its collections.

My bibliography on Sinkiang is about to be completed, but it does not seem easy to get a grant for its publication.

From the enclosed correspondence, you will note that I had to issue it in two parts. For the first part, I am hoping that a grant from the National Science Foundation may be possible. If you happen to know Dr. Burton W. Adkinson, you may see fit to write a letter on my behalf. There is a good deal of politics in the Foundation. My request was declined on the ground that it is outside the scope of activities of the Foundation.

This project was sponsored by the University of Washington, so I am asking Dr. Taylor to write a letter to the Foundation to support it.

I was rather disappointed with W. A. Douglas Jackson's Russo-Chinese Borderlands. Evidently, he did not know the existence of Chinese sources on the subject. So, I am to publish a monograph in Chinese about the treaties and agreements concerning Sinkiang.

〔University of Chicago Library, Yuan T'ung-li Papers, Box 3〕

按:11 月 13 日,拉铁摩尔致信"'驻美使馆'文化参赞办公室",订购《中国经济社会发展史目录》(*Economic and Social Development of Modern China, a bibliographical guide*)。该件为录副。

十一月十八日

先生致信香港新华印刷公司,寄上美金汇票、港币支票,并嘱校对务必仔细,另告拟印《新疆国界志》,请其寄下报价。

　　新华印刷公司大鉴:

　　　　本月十六日托刘国蓁先生寄上一函,请从速排印《中俄西北条约集》,兹奉上汇票美金一百元、港币支票叁百元,收到后请函告是盼。校对一事至关重要,望特别注意,希望收到末校时,不致有任何错字也。尚有一书名《新疆国界志》,一周后亦用航邮寄上,请即付排。此书拟印七百部,请按此寄下报价单,一切格式均照《中俄西北条约集》办理为荷。顺候时祉。

袁同礼谨启
十一月十八日

〔University of Chicago Library, Yuan T'ung-li Papers, Box 1〕

按:此件为底稿。

钱泰致函先生,告已照前单寄赠《中国不平等条约之缘起及其废除之经过》至各中文图书馆,并告钱家骐似未获得博士学位。

守和先生左右:

辱奉惠书,拙作过承奖励,愧谢交并。各中文图书馆已照前赐单寄赠,惟单中对于日本、高丽、南越未曾提及,如续有所得,尚乞见示。舍侄家骐似未得剑桥博士学位,已函询,得复再闻。专复,敬颂道祺。

弟钱泰上言
十一月十八日

〔袁同礼家人提供〕

按:钱家骐,1939 年毕业于上海交通大学物理系,后受李约瑟器重,介绍其获得剑桥大学奖学金,1944 年偕妻子顾菊珍和儿子前往英国留学,获该校物理学硕士学位,时在美工作。

十一月十九日

张公权致函先生,告行踪并附上支票。

同礼先生惠鉴:

前游华府,荷承招待,不胜感谢。满拟多多聆教,惜为时间所限,不获如愿,只可俟诸日后东来时再谋畅叙。弟自离美国即至维也纳开会,会毕则历游各埠,一昨始抵香港。承做资料照片,谢谢。兹随函附上支票美金六元零五分一纸,归还尊垫,尚请察收为荷。敬颂时绥。

弟张公权拜启
十一,十九

附支票。

〔University of Chicago Library, Yuan T'ung-li Papers, Box 2〕

按:是年 8 月,斯坦福研究所聘张公权为顾问,研究中国大陆物价制度,约定其赴港之后,每月给予顾问薪金及研究支出。8 月 27 日,张公权由纽约赴华盛顿,29 日离美飞往维也纳,9 月 1 日,国际经济学年会在维也纳大学召开。①

十一月二十一日

先生致信郭廷以,告除《新疆研究丛刊》十种外,拟重刊相关书籍三种。

量予吾兄著席:

正拟函候,又奉赐书,欣悉近况,至慰远怀。欣闻大著已付印,裨益学人,殊非浅鲜。希望明春可以问世,民国之部卷帙较多,亦盼早日能付剞劂,此种工具书造福学术界不浅,企予望之。弟鉴于时贤著述,对于中俄边界者语言不详,拟将下列三书予以重印,(一)钱恂:《中俄界约斠注》;(二)施绍常:《中俄国际约注》;(三)邹代钧:《中俄界记》。如贵所有重印史料之计划,可否由贵所予以影印,大约史语所、贵所、台大、"外交部"或有此书可否借出,最好交艺文印书馆予以影印,可免校对之劳。弟拟写一序文,说明此三书之重要,如贵所计划不便列入,弟则拟自行付印,但又无暇校对,亦盼予以影印。万一各机关均无此三书,则弟将印照本寄上以便排印。两周前已寄上钱、邹二氏之书之影照本。至于施氏书,正在研究,如台北无此书,望速示知,以便平邮寄上。弟意此三书可合印一册,西式装订,以便读者。一切务希赐予指示,不胜感祷。又,排印不但校对人不易觅,尚须加以标点,更费时间。如必须排印,能觅到负责校对及代予标点之人否?亦盼指示。弟编之《新疆书目》日文本,已寄商务二百五十部每部台币六十元,七折收款,另寄尊处二十五部,除奉赠吾兄及贵所各一部外史语所之一部,请代为转交,余者请交庶务代售,两所同人愿购者,每部收特价四十二元,但不宜使商务知之是盼。贵所刊物定价今后似可稍高,美人来买,未免太便宜也。《博士论文》系奉赠吾兄者,希教正。顺候教祺。

　　　　　　　　　　　　　　　　　　　弟袁同礼顿首

　　　　　　　　　　　　　　　　　　　十一月廿一日

又,排印不但校对人不易觅,尚须加以标点,更费时间。如必须排

---

① 姚崧龄编著《张公权先生年谱初稿》,北京:社会科学文献出版社,2014 年,页 1077-1078。

印,能觅到负责校对及代予标点之人否? 亦盼指示。

〔台北"中央研究院"近代史研究所档案馆,〈郭廷以〉,馆藏号
069-01-02-089〕

按:"又奉赐书"应指郭廷以 17 日复函。该信于 11 月 28 日送达。

十一月二十九日

先生致信钱存训,向其借书,并告知选印《新疆研究丛刊》计划,另请其撰
写跋文。

公垂吾兄大鉴:

昨奉惠寄新书目录,至以为谢。内中有《全国图书馆书目汇编》,
弟愿暂借一用,能寄下否? 大著近来销路如何,不识共印若干部。前
有芝大教授写一书评,如有存者,请再寄下一份是荷上次寄下者已遗失。
弟近印《新疆研究丛刊》,除自编五种外,拟选五种予以流传。内中
《新疆书目》中文本正在抄写,将来将序文写好,拟请吾兄写一跋文,再
送港付印,恐明夏方能出版也。专此,顺候教祺。

弟袁同礼顿首
十一,廿九日

三联杨端六著有《清代币帛金融史稿》,似可购买。

〔钱孝文藏札〕

按:《全国图书馆书目汇编》由冯秉文编(北京图书馆主编),1958
年 10 月中华书局出版。"书评"似指 *Journal of the American
Oriental Society*, vol. 82, no. 4, 1962, p. 618,该篇书评作者为
Edward H. Shafer。《清代币帛金融史稿》即《清代货币金融史
稿》,1962 年 7 月生活·读书·新知三联书店出版。

十一月三十日

先生致信香港新华印刷公司,请代为补入条约两种,并附上新目次,另嘱校
对务必仔细。

新华印刷公司大鉴:

本月十八日寄上美金汇票壹百元、港币支票叁百元,想已收到。
前托刘国蓁先生寄上之《中俄西北条约集》,兹又觅到条约两种,应即
补入,定为第二十七及二十八。原书内第二十七种应改为二十九,第
二十八种应改为三十,余如此类推,即希代为更改。附上新目次,即照

此排,而将以前所寄者作废为盼。又第二种条约之标题应为"中俄勘分西北界约记"应一"加"字。第二十一条约"读订喀什噶尔西北境界约"应改为"续勘",均望排印时予以注意。此书系国家所订之条约,千万不可有错字,务请详细校对。寄末校时每次以二十叶至二十五叶为限,并望用航邮寄下,尤盼能于阴历年前印好为荷。顺候时祉。

袁同礼拜上

十一月三十日

附上"目次"二页,"条约检查一览表"三页,余件日内即寄。

〔University of Chicago Library, Yuan T'ung-li Papers, Box 1〕

按:此件为底稿。

先生致信马克尔,告知《中国留英同学博士论文目录》即将在台北刊行,请其给予英国大学中国委员会委员名单以便寄赠。

November 30, 1962

Dear Mr. Morkill:

My survey of the doctoral dissertations by Chinese students in Great Britain was ready for publication last spring. The delay in having it published was due to my desire to issue it in one volume together with dissertations by Chinese students in France, Germany, Holland, Belgium and Switzerland.

Since the work of collecting additional material takes much longer time than I expected, I shall wait no longer, but publish immediately the dissertations approved by British universities. The survey consists of over 350 dissertations approved by British universities and will appear next spring as a Special Supplement to *CHINESE CULTURE*, a quarterly review published in English in Taipei.

Professor Simon suggested that it might be published as one of the Occasional Papers of China Society, but the present editor did not approve it.

Whenever you find it convenient, will you send me a list of names and addresses of those members of your Committee who may be interested in receiving complimentary copies. These will be mailed direct from the printer in Taipei.

Under separate cover, I am sending you a copy of my recent work entitled: *A Guide to Doctoral Dissertations by Chinese Students in America*.

Sincerely yours.

〔University of Chicago Library, Yuan T'ung-li Papers, Box 1〕

按：此件为底稿。

十一月

先生写定《重印〈西疆交涉志要〉序》。〔《西疆交涉志要》，1963 年初版〕

先生赴纽约哥伦比亚大学图书馆肯特楼（Kent Hall）查询文献。〔University of Chicago Library, Yuan T'ung-li Papers, Box 2〕

十二月一日

先生致信罗香林，请其从旁催促香港新华印刷公司排印《中俄西北条约集》《新疆国界图志》等稿件。

香林先生著席：

北平晤教忽忽多年，屡读大著，均属不朽之作，益深钦仰。当此世变日亟而台端专考学问，在文史界扬其异彩，足为青年之楷模矣。弟近拟编印一小丛书，以关于新疆史地者为主。承刘国蓁冯平山馆前任职员之推荐，已将《中俄西北条约集》及《新疆国界图志》稿件寄交新华印刷公司西营盘荔安里十五号，并预付定金港币八百余元，迄今尚未接到复音，颇为悬念。闻该公司承印大著，对于校对颇能负责，可否请吾兄致电该公司托其对于弟委托之件特别提前办理，如能于阴历年前印就，更所企盼。校对每次请寄二十叶，弟收到后即行寄回，亦盼能转告。又香港其他印刷公司能负责校对者，亦望推荐一二家。弟尚有《新疆书目》中文本亦愿早日付□□，感谢不尽。耑此，敬候□□。

十二月一日

□□□□

〔University of Chicago Library, Yuan T'ung-li Papers, Box 1〕

按：此件应为底稿，其左侧未能扫描全幅。

金问泗致函先生，提交《中俄西北条约集》序言初稿并略作说明，另请先生查询国会图书馆藏《元曲选》。

守和老兄惠鉴：

尊嘱之件顷已脱稿，颇觉太长，是序而非跋体，姑呈请览，俟审定后倘认为可用,则再付钞成清稿。兹有几点条列于下:(一)最近情形以尊定条列说明,俟公布后再补,故拙稿不提,免得复说,惹人注意;(二)《新疆研究文献》似可择印为丛书之一部分,故亦未提;(三)居民多属回教徒句,欲易为"汉回缠哈之人杂处其地"如何? 全稿统候我兄多多指教,再当面谈,其参考地图书报,亦容俟当面奉还不误。

再者,弟以有人嘱做貂蝉诗,需要参考元曲,不知贵馆有无明臧懋循辑《元曲选》一书,此书壬集下有《锦云堂暗定连环计》杂剧一卷(元无名人撰),此卷内有貂蝉之名,弟拟拜托读一遍,如无此书而有其他元曲本载有此剧者亦可。可否请兄便中先为一查,赐一电话见告,弟当往阅,因同时尚欲看看他书也。拜托拜托。敬候著祺,顺颂俪祉。

弟泗谨启
12-1-62
〔袁同礼家人提供〕

按:先生在该函左侧标注"湖北公安县人 迪化道""K521.76""T78.1""V.43"字样。

十二月四日

杨联陞覆函先生,婉拒为《新疆研究文献目录》(日文本)撰写书评的请求。

守和先生史席:

十一月十五日惠书早已诵悉,《新疆研究文献目录》(日文本)一册则前日始行收到,内容丰富,极为有用。惟书名虽题作"新疆",所收书籍、论文则绝不限于建省以后,其有关西域者亦不限于省境以内,作广告宣传时,此点似宜特别提出。人名索引拼音虽欠完全(人名多数略去)且有小误,然于日本学者笔名(或字、号)多能与其姓名用等号连系,殊为难得。又先生所谓日文本似指日文之部(即日文著作),而非目录本身有中英日文三种版本,此就英文书名观之,固甚显明,单看汉字则不免发生疑问也。晚学于新疆近代史事全无研究,关于拟印各书不敢妄发末议。至于短篇介绍,是否俟三种出全时再作比较相宜,因此时对其他二种之内容性质难以预定,若只讨论一种,可说之话太少,未必有多少广告效用。尊意如何? 专复,即请双安。

晚学杨联陞再拜

一九六二,十二,四

〔University of Chicago Library, Yuan T'ung-li Papers, Box 2〕

十二月五日

罗家伦覆函先生,谈购书、代订期刊、付款收据等事。

守和吾兄道鉴:

一、十月廿八日手教敬悉。吾兄大作《新疆文献目录》,东京出版人尚未寄来,一俟寄到,当为推销;售价若干,尚乞示知,以便遵办。

二、承代向美国国家档案局订制中东路文件胶片七卷,已寄到,正在办理提取手续。

三、十一月一日寄上一函,请代向纽约巴拉贡书店、康奈尔大学及伦敦克干保罗公司等三处分购书籍一批,谅邀惠察矣。

四、承代购史料书刊之付款收据,为年度报销关系,拟请吾兄费神检出早日寄下,无任感盼!

五、伦敦出版之《中国季刊》(*The China Quarterly*)已寄到第一、二及六至十期,共七册。Europe Publications 寄来 *The World of Learning 1962-3* 收据一份,计十九元六角。

六、十二月份征集费新台币五百元,已转存台湾银行,附上送金簿存根一纸。又附上一九六三年一月至六月份空白收据六张,请加章后寄下。

专此,敬颂著祺!

弟罗家伦敬启
十二,五

〔University of Chicago Library, Yuan T'ung-li Papers, Box 1〕

按:此件为文书代笔,落款处为其签名。

李霖灿致函先生,告知收到顾洛阜藏中国书画目录,并谈影印《书画书录解题》办法。

守和长者赐鉴:

先在这儿恭颂合府圣诞快乐,新年万福!

顾洛户(Crawford)的目录收到了,多谢多谢。正如长者所说,其中精品,都原是故宫之旧藏,尚未与《赏溥杰书画目》对照,然观其收藏玺印,皆《石渠》著录者无疑。在纽约时,曾往其寓所观画八次,今其展览既过，又得长者赐书，亦拟就当日记忆所及之观感，草一报道以告国人，使知我国珍宝流落何地，长者以为如何。因近得顾氏之亲笔函，亦提出此一意见，自当略加宣扬一番也。

关于《书画书录解题》，拟分两步手续办理，第一先向济老请问此书带出来否？然后问其是否准予影印流传。若史语所有此书，想不致成何问题。第二，向艺文严一萍先生商洽影印事，请其作一预算，渠近日正在影印《美术丛书》，想对此或有兴趣也。以上两节都得见济老面谈，容赴台北时详为请示后再作决定，当即有函专来报告也。济老近日目疾仍未完全复原，不便写信去打扰。然台北台中，时来时往，不需久候也。专此奉覆，肃叩福安。

后学李霖灿谨鞠躬

十二月五日

恕不再寄贺年片了。

〔University of Chicago Library, Yuan T'ung-li Papers, Box 8〕

按：严一萍（1908—？），浙江嘉兴人，东亚大学毕业，时应任艺文印书馆经理。

余又苏覆函先生，告台北商务印书馆愿意代售《新疆研究文献目录》（日文本），并表示有赴美进修之意，请代为寻找机会，另谈方豪近况。

守和先生道席：

大示奉到一周，但书尚未到，一俟书到，当即代拟广告，由商务刊登广告。书款由商务送存台湾银行尊户不误。近年来边疆问题研究之风甚盛，此间早有中国边疆历史语言学会之组织，有讲演会，又出版丛书。大著及拟印之《中俄边界》，必大受推崇也。

承示圣约翰大学事，据悉薛公及伊东之吴公，均系他系之教授而兼东方学院之职，并未有独立之经费。至于某主教，议论多而毫无力。就天主教大学而言，芝加哥为多，且无华人在焉。无华人先到，谋事似尚易也。

此间人士，对来美事，多讳而不言，但各有活动。台北"美领事"，对留学生之限制甚多，但对十年任职之教授，似尚宽松，如长居移民，则法令限制，故有受阻者耳（劳榦兄即此例）。

国务院短期视察之类机会，亦拟一试，统祈相机一助为感。

方杰人兄,近年为病魔所苦(心脏病),不敢行动。现住市外,唯上课到校耳。专肃,敬颂著安。

弟余又荪顿首

十二月五日

〔袁同礼家人提供〕

按:"圣约翰大学"即 St. John's University ,位于纽约近郊皇后区,是美国较大的天主教大学;"薛公"应指薛光前,"吴公"待考。1962 年,劳榦赴美国加州大学洛杉矶分校访学,内文所提应为申请赴美前的波折。

十二月六日

马大任致函先生,寄上康乃尔大学中国学生名录,询问何处藏有全套的《生活周刊》,并感谢先生对 1949 年以前出版的学术期刊所提的建议。

Dec. 6, 1962

Dear Dr. Yuan:

I am sending you the enclosed copy of *DIRECTORY OF CHINESE STUDENT CLUB AT CORNELL UNIVERSITY* which you want for reference.

Do you happen to know which library here or abroad has a complete set of the 生活周刊 and its successors edited by 邹韬奋、杜重远等?

Thanks to your suggestion in your previous letter concerning the learned journals, I have asked Professors Skinner of Cornell and Wilbur of Columbia to present this problem of Chinese journals published before 1949 to the Joint Committee on Contemporary China which will meet sometime this month. I hope something will come out of their discussion.

Best wishes.

Sincerely,

John T. Ma

Chinese Bibliographer

〔University of Chicago Library, Yuan T'ung-li Papers, Box 6〕

按:1925 年 10 月 11 日,《生活》周刊在上海创刊,翌年 10 月 24 日第 2 卷第 1 期改由邹韬奋主编,1933 年 12 月 16 日出版最后一期

（第8卷第50期）后被查封，1934年2月《新生》创刊。

十二月九日

郭廷以致函先生，商讨刊印中俄西北交涉史料。〔《郭量宇先生日记残稿》，页367〕

十二月十一日

先生覆信罗家伦，告知联系各书店购书情况及书款存余。

> 志希馆长吾兄尊鉴：
>
> 　　奉到十二月五日手教，拜悉种切，嘱购各书除伦敦克干保罗尚无回信外，余均分别寄上，想可陆续收到。兹将各项收据随函附上，即希查核。贵馆存款尚有149.04，应否继续申请外汇，即希尊酌。党史会尚有一百余元。前曾建议购买关于国父之资料，请将已入藏之西文资料开单见示，以免重复，仍希从旁一催，以利进行。目前美国军史编纂馆印出共四册，已函请连同他书赠送贵馆一份，收到后并盼函谢是荷。
>
> 　　　　　　　　　　　　　　　　　　　　　　十二月十一日
>
> 　　　〔University of Chicago Library, Yuan T'ung-li Papers, Box 1〕

　　按：此件为底稿，先生在其上作了三处标记，应为本年5月14日、8月23日、12月11日分批支出的购书款，合计为851.16。

何炳棣致函先生，称赞袁清论文，并谈返台参加第二届亚洲历史学家大会见闻。

> 守和先生：
>
> 　　夏间寄来清弟论文两篇，当时晚与芝大通信磋商频繁，并赶撰论文（为第二届亚洲历史学家大会），只得匆匆过目。上月内子及晚返温后，始得机会仔细重读。同盟会一文，能利用新出版史料，叙事清楚，在硕士论文中，自属佳作。阿古柏一文，能利用多量当时西文材料，头绪分明，论述皆有可取。惟惜因避免与朱文长论文重覆，中文史料（虽对阿氏之叛为比较边缘）引用太少，望将来能多加补充。即以左氏筹划饷运一节，即大有可作之处。但为西方学术刊物撰文，宜简不拟繁，能中肯要，正是清弟长处，可喜可贺。治史初步攻 events 最为稳妥，较易收效，以后乞其多多留意于 institutions，则逐步可以作到擒贼擒王之境界矣。清弟春秋方盛，语文基础良好，只要不怕"吃苦"，前程远大。

晚等在台居留四周,备蒙各方款待。亚洲史家大会,为台方国际学术空前盛事,以台湾标准而言,不能不谓为一大成功。惟日本主要史家均未赴会,东南亚史家学问还谈不到,国内亦有不甚像样文章,故距国际水准相差仍远。然此仅可为知者道,不可为外人言也。晚对治史原则曾被迫发表意见,居然见于各报章及新时代杂志。因措辞尚属婉转,不特未引起"中研院"史家之评击,且引起济老之共鸣,远非初料所及也。离台之前一日,黄"部长"召开茶会,文化界名流到者二百余人,当场颁晚以学术奖章。据说当初黄氏有意亦颁给简又文,遭"中研院"及台大人士反对,未果。总之,此行酬酢无虚日,完全未能读书。

拙著《明清社会史论》业经出版,年初即可发售。大约旬内可接到,必邮奉一本请正,并请清弟惠存。

再晚近一二年来对瓷器渐有兴趣,手头略有十来件,宋器中有钧碗一、龙泉双耳瓶(略补),龙泉双鱼小盘,刻花定窑小盘,明龙泉缸瓶几件及明建窑香炉一,明江南定香炉一,唐马、唐佣各一。但清瓷一件皆无。先生旅途之中,如遇明或早清(i.e.乾隆以前)单色瓶、盘、碗、罐,千乞代为注意为祷。如能先代买下,接示即行汇款。即使彩色之件,如精亦愿收一两件。此类物件,可遇而不可求。晚明夏迁芝大后,"交换情报"工作当比较容易矣。

敬请撰安,并祝佳节,阖府清吉!

晚炳棣再拜

一九六二年十二月十一日

景洛嘱代致候。

〔University of Chicago Library, Yuan T'ung-li Papers, Box 2〕

十二月十二日

先生致信郭廷以,寄上中俄外交史料,请其在台物色出版机构,并谈翻译《巴布阔夫回忆录》等事。

量予吾兄著席:

前上一书,并奉上《中俄约章会要》、《中俄界记》(影照本),谅不日可以寄到。兹又奉上施绍常之《中俄国际约注》,系在哈佛所照,或可影印,可否托艺文或其书店估价。此三书流传日稀,而对于研究近代史者可称原始资料,故弟愿为之印行,谅荷赞许。如能将《巴布阔夫回忆录》早日译成中文,可得更多之参证。至于译英一事,弟可委托英人为之,所需稿费较美人为廉。如贵所能在研究费拨出此款,即可进行,仍希尊酌示复是感。英国有 Central Asian Research Center,专研中亚细亚史地及边界问题,大约系英国情报部所支持,谅故对于此书亟为重视,但英国尚未收藏也。专此,敬候道祺,并贺新釐。

弟袁同礼顿首
十二,十二

英国出版之 *Central Asian Review* 为最有权威之期刊,贵所如愿购一全份,当代订也。

〔台北"中央研究院"近代史研究所档案馆,〈郭廷以〉,馆藏号069-01-02-089〕

按:*Central Asian Review* 由中亚研究中心和牛津大学苏联事务研究中心共同出版,1953 年创刊,1968 年停刊。

刘麟生覆函先生,谈诸事。

守和博士先生尊鉴:

(一)九日复示,如数家珍,感慰奚似。(二)承示拟传略名所应注意各点,敢不拜嘉。李士涛及傅吾康之书,前曾奉还邮架,可否再予赐寄一用,用毕归赵,如何? 如李书已将局部印下,弟当付印费,则不必寄下矣。(三)和钧兄亦熟识,渠学有本原,极为心折。(四)今诵大序及梁序,均雅洁动人。尊序尤清逸,有古文气息,知获教于新城先生为已多矣。重违雅意,擅易如干字,并将尊问一一奉答,请卓裁。(五)承告西士作文最重引用书目,诚然诚然。清代治学者亦如是也。存训兄近著 *Written on Bamboo and Silk: the beginnings of Chinese books and inscriptions* ,引用书及文达四百种,其精力诚可佩。弟尚未细读。(六)缘近来左目有"小尘埃",幢幢往来,不得不少憩息,以资恢复。即请著安。

教弟麟生谨上
十二月十二日

〔University of Chicago Library, Yuan T'ung-li Papers, Box 2〕

按:李士涛之书应指《中国历代名人年谱目录》,1941 年 4 月商务印书馆初版。"大序及梁序",应指《西疆交涉志要》中之自序、梁敬鐇跋,后者确撰于是年12月。

十二月十七日

先生致信钱存训,告知将协助查找冯承钧生平及著作目录。

公垂吾兄著席:

　　前奉手教,欣悉大著第一版已将售罄,足征不朽之作,可风行海内也。吾兄将继续翻译史之研究,亟感需要。冯君 1885-1945 晚年贫病交加,俱赖中基会及平馆予以维持。渠在巴黎时,伯希和或仍在河内 EFEO 研究,应查伯君传记或 Obituary notice。关于冯君何年在“教部”任职,当为代查,容再奉闻。北平沦陷之时,冯君著作散见于华北各期刊,弟之《新疆目录》收的不少,容得暇再行钞奉。向达之文似在 1946 年发表,容查到再行函达。先此,敬颂俪祺。

弟同礼顿首
十二,十七

〔https://www.thtsien.com/with-friends〕

　　按:时钱存训为 *Biographical Dictionary of Republican China* 撰写人物词条,以下各信所提《冯承钧小传》或《冯子衡小传》曾请袁同礼和吴光清校阅,后该书于 1967 年由哥伦比亚大学出版社出版。EFEO 即法国远东学院(École française d'Extrême-Orient)。向达之文似指《悼冯承钧先生》,刊于昆明出版的《民主周刊》。[1]

先生致信香港新华印刷公司,寄上《中俄西北条约集》金问泗序言及附录四,并催问《新疆国界图志》印刷报价。

新华印刷公司大鉴:

　　前寄数函,想均收到。兹奉上金问泗序及附录四:西北边界中西地名对照表,共十三叶,即希付排并将末校寄下是荷。对照表英文字颇多,务希校对时特为注意。前寄上之《新疆国界图志》望为估价,如需先付一部分之印价,亦请以航签函告。此致,并候时祉。

袁同礼拜上
十二月十七日

〔University of Chicago Library, Yuan T'ung-li Papers, Box 1〕

---

① 《民主周刊》(昆明)第 3 卷第 3 期,1946 年 3 月,页 9-13。

按：此件为底稿。

十二月十九日　纽约

先生赴哥伦比亚大学肯特楼（Kent Hall）查询期刊文献，请图书馆东亚馆藏负责人 Howard P. Linton 将《瀚海潮》杂志以馆际互借的方式送往国会图书馆。〔University of Chicago Library, Yuan T'ung-li Papers, Box 2〕

> 按：20 世纪 40 年代后期，《瀚海潮》由新疆省文化运动委员会出版。

十二月二十四日

伍藻池覆函先生，婉拒代售《新疆研究文献目录》（日文本）之请。

同礼先生惠鉴：

年柬并华翰拜收，感谢感谢。嘱代售大著，自当遵命，岂敢不为公效力耶。但此种著作，全用日文，且属新疆远地。此间华侨，知音太少。即偶有若干学生，能解日文者，亦少之又少。以其全此藏尘，何如物得其用。故今日收到后，即将全部廿本，用邮速为奉上，到时察收。方命之处，还请原宥。专此即覆，顺请年禧。

弟伍藻池顿首
十二月廿四日

〔University of Chicago Library, Yuan T'ung-li Papers, Box 3〕

十二月二十五日

刘麟生致函先生，感谢帮助复印资料。

守和先生博士勋右：

承影印《明代名人年谱目录》，已收到，感谢无量。印费二元，随函奉上，乞莞存。若有不足，乞示知为感。Prof. Goodrich 寄来该项计划 General Rules 一纸仅四小段，谓须参考"No. 24《八十九种明代传记综合引得》"云云。风雪频仍，伏维珍摄。敬祝迎年俪福！

教弟刘麟生谨颂
十二，廿五

〔University of Chicago Library, Yuan T'ung-li Papers, Box 2〕

十二月二十七日

李迪俊覆函先生，告前请转询徐铭信事未得确覆。

守和吾兄惠鉴:

手书敬悉起居佳胜,至以为慰。《博士论文目录》事,徐铭信君返
巴后,弟曾与谈及,并转致尊函,彼无表示,意似不属。两三月前,渠以
巴西时局不安,赴欧居住,一时似无返巴意,而此事亦迄无消息。有负
雅嘱,良用歉愧。然此事决定之权,操之自彼,实无可如何也。中俄西
北界务通商交涉,虽已陈迹,仍不失为重要史料。我兄加以蒐集,汇编
行世,不仅有功于学术,抑且有助于外交。承允出版后见赠一册,无任
欣幸,谨此预谢。专此奉覆,顺颂时祺,并祝年禧。

弟李迪俊敬启

十二月二十七日

粹如附候嫂夫人。

〔University of Chicago Library, Yuan T'ung-li Papers, Box 2〕

按:此件为文书代笔,落款钤李迪俊印。

十二月二十八日

先生致信郑通,补寄《中俄西北条约集》参考文献,并请早日寄下末校。

新华印刷公司郑经理大鉴:

十二月十七日寄上金问泗先生序文及附录四:西北边界中西地名
对照表十三页。兹又寄上参考文献五页,请付排列在附录四之后、末
叶之前。最末校样想已准备完备,即盼早日寄下为荷。顺候大安,并
贺年禧。

袁同礼启

十二月二十八日

〔University of Chicago Library, Yuan T'ung-li Papers, Box 1〕

按:郑通,即新华印刷公司经理,参见 1963 年 1 月 4 日刘国蓁覆
函。此件为底稿。

十二月三十日

罗香林覆函先生,略述新华公司之能力,并建议联系香港大学出版社彭锡
恩代为在港督促印刷。

守和先生道席:

数年来屡从留美各友通讯中得谂先生在美道履绥和,为中国学术
文化大力发扬,曷胜景佩。顷奉大教,承示正编印关于新疆史地之丛

书,此诚为极重要之工作,于中外关系史之研讨必有极大之引导与发展。关于新华公司承印《中俄西北条约集》及《新疆国界图志》等事,经即催促刘国蓁兄及该公司赶速将排字最后清样寄上覆校,据谓必可依照尊嘱办妥。香港之印刷公司关系复杂,版权页似当嘱其勿印上承印公司之名称为便。新华为第二流之印刷公司,仍须有在港熟于出版情形者为之督校、督印,始能达于理想。香港大学出版社有助理发行人(湘人)彭锡恩兄(出版主任为法国籍之魏智先生)富有印刷与出版经验,且乐为服务(耶路大学李田意兄及印第安那大学邓嗣禹兄在港所印各书,多由彼负责督促),谨为介绍。倘先生欲另觅其他公司刊印专书或交新华更印他书,鄙意或可托彼相助也。奉上拙作《蒲寿庚研究》及《香港与中西文化之交流》各一册,及拙作拙印书目一纸,乞赐教正。先此奉复,即请道安。

晚罗香林敬上

一九六二年十二月卅日

〔University of Chicago Library, Yuan T'ung-li Papers, Box 1〕

按:彭锡恩,湖南湘潭人。《蒲寿庚研究》,1959 年 12 月中国学社(香港)初版;《香港与中西文化之交流》,1961 年 2 月中国学社(香港)初版。邓嗣禹之书似指 *Japanese Studies on Japan and the Far East: a short biographical and bibliographical introduction* ,1961 年香港大学出版社出版;李田意之书,待考。

十二月三十一日

陈省身覆函先生,寄上修改后的《现代中国数学研究目录》导言。

守和先生:

前后得手书,并附各件,深为感谢。资料读后尤感兴趣,嘱撰序文,兹拟就呈改,不知有当否? 祈赐教为幸。匆此,即祝年釐。

弟陈省身上

十二,卅一

〔University of Chicago Library, Yuan T'ung-li Papers, Box 7〕

一九六三年　六十九岁

一月一日

徐家璧覆函先生,告知耶鲁大学图书馆日文文献为数不多,现只能够购入一册《新疆研究文献目录》(日文本)。

　　守和先生尊鉴:

　　　　敬肃者,昨奉手示,暨赐赠新编之《新疆研究文献目录》壹册,拜领之余,无任心感!

　　　　先生勤于编著,造福士林,深为敬佩!此编印行,其有裨于学术研究者,自不待言,甚望其姊妹篇中西文本两种,能早日获得经费,提前付梓,不禁馨香祷之!目前耶鲁日文部份甚小,尚未能全力发展,而所谓目录室,仅置西文书目,而东方语文不与焉!是以尊著恐只能暂购一部,且俟本年(一九六三)暑期新阅览室成立后,或可加购一部,置于该室,实情如此,当可鉴原!刻下 Tsuneishi 公尚在休假之中,一俟回馆,自当向渠征询意见,如璧推荐得售,能在此时立购二部,则更佳矣。草此布意,诸维亮察。耑此,敬颂崇安!

　　　　　　　　　　　　　　　　　　　晚徐家璧鞠躬

　　　　　　　　　　　　　　　　　　　元旦日晚

　　尊夫人前,乞为叱名叩安为祷!

　　　　　　　　〔University of Chicago Library, Yuan T'ung-li Papers, Box 2〕

一月二日

先生致信郑通,寄上《中俄西北条约集》部分校稿并谈字号等印刷细节。

　　新华印刷股份公司郑经理大鉴:

　　　　昨接十二月廿六日大札及初校稿,全部均拜收,除第二部分(条约)日内校改即寄上外,兹将第一部改正后奉上,即希改用四号字重新排版,因所用之老五号字太小,不雅观也。又条约检查表应按年月先后排列次序。兹一并改正,望特别注意。至于王伊同总序、金问泗序及附录——附录四均是《中俄条约集》的(见目录),亦请速排寄下。

王、金两序用四号字,附录用老五号字。为更明了起见,另附一单注明先后次序,即祈照办是荷。顺颂时祉。

袁同礼再启
一月二日

〔University of Chicago Library, Yuan T'ung-li Papers, Box 1〕

按:此件为底稿。

刘麟生覆函先生,告目力昏花及刘体智逝世等事。

守和尊兄勋鉴:

(一)两奉廿七、八日手教,指示多端,宜铭座右。今日有假,爰往哥大阅读。移时便觉目力昏花,遂尔中辍。本月八日,当就医检验也。(二)在图书馆,晤同学高肇源兄,始知馆长已易 Dr. Evans, Dr. Linden 似为副馆长。(三)晦叔闻已在沪逝世,享年八十又四。(四)一年容易,岁又更始。维祝著述日新,迎年俪吉!

教小弟刘麟生敬上
一,二

〔University of Chicago Library, Yuan T'ung-li Papers, Box 2〕

按:高肇源,1923 年上海圣约翰大学毕业,获文学士。① "晦叔"即刘麟生从叔刘体智,参见 1 月 10 日刘麟生覆函。

一月三日

先生致信福克司,对未能与其晤谈表示抱歉,寄上《新疆研究文献目录》(日文本)五册,请其在德国宣传并销售。

January 3, 1963

Dear Professor Fuchs:

I was so disappointed to have missed you when you came for a brief visit. I had hoped that we may discuss matters concerning Sinkiang in which you were particularly interested.

I am sending you herewith a copy of my recent work. I hope you may write a short review in one of German journals. As only five hundred copies of each work are printed, I hope copies may be available in

---

① 《圣约翰大学史》,上海人民出版社,2007 年,页 465。

German libraries.

I am also sending four more copies and I hope you could sell them for me at 12 marks per copy.

With Season's greetings and warm regards,

Yours sincerely,

T. L. Yuan

〔University of Chicago Library, Yuan T'ung-li Papers, Box 2〕

吴文津覆函先生,告知《蚕桑萃编》序言并未找到,《金韬筹笔》已付邮寄上。

守和先生赐鉴:

十二月二十七日惠书敬悉。前由渡边宏君寄来《新疆文献目录》一册,业经查收,感谢之至,并已为敝馆代购矣。嘱查《蚕桑萃编》事,光绪二十六年本仅载圣谕及徐树铭、裕禄奏片,并无魏序。《金韬筹笔》已另邮奉上,用竣后尚希挂号掷下为感。专此奉覆,并贺年禧。

弟吴文津敬上

一,三

〔University of Chicago Library, Yuan T'ung-li Papers, Box 2〕

按:先生在该函左下标注"一,廿一寄还"。

一月四日

先生致信叶公超,告已请江易生携带《退庵谈艺录》,并请惠赐画作。

公超吾兄左右:

前奉手教,深慰饥渴。退公近著《谈艺录》,前嘱香港书店径寄尊处,该书店以北平所印者不敢邮寄。兹托易生兄设法奉上,即希惠存。尊绘竹梅素所羡慕,如承赐一小幅,尤所感盼。临颖依依,未尽所怀。敬颂新釐。

弟同礼顿首

一月四日

〔University of Chicago Library, Yuan T'ung-li Papers, Box 2〕

按:江易生(1908—?),江苏无锡人,曾任中华民国驻洛杉矶领事。

先生致信钱存训,请影照《沅湘通艺录》中篇目,并委托销售《新疆研究文献目录》(日文本)。

公垂吾兄:

贵馆藏有《沅湘通艺录》,其中卷四 p.71 有《书〈金轺筹笔〉书后》,想不太长,请用 Xerox 照一副本,奉上一元备用。《新疆目录》日本之部想尊处业已收到,得暇时可否写一短篇介绍登载 *Library Quarterly*,因美人对此区域毫无所知,而日人对于中西史地考古、语言之研究颇有成绩。兹另邮寄上五部每部三元(直接寄贵馆),请为介绍,想贵馆可购两部,美术系及 Chicago Museum of N. H.或可各购壹部俟决定后再寄发票,至于 Art Inst. of Chicago 已由弟直接寄奉矣。顺颂教祺。

弟同礼顿首

一月四日

又芝城《中国同学录》如有印行者,盼代索一份。

〔钱孝文藏札〕

按:《沅湘通艺录》为清末湖南学政江标编,《书〈金轺筹笔〉书后》即《书曾惠敏公〈金轺筹笔〉后》,汪都良撰写。钱存训本拟为该书西文本撰写书评,但因西文本在先生生前并未出版,此计划亦随之落空。

钱存训覆函先生,寄出所需书籍并告知台北历史学者曾在彼处聚会,另谈其著作再版修改细节。

守和先生:

两奉手教,敬悉种种,并蒙见示冯君经厂等等,有劳清神,至为感幸。所要《中国内乱外祸厂史丛书》第二册,已嘱馆际借书处寄奉。该处请于下次借书时填用 LC 馆际借书之多联格式,较易办理云云,并以奉闻。又冯君著作目录已见《燕京学报》及《图书季刊》,想甚完全,请勿再费神钞录为幸。又日昨奉到自东京寄来大著《新疆研究文献目录》日文本,收罗广博,印刷精致,当极为有用,谨此致谢。中文本不知何时可以出版?又李孝芳(前芝大学生,谢义炳君夫人)所编西文《新疆地质目录》,想亦收入矣。前嘱写跋文,不知何时需用,请便中将序文及体例见示,当再一试。周前厂史学会在此聚会,刘崇鋐、张贵永、郭斌佳、邓嗣禹、张兴保诸君均来参加,张贵永及夫人均于卅一号返台,想已有所闻矣。小女在京承蒙优遇,并得有机会晤见诸兄姊,至为荣幸，并此道谢。拙作现已印第二版，拟将其中错误稍加修改：页139 曾述及高丽僧昙徵于 610 赴日传授制纸墨之法，据 Sansom 此人作 Dokyo，但据日文昙徵应读 Donchu，据韩文应读 Damjing，不知 Dokyo 之名从何而来，或 Dokyo 系另外一人而非昙徵？如 LC 有日本佛教史专家，乞代一询是所至感，否则请勿费时间为要。专此，即请著祺，阖府均此。

后学存训拜上

一月四日

〔University of Chicago Library, Yuan T'ung-li Papers, Box 2〕

按：信中各"历"字均被钱存训写作"厂"，似有意避讳，其原因待考。"冯君"即冯承钧。《中国内乱外祸历史丛书》由中国历史研究社编辑、神州国光社出版，该书在 1949 年前出版 3 次，分别为1935-1936、1938-1940、1946-1947，各版书目顺序并不一致，此处第 2 册应指《奉使俄罗斯日记》，内含《奉使俄罗斯日记》《与俄罗斯国定界之碑》《尼布楚城考》《俄罗斯佐领考》《俄罗斯进呈书籍目录》《伊犁定约中俄谈话录》，芝加哥大学图书馆确实藏有此册。[①] 昙徵，朝鲜半岛高句丽僧人，奉高句丽王之命与法定一同前往日本，他精通五经、善绘画，并向日本传播颜料及纸、墨、砚台的制造技术，*Written on Bamboo and Silk* 第 2 版第 139 页将其记作"Damjing"。

刘国荼覆函先生，谈先生转寄国内各物、在港账目及印书各事。

守和博士先生尊鉴：

敬启者，未修书敬候，瞬已月余，恭维撰祉延鸿，文祺纳燕，至以为颂。上月上旬拜奉手示，敬悉一一，内附汇单四十五元一张亦已收妥，代转令岳信亦已寄去矣。圣诞前奉到惠赐床罩一张，高谊隆情，寔深感纫。去年十一月十六日寄至美圖各亲友之圣诞礼物共七处，时至现在只得芝大采访部回信收到并致谢外，余六处皆未有回音，甚以为奇。尊处之茶叶两罐，想不会如去年打回头再寄方能收到也。汇单四十五美元找得港银二百五十六元一角半（即五六九二五计），当即由香港

① 芝加哥大学图书馆编目系统将此书记作第 6 册。

中国银行代汇港银一百四十二元至令岳处，汇费五角，但至今亦未见其回信收到；并代购德国听诊器成套价银卅七元，邮费二元二角；及代购英国多种(综合性)维他命丸三磲，每磲壹百粒，价银七元，共廿一元，邮费二元七角，包扎好用挂号邮分别寄松江令岳收及天津袁伯焘先生收。因由邮局寄发是未能完税者，而且听诊器是特别的，未知需纳若干，而维他命丸有好几种，及需要寄付多少，来示未有指明，是以问药房是寄大陆者则以此综合者为佳。晚已有信与伯焘先生说明一切也。月前收到令媛由美付来维他命丸两种，各一磲，经已即为改装包好，亦用挂号邮付去，邮费一元二角，计时当可到达，此项亦是未能完税者。尊账前存卅九元八角半，支二元信资两次共四元，五毛一次，四元一次，合共八元五角，比对尚存卅一元三角半，连此次二百五十六元一角半，合共二百八十七元五角，以上四项共用银二百〇六元六角，比对尚存银八十元〇九角在晚处也。新华印刷厂日前经已将《中俄条约集》全稿航寄奉尊处核校，想已办妥及直接交涉妥当。据他等云及尚有封面、扉页、版权稿等未收到，该书总可尽快完成也。至于《新疆国界图志》各稿尚未收齐，是以未能估价。该厂主理此事之人名郑通先生，甚为诚恳温和，亦是一能干者也。集古斋信经已交去，但其答谓该书尚未收到，如得收后当通知晚往取四册，并代分赠各人，因此未知日本方面寔在已将书寄来港否？去年十二月十四日为冯平山图书馆成立三十周年纪念日，晚趁此机会写一篇"有感"文字，刊登于《华侨日报》教育版内，以表感慨。迟日剪出奉呈，敬希指正，至所厚幸。专此，敬请钧安，并颂年禧。

愚晚国蓁顿首

一九六三年一月四日

〔University of Chicago Library, Yuan T'ung-li Papers, Box 2〕

徐传保致函先生，祝贺《新疆研究文献目录》(日文本)问世，并询问《新疆研究丛刊》有无附图画之可能。

同礼先生伟鉴：

违教日久，时深景慕。近维春节和风，道履康健，定符企颂。顷读《美洲日报》，知大作日文本《新疆研究文献目录》已在东京出版，纸贵洛阳、环宇誉诵，岂可测量？未知中英文本何日付梓，无任跂望。此后

《勘定回疆记》等书多种先后问世,晚拟一一备置,详细阅读。晚多年前曾购摄美京国会图书馆珍藏之 Conquêtes des Emperors Chinois 图画一套,又向 Honolulu 大学博物馆买到所印专册,互相参阅,颇觉法国教士画家绘品之精良,而巴黎(十八世纪)铜版更增美丽不少。至今摄件幸未遗失,至为欣慰。惟念上海土山湾耶苏会教士邸中壁上所悬多帧,尤为完全(内有一二图为美京及檀岛所缺)。当时即请该地大修道院院长(Henry)[姚氏赞唐]准许复摄一份,姚院长有求必应,垂命晚去禀明会长神父(Sarvini)。惟战鼓动地,迅惊歇浦,匆匆赴港,未竟所志,此系憾事。阁下新册中是否附示图画,如有意于斯,似可采访以益读者。书不尽忱,敬请钧安,并祝阖第春绥。

晚徐传保谨上
一月四日

〔University of Chicago Library, Yuan T'ung-li Papers, Box 2〕

按:徐传保(1901—?),江苏吴县人,法国巴黎大学法学博士,归国后历任复旦大学、东吴大学、中央大学法学院教授。Conquetes des Emperors Chinois 似应为 Les Conquetes de l'Empereur de Chine,即耶稣会来华画师集体创作的《乾隆皇帝平定准噶尔得胜图》。"姚氏赞唐"一般作姚缵唐(Yves Henry,1880-1963),法国耶稣会士,曾任震旦大学校长,并两次出任修道院院长。Sarvini 似应为 Louis Salvini(1889-1950),法国耶稣会士,中文名萨维义。

一月五日

先生致信郑通,再寄《中俄西北条约集》校稿。

新华印刷公司郑经理大鉴:

日前寄回《中俄西北条约集》第一部分校样,请改用四号字,在尊处寄下校样以前,务请仔细校对。兹寄上第二部分校样(条约部分),第一页至七十一页务请按照所改正者排版后再送下一看,方能付印(凡无改正之页可不必寄来)。有条文内有少见之字,如"哱""夃""嚪"均须刻好新字再将校样寄下,即希速为办理见复为荷。此颂时祉。

袁同礼拜启
一月五日

七十一页至一二〇页校样，明日寄上。

〔University of Chicago Library, Yuan T'ung-li Papers, Box 1〕

按：此件为底稿。

先生致信莫泮芹、莫余敏卿夫妇，请转托 Richard C. Rudolph 寄送其中国考古论文篇目，并请推销《新疆研究文献目录》（日文本）。

January 5, 1963

Dear Prof. and Mrs. Mok:

Thank you so much for sending us the Oregon pears which we enjoyed so much. It was very kind of you to remember us this way.

Prof. Chen Shou-yi was in town when I happened to be in Cambridge. I was so sorry to have missed him. Have you seen the Chens after their return? I hope Mrs. Chen has recovered after such a long journey.

When you wrote me about the collection of Chinese books offered by Mr. Meng, I thought of the University of Pittsburgh which has to start its oriental collection practically out of nothing. Did you make a copy of the catalog? How many volumes are there?

When you see Dr. Rudolph, will you ask him to send me a list of his articles on archaeology in China, as I should like to include all his writings on the subject in my forthcoming bibliography on Chinese art and archaeology.

Incidentally, there are two works on archaeology in Sinkiang. I list the titles below. If you are interested in obtaining xerox copies, I shall be glad to make copies for your library. They are very rare now, but L. C. has a copy each. The titles are given below:

I am sending you under separate cover six copies of my *Bibliography of Japanese books and articles on Sinkiang*. I hope you could recommend for their purchase. I have sent a complimentary copy to Professor Lao Kan, but I presume your Department of Art and some professors may like to buy a copy for reference. Each copy costs $ 3, and

I rely on your help in its wider distribution.

With cordial regards and many thanks,

Sincerely,

〔University of Chicago Library, Yuan T'ung-li Papers, Box 2〕

按:此件为底稿,空行处应为两种新疆考古著作书名,付诸阙如。

先生在该件下端标注"Jan 30 寄赖永祥《历代宝案》"。

先生致信马大任,寄送《新疆研究文献目录》(日文本),请代为推销。

January 5, 1963

Dear Mr. Ma:

I sent to you a list of Chinese journals on microfilm. Since then, another list with additional titles has been prepared by the photoduplication service. If you have not received it, I shall be glad to send it to you.

Herewith I am sending you two copies of a *Classified Bibliography of Japanese Books and Articles on Sinkiang* which I printed in Tokyo. I hope you would be able to recommend for their purchase by your Library. As soon as you decide how many copies you wish to have, I shall send you an invoice. Each copy costs ＄3.

Japanese scholars have made significant contributions in Central Asian studies, particularly in the field of art and archaeology. It is possible that your art library may wish to have a copy for its reference collection.

With Season's greetings.

Yours sincerely,

T. L. Yuan

〔University of Chicago Library, Yuan T'ung-li Papers, Box 2〕

按:此件为录副。

李田意覆函先生,告知已按要求核实账目及著作库存,并拟请耶鲁大学出版社作为先生著作的代售方。

同礼长者赐鉴:

前信寄出后,即请 Kono 夫妇详细清理账目,看是否有错误之处。田意亦随时加以注意,以防彼等疏忽。日前已清理完毕,大致无误。

当时即请 Kono 夫人奉上一函,报告一切,想已入览矣。尚未卖出之本数,经点验后亦与彼等所报告者相合。看情形彼等尚属老实,令人稍为放心。Far Eastern Publications 乃学校之印刷出版机关,款项皆由学校会计处经管,想 Kono 夫妇亦无法上下其手也。田意已嘱彼等今后务必按时寄版税,同时应尽量设法推销。过去在推销上未能尽最大努力,乃遗憾之事。田意现颇欲请 Yale University Press 代为推销,如能成功,则亦可解决一大问题也。如先生有何建议,随时告知,当请 Kono 夫妇尽量照办。专此,并颂时安。

晚学田意顿首
一九六三,一,五

〔University of Chicago Library, Yuan T'ung-li Papers, Box 2〕

一月六日

任以都致函先生、夫人,寄上任鸿隽遗墨一册,并告儿女近况。

　　袁伯伯、伯母:

　　　　多日未请安,想来您们近日都安好为祷。

　　　　现在另封寄上侄等编辑纪念先父的遗念一册,里面差不多全是先父的手笔。此书目的在保存其墨迹和一小部份诗文,所印只很少数几份。顷奉家母之命,特寄上一册送您们留念,以答您们多年之谊。敬希查收。

　　　　侄等在宾州各事依旧,小研今年已入小学一年级;小建很淘气,两岁多,颇费人力照顾他。

　　　　余后禀,敬请尊安。

以都谨上
一九六三,一月六日

〔University of Chicago Library, Yuan T'ung-li Papers, Box 2〕

　　按:“小建”即任以都和孙守全的二儿子孙建(Raymond),1960 年出生。[1]

庄泽宣致函先生,请转告牟复礼早日将书稿阅毕寄还。

　　守和兄:

　　　　上月中向兄拜年,曾附字及致牟教授函 copy,谅邀鉴及。弟与某

---

[1]《任以都先生访问纪录》,台北:“中央研究院”近代史研究所,1993 年,页 82、83。

出版商于十月初通信,得复愿考虑,弟允年底交稿,兹已再函稍延,但盼牟教授早日惠阅首三章。其他除一两章尚在他人审阅中外,均已收回(如蒋彝兄对弟关艺术部分,陈观胜兄关于佛教部分,均幸无大改)。如兄尚未与牟通信而兄认为可将上述各节告之,请转告盼他月内掷还,以便早日整理后付梓。一再渎陈,乞宥并谢惠助。即颂春祺。

弟宣

1/6

〔University of Chicago Library, Yuan T'ung-li Papers, Box 2〕

一月七日

徐家璧覆函先生,告知前寄三部《新疆研究文献目录》(日文本)皆已售出。

守和先生尊鉴:

　　敬肃者,顷接四日手示,藉悉种切。今日常石公 Tsuneishi 休假归来,谈及尊著日文本《新疆研究目录》,当蒙予允诺立购二册,为本馆之用。于上午已将订单打妥随函寄上,谅已寄达。中午回舍午餐,始收到周末手示,见所开书价又行更正,是以于回馆时乃将馆中订单存底(尤其 Fund 部份),按新价改正,将来烦寄馆中发票时,可否即按陆元计算,以资符合,不胜感盼之至! 至于李田意兄所主持之 Sinological Seminar,因有一单独阅览室,似可另购一册,俟与李兄晤见时,再为介绍,想无问题。如此则已寄之三部目录,皆有受主矣。吴讷孙兄方面,平日均到本馆借书参考,或无单购可能,似可不必进行推销,未悉以为然否? 此外耶鲁中国同学负责人,尚不悉为何人? 俟探听清楚后,当代询同学名单事,倘有印就者,自当索取一份寄上不误。崦此奉陈,敬颂崇安!

晚徐家璧鞠躬

元月七日晚

尊夫人前乞为叱名候安!

〔University of Chicago Library, Yuan T'ung-li Papers, Box 2〕

劳榦覆片先生,告因事未能撰写《新疆建置志》跋文,将于最近完成。

守和先生赐鉴:

　　大序及刘跋并已收到,因琐事纷忙,《新疆图志》只标点及半,而跋文尚未著手,至以为歉。奉到惠书,明日即到图书馆检书一次,本星期内当将跋文完成寄奉,敬乞赐予斧正为幸。专候,敬颂俪安。

后学劳榦敬上

一月七日

〔University of Chicago Library, Yuan T'ung-li Papers, Box 8〕

按:该片以航空信方式寄送。

一月八日

钱存训覆函先生,附《沅湘通艺录》一文复印件,并告知芝加哥大学图书馆购入两部《新疆研究文献目录》(日文本)。

守和先生:

兹将所需《沅湘通艺录》中一文复印奉上,计三页,合 45 ¢ ,尚存有 55 ¢ ,容后再为奉还。

大著《新疆目录》当由敝处留存二部,款即嘱馆中径奉,他处当俟洽妥再告。介绍文拟俟西文本出版后一并再写,因 *Library Quarterly* 仅评介西文刊物也。芝城同学录最近未有印行,并闻。专覆,即请著祺。

后学存训拜上

一月八日

〔University of Chicago Library, Yuan T'ung-li Papers, Box 2〕

王伊同致函先生,请协助评估马鉴藏书价值。

老伯大人尊前:

敬禀者,离都寸禀想邀青鉴。刻访院长长谈,于季明师藏书甚表欢迎,意欲烦老伯先阅目录、估行市,再与此间庋藏对核,未知能俯允否? 此事果成,公私咸便亦佳事。砚池已寄到,颇动目,惜木盒破裂,微感不足耳。舍亲章楚已函购大著,如赐复时告以东洋文库地址,尤感。专禀,敬请金安。

侄伊同再拜

元月八日

〔University of Chicago Library, Yuan T'ung-li Papers, Box 3〕

童世纲覆函先生,告普林斯顿大学图书馆只愿购买两部《新疆研究文献目录》(日文本)。

守公尊鉴:

顷奉手教,并《新疆研究文献目录》伍册,取材精当,内容详实,是为研究我国边疆问题之津梁,拜收之余,钦仰无似! 嘱向敝馆采访部洽购尊著一节,遵已照办;惟该部负责人 J. K. Fleck 氏只肯备置两部(一部存总馆,一部存葛库),良深抱歉! 至于其余两部究应如何处置,还乞示知,俾有遵循为盼为感! 肃此奉复,敬颂俪福,并贺新喜。

晚世纲拜上

一九六三,元,八

发票请写"P. U. Lib."

〔University of Chicago Library, Yuan T'ung-li Papers, Box 2〕

梁敬錞致函先生,告先生大著序言将在论坛刊出等事。

守和吾兄:

奉书,承赐新疆研究文献第二种,拜读之余,深感东洋学子之精湛。第一种尊著已否印出,何处可得,尚望见告,其余八种想当次第刊出也。

所附两序已转论坛,前次尊序、贱跋已得回信,云将于本月份论坛中刊出,特由港印寄,尚须时日耳。前途有函托致,谢恫并陈。专此奉覆,顺叩著绥。

弟錞启

元,八

再,如有来纽之便,千祈函知,当走谒。弟近亦有欲与日本朋友合研战史之意。有日人可介绍否? 望一思之。又及。

〔University of Chicago Library, Yuan T'ung-li Papers, Box 2〕

按:"论坛"应指纽约《海外论坛》月刊社,参见 1 月 15 日梁敬錞函。

一月十日

房兆楹致函先生,告澳大利亚国立图书馆有意延聘先生主持该馆东方馆藏,并请影照清代史料。

守和先生:

时序催人,又是一年了。祝您新禧。

此间国立图书馆需人主持东方书,我们已向白先生建议请您来一年或半年给作一全盘计画。此事若成,应日内即有消息,现请暂秘之。

钱恂《中俄边界图》此间有一幅,若要当可影为胶片给您寄去。

　　兹有事奉恳者,有同学急需宋恕《六斋卑议》(《敬乡楼丛书》第一集),可否请即日为照 Microfilm Copy 航邮寄来? 一切款需当即照还。谢谢。

　　近有 Yale 研究生 Spence 来跟我读满洲史料。现有的书不少,可惜重要的都没有。可否请您大约估计一下以下诸书 microfilm 费用?

　　　　1.《八旗通志初集》(Columbia)

　　　　2.《八旗通志续集》(L. C.)

　　　　3.《八旗氏族通谱》(L. C.)

　　　　4.《八旗文经》(L. C.)

　　目前无款,故此踌躇。但钱□应用若干,乞大略作估计。多谢多谢。

　　敬候俪安,新年百禧,合府安吉。

弟楹谨上

一九六二,一,十

　　再,书尚未到。五部代销可不成问题。又及。

〔University of Chicago Library, Yuan T'ung-li Papers, Box 2〕

　　按:"一九六二"当作"一九六三",此处应系房兆楹笔误,特此说明。《六斋卑议》,清末学者宋恕(1862—1910)著,全书抨击程朱理学,主张托古改制。收到此信后,先生即协助影印《六斋卑议》,并寄送。Spence 即美国汉学家史景迁(Jonathan D. Spence,1936-2021)。

刘麟生覆函先生,谈目疾及晦叔逝世等事。

守和尊兄博士勋右:

　　(一)承寄傅吾康明籍目录,感谢无涯。(二)弟已经纽约医院诊目疾,据云无甚病症,宜省目力,下月再查云云。(三)晦之叔闻已于上月中逝世,享年八十又四。(四)寒暄变幻异常,乞加珍重。敬祝俪绥。

小弟麟生谨上

一月十日

〔University of Chicago Library, Yuan T'ung-li Papers, Box 2〕

费正清致函先生,感谢寄赠《新疆研究文献目录》(日文本)。

January 10, 1963

Dear T. L.:

Many thanks indeed for sending me a copy of your latest bibliography, which seems to be very neatly done and will certainly be of use.

I am also hopeful that the Joint Committee on Contemporary China will be taking some interest in your letter to it, which was, however, necessarily referred to a subcommittee for eventual action.

I am sorry to have missed the Graves.

With cordial regards,

John K. Fairbank

〔University of Chicago Library, Yuan T'ung-li Papers, Box 3〕

一月十一日

先生致信王世杰,请"中央研究院"考虑补助《中国数学家著作目录》印刷费用。

雪艇先生尊鉴:

近年以来,我国数学家之贡献已引起各国学术界之重视,欧美专门杂志先后刊载此项论文,同礼曾编《中国数学家著作目录》,以资宣扬。在此刻正筹措印刷费,颇感困难。贵院能否预定若干部,藉资补助,至盼与数学所所长一商,早日赐覆为感。林所长在此时曾与商谈,业经表示赞助。兹准备付印,特奉商,亟盼贵院能预订一百四十部,内中以一百部寄贵院,四十部分赠各学术机关。事关学术宣扬,谅荷赞许,如承早日赐示,尤所……

一月十一日

〔University of Chicago Library, Yuan T'ung-li Papers, Box 8〕

按:"林所长"即林致平(1909—1993),江苏无锡人,1931 年毕业于交通大学土木工程学系,后赴英留学,时任数学所所长。此件为底稿,未写完,付诸阙如。

先生致信牟复礼,请速将庄泽宣书稿前三章寄回。

January 11, 1962

Dear Professor Mote:

When you were in Taipei, you probably had occasion to see the manuscript copy of the *Li Tai Pao An*　　　　which is the only existing copy as far as we know.

Sometime ago I sent the enclosed letter to Syracuse University which, as you know, is building up a research collection on Ryukyu. The letter has just been returned to me. I am passing it to you in the expection that you may be willing to order a copy for Princeton.

Dr. C. H. Chuang, in a recent letter to me, wishes me to convey to you his sincerest thanks for the time you had spent on his manuscript. As he is anxious to prepare for possible publication, he hopes that you will return to him the manuscript at your early convenience. May I also thank you for what you have done to improve the manuscript?

With season's greetings,

Yours sincerely,

T. L. Yuan

〔University of Chicago Library, Yuan T'ung-li Papers, Box 2〕

按:1962 应系先生笔误,实为 1963 年。*Li Tai Pao An* 后应填写汉字"历代宝案"。

一月十二日

先生致信钱存训,感谢芝加哥大学图书馆预约全部《新疆研究丛刊》,并告前询僧人译名可径函京都大学中国文化研究所。

公垂吾兄左右:

前寄下之论文目录极为有用。《新疆研究丛刊》承预约全部,至谢。此项书籍虽为大陆所需要,但不易出售,仅以一份赠徐森玉。中文资料截至 1962 年底较日文本多三倍,但内容远不如日人,现正候大陆出版之期刊,一俟全部稿件整理完毕,即将序文、凡例寄上,请写一跋。昙微译名,询此间日人(多土生)均不知之。加大有 Susumu W. Nakamura 教授,日文不识造诣如何? 似不如直接函询京都大学中国文化研究所,可获到准确之答覆也。此谢,顺颂时祉。

弟袁同礼顿首

一,十二

附发票请转交。

〔钱孝文藏札〕

按:《新疆研究丛刊》共计十种,但第一、三两种《新疆研究文献目录(1886-1962)》分别为中文之部和西文之部,先生生前并未完成。

先生致信马克尔,告知《中国留英同学博士论文目录》将由《中国文化季刊》登载,并寄赠《新疆研究文献目录》(日文本)。

January 12, 1963

Dear Mr. Morkill:

Referring to my last letter, I am glad to report that the *Guide to Doctoral Dissertations by Chinese Students in England* is to be printed in *CHINESE CULTURE*, Vol 4, No. 4, as a special supplement. I only regret that the checking of Chinese characters has taken much time and labour. A number of the older men had died, and to find out their Chinese names from their relatives is a laborious undertaking.

I am sending you herewith my latest bibliography on Chinese Turkestan, limited to books and articles in Japanese. I trust that you may like to have it for your Library.

With Season's greetings,

Sincerely yours,

T. L. Yuan

〔University of Chicago Library, Yuan T'ung-li Papers, Box 1〕

按:此件为录副。

一月十三日

田清波致函先生,告已找到唐努乌梁海地图,询问其是否仍然需要。

Arlington, le 13 janvier 1963

Cher Monsieur le Docteur,

Vous vous rappellerez qu'il y a quelques années vous m'avez demandé de vous envoyer la carte T'ang-nu Wu-liang-hai t'u, dont vous aviez besoin pour un travail sur la Mongolie, et qu'alors je n'ai pas pu rendre ce service parce que je ne retrouvais pas cette carte dans ma bibliothèque. Dernièrement j'ai dû faire transporter ma bibliothèque dans notre nouveau bâtiment. À l'occasion de ce déménagement j'ai retrouvé la carte. Si vous en avez encore besoin, je vous enverrai la carte avec plaisir, pour que vous en puissiez faire faire une reproduction, si vous le jugez nécessaire.

Agréez, cher Monsieur le Docteur, l'assurance de ma haute considération.

A. Mostaert

〔University of Chicago Library, Yuan T'ung-li Papers, Box 3〕

按:此件为其亲笔。

一月十四日

先生致信 Basil Gray,询问在大维德爵士资助《中国文化丛书》项目下协助出版《中国艺术和考古目录》的可能性。

January 14, 1963

Dear Mr. Gray:

May I write to you to ask your advice about the possibilities of publishing my *Bibliography of Chinese art and archaeology*?

A few months before illness, Sir Percival David informed me that he was to publish a series of books on Chinese culture under your able editorship. Being old friends since the old Peking days, he had insisted that my bibliography should be included in this series. He urged me to hasten the editorial work and promised that he would finance its printing.

I presume that his illness has upset all of his plans. Although I received a Christmas card from Lady David, I do not think it appropriate for me to write her at a time when she is so much disturbed with his illness. Since you are in touch with his plans, I shall be grateful if you could inform me how matters stand at the present time.

The first volume of my bibliography would be ready for the printer sometime in August. If Sir Percival's plans had to be postponed, I have to seek support elsewhere to get it published.

Any advice you would find it possible to give to me will be deeply appreciated.

Sincerely yours,

T. L. Yuan

P. S. Under surface mail, I am sending you my Bibliography of Japanese literature concerning Sinkiang. You will note that there is a considerable number of articles on the art and archaeology of Central Asia.

〔University of Chicago Library, Yuan T'ung-li Papers, Box 1〕

按：此件为录副。

徐家璧覆函先生，告收到《新疆研究文献目录》（日文本）及发票，并已转交耶鲁大学各处入藏。

守和先生尊鉴：

敬肃者，昨奉十日手示暨发票二种，诵悉一切。又日前另邮寄下《新疆研究目录》三部，业于馆中收到，诸乞释念！现已将目录暨发票，分别转致各单位收执，想于日内尊处定可收到书款支票。倘延迟过久，即请示知，以便代催为祷！耶鲁图书馆概况，仅见有 *This is the Yale Library* 一种，兹特随函寄奉一册，用备参考。倘此册非所需要，如能将书名开示，当行另为探问。此间购书费，似尚不恶，但用来亦速，更不知能长远如此否？余不多渎，敬颂崇安！

晚徐家璧鞠躬

元月十四日

尊夫人前乞叱名代为叩安。

〔University of Chicago Library, Yuan T'ung-li Papers, Box 2〕

劳榦致片先生，寄上《新疆建置志》跋文。

守和先生赐鉴：

承命作跋，迟迟至今始得写定奉寄，深以为罪，敬乞恕之，至以为叩。大著序文两篇及刘麟生先生序文一篇一同奉寄，大序及刘序高华扼要，相得益彰，榦文思迟钝，望尘莫及矣。宋书及祁书别包邮呈，并乞察收为幸。专此，敬颂著安，潭祺多福。

后学劳榦敬上

一月十四日

〔University of Chicago Library, Yuan T'ung-li Papers, Box 8〕

一月十五日

先生致信新华印刷公司，请代修改《新疆研究丛刊》次序，并催寄《中俄西北条约集》附录四种的校样。

新华印刷公司大鉴：

《中俄西北条约集》第二页之《新疆研究丛刊总目》之次序略有更动，第八种改为《金轺筹笔》，第九种改为《西陲要略》，第十种为《新疆建置志》，第十一种为《平定回疆记事七种》，第十二种为《戡定新疆记》，请代改正是盼。其总序、金问泗序、袁序等改用四号字重排，想已进行，惟附录四种迄今校样未到，深以为异，务希提前办理为荷。又香港新印之书应否呈缴香港政府，有无出版税，亦乞查明示知。兹寄上丛刊第七种之稿件全份（《中俄西北条约集》为第四种，请在版权页上代为□□，《新疆国界图志》为六种，第五种尚在编辑中），即希将结单寄下以便汇款。此书应与《新疆国界图志》从速出版，书前有序二页，书后有跋二页，日内即寄，并无附录。□上，顺候时祉。

袁同礼顿首
一月十五日

〔University of Chicago Library, Yuan T'ung-li Papers, Box 1〕

按：《新疆研究丛刊》最终付梓时，《西陲要略》为第五种，《新疆建置志》为第九种，《平定回疆记事七种》并未出版，《戡定新疆记》为第十种。"第七种之稿件"应指《西疆交涉志要》。此件为底稿，下沿未能全幅扫描，特此说明。

梁敬錞致函先生，转李和生函及剪报。

守和吾兄：

顷得《海外论坛》李先生覆书，特以转上。李书弟已另覆，不必寄还。

又前次尊序、贱跋均已在香港《天文台》见报，刊后有读者来函，叙钟镛获罪经过，颇足列为典故，特剪附，乞并察及。手此，顺候著绥。

弟錞叩上
一，十五

〔University of Chicago Library, Yuan T'ung-li Papers, Box 2〕

按：先生在该函左下标注"李和生 Homer S. Lee，《海外论坛》月刊社，221-41 Murdock Ave, Queens Village, N. Y. 29"，另附 1 月 4 日《天文台》剪报。

马大任覆函先生,感谢寄赠《新疆研究文献目录》(日文本)和中文期刊缩微胶卷清单,并表示将尽力向相关研究者、图书馆推荐先生大作。

Jan. 15, 1963

Dear Dr. Yuan:

Before I thanked you for the list of Chinese journals already microfilmed, your *Classified Bibliography of Japanese Books and Articles concerning Sinkiang* arrived. My debt of gratitude to you is really piling up.

I have checked your list against our holdings and have found that we have acquired all the microfilms listed. I certainly would appreciate your sending me the second, or latest, list so that I can be sure that we have everything which we should have.

I am now circulating your letter and the *Bibliography* among the faculty of China Program, and am trying to find out how many people will need it for themselves and how many copies the departmental libraries may need. I shall let you know as soon as I find out.

This is certainly a beautifully done reference work. Many thanks indeed for letting me have two copies of it. I am sure this bibliography will be needed by all university libraries and many research institutes. Have you advertised it? I shall mention it to all my fellow Chinese and Oriental librarians whenever I have a chance to tell them.

Thank you again. And my best wishes.

Sincerely,

John T. Ma

Chinese Bibliographer

〔University of Chicago Library, Yuan T'ung-li Papers, Box 2〕

按:此件为打字稿,落款处为其签名。收到该函后,先生于 21 日覆信致谢,因属具文,不再录入。

马克尔致函先生,附上英国大学中国委员会委员联系方式,并感谢寄赠《中国留美同学博士论文目录》。

15 Jan. 1963

Dear Dr. Yuan:

Please forgive me for delaying so long in replying to your letter of Nov. 30 and your kind offer to supply copies of the Special Supplement to *CHINESE CULTURE*.

I enclose a list of those who would much appreciate receiving a copy.

Thank you for the Guide to Doctoral Dissertations by Chinese Students in America. It is a monumental compilation and shows what a valuable contribution Chinese students make in countries which are privileged to have them pursue their studies therein.

With all good wishes for the New Year,

Yours sincerely,

A. G. Morkill

Secretary

〔University of Chicago Library, Yuan T'ung-li Papers, Box 1〕

按:此件为打字稿,落款处为其签名。另附 1 页英国大学中国委员会委员名单及联系地址。1 月 21 日、2 月 12 日,马克尔又分别致函先生,补充可以寄赠人员的地址。

一月十六日

李田意覆函先生,谈协助清查版税之事。

同礼长者赐鉴:

来示敬悉。诚如所言,版税一事,亟应清查。如有错误,应即改正,不然此间甚对不起先生也。此事当遵嘱与直接经售之人 Kono 夫妇一谈,然后请彼等详细报告。一切自当婉转为之,希勿念。圣诞节后因患病,未克至华府开会,缘悭一面,不胜怅怅。复承邀宴,未能前往,闻后益增不安。肃此,并颂时安。

晚学田意敬上

一九六三,一,十六

〔University of Chicago Library, Yuan T'ung-li Papers, Box 2〕

陈世骧覆函先生,询问《新疆研究文献目录》(日文本)售价,并告待将其最近刊发作品汇集后寄上。

守和先生惠鉴：

奉到《新疆研究文献目录》，各册当如嘱分着 Central 及东亚圖置购。每册订价多少？祈先示知，然后即使各□□机关再请正式发单。盖亦形式手续问题也。近年小有所作，分见"中研院"集刊、*China Quarterly* 及 *JOAS*，仍有即将出者，容将集起奉上。此候还云，并颂著安。

世骧

一月十六日

〔University of Chicago Library, Yuan T'ung-li Papers, Box 2〕

吴俊升致函先生，告前寄留学比利时名单已经王亚徽女士辨识，其中两人中文姓名确定，余者待查。

守和先生撰席：

敬复者，顷奉手教，敬悉一一。承示《留美博士论文目录》已编就付印，并将寄赠第一部，甚为感幸。留比学生之姓名，尊开名单弟已交请王亚徽女士查询，王长宝女士早经逝世。亚徽女士系其妹，现经本校聘为女生指导员兼教法文，伊之即可以确定之中文姓名计有下列两人：

T'ang Yu-hans 汤约翰；

Wang, Sypao 王锡民（福建人），亚徽女士之妹。

其他各人王女士正续查中，俟查实后续行奉告。恐劳廑念，先以所知者奉闻，尚乞察及。又尊编《留法学生博士论文目录》已编就否？并念。匆此奉复，敬颂撰祺。

弟吴俊升顿首

一月十六日

〔University of Chicago Library, Yuan T'ung-li Papers, Box 2〕

按：王亚徽，祖籍福建闽侯，生于北京，王景岐三女；王长宝，福建闽侯人，王景岐长女；"Wang, Sypao"似应为"Wang, Si-mine"，王景岐次女，姐妹三人均获布鲁塞尔自由大学（Université libre de Bruxelles）政治学博士学位。① "汤约翰"即汤于翰（1913—

① 王庆余著《留比学生史》，台北：光启文化事业，2011年，页474、481。

2014），浙江宁波人，医学家，1939 年获得鲁汶大学医学博士
学位。

庄泽宣覆函先生，告诸人协助审查其稿件情况。

　　守和学长道鉴：

　　　　昨接一、十大函，前已收到牟教授来函及拙稿首三章，承他每章略
　　示意见（首章指盘古及上古神话来自印度，次章引 Creel 认为孔子偶像
　　非如《史记》所载，三章以为最好将罗马政府组织与汉代者比较），是
　　否照改尚待考虑，昨已专函道谢。其他各章分得陈观胜（佛教）、蒋彝
　　（绘画）、杨庆堃、陈锡恩诸兄审阅，幸均无大谬之处。文学一章仅引
　　诗词数首及小说大要，原拟请陈受颐看，惜他赴欧，改得一在芝相识、
　　现任教南加之王正义兄看（他写新诗）。据云 Teresa Lee 即吴经熊，不
　　知应否在注脚中指明耳？复颂春祺。

　　　　　　　　　　　　　　　　　　　　　　　　　　　　弟宣

　　　　　　　　　　　　　　　　　　　　　　　　　　　一月十六

　　　　据弟发现蔡廷幹《唐诗英韵》*Chinese Poems in English Rhyme*，芝大出版所
　　译均押韵，比陈所引为佳（李白、杜甫等），惜不多。

　　　　据牟云，近乔迁，适台方友人寄来印有唐（？）画之小碟，拟寄他补
　　璧。与他不熟，承教，藉表微愧。

　　　　　　　　　　　　〔University of Chicago Library, Yuan T'ung-li Papers, Box 2〕

　　按：杨庆堃（1911—1999），广东南海人，社会学家，燕京大学毕业，
　　后赴美留学，时应任教于匹兹堡大学。陈锡恩（1902—1991），福
　　建永泰人，福建协和学院毕业，后赴美留学，获哥伦比亚大学教育
　　师范学院硕士，1929 年 9 月回福建协和学院任教，并任教务长，
　　1947 年任该校校长。蔡廷幹（1861—1935），字耀堂，广东香山
　　人，晚清民国时期政治、军事人物，《唐诗英韵》，1932 年芝加哥大
　　学出版社初版。

一月十七日

先生致信新华印刷公司，请估价《西疆交涉志要》《新疆国界图志》印刷费
用，并告印好后寄送邮资将另行补汇。

　　径启者：

　　　　日前寄上《西疆交涉志要》全部稿件，望将估价单从速寄下（共印

750部,四号字),以便进行,内有一错字,望代更改:卷三,页13,"二十六月"应改为"二十六日"。兹奉上《新疆国界图志》前一部分稿件及跋文,即希估价(共印750部,四号字),以便将应预之款如数汇上,估价并盼特别优待,因尚有其他稿件,其他印刷公司似较尊处为廉也。既有刘国蘖、罗香林两先生之介绍,务乞格外优待,至以为盼。将来每书印好,仍需代寄各处,另有住址单容再奉上,所需邮费自当另行计算也。此致

新华印刷公司

袁同礼拜上

一月十七日

〔University of Chicago Library, Yuan T'ung-li Papers, Box 1〕

按:此件为底稿。1月30日,新华印刷公司提交《西疆交涉志要》报价单,印750册须港币1655.5元,须付定金百分之五十。

刘麟生覆函先生,略谈《新疆研究文献目录》(日文本)之缺陷,并应先生之邀撰写题签。

守和博士先生史席:

（一）十二日雅翰拜悉。（二）承赐《新疆书目》日文本三册,精详堪佩,谢谢。检阅索引,日人多有姓而无名指英文,且校对亦多漏误也。然详审不易得,可断言耳。（三）顷正与此间图书主任夏震兄谈过,即以另二册由本圕购置。渠云"自无不可。惟'刘大使'已赴日内瓦,下星期返此。故须少俟。"云云。（四）承属题签,已照办。另纸呈教。（五）弟拟名为《西陲史料汇辑》,未识恰当与否?如有另撰之题目,当再行作篆也。（六）《新疆书目》题字,古朴俊逸,得未曾有。乃知椽笔深造有得,自然怡人。他日拙著印行,当求教于大君子之门也。敬颂迎春百福。

教弟刘麟生顿首

一,十七

〔University of Chicago Library, Yuan T'ung-li Papers, Box 2〕

按:"夏震兄"待考;"刘大使"应指刘锴,曾担任"常驻联合国代表"。

一月十八日

先生致信张群,请协助申请补助用以影印辛丑和约外交使团会议记录。

岳军先生钧鉴:

敬陈者,辛丑和约驻京外交团印有会议记录,流传日稀。近有美人收藏一份,不肯示人,经同礼奔走接洽,始允暂借一月以供影印,除要求印成后赠送壹百部外,并无其他条件。窃念我公对于外交史料素所关怀,用敢奉告,并附说明随函赍呈,应否转呈"总统"核阅,敬希尊裁。如承赐予补助,一俟出版再进全书,并可译成中文在台出版,想我公亦以为然也。临颖依依,未尽所怀。

一月十八日

〔University of Chicago Library, Yuan T'ung-li Papers, Box 3〕

按:该会议记录影印费用约在 3500 美金,先生拟申请补助应为 2500 美金。此件为底稿。

王伊同覆函先生,为重印新疆文献史料拟书系名称,并谈洽购古瓷经过。

老伯大人尊前:

敬禀者,一月十三日手谕奉悉,寻得稿本七种,所拟总衔"平定新疆记事七种"甚善。为切题计,如用"清乾道同光四朝勘定新疆纪事萃编"或"清代勘定新疆纪事辑要"似亦可取,唯遗"七种"两字略欠醒目耳。敬陈末议,尚乞尊裁。季明师所遗书已与此间院长议定原则,关键在:①目录;②售价(平允)能否分期付款;③复本。侄意如复本不甚多,则侄私人亦可购进数种如《四部丛刊》此间有初编,无二、三编,马藏初编,侄便可购。月下正编制豫算,请款倍去年,成否不可知,正为此事而发,承允校核议价,拜感拜感。建窑 Pole 据拍卖门市谓七十五元,不为昂,然阴青 140 元太贵,且建窑略残,代拟 50 元,经与物主函商,渠谓有人以 75 元求购时已心许。寄来未肯脱手,因减为 60 元,刻已成交矣。汝、哥、官窑诸书已托台湾之艺文公司严一萍先生代为物色,或较香港售价稍廉也渠常以九折优待。砚盒残破太甚,已将原盒寄去托照样重制,大抵五六元便成,唯王洪、启寿、冯焕文诸人迄不明身世为憾。石质不恶,篆铭书法亦挺秀,因刻意求全耳。命跋丛书未知指全集抑近寄七种,得暇乞谕为祷。敬肃,顺请福安,并候年釐。

侄伊同顿首拜
正月二十三日
夏历小除夕

高友工兄近病住院,二三周后始知无意迁馆,仍须他处物色,附闻。

〔University of Chicago Library, Yuan T'ung-li Papers, Box 2〕

按:王洪(1837—1912),字文命,号春澥,清同光间广东潮安人,擅长书法兼喜收藏;冯焕文(1898—1958),字翰章,江苏宜兴人,畜牧学家;启寿,待考。高友工(Yu-kung Kao,1929—2016),生于沈阳,文学理论家,1947年考入北京大学法律系,1949年后随家人赴台,同年入台湾大学法律系,后转入中文系,1954年毕业旋赴美留学,入哈佛大学东亚系,1962年获博士学位,后在普林斯顿大学任教三十余年。

刘国蓁致函先生,转呈袁慧熙函,并告先生书稿在港出版等事。

守和博士先生尊鉴:

敬启者,日前曾奉上芜笺,量邀尊览。日昨奉到令岳来示,并附嘱代转尊夫人函,兹特奉上,敬希察收为幸。本港与国内邮递经常八九日方能达到,渠信云及只收到港纸140元,折合人民券60元6角,未悉渠是否写错,因前次所汇款是142元,想银行不会交少也。兹奉回香港中国银行原币信汇便条一纸,祈为察收为荷。令媛付来之维他命丸两磅及听诊器一套,皆未得收,甚以为异,可能要经过海关检查及其他手续方能放行,递送阻延时日。此皆正当用途,想是纳税而已,可能并无其他留难也。日前得收集古斋交来大作《新疆研究目录》日文本四册,经已转送一册与罗香林教授、钱宾四院长及曾克崅教授,皆是用邮政寄去新亚书院,想当能收到。曾教授是到该院讲学,而其地址已问过多人,亦不知,故并寄新亚也。日前得接在澳洲学习会计之二小儿来信,云华人旅澳留学并不甚多,皆不相联系,同学录恐无刊行,而且各人皆是自私自利者,但他有暇当再调查也。如再有消息,当为奉闻。顷与新华郑通先生通电话,知该书初校稿已付回,但有些要改排或加排,是以尚要两三日后便可全部稿寄上,作最后校阅,并知各版皆付齐,恐不日可印刷出书矣。兹奉上拙作《冯平山图书馆成立三十周年纪念日有感》剪报一则,敬希指正,幸甚幸甚。茶叶两罐,未悉尚得收否,时在念中。匆匆,余当续陈。专此,敬请文安,敬贺春禧百福。

愚晚国蓁顿首

一九六三年一月十八日

再者,蒙惠赠大作,殊深感谢。至于汇款是427,计算港币142元,方能折合人民券 60 元 6 角也。

〔袁同礼家人提供〕

按：曾克耑（1900—1975），字履川，祖籍福建闽侯，生于四川，1920
年前后入北京财政商业专门学校，后在政府部门服务，1950 年南
下香港，时在新亚书院执教。

一月二十一日

裘开明致函先生，请补寄十五元支票，并告知哈佛燕京图书馆藏清代俞浩
著作情况。

守和吾兄著席：

去岁十一月五日尊函嘱转寄哈佛照相部《中俄边界记》相片，发
票因未收到，故未当急复书。兹将该发票附上，请再赐十五元支票一
张，以了此事。又嘱代查清俞浩《海月堂集》，敝馆无其诗文集，但藏
有其杂著六册，道光二十七年刊本，内容为《西域考古录》十八卷。若
需用此书，可由 Inter-library loan 寄上也。专复，敬候冬安。

弟开明敬上
一九六三，一，廿一

蒙赐大著《新疆目录》，已交图书馆收藏编目，以供众览耳。

〔University of Chicago Library, Yuan T'ung-li Papers, Box 2〕

刘麟生覆函先生，告诸事。

守和馆长先生勋右：

（一）十七日片示，谨悉。（二）书签三纸奉上，乞正。（三）新刊中
似有三种，见于《新疆研究丛刊》。前已将书目奉还，并用红铅笔为记，
谅荷察及。（四）弟目疾稍愈，下次检查后再奉告。（五）承示红萝卜可
多食，谢谢。弟不甚笃嗜之，然深信此物富营养料。日人呼为人参，殆有
由也。（六）弟作篆书用朱丝阑。尊著刊行时，或用乌丝阑，亦不妨耳。
（七）昨晚浦君来访，彼谓尊辑如交其印行，当乐于效劳云云。（七）偶阅
大著《留美博士论文索引》，乃发现堂弟圉生 即晦叔之幼子于 1960 年在
Ohio State U.获得博士衔。彼与弟无甚往还也。敬颂春禧俪吉。

教小弟麟生谨上
一，廿一

〔University of Chicago Library, Yuan T'ung-li Papers, Box 2〕

香港大学出版社彭锡恩覆函先生,略述香港印厂情况,建议先生与万有图书公司联系。

同礼教授赐鉴:

一月十七日华瀚奉悉,辱承过誉,愧不敢当。罗香老日前方再次吩咐,嘱有机会应为教授之大著尽力,后学唯恐力有不逮,今能效劳,当认是无上之荣光也!敬将管见分叙于左:

一、香港之印刷厂除中华、商务外,似无其他能负起校对之责任,而中华、商务立场欠妥,无庸考虑。后学有见及此,年前商诸万有图书公司徐炳麟兄,劝其逐步填补此一空虚,顷得徐兄来电,彼对教授亦心仪已久,并云如承认可,一切均愿援李田意教授已行之出版方式进行。如此,教授是否可径函万有洽商?后学定当从旁催促,期能符合标准。

二、敝社长魏智先生今闻教授愿以钜著交其印行,不胜欣悦,彼嘱后学转呈教授,宜先将大著之纲领目录邮交与彼,以便具体作进一步之安排云。

匆匆,崘此奉覆,并请年禧。

后学彭锡恩顿首

一月廿一日

〔University of Chicago Library, Yuan T'ung-li Papers, Box 1〕

按:"钜著"似指《中国艺术和考古目录》,待考。

一月二十二日

王世杰覆函先生,告此前申请补助已转"国家长期发展科学委员会"并获初步同意,请寄送申请书以利办理资助手续。

守和吾兄惠鉴:

久阔,至念。接来书,承嘱"中央研究院"订购《中国数学家著作目录》一节。此事已移请"国家长期发展科学委员会"(该会由"中研院"院长兼任主席)设法办理;经其专门委员会初步审查,认为订购方式不甚合适,大约可改为补助印刷费台币一万五千元;出版后寄赠一百册,由该会支配转赠,以每册定价美金三元五角计算,一百册约合台币一万四千元,其余一千元可作为寄递邮费之用。……备文航寄该会申请,以便办理。顺颂时祺,不尽。

弟王世杰敬复

□□□□

〔University of Chicago Library, Yuan T'ung-li Papers, Box 8〕

按：1962年5月，王世杰担任"中央研究院"院长，"国家长期发展科学委员会"主席亦由其兼任。该函破损部分以……标识，由2月5日先生覆信可知该函撰写时间为1月22日。此件为打字稿，落款处钤王世杰印。

一月二十四日

任以都覆函先生，告收到《新疆研究文献目录》（日文本）并将向校内相关教授推介。

袁伯伯：

您的手示和新疆研究文献目录一册都奉到，谢谢！目录我最近就会介绍给此校教亚洲史的同事，促他订购。这一部丛刊，里面搜集的资料这样丰富，对研究中国西北史地的人实在有绝大的帮助！日后中文、英文本若均能继续出版，则更可贵了。

知道清弟在宾大研究，十分高兴。袁伯母想来也很忙。谨此道谢，即请尊安。

并请袁伯母安。守全附笔问候。

晚以都谨上

一九六三，一月廿四日

〔University of Chicago Library, Yuan T'ung-li Papers, Box 2〕

王鸿益覆函先生，告知所询哥伦比亚大学图书馆馆藏书刊情况。

守和先生道席：

接奉廿日手教，当即代为查询，适 Linton 与鲁光桓兄均先后有小恙，未及随时答复，尚祈原宥。

《瀚海潮》现既不在书架上，而 Linton 先生谓似已付邮寄出，但又查无纪录，鲁现将此事交请副馆长 Miss Kai 继续追查，想不久必会另有报告也。

至《义和团》一书，计有四册，其号码为2913/8222，并非二册；此外有《义和团》史料号码为2913/6343，二书均在架上，并未有人借阅。

现在 Dr. Evans 为 Acting Librarian，新馆长为谁现尚未知。

日内此间天气极寒,预报今晚可能降至华氏零度,不知美京情形如何? 诸希珍摄。专此奉复,并请年安。

王鸿益敬上
国历除夕

〔University of Chicago Library, Yuan T'ung-li Papers, Box 2〕

按:Miss Kai 应指 Miwa Kai(1912-2011),日裔,生于旧金山;Dr. Evans 应指埃文斯,"国历除夕"即是年 1 月 24 日。
Dorothea Scott 致函先生,告因其丈夫教职变动遂辞去康乃尔大学 Bibliography of Asian Studies 编辑工作。

January 24, 1963

Dear Dr. Yuan:

I think this is the first (and most probably the last!) letter I have written to you as Editor of the Bibliography of Asian Studies. I did tell you when I saw you at the Cornell dedication, how much I appreciated your continuing to send cards for the Bibliography. Although there is a good deal of duplication between your cards and the proof slips Gussie saves, there are always some cards which are not duplicates. I hope you will continue to send them for 1962 publications, and I would like to receive them as quickly as possible as far as you have them collected.

Now for the explanation of my opening sentence. I am sure you will be pleased to know that Scottie has been appointed Professor of Oriental Drama at the University of Wisconsin and Acting Director of their International Theater Program, part of their University wide International Studies Program. He will probably go there for this coming term although his permanent post will not take effect until the new academic year.

I am therefore resigning my post at Cornell and also from the Editorship of Bibliography. I know it is a nuisance for all the people concerned, especially as I was destined to inherit Gussie's post here, but it's one of those things that can't be helped. Scottie's speciality is so special that he can't hope to find many such jobs and we both feel this is an opportunity not to be missed.

I don't know what I shall do yet. I am exploring possibilities. I shall probably stay on there until the meeting of the Association in March and then go to Madison. Will you be at the meeting? I hope that Scottie will be able to get there as well and that we shall both have the chance of meeting you them. We were sorry not to be able to entertain you while you were here-we had only just moved and were living with packing cases. And I know you were every rushed.

With best wishes for the year of the Rabbit,

Yours sincerely,

Dorothea

Editor, Bibliography of Asian Studies

〔University of Chicago Library, Yuan T'ung-li Papers, Box 2〕

一月二十五日

先生致信郭廷以,再商译印有关中俄西北交涉史料事,并告拟推荐郑宪前往匹兹堡大学执教。

量予吾兄著席:

近闻骝先先生突然作古,至为伤痛,想治丧委员会成立后,一切定可办理妥协也。前代购之俄文《汉学书目》及《中共今日》两书,日前交邮寄上,其发票俟下次通讯再行寄上。又美国务院印行之白皮书(1949年印行者)此间市上偶有发现,需十元原价七元,想贵所业已入藏,未敢代购,恐重复也如需要望示知。上月寄上之施绍常之《中俄约注》影印本,想已收到,能否用此本加以影印,想已在考虑之中,如何之处并盼示覆。又关于光绪六年伊犁交涉一案,俄方主持者为吉尔斯外部尚书及热梅尼外部总办,前二年热梅尼致吉尔斯时在黑海信札在荷兰印行出版,全系法文,弟拟为之印行曾之《金轺筹笔》,弟已为之印行,但国内读法文史料者实不太多,自应译成中文,可否请兄代觅精通法文而又对于当时历史有兴趣者从事譒译有若干史料为中文图籍中所未载,即作为贵所丛书之一,望觅妥相当人之后予以示知。当代贵所购一部,由荷兰径行寄上也。应翻者仅数十页,并不难也。如晤梁实秋,渠或能推荐相当之译员也。亚洲学会年会定于三月廿五日在费城举行三天,大驾来美计划已定否？不胜企念。顺候时祉。

弟袁同礼顿首

一月廿五日

又 Shelley Cheng 在 Iowa State 教书，比较闭塞，又无资料可资研究，弟拟推荐于 Pittsburgh 大学，但不识渠愿转职否？

前托日人寄上之《新疆研究文献目录》日文本已收到否？此书过于专门，恐无人问津也。

〔台北"中央研究院"近代史研究所档案馆，〈郭廷以〉，馆藏号 069-01-02-089〕

按：1月3日，朱家骅去世。"吉尔斯"即 Николай Ка́рлович Гирс（Nikolay de Giers, 1820-1895），1882 年起担任俄国外交大臣；"热梅尼"即 Александр Генрихович Жомини（Aleksandr G. Jomini, 1814-1888）。此信于 2 月 1 日送达。

马大任覆函先生，告康乃尔大学图书馆有意购买《历代宝案》的缩微胶片，但嫌价格略高；毕乃德教授将前往台湾地区，如需请他在台查看文献可直接与之联系，另告已根据国会图书馆《信息公报》订购了所缺胶卷，此外愿订购一部《新疆研究文献目录》（日文本）。

Jan 25. 1963

Dear Dr. Yuan:

Thank you very much for your letter of January 21.

The information about *Li Tai Pao An* is most appreciated. We are considering purchasing a set of its microfilm. But the price is a little high. Do you think if both L. C. and Cornell order for it, they may reduce the price? Do you happen to know whether any other library is interested in purchasing this too?

Professor Biggerstaff is going to Taiwan next week. He will be spending some time at "the Academia Sinica". If you want him to examine the documents for you, I think he may be willing to do it.

I appreciate very much your kindness in sending me the new list of periodicals on microfilm. I shall check it against our holdings immediately.

I have already checked the list in the L. C. *Information Bulletin*, Dec.

10, 1962, with our holdings and have ordered for all those microfilms which we do not already have.

We shall be happy to have a copy of your *Classified Bibliography of Japanese Books and Articles concerning Sinkiang, 1886 - 1962*, in our Japanese collection. Please send us a copy and bill us in triplicate. I have also written to Suzuki of Michigan about your book.

I am returning to you Mr. Lai's article which is very informative and useful. Many thanks for letting me see it. I have made a xerox copy of it and it will be cataloged in our Wason Collection.

Many thanks again for all your help.

Sincerely,

John T. Ma

Chinese Bibliographer-Cataloger

〔University of Chicago Library, Yuan T'ung-li Papers, Box 2〕

按：Mr. Lai 应指赖永祥（1922—），时在台湾大学图书馆工作。

一月二十六日

先生致信马克尔,感谢其发来委员会人员名单,待收到台北寄赠的样刊后即按名单寄出。

January 26, 1963

Dear Mr. Morkill:

Thank you so much for your two recent letters giving me the names and addresses of the members of your Committee interested in receiving copies of *Guide to Doctoral Dissertations by Chinese Students*. I shall send them immediately as soon as copies are received. So far, I have not yet received the final proofs but I have urged for its early publication.

I was not quite sure that I had sent you a copy of my *Russian Works on China: a selected bibliography* published in 1959. If not, I take pleasure in enclosing a copy.

Yours sincerely,

T. L. Yuan

〔University of Chicago Library, Yuan T'ung-li Papers, Box 1〕

按：此件为录副。

劳榦覆函先生，商《新疆建置志》跋文付印事。

守和先生赐鉴：

　　奉到惠函，诸承奖誉，愧不敢当。大序言简意赅，详及宋生平及成书始末，嘉惠读者匪浅，诚不敢妄加雌黄也。拙跋诸承评定即可付刊宋联奎跋之后，贱名亦宜依旧例，写"壬寅十二月劳榦谨跋"。《大陆杂志》等刊登亦仍乞删定后径寄该处，多费清神，深用拜托之至。大序似亦宜置拙跋之前同时付邮，因刊登时有大序为之介绍宋氏生平，更为有意义也。（宋联奎之生卒未知，陕西省志书又记载否？后学但知宋联奎字聚五，民国成立曾任陕西民政长——即省长——其后退休住西安东关。）大跋及宋联奎跋并附寄，大函因涉及鄙跋修改事，亦谨附入，俾先生作为参考。专此敬覆，顺颂俪安。

后学劳榦敬上

一月二十六日

〔University of Chicago Library, Yuan T'ung-li Papers, Box 3〕

　　按："大跋"似当作"大序"。宋联奎（1870—1951），赋闲后曾编《咸宁长安两县续志》。

一月二十八日

Basil Gray 覆函先生，告大维德爵士身体状况转好，并表示《中国文化丛书》项目难以出版异常宽泛的《中国艺术和考古目录》，另询问该目录的范围、内容、汉字使用情况等细节，将与大维德爵士商讨。

28th January, 1963

Dear Dr. Yuan:

　　Many thanks for sending me a copy of your *Bibliography of Japanese Literature Concerning Sinkiang*, which I look forward to studying.

　　I am glad to say Sir Percival David is in slightly better health and I now hope that he will have the strength to finish his annotated translation of the *Ko Ku Yao Lun*. But he has wisely decided to abandon, at any rate for the time being, his project for collections of essays and other material, extending to several volumes to accompany this publication.

Consequently, I now expect it to appear as a single volume. The publisher, Messrs. Faber, will be prepared to consider later on, the possibility of one or even two volumes of essays, but I do not think in any case that your bibliography, which I imagine is very extensive, could be included in this project.

If you will let me know something about its scope and extent, use of Chinese characters, and other particulars, I will make enquiries as to possibilities for publication in this country. Meanwhile, when I see Sir Percival next, I will let him know what you have written.

With kind regards,

Yours sincerely,

Basil Gray

Keeper

〔University of Chicago Library, Yuan T'ung-li Papers, Box 1〕

按:此件为打字稿,落款处为其签名。

一月二十九日

先生致信 Miwa Kai 女士,请其协助查找《瀚海潮》并将此刊寄送国会图书馆。

January 29, 1963

Dear Miss Kai:

I would appreciate your help very much if you could trace the whereabouts of a Chinese journal entitled: *Han Hai Chao* which I requested for temporary loan since October. The men in charge of your inter-library loans reported that this journal was lost. But when I went to Kent Hall in November and December, this journal was placed in its proper place on the shelf.

On December 19 I took it from the shelf and left it with Dr. Linton who promised to send it to me through the Library of Congress the next day. But so far it never came.

Since no one used this journal for so long as your record shows, could you make a special effort to search it? It might be still found in Dr.

Linton's office. I am asking the Library of Congress to send a third request.

Thanking you for an early reply,

Sincerely,

T. L. Yuan

P. S. Thank you for your order for *Sinkiang Bibliography* . Enclosed please find the invoice.

〔University of Chicago Library, Yuan T'ung-li Papers, Box 2〕

按：此件为录副。

一月三十日

先生覆信马大任,建议其联系莫余敏卿女士,与台湾大学商洽一并购买《历代宝案》缩微胶卷。

January 30, 1963

Dear Mr. Ma:

Thank you for your letter of January 25. Concerning the microfilm copy of *Li Tai Pao An* , the Library of Congress hopes to get a set in exchange. I have asked the Oriental Library of the University of California at Los Angeles to consider the possibility of acquiring a copy. Perhaps you may like to write to Mrs. P. K. Mok and to see if both libraries can write to Taipei requesting for reduction of its price.

As there are very few copies printed of my Bibliography of Sinkiang, it would be to your advantage to buy two copies which I had sent to you. Only fifty copies were sent to the United States, while the rest were sent to China and Japan.

With many thanks,

Yours sincerely,

T. L. Yuan

〔University of Chicago Library, Yuan T'ung-li Papers, Box 2〕

按：此件为录副。

邓嗣禹覆函先生,按嘱寄上《新疆研究文献目录》(日文本)书评底稿,并告本年秋拟前往华盛顿任教一年。

守和先生赐鉴：

　　辱承惠赠大作《新疆研究文献目录》，并命为文介绍，受宠若惊。因人事牵联，迟至昨晚方有暇略握笔，今朝打出，不知能合尊意否？印大圕已介绍购买二部，想能照办。今年九月底嗣禹将去 American University 任客座教授一年，盼能长聆教益。即叩著安。

后学邓嗣禹拜复
正月卅日

　　华府租 apt. 或住宅，若知有价廉物美之处，便请示知，否则乞不必劳神回答。

〔University of Chicago Library, Yuan T'ung-li Papers, Box 8〕

　　按："印大圕"即印第安纳大学图书馆；American University 即位于华盛顿的私立大学，由基督教卫理公会教派联合会创办。

一月三十一日

王伊同覆函先生，寄上《新疆建置志》短跋，并就丛书名称提出意见。

老伯大人尊前：

　　敬禀者，昨奉手谕，知贞一兄为《新疆建置志》作跋，饱学宏才，定多创见，侄得附骥为厚幸。季明师遗书及王洪砚池承专函探询，甚感甚感。季明师之儿名"蒙"，刻任教港大，亦侄旧识也。来日果成交，公私两便，其重板书如为数不多，侄自当购入数部，以成其美，尊见何如？唯为数不可过昂耳，一笑。

　　命作短跋，昨忽忽草就奉缴，中"治舆地者曰禹贡，倡丛刊者曰边疆"两句自指顾颉刚先生，渠刻在京标点古舆地书承命侯仁之，一返旧制，可叹，甚不得意，要否删去，乞尊裁。又是书总名，尊旨"西陲史料汇辑"自佳，"汇辑"要否改作"萃编"，亦请明断。至惠稿"标准"两字擅改为"识见或异今日"，余悉无可无不可间。承厚爱不敢方命，聊复为之耳。敬请金安。

侄伊同顿首
三十一日

〔University of Chicago Library, Yuan T'ung-li Papers, Box 2〕

二月四日

先生致信渡边宏，请其代问日本三家书店可否将今后出版的著作行销中国大陆。

February 4, 1963

Dear Mr. Watanabe:

I am grateful to you for the trouble I have given to you in mailing copies of our bibliography to various places. I hope the check I sent to you would cover all the postal charges. If I owe you any amount, will you be good enough to let me know?

To-day I received with much appreciation the following two books which you were good enough to have sent to me. They are very useful to my work and I thank you most warmly for your thoughtfulness.

In the next few months, I shall publish my bibliography of Chinese Books and Articles concerning Sinkiang. I shall send you a copy of it as well as other titles in the series known as　　　.

Since books of this kind will be much use to the scholars in Mainland China, I wonder if you could advise me which booksellers in Tokyo have close business connections with bookstores in China. I understand that a trade agreement has recently been concluded between Japan and Communist China. Would it help a little in bringing about closer trade relations?

I am thinking of asking the following bookstores to sell my forthcoming publications. If you happen to visit any of them, will you check whether they can send my books to Communist China? I give their names below:

　　Rinrokaku Bookstore, 71 Morikawa-cho, Bunkyo-ku, Tokyo

　　Yamamoto Bookstore

　　Dai An Co., No. 14 2-cheme, Tokyo

With many thanks,

Yours sincerely,

T. L. Yuan

〔University of Chicago Library, Yuan T'ung-li Papers, Box 10〕

按：Rinrokaku Bookstore 即琳琅阁书店，Yamamoto Bookstore 即山

本书店，Dai An Co.即大安株式会社。此件为录副，空白处付诸阙如，应填写"新疆研究丛刊"。本年4、5月，先生分别致信此三家书店，请其代售《中俄西北条约集》。

徐炳麟覆函先生，谈推销《新疆研究文献目录》（日文本）情形和代购书籍进展。

守和先生：

一月廿六日惠书敬悉，至慰。

《新疆研究文献目录》（日文本）50本业已收到，经向左右各书店推销，销数不甚合理想，和平书店已作样本，看将来何如？

承订购书——三种另邮寄，四—六尚未到港，俟到港时取寄。

关于印书事，刘、彭两兄曾来谈及，俟稿件寄到，当尽力与彭兄研究，该印件价廉质优，达到港大出版物水准，不负□期。敬颂时绥。

弟徐炳麟上

二月四日

〔袁同礼家人提供〕

郭廷以覆函先生，谈《新疆研究文献目录》（日文本）代售、朱家骅去世等事。

守和尊兄道席：

元月廿五日手书及惠寄《中俄国际约注》均收到，至感。

大著《新疆文献目录》（日文）十五册，亦于昨日邮到。关于《中俄界记》、《中俄界约斠注》、《中俄国际约注》及《中俄约章会要》各书重印事，已商得此间文海书局同意，由其承办，出版后以原书若干部分赠吾兄及近史所，此外无何条件。惟《中俄约章会要》一书尚未收到。艺文书局早已关闭。《巴布阔福回忆录》决定由孙桂籍（东北人，俄文法政毕业，现任"立法委员"）译汉，前寄原书缺472—473页，务希设法补齐掷下。《热梅尼致格尔斯函札》近史所亦愿译出，请即代向荷兰购买原书。

《俄文汉学书目》及《中共今日》两书价款，俟发票收到，即奉上。国务院一九四九白皮书已有，不需另购，谢谢。

朱骝公年来健康不佳，但始终不知患有心脏病。元月三日中午尚出外访友，下午四时许病发，不五分钟，即溘然辞世。一年之内，胡、梅、朱三前辈相继作古,洵教育学术界之至大不幸,伤怆曷亟!

郑宪(Shelley Cheng)确为一不可多得之才,渠亦有意他就,尚望鼎力为助。其通讯地址:

Dr. Shelley H. Cheng

2303 Franklin St.

Cedar Falls, Iowa

三月廿日前弟可到纽约,除参加费城之会议,将有三四个月停留。一切容再面陈。匆此,祇颂时福。

弟郭廷以谨启

二、四

〔University of Chicago Library, Yuan T'ung-li Papers, Box 2〕

按:"文海书局同意",此处有误,据本月 18 日郭廷以覆函可知诸书实际系广文书局影印,《中俄界记》《中俄界约斠注》《中俄国际约注》版权页均标注 1963 年 3 月初版。孙桂籍(1911—1976),祖籍山东掖县,生于海参崴,国立北平大学俄文法政学院经济系毕业,曾任旅顺、长春市长,1949 年去台。

莫余敏卿覆函先生,告知该校愿意购买两本《新疆研究文献目录》(日文本),并谈马鉴藏书及购买《历代宝案》胶片等事。

February 4, 1963

Dear Dr. Yuan:

Thank you for your letters of Jan. 5, 11 and 30th. I am sorry not to write to you earlier. My work has been far behind. Will you please excuse me?

Thank you also for sending us the complimentary copy of your bibliography. As it is on very specialized field, I am unable to sell the copies to individual persons except a few special libraries. Both my library and the Dept. of Oriental Languages will buy one each. Would you be kind enough to send me 2 invoices (in triplicate copies)? I shall arrange for their payment as soon as possible. I have also asked Chen Shou-I to buy one for his library, but he has not informed me yet. I will let you know when he does.

I understand that the books offered for sale by Mr. Ma in Hong Kong have been sold but I do not know whether it is true or not.

I have asked Mr. Rudolph to send you a list of his articles on Chinese archaeology as you requested. Have you heard from him yet? I am sorry we do not keep any of his reprints, as they are in the main Library. I am very much interested in your forth-coming bibliography on Chinese art and archaeology. Would you let me know when it is published?

I would like to obtain xerox copies of the two works on archaeology in Sinkiang which you mentioned about. How much the cost will be?

There is no official directory of Chinese students at UCLA this year.

As to the *Li Tai Pao An*, I am finding out what fund I can have in order to buy it. May I return the article about this work to you next time?

Our Main Library will buy the Library Catalog of the School of Oriental and African Studies but not the Oriental Library because we do not have enough fund.

I believe I have answered all your questions now. Mr. Mok and I want to thank you for your kind thought of us at Christmas and for the delicious box of fried meat which you and Mrs. Yuan gave us.

　　　　　　　　　　　　　　　　　Yours sincerely,

　　　　　　　　　　　　　　　　　Man-Hing Mok

　　　　〔University of Chicago Library, Yuan T'ung-li Papers, Box 3〕

　　按：此件为打字稿,落款处为其签名。

二月五日

先生致信王世杰,请酌情增加《现代中国数学研究目录》编印补助费。

　　雪艇院长钧鉴：

　　　　奉到一月二十二日赐书,藉稔申请印刷费一案业承移请"国家长期发展科学委员会"予以审查,荷承赞助,感荷良深。顷与此间数学家商谈,渠等建议各国科学院及数学会均应寄赠,可否转请"发展科学会"酌增补助费,以便出版后即用贵院名义直接寄出,附上一单以供采择。在国家所费有限而收效较宏,是否有当仍希尊酌,如汇寄美金不无困难,即希就近将该款送交台湾银行总行 7332 号,收入同礼账内为感。又适之先生……

〔University of Chicago Library, Yuan T'ung-li Papers, Box 8〕

按:此件为底稿,未写完。

二月七日

先生致信郑通,嘱校对人甚须仔细,否则耽误时间太多,并谈《新疆国界图志》《西疆交涉志要》印刷费用问题。

新华印刷公司郑经理大鉴:

日昨接到一月三十一日大札,敬悉——。兹将各事开列于后:

(一)《中俄西北条约集》:(1)内封面篆字须缩小,放在该页之中央。兹另寄一纸备用。(2)页数用Ⅰ、Ⅱ、Ⅲ,应放在每页之下,今全书页数不易改动,则仍改用一、二、三、四较为好看。(3)校样错字太多,兹先将总序、总目、目次、金序、袁序、凡例、一览表寄回,其余者日内即寄还,以后对于校对人仍盼托其注意,务再印错,彼此时间均不经济也。

(二)《新疆国界图志》及《西疆交涉志要》稿件,寄上时未将总页数注明,望代注出,以免次序弄错。

(三)《新疆国界图志》报价单总数为 HK $ 1511.50,请速付排,其定金七百五十五元已告东亚银行即日寄上。

(四)《西疆交涉志要》总页数共 109 页,比《新疆国界图志》页数 196 页少一半,贵局估计价目恐有错误,请再详细计算,俟得到新估价单再寄定金。

统希查明示复为荷。顺候时祉。

袁同礼顿首

二月七日

〔University of Chicago Library, Yuan T'ung-li Papers, Box 1〕

按:此件为底稿。2 月 14 日郑通覆函先生,表示《西疆交涉志要》估价并无错误,因该书小字甚多而致。

房兆楹覆函先生,感谢影印《六斋卑议》并赐书,所嘱跋文不日寄上。

守和先生:

承费神为影印《六斋卑议》航邮寄来,至感至感。又承惠赐大著

《新疆日文文献目录》,多谢多谢。兹附上美金支票一纸＄25.00之数,其中十五元为代售书价,余为影印、邮寄诸费,若不足请即示知为荷。《勘定新疆记》跋,原写的太长,殊觉辞费,故正删节,下星期内当可钞好奉寄。数月因人事关系及同人冠盖往来颇形忙碌,念来此一年半毫无成绩,不觉苦笑,不知何日得返 L. C. 读书也。谨此奉覆,拜祝俪安。

弟楗拜启

一九六三二月七日

〔University of Chicago Library, Yuan T'ung-li Papers, Box 2〕

余又荪致函先生,告收到渡边宏寄来的二百册《新疆研究文献目录》(日文本),并介绍美籍耶稣会士牧育才请与之接洽,另建议《新疆研究丛刊》在东南亚一带销售。

守和先生道席:

渡边宏先生先后寄来新疆研究文选目录二百册,皆为日文本,均已由商务收讫。

此间人士所需者为中文本,日文本甚不易售出。前商定中文本每本定价为台币六十元;日文本每本售价若干? 尚祈速示! 是否尚有中文本、西文本寄到? 倘三种均有,则更佳! 商务待得大示后,方刊登广告及发售。

台大教授牧育才(Ed. J. Murphy S. J.),在华十八年,曾在京沪一带久住。上月来美,访问留学生,考察教会教育,并为学生中心募捐,现尚在 San Francisco,将在美东西各埠访问,到华盛顿时,介绍其访先生,请惠予接□,彼甚愿了解中国留美学人及留学生情形。

大著似可在东南亚一带销售,不知已有委托书店否? 似可委托九龙集诚图书公司代售,该公司为正中书局之支店,近年向东南亚销售书籍甚多。该公司负责人亦系旧友,拙著即由其代售也。

专肃,并颂研安。

余又荪敬上

二月七日

〔University of Chicago Library, Yuan T'ung-li Papers, Box 8〕

按:牧育才(Edward J. Murphy, 1912-2005),美国耶稣会士,1937年来华在上海公萨格公学(Gonzaga College)学习语言,1943 年

在徐家汇晋铎，1951 年抵台，同年 11 月 23 日受聘台湾大学。①
"学生中心"似指耕莘文教院，即本月 28 日余又苏覆函中的
Catholic Students Center，该馆位于台北市辛亥路，由牧育才等牧
师募集善款筹建的文教活动中心，用以纪念中国第一位枢机主教
田耕莘。该函略有破损。

二月八日

马蒙覆函先生，告知其父遗书早已售出。

守和先生赐鉴：

顷奉一月卅日手示，诵悉种切，并承垂询先父藏书可否出让一节。
按先父藏书早于一九六〇年售予美国维几尼亚大学，去年复有友人廖
君遗书约七千余册，经蒙居间售予美国伊利诺亚大学。目前就蒙所
知，香港稍具规模之藏书实已不多见，而内地亦禁旧书出口，故此间书
肆所存中文旧籍为数甚少，且多残缺，实不足以供一般图书馆之用，俟
后一有发现，当即专函奉闻，藉释廑念。年来旅美我国学人东来者渐
众，间亦谈及先生况，今悉先生亦有意抽暇来港一游为慰。如有定期，
务祈早日赐示为幸。家母年来一直在港与蒙同住，身体托庇尚健，知
注谨闻。专此，即颂时绥。

晚马蒙敬上

一九六三年二月八日

〔University of Chicago Library, Yuan T'ung-li Papers, Box 2〕

二月九日

哥伦比亚大学艺术史和考古系副教授 John F. Haskins 致函先生，告该校已
将此前收到的《新疆研究文献目录》（日文本）转售予他，并询问有关新疆
考古类书籍信息。

9 February 1963

Dear Mr. Yuan:

Mr. Adolf Placzek, the Avery Librarian, has turned your book and
letter over to me, and I am enclosing my check for three dollars ($ 3.00)
in payment for your book: *A Bibliography of Japanese Literature on*

---

① 天主教辅仁大学神学院《神学论集》第 153 期，2007 年 10 月，页 332。

Chinese Turkistan . I shall certainly apprise my colleagues Mrs. Mahler and Mr. Samolin of your work and they might wish to purchase copies of their own.

The Avery librarians felt that since there was another copy in the East Asiatic Library, and that since the new bibliography was in Japanese, that it would be duplication for them to keep the copy that you had sent to them. While Avery has an archaeological section, they have very little in Asiatic languages, and no facilities for cataloguing, which for Chinese and Japanese works must be done in the East Asiatic anyway.

I assume that you are familiar with the work that has been done by the present government in Hsin-chiang archaeology and have seen the references that occur from time to time in *Wen-wu* 文物 and *Kaogu* 考古, in addition to the book edited by Huang Wen-pi 黄文弼, "*Ta-li Mu-pen-ti K'aogu Chi*" 塔里木盆地考古记, Peking (1958).

I hope that the decision made by the Avery Librarian is agreeable to you.

Sincerely yours,

John F. Haskins, Ph. D.

Assistant Professor of Art History and Archaeology, 806 Schermerhorn Hall

〔University of Chicago Library, Yuan T'ung-li Papers, Box 3〕

按:John F. Haskins(1919-1991),二战时加入美国空军,在中国、缅甸和印度服役,1958 年担任哥伦比亚大学艺术史和考古系讲师,1963 年离开该校前往匹兹堡大学执教。《塔里木盆地考古记》,中国科学院考古研究所编辑,考古学专刊丁种第三号,1958 年科学出版社初版。此件为打字稿,汉字和落款处签名为其亲笔。

二月十日

童世纲覆函先生,告知推销书籍进展。

守公尊鉴:

手教奉悉,因事稽复为歉! 承嘱各事,遵已先后办妥如下:一、《新疆目录》两部,已由陈观胜教授私人认购乙部,其支票随函附呈;另乙部已蒙方闻兄惠乞代向馆方推销,其书款未知业已送寄尊处否? 二、《博士论文目录》六册,因遍求本市书店代销不果,已交本校合作社予以寄售矣。肃此奉陈,敬请双安。

晚世纲谨上

一九六三,二,十,星期日

内子仝候请安

恕用铅笔,因原子笔突然无锭也!

〔University of Chicago Library, Yuan T'ung-li Papers, Box 2〕

二月十一日

先生致信莫余敏卿,告知将等候哈佛大学、伦敦大学相关目录的问世,并随之推迟《中国艺术和考古目录》的出版,并建议加州大学洛杉矶分校在两册外再多购藏《新疆研究文献目录》(日文本)。

February 11, 1963

Dear Mrs. Mok:

Thank you for your letter of February 4 and for your help in disposing of my bibliography of Sinkiang.

You probably heard that the Peabody Museum at Harvard is printing its catalog at a cost of $ 2970 (prepublication price). This catalog and the Catalog of the London School of Oriental & African Studies will be very important bibliographical contributions.

In view of the forthcoming appearance of these two catalogs, I shall wait the publication of my bibliography on Chinese Art and Archaeology until next year. So, there is no hurry for Professor Rudolph to send me a list of his articles.

My three bibliographies on Sinkiang are tools of research in Central Asian studies. At present the Americans are not yet ready for books of this kind. But since it is printed in limited editions, all East Asiatic libraries have bought two copies and have a standing order for the other two now in preparation. I would suggest that your Library keep two copies for future use, though at present your faculty members do not realize the importance of Central Asian studies.

　　Dr. Ting Su has travelled extensively in Sinkiang and would be interested in having a copy for reference. As I have forgotten his address, will you kindly send him a copy with my best compliments?

　　With cordial regards and many thanks,

Yours sincerely,

T. L. Yuan

〔University of Chicago Library, Yuan T'ung-li Papers, Box 3〕

　　按:Peabody Museum at Harvard 即 Peabody Museum of Archaeology and Ethnology,通译作"皮博迪考古与民族学博物馆"。此件为录副。

曾约农(台北)覆函先生,婉拒撰序之请。

　　守和先生惠鉴:

　　　　流光易逝,又换卯年,正切驰思,忽于抽屉夹缝中发现去岁十二月廿八日大示,敬谂起居安适为颂以慰。因尊函顷始发现,致羁奉答,至深歉忱。先惠敏公《金轺随笔》具有历史价值,荷列入丛书,极感。仍求先生赐序,较弟自行执笔权威多矣,叩谢叩谢。任叔永兄仙逝,可惜之至,幸其子女皆贤,至以为慰。舍间故园久未通讯矣,多人生死莫明,亦人寰惨剧也。李秀成亲供影本一册,另邮寄供存览。专此奉复,顺颂台绥,并贺岁釐。

弟曾约农谨启

二月十一日

〔University of Chicago Library, Yuan T'ung-li Papers, Box 1〕

　　按:《金轺随笔》即《金轺筹笔》。此件似为记室手笔,落款处钤曾约农印。

二月十二日

先生致信郭廷以,告在美发现辛丑和约驻京外交团会议记录及各国驻京公使往来文件,拟筹款影印,请从旁催问张群前请是否有确定答复。

　　量予尊兄著席:

　　　　奉到本月四日手教,欣悉大驾将于下月来美,晤教有期,无任神驰。《中俄约章会要》系总理衙门所印,弟搜求数年,迄未获到,如"外

"交部"无此书,只得先印钱、邹、施三书,谅荷同意。不需要之影印本指钱、邹二书言,仍盼便中交邮寄还。此间美国友人藏辛丑和约驻京外交团会议记录及各国驻京公使往来文件,全书五百八十页,为最重要之原始资料,中西著作均未引用,盖秘件也。弟极盼能予影印。此间友人已凑壹千元,仍不敷用。弟曾上书张岳军先生,希望政府酌予补助,如能再凑成壹千元至一千五百元即可付印,惟念政府对于外汇管理极形严格,尚乞吾兄从旁一询,如不能补助,只得作罢矣。倘承早日示知,俾有遵循,尤所感盼。顺候著祺。

弟袁同礼顿首
二月十二日

附回忆录所缺 472—473 两页。

〔台北"中央研究院"近代史研究所档案馆,〈郭廷以〉,馆藏号069-01-02-089;《郭量宇先生日记残稿》,页381〕

按:"回忆录所缺 472—473 两页"之事,参见 1962 年 10 月 21 日先生致郭廷以信。该信于 17 日送达。

二月十四日

王伊同覆函先生,感谢寄赠玉器图录并告将赴费城参加亚洲学会,并谈购置家具、章楚函购东洋文库书籍等事。

老伯大人尊前:

敬禀者,予奉玉器目录两册,甚感,嗣有所购乞示价格,否则甚不当承也。玉器一书,曾见广告,恨为价太昂,不敢问津耳。亚洲学会三月底在费城举行,侄以招聘教习拟前往,廿八归,其地多古董商铺,或可乘便一看,如有可靠铺名,乞见示。又尊驾是否亦往,甚盼良聚也。舍亲章楚来信已得东洋文库回音,《宋史》135 元,《敦煌》、《明史》两书缺货,正重板中,渠已函定矣,费神谢谢。安吉之妹梅博刻在泰国,秋后便归,三月中拟赴港购硬木家俱数件,其 rest table, cocktail table 在美旧货铺约为若干,得便略示价格为感。安吉颇思购置一二件,恐远东运来为价或视在美购买更昂,因求讯耳。拙稿"经师老儒"句,"老"乞改"宿",又末句"倘吾丈……","倘"下要否增一"又"字,乞尊裁。专谢,敬请金安。

侄伊同敬禀

二月十四

〔University of Chicago Library, Yuan T'ung-li Papers, Box 1〕

　　按:"安吉"即娄安吉,王伊同之妻,燕京大学毕业,在美研究艺术史。

徐高阮致函先生,请就胡适全集出版方式和编列体裁给予建议。

　　守和先生道鉴:

　　前请先生主持续编《胡适之先生西文著作目录》,早应函请寄下,乃延搁至今,歉甚。顷见先生致王雪艇先生函,藉悉已成稿,极感。史语所集刊纪念胡适先生论文集上册本月内出版,下册拟月内开始发排,著作目录列在最后,仍祈能早日寄来能于下月中寄,不迟。打字费及航邮费多少,请函示,自当照付。在美仍可由王方宇先生处拨付,在台北付台币亦可,并祈示知何者为宜。再者,胡适先生西文零篇著作,除尊处前已代拍照寄来者外,几全部皆此间所无,亦请分神代为拍照为感。胡先生遗著整理委员会成立以来尚无成绩可言,仅先将未发表遗稿已作一草目,全集印行亦未定方针。毛子水先生主持编辑委员会,甚盼先生多所匡助。高阮尤盼先生就两事指示,一此全集出版方式宜由院方筹印或交由出版家发行,二此全集内容编列宜仿何人全集体裁,想先生熟悉胡先生著作全豹,自有南针可示。此间编委会甚仰盼也。又既名为全集,西文著作自应收入,而编列方式又如何,亦祈先生指示此间人士对诸事大纲及细务多欠方策,高阮人微不敢多主张,然深知非得高明指示不可也,感甚。专上,不一。顺请道安。

　　　　　　　　　　　　　　　　　　后学徐高阮敬上
　　　　　　　　　　　　　　　　　　二月十四日

　　胡先生在《独立评论》中提及民国十八年在英文《基督教年鉴》著有 The Cultural Conflicts of China 一文,先生已查及否? 此《年鉴》恐系上海出,是否? 又及。

〔University of Chicago Library, Yuan T'ung-li Papers, Box 2 & 9①〕

　　按:《基督教年鉴》英文名为 *The China Christian Year Book*,The Cultural Conflicts of China 实为 Conflict of Cultures,确实刊登于

━━━━━━━━━━

① 该函第 1 页存于 Box 2,第 2 页存于 Box 9。

1929 年,该文收录于《胡适先生西文著作目录》,编号为 12,但归于 Articles from parts of Books 类下,因之标注 Also in: *Problems of the Pacific, 1931*, Chicago, University of Chicago Press, 1932. p. 471-477,该文的两个出处信息均准确,但彼此内容则有相当出入和调整。①

二月十五日

于震寰覆函先生,告哈佛燕京图书馆所藏两种《金轺筹笔》版本信息。

> 守和先生尊鉴:
>
> 敝处《抱秀山房丛书》第十七至二十册为《金轺筹笔》,无封面无序无刊年,但首有光绪十一年(一八八五)和约十款条程,中法新约四叶,全文未完,想系装钉时脱漏,故其刊刻当在光绪十一年以后。丛书封面有光绪甲午(二十年,一八九四)朱氏重刊木记,随后目次中不载《筹笔》,则《筹笔》之收入丛书必不早于光绪二十年,丛书其他部分每半叶九行各廿二字,独《筹笔》半叶十一行,行廿二字。敝处又有光绪十三年(一八八七)刊单行本,可信为最早刊行之本。丛书是否即利用此十三年原板,因此单行本刻下失踪,一时未能查对为憾。专肃奉闻,虔颂道绥。
>
> 　　　　　　　　　　　　　　　　　　于镜宇拜上
>
> 　　　　　　　　　　　　　　　一九六三年二月十五日

〔University of Chicago Library, Yuan T'ung-li Papers, Box 8〕

李霖灿覆函先生,告知查得《书画书录解题》藏于"中央研究院"图书馆,但不能提出影照,并谈其返台后近况。

> 守和长者赐鉴:
>
> 二月八日来示捧领,所嘱《书画书录解题》一事,前日赴"中央研究院"图书馆细查,访得此书已带来台湾,亦未改作洋装,但据告知,依照规定,不得携出室外,故此事须书店移樽就教在南港拍摄,且在此之前,长者似以与济老先通一信为好,因无济老同意,圕中人必不敢借照,则印刷更无从谈起矣。若能就便托史语所朋友代拍代印,南港台

---

① 1930 年 1 月 23 日,胡适日记附有剪报一则,为其针对美国大学妇女联合会(American Association of University Women)的演讲要点,题目为 The Cultural Conflicts in China,与 Conflict of Cultures 两版本皆有出入。《胡适日记全集》第 6 册,页 6-13。

北,近在咫尺,当更方便,须霖效力之处,必不敢推辞,只恐台中、台北距离遥远,多有延误耳。谨将细情告知,俾便卓夺。

美京生活当忙迫如昔,近日台湾亦渐染上此等风气,除若干书呆子之外,大家都较以往紧张(博物院属于骨董一类,台北新建事又停摆,故尚乡居清净),中西文化如此交流,人类文明如此进步,不知为得为失也。归来已半年,只写得《美国展览日记》一书,约二十二万字,拟为此一美展留一较详细之纪录,鉴于伦敦艺展之缺此一笔也。但今日印书情况迟滞,亦不知何时方能印行供世,只算了却一桩心愿而已。余再奉陈,顺叩福安,合府吉祥。

晚李霖灿谨鞠躬
二,十五日

〔University of Chicago Library, Yuan T'ung-li Papers, Box 2〕

按:《美国展览日记》即《国宝赴美展览日记》,后于1972年初版。刘国蓁覆函先生,谈其撰写《冯平山图书馆成立三十周年纪念日有感》初衷和经过,并告知代寄信札、各物的反馈。

守和博士先生尊鉴:

敬启者,拜奉手示敬悉。叨蒙赐誉,愧不敢当,寔深感谢。晚以为既有此如事,寔不妨向社会报道,是以趁此良机发泄积冈。港中各亲友得见拙作后,皆谓必是冯氏授意所写,但确非事寔,完全是鄙意而已。初稿时,曾就正于秉华东翁并得其同意,而此事之效果是冯馆本身之主持人极为重视,并追查五年前之冯馆服务回忆一文以为研究,想亦可用来为该馆之历史资料也。昨日又得奉令岳来示,似乎以未有得接覆函为憾,亦未有提及收到代转维他命丸前后两包,故未知情形如何。此次接奉代转令岳及令嫂两信,经已即为付邮,想不久当可收到也。兹将代转尊夫人信附呈,敬希察收为幸。日前曾接伯焘先生来信,云及收到代寄维他命三瓶,并谓大陆亦有发售,以后不必再寄云云。顷与郑通先生通电话,问及最后校对情形,据谓最后之一次现已校正,待改好电版时则于一二日内当可付呈,并谓校书工作甚难,而且原稿亦有错。至其余两部,有一部即将开始排版也。春寒料峭,伏祈珍重。秉华东翁嘱笔敬候。专此,敬请撰安。

愚晚国蓁顿首

一九六三年二月十五日

〔袁同礼家人提供〕

二月十八日

王华隆(海厄茨维尔)致函先生,寄赠专著二种,以利编撰《新疆研究文献目录》(中文本)。

同礼博士吾兄勋鉴:

有疏函候,时切驰慕。上年曾拜读大著《博士论文详目》,至深钦佩。兹阅报载近正在编著《新疆研究文献目录》(中文本)等书,弥增敬仰。兹检呈拙稿两种,但均系小品稿本也。一为《俄帝侵华地志》,又名《中俄边疆问题》,内容注意对俄失地之地略形势,即其在国防上之重要性也。并罗举出失地确系中国领土之证明等。一为《我们的河山》(此书存数不多,仅有盖章之旧本,请原谅),内容分三编:上编述列祖列宗开疆拓土之艰钜;中编述列强侵占我之领土与其地在国防上之重要形势;下编则依照弟拟之"中国八大地理区"略述各区地形与人文之概况。内容简陋,谨以奉上。敬祈指正! 顺颂勋祺!

弟王华隆敬上

二月十八日

外寄呈书二册。

〔University of Chicago Library, Yuan T'ung-li Papers, Box 2〕

按:王华隆(1894—?),字阶平,辽宁黑山人,北京高等师范学校毕业,后入该校研究院,曾历任奉天教科书编审处主任、通志馆编纂、北平师范大学和辅仁大学讲师。[1]

郭廷以覆函先生,告广文书局影印三书即将出版,并告与各机构主事者洽商资助印书进展及来美日期。

守和尊兄道席:

十二日大教敬悉。钱、邹、施三书正由广文书局印影(前函误为文海书局),日前见该局广告,定于三月下旬出书,相当迅速。惟售价稍昂,每册约台币八九十元。一俟出版,当以每种五册奉赠长者。至原影印本,日内即通知该局于出书后寄还。

---

① 《我存杂志》第 4 卷第 8 期,1936 年 10 月,页 506。

辛丑和约驻京外交团会议记录及各国公使往来文件,自为极重要
资料,应及早刊布。关于政府补□事,日昨曾与罗志希先生谈及,请其
便中一询张岳军先生。今日拟再与王雪艇先生一商。弟准于三月三
日动身,过日本将约有十日停留,廿日前后可抵纽约。

赐书可由淬濂兄收转。匆覆,敬颂双福!

弟廷以拜上

二、十八

〔University of Chicago Library, Yuan T'ung-li Papers, Box 2〕

按:"钱、邹、施三书"即钱恂《中俄界约斠注》、邹代钧《中俄界
记》、施绍常《中俄国际约注》,所依底本应为光绪二十年(1894)
三月上海醉六堂、宣统三年(1911)武昌亚新地学社、光绪三十一
年(1905)上海商务印书馆。2月19日,郭廷以访王世杰,后者表
示可以资助先生所议印行庚子外交团会议纪录等文件。①

罗家伦致函先生,请与国会图书馆摄影服务部沟通复制文献。

守和吾兄道鉴:

本馆为搜集有关抗战史料,前在 Japanese Monographs 文献目录内
选录 Homeland Operations Record 八十五种,函请美国驻华武官处转
由美军史政局检赠四十八种到馆,其余四十五种,嘱径函美国国会图
书馆洽购,经于去年十一月间函据该馆复摄服务部复称,其中有
History of the Southern Army 二十九种,可代为复制微影胶片,需复制
费用美金一一八.五〇元。兹开具清单,除径函该馆复制外,特检奉一
份,请吾兄费神,就近向该馆洽办,所需价款,请在前存购书款项内支
付,单据请寄下,以便报销。专此,顺颂道祺!

弟罗家伦敬启

二,一八

〔University of Chicago Library, Yuan T'ung-li Papers, Box 1〕

按:"四十八种"似应为"四十种"。此函为文书代笔,落款处为其
签名。

---

① 《郭量宇先生日记残稿》,页382。

二月十九日

王世杰覆函先生,告知"国家长期发展科学委员会"决定补助印刷费,并告《纪念胡先生论文集》下册即将发稿。

> 守和吾兄惠鉴:
>
> 　　二月五日手书敬悉。关于《数学家论著目录》一事,"国家长期发展科学委员会"已决定补助台币一万五千元,估计除开支印刷费外,尚稍有余款可作邮费之用。此项补助款,系请美援拨付,故须照规定办理填表手续,已由"科学委员会"径函奉达。承开示若干外国学术机构及数学界学人名单,俟目录印成,当由此间径行寄赠。至所询胡适之先生西文著作目录应于何时寄台,据本院历史语言研究所经办人报告:"史语所集刊《纪念胡先生论文集》下册,二月内开始发稿,胡先生西文著作目录排在最后,又打字费自应照付,集刊编辑委员会当一并径行函告"等语。特函奉复,顺颂撰祺。
>
> 　　　　　　　　　　　　　　　　　　　　弟王世杰复启
> 　　　　　　　　　　　　　　　　　　　　二月十九日

〔University of Chicago Library, Yuan T'ung-li Papers, Box 8〕

　　按:此件为打字稿,落款处为其签名。

二月二十日

马克尔致函先生,感谢寄赠《新疆研究文献目录》(日文本)、《俄文汉学简目》。

> 20 February 1963
>
> Dear Dr. Yuan,
>
> 　　Thank you very much for your *Bibliography on Chinese Turkestan* and *Russian Works on China: a selected bibliography*.
>
> 　　These will be most valuable books of reference.
>
> 　　With best wishes,
>
> 　　　　　　　　　　　　　　　　　　　Yours sincerely,
> 　　　　　　　　　　　　　　　　　　　A. G. Morkill
> 　　　　　　　　　　　　　　　　　　　Secretary

〔University of Chicago Library, Yuan T'ung-li Papers, Box 1〕

　　按:此件为打字稿,落款处为其签名。

二月二十一日

郑宪覆函先生,婉拒介绍教职并附购书支票。

　　守和先生赐鉴:

　　　　本月十一日大函奉悉,承厚爱向 Pittsburg 推荐工作,无任铭感。惟
宪对于语文毫无研究,且乏兴趣。该校历史课程既已有人担任,此事似
可作罢也。大作《论文目录》昨已寄到,拟留下自用,书费支票乙纸兹随
函奉上,乞察收。此间图书馆尚无此书,已通知主管人员径行添购矣,并
此奉闻。下月费城之会,宪亦拟前往参加,一切面馨。专此,复请撰安。

　　　　　　　　　　　　　　　　　　　　　　　　郑宪谨上

　　　　　　　　　　　　　　　　　　　　　　　　二月二十一日

　　　　　　　　〔University of Chicago Library, Yuan T'ung-li Papers, Box 2〕

　　按:“费城之会”即 3 月 25 日举行的美国亚洲学会年会。

刘麟生致函先生,告富路德已聘其参加临时工作。

　　守和先生勋右:

　　　　昨访 Prof. Goodrich,允以临时工作借重,以五个月为限,月薪同于
华昌,即去冬所言之职,原职已有人矣。渠又指出“原表”,请弟在书
法家中撰述(见另纸),多承将护,只益裹惭而已。三月一日开始工
作,即在图书馆中也。专此申谢,并颂双祺。

　　　　　　　　　　　　　　　　　　　　　　　　小弟麟生顿首

　　　　　　　　　　　　　　　　　　　　　　　　二,廿一

　　　　《新疆研究目录》一册已赠渠,并代道意。

　　　　　　　　〔University of Chicago Library, Yuan T'ung-li Papers, Box 2〕

　　按:后附明代书法家清单一纸。

二月二十二日

先生致信张群,告前请补助影印费因原书已售只得作罢。

　　　　一月十八日曾上一书,述及辛丑和约驻京外交团会录记录一案,
谅荷垂察。昨该收藏人来长途电话,谓此书渠已售出,不便借照,前议
请作罢□。同人等因念筹款匪易,只得允其所请,用敢将最近接洽经
过专函奉陈,敬希鉴察。

　　　　　　　　　　　　　　　　　　　　　　　　一,廿二日

　　　　　　　　〔University of Chicago Library, Yuan T'ung-li Papers, Box 3〕

按:"一,廿二日"当作"二,廿二日"。此件为底稿。

二月二十三日

先生致信马克尔,向英国大学中国委员会提交资助《中国艺术和考古目录》编纂的申请。

23rd February, 1963

Dear Mr. Morkill:

For some time, I have been engaged in a comprehensive bibliography on Chinese Art and Archaeology. Though it is a labor of love, it could drag on for many years unless some financial support could be obtained.

Last year Sir Percival David would like to have me complete this bibliography and have it published simultaneously with his annotated translation of a Chinese work on archaeology entitled *Ko Ku Yao-Lun*. He even wrote to one of the American Foundations on my behalf. Although I was not able to get any grant, the work continues steadily.

In view of the growing interest in Chinese art in England, I wonder if your Committee would like to consider the possibility of a subsidy for a project of this kind. I now enclose a statement about the scope of this bibliography and I hope I may count on your interest and assistance.

I shall be grateful if you could bring this request to the attention of your Committee.

Sincerely yours,

T. L. Yuan

〔University of Chicago Library, Yuan T'ung-li Papers, Box 1〕

罗家伦覆函先生,谈代购书籍、书款各事,并告收到寄赠的《新疆研究文献目录》(日文本)。

守和吾兄道鉴:

一、一月十一日复示暨帐单收据,均敬奉悉。除加州大学 T. A. Hsia: *The Enigma of the Five Martyrs* 一书,尚未寄到外,其余承订购之书籍胶片,均已先后寄到,帐单数目相符,有渎清神,无任感谢!

二、伦敦克干保罗书店已寄到书籍十一种,书款请兄处代为支付,所需邮汇费,请在本馆购书款内扣除。

三、尊处购书款所存不多,稍后当再申请汇奉,请兄尽本馆及党史会存款支付。

四、本馆及党史会所藏有关国父之西文资料,当分别一查,俟整理好寄奉。

五、美军部陆军史编纂会印行 *Strategic Study of Manchuria: military topography and geography* 四册,尚未寄到,俟寄到后,当即函谢。

六、《新疆研究文献目录》(日文本)廿五部,已由东京寄到,承惠赠本馆及党史会与弟各一部,敬先致谢! 其余当由总务处托书店代售。此书弟因本人奉使在新三年,怵目惊心,饱经忧患,故尤多欣赏。兄自序中"他人知我,胜于我之自知"一语,真使我一唱三叹。

七、北京大学台湾同学会同学录,已请孙德中兄寄奉。

八、兹将吾兄一月及二月份征集费新台币壹千元台湾银行存款收据二张附上,请察收。

专此,顺颂道祺!

弟罗家伦敬启
二,二三

〔University of Chicago Library, Yuan T'ung-li Papers, Box 1〕

按: *The Enigma of the Five Martyrs* ,夏济安著,全称为 *Enigma of the Five Martyrs: a study of the leftist literary movement in modern China* ,通译作《五烈士之谜》。孙德中,浙江天台人,1926 年北京大学英文系毕业,后赴美留学,入哥伦比亚大学并获教育学硕士学位,曾任河南大学教务长。此件为文书代笔,落款处为其签名。

二月二十四日

先生寄送美金支票与国会图书馆照相复制部,请其尽速完成"国史馆"复制缩微胶片的申请。〔University of Chicago Library, Yuan T'ung-li Papers, Box 1〕先生覆信罗家伦,告知"国史馆"购书款已尽,并请开列其馆藏西文文献目录,避免重复购买。

志希馆长仁兄道席:

奉到二月十八日手教,嘱在贵馆所存购书款内拨付国会图书馆美金一一八.五〇元,以备复制胶片二十九种之用,自当照办。兹将弟函及该馆收据随函奉上。又上年寄下一千元,现已无存见附单,超出之十一元三角八分,暂在党史会余款内拨付。该馆所藏西文资料想已甚多,恐有重复,未敢购买,如承将此项资料开单见示,当即进行采购。除国父西文传记外应购何书,亦望示知,俾有遵循。

二月二十四

〔University of Chicago Library, Yuan T'ung-li Papers, Box 1〕

按:此件为底稿。

刘麟生覆函先生,告接到收据及工作近况诸事。

守和博士先生著席:

(一)廿日明教拜诵,感甚。(二)小恙料已全愈,近日人士患此甚众,内子已恢复健康矣,承询,至感至感。(三)收据一纸奉到,大君子治事之不苟如此。(四)Prof. Goodrich 已有书至,云因经费关系,仅可约弟工作四个月,三月一日开始,月薪 370 元乞秘之,即在图书阅览室中治事,弟已书面答复(同意)。(五)《明人传记引得》港中缺货,舍弟复书亦如是说。"综表"当不日可到。敬谢敬谢。谨祝痊福。

小弟麟生敬上

二月廿四日夜

〔University of Chicago Library, Yuan T'ung-li Papers, Box 2〕

按:"综表"似指《历代人物年里碑传综表》,姜亮夫纂定,1959 年中华书局初版。

二月二十五日

先生致信徐炳麟,商影印《新疆建置志》《西陲要略》两书事。

徐经理大鉴:

前上一函,计达座右。弟拟印下列两书,拟改为照相石印(影印),其尺寸大小及纸张装订等均与罗香林教授《蒲寿庚传》相等,每种印七百部。兹交邮寄上,请费神觅一可靠商店,先行估价,便中示知。每书之前有弟之序文,每书之后有一跋文,以后再寄。台端对于文化事业素所提倡,想必乐为赞助。先此申谢,敬候时祉。

弟袁同礼上

二月廿五日

①《新疆建置志》,宋伯鲁撰,四册,共装订为一册。

②《西陲要略》,祁韵士撰,二册,共装订为一册。

以上二书均借自公家,望告工人特别注意,影印时如须将书拆散,用完后仍须归还原状。尤应注意者,即该书之前后次序,不可错乱。

〔University of Chicago Library, Yuan T'ung-li Papers, Box 8〕

按:《新疆建置志》《西陲要略》二书均由台湾商务印书馆影印,非香港书局承印。《蒲寿庚传》,罗香林著,台北"中华文化出版事业委员会"1955 年初版。此件为底稿。

先生致信郑通,告以后寄送校样须附先生此前改正者,并告《西疆交涉志要》改为影印。

新华印刷公司郑经理大鉴:

接到校样,适本人患病未能详细校对,兹分两批寄回,凡内中有错字者仍请改正后连同原稿寄下,凡无错误者即不付印,不必寄回。此次寄回之件,未将弟原改正者寄下,以致又重新校对一次,费去时间不少。今后为节省时间计,望将弟改正者与新稿一齐寄下。关于《西疆交涉志要》,今拟改为影印,请为估价,当较排印公道,今日交邮寄上,即希查照办理见复为荷。东亚银行之款想已收到,否则请速函告,以便汇上。近日信件甚慢,且有遗失,故颇悬念也。此上,顺颂时祺。

弟袁同礼顿首

二月廿五日

〔University of Chicago Library, Yuan T'ung-li Papers, Box 1〕

按:此件为底稿。

先生致信 Basil Gray,告因为汉字数量较多,《中国艺术和考古目录》拟在香港印刷、出版,虽有大维德爵士、史克门的支持,但并未获得美国各基金会的资助,正在向英国大学中国委员会申请获取资助。

25 February, 1963

Dear Mr. Gray:

I am deeply grateful for your letter of 28th January. I am particularly happy to learn that Sir Percival is to finish his monumental work on the *Ko Ku Yao Lun*. Please convey to him my very best wishes when you see him next time. I am also to send him some new Chinese works as soon as I receive them from Peking.

The printing of my bibliography on Chinese art and archaeology does not give me much headache since I wrote to you last, as the Chinese Government has given me assurances that I can count on its support when materials are ready for the printer. Because of the large number of Chinese characters, it would be much cheaper to have it printed and distributed in Hong Kong. Mr. Vetch, the Manager of the University of Hong Kong Press, is able to do first class job, if he is given some subsidy.

What worries me at present is the lack of support from the United States, although everyone says he is most eager to see the manuscript published. In spite of the strong recommendations from Sir Percival and Laurence Sickman, my application for a research grant was turned down for the second time. As you know, a large portion of available grants have been awarded to projects dealing with Communist China, while basic research in the humanities has been neglected. In a way this is sad, but this is true of American academic interest at this moment.

I trust that the situation in England might be quite different. I have just written to the Secretary of the Universities' China Committee to explore the possibilities of obtaining some support there. As I promised to Sir Percival, I should like to do some research in British museums and libraries to gain access to materials not available in this country. If you should be consulted about my request, I trust that you will do something on my behalf.

There are over two hundred serial publications which I have to analyze. This is in itself a gigantic task. For monographs, it is quite easy to make a survey.

I have analyzed the *British Museum Quarterly* and other British journals. I have quite a number of your scholarly articles listed. But if you should have reprints from other journals, I hope you could set them aside for me until I come to London in the not too distant future.

〔University of Chicago Library, Yuan T'ung-li Papers, Box 1〕

按：此件为底稿。

二月二十六日

蒋复璁致函先生,请将胡适纪念亭募集款项尽快汇台。

> 守和先生赐鉴:
>
>   顷上芜函,谅蒙垂察。去年为适之先生筹建碑亭事,曾向旅外学
> 长寄发捐启多份,数月以来极蒙各方鼎力协助,多已将捐款寄下。碑
> 亭工程业于本月二十四日开工,惟尚未奉执事赐示,未审募集若干,至
> 祈早日寄下为感。耑此,敬请大安。
>
>   弟蒋复璁顿首
>   二月二十六日
>   〔University of Chicago Library, Yuan T'ung-li Papers, Box 2〕

　　按:此件为文书代笔,落款处为其签名。

刘茂才(波恩)覆函先生,感谢赠书,并告知波恩东方语言学院将订购《新疆研究丛刊》全套。

> 同礼先生台鉴:
>
>   兹蒙惠赐《新疆书目》,不胜感激,对于新疆研究工作将裨益匪
> 浅。另外一部敝研究院留下,发票至后必将书价电汇不误,所予告诸
> 丛刊,敝院亦拟全部订购,务乞随时寄下为盼。辱蒙阅读敝著,愧甚,
> 尚望加以指正为荷。弟自著《东突厥史》以来,数年间搜集关于龟兹
> 政治、佛教、音乐史料,幸于本月稿成,题为《龟兹及其与中国关系》
> *Kutscha und seine Beziehungen zu China*,然尚待校正,出刊日期尚无一
> 定。耑此鸣谢,顺祝冬安。
>
>   弟刘茂才敬上
>   一九六三年二月廿六日
>   〔University of Chicago Library, Yuan T'ung-li Papers, Box 3〕

　　按:刘茂才(Liu Mau-tsai,1914—2007),1935 年赴德国留学,时在
联邦德国波恩大学东方语言学院工作,并在波恩大学汉学系兼职
授课。《东突厥史》即 *Die chinesischen Nachrichten zur Geschichte
der Ost-Tuerken*,1958 年出版。1969 年 Harrassowitz 出版《龟兹及
其与中国关系》。

马克尔覆函先生,告收到《中国艺术和考古目录》的资助申请函并已提交给专家委员会主席。

26 February 1963

Dear Dr. Yuan,

Thank you for your letter of February 23rd and particulars of your proposed *Bibliography of Chinese Art and Archæology*. It would be a most valuable contribution and I hope it goes through. I have put it to the Chairman of the Expert Committee.

With best wishes,

Yours sincerely,

A. G. Morkill

Secretary

〔University of Chicago Library, Yuan T'ung-li Papers, Box 1〕

二月二十七日

张群覆函先生,略述转陈购买辛丑和约外交团会议纪录之经过,并对未能购入该史料表示遗憾。

同礼吾兄惠鉴:

别来音问疏隔,至念近况。上月接奉一月十八日手书,附影印辛丑和约外交团会议纪录说明,敬悉近来国际关系益趋密切,外交资料至关重要,此间正从事于搜集整理。承示一节自属要图,当即转陈奉谕交"外交部"办理,即由"外交部"呈"行政院"核拨款项,正在办理手续中,闻日内即可办妥。弟原拟俟办妥后再行覆闻,不意顷间接到二月廿二日大函,前途因已出售,不便借照、前议作罢,至深惶歉,亦觉十分可惜,然此事时间限制如此之促,亦非始料,所及除再陈明经过并通知"外交部"外,特此布复。顺颂时祺。

弟张群拜复

二月廿七日

〔University of Chicago Library, Yuan T'ung-li Papers, Box 3〕

二月二十八日

余又苏覆函先生,告商务印书馆遵嘱将《新疆研究文献目录》(日文本)订价为每册台币五十元,并谈其赴美进修计划等事。

守和先生道席:

二月十八日大示敬悉!

已通知商务将日文本订价为每册台币五十元,将来七折缴款。将来中文本出版,请即照此法寄书,照此法经售。商务当愿为服务也。

台大历史研究室之五十部收到时亦当送至商务,祈释念!

台湾读书人不少,但确如尊函所云,购买力则甚弱!

承询来美计划有无进展,各种基金会虽有补助者,但其款额少而限制严,譬如 China Foudation 补助,限制一年后返国、原机关服务二年,种种限制近乎侮辱。

苏望得一聘请之工作,来美住二年。牧育才神父(E. J. Murphy)到美各大学视察,并为 Catholic Students Center 募捐,已请其代为注意。顷已函彼(尚在西部 San Francisco University)到华府时访先生,见面时仍请就近促成此事。

华盛顿及纽约方面现有华人所在之单位,经查悉无法可入,彼等门户紧严。芝加哥方面则机会尚有,西部亦有,能有新地盘则甚善也。能有两年时期住美,观摩进修,当可获益不少。

台大已开学,此期任中国通史、魏晋南北朝及近世中日关系史三课程,华侨生外国学生杂处一堂,近年台大甚繁荣也。

今年美国对来美者尺度放宽,留学生或较增多。

小儿承一(Yu Tsen-i),台大经济系毕业,去年经过若干度考试,已来美洛杉矶,入研究院,攻读工商管理。子女众多,此子只能靠半工半读耳。专肃,敬颂旅安!

余又荪敬上
二月廿八日

〔University of Chicago Library, Yuan T'ung-li Papers, Box 8〕

刘麟生覆函先生,感谢寄送《历代人物年里碑传综表》并谈该书校订问题等事。

守和先生勋右:

(一)廿五日赐书,拜诵为感。(二)承寄《历代人物年里碑传综表》一册,如启"总钥",曷胜感戴。尊处如需用,当即奉还。(三)此表体大思精,自属有功文艺。然校订之处,仍不厌求详也。譬如(甲)索引中先文庄公讳,"璋"字误作"章"。(乙)张飞下注益州涿郡人。涿郡似不属益州也。(丙)无叶小鸾、小纨名字。大君子以为然否?(四)属抄跋文,谨当遵照缮写。惟弟不长小楷,故拟作行楷。照原纸尺寸,分为每页(page)六行,过小则拙书更拙矣。俟缮毕,即奉上呈教。(五)尊书朴茂,颇为内子所称誉。今乃见推崇拙书,徒增颜汗耳。敬颂著绥,无任瞻依之至。

弟麟生上书

二,廿八

〔University of Chicago Library, Yuan T'ung-li Papers, Box 1〕

按:"先文庄公"应指刘麟生伯祖父刘秉璋(1826—1905),晚清重臣,淮军将领,谥号"文庄";叶小鸾、叶小纨均为明代女作家,有作品传世。

二月

先生校订的《中俄西北条约集》出版。〔University of Chicago Library, Yuan T'ung-li Papers, Box 2〕

按:该书问世后,先生向"中央研究院"历史语言研究所图书室、"国立中央图书馆"、台北图书馆等处捐赠。

先生撰写《重印〈新疆建置志〉序》。〔《新疆建置志》,1963年6月〕

先生撰写《重印〈西陲要略〉序》。〔《西陲要略》,1963年6月〕

三月四日

先生致信郑通,请其在《中俄西北条约集》参考文献部分增改两处细节,并嘱将《新疆国界图志》校样分四次寄送。

新华公司郑经理大鉴:

旬日前寄回之稿件,凡应校正者,望速寄回。兹有下列两件,望代为添入及改正是荷。东亚银行之款想已收到,《新疆国界图志》想已付排,校样望分四次寄下,万勿一齐寄来,因只能抽暇为之,如分四次则方便多矣。《西疆交涉志要》改用影印原书,想已寄到,望估价示知以便决定,即希示复为荷。顺候大安。

袁同礼顿首

三月四日

"参考文献"内有《宣统条约》一书,著作人为汪毅、张承棨二人,并无许同莘,望代为删去。在最后之页,倒数第二书之前,望代加一书,书如下:*Krasnyi Arkhiv*, Moskva, 1922–1941, 106 v.

〔University of Chicago Library, Yuan T'ung-li Papers, Box 1〕

按：《宣统条约》，1915 年外交部排印本；*Krasnyi Arkhiv* 实为期刊，直译为"红色档案"，由苏联国立中央档案馆出版。此件为底稿。

三月五日

余又荪致函先生，告知台北商务印书馆愿承印《新疆研究文献目录》（中文本）。

守和先生道席：

二月二十八日寄上一函，已通知商务照每册五十元发售。台大历史系研究室之五十部亦收到，均交商务（共 250 册，遵示赠书二册）。

日昨与商务经理赵叔诚先生面晤，谈及大著中文本印刷事。前函谓拟俟日文本售出后将款作中文本之印刷费，事实上不易办到也。可否交商务代为印行？台湾印刷水准尚佳，商务可为先生服务。先生如同意，请即将稿寄下，并示知用何种纸、何号字等等。如照日文本样式付印，则更为方便。

哈佛燕京之引得，亦在接洽由商务印行（董同龢兄商洽，因杨联陞先生前次未到台湾而停滞），此类学术性书籍，销路未必广；自然商务为业务计，未必有利，但亦应印行学术性之著作也。

近年以小股东而当选参预商务业务问题，历年均劝其翻印及出版一点有价值之书，惜商务局面太小，不能如愿！

Fr. Murphy 近尚在 San Francisco，已函其到华府时访先生候教。西部各大城市彼均将往视察，晤面时尚祈一谈代觅来美机会问题，至感至感！肃颂旅安！

余又荪敬上
三月五日

〔University of Chicago Library, Yuan T'ung-li Papers, Box 8〕

杨家骆致函先生，请教《永乐大典》存世情况。

守和先生有道：

十数年未得修书奉候，去岁严文郁先生来台，曾为道及尊况，以是驰仰之忱实未尝一日间也。骆早岁妄事辞典之业，当时急于刊行，实无一当，然后知俟方域以壮悔名集之意。此后廿年间，日日为补过之计，编检群籍，重写旧稿。岁月既积，遂复盈几充栋，多达一百卅余万条，窃虑不能更有所进，于是又萌刊行之念。然以生值板荡，屡经播迁，条文既有散失，次序尤极凌乱，他日幸能条理成书，终冀先生能一定其是非耳。前曾试刊《释且》一册，谨另邮寄呈指正。民国廿年时，舍下为刊行拙编事，曾投资于世界书局，此后遂得屡主局务，前见上海所刊《永乐大典》，固多为骆所未见，然骆所得胶卷印本为沪本未收者亦达七八十余卷，且以时时引用，故曾编引得并撰考证百余卷，近遂由世界书局重为汇印，顷已竣事。关于《大典》存世情形，骆原得自先生所撰诸文，此点尝敬志于卷首"辑略"中，不日"辑略"抽印本装成，当以邮呈。惟先生所撰《大典存目》，除民十四、十六、民十八、民廿一、民廿二诸篇外，未识其后续有发表否？倘承不吝见示，实所深感。再者，拙撰《永乐大典考证》，其中《据本探源》一卷，曾考五代十国书之归于北宋，辽及北宋书之归于金，金及南宋书之归于元，元书之归于明，此五百年来中秘之藏又悉萃于《大典》，窃以今所集印存本八百余卷，虽仅当于《大典》廿八分之一，然可代表五代十国宋辽金元五百年中秘旧藏者，亦正在此。至明文渊阁书之渐次散失，从杨士奇《文渊阁书目》、张萱《内阁藏书目录》，犹可考见其幸存内阁大库，后卒为京师图书馆创立时之基本藏书，亦世所共知，故先生向所典领者，实为我国中秘书千年来一系相承之正统，而复继续长以居世界上中文书藏之首位，骆之撰《大典据本探源》，固在推尊《大典》之价值，然亦欲明此千年传统实未间断，未识先生以为此说尚不谬否？窃愿一质定也。顷接散友王文山先生自日惠函，谓将于本月九日抵华府，嘱以文件寄至尊处留交。昨已寄出，今更附一函，统祈费神代转为叩。专肃，敬叩道绥，不一。

弟杨家骆顿首

三月五日

〔University of Chicago Library, Yuan T'ung-li Papers, Box 1〕

按：杨家骆（1912—1991），江苏南京人，少年时代随祖父杨星桥编纂《国史通纂》，1928年东南大学附中高中部毕业，后入国学专修馆肄业。1930年春，创办中国辞典馆和中国学术百科全书编辑馆并任馆长。1948年赴台，在世界书局和鼎文书局任职。

王华隆致函先生，感谢赠书并称赞其价值。

同礼博士吾兄勋鉴：

　　敬启者，奉读大著日文本，搜集宏博，内容精审，而印刷尤为精良，诚宜人手一编者也，至深感佩。大著如此讲究，成本自高，未识定价若干，弟应奉上也。以后中文本出版，请万勿客气，弟当先行寄款也。大著中文本如尚未付印，而时间来的及时，弟日前赠之两种小书的书名倘能附骥尾，得以列入，则藉增声价多矣——一笑！专布谢忱，敬祝撰安。

弟王华隆敬上

三月五日

〔University of Chicago Library, Yuan T'ung-li Papers, Box 2〕

　　按：王华隆的住址应为 2109 Chapman Rd. Hyattsville, Md。

刘麟生覆函先生，感谢赠书并寄送题签。

守和尊兄学长勋右：

　　（一）二日手教谨悉。（二）承赐《人物年里综表》，深裹厚谊为感。（三）《明代传记引得》Kent Hall 有之，极重要之门径书也。（四）尊序大体极佳妙，略易数字，请再酌。（五）题签四纸奉上，乞政。（六）拙序已易一字，不识控补工夫能合格否？（七）前寄下图书室中应补之书画参考书目，已给 Dr. Goodrich 一阅，渠云可交主管者阅，弟已与鸿益兄谈过，随时设法补充。（八）弟近探讨张凤翼生平，尚属有兴趣。敬请双安。

小弟麟生顿首

三，五，夜

〔University of Chicago Library, Yuan T'ung-li Papers, Box 8〕

　　按：该函封上，刘麟生补写"鄙意，印时各签上应加乌丝阑，仍候大君子卓裁"。

三月六日

先生致信裴开明，请核实《挹秀山房丛书》第十七至二十卷是否交送馆际互借或有人借出，并询问陈芳芝在《燕京社会学界》发表文章的情况。

March 6, 1963

Dear Dr. Chiu:

　　May I solicit your personal help in locating the following book?

In the *I Hsiu Shan Fang tsung-shu*, there are four volumes (v. 17 – 20) entitled: , which I borrowed from your Library through interlibrary loan about three weeks ago. As it has never been received, I was informed that these volumes are missing! Could you find out who had borrowed these volumes and arrange to send them to me?

Will you also please check if your Library has the last issue of the *Yenching Journal of Social Studies* published in 1949 or 1950. In this issue there was an article by Miss Agnes Fang-chih Chen. If you have this particular issue, could you check the title of the article, the inclusive paging, the volume number and the issue number, as well as the date of its publication.

Thanking you for your assistance,

Yours sincerely,

T. L. Yuan

〔University of Chicago Library, Yuan T'ung-li Papers, Box 8〕

按：*Yenching Journal of Social Studies* 即《燕京社会学界》,1938 年 6 月创刊,燕京大学出版的英文半年刊,后因太平洋战争爆发停刊,1948 年 8 月份复刊,至 1950 年出版至第 5 卷第 1 期后停刊。Miss Agnes Fang-chih Chen 即陈芳芝（1914—1995）,燕京大学毕业,后赴美留学获博士学位,1940 年底回国并在母校任教,担任政治系主任,并任《燕京社会学界》主编。该件为录副,空白处付诸阙如,应为"金轺筹笔"。

三月七日

先生致信金问泗,请为重印《金轺筹笔》撰写序文。

纯孺"大使"道席：

昨在荷兰购到 *Russia in the East* 一书,其第二段专述伊犁交涉经过附录另有外长吉尔斯致该部总办热梅尼信札,内中可与曾纪泽《伊犁交涉谈话录》（原名《金轺筹笔》）相参证,可称新资料,为国内研究外交史者所未见,因此拟将曾侯谈话录早日出版,并利用此项新资料,将重要者列入附录。兹将两书附上,请参阅,并盼得暇时赐一序文,以光篇幅,先此申谢。敬候道祺。

　　　　　　　　　　　　　　　　　　同礼再拜
　　　　　　　　　　　　　　　　一九六三年三月七日
　　附书两部。

　　近代史研究所郭量宇现来纽约,已请渠将法文资料译成中文,由该所出版。

　　　　　　　　　　　　　　　〔《传记文学》第 8 卷第 2 期,页 36-37〕

　　按:*Russia in the East, 1876 - 1880*, 作者为 Charles、Barbara Jelavich,1959 年莱顿初版。后金问泗答应作序之请,参见 4 月 10 日郭廷以致先生函。该函亦存于《思忆录》,但有别字。

三月八日

先生致信郑通,再汇上美金支票。

　　新华公司郑经理大鉴:

　　顷奉三月二日大函,知前托东亚银行寄上之款,尚未送到,甚以为怪。兹致该行一函,请代发出,或派人持贵公司公函前往走取。兹又奉上美金壹百元支票一纸,即希于收到后示覆为荷。此颂大安。

　　　　　　　　　　　　　　　　　　袁同礼顿首
　　　　　　　　　　　　　　　　　　三月八日

　　校样望速寄下,因月杪拟离华京数日也。

　　　　　　〔University of Chicago Library, Yuan T'ung-li Papers, Box 1〕

　　按:此件为底稿。

陈祚龙覆函先生,谈其所知中国留法博士生及巴黎代售英文著作之机构情况。

　　守和先生道右:

　　拜读来示(三、五),敬悉各节。龙对“汉学”究讨之文稿,为数固属不少(即使单以龙对“燉煌学”研究之中外文献目录来讲,至今犹在增补中),惟以一直无钱付印,故仍只有束置高阁而已。至于先生之《敦煌艺术研究目录》能得早日印行,诚为龙所乐闻。

　　Wei Tsing-Sing Louis 之中文实为“卫青心”。关于近年中国朋友在法究有若干已获博士学位,龙确不得其详。巴大中院从无中国留法同学深造之名目,即使某人已获博士学位,如其论文全与“汉学”无关,实际中院照例不加购藏。先生果欲补全巨制,最好径函法国诸大学之 Service des Doctorats，请其开送详单，次即函求使馆，列举中国"学生"或"学人"之中西文姓名与地址，以便先生进行核对。如依口传耳闻，殊恐难予凭信也。

承告暑季莅此重游，此实一大好讯，届时如龙仍在巴黎度假，自当竭力接应。

关于先生之大作《中国数学研究目录》，将来问世，自当继为中院照例径向纽约 Paragon 书店函购一份。至于在法销售先生之著述，愚意最妥则为径函此间之 Presses universitaires de France, Rue Soufflot, Paris 5e 当局洽办，爰以该店实为巴黎经售代理外版外文（特别是在美印行之书籍）之总汇。Maisonneuve 故已无须讲，而 Paul Geuthner 实际亦不足道也。崀此布复，恭颂道安！

愚陈祚龙拜上

六三，三，八于巴黎

〔University of Chicago Library, Yuan T'ung-li Papers, Box 2〕

按：《中国数学研究目录》即《现代中国数学研究目录》。信纸左上角标有陈祚龙的地址——Chen Tsu-lung, 35, Rue Montéra, Pairs-XII。

裘开明覆函先生，确认已将《挹秀山房丛书》所需各卷交馆际互借寄出，并附陈芳芝在《燕京社会学界》发表文章的信息。

March 8, 1963

Dear Dr. Yuan:

In answer to your letter of March 6, we have sent the book: *I Hsiu Shan Fang Tsung Shu* 挹秀山房丛书, vol. 17 - 20 to Widener for forwarding to L. C. on inter-library loan.

As to the two articles by Miss Agnes Fang-chih Chen 陈芳芝 in *Yenching Journal of Social Studies*:

1. "Chinese Frontier Diplomacy: the Coming of the Russians and the Treaty of Nertchinsk." Vol. IV, No. 2, pp. 99-149, Feb. 1949.

2. "China's Northern Frontiers: Historical Background." Vol. IV, No. 1, pp. 15-87, August 1949.

Sincerely yours,

Kaiming

Librarian

〔University of Chicago Library, Yuan T'ung-li Papers, Box 3〕

三月十一日

蒋复璁覆函先生,感谢协助"中央图书馆"获取中国政治学会基金利息,并谈其宋史研究的进展。

守和先生大鉴:

上月廿六日及本月四日手示均敬悉,所寄捐启竟致浮沉,至为歉憾。建立碑亭工程是否须劳神重捐,已函询同学会斟酌,容再奉闻。关于前北平政治学会基金利息,承鼎力建议拨助敝馆,至以为感。"教育部"拟拨敝馆一万元,拟以五千元购政治经济西书,此间已有一法学室及社会科学参考室,略加充实,即可应用矣。大著《中俄西北条约集》,承允出版后惠赠,敝馆至感。嘱告宋晞先生事,业已去函,祈即释注。拙著关于宋史之作,现有《宋史新探》一书,即可交由正中书局出版,至宋史则非短时可办也。敝馆新印《机关录》一书,寄上一册,即请查收指正为祷。顺颂大安。

弟蒋复璁顿首

三月十一日

〔University of Chicago Library, Yuan T'ung-li Papers, Box 1〕

按:"同学会"应指台湾地区北京大学同学会,"碑亭"即胡适纪念公园中的碑亭。《宋史新探》后于1966年2月在台北出版,发行及印所确为正中书局。此件为文书代笔,落款处为其签名。

徐炳麟覆函先生,告知筹划影印《新疆建置志》《西陲要略》的想法。

守和先生:

二月廿五日惠书暨《新疆建置志》四册、《西陲要略》二册均先后收到。经与港大彭锡恩兄数度会商,认为《蒲寿庚研究》印刷编排尚欠理想,将来印时除尺寸大小照样外,其余希望能更臻完善。俟序文及跋文寄到,当即估价奉闻。序、跋盼早日寄下。敬复,并颂时绥。

弟徐炳麟上

三月十一日

〔University of Chicago Library, Yuan T'ung-li Papers, Box 8〕

莫余敏卿覆函先生,告知已售出四册《新疆研究文献目录》(日文本),并告该校已购有关中文期刊卡片(索引)情况,另愿意通过先生在国会图书馆获取《西域考古录》的复印本。

March 11, 1963

Dear Dr. Yuan:

Thank you for your letter of February 11th. I am sorry not to have written to you earlier. I sold only 4 of your Bibliography of Sinkiang. They are from

1. Oriental Library

2. Dept. of Oriental Languages

3. Pomona College Library (I gave this copy to Prof. S. Y. Chen and he said he will ask his Library to send remittance direct)

4. Dr. Ting (He already paid me before your letter came)

Payment for the first 2 copies will be sent to you direct from this University. I am enclosing a check for $ 3.00 which Dr. Ting paid me.

The oriental Library would be glad to keep two copies as you suggested but we already had a copy sent to us from the Oriental Book Co. in Hongkong. We have a blanket order from them and we cannot return any book back. How about the 2 copies now left in my possession? Do you want me to send them back to you or do you want me try again?

Thank you for informing me about the forthcoming catalog of the Peabody Museum. I do not think we can afford to buy. Maybe our Art Dept. will. However, we bought the catalog of the London School of Oriental & African Studies and *Index Sinicus* which is also issued by the same place. We also bought the received Columbia's Index to Learned Chinese Periodicals.

We are very much interested in obtaining a copy made of the *Hsi Yu K'ao ku lu* by Yu Hao. I have asked Harvard to borrow a copy through interlibrary loan so that we can make a Xerox copy of it. But if we cannot get it from Harvard, I will have to bother you to order it from L. C. for us. I shall let you know.

Are you going to attend the Conference at Philadelphia? If you go, I shall see you there.

With kindest regards to you and Mrs. Yuan,

> Yours sincerely,
>
> Man-Hing Mok

〔University of Chicago Library, Yuan T'ung-li Papers, Box 2〕

按：*Hsi Yu K'ao ku lu* 即《西域考古录》，清代俞浩著。此件为打字稿，落款处为其签名。

三月十二日

钱存训致函先生，告知代售《中国留美同学博士论文目录》进展，并表示将于三月中下旬途经华盛顿时前来拜会。

> 守和先生钧鉴：
>
> 　　前承寄下《博士论文目录》二十本，除遵嘱送赠桑女士一本外，尚存十本。除前结奉七本书款外，现又续售二本，又《新疆书目》收得现款一本（三本已径汇承），两共九元，奉上清单一份、支票一纸，即请查收，如有错误，并请示知是幸。训携内子拟下周过华京小留，再转赴费城之会，届时当到馆来候。专此，即请双绥。合府均此道候。
>
> 　　　　　　　　　　　　　　　　　　后学存训拜上
> 　　　　　　　　　　　　　　　　　　内子附候
> 　　　　　　　　　　　　　　　　　　三月十二日

〔University of Chicago Library, Yuan T'ung-li Papers, Box 2〕

刘麟生覆函先生，感谢代为抄录张弼传记资料。

> 守和馆长勋鉴：
>
> 　　顷奉到十一日雅训，拜感殊深。承椽笔抄录《张汝弼传》二条，尤用惶汗，大君子治事不苟如斯，谨谢谨谢。赐示谓此后如向尊处借资料影印，最好照表申请预付若干一节，拟俟便与 Dr. Goodrich 一谈。弟之第一篇传记承其修订，已缮清交稿。今日彼谓楼上有书桌可给弟使用，敬谢，并颂著安。
>
> 　　　　　　　　　　　　　　　　　　教小弟刘麟生谨上
> 　　　　　　　　　　　　　　　　　　三月十二日

〔University of Chicago Library, Yuan T'ung-li Papers, Box 3〕

按：张弼(1425—1487)，字汝弼，明松江府人，成化朝进士，授兵部主事，擅长草书。

三月十三日

先生致信 Richard G. Irwin，请复制加州大学伯克利分校所藏《同文馆题名录》各版本。

March 13, 1963

Dear Mr. Irwin:

When I was doing research in your Library some years ago, I made use of the directories of Tung Wen Kuan, but I have forgotten the exact title. Could you be good enough to check this for me and make zerox copies of all available editions? Please ask the duplication service of the University to send me the bill.

If I remember correctly, there are four editions, namely, 1879, 1888, 1893, 1898. Possibly your Library has only three editions.

Thanking you again for your help.

Yours sincerely,

T. L. Yuan

P. S. I enclose a circular about my new bibliography. Possibly your Library may like to have a copy for your reference collection.

〔University of Chicago Library, Yuan T'ung-li Papers, Box 3〕

按：先生对《同文馆题名录》版本的描述并不准，现可以确定 1887 年本为第 4 版、1896 年本则为该题名录的第 6 版。该件为录副。

三月十四日

先生致信新华印刷公司，商影印《西疆交涉志要》纸张问题，并告《中俄西北条约集》校样仍有错字，请务必改正。

新华印刷公司大鉴：

前复一函，内附美金支票一百元并附致东亚银行一函，请尊处持函取款，想该款业已收到，即希函示为荷。影印《西疆交涉志要》估价单，尚未承寄下，想尚在途中。影印书之纸张是否应用稍软之纸（如道林纸），想尊处当可根据已往之经验予以指示也。兹接到三月五日大函，已将最后校样重校一次，仍有错字。兹开列一纸，又在各页上贴上应改正之字,如尊处能负责校对,即可不必再行寄下,尊处改正无误后,即可付印。该书印成,拟请暂存尊处壹佰,以便他日寄往大陆图书馆,余九百部应寄各处之住址单,下次再行奉上。顺候时祉。

袁同礼顿首
三月十四日

　　寄还附录一、附录三、附录四、参考文献,共装一信封。附录二另装一信封,明日即寄还。

〔University of Chicago Library, Yuan T'ung-li Papers, Box 1〕

　　按:此件为底稿。

先生致信拉铁摩尔,请其作为向社会科学研究委员会申请资助的评议者,并告知将寄赠《中俄西北条约集》。

March 14, 1963

Dear Professor Lattimore:

　　The Social Science Research Council is administering a research grant on contemporary China. Since I am most anxious to bring my Bibliography of Sinkiang to early completion, I am applying for such a grant.

　　Since you are an outstanding scholar on Inner Asia, may I ask you to serve as one of my Respondents? I am confident that any recommendation from you would carry considerable weight.

　　For your information, I now enclose a copy of my application. If you could mail your report to the Council in a day or two, I shall be most grateful. The closing date is March 15, but a few days' delay would not matter.

　　My new book on *Russo-Chinese Treaties and Agreements Relating to Sinkiang, 1851–1949* will be published in Hong Kong this month. I have asked the printer to mail you a copy. As you will note, a number of the agreements are published for the first time.

　　With cordial regards to you and Mrs. Lattimore,

Yours sincerely,
T. L. Yuan

〔University of Chicago Library, Yuan T'ung-li Papers, Box 3〕

按：该件为录副。

先生致信罗文达,请其就向社会科学研究委员会申请资助的研究计划给予支持。

March 14, 1963

Dear Dr. Loewenthal:

As we talked over the phone the other day, I am submitting my application for a research grant from the Social Science Research Council under its program of "Research on Contemporary China".

Since you are an outstanding scholar on Central Asia, any recommendation from you would carry considerable weight. On my application, I put down your title as Editor of *Central Asian Collectanea*.

For your information, I now enclose copy of my application. If you could mail your report to the Council in a day or two, I shall be most grateful. (closing date: March 15)

Thanking you for your help,

Sincerely yours,

T. L. Yuan

〔University of Chicago Library, Yuan T'ung-li Papers, Box 3〕

按：*Central Asian Collectanea* 应指《新疆研究丛刊》,该件为录副。

刘国蓁覆函先生,告新华印刷厂排印书籍进展。

守和博士先生尊鉴：

敬启者,月前拜奉手教敬悉,并代转令岳信等均已办妥。昨日又得奉令岳来示,嘱代转尊夫人信一函,并附呈左右,敬希察收为幸。此次该函较重,多付邮费一倍也。令岳手示未有提及代转寄两次维他命丸,可能收到否,时在念中,想渠当有回覆。尊夫人知之,便中希为示知为幸。新华校对工作尚未完成,故未能印就,出书时间大有关系,而"校书如扫落叶"亦是一困难事也。最近有与郑通通话,知前书最后校对尚未完成,而每次往返时间要两星期,虽用航空邮亦是迟滞。又闻先生再另印《新疆边境图志》一书,现已排版并已初校,迟日又可付上。至另一影印本,似先影两三幅寄呈看情形再定。关于付款事,该银单尚未收到,惟已与东亚银行接洽矣。又悉他与先生时有信来往也。春寒料峭,敬希珍重。专此,敬请撰安。

愚晚国蓁顿首

一九六三年三月十四日

〔袁同礼家人提供〕

三月十五日

先生致信莫余敏卿,请其在将《新疆研究文献目录》(日文本)退还前再向南加州大学图书馆推销,并告将寄上《现代中国数学研究目录》。

March 15, 1963

Dear Mrs. Mok:

　　Thank you for your letter of March 11. The Peabody Museum Catalogue is an indispensable tool for research, as I used it very often in my bibliographical tours in the Boston area. Professor Rudolph would regret it later on if he wishes to continue his studies on Chinese archaeology.

　　Before returning to me the unsold copies of the Sinkiang bibliography, will you check with the University of Southern California Chinese library if a bibliography of this kind would be needed. You may send her the enclosed clipping.

　　In a day or two I shall send you two copies of my *Bibliography of Chinese Mathematics*, just off the press; one for your Library, the other for your general reference collection.

　　I shall be at Philadelphia March 25 and 26 and New York 27 and 28. If you could arrange to come to Washington, be sure to stay with us.

　　Looking forward to seeing you,

Sincerely yours,

Mr. Ma Meng wrote me recently that his father's collection was sold to the University of Virginia in 1960, and it was through his afforts that his friend Mr. Liao's collection was sold to the University of Illionois at US $7,200.

〔University of Chicago Library, Yuan T'ung-li Papers, Box 2〕

　　按:该件为录副。

三月十六日

先生致信香港新华印刷公司,询问《新疆国界图志》付排进展,并附《中俄西北条约集》附录二请改正后付印。

新华印刷公司大鉴:

前寄美金支票壹佰元,想已收到,东亚银行之款已收到否?《新疆国界图志》如尚未付排,可改影印,望估价示知。如已付排,望将校样分六次寄下,当在最速时间内寄还也。兹奉上《中俄条约集》附录二,因原稿不清楚,故遗漏之字颇多。兹校好,望尊处负责改正,即不必再行寄下。改正无误后,即付印可也。顺候大安。

袁同礼顿首

三月十六日

〔University of Chicago Library, Yuan T'ung-li Papers, Box 1〕

按:附录二为"中苏合办独山子油矿协定草案三种"。此件为底稿。

谭旦冏致函先生,告知已遵嘱寄上《故宫藏瓷》二册,并告拟付印的各书情况。

守和先生赐鉴:

久疏函候,殊为歉仄。

前承嘱寄故宫藏瓷之汝窑及钧窑各二册,谅早经先后寄上?刻官窑即将出版,而明青花亦将分四册出版,正编印中。

故宫瓷器录明乙,亦在月内印行,届时当寄呈一册。

目前,冏等从事历代书画家及收藏家款印谱编制,计划分四册印行,第一册晋迄宋元,将在四月后付印。

前托留法博士论文姓名探询,闻已由郭有守先生查明径寄,想蒙收阅矣。余容续陈,耑此,敬叩道安,并候潭福!

后学谭旦冏谨上

三月十六日

〔University of Chicago Library, Yuan T'ung-li Papers, Box 2〕

按:《故宫藏瓷·明青花瓷》根据时间分为洪武永乐、宣德、成化,似并未如计划分为4册,只有3册面世,仍由香港开发股份有限公司出版发行。《故宫瓷器录·第二辑明(乙)》题名页标注出版时间为 1963 年 1 月。《历代书画家及收藏家款印谱》应指《晋唐以来书画家鉴藏家款印谱》,分为 6 册由香港艺文出版社出版。

三月十七日

先生致信 Mrs. Shih,对外借其馆藏期刊太久表示歉意,告拟于四月中旬归还。

March 17, 1963

Dear Mrs. Shih:

May I thank you for your indulgence in letting me keep your journal for such a long time. I should have returned it to you earlier, but as I have been kept busy in proofreading my manuscript during the last two months, I did not find the time to glance over your journal. As soon as I return from the Philadelphia meeting of the Annual meeting of the Association for Asian Studies, I shall spend some time on it. In the middle of April, I shall be able to return it to you.

I have sent the enclosed circular to the Department of Mathematics at M. I. T. It is possible that your Library may like to have a copy in your reference collection.

With cordial regards to you and Mr. Shih.

Yours sincerely,

T. L. Yuan

〔University of Chicago Library, Yuan T'ung-li Papers, Box 2〕

按:Mrs. Shih 似指施友忠夫人,时或在华盛顿大学图书馆工作。

三月十八日

先生致信徐高阮,告知《胡适先生西文著作目录》收录篇目数量,并谈对胡适著作出版的意见。

高阮先生著席:

奉到二月十四日手教,拜悉一一。《适之先生西文著作》共收 160 种,惟尚须整理方能交人打字。前胡先生面告,谓许多文字毫无价值,不宜列入目录,此事记在心中,因之迟迟未决。至于尊处拟印全集,曾与联陞兄谈过,我们颇主张将尚未发表先行整理予以出版,其余稍稍无妨也。至于西文著作,似应选有关学术性者先行出版,与中文本分别印行较为经济。惟台端出版之西文书不合国际标准,在国外销售颇感不易,如改在美出版则又无人可托,亦有种种困难。弟对此事虽时在念中,亦想不出解决办法。院中拟影照胡先生西文著作,自当赞助,已交馆中陆续影照。惟前寄尊处之件未留目录,恐有重复,望将已有之论文开单见示是盼。顺候著祺。

弟同礼顿首

三月十八日

附上序跋,可否转交《大陆杂志》编辑部?

〔University of Chicago Library, Yuan T'ung-li Papers, Box 9〕

按:"前胡先生面告,谓许多文字毫无价值,不宜列入目录"应属实情,亦可参见 1956 年 8 月 27 日胡适覆先生函。此件为底稿。先生致信裘开明,商借哈佛燕京图书馆所藏一八八六年版《金轺筹笔》用作影印底本。

March 18, 1963

Dear Dr. Chiu:

Thank you so much for the loan of the four volumes of *Chin chao chou pi* (　　　) included in the *I hsiu shan fang tsung shu* . (1886.ed.)

After checking with the texts of other editions of the same work, I find that your edition marked the hour of each interview which Marquis Tseng had with Russian authorities. This is a point which had been omitted in other editions. For this reason, it would add scholarly interest if this edition could be reprinted.

I am therefore writing to ask your special permission to have photolithographed edition made for this work. Under my custody, I shall take best care of it. I shall also arrange to send ten copies of the reprint as soon as it comes off the press.

I have here a zerox copy of the 1887 edition. I shall be glad to send this copy to your Library in case some research scholar may need to consult it. The texts of these two editions are exactly the same, except the hours of each interview are not recorded in the 1887 edition.

Since your Library is always ready to help scholars in their research, I hope the present request will meet your approval.

Looking forward to hearing from you,

　　　　　　　　　　　　　　　　　Yours sincerely,

　　　　　　　　　　　　　　　　　T. L. Yuna

　　　〔University of Chicago Library, Yuan T'ung-li Papers, Box 8〕

　　按：此件为底稿，括号处付诸阙如，应填写"金韬筹笔"。Marquis Tseng 即曾纪泽。

孙德中致函先生，请再为胡适讲座基金在美东地区募捐，并告台湾最近刊登纪念胡适、蔡元培的报纸文章。

　　守和先生赐鉴：

　　　　奉诵三月四日寄慰堂学兄之华翰，藉谂美东友人为筹募胡先生讲座基金事多所尽力。台北报纸亦普遍登载是项新闻及照片，并谓总数已超过十万美元云。此间校友，同感佩慰。至纪念亭之捐款，已收到新台币九万元，工程已于上月开始，六月间可以完工。美西赵元任先生夫妇合捐美金百元，黄文山兄四十元，余天休先生经募百余元云。先生原被推为美国东部经募主持人，惜捐册邮局遗失，歉甚。讲座与纪念亭，虽属两事，意义则同为纪念适之先生。先生等既已捐款在前，在理不应再以此事烦渎，惟如征信录上无先生等大名，恐失众望。因再补奉捐册三份，请就北大师友中，托其再捐些须，并注明已捐数目（胡氏讲座），同在征信录上发表，庶可彰盛德、励众志也。

　　　　前承嘱寄北大同学录，曾托慰堂兄寄上二本，并附《德育讲义》一册，谅早收到。新同学录或可在五月间印出，届时当再邮奉。先生与在美东校友，如愿附入，当即遵办。

　　　　三月十六日《新时代》登有毛子水兄撰之《胡适传》校正本，三月一日《文星》登中撰纪念胡先生逝世周年文，一月十一日《"中央"日报》登纪念蔡先生文，未悉先生有机会看到否？如没有，亦可寄奉请指教也。

　　　　专此，敬颂道安。

　　　　　　　　　　　　　　　　　孙德中拜上

　　　　　　　　　　　　　　　　　三月十八日

　　回示请仍寄"中央图书馆"蒋慰堂兄。

　　　〔台湾省立师范大学用笺。University of Chicago Library, Yuan T'ung-li Papers, Box 2〕

按:黄文山应指黄凌霜(1889—1988),广东台山人,社会学家,清
华学校毕业后转入北京大学,后赴美留学,获哥伦比亚大学硕士
学位,时应任洛杉矶中国文化学院院长。余天休(1897—1969),
广东台山人,社会学家,早年随家人赴美,获克拉克大学(Clark
University)经济学硕士和社会学博士学位,归国后在北京大学执
教,曾主办英文《中国社会学报》(*The Chinese Sociological
Bulletin*)。《胡适传》校正本似指该文先在《文星》1963 年 11 卷 5
期刊行,后又在《新时代》1963 年 3 卷 3 期有所修正;"纪念胡先
生逝世周年文"全称应为"纪念胡适之先生逝世周年文"。收到
此函后,先生又联系熟悉之人为胡适讲座及纪念碑亭募集款项。

刘茂才覆函先生,告知已请波恩大学东方语言学院汇上书款,并表示因八
月偕眷旅行无法在西德恭候先生。

同礼先生台鉴:

兹接大札并发票贰份,即付敝院会计科使火速汇款矣。此后请直
接寄至敝院——Ostasiatischen Seminars der Universität Bonn, Bonn,
Liebfrauenweg 7——免生错误为盼。其间翻阅大著,多受神补,感甚。
藉知将于八月间台临西德,欢迎之至。奈弟已定于八月携眷旅行,八
月末始能回德,将不能尽地主之谊,歉甚。闻 Le Coq 发掘文物得脱战
祸者,已尽运回柏林,仍由 Lessing 女士保管云。此祝春安。

弟刘茂才敬上

一九六三年三月十八日

〔University of Chicago Library, Yuan T'ung-li Papers, Box 3〕

按:Le Coq 即 Albert von Le Coq(1860-1930),德国探险家,通译
作阿尔伯特·冯·勒柯克,曾对吐鲁番柏孜克里克千佛洞的佛教
和摩尼教壁画进行野蛮切割。

三月十九日

张光直覆函先生,告知将寄送*COWA Surveys and Bibliographies* 第一期,并
谈在美国学习考古人类学的台湾学生情况。

同礼先生足下:

顷奉先生十三日大函及赐赠《新疆书目》,谢谢。另外一本书目,
因博物馆图书室不收中日文书,已转寄校图书馆,嘱其购买。倘图书

馆已有,当再寄还。

COWA 之远东部分,至今仅出二期,第二期即先生已有者,第一期
(1957)晚自己只留了一本,为学生写论文借去不还,正在追索中。一
俟取回,当即奉上。倘先生亟需,不妨径向 COWA 索要一册,大概该
处所存,亦已不多矣!

台大考古人类学系毕业生在美攻读者,晚只知前几届者,如加大
(Berkeley)之唐美君兄,NYU 之任先民兄,及康耐耳之乔健兄,此外必
定还有,且恐有政大边政系毕业学人类学者,则晚所不悉者也,"大使
馆"文教处或有较详之资料?

承索晚用英文所写的关于中国考古论文,已打了一份,附函中寄
上。晚将于廿六日去费城参加亚洲学会,廿七日即归,住同一旅馆内。
倘先生有暇,盼能谒见!

谢谢先生的信! 并祝近安。

晚张光直敬拜

三月十九日

〔University of Chicago Library, Yuan T'ung-li Papers, Box 1〕

按:张光直(1931—2001),1954 年台湾大学毕业,旋赴美留学入哈
佛大学。"COWA 之远东部分"即 *COWA Surveys and Bibliographies:*
Area 17, Far East,其中 COWA 则指 Council for Old World
Archaeology,该学术社团由人类学家 Lauriston Ward(1882-1960)筹
组,1957 年创办 *COWA Surveys and Bibliographies* ,该刊汇集考古
信息、出版书刊内容摘要等,将世界分为 22 个区域,其中远东为
第 17 区,张光直长期担任该份刊物的合作编辑,[1]第 2 期约在
1961 年刊行。唐美君(1927—?),浙江鄞县人,1953 年台湾大学
考古人类学毕业,导师即凌纯声,后赴美留学获伯克利分校人类
学硕士学位,随后返台回母校执教。任先民(1928—2020),师从
凌纯声。乔健(1935—2018),山西介休人,1954 年入台湾大学历
史系,翌年转读人类学系,1958 获台湾大学考古人类学学士学
位,1961 年获硕士学位,后赴美留学。

---

[1] Bibliography of the Publications of Kwang-Chih Chang.

三月二十日

先生致信大维德爵士夫人，对爵士身体逐渐康复感到高兴，并告将寄赠瓷器目录。

March 20, 1963

Dear Lady David:

I have been much concerned over Sir Percival's illness. From Mr. Basil Gray's recent letter, I am most delighted to learn that he is now enjoying better health and is working daily on his translation of *Ko Ku Yao Lun*. I am very happy at this turn for the better, though I hope he will not work too hard.

A week ago, I sent to you by registered parcel post a copy of *Ch'ün Yao*, recently published by "the National Palace Museum". I shall send you shortly another catalogue of Chinese porcelains preserved at the Mukden Museum. As I have not seen this catalogue, I have no idea how good it is. I shall forward it to you as soon as it arrives from Hong Kong. Both volumes contain specimens of some interest, so I trust you and Sir Percival may like to have them for your Foundation.

The monumental catalogue of your great collection compiled by Mr. Hobson has long been out of print. It is not likely that a copy can be found in the market here. Since London is a better place for out-of-print books, it is possible that you might know the availability of a copy from time to time. If you do, will you be good enough to let me know, so that I may acquire it, needed constantly in my research.

Everything goes fine with my bibliography on Chinese art. The work of analyzing journals and other serial publications takes much longer time than I had anticipated. Though a labour of love, the anxiety it has involved can only be appreciated by those who have experienced a similar ordeal.

With sincere greetings to you and Sir Percival,

Sincerely,

〔University of Chicago Library, Yuan T'ung-li Papers, Box 8〕

按:Chün Yao 应指《故宫藏瓷:钧窑》(*Chün Ware of the Sung Dynasty*),该书版权页标注为 1961 年 12 月初版,实际刊行日期应为 1962 年秋。Moukden Museum 即奉天博物馆,信中所指瓷器目录待考。此件为底稿。

王伊同覆函先生,谈匹兹堡大学虽有购书经费但操作不易,并谈拟延聘郑宪或劳延煊等事。

老伯大人尊前:

手谕及马蒙来信奉悉。季明师藏书易主,可憾可憾。近争得购书费九百元,然采购部无(华)人负责,不能以常法添置,嗣有私人藏书出让,乞示最盼。费城之会得会欣然,郑君自可面商,唯出身史学,若专教语文,不无遗憾耳。贞一兄长子延煊亦商洽中。近表叔陈季鸣名珂以篆书名海上代治章五方,寄呈一看,印泥仍西泠所制佳品也。承示家俱行市,甚感。敬请金安。

侄伊同顿首拜
二十日

〔University of Chicago Library, Yuan T'ung-li Papers, Box 2〕

按:陈名珂(1892—1972),字季鸣,号文无,江苏江阴人,书法篆刻家,定居上海,尤以铁篆闻名。

裘开明覆函先生,允借用该馆所藏《金辂筹笔》作为影印底本。

March 20, 1963

Dear Dr. Yuan:

Thank you very much for your letter of March 18. It is all right for you to keep our copy of *Chin shao chou pi* 金辂筹笔 for a longer period than the normal period of two weeks.

For bringing out a photolithographed edition of that work, an acknowledgement should be made for the existence of the original in our Library.

When we need the text, we shall ask you to send us the Xerox copy of the 1887 edition, which we also have.

With best wishes and hope to see you in Philadelphia,

Sincerely yours,

A. Kaiming Chiu

Librarian

Please submit your acknowledgement for Dr. Baxter to see it before the publication of the book.

〔University of Chicago Library, Yuan T'ung-li Papers, Box 8〕

按:Dr. Baxter 即 Glen W. Baxter(1914-1998),美国汉学家,中文名白思达,曾任哈佛燕京学社副主任。

三月二十三日　费城

先生参加美国亚洲学会年会。

按:会期为 23 日至 24 日。

三月二十四日

先生致信新华印刷公司,告支票已寄并请替换封面题字。

新华印刷公司大鉴:

昨奉三月廿日惠书,知东亚银行之款仍未取到。兹又致该行一函,请其查照,前函将支票 755 元港币径寄尊处,想不久可以寄到矣。校样寄还,惟封面题字似稍歪。兹又写一纸,请重新制版改用此纸印,不必再寄还矣。顺候大安。

袁同礼顿首

三,廿四

前寄还"附录二"等,想已收到。书印成后,将用航空寄下一部。

〔University of Chicago Library, Yuan T'ung-li Papers, Box 1〕

按:此件为底稿。

刘麟生致函先生,谈撰写《陈道复传》等事。

守和尊兄博士著席:

(一)莆老于昨日偕夫人赴英,弟曾往船边握别。(二)弟已将《陈道复传》交富先生。渠不日赴美里兰,参加会议,尚未修订此稿也。(三)借撰此文,参阅书目,达十余种。惟《皇明文海》所载之张寰撰《白杨先生墓志铭》,未及见。然其若干评语,则已于他书见之。《皇明文海目录》,则此间已有,京都版也。(四)弟现在 502 室治事,周、黄二君亦同室,富公之治事室,则为 502 室也。(五)台驾来此,当图良晤,并候教。敬请俪安。

教小弟刘麟生谨启

三,廿四

〔University of Chicago Library, Yuan T'ung-li Papers, Box 1〕

按:"白杨先生"应即白阳山人陈淳(1483—1544),明代书法家、
画家,文徵明弟子。周、黄二君应分别指周道济(Chou Tao-chi,
1927—1994)、黄养志(Huang Yang-chih),时均参与 Dictionary of
Ming Biography, 1368-1644 编纂计划。"则为 502 室也"照录。

三月二十七日

陈祚龙覆函先生,告知巴黎在售《论文和学术著作目录》各卷期及价格,并
感谢帮助联系台北商务印书馆筹印著作等事。

> 守和先生有道:

> 大示(三、十三)早经收到,关于 *Catalogue des thèses et écrits
académiques* ,兹经 le Cercle de la Librairie, 117, Bd. St.-Germain, Paris
6e, 经理函告:1933-1962(除却:1933,1934,1938,1950,1960 已属绝
版以及 1961,1962 尚未出版不计外)共值 66.50 F 正。

> 承示已向台北赵叔诚先生函荐承印龙所草就之长篇,盛情优谊,
感且不朽! 一俟赵先生来信提及此事,自当详与商定有关事宜。

> 关于接替陈缺,据闻已故"驻比大使"之胞弟很有可能。并此奉
闻,敬颂潭安!

> 愚陈祚龙拜上

> 六三,三,二七。

〔University of Chicago Library, Yuan T'ung-li Papers, Box 6〕

> 按:"陈缺"似指本年陈雄飞离任"中华民国驻法大使",接任者应
> 为高士铭;"驻比大使"应指钱泰。

三月二十九日　华盛顿

中午,先生设宴款待郭廷以,金问泗作陪。〔《郭量宇先生日记残稿》,页 390〕

三月三十日

晚,郭秉文在北宫楼设宴,先生、郭廷以、李惟果、顾翊群、吴光清夫妇同席。
其中,郭秉文谈"中美文化教育顾问委员会"事,并对黄季陆表示不满。
〔《郭量宇先生日记残稿》,页 390〕

> 按:李惟果(1903—1992),四川人,1923 年入清华大学政治学系,
> 1927 年赴美留学,先后在加州大学伯克利分校、哥伦比亚大学学

习,并获博士学位,归国后历任四川大学、武汉大学教授,1936 年1 月,任蒋介石侍从室第二处第五组组长,1942 年 6 月正式出任国民政府外交部总务司司长,1947 年任中宣部副部长,时应在乔治敦大学任教。

三月

Chinese Culture 刊登先生文章,题为 Doctoral Dissertation by Chinese Students in Great Britain and Northern Ireland, 1916~1961(《中国留英同学博士论文目录》)。〔*Chinese Culture,* Vol 4. No. 4〕

四月一日

汪敬熙覆函先生,谈家事并告已为建造胡适纪念碑亭捐款五十元。

> 守和吾兄惠鉴:
>
> 三月廿九日惠示敬悉。内人久不来信,弟疑其有再来美之企图。他不能在美多住,社会环境使他发精神病。他人不知,代他胡出主意。他如来,我又须费四五千元。我没有多少钱,此款我出不起!出主意人绝不后悔,只是我吃不消而已!只有死亡一途!匆此奉复,顺颂俪安。
>
> 弟敬熙拜上
六三,四,一
>
> 捐款附件,附此信内寄上。已捐五十元纪念适之先生,不够再捐。
>
> 〔University of Chicago Library, Yuan T'ung-li Papers, Box 1〕

按:"内人"即何肇菁,因与汪敬熙性格不合,分居台湾、美国两地,后因精神疾病去世。

四月四日

先生致信李书华,告知馆藏《赛金花本事》暂被借出,并寄赠《现代中国数学研究目录》一册。

> 润章先生:
>
> 商鸿逵所印《赛金花》一书,馆中业已入藏,惟近月以来不在架上,想为他人借阅,未经负责人之手擅自取去。除告负责人随时注意外,特先奉达。拙编之《数学目录》,其页数之尺寸经印刷公司翦裁过多,极不雅观,故不愿赠送他人。兹奉赠一册,幸勿转示外人是幸。顺候著祺。
>
> 弟同礼顿首

四，四日

〔Columbia University Libraries Archival Collections, Shuhua Li Papers, 1926-1972, Volume II: Modern Eminent Chinese Leaders〕

按："《赛金花》一书"应指《赛金花本事》,刘半农初纂、商鸿逵纂就,1934 年 11 月初版,北平星云堂书店发行。

四月五日

先生致信郭廷以,谈代"中央研究院"近代史所购书等事。

量予先生教席:

日前落雨,未见驾临,弟亦未能到站送行,为怅。关于与馆方交换刊物一案,兹附上信稿,仍希尊酌,何时信纸寄到,即可发出也。俄国档案全书共 106 本,想贵所尚未入藏,此书颇不易得,幸有美人为之编一撮要,可供参考。*Digest of Red Archives* 仅八元五角,如愿订购,并盼示知。弟拟自购一部也。匆上,敬候俪祺。

弟同礼再拜

四月五日

嫂夫人同此致意。

"金大使"之序文请改正后寄下是盼。

桂荣、塔克什讷之履历均已查到,勿须函请贵所再查矣。

〔台北"中央研究院"近代史研究所档案馆,〈郭廷以〉,馆藏号069-01-02-089;《郭量宇先生日记残稿》,页 393〕

按:桂荣、塔克什讷均为京师同文馆俄文馆翻译官,光绪三年(1878)曾随崇厚出使俄国,后曾纪泽交涉伊犁问题时,二人充当翻译。该信于 8 日送达。

牛满江覆函先生,告知孙兆年联系方式,并为胡适讲座和纪念碑亭捐款五十元。

袁先生钧鉴:

顷接来示,得悉先生为胡先生纪念亭事多为辛劳。北大同学,晚并不知很多。孙兆年(Dr. C. N. Sun)在 St. Louis 大学医学院教书,先生可直接同通信:

Prof. C. N Sun

Department of Pathology

St. Louis University School of Medicine

St. Louis, Mo.

晚随信寄来支票伍十元,作为胡先生讲座及纪念亭事,微微小款,稍表心意,望勿见怪。专此,即颂教安。

晚牛满江拜

四月五日

〔University of Chicago Library, Yuan T'ung-li Papers, Box 2〕

按:该函右下角标有"顾40,瞿,孙"字样,应为先生标记捐款人信息,其中"孙"为孙兆年。

四月七日

余又苏覆函先生,告商务印书馆表示可以协助校对《新疆研究文献目录》(中文本)书稿,并感谢先生与澳大利亚国立图书馆商洽介绍其前往筹建中日文馆藏事。

守和先生道席:

四月一日大示敬悉。大著《新疆目录》(中文本)交商务印行,先生注意者为校对问题,甚佩忠实于学术之至意!商务过去在大陆印书,校对认真,近年在台印书,最后赵叔诚先生尚亲手逐字逐句核校一次,故成绩尚佳。先生同意后,当另正式签合约,照例抽版税百分之十五,抽取百本,当无问题。大著已杀青,当以早日出版,公诸学术界为宜;自行印行,不唯须付出一笔费用,且经理甚烦。故建议交商务也。赵叔诚先生当另覆。

日文本已出售,由商务与先生结账,款存台银先生户。

承绍介至澳大利亚国立图书馆,其事为中日两国官书及学术出版品之搜集及采购,甚感兴趣。遵示附呈略历表,祈径与 Dr. White 洽谈为感。名义为何?待遇若干?聘期如何?可否携眷同往?均祈进一步洽谈后示知!如能在该处大学兼课,则既不使多年教学研究中断,而请出境尤为方便。

牧育才神父迄无信来,不知近在何处考察。彼此行为视察天主教留学生及为台北学生中心大堂建筑费募捐,在美各地视察后,再绕道欧洲返国,大约在九月开学时到台北。

澳大利亚与加拿大相似,当较香港、新加坡为佳。倘得一相当待遇及安定工作环境,当能有所成就,不负雅意也。专肃,并颂著安。

余又荪谨上

四月七日

〔University of Chicago Library, Yuan T'ung-li Papers, Box 8〕

按:Dr. White 即 Harold F. White(1905-1992),1923 年进入澳大利亚国会图书馆服务,1927 年任该馆副馆长,后长期职掌该馆及后来的澳大利亚国家图书馆。

四月八日

徐炳麟覆函先生,告知收到寄送书籍四册并已就其中两册刊印代为估价。

守和先生:

《新疆建置志》及《西陲要略》序跋、《勘定新疆记》四册均先后收到。经与彭锡恩兄数度洽商,除《勘定新疆记》一种俟序跋到再估价外,谨先将《新疆建置志》及《西陲要略》两书估价单附呈参考。《中国丛书综录》之索引,四月三日已附 y8-0013 发票挂号邮寄,并闻。敬颂台绥。

弟徐炳麟上

一九六三年四月八日

〔袁同礼家人提供〕

四月十日

郭廷以致函先生,谈近代史研究所欲与国会图书馆交换书刊及购书事,并请金问泗删减其为重印《金轺筹笔》所拟序言。

守和先生有道:

华府畅叙,至为快慰。终以为时仓促,未克于国会图书馆多事盘桓为憾。关于交换书刊之事,多承费神,公私均感。代拟函稿,经已拜读,极为得体,一俟所内将信笺寄到,即可照缮发出。今后相烦之处正多,谨先预谢。俄国档案全书,即希代订购,价款可否先为垫付? 容积有相当数目,一并开具支票奉璧。"金大使"序文,似以请其再加斟酌为是,最好删繁就简,不必多事发挥,不学如弟,焉敢妄参末识,务乞宥谅。原稿随函附还。弟在哥大工作,以审核文稿,指导论文,交换中国文史研究教学意见为主,尚不算忙。月内当须去哈佛一行,五月下旬,再携眷前往,作较长时间停留。如有赐教,仍盼不时示知。匆此,祗颂研安!

嫂夫人同此问候。

弟廷以谨启

四，十

内子附候

〔University of Chicago Library, Yuan T'ung-li Papers, Box 2〕

按:《金轺筹笔》前冠金问泗序,标注于 1963 年 5 月写定。

四月十三日

徐高阮覆函先生,请就胡适全集编辑方针给予意见。

守和先生道鉴:

三月十八日尊示敬悉。《新疆建置志》序跋已交《大陆杂志》,即可刊出,编者赵铁寒君甚为感谢先生赐稿之盛意。胡先生西文著作目录,仍甚企盼。胡先生谓若干文字不收入文存、不列入目录,高阮等亦闻其言。此点现应如何决定,尚祈指示。惟胡先生所谓不宜列入目录者,其实往往亦甚重要,如就全集而论自绝不可舍去,此点先生谅亦同意。现下此间之编辑委员会仅作一初步工作,即将胡先生所遗未发表之稿件点清,并已计划将此等稿件一律拍照,以后阅看、编辑、排印,全用晒出之照片。大约遗稿亦有百万余字。拍照稍迟即作。至于全集编辑方针,西文部分如何付印,尚未议及。敢请先生先就整个编辑方法作一种方案之草稿,俾此间人讨论有所遵循。此亦甚为重要。又,前曾提及民国十八年胡先生在 *Christian Yearbook* 发表之 Cultural Conflicts of China 一文,系后来在《独立评论》上提及者,此《基督教年鉴》不知系何处出版,甚祈先生注意及之。专上不一,顺请道安。

后学徐高阮敬上

四月十三日

附上前寄来之胡先生西文著作照像一批之目录二页。

〔University of Chicago Library, Yuan T'ung-li Papers, Box 9〕

按:赵铁寒(1908—1976),河北青县人,时应任《大陆杂志》主编。

四月十五日

刘麟生覆函先生,告诸事。

守和馆长勋右:

(一)十日诲言,雒诵快慰。(二)弟已拟撰第五传记,即彭年之传记。因此又需要过庭训之《本朝分省人物志》。上次承抄示,惶悚感戴,至今未泯。今又欲烦大贤设法影印,或烦友人代抄关于彭年之记载,其叶数为廿四卷第29叶(24/29a)。沈度见同书25/3a,亦烦代查示知。费用请勿吝指示,以便奉赵。长期交易,自应尔尔。一笑。(三)Kent Hall 治学,当属顺利。知注,谨以复陈。(四)"金大使"大作,约1900字。弟已遵示另写一文,约一千字,似少简练,仍请椽笔再加厘定。(五)《南明画家忠烈传》除黄石斋外,似均为清初名家。ECCP 已有所述,故此书拟暂不复制。异时需用,当再奉告。(六)承属查《大清搢绅录》,另纸答复。(七)廷以先生在此,已晤叙。渠言明公身心俱健,尤用欣悦。春明景和,伏维为道珍重。

　　　　　　　　　　　　　　　　　教小弟刘麟生谨复

　　　　　　　　　　　　　　　　　　　　15/4/63

　　　　　〔University of Chicago Library, Yuan T'ung-li Papers, Box 1〕

　　按:彭年,明代学者、书法家。"黄石斋"即黄道周(1585—1646),字幼玄,号石斋,明末学者、书画家。ECCP 即 *Eminent Chinese of the Ch'ing Period*(《清代名人传略》)。

四月十六日

先生致信赵叔诚,谈《金轺筹笔》影印之细节问题。

　　叔诚经理先生惠鉴:

　　　　近接余又荪先生来函,欣悉贵馆拟刊印文史书籍,为学术界服务,有功载籍,曷胜钦仰。兹有曾纪泽《金轺筹笔》四卷,在今日已成罕见之本,弟商得哈佛大学同意,准予影印以广流传。原书有模糊之处,照相时似须用较大之光度,印出后方能清晰,原书内圈点如承能用纸遮盖,最所企盼,否则照原书影印亦无不可。除原书外,尚有序文二篇及附录五种,均须排印。兹先将原书四册及曾纪泽照片二件(一底片,一照片)先行寄上,请先交技术专家加以研究,将样张寄下一阅。此书如贵局愿为发行,极所欢迎,否则由弟自印,委托贵馆代办一切。除附录五种下周寄上外,先此奉达。顺候

　　　　　　　　　　　　　　　　　　　　四月十六日

　　　　　〔University of Chicago Library, Yuan T'ung-li Papers, Box 1〕

　　按:此件为底稿。

郭廷以致函先生,请协助近代史所与国会图书馆交换出版物,并告知将赴哈佛大学。

　　守和先生道席:

　　　　前函谅已邀鉴。致国会图书馆交换赠送部 Wood 主任信,已缮就付邮,敬烦便中再与面洽,赐覆请径寄 619 Kent Hall, Columbia University, New York 27, N. Y.。如尚有其他手续,仍恳随时示知。下周去哈佛,逗留三数日即归。多劳清神,谨再谢。祗颂双福!

　　　　　　　　　　　　　　　　　　　　　　弟廷以拜启

　　　　　　　　　　　　　　　　　　　　　　　四,十六

　　　　　〔University of Chicago Library, Yuan T'ung-li Papers, Box 2〕

　　按:4 月 22 日至 24 日,郭廷以赴哈佛大学参加费正清近代史讨论班。[1]

四月十八日

先生致信梁实秋,请帮助物色合适人选翻译法文史料。

　　实秋吾兄著席:

　　　　上月晤浦家麟先生,欣悉吾兄健康如恒,忙于著述,引企贤劳,至为钦佩。浦君赠尊编《中英字典》,融会贯通,实为交换中西学术之津梁。闻以后并拟编辑辞典,敬祝早日完成,以压社会之需求。兹有一事奉商,即翻译一部分之法文书,敬求赐助。闻贵同事或台大教授精通法文之人颇多,兹拟请翻译 *Russia in the East* 第 91 页至 139 页及附录一 p. 143–156,(信札)则选于中国有关者译成中文,于中国无关者则不译,稿费若干并祈代为决定,如须先付一部分稿费,亦盼示知,如能于六月二十日左右交航邮寄下,尤所企盼。原书不必寄还,用毕并请将该书交邮寄"南港'中央研究院'近代史研究所图书室"是感。琐事渎神,不安之至。专此拜托,敬候教祺。

　　　　　　　　　　　　　　　　　　　　　　弟袁同礼再拜

　　　　　　　　　　　　　　　　　　　　　　　四月十八日

　　附 *Russian in the East* 一本。

　　　　　〔University of Chicago Library, Yuan T'ung-li Papers, Box 8〕

─────────────

[1]《郭量宇先生日记残稿》,页 396–397。

　　　　按：浦家麟（1916—？），字公展，江苏无锡人，记者、报人，时应任
　　　　远东图书股份有限公司董事长，梁实秋好友。此件为底稿。

四月二十三日

罗香林覆函先生，建议《新疆研究丛刊》交香港万有图书公司代理销售，并
谈清人王洪简历及家人近况。

　　守和先生道席：

　　　　前奉三月二十日大教，诸承奖誉，感甚愧甚。拙作《香港与中西文
化之交流》承东京东亚文化研究中心（东洋文库与联合国文教处合组
者）约为翻为英文交该处出版，大约下月底或可译毕。关于何启留英
事迹已依照尊示各节于译文内更正，出版后当为奉呈请正。承示尊编
《新疆丛书》在港印成部分如何推销问题，鄙意即交万有图书公司经
理亦无不可。盖香港旧日有名书局如中华、商务等皆受控制色彩甚
深，集成图书公司则为正中书局之分铺，经营方面皆有限制，惟万有图
书公司则仅作出口与分发生意，无零售门市，台湾新书与大陆新书皆
一律经营，其所经理各书亦一律能发交中华、商务门市出售（另有智源
书局亦有门市，则与日本关系较深）。至直接寄至大陆则似困难甚多，
因彼处书店无摆卖香港所出各书者，有之唯高级机关或研究院所函请
中华、商务或智源搜寄参考耳。鄙意如《新疆丛书》一类专门书籍出
版时，每种当可外销三百部左右，其余须俟二年左右始能售清，故存放
地址不能不预为筹划。如万有图书公司愿为经理，则存放地址自亦由
彼负责（彼公司办公室则不甚宽广），想此类问题彭锡恩兄或亦曾径
向先生报告也。

　　　　承示贵友近购得王洪旧藏端砚，敝知王洪等略历。按王洪字春
澥，为清同光间广东潮安人，擅长书法兼喜收藏，在潮属各县略有文
名，今其孙王显诏仍为岭东画家，寄居汕头。惟启寿则迄未查出其姓
氏耳。门人王文卓君，其父与王显诏为好友，据云显诏在潮亦藏一王
洪旧遗类似之砚，或当日以同一端石剖制为二砚也（粤人则称之曰双
砚），容查有更详资料时当另为报告。承询内子及小儿辈情况，至感。
香林自一九四九年秋避地香港，初住新界粉岭，内子朱倓即在其地从
谦学校（政府津贴）任教越二年，香林始受港大聘约讲授中国历史，三
子一女则随在九龙、香港上学。现长小儿罗文已于去年毕业港大历史

系,随即获得哈佛燕京学社奖学金赴哈佛大学远东学系攻读硕士学位（正选读蒙古文与蒙古史）,二小儿罗武则尚在港大医科肄业,三小儿罗唐及小女罗瑜则准备投考港大,生活勉可维持,差堪奉慰。本年七月至十二月,香林在港大有短期休假,如能筹得旅费（因决定过迟,故筹划不易）,则拟赴日本及美国,研究各大图书馆所藏之中国人族谱,此刻尚未能全定也。专此奉复,并请道安。

后学罗香林敬上

一九六三年四月廿三日

〔University of Chicago Library, Yuan T'ung-li Papers, Box 8〕

按：王显诏（1902—1973）,原名观宝,广东潮州人,现代画家,上海大学美术专科毕业,后任教于广东省省立第二师范学校,兼金山中学教员。该函应于 4 月 27 日送达。

四月二十四日

先生致信澳大利亚国家图书馆 Harold F. White,表示期待访问澳大利亚并力荐余又荪协助该馆建设东亚馆藏文献。

April 24, 1963

Mr. Harold F. White, Librarian

Commonwealth National Library

Canberra, A. C. T.

Australia

Dear Mr. White:

During our conversation in Washington, I expressed to you my sincere appreciation for your invitation to visit Canberra. I hope that in the not-too-distant future I might be able to arrange a visit to your beautiful country.

As promised, I have been thinking of recommending a qualified person to assist you in the building up of your collections on East Asia. Since experts in Chinese and Japanese source materials are not so easy to find these days, I have given the matter a considerable thought.

I now enclose a statement from Professor Yu Yu-sen of the Department of History of the Taiwan University, Taipei, Taiwan. He would probably meet your requirements and would be able to carry out your plans. But he is not trained librarian in cataloging and classification compared with a graduate of a library school.

When I had charge of the National Library at Peiping, I preferred to use men of this type to build up collections. I wonder if you would agree.

After you have been promised the grant from the Rockefeller Foundation, perhaps you could let me know the details of your position, including salaries, travel allowances, etc. You may like to communicate with Professor Yu direct.

With best wishes for your success,

Yours sincerely,

T. L. Yuan

〔University of Chicago Library, Yuan T'ung-li Papers, Box 1〕

按:National Library 应为 Commonwealth Parliamentary Library 或 Parliamentary Library of Australia,澳大利亚国家图书馆的前身。该件为录副。

刘麟生覆函先生,谈代查《搢绅录》诸事。

守和尊兄博士勋鉴:

　　(一)十九日雅教,百读不厌。改文乃蒙过奖,非所克当。谨当自勉而已。(三)连日上午查《搢绅录》达二小时,仍未能寻出,歉仄万状。光绪元年,仅有一册,余三册或四册不等。弟遵示,在五年以前,即四、三、二、元年各《搢绅录》,均检阅户部,并无二人之名。缘上次明公便条中曾言"塔克什纳在五年前任户部员外郎"也。五年春季《搢绅录》户部门,有荣桂无号,系笔帖式,满洲正蓝旗人,或非其人。如再给予其他线索(Clue 或 Data),当乐于再查也。(四)蒙橡笔代抄彭年父子小传,及速印下沈度小史,感激非常。印费＄2.50 之收据,富先生云:可由公家付。已交其女秘书。女秘书云:当如数寄贵馆不误也。(五)今岁农历五月十八日莘老八旬俪寿。弟于其临行前,曾写百字令一阕赠之。顷闻友言,台湾将有手册到此,由友人书贺。届时弟当缮入拙作。(六)《文艺周刊》一卷,另寄,阅后仍请赐还为荷。敬颂著绥。

教小弟麟生敬肃

四月廿四日

〔University of Chicago Library, Yuan T'ung-li Papers, Box 1〕

四月二十五日

Felix Reichmann 致函先生,请教中国图书馆发展史和现状,并欲了解中国图书馆如何对中西文文献分类、编目。

April 25, 1963

Dear Dr. Yuan:

My colleague Mr. Ma gave me your name as the best man to give me some advice. I would like to read one or two good books about Chinese libraries. I am interested both in the historical development of Chinese librarianship and at the moment I am especially interested in the present-day conditions in Chinese libraries.

Unfortunately, I do not read Chinese, but I can handle in a certain fashion most of the Western European languages.

If in addition to this bibliographical advice you could tell me something about the National Library of Peiping, I would appreciate this very much. My interest with regard to this question is confined to the catalogs. What I want to know is: classification, both for Chinese books and Western European books; arrangement of the catalog; author and subject approach.

With best regards,

Yours sincerely,

Felix Reichmann

Assistant Director

〔University of Chicago Library, Yuan T'ung-li Papers, Box 10〕

按:Felix Reichmann 时任康乃尔大学图书馆馆长助理,Mr. Ma 即马大任。此件为打字稿,落款处为其签名。

四月二十六日

蒋廷黻覆函先生,告中基会已同意资助先生编撰《中国留欧大陆各国博士论文目录》。

April 26, 1963

Dear Dr. Yuan:

Further to your application of August 30, 1962 I have the pleasure to inform you that the Executive Committee of the China Foundation has voted to grant you a sum of $1,200 for the compilation of a guide to doctoral dissertations by Chinese students in Europe.

Our check for payment of the grant will be sent in about a week.

Yours sincerely,

Tingfu F. Tsiang

Acting Director

〔University of Chicago Library, Yuan T'ung-li Papers, Box 2〕

按:此件为打字稿,落款处为其签名。

刘麟生致函先生,告知富路德将辞退其并请代为谋事。

守和尊兄勋右:

昨奉一书,谅尘燕几,上文为富教授所给手札,弟已函复同意。弟意彼早已另约一人,是否为闽中王君(?)不及知,以彼曾一度绍介也。拙事仍烦异日代为留神,至托至感。素荷厚意,故敢密陈。敬请双安。

弟麟生顿首

四,廿六

〔University of Chicago Library, Yuan T'ung-li Papers, Box 1〕

按:"上文"为"April 24, 1963. I find that we have sufficient funds to extend your service for $1\frac{1}{2}$ months, or until August 15, at the same rate and under the same conditions as before, except that you are to take a week's vacation any time in July or the first half of August. Let me know if this is agreeable to you. It has been a pleasure to have your cooperation in this venture up to now. Yours sincerely"。

"闽中王君"待考。

四月三十日

宋晞覆函先生,告知文章已刊印并寄出抽印本,此外就影印事已与商务印书馆接洽。

守和先生道鉴:

四月十一日手书祗悉。大稿《留英中国学生博士论文名录》校样收到后即付印,统计表亦印入。《文化季刊》四卷四期已出版,抽印本二九〇本(分五包)另付平邮挂号寄上,请查收。关于影印新疆史地之书,曾访此间商务经理赵叔诚先生,据告该馆已有函复先生,谅已阅及。该馆愿意合作,惟影印之书,如原版不清楚,或纸张褪色变黄,或深度不一,均可影响制版。至于美观与否,是在成本上考虑,如不太计成本,当可印得精美些,装得精致些。世界、文海等书店,目的在赚钱,因此把美观列为次要了。专此奉复,祗颂撰安。

后学宋晞敬上
四,卅

〔University of Chicago Library, Yuan T'ung-li Papers, Box 2〕

按:"影印新疆史地之书"事,应指 1963 年台湾商务印书馆刊印《西陲要略》《西疆交涉志要》《金轺筹笔》《新疆建置志》《戡定新疆记》。

是年春

先生所编*Bibliography of Chinese Mathematics, 1918-1960*(《现代中国数学研究目录》)刊行。

按:该书似由 American Mathematical Society 出版。

先生赴加拿大温哥华开会,宿彭世美家。〔《思忆录》,中文部分页 108〕

按:彭世美即彭昭贤之女,称先生为三舅。

五月一日

先生致信蒋廷黻,感谢中基会的赞助。

May 1, 1963

Dear Dr. Tsiang:

With grateful appreciation I beg to acknowledge the receipt of your letter of April 26 informing me that the Executive Committee of your Foundation has made a grant of $ 1,200 for the compilation of a *Guide to Doctoral Dissertations by Chinese Students in Europe* .

I am highly sensible of the honor and support which the Trustees have accorded me. May I ask you to convey to them my hearty thanks. Although the work is not going to be an easy one, I hope that my labors will be of some use to those interested in the history of modern education in China.

Sincerely yours,

T. L. Yuan

〔University of Chicago Library, Yuan T'ung-li Papers, Box 2〕

按：5 月 2 日，叶良才亦致信先生通知赞助事宜，因属具文，笔者未录。

五月二日

先生致片郭廷以，告已为近代史研究所选书二十三种。

量予吾兄：

预计大驾已返纽约，所嘱之件自接到负责人电话后，即前往选择，共得二十三种，均关于中国近代史之英文书中文书多台北出版的，故未选，内有 MacMurray《中国条约集》两大册，在今日已不易得，已于昨日由馆方邮寄贵所。请其开一书目，据云无暇为之，故寄出后并无书目，亦无记录，可见美人办事之糊涂，便中并望转告贵所是盼。顺候旅祺。

弟同礼

嫂夫人同此问候。

〔台北"中央研究院"近代史研究所档案馆，〈郭廷以〉，馆藏号 069-01-02-089〕

按：MacMurray 即本谱中的"马慕瑞"，《中国条约集》即 *Treaties and Agreements with and Concerning China 1894-1919*。该片于 1963 年 5 月 2 日由华盛顿寄出，收件地址为 Mr. Ting-yee, Kuo, 619 Kent Hall, East Asian Institute, Columbia University, New York 27, N. Y.

先生致信赵叔诚，商洽《新疆研究丛刊》待出各书之印行办法。

台湾商务印书馆赵经理台鉴：

奉到四月廿五日第 65-1 及 65-2 号两函，拜悉种切。兹分别答覆如左：

（一）《新疆文献目录》中文本贵局愿为印行，至为感谢。末校由本人负责，至于补贴排印费用，亦愿查照来函所示办法予以采纳，惟该稿虽已完成，但无暇抄录清本，恐须至秋间方能寄上，届时再行函达。

（二）《金轺筹笔》此间有三种版本，但以寄上之本为最罕见之本，故决定以该本影印。承寄下影印样本,足征技术精良,虽不能与《四部丛刊》相比,但原书字迹不清,有此成绩已属不易,望即照此进行。书前有序文六张或四张,书后有附录四种,均需以四号字排印,将分两批航邮寄上。此书为中俄外交史重要资料,销路极佳,拟请贵馆发行出版。敝处可按定价之六成一次购取壹百部藉作补贴,或印六百部,或印七百部,均由贵局决定。惟此书列为《新疆研究丛刊》之一,其尺寸大小须与其他各书完全一致九英寸长,六英寸宽,每页之天地头务必宽大较为美观。承寄下之《樵歌集》印刷精良,至为钦佩,惟尺寸太小耳。

(三)敝处尚有《西陲要略》《新疆建置志》《戡定新疆记》序跋以后再寄及《西陲交涉志要》四种,均请贵局影印发行,由敝处补贴若干部以资调剂。惟今日读书人购买力薄弱,希望定价低廉可以畅销,如各书能同时印出,则购者愿购全份,于销路有所补助,谅荷同意。

(四)以上五种均系影印,惟序跋等均系排印,其末校由本人负责,收到尊处寄到校样后,于短期内即可寄还。

(五)不日由香港新华印书局寄上贵馆各同人及余又荪教授代收《中俄西北条约集》二百五十部,请予代售按七折收款,每册定价台币七十元,将来中文本《新疆目录》出版后,凡购日文本者可予优待(如改五折出售),亦可略销若干本也。不日拟汇上台币壹万元,作为贴补一部分之费用,届时当再函达,至盼提前进行。各种校样务希于六月底以前寄到敝处,因七月间□事赴欧,在旅行中无……

〔University of Chicago Library, Yuan T'ung-li Papers, Box 1〕

按:"查照来函所示办法"即先生于该书出版时,按定价之六折一次购取四百册;如无需四百册之数,可以减少,但须贴补若干排印费用,而其余之六百册按实际销售数量与定价的百分之十,分期结算版税。另,实际寄到商务印书馆由其代售《中俄西北条约集》的数量是二百四十八部,特此说明。此件为底稿,未写完。

谭旦冏覆函先生,告知购书款虽有不足但无须补寄。

守和先生有道:

四月一日手教,早经拜读,因事稽覆,殊为歉仄。

蒙建议丛书次第,经转陈,当尽量采纳。

前承嘱代向香港开发公司所购《汝窑》及《钧窑》各二册,七折计为美金七十七元,经商妥以台湾官价折合新台币为三千零八十元,是先生所寄之支票新台币二千五百元,不足五百八十元,已由此间代垫付,请不必寄来,将来如有所需,再行函陈,暂存尊处,为感。

《故宫藏瓷:官窑》在装订中,明青花第一册,洪武、永乐两窑,将在本年六七月间出版,第二册宣德窑在年底。已嘱该公司出版后即寄两册,仍按七折优待。

《故宫瓷器录》第二辑明(乙),想已蒙收阅矣。明(丙)将为御窑之无款者,正编制中。耑此,敬请道安,并候潭福。

后学谭旦冏拜上
五月二日

〔University of Chicago Library, Yuan T'ung-li Papers, Box 10〕

按:《故宫藏瓷:明青花瓷一(洪武永乐)》版权页标注的出版时间为 1963 年 3 月。

徐炳麟覆函先生,告寄送书籍和稿件均已收到,并谈《中俄西北条约集》推销计划。

守和先生:

四月廿二日惠书敬悉。

前嘱估价印刷图书三种及稿件已请彭锡恩兄取回,并点交刘国蓁兄接收办理,彭兄处已代致意。

《中俄西北条约集》本港推销问题,国蓁兄曾电话商谈,已将港九主要书店提供参考,想能发行顺利。弟能尽力处当尽力办理。书款容另清结,送银行。敬颂台绥。

弟徐炳麟上
五月二日

〔袁同礼家人提供〕

五月三日

先生致信王世杰,请将补助印刷费改拨台币,并告《中国数学书目》已寄出。

前奉二月十九日赐书,欣悉尊处补助《数学家著作目录》(今改题《中国数学书目》)之款系请美援拨付,该款迄未寄到,谅以外汇关系筹措不易。兹请改拨台币,即希以一万五千元径寄台湾银行,收入同礼存款账内第 7332 号,倘荷赞同,无任感盼。该书以印刷人未得同礼之同意,将尺寸缩小,因之印费亦随之减少。按照尊处补助费之数比例分配,共得 150 部,已由印刷人交邮寄至"国家长期发展科学委员会",预计四星期内可以寄到,并盼转告该会负责人查照,至感。专此,敬候道祺。

五月三日

该款于送到台湾银行后,望告该行以航邮示知。

〔University of Chicago Library, Yuan T'ung-li Papers, Box 8〕

按:此件为底稿。

耶鲁大学地理系教授 Herold J. Wiens 致函先生,询问《新疆研究丛刊》各书出版情况,尤其关注有关地理的史料。

May 3, 1963

Dear Dr. Yuan:

I have been informed that you are editing a series of studies in Chinese on the history of Sinkiang, including subjects of geographical interest.

Would you kindly inform me where these are being published and when various volumes are to be published? I am much interested in the historical geography of Sinkiang and have been doing some research in this subject. Recently, I finished a 39-page manuscript on the historical and contemporary development of Urumchi or Ti-hua which I hope to publish. I shall give a paper this fall on the subject at the annual meetings of the Association of American Geographers in Denver.

I would appreciate information on your series.

Sincerely yours,
Herold J. Wiens
Professor of Geography

〔University of Chicago Library, Yuan T'ung-li Papers, Box 3〕

按:Herold J. Wiens(1912-1971),美国地理学家,生于上海,14 岁前一直在中国生活,后随父母回国,毕业于加州大学伯克利分校,

1936 年回到中国并在燕京大学继续学习,抗战期间曾在重庆美国驻华使馆服务,1949 年获得密歇根大学博士学位,后长期在耶鲁大学执教,对中国历史地理颇有研究。Urumchi 即乌鲁木齐,Ti-hua 即其旧称迪化。信中所提论文,除应在美国地理学家协会年会宣读外,另以 The Historical and Geographical Role of Urumchi, Capital of Chinese Central Asia 为题目刊登在 *Annals of the Association of American Geographers*, vol. 53, no. 4, 1963, pp. 441-464.

五月四日

先生覆信 Felix Reichmann,就其所询问题做简要回答,并告其可参考平馆《年度报告》《图书季刊》英文本。

May 4 1963

Dear Mr. Reichmann:

Owing to my absence from Washington, I was not able to see your letter of April 25 until yesterday.

With reference to books on Chinese libraries, I enclose herewith a list. I trust that all of them are on file in your Library.

Concerning the work of the National Library of Peiping, the most informative literature would be its *Annual Reports, the Quarterly Bulletin of Chinese Bibliography*, etc. which I sent to the Wason collection while I was in Peking. We adopted L. C. system of classification for Western literature, while a rather modified Chinese system of classification was applied to Chinese and Japanese material. Separate author and subject catalogs were maintained following the example of the catalogs maintained by the School of Business at Harvard.

Hoping that the above information will prove useful to you,

Sincerely yours,
T. L. Yuan

〔University of Chicago Library, Yuan T'ung-li Papers, Box 10〕

按:该件为录副。

孙兆年覆函先生,为筹建胡适纪念亭捐款三十美元。

同礼先生惠鉴：

弟因事外出，刻归来拜读四月十二日大札。关于筹建胡适之先生纪念碑亭募款事，弟甚表赞同。兹随函奉上卅元，请转交台湾北京大学同学会。耑此，顺颂台安。

弟孙兆年谨启

五月四日

〔University of Chicago Library, Yuan T'ung-li Papers, Box 2〕

刘国蓁覆函先生，告知已将三种书稿邮寄台北，并谈在港印刷各书的进展。

守和博士先生尊鉴：

敬启者，上月廿七日拜奉廿二日手教，敬悉一一。日前奉上令岳信及芜笺与本港各书局名单，量邀尊览。承命向万有徐经理取回《戡定新疆纪》四册、《新疆建置志》四册（另附文件：封面题字、次序表、题字、总序（2）、袁序、宋跋、劳榦跋）、《西陲要略》两册（另附封面题字、次序表、题字、版权页、序、跋），经已签回收据一纸与徐经理。再为扎好一包，于昨日用航空包裹邮寄至台北重庆南路一段卅七号，商务印书馆赵叔诚经理收，想当可收到。该书共重两磅，邮费十四元，以此种寄法较为廉宜及安全，若用印刷航空挂号邮则需款十八元四角，而仍不能封密口，经已领回收据矣。闻徐经理云及该三种书如在港影印则水准较好，他为此事办采访工作已有多时也。关于《中俄条约集》出版事，已与郑通君通电话，据其回答谓该书在装订中，约下星期可全部竣工，决不有误。如一装好即送一部与晚，先此敬谢。如收到后及其情形如何，当另函奉陈。《新疆国界图志》有八卷之多，一二卷已再改正，不日连同三四卷稿付上校阅，五至八卷亦将排好，只须校对而已。《西疆交涉志要》之影印样本，他认为不甚好，拟再制妥后，便可付上也。港中天气十分干旱，食水无着，现已再加限制，如两周后再无雨，则可能隔日供水云云。专此，敬请撰安。

愚晚国蓁顿首

一九六三年五月四日

〔University of Chicago Library, Yuan T'ung-li Papers, Box 2〕

五月五日

先生覆信叶良才，告收到中基会支票并附上收据两份。

May 5, 1963

Dear Mr. Yip:

Thank you so much for your letter of May 2 enclosing check for $1,200.00 in payment for the grant from the China Foundation in connection with the compilation of a Guide to Doctoral Dissertations by Chinese Students in Europe.

I enclose my letter of thanks to Dr. Tsiang and the two copies of receipt.

With sincere thanks,

Yours sincerely,

T. L. Yuan

〔University of Chicago Library, Yuan T'ung-li Papers, Box 2〕

按：此件为录副。

梁实秋覆函先生，禀告拟请黎烈文翻译法文史料，但后者提出两个条件，请先生酌情考虑。

守和先生：

四月十八日赐书敬悉。师大无外文系，只有英语系。故法文人才不易觅得。经询台大外文系黎烈文教授，伊系专攻法文者，翻阅之后认为可以担任翻译，但有两个条件：

（一）六月十日之限期太迫，拟请延至七月十日。事实上一般人都很忙，所请亦不无理由。

（二）稿费不能按美国标准，亦不可按台湾标准，希望折衷从优致送。可否请先生酌定示知，如能早惠，更好。

以上两点，盼即赐示。如荷同意，即可进行，否则当另行设法，惟日期益迫，殊为困难耳。尚复，敬颂教安。

受业梁实秋谨拜上

五月五日

〔University of Chicago Library, Yuan T'ung-li Papers, Box 2〕

按：黎烈文（1904—1972），湖南湘潭人，作家、翻译家，早年赴日、法留学，归国后曾任《自由谈》主编，1946年赴台，时在台湾大学文学院执教。

陈祚龙覆函先生,谈在法购书等事并感谢赠书与巴黎中国学院。

守和先生道右:

大函(四、廿九)收到。

(一)关于先生已经汇款至 Le Cercle de la lib. 购买 *Cat. des Thèses et Éc. Acad*,而迄今仍未收到有关是目事,龙固可以就近代为查询,惟先生实得径函收款人自加催促也。

(二)Hambis 整理之 *Toumchouq* 一书,其第一本均为图版(龙曾亦对是书草有评介,刊在 *Bull. des Bib. de France*, No. 5, Mai, 1962 之中,只惜手头已无是评之抽印,是故未能寄奉参阅)。该书系由 Lib. Adrien-Maisonneuve, 11, Rue St. Sulpice, Paris VIe 经售,当前售价,每本想必至少得为 175F(外得另加邮费)。先生如欲购置,而不愿与该店往来,似以直接函托此间其他与先生熟悉之书店,如 Paul Geuthner 办理,最为便当。

(三)承告《敦煌遗书总目索引》已经问世,谢谢。事实是书早经龙向香港书商为馆预订,想必不日即可见到。

(四)大作《数学书目》,今蒙邮赠中院图书馆一部,至感。将来到达,自当遵嘱存馆。事实关于先生历来之专著,即使先生不予赠送,而龙向即特为中院购藏一份也。专此布复,敬颂潭祺百福!

愚陈祚龙拜上

六三,五,五于巴黎。

〔University of Chicago Library, Yuan T'ung-li Papers, Box 1〕

按:"汇款至 Le Cercle de la lib. 购买 *Cat. des Thèses et Éc. Acad*"实际是为 Le Cercle de la Librairie(书业协会)购买 *Catalogue des Thèses et Écrits Académiques*。Hambis 即 Louis Hambis(1906 - 1978),法国汉学家,中文名韩百诗;*Toumchouq* 即 *Mission Paul Pelliot: Documents Archeologiques*(《伯希和考察队考古资料丛刊》)第 1 卷,通译作《图木舒克》,包括托古孜萨来(Toqqouz-Sarai)发掘所得的佛教雕像图片,以及喀什(Kashgar)等地发掘的地形图。《敦煌遗书总目索引》,商务印书馆编,1962 年 5 月初版。

普实克致函先生,询问《辅仁文苑》第一期有关刘鹗生平的文章,并请协助复制文献。

May 5, 1963

My dear Professor YUAN:

I was extremely sorry that I was unable to visit Washington and your Library during my visit to America, but my program was too crowded, and I had to reduce it. Still, I was so glad to receive your kind letter, it was the proof that our old friendship continues.

This time I am obliged to beg you for a kind help. During my stay in America, I was looking for the magazine *WEN YUAN* published at the Fu Jen University, Peking, 1939. In the first number of this magazine there has been published a biography of Liu O prepared by his son Liu Ta-shen / I gathered this information from the translation of Liu O's *Lao Ts'an Yu Chi*, by H. Shadick, p. 233/. I need this article very badly as I prepare a study on Liu O and his work. I was unable to locate this magazine and therefore I take the liberty to beg you in case that this magazine exists in the Congress Library to kindly make for me a photo or xerographic copy of this article. I should be very much obliged to you therefore and in case that I could help you in any similar case, it will be a great pleasure for me.

It is possible that I shall visit the United States again in Summer. Meanwhile I wish to you, dear Professor Yuan, much success in your work and a very good health.

Sincerely yours,

Professor Jaroslav Průšek

〔University of Chicago Library, Yuan T'ung-li Papers, Box 3〕

按：a biography of Liu O prepared by his son Liu Ta-shen 应指刘大绅(笔名"绅")所写的《关于〈老残游记〉》,其为刘鄂的四儿子；此外,该期另有一篇文章《一个外国人对〈老残游记〉的印像》,由谢迪克(Harold E. Shadick)撰、杜阳春译。

五月七日

先生覆信 Herold J. Wiens,附上《新疆研究丛刊》出版信息,并谈曾将《新疆研究文献目录》（日文本）寄至耶鲁大学地理学图书馆但被退回。

May 7, 1963

Dear Professor Wiens:

　Thank you for your recent letter.

　I enclose herewith a statement about a series of studies which I am publishing. This is a writing for the NEWSLETTER of the AAS.

　At the beginning I did include a number of geographical works, but experience has shown that books of this type are difficult to sell unless they are subsidized.

　Therefore, I am printing in limited editions and hope they will meet the immediate need. When my Japanese bibliography on Sinkiang was sent to your Geography Library, it was returned. This led me to think that there is no interest even in an institution where Ellsworth Huntington had taught for many years.

　I shall be glad to put your name on the list to receive notices of these publications.

　With all good wishes for your work,

Yours sincerely,

T. L. Yuan

〔University of Chicago Library, Yuan T'ung-li Papers, Box 3〕

按：Ellsworth Huntington（1876－1947），美国地理学家，通译作埃尔斯沃思·亨廷顿，20 世纪初曾赴中亚考察，著有 *The Pulse of Asia, a journey in Central Asia illustrating the geographic basis of history* 等专著，后在耶鲁大学地理学系执教。该件为录副。

张馨保致函先生，已遵嘱联系本校图书馆订购《新疆研究文献目录》（日文本）及《新疆研究丛刊》各书。

守和先生赐鉴：

　上次费城开会，馨保本拟赴席，藉便请益问候，临时以事务烦杂不得脱身，怅惘何似。顷蒙赐寄近中出版大作《新疆图书目录》（日文本），感愧不已，多谢多谢。展卷快览，甚叹广征博采，收揽之富，学者得益不能胜言。附寄《中国数学目录》一册，当交梅先生处，现已得到书款,兹附寄上。另两册《新疆目录》已交圕采购部矣,虽其手续较缓,大约不日即可将书款径自寄上,日内当再去探询。再者,敝校不论何系购书,统由圕之采购部办理,以后出版书籍,或有旧书出售,请先将书名赐知,由教员建议,然后由圕函购。如此较省手续,多免周折也。顷已书面建议采购部将尊处已出版或将出版之《新疆研究丛刊》全部订购,谅订单不日即可收到。

贻宝先生本周末将赴华府出席 Maryland 大学之会,当可晤面。馨保今年暑假在此教暑校,九月间或可至华府一行,当面谒一倾衷肠。此间在港购书多由交流、古今两家处理,其地址附上。又此间圕采购部负责人姓名地址为: Mr. Frank Hanlin (Director), Dept. of Acquisitions, University Library, State University of Iowa, Iowa City, Iowa. 余容再陈。祇颂撰安。

伯母及清兄不另。

后学张馨保拜上

一九六三,五,七日

〔University of Chicago Library, Yuan T'ung-li Papers, Box 2〕

按:"Maryland 大学之会"应指第九届"中美文化关系圆桌会议"。交流书报社(Chiao Liu Publication Service),地址为 P. O. Box 5734 Kowloon, Hong Kong;香港古今图书公司(C. M. Chen Book Company),地址为英皇道 324 号 2 楼。

五月十三日

王世杰覆函先生,告知《中国数学家著作目录》印刷费已嘱科学会垫拨。

守和吾兄台鉴:

接诵本月三日大函,敬悉种切。《中国数学家著作目录》印刷费,前已由科学会转请美援补助,惟美援申请案件,向须待六月间方能确定。既急需款支应,已嘱科学会先行垫拨,并由"中研院"具领转付。因科学会接受申请,须以机关为对象,上次系用"中研院"名义代请,故领款手续亦须由院转付。专复,祇颂箸祺。

王世杰敬启

五月十三日

〔University of Chicago Library, Yuan T'ung-li Papers, Box 2〕

　　按:该函为打印件,落款处铃王世杰印。

匹兹堡大学图书馆学院院长 Harold Lancour 致函先生,请为 *Library Trends* 特刊撰写文章,以中华人民共和国图书馆学教育为主题。

May 13, 1963

Dear Dr. Yuan:

　　Professor J. C. Harrison and I are editing an issue of *Library Trends* on "Education for Librarianship Outside the United States and Canada." It is our hope to present in this issue a reasonably detailed account of the method by which librarians, documentalists, and information officers are professionally prepared and qualified in various parts of the world. An outline of the issue is attached.

　　We are happy to invite you to join us in this undertaking, specifically to prepare the article on Education for Librarianship in People's Republic of China.

　　We feel that you are eminently qualified to carry out this assignment and sincerely hope that you will be able and willing to accept it.

　　There is no specific number of words to which the paper must be limited, although conciseness of expression is desirable. The important thing is to cover the subject adequately. We will need, however, to reserve the right to do some editing of your paper in the event of compression becoming necessary.

　　We assume that you are familiar with *Library Trends* and its format and will therefore know of the regular inclusion of a list of references at the end of each article. This is a valuable feature and should include all relevant material regardless of language.

　　This issue, we feel, should bring together authentic descriptions of the historical development, current situation, and probable future trends in library education throughout the world.

　　The issue is scheduled to appear in October, 1963, and we shall need to set the coming June 30 as our deadline for the receipt of your manuscript.

An early reply, indicating whether you are in a position to accept this invitation, will be appreciated.

Sincerely yours,

Harold Lancour

Dean

〔University of Chicago Library, Yuan T'ung-li Papers, Box 10〕

五月十四日

先生致信李书华,感谢赠书,并告张秀民两篇文章的出处。

> 润章先生著席:
>
> 　　承惠寄近著,至为感谢。吾兄治学谨严,资料丰富,致力之勤,至为钦佩。此书应多印若干部,分送各机关,以其系不朽之作,足以传世也。弟近日因事离京,以致未能早日作书。专此申谢,敬候俪祺。
>
> 弟同礼再拜
十四日
>
> 关于活字之资料,近见两文,不识尊处已见到否?
>
> (一)张秀民:《元明两代的木活字》,《图书馆》,1962第一期。
>
> (二)张秀民:《清代泾县翟氏的泥活字印本》,《文物》,1961第三期。

〔Columbia University Libraries Archival Collections, Shuhua Li Papers, 1926–1972, Volume II: Modern Eminent Chinese Leaders〕

五月十五日

《大陆杂志》刊登先生文章,题为《重印〈新疆建置志〉序》。〔《大陆杂志》第26卷第9期,页1〕

> 按:该刊在先生文后附劳榦《重印〈新疆建置志〉跋》。

五月十六日

徐高阮致函先生,催寄《胡先生西文著作目续编》之稿。

> 守和先生:
>
> 　　前上一函,又复多时,《胡先生西文著作目续编》不知已付打录否? 此间之集刊候排此稿,故嘱高阮专函询问。先生提及何者应列入、何者不列入,自是一问题,想凡胡先生亲自著作者自以求全为上。中文方面,凡笔录者均未列入,但拟另编一目。尊见如何,仍希见示。

又前乞注意之民国十八年英文《基督教年鉴》中《论文化冲突》一文，已查得否？念念。《非留学篇》可得否？又《甲寅》杂志，美何处有存，亦乞见示。诸多渎神。谢谢。专上，顺祝道安。

后学徐高阮敬上
五，十六
（University of Chicago Library, Yuan T'ung-li Papers, Box 9）

按：《非留学篇》即《非留学议》。

余又荪致函先生，告知牧育才教授已与乔治敦大学商洽谋求教职事，但因无法联系故希望渺茫，另告前请书评已撰写并发表于《新时代》。

守和先生道席：

□Murphy 自旧金山来一信，谓已于华盛顿之 Georgetown 大学友人谈及，"he can offer you a position, maybe you will hear him directly." 他在各地旅行中，现在何处亦不得而知，他募捐事很忙。此事不存希望，无从接头。

前函谓如来美，年龄可少填。此间友人皆谓面貌如四十余岁。如与先生见面，谅亦有未变老之感觉。我自思大约是不用脑筋之故。如求方便，当遵示少填，面貌体力都不老，说得过去。

闻燕京大学有位方教授在雪梨，不知是在雪梨大学，或在 Dr. White 的图书馆？澳洲安定，如条件适合，举家而去，□为得计。

□撰《新疆研究的新文献》一文，《新时代》本期已发表，本日出版。文内提及十种丛刊事，前至商务，得见自港寄来之影印书，即在其中。甚愿早日出版。一俟先生复函，该馆即可着手交印。

Murphy 如到华府，谅必访先生也。前已将尊址开示。因彼函告 Georgetown University 事，故函陈其事。

专肃，并颂著安。

余又荪敬上
五，十六
〔University of Chicago Library, Yuan T'ung-li Papers, Box 8〕

按："方教授"应指房兆楹。该函四角破损。

五月十七日

严文郁致函先生，告知将尽力为胡适奖学金及纪念碑亭再次募集捐款。

守和先生大鉴：

去冬寄上圣诞贺片，因地址错误，致遭退回，至以为罪。月前章楚君出示大箸《日文新疆书目》，当即转请敝购书科照购，早已编目上架矣。近奉大示及捐册，敬悉。此刻捐款正如先生所言，非常困难，因前次为适之先生讲学金与北大有关人士诸已捐过，颇难再引劝募，但当尽力为之，成否则不敢必也。专此，敬颂撰祺。

弟严文郁谨上

五，十七

〔University of Chicago Library, Yuan T'ung-li Papers, Box 2〕

五月十九日

梁实秋覆函先生，告知黎烈文翻译的稿费标准及叶公超近况。

守和先生：

赐书敬悉。

（一）黎烈文教授已允即日动手翻译，于七月中交稿。稿费定为每千字美金五元，此数较台湾标准略高，但尚合理。全稿估计约有五万字左右。如荷先生同意，仍乞再赐答，以便通知黎先生，促其切实开始进行。（支票台币壹千元，现存秋处。）

（二）公超近已心情安定，颇忙，半年来不常见面，先生索兰竹，已转告。

（三）狼毫笔两枝，秋得便当即购来邮上，不需托人携带也。

匆复，敬颂旅安。

受业梁实秋顿首

五，十九

盼覆。

〔University of Chicago Library, Yuan T'ung-li Papers, Box 2〕

按：先生在该函左下角标注"五、廿三复函同意"。

五月二十日

先生致信郑通，寄上《中俄西北条约集》分配单，并请速寄《新疆国界图志》校样。

新华印刷公司郑经理大鉴：

前委托贵公司所印二书，月余以来，迄未接到只字，不识何故！兹将两事列后：

（一）《西北条约集》，日内想可装订完竣，弟处需用壹百部，除请航邮寄下二部外，余九十八部请用平邮寄下。

（二）奉上分配单四纸，共 712 部。请照单寄出，邮费若干，请暂垫，俟收到清单后，再行奉还。包装务须坚固，以免损伤书籍，包内用厚纸，每包十五部左右。

（三）《新疆国界图志》之校样，请速寄下。

收到此信后，望速覆，以免惦念。顺候时祉。

袁同礼顿首
五月二十日

余书暂存尊处。谢谢。

〔University of Chicago Library, Yuan T'ung-li Papers, Box 1〕

按：此件为底稿，另附四张邮寄单，分别为寄台北者、寄香港及新加坡者、寄澳洲者、寄日本东京者。

五月二十一日

先生覆信普实克，告知美国各大图书馆均无《辅仁文苑》第一期，请尝试联系北京图书馆，此外请其向布达佩斯询问匈牙利语中有关新疆的学术文章或著作。

May 21, 1963

Dear Professor Prusek:

I am glad to have your letter of May 5 and to know that you are working on Liu O and his work. The title of the magazine is entitled: *Fu Jen Wen Yuan*. Since we have a union list of Chinese periodicals in American libraries, I checked the holdings of these libraries, but sorry to report that none of them have this particular issue, though nos. 2 and 3 are kept in the Library of Congress, Harvard, Columbia, etc. Since it is rather easy to communicate with Peking, may I suggest that you write to the National Library there to make a duplicate copy for you? I am sure you will get a quick answer soon.

If you come to the States in the summer, I hope you will be able to come to Washington. I shall be away in Europe for six weeks from July 15th on, but will be back in Washington at the end of August. I have been working on a bibliography on Chinese Turkestan from 1860 – 1963. I wonder if there are any articles written by Czech scholars. There is a considerable literature on Sinkiang in Hungarian, but it seems difficult to obtain information from Budapest at present.

I have been wondering whether it would be easier to obtain a list of articles on Chinese Turkestan in Hungarian from Budapest, if the request comes from your librarian. May I rely on your judgment in this matter? So far, I have the titles of Hungarian monographs on this region.

Sometime ago I mailed you the two volumes of Watson's *Records of the Grand Historian of China*. In one of my letters, I suggest that you be good enough to send the cost of this book ($ 20.00) to my brother, Professor of Geology, Peking Institute of Geology and Mineral Sciences, West Peking. His name is Philip L. Yuan. As he has not received it, it is possible that my letter to you may have been lost. If you have not remitted it, you may give it up, as you may have difficulties in remitting money to Peking. You may find it easier to send it to my friend in West Germany. With all good wishes for your work,

　　　　　　　　　　　　　　　　　　　Yours sincerely,

I list below references for 4 articles on Liu O which you may have seen already:

　　　　　　　　〔University of Chicago Library, Yuan T'ung-li Papers, Box 3〕

　　按: *Records of the Grand Historian of China* 即 Burton Watson 节译的《史记》,1961 年哥伦比亚大学出版社初版。4 articles on Liu O 应分别指: 顾颉刚《〈老残游记〉之作者》(《小说月报》)、胡涤《〈老残游记〉考证》(《中华月报》)、赵景深《〈老残游记〉及其二集》(《新小说》)、刘鹗《〈老残游记〉二集序》(《人间世》)。此件为底稿,空白处付诸阙如,应填写"辅仁文苑"四字。

郑宪覆函先生,感谢为其妹郑华介绍工作。

　　守和先生赐鉴:

　　　前承介洽匹茨堡大学工作,以兴趣不合未敢申请,嗣于三月费城开会时面向令亲王斯大先生转介舍妹华前往申请,近得舍妹函称申请已邀准,并去函表示接受云云。此事全仗鼎力玉成。敝兄妹同深感激。专此函谢,顺颂大安。

郑宪谨上

五月廿一日

〔University of Chicago Library, Yuan T'ung-li Papers, Box 2〕

余又荪致函先生,告知其拜访曾约农,并得确认《金轺筹笔》未存原稿。

守和先生:

拙撰《研究新疆问题的新文献》一文,无内容,甚惭歉! 已另邮寄上一册。十五日《新时代》杂志出版,十七日晚即有人来访,谓将出版《曾纪泽全集》,拙文中谓将单独影印《金轺筹笔》一书,非全豹;又谓曾约农先生藏有《金轺筹笔》原稿云云。

木刻《金轺筹笔》,此间"中央研究院"有之(台大有全集),先生自哈佛借来者同,但未闻有原稿。昨特访曾约农先生,方知并无原稿,对先生影印此书,甚表赞同,谈及先生所编之三种目录及十种丛书,更为钦佩。(广禄先生亦深赞佩。彼近年在台大教满文,并热心于边疆语言历史学会。)

初意以为如有原稿,当校对其同异;或请影印一二页插入木刻影本中。

曾惠敏有日记,未在台,约农先生谓将寄来台北付印。他也没有印全集的计划。

年来台湾各书印书之风甚盛,亦有销路。廿四史印得很多了,但去年冬尚有启明等两家再印,闻亦未亏本。因国外亦有购者。

甚望先生之十种丛书早日出版!

专肃,并颂研安。

余又荪敬上

五,廿一

赴欧行期定否?

〔University of Chicago Library, Yuan T'ung-li Papers, Box 8〕

按:"年来台湾各书印书之风甚盛"当作"年来台湾各书店印书之风甚盛"。

五月二十二日

先生致信富路德,建议补全《台湾文献丛刊》中有关晚明史料,并恳请留用刘麟生。

May 22, 1963

Dear Professor Goodrich:

　　The Economic Research Department of the Bank of Taiwan has published a considerable number of monographs dealing with the men and events of the Southern Ming period. Included in a series known as *Tai-wan wen-hsien tsung-k'an*　　　　, much biographical data can be gathered from these sources.

　　If your file of this series at Columbia is not complete, may I suggest that you write to the Bank of Taiwan to supply the missing volumes? I am sure you would get them gratis if you would indicate that they are needed for your project.

　　Mr. L. S. Liu would be a most suitable person to go over these volumes and call your attention to the biographical data suitable for inclusion in the biographies. With the financial support now assured, your project would be a great success. I hope you could arrange to keep Mr. Liu on your staff, as he can locate important sources of information often overlooked by other scholars-an asset indispensable for a project such as yours.

　　I trust that you have gone through the titles of works listed in the *Wan-ming shih-ch'i kao*　　　　compiled by Hsieh Kuo-chen and published by the National Peiping Library. Much information can be obtained in these works.

　　With cordial regards,

Sincerely yours,

T. L. Yuan

〔University of Chicago Library, Yuan T'ung-li Papers, Box 1〕

按:The Economic Research Department of the Bank of Taiwan 即台湾银行经济研究室。*Tai-wan wen-hsien tsung-k'an* 即《台湾文献

丛刊》,其中确有相当与南明历史相关者,如《南明野史》《鹿樵纪闻》《郑氏关系文书》《郑氏史料续编》等。*Wan-ming shih-ch'i kao* 即《晚明史籍考》,Hsieh Kuo-chen 即谢国桢。此件为底稿。

五月二十三日

邵毓麟(伊斯坦布尔)覆函先生,询问《新疆研究文献目录》各书细节,并表示不便将《中俄西北条约集》及函件转交与在土异己人士。

　　同礼吾兄道鉴:

　　　接奉四月三日华翰,敬悉台驾今夏或能便道来土观光一节,至表欢迎。承赠《中俄西北条约集》一册,业已拜读,获益良多,其中列有《新疆研究丛刊总目》之(一)(二)(三)项,《新疆研究文献目录》中、日、西文之部,未悉此三种书刊亦系香港新华印刷股份公司承印,可否向该公司购买,或有代售处,均请示知。查同时寄有致伊敏一函及《中俄西北条约集》一册,嘱为转发一事。查伊敏在土十数年来从事新疆独立运动,不仅对我政府不利,且有侮辱我"元首"之词句。经弟曾一再劝告并印有驳覆伊敏荒谬之英土文小册,兹特另寄上英土文小册各一本,敬请察阅。伊敏之态度如此,久已与其无往来,嘱代交函书是否仍有查明转寄必要,尚乞指示。至于艾沙情形与伊敏同出一辙,但艾之活动情形并非表面化,乃系暗中工作。弟在此处境非常困难也。专复并谢,敬颂撰祺。

弟邵毓麟拜上

五月廿三日于土京

　　　　　　〔University of Chicago Library, Yuan T'ung-li Papers, Box 2〕

　　按:邵毓麟(1909—1984),浙江鄞县人,早年赴日本留学,归国后任四川大学教授,1957年1月至1964年10月任"驻土耳其大使"。

五月二十四日

福克司致函先生,感谢寄来《新疆研究文献目录》(日文本)并汇上书款。

den 24. 5. 1963

Dear Director Yuan:

　　Thank you very much for the five copies of your classified bibliography on Sinkiang. I am much pleased to have this valuable contribution in my library. By the same mail I am remitting DM 48 to you.

It was indeed a disappointment to me, too, that I was unable to meet you during my last visit to Washington, but let us hope that we'll have another chance in the future.

With kind regards,

Yours sincerely

W. Fuchs

〔袁同礼家人提供〕

按：福克司时任科隆大学东亚研究系主任（Ostasiatisches Seminar, Universität Köln）。此件为打字稿，落款处为其签名。

五月二十五日

先生致信台湾商务印书馆，谈《新疆研究丛刊》各书印行注意事项。

台湾商务印书馆大鉴：

昨接台 52 西字第 79 号大函，拜悉种切。兹将各项分答如次：

（1）《金轺筹笔》影印问题，原书黄色纸张字迹不清，只得将淡墨字迹在印版上重行写出，抗战前张菊生影印《四库丛刊》即用此法，惟修工校工成本较高，故敝人愿略补贴（按贵局定价之六成购取壹百部），至于出版发行仍请贵局完全办理，敝意此书可以畅销。

（2）除《西陲要略》《新疆建置志》《戡定新疆记》三书外，又请港友刘君寄上《西陲交涉志要》，此四种书字迹清晰，制版印刷均无困难，拟请贵局予以出版。敝处按定价之六成购取五十部，每种印制数量统由贵局决定，惟尺寸用纸均须一律九英寸长，六英寸宽。

（3）胡适之先生及"中央研究院"委托贵馆影印及排印各书之办法，可供参考，敝处亦愿遵照办理，一切请尊处决定。

（4）《戡定新疆记》及《金轺筹笔》之序文等正在清抄，一星期内即可奉上。

（5）承寄赠《石遗室诗话》，至为感谢，一俟寄到当再函达。

专复，敬颂时祉。

袁同礼拜上

五月廿五日

〔University of Chicago Library, Yuan T'ung-li Papers, Box1〕

按：此件为底稿。

先生致信 Denis Twitchett，告知将寄赠《新疆研究文献目录》（日文本），并希望其能够为《中俄西北条约集》撰写书评。

May 25, 1963

Dear Professor Twitchett:

　　Sometime ago I read with much interest your article on the fragment of the T'ang Dynasty Ordinances of the Department of Waterways Discovered at Tun-huang. Knowing your interest in the literary finds of Tun-huang, I asked one of my printers to mail you a copy of my bibliography of Japanese literature concerning Sinkiang. Two more bibliographies on Sinkiang, one in Chinese and the other, in Russian and western languages, will be published next year. I shall be glad to send you review copies upon their publication.

　　My printer in Hong Kong has mailed to you a copy of my recent work entitled: *Russian-Chinese Treaties and Agreements Concerning Sinkiang, 1851 – 1949*. As you will note, it contains a number of documents which have not been published previously. I hope you could write a review for *BSOAS*.

　　I have been engaged in compiling a comprehensive bibliography of Chinese Art and Archaeology, and I have already analyzed a considerable number of Sinological and art journals and serial publications. It is a laborious undertaking and I presume that it will take another two years before it is printed. In February I applied for a research grant from the UCC and I hope it would receive due consideration from the Committee. I am particularly anxious to gain access to materials not available in this country.

　　With cordial regards,

Yours sincerely,

T. L. Yuan

〔University of Chicago Library, Yuan T'ung-li Papers, Box 1〕

按：Denis Twitchett(1925-2006)，英国汉学家、历史学家，中文名杜希德，时任伦敦大学亚非学院汉学讲座教授，your article 应指

The Fragment of the T'ang Ordinances of the Department of Waterways Discovered at Tun-huang，刊*Asia Minor*，New Series 6, 1957, pp. 23–79.*BSOAS* 即 *Bulletin of the School of Oriental and African Studies* 。此件为录副。

蒋复璁覆函先生，告收到募捐支票两张，并询问溢出之款为何人所捐。

> 守和先生大鉴：
>
> 　　奉到五月四日大函，敬悉一切。胡先生纪念亭，承慨解义囊，并多方募捐，此间同学均极铭感。惟尊示列举捐款者四人共美金为九十元，乃该款经汇到后实为美金一百一十九元五角，一支票为九十二元，另一支票为二十七元五角，不审溢出之款为何人所捐？兹先将尊函所列九十元之收据附函寄上，其余款收据，俟奉函示后再行补寄。谨先申谢，顺颂大安。
>
> 弟蒋复璁敬启
五月二十五日
>
> 〔University of Chicago Library, Yuan T'ung-li Papers, Box 2〕

　　按："捐款者四人"中可以确定者为牛满江、孙兆年，其余二人，先生在该信纸底部标注"顾、瞿"，具体姓名待考，另由美汇台及在美各银行间转账似均有汇水损失。此件为文书代笔，落款处为其签名。

五月三十日

先生致信渡边宏，感谢寄赠图书，并请其将二十册《新疆研究文献目录》（日文本）寄送中国大陆图书馆，告知因为经费问题，暂时无法出版该目的中文本和西文本。

May 30, 1963

Dear Mr. Watanabe:

　　Owing to my absence from Washington, I have not been able to write to you earlier. I wish to thank you for the book you so kindly sent to me. I am glad to hear the exhibition of the Central Asian objects from the Otani Mission. You are very fortunate to have seen this interesting and instructive exhibition.

　　As to the twenty copies of our bibliography which were returned from Hong Kong (China Book Company), please mail them to Chinese libraries according to the enclosed list. Since you have already sent 10 copies by Naigai-Boeki, there will be some duplication.

Please let me know how much you have advanced for me for the postage, I shall refund.

My bibliography on Sinkiang in Chinese and European languages will not be published this year, as I have not much money now. The Japanese edition has cost me too much, and the sales from this bibliography are not very encouraging. As soon as I have more money, they will be published.

I am sending you from Hong Kong, a new book of mine on the *Russo-Chinese Treaties and Agreements Relating to Sinkiang*. I hope you may find it useful to you.

With cordial regards,

Yours sincerely,

T. L. Yuan

〔University of Chicago Library, Yuan T'ung-li Papers, Box 2〕

按：Otani Mission 即大谷光瑞考察队，二十世纪初曾三次至中亚、中国西部考古。Naigai-Boeki 直译为"内外贸易株式会社"，但具体指向何所，待考。该件另附一张寄送清单，包括北京、上海、天津、南京、济南、青岛、杭州、武昌、南昌、成都、广州、迪化的二十家图书馆。该件为录副。

余又苏致函先生，告知台北商务印书馆已对《新疆建置志》排版，并请在美就近与牧育才教授洽商乔治敦大学教职。

……道席：

六月廿二日大函及 Dr. White……。Dr. White 同日亦寄下一函，语气较致先生函更为客气，谓 Mr. Paul Chen 及其夫人尚留澳二年，目前尚未考虑加人。细思之，他所谓 Trained Librarian 之标准确不合，他是对的。敬谢雅意！

前日赴商务，《建置志》序跋已排印，影印甚快。本日赵叔诚先生面告，已有函及排印稿寄尊处，决于七月大驾赴欧前将校对及出版事办妥,以后即由商务照办,尚祈释念!

《大陆杂志》发表尊序及贞一兄跋,亦已拜读。

Georgetown 情形,承示知,至感。李惟果先生,同乡,舍表兄徐敦璋之同学,在重庆时常见面,他侄女李恕敏在台大作助教,近方到美。便中请代道候! Murphy 前函所谈,如系先生想像之任日本史及日语,或逐鹿之人少。昨日赴教堂查询 Murphy 近址,得知彼现尚在西部,通信处为 University of San Francisco。已去一函,询其与 Georgetown……,可否请先生就近咨询。唯未……教日本史之类事,恐有夺人位置之嫌,且不知其前谈……履历,谅 Murphy 已交去。

E. J. Murphy 为耶稣会,此间美籍耶稣会美籍神父,告以其事很可能。并谓该校图书馆及国会图书馆所藏耶稣会在东方活动史料甚丰。近年注意 The Story of the Jesuits in China and Japan,他们知之,故亦鼓励来 Georgetown。

Murphy 如有信到,拟请先生就近与该校洽谈,至感。为时尚不迟也。(《留美学生论文目录》,尚未到。)

专肃,并颂研安。

余又荪敬上
五月卅日晚。

〔University of Chicago Library, Yuan T'ung-li Papers, Box 1〕

按:"六月廿二日"当作"五月廿二日"。徐敦璋(1904—?),四川垫江人,清华大学毕业,1926 年赴美留学,威斯康星大学硕士、博士学位,归国后曾任南开大学、四川大学教授。[1] 该函四角破损,部分文字无由得见。翌日以航空信方式寄送。

刘麟生覆函先生,谈诸事。

守和先生馆长座右:

雒诵廿七日详示,多承厚谊,惭感深矣。椽笔亲抄,尤增弟之悆戾也,勿罪勿罪。富先生处能蝉联最佳,然不敢必闷葫芦贮药不可解也。前此曾奉一英文书,并有附件中文,谅入览,该函千祈付丙,附件当已存查,便希示及,尤感。昨日富先生示弟大陆刊印之《文物》,内有文论

---

① 《清华同学录》,1937 年 4 月,页 208-209。

米书,亦推重张丑之考证也。敬申谢悃,祇颂著作之兴日浓。

教小弟刘麟生谨上

30/5/63

〔University of Chicago Library, Yuan T'ung-li Papers, Box 1〕

五月三十一日

王伊同覆函先生,感谢寄赠陈衍诗话并谈所知学人存《四部丛刊》情况,另询金问泗所撰序言是否须请其重写。

老伯大人尊前:

敬禀者,刻奉五月廿九日手谕及《陈石遗诗话》一本,极见关爱,汗颜拜领。《四部丛刊》赵元任先生即有一部,往年张充和女士以三百金代购别一部转售卞学鑨夫人,价同,未必肯以原价出手。世骧兄本人亦有一部,更未必肯售矣。台湾艺文书局近刻《四库善本丛书》,拟将《四部丛刊》初、二、三编收入,然以商务版权关系不敢用《丛刊》旧名,实亦改头换面之事,未必能成否。近曾函“教部次长”邓传楷兄亦江阴人,南菁中学校友,早侄三二年代访《丛刊》,果得佳遇,价当略平,且看陈兄复音何如? 拙稿所存约十余本,非定稿,亦非卖品,只以 Boorman 君全书问世无期,因先印送国会图书馆,拟搜存自当寄呈,或酌以复本一二种互易何如? 公事不可私办也,一笑。又“金大使”原序晦涩嫩弱,且极芜乱,如需重写,乞示,否则无改削地,甚可憾耳。敬肃,专请金安。

侄伊同百拜

三十一日

〔University of Chicago Library, Yuan T'ung-li Papers, Box 1〕

按:《陈石遗诗话》即《石遗室诗话》。“拙稿”所指,待考。1961年3月,邓传楷(1912—1999)出任“教育部政务次长”。

马大任致函先生,请教《通志》《永乐大典》《史记》等书在国会图书馆分类法中主题分类问题。

May 31, 1963

Dear Dr. Yuan,

We are not quite sure of what the best place for Cheng Ch'iao's *T'ung Chih* in the L. C. classification should be. Could you give us your expert advice on this? Enclosed please find a stamped postcard with return address. Many thanks.

By the way, we are wondering why the *Yung-lo ta tien* is classified under AE17, which is a number for modern encyclopedias, instead of AE2 which is the early works. Could you enlighten us on this?

Also, *Shih Chi* of Ssu-ma Ch'ien is classified under DS748 which is Han Dynasty, i. e., the dynasty of the author, not the dynasty covered by the book. The *Shih Chi* covers more territory than the Han Dynasty. It seems to us this classification is a deviation from the usual practice. Probably there are some new rules concerning classifying Chinese books which we do not know. Could you also advise us on this matter? When convenient? Many thanks.

Sincerely

John T. Ma

Chinese Bibliographer

〔University of Chicago Library, Yuan T'ung-li Papers, Box 9〕

按：该函寄送国会图书馆，于 6 月 4 日送达。

五月

先生撰写《重印〈金辂筹笔〉序》。〔《金辂筹笔》,1964 年 5 月〕

先生撰写《重印〈戡定新疆记〉序》。〔《戡定新疆记》,1963 年 6 月〕

六月一日

王世杰致函先生,告知"国家长期发展科学委员会"补助款已经遵嘱存入台湾银行账户。

守和先生惠鉴：

"国家长期发展科学委员会"补助《数学家论著目录》印刷费台币一万五千元,现已由本院代为领到,如嘱存入台湾银行七三三二户内。是项目录,承五月三日函示已由印刷商以一百五十部交邮径寄"国家长期发展科学委员会",谅近日内可望寄到;届时当参酌前示外国学术机构及数学界学人名单,径行寄赠。知注特达。顺颂撰祺。

王世杰敬启

六月一日

〔University of Chicago Library, Yuan T'ung-li Papers, Box 8〕

　　按:"本院"即"中央研究院"。该函为打印件,落款处钤王世
杰印。

六月四日

余又荪致函先生,请在美代为谋划赴乔治敦大学任教事。

　　守和先生道席:

　　　　顷接牧育才神父自旧金山来函,谨转呈,恳祈就近代为接洽乔治
汤大学事。前承示李惟果先生在该校,杨君去日本。如杨君不返,则
其日本史及日文当可接替。不然,中文、中国史之类,与李、杨不冲突
之下,亦可任之(该校尚有研究部)。统祈就近相机洽办为感!

　　　　台大,因刘崇鋐将到 Fulbright Foundation 去,下年责任已决定加
到头上。一为历史学系主任,一为历史学研究所主任。只任教授,离
去容易。任此两个主任,则不便说走就走。刘寿民表示在台大维持至
六月底止。

　　　　目前乔治汤大学事未定,提不出强硬理由拒绝作两个主任事。台
大与北大、清华传统习惯同,人事有一定不成文规律也。

　　　　来美,一为经济上调济,一为更易环境,图获研究之益。甚盼其成也。

　　　　Dr. White 致先生函,谨附还。商务每次致先生函,均有副本交
来。印刷事已定夺矣。专肃奉恳,敬颂著安。

　　　　　　　　　　　　　　　　　　　　　　余又荪谨上

　　　　　　　　　　　　　　　　　　　　　　六,四

　　　　　　　〔University of Chicago Library, Yuan T'ung-li Papers, Box 1〕

六月七日

先生致信牧育才,期待来华盛顿面谈,并希望其建议乔治敦大学考虑聘请
余又荪担任日本史教职。

　　　　　　　　　　　　　　　　　　　　　　　June 7, 1963

Reverend Edward J. Murphy, S. J.

American Jesuits in China

284 Stanyan Street

San Francisco 18, California

Dear Reverend Murphy:

　　Professor Yu Yu-sen informed me that you expect to visit

Washington sometime in the summer, and I have been looking forward with much pleasure to seeing you. I know that you are now engaged in an important educational campaign for China, and I wish to extend to you my best wishes for your success.

As to the vacant chair in Japanese history at Georgetown, it looks that the University is looking for someone who can teach European history and also Japanese history. Since the number of students taking the latter course is limited, it does not seem easy for Professor Yu to be considered for this post. However, much can be accomplished after you talk with the authorities at Georgetown. It is therefore my hope that you could arrange to be here before his application is decided.

A considerable number of universities have offered courses in Japanese language as a result of the National Defense Act. If you should go to Los Angeles, you might ascertain the possibilities of openings at Loyola University there.

With sincere greetings,

Yours sincerely,

T. L. Yuan

〔University of Chicago Library, Yuan T'ung-li Papers, Box 1〕

按：Loyola University 即加州私立天主教罗耀拉大学。该件为录副。

杜希德覆函先生，感谢寄赠《新疆研究文献目录》（日文本），将撰写相关书讯并刊登在伦敦大学亚非学院公报。

7th June, 1963

Dear Dr. Yuan,

Thank you very much for your letter of the 25th May and also for the copy of the Bibliography of Japanese Works on Sinkiang. This looks very useful and I look forward to receiving the other bibliographies on Sinkiang which you mention in your letter. I will indeed write a notice of these notes in *BSOAS*, but at the moment we are very short of space, and the notice will probably be some time before appearing.

I shall be writing to you separately about your application to the U. C. C. after the Committee have met.

With very best wishes,

Yours sincerely,

Denis Twitchett

〔University of Chicago Library, Yuan T'ung-li Papers, Box 1〕

六月八日

先生致信马克尔,告知将寄赠《中国留英同学博士论文目录》给英国大学中国委员会委员,并询问英国大学中国委员会是否已就资助《中国艺术和考古目录》的申请予以讨论。

June 8, 1963

Dear Mr. Morkill:

About five weeks ago I was informed that copies of my *Guide to Doctoral Dissertations by Chinese Students in Britain* were mailed to me from Taipei. Although I have not yet received them, I am expecting to have them one of these days.

After their arrival, I shall send you a copy by air-mail, and shall post the rest to members of the UCC according to the addresses you gave me. I am afraid that when they arrive at their destinations, most of your members would be away for the summer.

In February I applied for a research grant from your Committee in connection with my work on a comprehensive Bibliography on Chinese Art and Archaeology. I wonder if members of your Expert Committee have had time to discuss it.

With sincere greetings,

Yours sincerely,

T. L. Yuan

〔University of Chicago Library, Yuan T'ung-li Papers, Box 1〕

按:该件为录副。

六月十日

先生致信赵叔诚,嘱《金铎筹笔》序言和附录各节印刷注意事项,并谈订购及支票等事。

台湾商务印书馆赵经理大鉴:

连奉五月十七日 83 号及五月三十日 89 号大函,拜悉——,并承惠赠《石遗室诗话》,尤感厚意。兹将各事列后:(一)《金铬筹笔》序文及附录三种连同《戡定新疆记》之序文、版权页等已于前日挂号寄上。此书因有附录四种,页数增多,其书价似须调整。凡字迹不清处,或在书上加以描写再行影印,或另行铅印一张附于该页之后,请尊酌。又"中央研究院"藏有一部,如系白纸字迹清楚,则改印该院藏本亦可,已请徐高阮君查明径告尊处矣。(二)《金铬筹笔》因工料较多,由敝处订购壹百部,其余三种印刷成本较低,敝处原拟每种订购五十部,兹改为七十五部,以副雅嘱。既作国际交换之用,应请改用穿线钉精装较为适合。(三)兹奉上新台币壹万元支票一纸,作为一部分之订购费,即乞查收示复。旬日前寄上《留美博士论文目录》八部,每部特价新台币壹百元(七折收款)。并乞《石遗室诗话》二部……

六月十日

〔University of Chicago Library, Yuan T'ung-li Papers, Box 1〕

按:此件为底稿,未写完。

杜希德致函先生,告知英国大学中国委员会专家委员会讨论后,拒绝资助编纂《中国艺术和考古目录》的申请。〔University of Chicago Library, Yuan T'ung-li Papers, Box 1〕

六月上旬

先生赴波士顿。〔University of Chicago Library, Yuan T'ung-li Papers, Box 1〕

六月十一日

刘麟生致片先生,告胡适所撰序文之信息,并寄送《艺林》。

守老馆长座右:

昨奉小札,谅登燕几。"董大使"所著《扶桑谐谭》已寻得。胡博士序文共五页半,时期为 Nov. 14, 1955,叶数为 ii 至 vii,俟印好后再承奉。附寄《艺林》三四月,乞存览,览后赐还。旧者已收到。敬请节劳憩游。

小弟麟生谨上

11/6/63

〔University of Chicago Library, Yuan T'ung-li Papers, Box 1〕

按:《扶桑谐谭》即董显光所著 *Japanese Sense of Humour*,1956 年东京印行。

六月十二日

先生覆信马大任,解释国会图书馆分类法中对中国古代文献并未留有充足的空间,并请补寄胡适文章的题名卡片。

June 12, 1963

Dear Mr. Ma:

On my return from a trip to Boston, I was glad to have your letter of May 31.

As I told you before, there is no adequate provision for Chinese old literature in L. C. classification schedules. I attach a list to answers to your questionnaire, although I do not believe there answers are satisfactory.

Sometime ago you supplied the title of Dr. Hu Shi's essay on Robert Browning. But your letter had been misplaced. Will you kindly copy the card for this title and send it to me at your early convenience?

Your sincerely,

T. L. Yuan

In order to avoid delays, please send your letters to my private address.

〔University of Chicago Library, Yuan T'ung-li Papers, Box 1〕

按:Dr. Hu Shi's essay on Robert Browning 应指 A Defense of Browning Optimism,参见 1962 年 3 月 29 日马大任覆先生函。该件为录副。

六月十三日

刘麟生覆函先生,告诸事。

守和尊兄勋右:

(一)顷诵十日翰教,祗承一是;(二)伊同先生五律遵命酌易数字,敬候两公裁择为幸;(三)胡博士序文已印就奉上乞察,收据小纸亦乞备案;(四)此书无出售地点及铺名,当时系赠送性也;(五)题名录仅有光绪 5、13、19、24 年,并闻。匆匆,敬请俪安。

教小弟刘麟生谨上

13/6/63

伊同兄统此问候。

〔University of Chicago Library, Yuan T'ung-li Papers, Box 1〕

梁实秋覆函先生,告此前支票因故无法兑现,并建议预开一万元支票,将来多退少补。

守和先生:

接奉赐示,即趋访黎烈文教授,译稿已在进行,可以如期完成,不至误期。前收到之支票(台币壹千元)一纸亦已转交。惟前日黎先生将支票返还,谓在银行不能兑现,因签盖不符之故。兹将支票及退票单附上,乞察收。往返写信费时,此款不必再寄。黎先生提议可否请先生开一支票,票面开一万元台币,将来多退少补,支票兑现日期可写七月十日,交由秋暂为保管,届时全稿译成,即由秋交付支票,钱稿两讫,稿件可以及时邮上,不至误时日。不知是否可行,乞赐示。

毛笔四枝已买好,日内寄上。匆上,即请大安。

受业梁实秋顿首

六,十三

〔University of Chicago Library, Yuan T'ung-li Papers, Box 8〕

六月十七日

先生致信马克尔,告知寄出《中国留英同学博士论文目录》。

June 17, 1963

Dear Mr. Morkill:

I have mailed over 60 copies of the brochure on Doctoral Dissertations to British institutions, including those addresses which you kindly gave me. I hope that it may be of some use to these interested in the promotion of Sino-British cultural relations.

I expect to stay in London for a week beginning July 16 on my way to Germany. I shall look forward with much pleasure to seeing you.

With sincere greetings,

Yours sincerely,

T. L. Yuan

〔University of Chicago Library, Yuan T'ung-li Papers, Box 1〕

按:该件为录副。

六月十九日

先生致信郑通,寄上美金支票一张,并告《新疆国界图志》有两卷错字太多,请务必仔细改正且加紧印刷。

> 新华印刷公司郑经理大鉴:
>
> 　接到6、10大函,详悉种切。制成纸型,前已同意,今后再版,当请贵公司上机印刷,其他估价似较过昂,容再函达。兹先寄上美金壹百元支票一纸,即希查收示复。《新疆国界图志》卷七、卷八错字甚多,务请查照敝人所改者,一一改正。如能负责校对,即不必再行寄下矣。上次《中俄西北条约集》末校改完后,相隔许久时日,方始印出。订购人颇为不满。兹《新疆国界图志》全部末校,均已改正,即希照改后,即行付印,万勿耽搁过久,是为至要。此书印好,全部印刷费均可付清矣。顺候时祉。
>
> 袁同礼顿首
>
> 六月十九日

〔University of Chicago Library, Yuan T'ung-li Papers, Box 1〕

　　按:此件为底稿。

六月二十日

宋晞覆函先生,告知所询信息并寄赠《中国留英同学博士论文目录》抽印本。

> 守和先生道鉴:
>
> 　五月卅日手示祗悉。本院出版之期刊论文索引,已出版者至三卷六期,七至十期均已付印,为印刷厂所搁。据经办人员称,正催印中,不日即可出版。附来嘱查之索引,除四条无法查到外,均已注明。兹将原件奉上,请查收。关于尊著《留英学生博士名录》之抽印本,免费奉赠,不另收费。《文化季刊》之论文英文欠佳,恒慕义先生之建议甚为感激,今后尽可能请外籍学者或神父先为润色,以求完美。承示荷兰出版宋史专刊两种,至以为感。余不尽陈。专此,祗颂撰祺。
>
> 后学宋晞敬上
>
> 六月二十日

〔University of Chicago Library, Yuan T'ung-li Papers, Box 1〕

　　按:"本院"应指"国防研究院"。

六月二十二日

闻汝贤致函先生,请在美代为推介《词牌汇释》。

> 同礼先生道席:
>
> 　　久闻先生典校兰台,饮誉盟邦,宗仰之余,时驰向往之忱。项晤"教部"刘首席参事英士先生谈及先生,嘱径函请益。缘鄙人于此间各大学讲授词学之余,纂辑《词牌汇释》一书,其旨趣悉载是书叙例,兹寄奉一册,恭候郢政,并乞赐予多方推介,至为感幸。兹将此间报纸披露消息及广告附寄二份,俾便游扬。以先生之清望,如获鼎助,庶不致使此冷门著作□罹覆瓿之厄,幸甚幸甚。耑此,敬候旅安。
>
> 　　附广告及出版消息各一则,至拙书《词牌汇释》一本,统希察收。海天在望,企候佳音。
>
> 愚弟闻汝贤顿首
> 六,廿二
> 〔University of Chicago Library, Yuan T'ung-li Papers, Box 8〕

　　按:闻汝贤(1902—1986),湖北人,早年留学日本,抗战胜利后曾任南京《和平日报》主笔,1950年由香港赴台。《词牌汇释》,1963年5月初版,售价新台币贰佰元。该函于6月26日送达。

六月下旬

先生赴医院检查身体。〔University of Chicago Library, Yuan T'ung-li Papers, Box 1〕

六月二十九日

先生致信赵叔诚,寄上《金轺筹笔》序跋末校并谈附录注意细节。

> 台湾商务印书馆赵经理大鉴:
>
> 　　奉到6月11日第95号及6月24日103号大函,拜悉种切。兹将各事分别列后:
>
> 　　(一)序跋末校又重校一次,随函奉上。《金韶筹笔》附录四种文字较多,其末校请于八月二十以前寄到,以便返美后即可校阅,再行奉上。
>
> 　　(二)各书页内版口大小,请参照《石遗室诗话》及《中俄西北条约集》已由香港邮寄。
>
> 　　(三)第二批印制费拟交纽约中国银行汇上美金250元,收到后望示知。

（四）《金韶筹笔》附录四有关人物履历简表及后记，另邮寄上。

（五）《金韶筹笔》正文卷四之后，应有和约专条及改订陆路通商章程，寄上哈佛藏本《挹秀山房丛书》本。有无和约专条及改订陆路通商章程，请在该书内代为一查，如万一无此种资料，只得排印。兹将无锡杨氏刊本所载者予以照相，与附录四一并寄上，以备万一_{如哈佛已有，则作废}。

六月廿九日

〔University of Chicago Library, Yuan T'ung-li Papers, Box 1〕

按：《金韶筹笔》当作《金轺筹笔》。此件为底稿。

刘麟生致片先生，告房兆楹、杜联喆夫妇将来哥伦比亚大学参加《明代名人传》项目，其职位因此不保。

守老馆长著席：

兹密陈者，金山学友见告，谓房君伉俪将来纽任明史事，则弟与周君之不克蝉联，自在意料之中。旌节莅此，乞先示知，以便约谭候教。敬请双安，并盼珍摄。

小弟宣阁上肃
六，廿九

〔University of Chicago Library, Yuan T'ung-li Papers, Box 1〕

七月一日

徐高阮覆函先生，商讨排印《胡适先生西文著作目录》细节及与台湾商务印书馆印书事。

守和先生：

月来迭奉三示，附胡先生日记片断、《胡先生西文著作目录》及增改数页、《金轺筹笔》序诸件，深为感幸。乃中间未能早覆，至乞赐谅。

《金轺筹笔》，此间竟无挹秀本。经查台湾各处，未得此丛书，然后始与商务赵叔诚先生见面，于彼处得见先生寄来挹秀黄纸本。此本自不能印得甚好，又字迹有模糊处，须描补。赵先生云将先印尊处所寄其他数种，最后印此《筹笔》，当在二个月后。挹秀白纸本既不可得，《小方壶舆地丛钞》本为白纸本，不知可用否？先生不用此本，谅有理由。万一此本可用，此间所藏之本自可借用，先生可来一信给蓝乾章君（在此间图书馆负责），由高阮代为借用，只按例赠书十册即可。此等事务,高阮应当尽微力,先生请勿客气。唯恐先生不愿用小方壶本耳。

《胡先生西文著作目录》,先生与 Delafield 增补之工作,极令人感佩。Delafield 先生前请特为致谢。兹有数小节须与先生商之。一、最后增翻译(成德文)之作品一节,然前面亦有译成英文之若干篇,是否可予抽出,改列在此最后一节内? 二、此最后一节内有法文之评论项,为数不多,是否可以省去? 三、Books 及 Periodical articles 部分有若干演说评论等,且有 extract, gist,是否可以抽出,另成一节,标 Addresses, Statements & Comments Speeches? 若如此分类,用何字样,请注意示及。因先生亦曾提到,有若干篇目,胡先生不欲列入著作目录。据高阮所知,胡先生对他人所录演讲词,颇不愿列入,今为保存资料,似应列入,然以分别开来为宜。然而如此作法,似又不得不将胡先生自写之稿、记录稿及摘要等列在一起矣。此处,若如此办法,又当如何? 仍祈见示。尊稿 11 页之一项:My people and the Japanese 注"译自 The *People's Tribune*",此系何刊物? 乞示。因有英文刊物名 *People's Tribune* 也。

又,胡先生一九五九在夏威夷东亚哲学会所提之论文,当列入何栏? 演说? 期刊文字,书之一部分? 请示。尊目此题分见九卷一、二期之《东亚哲学》及一九六二之《哲学与文化:东方与西方》。惟九卷一、二《东亚哲学》所载仅四面,想系一种摘要。然否? 亦乞分神及之。

此间为时间上种种要求,或者先付排。高阮大胆先按上陈宗旨付排,但排字亦要相当时间,仍候尊示为决定。乞即覆示为感。《金辂筹笔》序稍迟即送《大陆杂志》发表,请勿念。匆草,乞赐谅。迟迟奉覆,尤乞赐谅。专上,敬请道安。

后学高阮敬上

七月一日

如□所□改动,目次是否如下:

1.Books

2.Articles forming part of books

3.Pamphlets

4.Periodical articles

5.Book reviews

6.Forewords

7.Addresses

8.Translations of Hu Shih's writings

乞示。

〔University of Chicago Library, Yuan T'ung-li Papers, Box 2〕

按：Bibliography of Dr. Hu Shih's Writings in Western Languages（《胡适先生西文著作目录》）目次名称及顺序大致如信中所列，只是 Forewords 改为 Introductions, Forewords and Prefaces; Adresses 改为 Addresses, Statements, Comments, Etc., 后又加上 Addenda（附录）。

刘麟生覆函先生，谈诸事。

守和尊兄博士勋右：

（一）顷诵廿六日明教，敬审大贤入院检查，健康如昔，引为快慰。（二）《何翰林集》及《四友斋丛说》，此间均备，故弟写《何良俊传》，尚可尽情发挥也。（三）承椽笔抄示王兆云书所载《都穆传》，甚可珍视，感谢之至。（四）富先生已往 N. H.避暑，为时一月，弟拟于本月十五日休假一周。（五）如房君伉俪来此乞暂秘之，弟与周君自不易蝉联，已托友留意，仍盼贤者随时观察也。（六）轺驾将由波城出发，远违教诲，盼归时可在此承训耳。敬颂双绥。

小弟麟生谨上

七月一日夜

〔University of Chicago Library, Yuan T'ung-li Papers, Box 1〕

普实克致函先生，告知其仍无法从北京获得先生所需书籍，而派人前往北京似乎又无希望。

July 1, 1963

My dear Professor YUAN,

I am extremely sorry that until now we were not able to procure for you the book you needed from Peking. We hoped that a member of our staff will go to Peking and arrange the matter personally, because this seemed to us the only way to do it. Sorry to say that due to the circumstances until now we are not in a position to send anybody to Peking, even if we still have some hope for September next.

If our attempts are futile, I shall pay you the price of the book in US Dollars. We were trying our best, but you know how the things are.

I wish you much success in your work and remain with my very best wishes.

Very sincerely yours,

Professor Jaroslav Průšek

〔University of Chicago Library, Yuan T'ung-li Papers, Box 3〕

七月二日

王伊同覆函先生,感谢寄赠《中国留英同学博士论文目录》。

老伯大人尊前:

敬禀者,晨甫发寸禀,尔后返舍得《国人留英博士论文目录》。昨读拙稿,除留美外,大人手增"留英"两字,因知此书已传世,初不意厚赐若是之速也。郑老先生序不卑不亢,英文尤老练,甚可佩。留英国人究不若留美之众,且杂然其中不乏旧识,略晚辈如邱绪瑶、崔枋、黄昆(以上皆燕京校友),久不知其下落,且前闻有意出国,初不料已学成多年,刻或返国矣,则意外安慰也。拜谢拜谢。敬请旅安。

侄伊同再拜

七,二

〔University of Chicago Library, Yuan T'ung-li Papers, Box 1〕

按:"拙稿"应指先生嘱王伊同撰写的书评介绍类文字。邱绪瑶(Chiu Hsu-yao),女,1953 年在伯明翰大学获博士学位,其论文题目为 The development of the foreign trade of China and her trade with the United Kingdom。崔枋(Tsui Fang),1954 年在利物浦大学获博士学位,其论文题目为 A study of spark channels。黄昆(Huang Kun,1919—2005),生于北京,物理学家,1941 年毕业于燕京大学,后入西南联合大学攻读研究生,1948 年获布里斯托大学(University of Bristol)博士学位,其论文题目为 Some consideration in the theory of alloys, together with a discussion of the binding energies of the lightest nuclei,1951 年归国并在北京大学执教。

七月三日

先生致信赵叔诚，谈《金轺筹笔》印刷各细节，并告赴欧行期。

台湾商务印书馆赵经理惠鉴：

近奉 6 月 11 日第 95 号及 6 月 24 日第 103 号大函，拜悉种切。兹将各事分陈如下：

（壹）承寄下各书序跋末校，业经重校随函奉还，即希尊处照改后再校一次，以资审慎。

（贰）承询各书页内版口大小，请参照《石遗室诗话》及《中俄西北条约集》之样式已函香港寄上，收到后示知为盼。

（叁）《金轺筹笔》正文卷四之后应有（一）合约（二）专条（三）改订陆路通商章程。前寄上哈佛所藏《艳秀山房丛书》本，不识有无此项文件，务请在该书内代为一查，如未刊载，则用本日寄上之件由他本照的，惟须排印。

（肆）《金轺筹笔》除正文及上项文件外，另有附录四种，其附录一、二、三前已寄上，兹将附录四十一页及后记二页另邮寄上，即希付排，并乞于八月二十日左右将末校寄下一阅。

（伍）第二批印制费已委托纽约中国银行汇上美金贰百伍拾元，收到后并盼示知。

（陆）每书出版后，请查照前函规定之部数交邮寄下，其邮费应由尊处担负，惟每包不得超过十五部，并乞包装坚固以免损坏，如装入坚固纸盒，再用报纸填满更妥。

（柒）各书影印完毕，即希用平邮挂号寄下，内中有借自他人者，必须早日归还也。专此，敬候时祉。

袁同礼拜上
七月三日

又弟十三日离美赴欧，八月二十日返美，如有信件书籍，均请寄至华京舍下。万一有特事须商榷者，请于七月廿三日以前寄至伦敦旅馆留交（七月廿三日以后住址不定，请寄华京），T. L. Yuan, Gresham Hotel, 36-38 Bloomsbury Street, London, W. C. 1, England.

〔University of Chicago Library, Yuan T'ung-li Papers, Box 1〕

按：此件为底稿。

七月四日

罗家伦致函先生,寄上书单两份请分别办理购书。

> 守和吾兄道鉴:
>
> 多时未能函候起居,甚为悬念!兹汇奉美金五百元,并书目名单两份,烦请照单订购。因各书内容及分别采购地点不同,将单分为(1)(2)(3)(4)号。其中(1)号单内所开 *The War Against Japan* 为英国新闻处出版,地址为 British Information Services, 845 Thrid Avenue, New York 22, N. Y.(附该处来卡一纸)。此书共为五卷,单上仅开列已出版之第一、二、三三卷,如第四、五卷亦已出版,即请一并订购。至第(4)号单所开向英伦购买诸书,为节省时间计,如能在美就近购得(尤其是单上开明原在美国出版),请即在美订购。为赶速办理本年会计年度报销手续,盼能将此批购书尽速购妥,并烦清神将发票尽先航空邮递寄下,书籍仍用挂号海运为荷。诸事多承劳神,不胜感谢之至!专此,敬颂道祺!
>
> 　　　　　　　　　　　　　　　　　弟罗家伦敬启
> 　　　　　　　　　　　　　　　　　　七,四,台北
>
> 附奉台湾银行 C72544 美金五百元汇票一张,本年三月至六月份征集费缴款台币二千元收据一张。

　　　　　　　〔University of Chicago Library, Yuan T'ung-li Papers, Box 1〕

　　　　按:此件为文书代笔,落款处为其签名,于 7 月 11 日送达。

刘国蓁致函先生,转寄袁道冲信,并告知与新华印刷厂交涉款项经过和问题。

> 守和博士先生尊鉴:
>
> 敬启者,月前拜奉手教敬悉,并新华估计单及发票并代寄令岳信一函,均已妥收及代邮转去。日前得奉令岳来信嘱代转呈,兹特奉上,敬希察收为幸。关于新华印费事,该经手人郑通甚为狡侩,态度不好,而且现时情形是俗语有云"打死狗正讲价"甚为切合。初时与其交涉,则说晚等"不在行",如再不明白可问罗香林教授,当可清楚。因估价单内有注明页数多少,待印成时方能计实及其他开销,俱是后来件所加入。晚询问及"纸型工料"一项一百九十六元之多,此项不入估价单内,他取出与晚看,原来是一大叠纸皮,是制版时用以造模者,

若留存,如再版时不必再造,如不再版大可不用,而是可有可无。他不对晚讲明,但他对罗教授则有谓,曾写信问及先生需要否? 而先生未有答覆,是以将其保留。晚与罗教授通电话并着人交两单与其审查,请他与其接洽并帮忙着其减低价钱,随后他答谓该价目比之港大则相宜,比之普通刊物则较贵,他允与新华交涉。但经其与郑通商谈后,晚再与郑通交涉,他仍肯定的谓一文不减,更兼付款如此迟慢,亦有阻碍也,正是莫奈他何。当初晚以为该公司刊件亦可靠得住,但事情演变不甚满意,晚亦觉惭愧也。付来新华单两张,本拟奉回,但因重量关系,是以未果。此乃大概情形,特此奉闻。尊意以为如何? 敬希示知为幸。尚有如书背大名印得高及漏字等,他谓事前皆有付稿与尊处校对,似乎有些卸责。总之,是他是合而驳他是不合而已。又闻尊处另有一部交其代印,又未知如何处理也。港中水荒稍为解困,因连日皆有雨落,而且前日下豪雨六小时,得水逾六亿加仑,更兼政府已动用运油船三艘,穿梭式到珠江运淡水,虽然不多,但可救燃眉之急也。现仍四日供水一次,每次四小时而已。专此,敬请撰安。

愚晚国蓁顿首

一九六三年七月四日

〔袁同礼家人提供〕

七月五日

先生致信钱存训,寄书两种请芝加哥大学图书馆订购并告知去欧计划。

公垂吾兄:

小书两种,均系宣传品,请转总馆采购处,想可订购。因印刷太坏,故不愿赠送,而成本一时又无法收回也。一周内因事赴欧,八月杪可返。顺颂暑祺。

同礼顿首

七,五

〔钱孝文藏札〕

按:“小书两种”,一种应为《中俄西北条约集》,另一种应为《现代中国数学研究目录》。

七月六日

先生致信 Wolfgang Seuberlich,感谢寄送《日本法律书目补编》,并告将赴欧洲收集有关中国新疆、艺术品资料,请便中告知此方面收藏丰富的图书馆及特色馆藏。

July 6, 1963

Dear Dr. Seuberlich:

　　I am much obliged to you for your kindness in sending me the Third Supplementary List to the Bibliography of Japanese Law complied by Miss Koschel. Since writing to you last I wrote to a Japanese editor to explore the possibilities of having it published, but so far there is no answer.

　　I plan to pay a short visit to Europe for the purpose of gathering material on Sinkiang and on Chinese art in German collections. If it is convenient to you, could you send me a list of leading libraries in which material of this can be found. I have to give up my trip to Berlin because of pressure of time, but I would appreciate the address of Miss Lessing (now married) and her Museum.

　　My address up to July 23rd will be care of Gresham Hotel, 36 Bloomsbury Street, London, W. C. 1.

　　Thanking you once more for your courtesy,

Yours sincerely,

T. L. Yuan

〔袁同礼家人提供〕

七月七日

先生致信牟复礼,再次推荐刘麟生前往普林斯顿大学协助编撰中文善本书目。〔University of Chicago Library, Yuan T'ung-li Papers, Box 1〕

七月八日

先生致信大维德爵士夫妇,感谢寄赠藏品目录,并告知将于七月中旬抵达伦敦,届时拜访。

July 8, 1963

Dear Sir Percival and Lady David:

　　Words fail me to express to you my deep gratitude for your kindness in sending me a copy of your monumental catalogue which arrived while I was touring in the west coast. Receiving such a magnificent gift, I can think of no appropriate words to express my feeling. All I can say is that I shall always treasure it as a token of our friendship.

In connection with my work on a comprehensive bibliography on Chinese art and archaeology, I applied for a research grant from the Universities' China Committee in London. Although the competition is rather keen, I had hoped that my application might be favorably considered in view of the fact that Mr. Gray is a member of the Expert Committee. Although it was finally turned down, I have decided to come to London for a brief visit.

I have just □□□□ the British visa and shall arrive July 16th. I shall remain about a week in London and am looking forward with much pleasure to seeing you. Meanwhile please accept my heartfelt thanks for your generosity and kindness.

Sincerely,

Yuan T'ung-li

〔University of Chicago Library, Yuan T'ung-li Papers, Box 8〕

按：此件为附录，□□□□处有涂抹，无法辨识。

朱文长致函先生，意欲订购《新疆研究丛刊》。

守和老伯赐鉴：

五月间华府匆匆一面，未及畅谈为憾！世侄之论文前经荷兰Mouton Co.承印，最近已可望出书，然延搁经年，不免有需要增订处。老伯主编之《新疆研究丛刊》，其中材料极富，而世侄处仅有第二种《日文文献目录》一种。不知其他九种，已否出书？何处可以购买？书价若干？能否由世侄将款寄呈尊处代购？便中请见示为感！斯大兄朝夕聚首，常道及盛德，景仰更深。而对西疆之兴趣如此之浓，尤使后辈兴奋。拙作成形后尚寄呈斧正！肃此，即请撰安！

世侄朱文长敬上

七月八日

〔袁同礼家人提供〕

按：朱文长的博士论文题目应为 The Moslem Rebellion in Northwest China 1862-1878: a study of government minority policy，1966 年由 Mouton & Co 出版，为该社《中亚研究丛书》第五种。

七月九日

杨联陞覆函先生，感谢寄赠《中俄西北条约集》并告身体已经复元。

> 守和先生史席：
>
> 今日收到六月廿七手示，并大著《中俄西北条约集》乙册，多谢多谢。贱恙经手术后已全恢复，步履如常，承关注，不胜感激。大著搜罗宏富，王序文字甚佳，金序与先生自序则语重心长，发人深省。参考文献似可加列近代史所之《中俄关系史料》，其《新疆边防》一册尤为重要。匆此布谢，即请暑安。
>
> 晚学联陞拜
> 一九六三年七月九日
> 〔University of Chicago Library, Yuan T'ung-li Papers, Box 8〕

七月十日

先生致信钱存训，介绍委托香港印刷所排印经验。

> 公垂吾兄著席：
>
> 昨奉手教并 Crawford 艺术目录书评，发挥尽致，佩甚佩甚，大著译成中文定可风行一时。惟香港工人中文程度太低，末校改正后仍有错字，真不知如何改进，故《新疆丛刊》后五种改为影印，惟不能加以标点，是可惜耳！香港排工印价，如印七百五十部，每页印价港币二十四元，最好找二三家同时估价，选其肯负责校对者，可省精力不少也。中文译本将内容稍加更动，极表赞成，或用李润章前例，委托新亚书院出版，由院负校对之责以及与印工接洽一切，亦良法也。新华印刷公司不太负责，去年十月交稿，今年六月始印出，实太迟缓。余俟再函。敬候暑棋。
>
> 弟同礼顿首
> 七，十日
> 〔钱孝文藏札〕

按："Crawford 艺术目录书评"即钱存训对史克门编 *Chinese Calligraphy and Painting in the Collection of John M. Crawford. Jr*

所作之书评,刊登于 *Papers of the Bibliographical Society of America*, 1963。《新疆研究丛刊》后五种为《新疆国界图志》《西疆交涉志要》《金轺筹笔》《新疆建置志》《戡定新疆记》。"李润章前例"应指李书华所著《中国印刷术的起源》,1962 年 10 月由香港新亚研究所出版。

先生致信香港新华印刷公司(郑通),寄上美金支票一张。

　　……十五部为要,又新书出版时应呈送表格,想稍缓呈送无妨也。关于《西北条约集》每页正文工料,请按每页二十四元计算,与《新疆国界图志》相同,谅荷同意。代邮寄各书于台北、日本者,均尚无信来,不识何日付邮,即希一查。兹奉上美金一百叁拾元($130)支票一纸,即希查收示复为荷。顺候大安。

袁同礼顿首
七月十日

附邮寄单一纸。

〔University of Chicago Library, Yuan T'ung-li Papers, Box 1〕

　　按:此件为底稿,仅存最后 1 页,先生在末尾处标注"前页述总序、总目退,封面重写,另制板,不要纸型,印 750 寄来 100,包装不严。"

七月十一日

先生覆信罗家伦,告知将赴英伦,并建议部分书籍可在英国购买。

　　日前寄一航签,谅登记室。顷奉七月四日手教并美金五百元汇票一纸、书目名单两份,均已拜收。所需各书系尊处选目,虽系 Paragon 书店目录普通书籍,但该店系犹太书商,索价过昂,除美国出版之书不得不在此购买外,其欧洲出版者,拟日内到伦敦后,分交两家配购径行寄上将发票航邮寄上,可节省若干外汇,谅荷同意。弟八月二十日返美,在欧通讯处由郭有守兄收转。余容再陈。

七月十一日

〔University of Chicago Library, Yuan T'ung-li Papers, Box 1〕

　　按:此件为底稿。

先生致信芝加哥大学出版社,为"国史馆"续订 *Journal of Modern History*。

〔University of Chicago Library, Yuan T'ung-li Papers, Box 1〕

七月十二日

先生致信富路德,就房兆楹、杜联喆夫妇将加入哥伦比亚大学协助开展《明代名人传》项目表示祝贺,并希望其能够继续聘用刘麟生协助编纂。

July 12, 1963

Professor L. Carrington Goodrich

640W. 238th Street

New York 63, N. Y.

Dear Professor Goodrich:

　　Dr. Hummel called me up the other day informing me that you have asked the Fangs to join your staff. This is good news to all of us, as we feel the Fangs will make valuable contributions to your project.

　　I told Dr. Hummel about Mr. L. S. Liu's scholarly accomplishments. From what I told him, he feels that men of Mr. Liu's type are getting rare these days and you are to be congratulated for his collaboration. We are confident that if you would keep Mr. Liu to work on the project, the "Trio" will work harmoniously under your able leadership. You certainly had a better start than Boorman's who has wasted much unnecessary effort.

　　I am off for Europe for five weeks. Meanwhile, let me thank you for your courtesy extended to Mr. Liu.

　　With best wishes for a pleasant summer.

Sincerely,

T. L. Yuan

〔University of Chicago Library, Yuan T'ung-li Papers, Box 1〕

按:Boorman's who has wasted much unnecessary effort 应指其主持的 *Biographical Dictionary of Republican China*(《中华民国名人辞典》)项目。该件为录副。

梁敬錞致函先生,感谢寄赠《中俄西北条约集》,并询王伊同生平履历及书籍印刷等事。

守和学长兄大鉴:

　　前周奉到《中俄西北条约集》,因适有山中之行,带往山上循读至暮。此书材料翔实,最为可贵,治疆史者必不能不早置一编,有功士林,此亦最著,非敢阿所好也。王伊同先生之序,亦甚可读,因其胎息甚厚,知其为宿学,而不知其人在何处,系何作业,便中乞示之。又此书由新华承印,工价如何,校对方法如何,弟年底或有一书出,愿得指示。闻现时影印比铅印更廉,确否? 专此奉谢,并请著安。

弟鋕叩上
七,十二

〔University of Chicago Library, Yuan T'ung-li Papers, Box 2〕

按:“王伊同先生之序”即书前所冠《新疆研究丛刊总序》,为王伊同1962年(壬寅)冬以文言撰写。“新华”即此书承印公司——新华印刷股份公司(香港西营盘荔安里十五号)。

汪季千致函先生,告已将《中俄西北条约集》转校图书馆,并询问有无可能协助其将在香港购得书中之复本售与该馆。

守和先生惠鉴:

书已收到,即转图书馆,惟外人办事松懈异常,时值暑令,签字人多不在,付款恐在九月后矣。第一次书单已查明,移交经办书记,想不久必有通知也。晚前在香港、东京购书甚多,因指挥不灵,若干书籍迄未购到,而购得者常有重复,兹拟将其中若干转卖图书馆,而未便自卖自买,是否可用我丈名义。如蒙俞允,请寄空白发票六纸(一式须三份也),将来手续完毕后,当即函陈,俟款到尊处再行拨下。事并不急,如有不便之处,无所容心也。即颂旅绥。

晚汪季千顿首
七,十二

〔University of Chicago Library, Yuan T'ung-li Papers, Box 2〕

按:时,汪季千在北卡罗来纳大学(The University of North Carolina)任教。

七月中上旬

先生致信郭廷以(美国),告知将赴欧洲搜集史料。〔《郭量宇先生日记残稿》,页422〕

按:此信于15日送达。

七月十三日

先生离开美国前往英国。

七月中旬　伦敦

先生致信郭廷以,对《中华民国史事日志》颇为赞许。〔《郭量宇先生日记残稿》,页423〕

　　　　按:此信于18日送达。

七月十六日

朱文长致函先生,请告知其父朱经农著述信息,并请核对细节。

　　守和老伯赐鉴:

　　　　七月十一日赐示敬悉。今谨寄奉订书单一份,乞查收。

　　　　承告先父遗作两种,《中学国语课程的讨论》一文未见到。可否请将《新闻报教育特刊》之出版年月及地址,以及何处图书馆藏有此书,于便中见示?又《初中课程的讨论》一文虽收入,但系《教育杂志》十六卷三、四、七号及十七卷五号等共八篇,而非十六卷五号,不知是否由于笔误?

　　　　欧行必甚愉快,望旅途保重。

　　　　即请撰安!

　　　　　　　　　　　　　　　　　　　　　世侄朱文长敬上

　　　　　　　　　　　　　　　　　　　　　七月十六日

　　　　　　〔University of Chicago Library, Yuan T'ung-li Papers, Box 3〕

七月下旬

先生离开英国前往欧陆游历,曾在法国、瑞士等小住。〔《思忆录》,中文部分页138〕

　　　　按:此时,袁澄夫妇正在南德度假,请先生及夫人前往巴特海新哈尔(Bad Reichenhall)休息,先生本已答应,后又因无暇婉拒。

七月三十日

梅贻宝覆函先生,告知已按先生所托购书、赠书,并谈编排《清华学报》哲学论文专号进展。

　　守和吾兄台鉴:

　　　　手示敬悉。家嫂久无信来,现仍住台北。据闻有意动身由英转美,但无确讯。

　　　　承寄近著二种两份。一份已转学校圕,并嘱照发票付款,盼无窒碍。通常手续,教员只可提荐书名,购置应由圕直接处理也。

另一份书款 4.50,弟附奉支票一纸。《西北条约》则已赠送张欣宝君。此间中国中心购置图书,仍应由大学圕办理也。

今年暑期较热。弟正赶编《清华学报》哲学论文专号,日内盼能交稿付邮,当较清凉多矣。此候合府钧吉。

弟贻宝上

七月卅日

明春亚洲学会在华京举行,届期当携逢吉登府候安。

〔University of Chicago Library, Yuan T'ung-li Papers, Box 2〕

按:"张欣宝"即张馨保。"中国中心"应指爱荷华州立大学(Iowa State University)中国语言文化中心(Chinese Language and Area Center)。

七月三十一日

李书田致函先生,寄上旧作两种。

守和吾兄道右:

顷悉吾兄又有 *Bibliography of Chinese Mathematics 1918-1960* 之作。兹特附奉弟"一九六〇"年以前旧作二则。上述《中国数学论文目录》,不知售价几何? 专此,并请暑安。

弟李书田顿首

七,卅一

另一另寄。

〔University of Chicago Library, Yuan T'ung-li Papers, Box 9〕

八月八日

王伊同致函先生,问安并告郑华即将来匹兹堡大学任教。

老伯大人尊前:

敬禀者,英伦归来,谅多新获,不悉曾晤郑德坤、吴世昌诸兄否? 此间公事房以郑华女士即到,顿不敷用,因迁入四楼,电话仍为 621-3500 Ext. 7474。寒舍赁约月底到期,正勘居中,一俟定夺再闻。敬禀,并叩金安。

侄伊同再拜

八月八日

〔袁同礼家人提供〕

刘国蓁致函先生，寄上代转书札并告新华印刷厂暂停排印等待付款等事。

> 守和博士先生尊鉴：
>
> 　　敬启者，未修书敬候又已月余，恭维文祺纳燕，撰祉延鸿，至以为颂。上月四日奉上芜函，并附令岳丈大人信，量邀尊览矣。日前接到上海市松江袁鹏先生来信，日昨又奉到令岳来函，兹一并奉上，敬希察收为幸。前函有说及关于新华印刷事，想已亮察。昨接新华来电话，云及前印妥之书，至今尚未结算清楚，而第二部亦已排好，如有款付来，即可开工印刷，倘若不收到款项，则将其停顿而已，故顺为奉闻。又悉先生可能往欧洲一行，未悉已返回美京否也？便中敬希示知为幸。尊账四月时存六十三元二角五分，支寄台北空邮费第一次十四元，第贰次六元一角五分，寄令岳邮费五角，前后三次（连此次）空邮费共六元，总共支廿六元六角五分，比对尚存卅六元六角在晚处也。港中天气真热，仍是四天一次供水，十分难捱，虽然已有雨落，但仍是不足，另有十艘运水船载运珠江水接济，不无少补矣。匆匆，余当续陈。专此，敬请撰安。
>
> 愚晚国蓁顿首
一九六三年八月八日灯下
>
> 〔袁同礼家人提供〕

八月九日

刘麟生致函先生，告《明代名人传》项目已结束，工作无法延聘。

> 守和先生博士勋鉴：
>
> 　　盛暑远游，必多建树，甚佩，甚颂。富先生于前日告弟等三人，以经费有限，工作只得至本月底为止云云。黄君谓自系迎房君也。黄君将往 N. C. 授课，并以奉闻。伫候台旌，无任延企。敬请旅安。
>
> 夫人前候安。
>
> 小弟麟生顿首
八，九
>
> 〔University of Chicago Library, Yuan T'ung-li Papers, Box 1〕

八月十五日

钱思亮致函先生，告知中基会执委会已批准补助《中国留欧大陆各国博士论文目录》出版费。

守和先生道鉴：

　　四月十日手示,早经奉悉。关于先生向中基会申请补助尊编《中国留欧博士论文目录》之补助出版费用,业经该会执委会通过补助美金一二〇〇元,想已接获该会通知矣。兹编之作,搜证工作固大为艰勤,其于近代中国学术史之文献征考,实具殊价,钦仰无量。近以事冗,久稽裁答,尚乞见谅为幸。耑此,并颂道祺。

弟钱思亮敬启
八月十五日
〔University of Chicago Library, Yuan T'ung-li Papers, Box 1〕

　　按:此件为打印稿,落款处为钱思亮签名。

八月中下旬

先生及夫人乘坐飞机回到美国波士顿,后前往哈佛大学怀德纳图书馆(Widener Library)查阅馆藏文献。〔《思忆录》,中文部分页 138〕

八月二十二日

先生回抵华盛顿。〔University of Chicago Library, Yuan T'ung-li Papers, Box 3〕

八月二十五日

先生致信赵叔诚,询问美金支票是否收到及《金轺筹笔》杨楷刊本试照结果等事。

台湾商务印书馆赵经理台鉴：

　　返美后接奉七月十日大函,拜悉种切。寄上之美金贰百伍拾元已经中国银行查复,系于七月九日由纽约汇出,想已收到。《金轺筹笔》挹秀山房本前以其字迹不清,曾于七月初旬寄上光绪十三年杨楷刊本之影印本,以之代挹秀山房本,必较清晰,不识已试照否? 王云五先生所藏者系小方壶斋王氏本,欠佳。并盼见示。《戡定新疆记》之跋文,前请房兆颖担任,久未寄到,即不必再候矣。各原书影印后想不需要,即希寄还为荷。《金轺筹笔》之附录四种想已付排,并盼将末校寄下一阅是荷。本日收到《石遗室诗话》两部,内中未附发票,并盼补寄。专此,顺候大安。

弟袁同礼拜上
八月廿五日
〔University of Chicago Library, Yuan T'ung-li Papers, Box 1〕

按：此件为底稿。

先生致信郑通，寄上美金支票一张，并告《中俄西北条约集》《新疆国界图志》寄美数量。

新华印刷公司郑经理大鉴：

七月十日寄上一函，内附美金支票壹百叁拾元，迄今多日未奉复函，亦未接到收据，至以为念。前托尊处代寄《中俄西北条约集》于台北、香港、新嘉坡等处，各处均尚无信来，不识是否照单寄出。新嘉坡中华书局来信谓仅收到十五本（前请寄三十部），究竟寄出若干部，亦请一查是盼。《新疆国界图志》早已印出，何以装订如此之久，尚未印出。兹随函奉上美金支票壹百贰拾元，即希查收见复为荷。《中俄西北条约集》弟处需用陆拾元，前曾数次函请寄下，迄今未收到，究竟已全部装订否？《新疆国界图志》弟处需用壹百部，亦盼从寄下，每包以十五部为宜，纸盒内多塞报纸，以免书籍损坏为要。顺候大安。

袁同礼顿首

八月廿五日

〔University of Chicago Library, Yuan T'ung-li Papers, Box 1〕

按："陆拾元"当作"陆拾部"。此件为底稿。

八月二十六日

先生致信渡边宏，告知有关马可波罗的书目即将编制完成，希望其协助将日文中有关该主题的主要书籍、论文搜集并在去往近东地区前发来，并请告知垫付寄送《新疆研究文献目录》（日文本）至中国大陆图书馆的邮费。

August 26, 1963

Dear Mr. Watanabe:

Thank you so much for forwarding to me my letter to Mrs. Wei.

I have been wondering if your plan to continue your research on Islam in the Near East has been realized. I send you my best wishes for your success.

My work on a Bibliography of Marco Polo is almost completed. I wonder if you would be kind enough to send me a list of Japanese books and articles on Marco Polo when you can spare your time. It needs not be comprehensive, but you will certainly include all important works. I shall be very grateful if you could assist me in this work. Could you arrange to send me this list before you leave for the Near East?

I just spent five weeks in western Europe, visiting museums and libraries. The weather was very nice, having had no rain at all. It was a fruitful trip, but a little too tired.

Trusting that you have had a pleasant summer and with all good wishes,

Your sincerely,

T. L. Yuan.

P. S. Sometime ago I requested you to mail 20 copies of our Bibliography to Mainland Chinese libraries from the copies returned to you by a book-dealer in Hong Kong. If you have mailed them, please let me know the amount of postage you had advanced for me.

〔University of Chicago Library, Yuan T'ung-li Papers, Box 2〕

按：Mrs. Wei，待考。该件为录副。

八月二十八日

徐家璧覆函先生，告《西域考古录》卷七首页已特装寄上，并介绍前哥伦比亚大学图书馆同事袁道丰前往国会图书馆拜见。

守和先生尊鉴：

敬肃者，顷奉月之二十五日手示，藉悉先生已由英伦返美，虽云劳顿，想收获必甚丰富，至希稍事休息，再行工作为祷！嘱寄俞浩撰《西域考古录》卷七首页，以便印制卷一至六，自应遵办，惟因原件付邮恐遭损坏，乃改用白纸裁成一式大小，并画出书框行格，随函奉上，谅可合用。璧自来耶鲁后，已十五阅月未曾休假，下月初常石公归来，当可略享假期之乐。

先生拟于十月底莅此观书至佳，彼时璧早已回书案，恭迎尊驾不误。上星期日（二十五日）前去康桥观礼，得晤令嫒，至感快慰！想伊刻已携孙回府矣。耑此奉呈，敬颂崇安！

晚徐家璧鞠躬

八月廿八日

尊夫人暨令嫒等前，乞代候安为感！

再者:前哥大同仁袁道丰兄拟择日前来 LC 参观,并拟晋谒先生,藉聆教益。如其得便,尚乞赐予接见指示一切为感! 袁君闽人,早年曾留学巴黎,专攻国际关系,归国后执教于复旦、上海商学院等校,颇有著述。战后转入外交界,曾任古巴夏湾那"总领事"多年,故西班牙文亦颇精通。一九五九年由古巴撤退后,乃在哥大东亚圕任出纳员,继又转纽约长岛大学圕任职迄今。现渠自行钻研圕学,一般基本图书,均已阅过,颇有心得,实可钦也! 故愿略作介绍如右。

晚徐家璧又及
八月廿八日

〔University of Chicago Library, Yuan T'ung-li Papers, Box 9〕

按:时耶鲁大学图书馆拟将馆藏《西域考古录》补齐,委托先生在国会图书馆拍摄前六卷。

刘麟生覆函先生,感谢再次代为谋事。

守和尊兄博士勋右:

辱荷廿二日嘉翰,备谂旌节安抵华都,曷胜欣慰。鄙事又蒙眷注,爱人以德,真有古风。抄稿尤具委婉之妙用也。弟在此已托友人设法,惟需二周后始知分晓,因其人不在纽约市耳。敬请俪安。

小弟麟生谨启
八,廿八

〔University of Chicago Library, Yuan T'ung-li Papers, Box 1〕

八月二十九日

马克尔致函先生,很高兴与先生再次见面,感谢告知梅镇岳、黄昆等人近况。

29 August 1963

Dear Dr. Yuan,

It was a real pleasure to see you again and I was most interested in all you told me. The nuclear physics students did well here; Mei Jeann Yueh had a bad mental breakdown but took his degrees notwithstanding this handicap and went to some nuclear station in Canada. I was not altogether surprised to hear that he was working at this in China along with Huang Kung and another. I should be most interested to hear more about their achievements and to know where I could read about them.

I hope that you had a successful visit to the Continent of Europe and that you returned home safe and well. Do please let us know when next you visit these shores.

My wife and I are enjoying your delicious tea.

With best wishes,

Yours sincerely,

A. G. Morkill

P. S. The Annual Report is now published and I enclose a copy.

〔University of Chicago Library, Yuan T'ung-li Papers, Box 1〕

按：Mei Jeann Yueh 即梅镇岳（1915—2009），浙江杭州人，核物理学家，1939 年毕业于西南联合大学，随即留校任教，1945 年赴英国伯明翰大学留学，1949 年获得博士学位，论文题名为 Search for nuclear isomers with half-lives between a millisecond and a second，后的确曾去加拿大，但并非在核电厂，而是在加拿大国家实验室从事研究，1953 年归国，在中国科学院近代物理研究所工作。此件为打字稿，落款处为其签名。

八月三十一日

先生致信李书华，略述在巴黎盘桓情况，并告《中国留欧大陆各国博士论文目录》法国部分编纂已近完成。

润章先生著席：

弟近因事赴欧，在巴黎仅住六日，得晤上海楼赵经理，渠对吾兄钦佩无已。又承赵明德夫妇约请午餐，均嘱代致拳拳之意。赵君夫妇现研究针灸之学，颇愿于一二年后来美。弟告以李济欧先生对于美国医学界情形较熟，似可与之通讯，故盼将李君住址示知为感。弟编之《留法博士论文目录》大致业已编成，此次略加补充，想无遗漏。惟圣章系何年获得学位，兄知之否？ 其论文则各馆均未入藏也。将来编就，拟请赐一序文以光篇幅，至盼至盼。顺候俪安。

弟同礼顿首

八，卅一日

又附上一同学名单,其中文姓名请就所知者赐予注明,其不详者能否托友人中代填,无任感谢。法国各馆之目录以名为姓者甚多,并乞代为改正。

〔Columbia University Libraries Archival Collections, Shuhua Li Papers, 1926–1972, Volume II: Modern Eminent Chinese Leaders〕

按:赵明德,1939年在里昂大学获医学博士学位;李济欧,1933年在里昂大学获医学博士学位。李麟玉,应未获得博士学位。

九月一日

钱存训致函先生,请协助校阅《冯承钧传记》初稿。

守和先生:

前闻大驾有欧洲之行,想必快游归来,至为欣羡。《冯承钧小传》月前已经交卷,惟材料不多,对其早年及在欧洲求学时代生活多不甚详,细阅其译著亦少及其生平。兹将初稿副本奉呈一阅,如有遗误,仍乞指正,尚可更改也。原稿阅毕仍请掷还,是所至幸。专此,敬请著安。

后学存训拜上

九月一日

〔University of Chicago Library, Yuan T'ung-li Papers, Box 2〕

渡边宏致函先生,告知将在九月底前收集完有关马可波罗(日文)资料,并称赞《中俄西北条约集》的学术价值。

Tokyo, le 1er septembre 63

Cher Monsieur Yuan,

Merci mille fois pour votre lettre qui m'annonçait votre bon retour à Washington.

Le concours d'étudiant résidant à étranger n'est fait pas encore.

L'étude de Marco Polo n'est pas beaucoup, mais je la rechercherai en détail. (ci-joint un spécimen) Ce travail finira à la fin de septembre.

Les frais de poste sont / 200 yen (= 3.3 U.S. $) (Une copie est 65 yen)

Je voyais votre nouveau livre, 中国西北条约集, dans les librairies. Je me le sens très excellent. Mais je ne le reçois pas encore. (Selon votre lettre de 30 mai, vous déjà m'envoyait de Hong Kong.)

Votre tout dévoué,

H. Watanabe

〔University of Chicago Library, Yuan T'ung-li Papers, Box 2〕

　　按：此件为其亲笔。

九月四日

刘麟生致函先生,告其在哥伦比亚大学研究工作结束时情形,并谈西人治学优点。

　　守和尊兄馆长勋右：

　　　　（一）兹将仆离别情形奉告,以资轩渠。（二）廿九日散值时富氏谓"工作既毕,明日可不必来",弟谓"今日携打字机归,尚有若干书籍拟明日上午携返"。卅日上午十时,弟告辞时,彼谓"尚有若干问题请教"。（三）（此段请秘之）彼取出译稿陈援庵《元西域人华化考》,谓"其中诗句请校"。彼阅稿,弟阅原文,对于译文时加赞美,有若干漏略或不准确者,则贡献意见,最后问"筮观之益"作何解,弟答"须检阅《周易》"。弟往书库取得《周易王弼注》,告以"此系卦变俗语变卦本此,观为巽上坤下☷,益为巽上震下☳,仅初爻一变而已"。富公大笑,临行时谓"获益甚多,他日有机会再谈"云云。（四）西士治学脚踏实地且富于参考资料与工具,弟此次在哥大研究获益不少,皆明公之赐也。（五）工作方面,弟亦另托人留意,仍盼贤者代为留神。弟深信经过此番训练,亦勉为称计工作矣。（六）《文学副刊》另邮呈奉。即颂著余双胜。

小弟麟生谨上

九,四

〔University of Chicago Library, Yuan T'ung-li Papers, Box 1〕

九月五日

张馨保致函先生,告知在纽约见闻,并告房兆楹已经抵达哥伦比亚大学协助开展《明代名人传》项目。

　　守和先生赐鉴：

　　　　上周在华府又承招待,感愧无已,歆保于劳工节抵纽约,现在哥大圕阅览,拟于周末赴波士顿留一周再返校。日来在此得见中外汉学家数人,实为幸事。房兆楹先生昨日方抵此主持明史之事,今日与之午餐,连喆夫人日内亦可赶到。伦敦大学亚菲学院之李棪先生亦在此研究。前在英伦、欧陆与之数度相晤,每逢倾谈获益匪浅。李先生系岭南名宿文田公之孙,前在大陆时代精研明史,其旧作东林党籍考,于一九五七年中共为之出版。李先生近年转攻甲骨文字,十余年来在伦敦研究,甚有发见,现来美住一年搜集材料,拟出版 *Catalogue and Transcription of Oracle Bones from North America and Western Europe Collections*,日后难免有函询请益之处,尚恳照拂为祷。专此,祗请撰安。

后学歆保鞠躬

九月五日

伯母及清兄不另。

〔University of Chicago Library, Yuan T'ung-li Papers, Box 2〕

　　按:"明史之事"即富路德主持、房兆楹夫妇协助 *Dictionary of Ming Biography, 1368-1644*(《明代名人传》),该书于 1976 年由哥伦比亚大学出版。*Catalogue and Transcription of Oracle Bones from North America and Western Europe Collections* 似指《北美所见甲骨选粹考释》。

普实克致函先生,告知将委托其在北京学生将款项转给袁复礼,并告在美停留日期及通信地址。

New York, September 5th 1963

My dear Professor Yüan,

　　Having returned for a conference to the United States I am writing you again about our dealings with Peking. Before my departure from Prague, we received from Peking a permission to send one of our collaborators to Peking with purpose of checking our materials for the Czecho-Chinese Dictionary we are preparing. It is a lady, pupil of mine, who shall stay in Peking several months. I entrusted her with carrying out the transmit of the sum for your brother and, of course, I advised her to take all the precautions and better to drop the matter entirely if it could mean any complications for your brother. I shall inform you —in a most discreet way— what will be the result of it. In the negative case, I shall ask our bookseller here to return you the amount.

I am sorry that I could not fulfil your wish earlier, but, as you see, the things are becoming ever more complicated. But let us hope that we will succeed.

I stay here until September 20th when I go to Mexico City for a meeting of CYPSH.

I wish you very much success in your work and remain,

Very sincerely yours

J. Průšek

My address here is:

Kent Hall, 408, Columbia University, New York

I am looking through the library journals of the pre-revolutionary period. Of course, I could find much more in Washington, but my time is too short.

〔University of Chicago Library, Yuan T'ung-li Papers, Box 3〕

按:此件为其亲笔。

九月七日

何日章(台北)致函先生,请协助友人在美出售古籍两种。

守和吾兄惠鉴:

违教以来,倏忽十余年,驰念无已。弟自别后展转来台,初在省立图书馆,继主政治大学图书馆事,迄今坚守岗位与我兄同。现今正修订拙著《分类法》,俟藏事后,当再请益。兹有敝友徐庭瑶将军之公子先汇君,在美藏有明版《事文类聚》及《文献通考》各一部,每部均在百本以上,现拟就近出售,苦无门径。吾兄久居彼邦,熟友较多,拟恳推介贵馆或其他处,务祈推爱促成,感同身受。如风便惠示近况,尤为盼祷者也。耑此,敬请旅安。

弟何日章启

1963. 9. 7

〔University of Chicago Library, Yuan T'ung-li Papers, Box 9〕

按:1948 年何日章赴台,先在台湾省立图书馆研究室工作,1959年 10 月起任台湾政治大学图书馆馆长。"拙著《分类法》"即《中国图书十进分类法》,1965 年第三版在台北出版。此件为打字稿,落款处为其签名,并钤印。

九月九日

罗家伦致函先生,谈代购书籍等事。

守和吾兄道鉴:

奉读复教,敬悉前汇上之美金五百元,已荷察收。吾兄欧洲之游,想必旅途愉快,现已返华府矣。兹有数事奉托于后:

一、最近收到吾兄在英及在美付邮寄来书籍三包。(一)North & Eudin *M. N. Roy's Mission to China* 及《九一八事变真相》各一册,附 **Park Book Shop** 发票一张,计书价美金七.五〇元,邮费二.四三元,共九.九三元。惟经手人未签名,兹再将原发票寄还,再烦吾兄转寄该书店签名寄下为托。(二)自伦敦寄来书籍一包,计 Collier,*Manchoukuo*; Strabolgi,*Singapore*; Curzon,*Problems of the Far East* 三书,发票一张,计英金一镑十先令,均已收到。(三)英国 W. Heffer & Sons 寄来 *Documents on British Foreign Policy, 1919-39* 一书,附上空白发票一张,书款及邮费计英金四镑四先令。以上各书价款均烦吾兄代付,为荷感。

二、Facts on File 寄来 *Yearbook 1962* 一册及空白发票一张,计美金三〇.七〇元,兹将发票寄上,烦请费神代为付款是托。

三、前在伦敦 Arthur Probsthain 亚瑟普若布斯坦书籍目录内选定书籍一批,计五十三种,共需英金四十九镑四先令六便士,折合美金约一百四十元左右,检附书单二份,烦请费神代为订购,书籍请其以印刷品挂号分包直接交邮寄运。

敬将本年七、八、九月份吾兄征集费壹仟伍百元送存台湾银行收据一纸奉上,即请察收。有渎清神,无任感谢。专此,顺颂道祺!

弟罗家伦敬启

九,九

〔University of Chicago Library, Yuan T'ung-li Papers, Box 1〕

按:*M. N. Roy's Mission to China*,Robert C. North 与 Xenia J. Eudin 合著,1963 年加州大学出版社初版;*Manchoukuo* 即 D. M. B. Collier 所著 *Manchoukuo, jewel of Asia*,1936 年伦敦初版;

Singapore 应指 *Singapore and After: a study of the Pacific campaign*，第十一任 Strabolgi 男爵 David Montague de Burgh Kenworthy（1914-2010）著，1942 年伦敦初版；*Problems of the Far East*，寇松侯爵著，1894 年伦敦初版。该函为文书代笔，落款处为罗家伦签名。

九月上旬

先生邀郅玉汝到国会图书馆左侧餐馆吃饭，饭后，先生送其至公交车站。

〔《中国图书馆学会会讯》第 3 卷第 4 期，1995 年 12 月，页 9〕

> 按：郅玉汝（1917—2016），卫立煌的大女婿，印第安纳大学执教，时赴华盛顿查阅资料，但对街道不熟，先生遂待其上车后才步行回馆。

九月十一日

刘麟生覆函先生，谈诸事。

> 守和馆长勋右：
>
> （一）辱惠七日手谕，深裹垂注之雅。（二）今晨往 Kent Hall，查无正德《进士录》，略阅他书，亦无所得。正苦无以报命，归阅《辞海》，乃有一条，爰另纸抄奉，以博轩渠。（三）此后如有下走可效劳之处，乞源源赐教也。（四）德刚兄之太夫人，为三沙镇刘伯龙先生之妹。伯龙为弟之族兄，仅晤一面。弟当时告德刚兄，系本家，不敢详陈，自居高位。后者唐君似有所觉，一次称弟为"舅太爷"。上月中，曾作书与彼，请其相助，未获复音。明公如能致书与 Dr. Evans，自系佳构。爰写 Resume 一份呈政。（五）同学高肇源君系纱业商，去秋来 Kent Hall 任事，系 Dr. Linton 所用。今春因治事不快，辞职。弟与德刚书，曾询及此点也。（六）三沙位巢湘西岸，乃湘西农产出口所。家舍旧居此，嗣移居无为，并以奉闻。敬请俪安。
>
> 弟麟生谨上
>
> 九，十一

〔University of Chicago Library, Yuan T'ung-li Papers, Box 1〕

> 按：后附抄录《辞海》梅鷟生平一纸。

九月十四日

先生致信中基会，汇报《中国留欧大陆各国博士论文目录》编纂情况。

September 14, 1963

Dear Sirs:

Thanks to the support from the China Foundation, I have been able to bring to completion my work on the *Doctoral Dissertations by Chinese Students in Europe*. This bibliographical guide includes about 2,000 dissertations submitted by Chinese students and approved by various universities in ten European countries from 1907 to 1963. (England, France, Germany, Austria, Belgium, Switzerland, Holland, Italy, Spain, and Poland)

Under each country, the dissertations are grouped alphabetically by author under four faculties of Letters, Law and Social Sciences, Natural Science and Engineering, and Medicine and Pharmacy. There are indexes and statistical tables at the end of the volume.

This work indicates whether a dissertation is available in book form, or printed in a scientific journal with its date of publication, volume number and pagination, so that it could be located without any delay. Though a laborious undertaking, it is an authorative record of scholarly achievements of Chinese students in European universities.

The manuscripts are being typed, and it will soon appear as special supplement to *Chinese Culture*, a quarterly review published at Taipei.

Assuring you once more my sincere appreciation for your interest and assistance,

Sincerely yours,

T. L. Yuan

〔University of Chicago Library, Yuan T'ung-li Papers, Box 2〕

按:此件为录副。

王伊同覆函先生,告知匹兹堡大学新聘华人教授及迁居等事。

老伯大人尊前:

敬禀者,日前奉手谕,欣悉英伦之行收获甚富,且得与郑、吴两君抱聚,甚慰。舍甥女迄无信,未知已分娩否? 闻吴君收藏钟鼎彝器兼及书画,数年前曾到美,与 John Pope 亦常通讯,想来颇精此道,然未尝一晤为憾耳。台湾之行,仅见报章,"教部"无信,国人办事素重宣传,此似不能例外。据闻敝校被邀者三人,优生学之李景均含大同年、电机系施增玮,侄亦陪末席。闻近又邀副校长 Peals 先生亦在,未可知之数矣。开学二周,郑华女士已到校,常相遇,从今年算学系增国籍教授二人一为赵中云,一为 Wang 君(未晤),争光上邦,可喜可慰。

承赐玉器目录一册,至感。别购《故宫藏瓷》均、汝两窑,均窑到,汝窑在途中,大增见闻。迁居事仍进行中,东屋太多转不易遽定。Pgle 四散,冬季多雪,又不愿远寓乡间(刻按月付租,万一出手仍可寓三月),诚一问题也。舍表兄章楚过金山,得晤陈景颜表兄,近况似佳。附闻,敬请金安。

侄伊同顿首再拜
九月十四

〔University of Chicago Library, Yuan T'ung-li Papers, Box 2〕

按:"郑、吴两君"应指郑德坤、吴权。

九月十五日

徐家璧覆函先生,告知将休假外出,前请代摄《西域考古录》之垫款须等归时方能结清。

守和先生尊鉴:

敬肃者,日昨接奉十三日手示,暨发票二纸(耶鲁例需三份),拜悉一一。璧休假自九月四日开始,为期一月,故须俟十月四日始行销假复工。

先生代摄《西域考古录》卷一至卷六,业已完成,至感!现该件既已邮寄馆中,当有人代为收下。璧现因事,须去波斯顿一行,未悉可否俟回埠后,再行通知常石先生径行归垫清结?稽延之处,统乞谅鉴为祷!函内所附另一书单,确至有用,各书购置事宜,恐须俟下月初璧回馆后再行函洽。耑此奉陈,敬颂崇安!

晚徐家璧鞠躬
九月十五日夜(星期日)

尊夫人前,并乞叱名候安为感!

〔University of Chicago Library, Yuan T'ung-li Papers, Box 9〕

九月十六日

先生致信中基会,申请补助《新疆研究文献目录》(西文本)印刷费。

〔University of Chicago Library, Yuan T'ung-li Papers, Box 2〕

按：该信并附备忘录一页，共申请 1250 美元。

九月十七日

先生致信郭廷以，建议其与费正清沟通延长福特基金会赞助。

> 量予先生著席：
>
> 　　七月间荷承赐赠大著，在伦敦时曾奉一书，谅达记室。返台北后，所务繁忙，贤劳可想。Ford 补助之款转瞬将届三年，自当设法延长，惟该会请款手续颇不简单。此次费正清君来台北视察，似可与之详商，想已在考虑之中。弟在欧月余，走马看花，惟所获资料颇多，聊以自慰耳。此上，顺颂俪安。
>
> 　　　　　　　　　　　　　　　　　　　　　　弟袁同礼顿首
> 　　　　　　　　　　　　　　　　　　　　　　　九月十七日
>
> 　　弟所印《新疆丛书》已告印刷人径寄贵所及吾兄各一份，希教正。

〔台北"中央研究院"近代史研究所档案馆，〈郭廷以〉，馆藏号069-01-02-089〕

按：该信于 9 月 24 日送达。

九月十八日

先生致信钱存训，告稿件已修改，并告在欧访书收获不少。

> 公垂吾兄著席：
>
> 　　返美后得读大函及《冯子衡小传》，以信件积压过多，未能早日拜读。兹酌易数处，是否适宜，仍希尊酌，又请子明兄看过（铅笔更动者），均以为资料充实，言之有物，仅在文字上酌改数处而已。此次欧行，适值天气凉爽，虽在休假中，亦获到若干资料为北美各处所无者，亦可宝贵也。顺候教祺。
>
> 　　　　　　　　　　　　　　　　　　　　　　弟袁同礼再拜
> 　　　　　　　　　　　　　　　　　　　　　　　九，十八

〔钱孝文藏札〕

九月二十日

程其保覆函，告其子已赶回巴黎，所须注明之留法博士中文姓名须请教郭有守。

> 守和先生道席：
>
> 　　奉示敬悉。小儿纪贤因须赶回巴黎任课，已于月初离美，嘱件弟

只知二人,其余势须寄法,请子杰兄注明也。

大千画展,此间(纽约)应邀请名单,仍遵子杰兄嘱寄法,如此弟方更省事也。

耑复,敬颂日祺。

弟其保拜

九,廿

〔University of Chicago Library, Yuan T'ung-li Papers, Box 9〕

按:"纪贤"即程抱一(François Cheng,1929—),江西南昌人,1947年入私立金陵大学英文系,翌年随其父赴法国,后成为法兰西学院首位华裔院士。

九月二十二日

罗文达覆函先生,感谢来信及所赠目录卡片,并告知新公司地址。

608, Congressional Towers, Rockville, Md. Phone 427-4728

22 Sept. 63

Dear Dr. Yuan:

Many thanks for your kind letter & the enclosed catalog cards. Please note above our new address. Meantime, my wife & I established with our partner & financier Information Systems, Inc. 7720 Wisconsin Avenue Bethesda, Md. Phone 656-9033. We are hard at work putting our new system on the machine.

I am glad that you were able to collect data in Europe & meet old friends.

With all good wishes for the success of your work & kindest regards,

Sincerely yours,

Rudolf Löewenthal

〔University of Chicago Library, Yuan T'ung-li Papers, Box 9〕

按:此件为其亲笔。

九月二十六日

先生致信台湾商务印书馆,告《金轺筹笔》或可改用杨楷本,并请将附录寄下以便校对,另谈寄书细节等事。

径启者,顷奉九月四日137号大函,拜悉种切。《金轺筹笔》杨楷刊本如拍照结果较哈佛藏本为优,即改用杨楷本,其附录四种并盼早日寄下一校是荷。因请贵馆对于弟委托之事提前办理,爰将补助费尽先奉上,务希从速印就是荷。印制之书寄美时,务请包装坚固,每包以十册为适宜,并用厚纸包装以免书籍损坏,是为企盼。已照完之底本亦盼早日寄还,以便归还各馆也。此致
台湾商务印书馆

袁同礼再拜

九,廿六日

奉上《石遗室诗话》书款 198.30,希查收。

〔University of Chicago Library, Yuan T'ung-li Papers, Box 1〕

按:《金轺筹笔》最后所据底本确为杨楷刊本,即光绪十三年本,"附录四种"依次为"清廷致俄国国书及总署奏折""崇厚之自白""曾纪泽奏疏及书牍""有关人士履历简表"。此件为底稿。

九月二十八日

先生致信埃文斯,推荐刘麟生协助哥伦比亚大学图书馆整理中文馆藏。

September 28, 1963

Dr. Luther H. Evans

Columbia University Libraries

New York 27, N. Y.

Dear Dr. Evans:

In reorganizing special collections at Columbia, you would probably need more trained assistants as the program is well under way. May I therefore write to recommend a competent scholar Mr. L. S. Liu?

Mr. Liu is a writer of considerable experience and has a wide knowledge of Chinese bibliography. I am sure that he would be able to render useful service to you if he is given an opportunity to do so.

I am asking Mr. Liu to call on you and I sincerely hope that you would keep him in mind for any opening at Columbia.

With cordial regards.

Sincerely

T. L. Yuan

〔University of Chicago Library, Yuan T'ung-li Papers, Box 1〕

按：此件为录副。

九月二十九日

刘麟生覆函先生，谈诸事。

守和博士先生赐鉴：

（一）读廿六日谕言乃知驾游南州，声闻远播为慰。（二）鄙事又劳神思作书，感戴曷其有极。（三）今日《时报》（*Magazine*）刊十大女杰，内记述西后，乃将光绪帝误为宣统，可哂也。（四）傅吾康书另邮呈缴，久稽为歉。（五）大陆所刊文学史三册，约五十万字，港友寄此，尚未及细阅。明公如需参考，乞示知，不足为他人道矣。敬请俪安。

弟麟生敬肃
九，廿九

〔University of Chicago Library, Yuan T'ung-li Papers, Box 1〕

九月三十日

先生覆信马克尔，告知已请美国农业部图书馆寄送有关中国大陆农业研究的出版品，随信附上有关中国原子弹的文章，并告梅镇岳曾在苏联从事研究，另将寄赠《现代中国数学研究目录》。

September 30, 1963

Dear Mr. Morkill:

Thank you for your good letter and a copy of your Annual Report.

In addition to the two pamphlets I had sent to you, I am asking the Department of Agriculture Library to mail you some of its publications dealing with agricultural research in Communist China. They will be sent by surface mail.

I enclose an article dealing with A-bomb in China which might be of some interest to you. Mei Jenn Yueh did some research at the Dubna Research Institute, but I have not been able to get any literature relating to their work. It must be of classified nature and not yet published. There are several articles of purely scientific interest by Mei and Huang in the journal entitled: *ACTA PHYSICA SINICA*, copies of which may be found in the Science Library, South Kensington, or Cambridge University Library.

　　Under separate cover, I am sending you a copy of my Bibliography of Chinese Mathematics which includes a number of articles by Chinese students in Russia and published in Russian mathematical journals. Most of them have returned to China since 1961.

　　Thank you and Mrs. Morkill for the delightful evening I had with you. Both of you look young and in excellent health. I only regret that my time in London was too short. I can only hope that I may find myself again in London in the not too distant future.

　　With warmest regards,

Yours sincerely,

T. L. Yuan

〔University of Chicago Library, Yuan T'ung-li Papers, Box 1〕

按：Dubna Research Institute，杜布纳联合原子核研究所，位于今俄罗斯莫斯科州杜布纳市。*ACTA PHYSICA SINICA* 即《物理学报》，时由中国科学院物理研究所编辑出版，中文月刊。该件为录副。

叶良才覆先生两函。其一，请在《中国文化季刊》出版后寄赠三册至中基会保存。

Sept. 30, 1963

Dear Dr. Yuan:

　　Guide to Doctoral Dissertations by Chinese Students in Europe

　　Thank you for your letter of September 17, 1963. We note that your compilation of the *Guide to Doctoral Dissertations by Chinese Students in Europe* will be published as a special supplement to *Chinese Culture*, a quarterly review printed in Taipei.

　　Kindly send to this office 3 copies of the special supplement, when available, for file.

Yours sincerely,

L. T. Yip

Financial Secretary

其二，告知收到资助申请，表示将于中基会明年的例会上给予审议。

Sept. 30, 1963

Dear Dr. Yuan:

Bibliography of Sinkiang

We received your letter of September 16, 1963 to the Board of Trustees applying for a grant of $1,250.00 to cover half of the printing cost for *Bibliography of Sinkiang*. The request will be considered by the Board at its next meeting presently scheduled for April 1964.

Yours sincerely,

L. T. Yip

Financial Secretary

〔University of Chicago Library, Yuan T'ung-li Papers, Box 2〕

按:两函落款均为其签名。

九十月间

李书华覆函先生,告知其曾患急性盲肠炎入院治疗,并就所询人名告以所知。

守和吾兄大鉴:

八月卅一日及九月十八日两次手书,均敬悉。弟于九月一日突患急性盲肠炎,即入"纽约大学医院"割治,因病势较复杂,开刀后不能令伤口封闭,且接连不断有二度余之热度,故住院有十六天之久,始回寓。入院第十四天热度始退,伤口始渐封闭。现病已愈,惟身体尚未完全复元耳。此次入院开刀,尚未太晚,亦属幸事。住院十六天费用共八百七十余元,全可由健康保险支付。三个医生费用(包括开刀手术费 250 元)大约四百数十元或五百元,健康保险可担任一部分,弟个人担任一部分。知注并闻。

同学名单弟细阅一编,知姓名者有六人,已注明。此单不知兄曾问过赵明德夫妇否?又希就近一询凤举为盼。嘱编就时作一序文,谨当如命。

……

〔University of Chicago Library, Yuan T'ung-li Papers, Box 6〕

按:"凤举"应指张凤举,1948 年 2 月被国民政府委派担任驻日代表团顾问,约于 20 世纪 60 年代移居美国。该函仅存第一页。

九月

先生为《洪有丰遗著两种索引》撰写序言。

民国十年六月,洪范五先生卒业于纽约州立图书学校,访余于纽约旅次,畅谈竟日,相约以全力致力于图书馆事业,遂订交焉。范五返国后,主持东南大学孟芳图书馆,擘划周详,树全国之楷模。越三年,余亦返国,鉴于图书事业端赖群策群力,方易收效,乃联合斯学专家及学术界人士设立中华图书馆协会,以为倡导。又念新旧图籍,日增月益,商之范五,首先编辑专科目录及索引,藉以统系贯穿,内中如《老子考》《国学论文索引》《文学论文索引》《地学论文索引》等,均由协会印行,列为丛书。将当时散见于各期刊之论文分类编辑,承学之士因类求目、因目寻篇,探囊取物,莫不称便。范五又念古今丛书卷帙浩繁,且多已佚之本,而子目众多,检查不易,爰将子目书名编为索引。此项艰钜工作于二十三年五月完成,考订赅赡有如提钥在握,文学宝藏举手而得,于是风行一时,不胫而走。余又嘱王君有三,摘录清代文集四百余家之篇目,汇编分类索引,与范五之书相辅而行。流风所被,国内工具之书彬彬而出。未几,芦沟变起,烽火连天,已编就之《清代笔记索引》《国学论文索引五编》等,虽交由开明书局接收印行,迄今未能问世,识者惜焉。近二十余年来,国家频经祸患,人事又多变迁,星霜屡易,旧友日稀,而范五竟于今年二月遽归道山,追维往事,曷胜怆悼无涯! 其哲嗣余庆兄搜集先人遗文,行将印行,征序于余。余与范五为莫逆交,一生夙好,雅在书林。鉴于四部二乘,浩如渊海,辄以编辑工具书相勖勉。今读其遗著,顾念前徽,益增怀旧之感。惟望从事图书馆事业者,能用科学方法输入新知,并能致力于工具书之纂辑,以完成范五之夙愿,而应学术界之需求,此则余殷殷企望者也。

九月

〔University of Chicago Library, Yuan T'ung-li Papers, Box 2〕

按:本年1月27日,洪有丰在上海去世,生前担任华东师范大学图书馆馆长。《洪有丰遗著两种索引》似并未正式发行,极有可能是极小数量的私印本。该件为初稿,上有他人改动之处,且将落款日期改为"十一月"。

十月二日

刘麟生覆函先生,告与埃文斯面洽求职经过,并谈海陶玮覆函等事。

守老馆长勋鉴:

（一）承赐廿一日手教并介绍书,用情深挚,感何可言。（二）今日下午已访晤 Dr. Evans,渠谓"阁下必识唐君",弟答"唐君之太大人系族人也"。彼微笑,又谓"富先生系老友",问弟欲就何职,弟告以"研究及书庋事",彼言"当与执事者商谈再告"。弟之履历已面交,有住址及电话也。（三）哈佛高塔君复书,略如下文:-------There does not appear to be any opening just now. I will keep your resume on file, and if I hear of anything I shall get in touch with you. I owe you a real debt, for it was from your book on Parallel Prose that I first learned about this fascinating style. I am taking the libety of sending you a copy of my article which I wrote on the subject a few years ago.(September 30, 1963.)（四）原书略有误点,如《滕王阁序》滕字误腾,"飞燕长裾"《玉台新咏序》,飞燕作专门名词之类,弟尚未及复知也。（五）艺林又有新者,容再奉寄。（六）舍亲陈君明之往哥大读博士科,另有小职,故属弟代理其通运公司事,所入正微且该公司亦多□□,故弟未向伊先生说,乞勿向他人道及之。敬谢,并祝俪禧。

弟麟生顿首

十,二

癸卯中秋

〔University of Chicago Library, Yuan T'ung-li Papers, Box 1〕

按:"高塔君"即海陶玮。your book on Parallel Prose 应指《中国骈文史》。my article 似指 The Wen Hsüan and Genre Theory。[1] "通运"应指卢芹斋、张静江、李煜瀛等人开办的通运（Ton Ying）公司在纽约的分店。

十月四日

刘麟生覆函先生,感谢举荐,并寄上修订序言。

---

[1] Hightower, James R. "The Wen Hsüan and Genre Theory." *Harvard Journal of Asiatic Studies*, vol. 20, no. 3/4, 1957, pp. 512-533.

守和先生学长史席:

(一)诵一日台简,附赐介绍书,迭承嘉惠,无以为报为愧。(二)尊序纡徐为妍,所叙皆事实,甚佩甚佩,略加订正,仍请卓裁。(三)弟去夏离华昌时,曾访孟君,并赠拙著。今夏莆老亦作书,尚未及奉访也。(四)弟有意于文化教育,对于政治论文殊无兴趣也。敬谢,并颂著席。

小弟麟生谨启
十,四

〔University of Chicago Library, Yuan T'ung-li Papers, Box 1〕

按:"孟君"应指孟治。

十月五日

先生致信李书华,慰问病情并告《中国留欧大陆各国博士论文目录》编纂进展。

润章先生著席:

奉手教,知住院及医生费用可由健康保险支付一部分,心始放下。弟前未保险,后经适之力劝始行加入。春间有小手术,亦由健康保险支付。吾兄病后,亟须修养,望多受日光,住楼花园内有座位似可享受也。《论文目录》法国部分正在打字中,兹先将瑞士部分五十余人送上一阅,内中有研究理化者,或知其姓名又附上宣统年间留德博士名单。弟曾遍查"学部"官报,迄无所得。留德者约850余人,拟一并付印,内中以医学为最多。余俟续陈,顺候愈安。

弟同礼再拜
十,五日

〔Columbia University Libraries Archival Collections, Shuhua Li Papers, 1926–1972, Volume II: Modern Eminent Chinese Leaders〕

先生致信香港新华印刷公司,送上《新疆国界图志》邮寄单,并嘱妥为包装。

新华印刷公司大鉴:

前委托贵处排印之《新疆国界图志》想已装订完竣,请用航邮先寄下一部为盼,送上邮寄单二纸,即希照单交邮寄出,所垫邮费连同上次者共计若干,请示知以便奉还。包装须用厚纸,每包以十本为限,以免书籍损失。请于收到此信后从速作复,并将七月汇上之壹百叁拾元及八月汇上壹百贰拾元收据一并寄下为荷。顺候时祉。

袁同礼拜上
十月五号

〔University of Chicago Library, Yuan T'ung-li Papers, Box 1〕

按:该件为底稿。

马克尔致函先生,感谢寄赠《现代中国数学研究目录》。

5th October 1963

Dear Dr. Yuan,

How very kind you are to send me the volume of *Bibliography of Chinese Mathematics 1918-1960*.

I admire your enterprise and industry in this-it must entail much thought and effort.

With best wishes from my wife and myself. We are glad to know that you are safely home from your travels.

Yours sincerely,
A. G. Morkill

〔University of Chicago Library, Yuan T'ung-li Papers, Box 1〕

十月十日

郭廷以致函先生,告其与出版社商讨赠书结果并谈近代史研究所研究计划。

守和先生道席:

费城、华府两度畅叙,获益良多,快慰莫名。离美之前,复奉手札,以行色匆匆,未即作覆。返台之后,复因琐事待理,炎暑逼人,一再迟迟,罪甚罪甚。日前续获赐示,欣悉已自英伦归来。近年先生对于文献搜寻,用力之勤,贡献之大,士林共钦。此行收获,谅亦不少。关于中俄西北交涉史料三种,以付印之前未与承办者说明条件,商人重利,事后再提,难期就范。经一再交涉,始勉允另以原书四部见赠,连同前寄五部,共为九部,价值约在八十元左右。日内即可付邮。有负雅命,颇觉不安,敢祈谅之。近史所以限于人力财力,所成有限,有负先生及各方嘱望,深为愧汗。今后四五年内,决集中力量于有系统的专题研究,而以近代化之成败为中心,俟此项计划告一段落,如力能胜任,再事全部近代近之撰写。史料编纂自当赓续进行,然亦以事实所限,困难重重。但无论如何,必设法将中俄关系及近代中国之西方认识完成。民国史研究此时此地确有其必要与便利之处,不过亦有若干顾忌,目前只好仍从事于有关资料之搜集。四年以来,访问人数约四十位,纪录近三百万言。此事王雪艇先生亦深感兴趣,或可渐趋好转。福特补助计划为期尚有三年,拟待一九六五年再与商洽延展,多承关注,至感。拙编《近代中国史事日志》仅属于工具之书,俾备史家参考之需,说不上有何重大价值,谬蒙过奖,实不敢当。华府或其他各地学者及图书馆,可否便为推介,以广流布? 如属可行,当先邮上数部。王雪艇先生近日将去华府,此间情形,想可知其梗概。金纯儒先生晤及,将请代为致意。国会图书馆复本书刊,至希继续费神留意。匆此,敬颂时福!

弟郭廷以拜上
十、十

〔University of Chicago Library, Yuan T'ung-li Papers, Box 2〕

按:"近代近"似当作"近代化"。"商人重利"应指广文书局影印《中俄界记》《中俄界约斠注》《中俄国际约注》事。另,《近代中国史事日志》(清季),版权页标注为 1963 年 3 月初版。

十月十一日

刘麟生致函先生,告向哥伦比亚大学图书馆谋事的结果。

守和先生学长赐鉴:

兹奉上德刚兄复书一通,乞阅后掷还为感。此殆系上次弟转尊简谒伊文思先生之结果,文字之感人深矣,一笑。敬谢,并请著安。

教弟刘麟生谨颂
十,十一

〔University of Chicago Library, Yuan T'ung-li Papers, Box 1〕

十月十二日

李书华致函,感谢寄赠《中俄西北条约集》。

守和先生惠鉴:

承惠赠大著《中俄西北条约集》一册,业经收到,极深钦佩。此书内容,经兄搜寻加以校订,诚为研究中俄边务者最有用之参考文献也。特此鸣谢。顺请双安。

弟李书华敬启

10/12/63

〔University of Chicago Library, Yuan T'ung-li Papers, Box 9〕

十月十三日

洪余庆覆函先生,感谢撰写序文,并告纪念文集印行后拟赠送美国各校,并请校对洪有丰事略初稿。

守和老伯赐鉴:

昨接奉九月三十日训示及附序文与先父序文等件,均经拜读。时当乱世,而能得老伯辈之助,稍待时日或可多得一二篇也,此种大恩,亦非徒言可报,故亦不言谢矣。承告《东南大学图书馆述要》一文,载在《新教育》六卷一期,仅有胡佛图书馆收藏一份。前接周之南兄函,曾言及在接老伯函时,即已去函,现尚未见掷下,不知胡佛图书馆已寄周兄否? 可否便中请老伯再为一索,或可早日收到也。

前为统计所印数量,曾函此间美国新闻处,美国有图书馆系之学校数字,承告共有三十九所。侄拟出版后,各赠一册,又其曾在国会图书馆服务,亦拟赠一册。此书印后,仅送父执及若干处所作为纪念,不拟出售,诚恐有误会,以为图利,但因不发售,则不易流传,为此亦颇志忑未决。

关于事略,因系取自《中华图书馆协会季刊》及各父执处,以记忆所及,有所错误,如是侄更感人子之责。而今既印专集,自当改正。承示先父在美年月,确可作为根据也,至谢。惟其他之处,仍有错误,在所难免,兹再附上事略一份,敬请为改正赐下。以老伯与家父为莫逆之交,故敢一再相求也。又其在国会图书馆工作年月,亦请为一查,一并示覆为叩。

慰堂老伯之序文亦已掷下,此次得其助者至钜。不意志骞老伯亦已作古,是以可求助者又少一处矣。专此,敬请崇安。

洪制侄余庆叩

十,十三

〔University of Chicago Library, Yuan T'ung-li Papers, Box 9〕

按:周之南,江苏如皋人,中央大学毕业,曾任国民教育辅导研究
委员会委员、教育部台湾省督学。①

十月十四日

刘国蓁覆函先生,告知接洽新华公司代印著作进展及印制圣诞贺卡所需各
种费用。

守和博士先生尊鉴:

敬启者,日昨拜奉手教,敬悉种切,并附代转令岳信亦已投寄,想
当可收到也。日前得接令岳来示嘱代寄尊夫人信,兹附呈左右,敬希
察收为幸。新华公司代印尊著事,经已与郑通先生通电话,渠谓已收
到汇单二百五十美元,但仍有欠数,并已有信回答尊处也。至于代印
制圣诞咭事,经已购妥赵少昂所写花鸟咭八种,如晚昨年所用者,共四
百个,连信封价银每百廿五元(原价三毛一个),共壹百元,印工每百
五元,共贰十元,要二三日后方能印好。如印好即分两包包妥(每包重
五磅半),用印刷挂号邮奉上,邮费共银九元七角,三款总共壹百廿九
元七角,连邮费前次贰元、今次四元,合共壹百卅五元七角。尊帐前存
卅六元六角,比对寔支长九十九元一角也。港中供水仍继续四日一
次,每次四小时,寔为大不方便,但为长远计,亦无可如何也。月前承
秉华东翁命寄奉其先师李景康先生诗文集,想已到达矣。已凉天气未
寒时,敬希珍重。专此,敬请钧安。

愚晚国蓁顿首

一九六三年十月十四日

再启者,如尊处不存旧邮,请赐回此次信封面旧邮,至所厚幸。

〔University of Chicago Library, Yuan T'ung-li Papers, Box 2〕

按:李景康(1890—1960),字铭深,广东南海人,香港大学文科毕
业,后长期担任香港官立汉文中学校长,提倡中文教育。

十月十五日

范一侯致函先生,询问袁静联系方式及《国会图书馆藏中国善本书录》等
书的购买方式。

---

① 《教育部职员录》,1947年,页70。

守和先生：

　　久疏奉候，至以为歉！项因修改旅美南开校友录，拟祈将令媛袁静谅已自英返来之最近住址、工作及电话见示为感！

　　先生所编善本书目及现代中国数学研究目录，是否可用机关名义函索？或可由私人购买？祈便示下。如可由机关出名函索，应写给何机构？用中英文何者较便当？

　　日内敝校友录改订妥当，必再寄奉一册，以供参考。耑此，敬颂道安！

范一侯（士奎）拜上

一九六三，十，十五

〔University of Chicago Library, Yuan T'ung-li Papers, Box 2〕

十月十六日

余又荪致函先生，告知台北商务印书馆因赶印教科书致《新疆研究丛刊》所余各种印刷迟缓，并谈台湾大学历史系学术近况。

守和先生道席：

　　商务近接先生两函，藉稔大驾已返美。欧游谅极圆满。

　　商务近因赶印教科书，故将尊著丛书短期迟印。但绝不致久延，最近当即出书。前撰短文介绍，先生与贞一又在《大陆杂志》发表序跋。故迩来常有购者向商务探询。将来出书，谅较前售之日文书目为广销也。

　　自七月以来，因台大兼职事，一度忙碌。现研究所及系均已上课，入正规矣。

　　本年度研究所毕业生萧启庆，已入哈佛研究，该生成绩尚佳。

　　历史研究所与中文研究所，上年度起，将研究生论文陆续出版，名曰《文史丛刊》，第一集已出版，日内当另行寄至贵馆 Gift and Exchange Division。

　　本年度，与刘子健先生（来台研究一□）共开设"国外史学讨论"一科，实际由彼主持。凡到台之外籍学者，均约请轮流参加，现已举行三周。谅可收良好"学术交流"之效。

　　小儿承一、小女承智二人现均在 New York，已将先生地址开示，彼等如到华盛顿，当前来拜谒也。

　　专肃奉候，并颂著安。

余又荪谨上

十月十六日

〔University of Chicago Library, Yuan T'ung-li Papers, Box 1〕

按：萧启庆（1937—2012），江苏泰兴人，1963 年硕士毕业后前往哈佛大学学习，1969 年获得博士学位，专攻元史，后在美国、台湾、新加坡等地教书，2000 年当选"中央研究院"院士。

十月十八日

先生致信郭廷以，表示愿意代为推介《近代中国史事日志》，并谈顾维钧将文书档案捐赠哥伦比亚大学。

量予先生著席：

奉到十月十日手教，欣悉近况，深慰饥渴。大著为重要参考书，承学之士必须购藏，请先寄下四部，当为介绍每部需发票三份，抬头处暂不填写，由购者代填，其书款当告其直接奉上也。纽约方面，犹太书店 Paragon 推销能力极大，但索百分之四十折扣，商人重利，亦无法也。此商印有代售书目，风行一时，似亦可先寄数部，委托代售地址列后。日前见《纽约时报》载"顾大使"将其全部文件赠送哥伦比亚大学，其条件为 copies of certain documents to be deposited in "the Academia Sinica"，想尊处已与之接洽矣。弟曾劝其将中文文件汇集成编，或用年谱方式，或用回忆录方式予以发表，渠仍在考虑之中也。大安书商事承代接洽，至感。雪艇先生今日抵此，定后日来舍下便餐，当可畅谈一切也。顺候俪安。尊夫人同此致意。

弟袁同礼顿首

十月十八日

国会馆复本书自当随时留意。Paragon 地址列后：

Paragon Book Gallery

140 East 59th Street, New York, 22, N. Y.

〔台北"中央研究院"近代史研究所档案馆，〈郭廷以〉，馆藏号069-01-02-089；《郭量宇先生日记残稿》，页 445〕

按：此信于 22 日送达。

先生致信赵叔诚，告知《新疆国界图志》已由香港寄出，请台北商务印书馆代售，并告《金轺筹笔》所用之底本与附录细节。

叔诚经理惠鉴：

　　前承代售各书,至以为感。兹告香港新华印刷公司寄上《新疆国界图志》贰百伍拾部委托代售分寄叶、张、余、尊处及台大史学系,其书价应与贵馆承印五种之价目按叶数多寡比例决定,即乞于发售前代为决定为感。至于《金轺筹笔》,如已决定用杨楷刊本即影照之本,则将哈佛藏本从速交邮寄下为荷。其附录四种之末校,按照九月四日大函,应于九月杪寄到,但迄今仍未收到,亦盼从速办理。其他已照完之底本,以借自公家,亦请即日寄还,不胜企盼。顺候大安。

弟袁同礼顿首
十月十八日

〔University of Chicago Library, Yuan T'ung-li Papers, Box 1〕

　　按:此件为底稿,上部标注"十月廿九又催"。

十月二十日

王世杰来访,先生及夫人在家设宴款待并畅谈。(University of Chicago Library, Yuan T'ung-li Papers, Box 2)

　　按:本月 18 日,王世杰乘飞机抵达华盛顿,29 日乘车赴纽约,在此期间有数次机会可与先生碰面,如 25、27 日应蒋廷黻、郭有守邀宴。[1]

刘麟生覆函先生,谈工作近况等。

守和先生馆长勋右:

　　(一)十六日赐谕拜诵,甚感。(二)《文学周刊》一卷已收到。(三)弟现在通运任事,虽所入不丰,精神上极愉快,且工作亦简也。(四)高塔氏寄一文 Some Characteristics of Parallel Prose,引用《北山移文》及《玉台新咏序》全文,有鲁鱼亥豕之处,弟已校正复书矣。文学史一事,他日当函商,弟未读受颐先生书,不知其如何也。(五)"顾大使"处蒙托"金大使"作书,感何可言。惟两年前迈群兄亦有此说,云将与弟合作,后此迄无所闻也。去夏荷台座荐言,"顾大使"复书亦甚予弟以佳印象也。(六)总之,通运虽小事,尚有永久性也。敬谢,并祝著述日新。

---

① 《王世杰日记》,页 1010–1012。

弟麟生谨上

十月廿日夜

〔University of Chicago Library, Yuan T'ung-li Papers, Box 1〕

按：Some Characteristics of Parallel Prose 即海陶玮为高本汉祝寿论文集（*Studia Serica Bernhard Karlgren Dedicata: sinological studies dedicated to Bernhard Karlgren on his seventieth birthday*）所撰文章，该论文集于 1959 年刊印。"迈群兄"似指徐汉豪（1907—1984），待考。

十月二十一日

先生致信渡边宏，感谢寄来有关马可波罗的日本作品书目，拟将其与自己搜集、整理的目录一并交图齐在意大利出版或在日本出版，另附上一信以便其获取《新疆研究丛刊》。

October 21, 1963

Dear Mr. Watanabe:

Thank you so much for compiling a Bibliography of Japanese works on Marco Polo which I received while I was away from Washington. It was an excellent bibliography and you have surprised me by sending the manuscript so promptly.

This work will be published together with my bibliography on Marco Polo which will not be published until next year. Due acknowledgement will be made in the preface of Professor Tucci who will undertake to publish it. Meanwhile, you are welcome to publish it in Japan, if you so desire.

I have been busy in publishing a number of titles in the series "*Sinkiang Collectanea*". Sometime ago I asked my printer in Hong Kong to mail you a copy. Since you have not received it, I am enclosing a letter to the Yamamoto Shoten Co. in Tokyo, asking that a copy be mailed to you. Please either mail it for me, or you pick it up whenever you go to visit this bookshop. It looks that this bookstore has a large collection of second-hand books.

Please accept my hearty thanks for your valuable help. I hope it has not taken too much of your valuable time.

　　　With warmest regards,

　　　　　　　　　　　　　　　　　　Yours sincerely,

　　　　　　　　　　　　　　　　　　T. L. Yuan

〔University of Chicago Library, Yuan T'ung-li Papers, Box 2〕

　　按：Yammaoto Shoten Co.即山本书店，先生嘱该店所寄之书具体为哪一种或哪几种，待考。该件为录副。

洪余庆覆函先生，感谢为洪有丰遗著作序并告仍有数篇文章尚未找到，请先生帮助搜集。

守和老伯赐鉴：

　　十六日训示、序文及附家父遗著一并于今日收到，毋任言谢。当遵嘱将此次掷下之序文付梓。在慰堂老伯处所摄得七十四页论文，已交照相放大，俟整理后，即可发排矣。俟印竣后，当即寄呈。胡佛图书馆藏《东南大学图书馆述要》已由周之南兄前日掷下之矣，请释念。尚有

　　（一）《我对于省立第一图书馆之希望》（《南京新报》，民十二年二月出版，又见《浙江图书馆年报》第八期）

　　（二）《大学图书馆》，中华图书馆协会十周年纪念论文

　　（三）《图书分类说明及其简表》

等篇，不卜老伯能为搜集否？以老伯与家父相交之深，敢以此请求也。训示中附有邮票乙张，兹附呈。专此，敬请崇安。

　　　　　　　　　　　　　　　　洪制侄余庆叩上

　　　　　　　　　　　　　　　　　　十，二十一

　　又前序：子目书名，编为索引，此项艰钜工作，完成于廿三年五月。此次之序：爰将子目书名，编次索引，体大而工钜，闻者有难色，而范五卒以二十二年春间成书。想以后者之年月为是也。

　　　　　　　　　　　　　　　　　　侄余庆又叩。

〔University of Chicago Library, Yuan T'ung-li Papers, Box 2〕

　　按："子目书名"指《丛书子目书名索引》，施廷镛编辑，1935年出版，洪有丰乙亥夏撰写序言。

十月二十三日

杨家骆向国会图书馆捐赠世界书局影印《永乐大典》100 卷，该馆特举办入藏仪式，国会图书馆执行馆长 Rutherford D. Rogers、负责远东事务的美国助理国务卿 Roger Hilsman、蒋廷黻、张乃维、王世杰、洪培克、恒慕义及国会图书馆东方部、参考部、交换部等代表出席，先生亦受邀到场。〔Library of Congress, *Information Bulletin*, Vol. 22, No. 43, 1963, pp. 577-578〕

> 按：杨家骆本人似未出席，《永乐大典》之影本应由王世杰携至美国并交 Roger Hilsman，由后者代为转赠国会图书馆。Rutherford D. Rogers（1915-2015），美国图书馆学家，曾在纽约公共图书馆服务，1957 年至 1964 年担任国会图书馆副馆长。Roger Hilsman（1919-2014），美国军人、政府官员，二战中曾在中缅印战区服务，1963 年至 1964 年担任助理国务卿。张乃维（1920—?），江苏宜兴人，中央政治学校外文系毕业，后赴美留学，入康乃尔大学、哈佛大学，获博士学位。

卫德明覆函先生，因未找到相关册页故无法回答前询有关留德中国学生的姓名问题，另告徐道邻现在西雅图华盛顿大学。

October 23, 1963

Dear Mr. Yuan:

　　Please forgive me for answering only today your good letter of September 24 concerning the directory of Chinese students who studied in Germany. As you know, all of my Chinese books went to our Far Eastern Library. Somehow this little pamphlet must have gotten lost in the shuffle. Our librarians went to great length in trying to find it, unfortunately however without any result. I am terribly sorry that I can't help you.

　　Dr. Hsu Dau-lin is still with us and will be here until at least the end of the academic year. It is a great pleasure to be able to consort with him again after so many years of separation.

Cordially yours,
Hellmut Wilhelm

〔University of Chicago Library, Yuan T'ung-li Papers, Box 9〕

十月二十四日

郭廷以覆函先生,劝写回忆录并寄上《近代中国史事日志》四部请代为推销。

　　守和先生有道:

　　　　奉十八日赐教,既慰且感。《史事日志》推销一事,复承多方代筹,益见爱护之深。兹谨先邮呈四部,可暂存尊处,不必勉强。Paragon 书店,前曾考虑,据淬廉兄云,收款颇为不易,未悉长者经验如何? 如属可行,当与试洽。顾少川先生文书,据幸伯兄来函,暂时只能以□□□□副本赠送近史所,其他部份,暂□□□□公开,如近史所需要,须预行商□顾先生许可,近日拟去函试探。先生得便,敢恳代进一言为幸。此项文献若能作有系统之刊布,其有裨于五十年来之外交史研究,自匪浅鲜,尚祈大力促成。今日收到金纯儒先生近作《华府会议与中国》,略事翻阅,弥为感佩,希先代致意。

　　　　长者公余之暇,可否亦就兴之所至,□写一二专篇? 如能完成一部回忆录,更为士林佳事。郭鸣声校长前亦屡以为请,或自行动笔,或出之谈话,均无不可,总望为史学上留下一部详实记载。王雪艇先生华府之行,观感若何? 专此,祗颂大安。

　　尊夫人同此问好。

弟廷以拜启

内子附候

十,廿四

　　　　　〔University of Chicago Library, Yuan T'ung-li Papers, Box 9〕

　　按:《近代中国史事日志》四部由该所职员周道瞻寄出。《华府会议与中国》即 *China at the Washington Conference, 1921-1922* ,1963 年由圣若望大学(St. John's University)出版。该函右上残破。

宋晞覆函先生,告知《中国文化季刊》将于明年三月出版《中国留欧大陆各国博士论文目录》。

　　守和先生道鉴:

　　　　十月十六日手示祗悉。《中国文化季刊》五卷二期延至本月底始能出版,五卷三期拟于明年三月印行。尊作《留法比瑞德奥博士论文目录》拟一并于五卷三期刊登,未悉尊意如何? 大稿已完成部分,如能早日寄下,更所企盼,盖可先行付排也。专此布陈,祇颂道安。

后学宋晞敬上

十月廿四日

〔University of Chicago Library, Yuan T'ung-li Papers, Box 6〕

十月二十五日

徐先汇致函先生,请协助在美出售其父所藏善本古籍。

同礼先生大鉴:

家父徐庭瑶平生嗜收集古藏,近年来托友人带散处宋版《事文类聚》及明版《文献通考》各一部,拟在美出售。唯本人与在美中国文学界学士交游欠广,入门无策。今承日章先生介诏,闻先生旅美多年,文学界上声誉海内外,如先生不厌本人之唐突,盼能助一臂之力。敖等当以薄礼聊表谢意。谨候秋安。

徐先汇上

十月廿五日

〔University of Chicago Library, Yuan T'ung-li Papers, Box 2〕

按:"介诏"当作"介绍"。

十月二十八日

范一侯覆函先生,感谢赠书并建议编纂其他学科的书目。

守和先生赐鉴:

月之十八日手示及赐赠《数学书目》乙册,业经收到,多谢多谢。

我国学人,除数学外,其他学科如物理、化学、生物,以及其工程技术方面之论文,以至于人文学科如经济(比较不少)与中国文化方面,或亦不无贡献,倘亦编成书目,便于我国学人之研究,功劳殊大,谅先生早已注意及之矣。按此类工作,费时而辛劳,然意义重大,特向先生致敬。

承示令媛袁静之最近住址,甚感,一俟校友录编就,自当寄奉晒纳。耑复,敬颂大安。

后学范一侯(士奎)奉上

一九六三,十,廿八

〔University of Chicago Library, Yuan T'ung-li Papers, Box 3〕

十月三十日

先生分别致信卜德教授、史克门教授,请二人作为向美国学术团体理事会申请《中国艺术和考古目录》出版资助的评审专家,并给予必要的支持。

〔University of Chicago Library, Yuan T'ung-li Papers, Box 3〕

> 按:这两封信与11月1日致毕乃德教授信,内容大致相同。在致史克门教授信中,先生表示大维德爵士曾承诺出版该书。

陈祚龙致函先生,感谢寄赠毛毯并附上近作两种。

> 守和先生有道:
>
> 　　客月廿七日寄下之名单,想必已经张兄馥蕊填还矣。今者接奉先生赐予小儿法中之毛毯,千里赠厚礼,感谢难言喻。随函附上拙译两种,请查收,祈教正。下况如常,希释远念。肃此。敬颂潭祺百福!
>
> 　　　　　　　　　　　　　　　　　　愚陈祚龙拜上
>
> 　　　　　　　　六三,十,三〇,于巴黎凡善之云楼。

〔University of Chicago Library, Yuan T'ung-li Papers, Box 9〕

> 按:张馥蕊(1914—?),山西安邑人,法国巴黎大学博士及法国高研院社会经济学博士,时应任教于巴黎大学。

十一月一日

先生致信李书华,寄上《中国留欧大陆各国博士论文目录》部分书稿请协助校对,并请将所撰序文于一月内寄下。

> 润章先生著席:
>
> 　　近数星期以来,想贵体已逐渐恢复,至念。雪艇先生昨日前往纽约,想已晤面。《留欧博士论文目录》已将法国部分打完,正在校对及补充之中,下周可以奉上。兹先将序文及比国部分随函奉上,即希教正。凡有不妥之处,均乞改正是祷。弟将《中法半月刊》及《北平研究院院务汇报》所载之人名先编成索引,由此得到不少的中文姓名。虽系苦肉计,亦可达到一部分之目的也。一笑。承允惠赐序文,望于一月以内送下,以便先行付排,至于全部稿件,恐须俟过年后方能打完内中以留德者为最多,查姓名最难。先此申谢,敬候痊安。
>
> 　　　　　　　　　　　　　　　　　　弟袁同礼顿首
>
> 　　　　　　　　　　　　　　　　　　十一月一日

〔Columbia University Libraries Archival Collections, Shuhua Li Papers, 1926-1972, Volume II: Modern Eminent Chinese Leaders〕

　　按：10 月 31 日上午，王世杰访问李书华，谈院士会议事宜，后者表示身体欠佳，否则极愿返台。①
先生致信某医生，询问留学瑞士的医学博士中文姓名。

　　达明大医士惠鉴：

　　久仰大名，亟愿识荆。弟今夏在瑞士小住，得悉台端在港执业，引企贤劳，至为佩仰。弟鉴于我国留欧学生成绩优良，已获得博士学位者已有二千余人，国内多不知之，不无遗憾，爰编印《留欧博士论文目录》以资宣传，大著业已收入，谅荷惠允。尚有少数研究医学之同学，其中文姓名迄未查明。因念台端为留瑞前辈，或有熟识者。兹奉上名单，可否就所知者注明中文姓名。素仰台端对于文化事业热诚赞助，谅荷惠允。先此申谢，顺候道祺，并盼赐覆。

弟袁同礼再拜
十一月一日

〔University of Chicago Library, Yuan T'ung-li Papers, Box 6〕

先生致信郑通，寄上美金支票，并请减低《新疆国界图志》印刷成本，另附第二次寄书单。

　　新华印刷公司郑经理大鉴：

　　两旬以来，因事赴加拿大，返后接到十月十日及十月廿一日来函，详悉一一。寄下之《新疆国界图志》二部亦已收到。兹随函寄上美金支票叁佰元，请查收赐据为荷。《新疆国界图志》前已奉上两笔定金（尊处收据第 3351 及 3358 号），此次来单未予列入，不识何故。又此书仅印 750 部，与《中俄西北条约集》（印 1000 部）略有不同，故正文工料，前请将单价减至二十三元，望即惠允是荷。又前次函内附第一次寄书单，共 360 部，兹又奉上第二次寄书单。尊处代垫邮费，亦望早日示知，以便归还。余书仍暂存贵公司为盼。此颂大安。

袁同礼顿首
十一月一日

〔University of Chicago Library, Yuan T'ung-li Papers, Box 1〕

　　按：工料一般包括封面、扉页、正文、纸型、电版，其中《中俄西北条

---

① 《王世杰日记》，页 1102。

约集》正文工料报价为 25 元。此件为底稿。

先生致信毕乃德，请其作为向美国学术团体理事会申请资助《中国艺术和考古目录》出版的意见征询者，并给予必要的支持。

November 1, 1963

Dear Professor Biggerstaff:

I trust that you have had a profitable and pleasant trip to the Orient. I wish I could join you on your important mission.

I thought I told you when I was in Ithaca a year ago that I had been engaged on a comprehensive bibliography of Chinese art and archaeology. In this work I have analyzed not only sinological and art journals, but also transactions of learned societies and journals of a fugitive character. As a result, I have brought together an immense amount of scientific literature dealing with this subject. I hope to publish it in four volumes. (Calligraphy and Painting, Pottery and Porcelain, Bronzes and Sculpture, and Minor Arts).

Last year I applied for a research grant from the American Council of Learned Societies. Owing to the competition among the applicants, my request was turned down. Now as the volume for Pottery and Porcelain is almost ready for publication, I thought I would try my luck once again. According to my own experience in matters of this kind, members of the Committee on Grants do not seem to give much consideration to the qualification of the applicant, but base their decision largely on the testimonials of the respondents.

Since this bibliographical survey deals entirely with the history of Chinese culture, I trust that you might be willing to give me your moral support. Would it be agreeable to you if I ask you to serve as my respondent?

With cordial regards to you and Mrs. Biggerstaff.

Yours sincerely,
T. L. Yuan

〔University of Chicago Library, Yuan T'ung-li Papers, Box 3〕

按：该件为录副。

十一月二日

龙章覆函先生,告所托查找留法、留瑞博士中文姓名进展。

> 和公馆长前辈赐鉴:
>
> 　　前奉手教,承嘱调查中国留学生在法国大学获得博士学位者之中文姓名,经查出大部分,其余本拟继续查访,俟齐全后一并奉上,旋奉"外交部"令出差奥京维也纳,继又出差西德,先后月余,遂致迁延,敬祈鉴谅。自德国归来,接奉手书及留瑞士学人名单,经去函陈延年兄,嘱其就所者填列中文姓名,尚现待覆中。瑞士中国留学生中尚有袁渊(Yuan Yuan)获博士学位,现身在大陆。兹谨先行奉上留法学人名单,其中未列中文姓名者当继续查问,一俟有结果当随时奉告。崀肃,并颂道安。
>
> 晚龙章敬上
十一月二日
>
> 〔University of Chicago Library, Yuan T'ung-li Papers, Box 6〕

　　按:"就所者填列"似应为"就所知者填列"。

十一月五日

王世杰致函先生,商洽居延汉简运台事宜。

> 叔和吾兄惠鉴:
>
> 　　在华府得与兄及嫂夫人岂晤,至以为快。汉简事承费神询明,甚善。杰现已与"中研院"同人电商,决定将该汉简十四箱运回,交"中研院"史语所管用(胡适之先生曾向该所声明可如此处置)。俟二三星期后,杰由纽约返台北时,即由院备函"驻美使馆",请其致函国会图书馆提取。至于运输办法,未审兄有无意见,可否交由招商局商轮在 Baltimore 取运,以及如何保险。倘承惠示尊见,尤为感盼。费神至谢,顺颂时祺。
>
> 弟王世杰敬启
十一,五
>
> 〔University of Chicago Library, Yuan T'ung-li Papers, Box 2〕

十一月六日

李书华覆函先生,告知韩咏华行踪,并询问《中国留欧大陆各国博士论文目录》各节以便撰写序言。

守和先生惠鉴：

接十一月一日手书，敬悉一切。弟近来大致已恢复原状。雪艇到纽后已见过数次。上周六月涵夫人由英飞抵纽，现住弟寓，数日后即将前往费城。"留欧博士论文目录"弟拟作之序言，仅为一短文，一月内想总可交卷。拟俟法国部分寄下稍加过目后，再开始起草。兄序文中称：留德理科论文以 Li Fo Ki 为最早（一九〇七）。不知大陆欧洲中国人之论文，以何人在何国者为最早？请查明示知。赵承嘏（原在英国留学，后在日内瓦大学得化学博士，任北平研究院药物研究所所长有年。）之论文在何年？（前在瑞士单中见过，但忘记。）亦请示知为感。寄下之比国单中，内有数人缺中文姓名，弟均不知。又大著 Preface 仅略修正一二字。比国单及 Preface 随信附还。匆此，顺请双安。

　　　　　　　　　　　　　　　　　　弟李书华敬启

　　　　　　　　　　　　　　　　　　11/6/63

〔University of Chicago Library, Yuan T'ung-li Papers, Box 9〕

按：赵承嘏（1885—1966），江苏江阴人，字石民，1905 年赴英留学，1910 年获曼彻斯特大学学士学位，后赴日内瓦大学获博士学位，毕业后在法国工作数年，1923 年归国，先后在南京高等师范学院、北京协和医学院等校任教，1932 年入北平研究院。

十一月九日

王伊同致函先生，感谢寄赠画展图录，并谈收藏张大千书画及郑华在校情况等。

老伯大人尊前：

敬禀者，昨奉手谕暨张大千画展一册，又蒙厚贶，良感良感。年前购进张老《黄山慈光寺山水》一幅全幅见《大千画集》，布局略有出入，早年笔势竟不及近作远甚，大抵吾国文人画家年老益工，诚古今同轨矣。郑华女士极负责，唯迩来移民局突有问题，正交涉中，而华府教署以议会方面迟迟不批准豫算，明年恐不能增款，亦一问题也。翁松禅之侄孙元庆君字龄雨，八月间染病，以十月十五日去世，年才五十有二，渠燕京前辈，教书梅贻宝先生处得讯怏怏。□师大今以师母入院休息，寿筵展开，康桥友好来信云尔。敬肃，并请金安。

　　　　　　　　　　　　　　　　　　侄伊同顿首拜

十一月九日

〔袁同礼家人提供〕

　　按:"翁松禅"即翁同穌。

十一月十日

先生致信李书华,询问数位留法学生情况并谈《中国留欧大陆各国博士论文目录》拟于一次出版,属撰序言并不亟需。

　　润章先生著席:

　　　　奉赐书,欣悉贵体逐渐恢复原状,至以为慰。国人在欧获得博士学位者,以马德润及李君为最早,附单备查。留法部份尚待补充,兹先将初稿奉上,仅五百六十余人,尚有遗漏。陆鼎恒、曾觉之曾得博士否,并盼示知,当再查。德国留学得博士者约九百余人,现正查中文姓名,颇感困难。昨接《中国文化》编辑部来函,谓拟将各国论文于一次印出,弟亦极表同意,故尊处序文不忙寄下也。此上,敬候时祉。

　　　　　　　　　　　　　　　　　　　　弟同礼再拜

　　　　　　　　　　　　　　　　　　　　十一月十日

　　月涵夫人想已赴费城,弟信寄交钟太太转。

　　　　〔Columbia University Libraries Archival Collections, Shuhua Li Papers, 1926-1972, Volume II: Modern Eminent Chinese Leaders〕

　　按:陆鼎恒(1902—?),字惟一,浙江萧山人,法国理学硕士,未获博士学位,曾任北平研究院动物研究所所长;曾觉之,并未获得博士学位。"钟太太"即钟安民的夫人梅祖杉。

十一月十二日

先生致信罗家伦,告知购书进展。

　　志希馆长学兄道席:

　　　　前奉手教,嘱向伦敦 Probsthain 及荷兰 Brill 两书店函购各书,当即分别订购,均有发票及收据寄来。兹连同其他单据一并送上,以便书籍寄到后可以根据点收,凡无正式收据者已告其补寄,容在奉上。汇下之五百元,现存六十壹元。前代订购之各期刊,下月满期应续订者,望早日示知,以免以后配补不易。党史会之款似需早日用完,前请将会中已入藏之西文资料开单寄下,以免重复,务请早日寄下,以便亲到各旧书店详细翻检。凡关于国父之资料,均拟设法购到或影制复本,谅荷赞同。先此,敬候道祺。

弟袁同礼再拜

十一月十二日

〔University of Chicago Library, Yuan T'ung-li Papers, Box 1〕

按:此件为底稿。

十一月十三日

王世杰覆函先生,谈汉简运台及向福特基金会申请资助事。

守和兄惠鉴:

七日来书,再悉。汉简事,兹决定于杰月底返台后,由"中研院"备公函致"驻美使馆",请其代为提取。至于运输、保险及改装诸事,我"使馆"如需人指告,想兄当不吝费神协助也。哥大教授 A. Doak Barnett 君,杰于日前曾在哥大公宴席上晤会,惜当时尚未接到兄之来信。福德基金会事,容详细研讨再行试洽。匆此,再候俪祺。

弟王世杰复启

十一,十三

〔University of Chicago Library, Yuan T'ung-li Papers, Box 2〕

按:A. Doak Barnett 即 Arthur Doak Barnett(1921—1999),生于上海,美国记者、社会活动家,对中美关系颇有研究。

Joseph F. Fletcher 致函先生,预订《新疆研究丛刊》全套,并称赞先生对于远东和中亚研究的巨大贡献。

15 Everett Street

Apartment 35

Cambridge 38, Mass.

13 November 1963

Dear Dr. Yuan:

I am writing so as to be sure to get copies of each of your publications in the *Sinkiang Collectanea*. Could you send them to me as they come out care of the following address?

Joseph F. Fletcher

c/o Society of Fellows

Widener Library W

Harvard University

Cambridge 38, Mass.

I shall be away from February until November of 1964; so I should like to send you payment in advance. Could you let me know what the price for them all will be? I shall send you a check as soon as I know the amount.

You and I have related interests. I am working on the modern history of Sinkiang and spent last summer in Europe exploring primary materials, mostly Turki and Persian manuscripts. Next year, I shall be looking for primary sources in the Far East, Central Asia, and Russia.

I look forward to meeting you and having a talk. Unfortunately, there is no time for me to get to Washington in the near future, but, if you should be in Cambridge before February, I hope you will give me a call.

The kind of thing you are doing is of the greatest importance for everyone interested in Far Eastern and Central Asian studies, and I, for one, should like to express my gratitude, especially for your bibliography of Japanese works on Sinkiang.

Sincerely yours,

Joseph F. Fletcher

〔University of Chicago Library, Yuan T'ung-li Papers, Box 3〕

按:Joseph Fletcher(1934－1984),哈佛大学中国史教授,对中亚研究领域有极其重要的贡献和影响。

十一月十四日

李书华覆函先生,就国人在欧获得博士学位清单中的错误予以纠正。

守和先生惠鉴:

接十一月十日手书及附单,均敬悉。陆鼎恒未得博士学位。曾觉之是否得过博士学位,弟则不知,希再查。荷兰华侨得博士者,似亦应列入单中。罗马教会大学不肯函告论文题目,可否转请谢寿康(字次彭,"驻教廷大使")或于斌代为说明编论文目录之用意,仍请其帮忙开列,何如?

留法部分初稿,弟曾细读一遍。有几处弟用铅笔略加修正。如:(一)Strassbourg 应为 Strasbourg(法文为 Strasbourg,德文为 Straßburg);(二)Wang Kono-Wei 为 Wang Kouo-Wei;(三)daus 应为 dans;(四)LI

SHU HUOA 应为 LI SHOU HOUA<small>(弟旅法时姓名如此写)</small>；(五)林融应为林镕。此外尚有下列可疑之处：(1)朱光潜之论文题目,是否系英文,抑系法文? (页 3);(2)Lou, Yei-Sen 中文名是否系卢郁文? (页七)<small>按"sen"与"文"其音相差颇远。又河北昌黎之卢郁文,非留法</small>;(3)谢东发(Paris, Droit 1926)是否系 1926? (页二五)是否系 1916 之误? <small>按此人系老资格,其父谢大明为旅法之古董商,母为法人。东发在"驻法使馆"任职多年</small>;(4)经利彬似兼有理学博士与医学博士。尊稿仅列其理学博士,希再查明其是否亦系医学博士?

以上(1)(2)(3)(4)希再一查,何如?

容闳为中国人在美留学之最早者。中国人在欧洲大陆留学之最早者,是否为马建忠? 马建忠字眉叔,马相伯之弟,马氏文通著者。马建忠于清光绪四年(一八七八)以郎中派赴驻法使馆留学,习政治法律。马建忠是否为欧洲大陆留学之最早者,盼示知。

月涵夫人已于本月十日由其女婿钟安民接往费城矣。此请大安。

弟李书华拜启

11/14/63

附"留法部分"原单一份。

〔University of Chicago Library, Yuan T'ung-li Papers, Box 6、7〕

按:林镕(1903—1981),江苏丹阳人,植物学家,1928 年获巴黎大学博士学位。经利彬(1895—1958),字燧初,浙江上虞人,生物学家、医学家,早年赴法留学,获理学及医学博士学位。马建忠(1845—1900),江苏镇江人,清末洋务派、外交官、学者,光绪二年(1876)被李鸿章派往法国,翌年成为第一个取得法国高中会考毕业证书(Baccalauréat en France)的中国人,1878 年入巴黎自由政治学堂(L'École Libre des Sciences Politiques),后获得法学士学位(Licences de l'École de Droit)。

十一月十六日

先生致信 Joseph F. Fletcher,告知《新疆研究丛书》出版计划,其中中、西文书目两种需要出版补助,预计在明年二、三月间向哈佛燕京学社递交申请。

November 16, 1963

Dear Dr. Fletcher:

May I thank you for your flattering letter and say how much I appreciate your interest in Central Asian studies. This is a new field of studies in America and I know you will be doing pioneering work in this field. May I look forward to numerous books and articles from your able pan in the not too distant future.

As to various works included in the *Sinkiang Collectanea*, seven of them will appear before next February, each costing ＄3.00. There will be considerable delay in the publication of the two bibliographies in Chinese and in Western languages. The University of Hong Kong Press has agreed to publish one of them but asks for a substantial subsidy. I am hoping that the Harvard-Yenching Institute may be able to make a grant next April, but I shall make the application in February or March. By that time, I hope you may like to write a testimonial on my behalf.

My primary object in publishing these works is to provide source materials for the study of Sinkiang and is intended for the use by Chinese students.

Harvard is my beloved university and I had spent a considerable time in Cambridge. If I do come in the future, I shall certainly call on you. Meanwhile, please accept my best wishes for your continued success,

Yours sincerely,

T. L. Yuan

P. S. I am sending you the two works under separate cover. Four more works have been published and on their way from Taipei.

〔University of Chicago Library, Yuan T'ung-li Papers, Box 3〕

按:此件为录副。

John Israel 致函先生,订购《中国留英同学博士论文目录》《中国留美同学博士论文目录》,并询问谭卓垣遗稿期刊目录有无出版可能。

November 16, 1963

Dear Dr. Yuan:

I have read of your recent publication, *A Guide to Doctoral Dissertations by Chinese Students in Great Britain and Northern Ireland* in the latest issue of *Asian Studies Newsletter*. Would you kindly send me a copy? I enclose a check for ＄1.50. May I also order directly from you your *Guide to Doctoral Dissertations by Chinese Students in America*? If so, please quote me the price.

In the preface to *China in Western Literature*, you expressed the hope that support might be found to complete and publish Dr. Cheuk-woon Taam's bibliography on articles in journals. I am one of many people who sincerely hope that your wish will be realized. Are the omens good?

Your truly,

John Israel

〔University of Chicago Library, Yuan T'ung-li Papers, Box 3〕

按:John Israel(1935-),美国汉学家,中文名易社强,时在 Claremont Men's College 任教。

十一月十九日

先生致信李书华,略述甄别留欧博士真伪情况,并告马建忠、陈季同为早期留法人士。

润章先生著席:

顷奉手教,承指示各节,至以为感,业已一一改正。凡此间无法查明者,均函请原校查覆,因之发现冒充博士者不少。关于欧洲留学自明末清初已有多人,另寄方豪论文,即希台阅。马建忠有著作,而《马相伯年谱》亦有记载(系光绪二年 1876 赴法者,公使为郭嵩涛)以上二书,想哥大均有。此外,尚有驻法使馆武官陈季同 Tcheng Ki-Tong,在光绪十年即以法文发表 *Les Chinois peints par eux-mêmes*,则在马氏之后矣。此上,顺候著祺。

弟同礼再拜

十一,十九晚

又留德学人已收入者将近千人,近年中共派往东德获得博士者亦有十人左右,并闻。

〔Columbia University Libraries Archival Collections, Shuhua Li Papers, 1926-1972, Volume II: Modern Eminent Chinese Leaders〕

按:陈季同(1851—1907),字敬如,福建侯官人,晚清外交家、作家,1878 年至 1880 年留学巴黎政治自由学堂(L'École Libre des Sciences Politiques),学习公法,1884 年出版 *Les Chinois peints par eux-m êmes*，今译作《中国人自画像》。

十一月二十日

余又荪覆函先生，告知商务印书馆前因台风致印书迟缓，寄送台大历史系所出《文史丛刊》，并表来美之议仍在念中请随时留意。

守和先生道席：

十月十八日及十一月八日两示均先后奉悉。本年度兼任两职务，而任课仍旧，未减少；研究所事务少，系则事烦。故较上年为忙。

商务已有函复先生矣，或未述明迟误之故。

暑中，台风豪雨，情况之怪，门外人很难信之。大约石门水库放水之故，顷刻之间，低区水淹及屋顶。死者不谈，物产损失甚巨。台大一同人，家藏善本书，有年矣，此次则随水而去。

商务为先生印之书，受此损失。——此事商务当已奉陈。

另一迟误原因，则九月、十月为教课书销售季节，商务此两月作季节生意，不得不将尊事迟缓。——此点商务或未便奉陈。

总之，请原谅，商务现已加速赶工矣。祈释念！

（商务，中华，仍保持往日信誉，较他书商为妥，请放心！）

《新疆图界国志》尚未寄到，到时当仍照前例交商务入账代售，定价若干，祈示知！

台大历史研究所印行之《文史丛刊》，系与中国文学研究所共同选硕士论文出版。现决继续出版，已寄七册至国会图书馆，另寄赠先生一份，今后当继续出版补赠。学位论文，当事人无力自印，由研究所筹款印行。甚为艰苦！

Murphy 已返台北，前日彼建筑之文教中心已开幕，耶稣会之力也。

来美事仍在计划之中，但不愿以教日文为主。自知才学不佳，不敢存"待价而沽"之志，但仍时时注意机缘也。

《新疆研究丛书》已引起此间学术界之重视，时时有询及者。此时出版，正值各方之需要，商务方面已赶工矣。

专肃，敬颂著安。

余又荪敬上

十一月二十日

〔University of Chicago Library, Yuan T'ung-li Papers, Box 1〕

十一月二十二日

黎东方覆函先生,谈新疆民族问题论战之隐情,并告嘱查留法学生姓名已转请在台友人代为询问、填注。

同礼先生道鉴:

昨晚敝校历史学系李君转到先生十月廿八日赐教,敬悉一切。此函被搁置在该系多日,始被李君发现。弟在此属于中文系,致有此误。

贱名及有关新疆之拙作,蒙分别惠列于大著之中,感何胜言。留法同学之姓名,弟竟一无所知。谨已代用 xerox 抄印一份(抄件附还,原件寄胡品清矣),寄"中国文化学院"之胡品清教授,托渠代找张兆智与台北留法同学会诸友,并告以填好径寄尊府。

新疆民族问题之论战,《"中央"日报》受了和事老陈果夫与尧乐博士之影响,未肯将弟之最后一篇对伊敏之答辩载出,以致伊敏占了上风。弟气愤之余,将该篇载在《国民公报》。此文现存台北舍下,如时间来得及,甚恳先生收入"丛刊"(《阿尔泰月刊》为伊敏、艾沙等人之刊物,彼辈乐得只抄《"中央"日报》之文章,而 ignore《国民公报》上之最后一篇也)。(伊、艾二人现均居住土耳其,入了土耳其籍。伊曾在南疆主持叛乱,与和加尼牙子相先后,曾被举为伪东土耳其斯坦共和国总统。)

丛刊弟拟自备一份(支票附上),本校图书馆方面已填了卡片去,大概两三月后方能完成 red tape。大著 *China in Western Literature*,弟已另行向 Yale 的 Far East Publication 订购,但该处谓只管批发,零购须经过书商,可否劳驾先从府上寄下一册,并盼赐寄《留美中国博士论文》一册,两册书价若干,当即补上支票。

中国之《申报》,不知何处图书馆藏有全份,务乞费神示下为感。

今秋在美京匆匆拜见,未及多多请益,极为怅惘。寒假颇想再来,不知先生其时离开美京他游否? 嵩此敬复,并颂撰安。

后学黎东方拜泐
十一月廿二日

〔University of Chicago Library, Yuan T'ung-li Papers, Box 5〕

按:"敝校"即威斯康星大学,时黎东方受邀前往该校访问并授课。

十一月二十六日

先生致信 Wenner-Gren Foudation,请该所寄下申请所需表格及该基金会资助范围公告。

November 26, 1963

Dear Sir:

For some time in the past, I have been engaged in a Bibliography of Prehistory and Anthropology of China. In order to bring the work to completion, I need clerical assistance and financial aid in the publication of this bibliography.

I understand that your grants-in-aid program provides a certain amount for research relating to the science of man. I shall indeed be grateful if you could send an application form and an announcement of your program.

Yours sincerely,

T. L. Yuan

〔University of Chicago Library, Yuan T'ung-li Papers, Box 8〕

按:此件为录副。

十一月三十日

先生致信郭廷以,惊悉董作宾去世,寄上挽联稿。

量予先生教席:

前奉手教,拜悉种切。大著四部,迄今尚未寄到,想仍在途中也。昨接"大使馆"电话,惊悉彦堂先生突然作古,无任痛悼,想后事有兄等照料,定必妥贴。兹奉上挽联稿,可否转托贵所同人代写一联,径送治丧处,所费若干,容再补呈。专此拜托,顺候道祺。

弟袁同礼再拜

十一月三十日

〔台北"中央研究院"近代史研究所档案馆,〈郭廷以〉,馆藏号069-01-02-089〕

按:11 月 23 日,董作宾去世。该信于 12 月 7 日送达。

先生致信郑通,请其将退回之《新疆国界图志》分别寄送台湾友人。

新华印刷公司郑经理大鉴:

十一月一日寄上美金支票叁百元,尚未奉到收据,请查复并赐收据为荷。十月五号请邮寄台北赵叔诚先生五人每人五十部《新疆国界图志》,曾由贵公司照寄在案,不意台北邮局以其不合进口手续,未获海关准许,以致原件悉数退回,想尊处不日可以收到,即希暂存为荷。据台北友人见告,谓每次寄书部数不可太多。兹拟每人暂寄六部,即希照下列所开分别寄出为荷。所垫邮费亦望示知。专此,即颂时祉。

袁同礼顿首

十一月三十日

〔University of Chicago Library, Yuan T'ung-li Papers, Box 1〕

按:250 部《新疆国界图志》并未退回香港。此件为底稿,左侧注有赵叔诚、叶友梅、张学训、余又荪等人地址信息。

刘麟生覆函先生,告诸事。

守和博士先生著席:

(一)承赐廿六日手翰,感慰无既;(二)大千先生画展,弟于第一日往观,并取得一纪念册,如台端未见此书,弟即当邮递,万勿客气为祷;(三)《唐伯虎传》弟未曾撰述,不知何人执笔;(四)项道济兄告弟,谓房君夫妇系五年合同,责其必须完成此巨帙也。匆匆,敬请双安。

弟麟生顿首

十一月卅日夜

〔University of Chicago Library, Yuan T'ung-li Papers, Box 1〕

按:"大千先生画展"应指本年 10 月 22 日至 11 月 2 日张大千(Chang Dai-chien)在纽约赫希尔·阿德勒画廊(Hirschl & Adler Galleries)举办的展览,该展确出版展览画册。"巨帙"即《明代名人传》。

十二月二日

吴俊升致函先生,告萧世言博士论文题目并寄讲演录。

守和吾兄撰席:

奉赐书,敬悉一一。陈静民先生之论文题,彼已径函奉达。萧世言先生之论文题已经查明如下,

El Problema de las Relaciones entre la Razón y la Fe en la Filosofía

Medieval, par Shiao Shih-yen.

萧世言:《中世纪哲学中的理性与信仰之问题》,马德里大学博士论文。

其他各位,因无法查明,已遵嘱停止调查,希望大作能早日出版,俾获先睹之快也。又弟最近在此讲演,以"中国大学教育之特色"为题,曾引尊编留英美中国学生得博士之人数,以证明中国大学教育之成就。兹另邮寄,乞指正为荷。匆此,顺颂撰绥。

弟吴俊升顿首

十二月二日

〔University of Chicago Library, Yuan T'ung-li Papers, Box 5〕

按:"陈静民"即陈敬民,1948 年在莱顿大学获得博士学位,其博士论文题名为 Over de lage valentie van lood en bismuth en loodcomplexen。萧世言,1947 年在西班牙马德里大学获得博士学位,此处所记论文题目与先生刊行之目录略有出入,待考。

十二月五日

李书华覆函先生,商榷马建忠派往法国时间。

守和先生惠鉴:

十一月十九日晚手书,敬悉。嗣承寄下方豪"中国初期留学拾遗"之 Photostats,业经收到,多谢多谢。该论文曾阅读一遍,本日另邮寄还,请查收。

张若谷编马良年谱,载:"1876 年眉叔(马建忠)以郎中派赴法国中国使馆学习洋务。"又载:"1877 年眉叔应试巴黎政治学院,获得优奖(时郭嵩涛任法使)。"然清史"交聘年表一"则载:光绪四年(1878)二月辛未命郭嵩涛(自光绪元年任出使英国大臣)兼为出使法国大臣,是法国正式设有中国使馆应自 1878 年始。则马建忠派往法国似亦应为 1878 年。

匆此,敬请双安。

弟李书华敬启

12/5/63

〔University of Chicago Library, Yuan T'ung-li Papers, Box 5〕

按:先生前信所言 1876 年准确,非 1878 年。

十二月六日

郭有守致函先生,告由留法同学确认此前寄来名单中数人之姓名。

> 守和学长兄:
>
> 　　纽约未及聆教为怅怅。顷奉十一月廿九日手教,今午与周麟、黄
> 家城及自台北来老留法同学陈翔冰同进午食。由黄家城就兄寄名单
> 又找出三四名,非常不易。因弟于 1928 年回国,1946 年来时对已往同
> 学不熟,若须找老人或可得知一二也。倘能得之,当随时奉达。先覆,
> 敬请著安。
>
> 弟郭有守再拜
> 十二,六

〔University of Chicago Library, Yuan T'ung-li Papers, Box 6〕

十二月八日

刘麟生覆函先生,告其现在工作地址,仍希代为谋职。

> 守和尊兄博士勋鉴:
>
> 　　雒诵二日明教,并承赐还邮票,非所克望,敬谢敬谢。郭君大维之
> 画展,并未见有目录。弟每日往通运治事地点为 Room 1603, 5 E.
> 57th. St.(Ncw 5th Avenue)。大驾来此,亟盼惠临,当介绍与鲍君一
> 谈,兼观所藏古玩,文衡山手卷尤为可贵,深冀大鉴赏家一赐评语也。
> 通运尚拟清理乞秘之,故不能视为久计,如晤嗣禹先生,祈为推毂为幸。
> 敬请著安。无任瞻企之至。
>
> 小弟麟生顿首
> 十二,八

〔University of Chicago Library, Yuan T'ung-li Papers, Box 5〕

　　按:"鲍君"和文徵明手卷,待考。

十二月九日

Lita B. Fejos 覆函先生,告知申请 Wenner-Gren Foundation 赞助的基本条件,并寄来制式文件。

December 9, 1963

Dear Dr. Yuan:

　　Thank you for your letter of November 26 concerning the possibility of Foundation support for your Bibliography of Prehistory and

Anthropology of China. We are enclosing herewith some general information about the Foundation's program of awards and activities, and our Information Requested sheet as a guide to the formal application for aid.

As we do not know from your letter whether or not you have completed your studies, may we point out that aid is extended to students only through our pre-doctoral fellowship program. To be eligible for this fellowship, the petitioner must be nominated by the head of the department in which he is officially enrolled as a doctoral candidate, and recommended by the faculty of that department with a status of Assistant Professor or above. The student's application is submitted to us by the department, accompanied by a cover letter of endorsement.

If, however, you already possess the Ph. D degree, you are eligible to apply for a grant-in-aid. We would suggest that, in either case, if you do wish to file a petition it should be done as quickly as is convenient for you. The procedure for processing petitions can be quite a lengthy one, and although the next meeting of our Board of Directors is as yet unscheduled, it is hoped that a decision could be given to you early in the coming year. We will look forward to hearing further from you in this regard.

Sincerely yours,

Lita Binns Fejos

Director of Research

〔University of Chicago Library, Yuan T'ung-li Papers, Box 8〕

按：该函附有文件 Information Requested from Petitioners for grants-in-aid、Wenner-Gren Foundation pre-doctoral Fellowships in Anthropology 和 Information Concerning Activies of the Foundation 三种。

十二月十一日

徐传保致函先生，代魏道明、王守竞订购书籍，并谈影印《四库全书》罕见本之设想。

守和先生钧鉴：

　　暌违尊范，时切景慕。今晨捧接大著三种，诵读诸序及目录，举世名作哀集无遗，诚经世治国之文，感佩交并，谢谢。兹附上支票一纸，计美金十元，敬求经售室邮寄魏伯聪"大使"二种（《中俄西北条约集》及 *Doctoral Dissertations in Great Britain*），又王守竞博士一种（《现代中国数学研究目录》）。伯公长于治国并善外交，诲延多士，邦洲之福利是筹，必以先睹为快。王博士吾乡硕彦、数学钜子，曾总裁中国物资供应委员会，亦必拜服（二公住址详后，如款额不足，当补不误）。

　　上月在中大校友会剧场幸遇郭秉文先生，藉知美京中华文化组织，晚乘机进言印行《四库全书》罕见本，似有必要，并谓务恳泰斗等之提倡始克有成，未识可荷郭氏赞许否？近闻杨家骆先生影印《永乐大典》（《今日世界》中曾提大名），各国争相订购，群儒称庆，但数仅百本，或未足与《四库》罕本同论。

　　光阴如驰，又值圣诞，依此邦习惯，谨备一书（《中国山水画册》）嘱 Brentano 书局递送，谅已邀览。此书虽于去年底出版，惟价值不昂（德国印刷），且著者为 Cleveland Museum 馆长，此君不独精通西方文化，且研置远东艺术（与 Nelson Gallery 馆长齐名，均为承福开森氏之余绪者），书中图画多示题识，于中国收藏家、鉴赏家、印鉴等问题之叙述，亦多发挥，故求者踵阶，或将售空，亦未可知。顾谫庸后学管见如斯，不值高明一笑。书不尽意，祗贺新禧，并祝阖第皆大吉祥。

晚徐传保率眷鞠躬

一九六三年十二月十一日

［附支票一纸计美金十元。］

"魏大使"通信地址如左：

Dr. T. M. Wei, 220 Lasky Drive-Beverly Hill, California

　　王博士地址为 Dr. S. C. Wang, 110 Garfield Street Watertown Mass （请经售室以寻常书报递寄方法寄出，不必挂号或用航空。）

　　又敬询者，尊著《改订国会图书馆藏中国善本书录》绝版后，已否重印，何处发售，均求吉便谕示，无任跂盼之至，之至。徐家璧先生所示大著《西文汉学书目》幸已托舍亲林君于耶鲁购到，亦云幸矣。

〔University of Chicago Library, Yuan T'ung-li Papers, Box 2〕

按:"Cleveland Museum 馆长"应指 Sherman E. Lee(1918-2008),
美国亚洲艺术史专家,1958 年起担任克里夫兰艺术博物馆馆长;
《中国山水画册》即 *Chinese Landscape Painting* ,1954 年该馆初
版。Nelson Gallery 馆长即史克门。

十二月十六日

恒慕义致片先生,寄上修改后的《中国留欧大陆各国博士论文目录》序言。

Dec 16, 1963

Dear Dr. Yuan:

Your preface seems to me inclusive and informative-very ably done.

You will have to judge for yourself the validity or not of my
changes.

Sincerely yours

A. W. Hummel

〔University of Chicago Library, Yuan T'ung-li Papers, Box 6〕

按:此件为其亲笔。

十二月十九日

先生改定 A Guide to Doctoral Dissertations by Chinese Students in Continental
Europe, 1907-1962 序言。

十二月二十七日

Delafield 覆函先生,告已收到《胡适先生西文著作目录》草稿,并拟增加部
分篇目,另告因出任陪审团无法如期前往华盛顿。

Dear Mr. Yuan,

Thank you for your letter and the list of Dr. Hu Shih's writings.

I have been going over it carefully, and will add to it a few more
titles. There are some titles I can't look up here. You may have them
buried in the Library of Congress.

I had expected to be able to come down to Washington this coming
month, and go over with you various matters. Very unexpectedly I have
been called to serve here in New York on the Grand Jury for one month
so that forces me to wait until February to come down to Washington. I
regret this very much, but it can't be helped. I hope that February will be

suitable for you to see me. I will write and tell you exactly when I will be coming. Till then my best wishes for the New Year.

Eugene Delafield

Dec. 27, 1963

〔University of Chicago Library, Yuan T'ung-li Papers, Box 9〕

按:此件为其亲笔。

十二月三十一日

余又荪覆函先生,告商务印书馆印书进展等事。

守和先生道席:

近奉大示,为商务印书事迟缓,深引为歉。已催促其速办。赵叔诚先生答覆,本周即寄上三种,余则元月内可印就,并嘱代致歉忱。

总之,此事绝促其早办清楚,祈释念! 台大历史研究所寄赠国会图书馆及先生之《文史丛刊》,均系平寄,因寄至国外者甚多,省寄费也。此次寄出者凡七种,今后陆续出版,陆续寄赠。——印刷费系向各方捐募而来者。

香港寄来之《新疆图志》,已收到一部份,当送交商务寄售。书到齐,始知总数。

半年来,任史学研究所及系事,较前为忙。但每日坐守研究室,亦得藉此整理文稿。近与商务谈妥,即将印行《中古中日关系史》一书。此亦可谓守办公室之收获。

子女二人,因纽约生活高,下学期均拟转至附近他校,盼能于一年内得一学位,然后再转至较大学校读博士学位。无力负担其学费,均由彼等自行活动耳。

除夕,谨奉此函,恭贺新禧!

余又荪谨上

除夕

〔University of Chicago Library, Yuan T'ung-li Papers, Box 1〕

按:"除夕"非指阴历,特此说明。《中古中日关系史》应指《隋唐五代中日关系史》,1964 年 6 月初版,隶属台湾商务印书馆《史地丛书》。

一九六四年　七十岁

一月四日

李书华致函先生,请协助查找国会图书馆藏北京大学教职员名录,并谈李大钊、陈独秀信奉共产主义的时间。

　　守和先生惠鉴:

　　　　弟为《传记文学》拟写一篇《七年北大》。弟系 1922 年八月到北大物理系任教,1929 年暑假时离开北大。弟初入北大一二年时,全校共有教授约七八十人,现就记忆所及,还可想出教授姓名,约七十人左右。国会图书馆是否藏有那时北大教职员录? 如有,敬请费神用 xerox 印一份寄下。用费若干务请示知,弟当如数归还。

　　　　弟初入北大时,北大图书馆主任(或称图书部主任)是李守常,大约一九二三? 守常离开图书馆,主任一职由皮宗石(皓白)继任。皓白之后,由兄继任。兄到北海图书馆,北大图书主任便由马叔平继任。守常离开图书馆是否在一九二三年? 彼为何离开图书馆? 守常在北大每周教课一二小时,其所任之课,系何名称? 是否属于政治系? 盼示知。

　　　　弟以为守常开始倾向共产主义是在一九一九年,或在"五四"稍后,亦未可知。陈独秀倾向共产主义则在一九二〇年春,彼由北方至上海以后。中共两位老祖宗:"南陈北李",北李倾向共产主义比南陈还要早半年到一年,兄意以为如何? 亦希示知。

　　　　特此奉恳,顺请双安。

弟李书华敬启

1/4/64

〔University of Chicago Library, Yuan T'ung-li Papers, Box 9〕

按:《七年北大》后连载于《传记文学》第 6 卷第 2、3 两期。[①]

---

① 《传记文学》第 6 卷第 2 期,1965 年 2 月,页 17–24;《传记文学》第 6 卷第 3 期,1965 年 3 月,页 27–30。

一月初

Joseph F. Fletcher 致函先生,愿为申请资助联系白思达,并告将赴远东和中亚地区,《新疆研究丛刊》可寄送其在马萨诸塞州的住所,另寄上购书支票。

Dear Mr. Yuan:

I hope you will forgive the long delay and the short note I am trying to pass off as a letter.

I shall certainly speak to Dr. Baxter and write a letter on your behalf if he advises me to do so in support of your request for a grant to help in the publication of your bibliographies.

At the moment I am in a great hurry trying to make all the necessary arrangements for my forthcoming trip to the Far East and Central Asia.

When the books come that you are going to send on to me, would you please use the following address:

6 Saint John's Road

Cambridge 38, Mass.

Anything sent to me care of that address will be held for my arrival.

I am sending a check for $24.00 to cover the seven forthcoming parts of the *Sinkiang Collectanea* (at $3.00 each) plus an extra copy of the Bibliography on Japanese works, which I hope you will forward to me at your convenience.

Best wishes for a good 1964. I look forward to seeing you in Washington in the fall of this year.

Sincerely yours,

Joseph F. Fletcher

〔University of Chicago Library, Yuan T'ung-li Papers, Box 3〕

按:该函无撰写日期。

一月六日

先生致信 Lita Fejos,向 Wenner-Gren Foundation 递交资助申请。

January 6, 1964

Director of Research

Wenner-Gren Foundation for Anthropological Research

14 East 71st Street

New York 21, N. Y.

Dear Madam:

I am grateful to you for your letter of December 8 enclosing your Information Requested sheet. Herewith I beg to submit my application for a grant-in-aid.

The clerical assistance of $750 which I requested would include the typing of the final manuscript for offset printing. If a research grant could be awarded, the bibliography should be published next fall.

As you will note, there is a considerable literature relating to Chinese archaeology and anthropology which has not received the attention from scientists it deserves. If a guide could be published, it would be a contribution to the Science of Man. In view of your Foundation's role in fostering scholarship, I hope I may count on your support.

Yours sincerely,

Tung-li Yuan

〔University of Chicago Library, Yuan T'ung-li Papers, Box 8〕

按：your letter of December 8 不准确，应指 12 月 9 日来函。此件为录副。

一月八日

先生致信李书华，就所询各事略作解答，建议联系伯克利东亚图书馆的参考馆员以获取北京大学教职员名录信息。

润章先生著席：

奉到手教，当即到书库详细检查，此间仅有民六所印《北大二十周年纪念册》，内有教授名单，想哥大已入藏。又《守常文集》最近在北平出版，此间有一部，适为他人借出，无法检查，想哥大亦购到矣。守常何年离开图书馆，弟已不记忆，但决早于一九二三年。当时弟在巴黎（时刘半侬、许德珩、周梅苏均在巴黎），故不知其详也。至于守常开始倾向共产主义，大概在一九一九年，记得加拉罕两次宣言影响最大。弟前在西岸时见加州大学藏各校同学录职员录甚多，兄可直接写信询问有无 1922－1929 之北大职员录，函寄 Reference Librarian, East

Asian Library, University of California, Berkeley 4, Calif.，不久可得复函
也。弟所编《留欧博士论文目录》，除意大利方面暂缓进行，其余大致
完成。前承惠赐序文，即希于一二星期内赐下是荷。顺候著祺。

弟同礼再拜
一月八日

或函询孟余先生，由 Center of Chinese Studies, Univ. of California,
Berkely 4, Calif.收转，必可收到。

〔Columbia University Libraries Archival Collections, Shuhua Li
Papers, 1926-1972, Volume II: Modern Eminent Chinese Leaders〕

按：1955 年，顾孟余由日本前往美国加州，担任加州大学伯克利
分校中国研究中心顾问。

先生覆信许烺光，请其担任申请 Wenner-Gren Foundation 资助的评议人并
支持该项研究计划，另请其审查论文篇目以免遗漏重要文章。

January 8, 1964

Dear Professor Hsu:

Thank you for your recent letter and for recommending the Sinkiang collectanea to your Library. So far three works have been sent to your Library, while three others are about to be published.

For the last two years I have been engaged in compiling a bibliography of Chinese archaeology and anthropology. The work in analyzing scientific journals has taken much longer time than I had anticipated. To try to secure some support, I hope you can serve as one of my references.

I enclose a statement which I hope to send to the Wenner-Gren Foundation for a research grant. If they ask for your comment, I hope I may count on your support.

Since you have a mimeographed list of your papers, could you be good enough to check against those titles which should be included in the bibliography? I shall greatly appreciate your help, so that no articles of importance will be overlooked.

With season's greetings to you and Mrs. Hsu,

Yours sincerely,

〔University of Chicago Library, Yuan T'ung-li Papers, Box 8〕

按:此件为底稿。

一月九日

先生致信 Joseph F. Fletcher,请其为申请哈佛燕京学社资助撰写推荐信。

January 9, 1964

Dear Dr. Fletcher:

Thank you so much for your letter enclosing check for ＄24.00. Under separate cover, I have sent you No. 6 of the Sinkiang Collectanea concerning the boundaries of Sinkiang. This work based on Chinese official documents contains much material for research.

As I am so anxious to have my bibliography on Sinkiang published, I shall submit my application for a printing subsidy to the Harvard-Yenching Institute. I shall send you a copy for your reference. If you could write a letter to explain the importance of these bibliographies, it would be of material help. Most of my western friends have never heard of the name of Sinkiang and do not realize its strategic importance.

With best wishes for your scientific work and a most productive year,

Yours sincerely,

T. L. Yuan

〔University of Chicago Library, Yuan T'ung-li Papers, Box 3〕

按:No. 6 of the Sinkiang Collectanea 即《新疆国界图志》。此件为录副。

王伊同致函先生,感谢寄赠《新疆国界图志》,并谈其年前赴纽约经过。

老伯大人尊前:

敬禀者,久未奉教,远念良深。刻奉丛刊第六种王晋卿先生《新疆国界图志》一册,考据精详,又不特以辞章胜,末附刘麟生跋亦古朴可爱,唯拙稿仍冠其首,甚不安耳。十二月廿一日全家到纽,廿八始归,与亲友畅谈,几忘寝食,亦快事。专肃并谢,敬请金安,并颂新禧。

侄伊同顿首拜

一月九日

〔袁同礼家人提供〕

Lita Fejos 覆函先生，告收到先生递交的申请，并请等待 Wenner-Gren Foundation 理事会的审查结果。

January 9, 1964

Dear Mr. Yuan:

This is to acknowledge with thanks receipt of petition for a grant from the Wenner-Gren Foundation for Anthropological Research. This will be presented for consideration at a meeting of our Board of Directors, as yet unscheduled. Please note that acceptance of an application does not insure that funds will be forthcoming, since all decisions concerning grants are made by our Board of Directors. You will be notified of its decision as soon as possible.

Sincerely yours,

Lita Fejos

Director of Research

〔University of Chicago Library, Yuan T'ung-li Papers, Box 8〕

一月十日

徐传保覆函先生，感谢寄赠《新疆国界图志》等书，并建议《新疆研究丛刊》加入"艺文志""访古录"等类型的文献。

守和先生钧鉴：

辱荷谕复，所示书名及所赐《新疆国界图志》一并珍藏架箧，以备随时检索。晚最近读剪 *National Geographic Magazines* 旧刊，关于中华西北之图说多种，益觉新疆等处塞外问题饶有经世及艺术意味。《新疆丛刊》络续增椠，匡协邦国、嘉惠儒林可断言也，敬佩敬佩。"魏大使"处亦蒙慨允赠送及售寄该册，有求必许，更见恩泽，中心感激，莫可言宣，祗谢祗谢。圣诞节，晚特赴哥大校长馆问询室，观瞻诸教席全年名著陈列厨，中获见某教师所撰《新近图书学之倾向》一书。窃谓为校刷印作品，或为公所爱阅。因当时大学校售书坊停业五日，亟录全名，嘱小儿家林及家勇试往 Brentano 或 Scribner 购就寄奉（晚当晚返乡），未识已先登递高斋否，念念。不敢云报，藉以聊表景慕至诚耳。书不尽怀，恭请钧安。阖第春岁皆大吉祥。

晚徐传保谨上

一九六四年元月十日

（前求随时注意利玛窦学生瞿氏作稿，似非仅涉混天仪一问题，又谨陈。）

西域考古自瑞典 Hedin 等以来，英法德日俄加均有钜士进行，坚忍不拔，多所究心，利益世界文化非浅。故《新疆丛书》中如有涉及"艺文志""访古录"种种之记载，务求随时示知，盖或可译成小品，以告天下儒林，又敬□。

〔University of Chicago Library, Yuan T'ung-li Papers, Box 2〕

按："瞿氏"似指瞿汝夔，字太素，江苏常熟人，曾跟随利玛窦学习，并将《欧几里得几何》第 1 卷译成中文。

一月十三日

宋晞覆函先生，告知已遵嘱面催孙宕越，并附上若干留学德奥意的在台学生之复信。

守和先生道鉴：

客岁十二月十四日惠示祗悉。嘱办各节，奉复如下：

一、孙宕越先生处已面催，承告即行函复。

二、留德奥意在台同学，照来示发出油印件十五件（即王震寰、朱仰高、吴静、沙学浚、段其燦、马熙程、陈琮、陈克诚、郭兆麟、郦堃厚、俞叔平、罗云平、叶东滋、倪超、张象贤），刻陆续收到回信者，计朱仰高、段其燦、陈琮、罗云平、叶东滋及倪超等六人。吴静已去美，函退回，余尚无回音。兹先将此等回件附奉，请查收。

三、其余地址不详，无法投递。

专此布复，祗颂道安。

后学宋晞敬上

元，十三

〔University of Chicago Library, Yuan T'ung-li Papers, Box 6〕

按：孙宕越（1907—？），广东梅县人，中山大学经济系毕业，后赴法获里昂大学地理学博士学位，归国后担任中山大学地理学系主任。

一月十五日

先生致信罗家伦，告 *War Against Japan* 一书因故购重，请告知如何处理。

志希馆长吾兄惠鉴:

　　十一月十二日寄上一函,内附单据,谅荷台洽。近月代搜集之资料有陈纳德两书,皆其夫人近著。关于缅甸战场之资料,已由英伦 Kegan Paul 寄上。惟 *War Against Japan* 一书,以该书店久不配购,乃交纽约英国新闻处寄上,该处书价较昂＄32.38,故又函告 Kegan Paul 取销此书,不意该店于十二月三日亦寄上一部,共£ 9.6.3.,因之重复。尊处如愿留两部或分让其他机关,统希尊酌。至于 Kegan Paul 之款,尚未拨付,候尊函到后再行办理,即希指示是荷。顺候道祺。

弟袁同礼再拜
一月十五日

　　　　　〔University of Chicago Library, Yuan T'ung-li Papers, Box 1〕

　　按:此件为底稿。

先生致信宋晞,建议将《中国留欧大陆各国博士论文目录》之法比瑞部分先行刊印,并寄上比利时、瑞士部分。

旭轩先生著席:

　　前奉十月廿八日手教,藉悉《留欧博士论文目录》拟一并于五卷三期刊登,极表同意。惟因托友人调查中文姓名,往往需时甚久,而结果又不圆满。兹论文已搜集完全,因留法比瑞三部分大致完成,而德奥荷义诸国之同学姓名多未查出,恐须俟三月底方能寄上,似不必再行等候,可先将法比瑞三部分共六十二页于五卷三期发表,谅荷同意。本日寄比瑞士部分,可先行付排,即希台洽是荷。专此,顺候时祉。

弟袁同礼顿首
一月十五日

　　孙先生迄无回信,望便中一催。前请代寄留德同学之信,想已发出,如有覆音者,望分批寄下是感。

　　　　　〔University of Chicago Library, Yuan T'ung-li Papers, Box 6〕

　　按:此件为底稿。

一月十六日

刘麟生致函先生,感谢寄赠《新疆国界图志》,并询问其所依照底本有无地图。

守和馆长先生勋右：

　　易岁后正念□踪，忽奉四日赐示，拜慰之至。承颁《新疆国界志》二册，印制甚美，似错字极少，谨谢盛谊。原著初版不知有无地图，因标题为图志也，复印自无图固无伤大雅耳。□□事甚简，闻亦可以攻读。《石遗室诗话》尚未读毕，略加眉注，恐无当于万一耳。敬请俪安。

　　　　　　　　　　　　　　　　　　　　弟麟生顿首
　　　　　　　　　　　　　　　　　　　　　一，十六

　　　　　　〔University of Chicago Library, Yuan T'ung-li Papers, Box 2〕

　　按："原著初版"应指清宣统元年（1909）陶庐丛刻本。

一月二十日

先生致信李书华，感谢其为《中国留欧大陆各国博士论文目录》撰写的序文。

润章先生著席：

　　承赐序文，考证精详，深佩深佩。辱奖过甚，殊不敢当。关于论文总数究有若干，此时尚无法统计义国资料暂无法进行，只得含糊其辞，仅提总数超过五千，谅荷同意。文字方面拟连同弟之序文一并送交Hummel，予以润色，一俟打后，再行奉上。先此申谢，敬候著祺。

　　　　　　　　　　　　　　　　　　　　弟同礼敬上
　　　　　　　　　　　　　　　　　　　　一月二十日

《北大七年》想已写就，教授名单中尚有高宝寿仁山，想已列入。
《磐石杂志》四卷一期，北平二十五年一月出版。

　　　　　　〔Columbia University Libraries Archival Collections, Shuhua Li
　　　　　　Papers, 1926–1972, Volume II: Modern Eminent Chinese Leaders〕

　　按：该篇"序文"落笔时间标记为 1963 年 12 月 30 日，实际应为1964 年初。

Lita Fejos 致函先生，告知 Wenner-Gren Foundation for Anthropological Research 批准资助先生三千美金用以编纂《中国考古人类文献目录》。

　　　　　　　　　　　　　　　　　　　　January 20, 1964

Dear Mr. Yuan:

　　It is my pleasure to inform you that the Board of Directors of the

Wenner-Gren Foundation for Anthropological Research approved the grant described in the Resolution set forth below.

There are no limitations or conditions attached to the conduct of projects aided by the Wenner-Gren Foundation, whose policy is to rely upon the integrity and scientific ability of its grantees. However, semi-annual reports on progress of grants and a final report on accomplishments of all projects are requested for presentation to our Board of Directors. It is understood that if the project is abandoned for any reason prior to completion, the amount of grant not theretofore expended in connection with the project shall revert, at its option, to this Foundation.

A list of publications reporting results of research supported in whole or in part should be submitted not later than the first week of January, for inclusion in the Foundation's Annual Report. In addition, acknowledgment of aid from the Wenner-Gren Foundation for Anthropological Research is requested in all material released for publication, as well as three or more copies of published material for the Foundation's Research Library.

I was instructed by our Directors to convey their best wishes for success.

> Sincerely yours,
> Lita Fejos
> Director of Research

RESOLVED that $3,000.00 be allocated for Tung-li Yuan, Library of Congress, Washington, D. C.-To aid compilation of bibliography of Chinese archaeology and anthropology.

〔University of Chicago Library, Yuan T'ung-li Papers, Box 8〕

一月二十一日

罗家伦覆函先生,感谢赠书并谈在美购买史料胶卷有重复者,请代为联系更换等事。

守和吾兄道鉴:

　　前奉十一月十二日大函及付款清单与发票,均敬收悉。兹奉复于次:

一、代付书款清单中，有 W. Heffer & Sons 4.4.0 ＄11.76 一项，收据未曾寄下，请费神查示所购书名，并嘱其补寄收据为托。其余各项书籍均已全部收到，数额亦均相符。尚有 Park Book Shop 邮费二元〇四分，单内未列，请补入。

二、现正申请外汇美金五百元，一俟办妥即汇请吾兄代为征购史料图书之用。查本馆去年续订之刊物为两年，故尚无到期者。

三、前由香港先后寄来吾兄赠送本馆与党史会《中俄西北条约集》及《新疆国界图志》各三册，均已收到。顷接此间商务印书馆来函，遵兄函嘱代送赠《新疆研究丛刊》《新疆建置志》《西陲要略》《西疆交涉志要》各三部，均照收到，除转送党史会一份外，先此一并致谢。吾兄在国外为祖国注重疆域之精诚，尤为钦仰。

四、开国文献会前承吾兄在美购置之国务院档案胶片 M329 中国内政档案二二七卷；M339 中美关系档案二卷；M341 中国与其他国家档案三四卷，因无 Checklist 可查，选用史料颇感不便，请费神就近代为查询。如有 Checklist 可购，请即代购各一册寄下，以资应用为感。

五、前承代购日本军部档案胶片，其中 R111 重复，而缺 R110，又外务省档案胶片 WT51 重复，而缺 WT82，请劳神代向原摄制单位洽询，是否可予更换。如万一不行，则请代为照价补制 R110、WT82 号各一卷为托。

六、去年夏间由伦敦寄来 Collier: *Manchoukuo* 等书三种，价目系壹磅十七先令，书及单据均已收到。

七、附奉吾兄一九六三年九至十二月份征集费台湾银行缴款书，请查收。又本年一至六月份空白收据六张，请加章寄下。

八、正复函间，接读一月十五日手教，暨购书发票，敬已奉悉。*War Against Japan* 一书，代购两部，不必汇回，其中一部可由党史会购，请代付款并将书价出在该会购书款内可也。

诸劳清神，无任感荷。专此，顺颂道祺！

　　　　　　　　　　　　　　　　　弟罗家伦敬启
　　　　　　　　　　　　　　　　　一，二一，台北

关于国父资料，如荷搜购，甚感。该项书单当嘱党史会开上，但甚少也。因所有无多,最后考虑,拟请兄择要斟酌购置。弟又及。

〔University of Chicago Library, Yuan T'ung-li Papers, Box 1〕

按:此件为文书代笔,落款和补语则为其亲笔。

一月二十三日

刘国蓁致函先生,转袁道冲函并告汇款单等事,另略述集邮爱好。

守和博士先生尊鉴:

敬启者,许久未修书敬候,抱歉殊深,恭维著述丰宏,撰祺迪吉,至以为颂。上月拜奉赐赠圣诞礼物,高谊隆情,寔深感谢(包裹内有银包、袖口钮、领带等均收妥)。十一月时奉上香茶两罐,想已及时到达也。十二月十八日手示早已拜读,内附汇单贰十美元一张,及代转令岳信亦已付邮。日前收到渠来示,嘱代转尊夫人信附呈左右,敬希察收为幸。书内并附其大作一首,嘱读后并附上。诗内有关于香港沦陷时,他有皮包稿件由孙述万先生手寄存冯平山圖,后被日人劫去云云。但此事当时并未有闻孙君说及,完成不知,而且孙君所做事皆秘密,只他自己知而已,深以为憾。汇单二十元找得港币一百十四元三角五分(五七一七五算),经即由中国银行汇寄一百十四元与令岳收,但其来信并未有谈及收到该款,想当在尊夫人信内提及。兹付回中国银行收据一纸,祈察收,并支汇费五角六,即由尊账内补一角五分,及寄信令岳处邮费五角,并此次信资二元,共代支二元六角半,前存四十四元六角,比对尚存四十一元九角半也。屡蒙赐寄美国纪念邮票,至谢。拙藏旧邮至今已有四十余年,积存至九千余枚,并无珍品,只是普通而已。少年时俱是搜集皆不购置,待至近年始有出资搜购,而以中共之纪念及特种新票为最齐全,故有欲向联合国补购各票之举也。港中天气寒冷,但仍是干旱,四日一次供水仍续进行,所幸天寒地冻,则用水较少矣。专此,敬请钧安。

愚晚国蓁顿首

一九六四年一月廿三日

〔袁同礼家人提供〕

一月二十六日

先生致信宋晞,寄上留法博士论文目录,并告可与此前寄送的比利时、瑞士部分一并刊行。

旭轩先生道席：

　　十五日寄上一函，内附比瑞博士论文目录，谅荷台察。兹将留法博士目录随函寄上，即希察收。此三批页数已不少，望于五卷三期登出。至于德奥荷义诸国，篇幅较多，而著者中文姓名一时不易查出，只得在五卷四期发表矣。承代发出留德奥义同学公函，并寄来第一批复函，极为感谢。其确有住址而不复函者，大约并未考取博士，只得不再等候矣。此次之单行本，请于印就后先寄下十五部，其余者候德奥荷义部分印齐后再装订成册，届时再行寄下可也。余详另纸。顺候时祉。

弟袁同礼再拜

一月廿六日

　　顷接孙宕越先生复函，大约系吾兄从旁催促之力，晤面时并代致谢意。

〔University of Chicago Library, Yuan T'ung-li Papers, Box 6〕

　　按：此件为底稿。

一月二十七日

先生致信 Lita Fejos，感谢 Wenner-Gren Foundation for Anthropological Research 给予三千美金用以编纂《中国考古人类文献目录》。

January 27, 1964

Dear Mrs. Fejos:

　　It is with grateful appreciation that I acknowledge the receipt of your letter of January 20 informing me the Board of Directors of your Foundation approved the grant in the amount of $3,000.00 to aid the compilation of a Bibliography of Chinese archaeology and anthropology.

　　I am highly sensible of the honor which the Board of Directors has thus accorded me. May I express to you and through you to your Board of Directors my heartfelt thanks? I only hope that with your timely aid my labors will be of some use to students and investigators in the field of archaeology and anthropology.

　　As required, I shall submit my semi-annual and final reports for presentation to your Board.

With renewed thanks,

Yours sincerely,

Tung-li Yuan

〔University of Chicago Library, Yuan T'ung-li Papers, Box 8〕

　　按:此件为录副。

一月二十八日

郭廷以致函先生。〔《郭量宇先生日记残稿》,页466〕

一月二十九日

先生致信余井塘,请其出面协商请台北海关将所扣《新疆国界图志》予以放行。

　　井塘院长勋鉴:

　　　　久未上书,时以起居为念。"内阁"改组,我公佐理院务,深为额庆,引企新猷,至为钦仰。同礼编印《新疆研究丛刊》,委托台北商务印行,内中第六种《新疆国界图志》则在香港付印。十一月初旬由香港新华印刷公司邮寄二百部于台大史学系主任余又荪先生等,原为赠送友人及各图书馆及各大学之用,而台北邮局内所附之海关误为营业性质,不合进口规则,全数扣留已逾三月,仍存海关仓库并未退回香港。因念我公对于边疆研究素所赞助,可否转托"财长",通知海关免予扣留,仍照所列地址交邮寄递。如承惠允,不胜翘企,仍盼赐覆为感。此上,敬候道祺。

弟袁同礼敬上

一月二十九日华盛顿

〔University of Chicago Library, Yuan T'ung-li Papers, Box 1〕

　　按:余井塘时任"行政院副院长"。此件为底稿。

先生致信赵叔诚,告《新疆国界图志》似仍在台北海关,并请将《戡定新疆记》底本航邮寄还。

　　台北商务印书馆赵经理大鉴:

　　　　顷奉西字第十四号大函,祇悉一一。关于《新疆国界图志》售价与《西北中俄条约集》相同均按七折结账,即希查照办理。又此书迄今并未由海关退回香港,大约仍在台北海关,已函请当局设法准予放行,仍照原包所开地址寄交尊处及叶、张两位先生,不识当局能照办否? 如收到后,并希示知。又魏光焘《戡定新疆记》底本借自胡佛图书馆,该馆屡次来催,务希以航邮寄下是荷。《金轺随笔》之序文两篇之末校,前已寄上,惟附录四种之末校,迄未收到,务希提前办理,并盼见复为荷。顺候时祉。

袁同礼再拜
一月廿九日

〔University of Chicago Library, Yuan T'ung-li Papers, Box 1〕

按:此件为底稿。

宋晞覆函先生,告知留德博士信息搜集进展。

守和先生道鉴:

顷接元月十五日大示,敬悉种切。关于留德同学之复信,已有六件于元月十三日奉上,谅邀鉴及。顷借得《留德奥瑞同学录》,又发出王云鹏、方学季、吴荣熙、沈承元、何清、陈克诚、郭兆麟、刘义光、谢喜安、张采为等人征询函。且已收到郭兆麟回信,沈承元已亡故,信退回。另洽得陈赓煜之纪录,一并附奉。其余俟收到后再陆续寄奉。孙宕越先生称,已有信覆上,未悉收到否?来稿将陆续付排,最后校样仍请过目。专此布复,祗颂道安。

后学宋晞拜上
元,廿九

〔University of Chicago Library, Yuan T'ung-li Papers, Box 6〕

一月三十日

恒慕义来访,送交润色后的李书华所撰《中国留欧大陆各国博士论文目录》英文序言。〔Columbia University Libraries Archival Collections, Shuhua Li Papers, 1926–1972, Volume II: Modern Eminent Chinese Leaders〕

郭廷以致函先生。〔《郭量宇先生日记残稿》,页466〕

一月三十一日

先生致信李书华,寄送《中国留欧大陆各国博士论文目录》序言打样。

润章先生著席:

廿六日赐书敬悉,尊处序文前交Hummel润色,昨日渠亲自送来,并参考若干书籍。此位老人年逾八十,对于中国文化仍感极大之兴趣。兹将该序重打一遍,仍请卓裁,如无大更动,拟即寄往台北,因三月杪必须出版也序文日期改写十二月,谅同意。弟根据东德发表之资料,1960 年中国学生获得博士者九人、1961 年八人,而 1962 及 1963 年均尚未发表,故将论文范围截至 1962 年为止。匆上,敬候撰安。

　　　　　　　　　　　　　　　　　　弟袁同礼再拜

　　　　　　　　　　　　　　　　　　一月三十一日晚

〔Columbia University Libraries Archival Collections, Shuhua Li Papers, 1926-1972, Volume II: Modern Eminent Chinese Leaders〕

二月三日

先生致信郭廷以,谈《金轺筹笔》在台印刷迟缓,并告在欧美代售《近代中国史事日志》情况。

量予先生著席:

　　正拟作书报告代售《史事日志》经过,适奉二十八日手教,藉悉所中研究进展近况,至以为慰。印刷问题最感头痛,《金轺随笔》等书于一年前改交商务,据云去秋台北飓风时被毁,弟亦不敢相信,大约商人谋利,先印教科书以致。弟委托之件迟迟不办,亦无可奈何也出版后即奉赠。弟处尚有《新疆目录》中文之部,约数千条,不知应交何处印刷(排印),能否不予资助且能赠送若干部,亦盼便中指示。尊著寄到后,正拟分寄各图书馆推销,不意有一美人(姓名俟查出再函告)费正清的学生曾到过台北,发出代售台北书籍之广告,将尊著书价列为美金 $5.50,下注系台湾商务交其代售者请向商务一询究竟。弟不得已只得改寄德国二部、意大利一部,其余一部则售于国会图书馆。兹将该馆寄来书款美金十一元支票,签字后随函奉上,即希察收。至于德、意之三部发票,仍请便中寄下,以便转寄。至于书款,当告其直接交邮寄上,附上格式一纸,以备参考前寄来之排印广告不能作正式发票用,即希打就寄下是荷。顺候时祉。

　　　　　　　　　　　　　　　　　　弟袁同礼再拜

　　　　　　　　　　　　　　　　　　二月三日

　　顷查明该人姓名为 Robert L. Irick,通讯处为 East Asian Research Center, Cambridge, Mass。其油印之广告名为 Taiwan Books.

〔台北"中央研究院"近代史研究所档案馆,〈郭廷以〉,馆藏号069-01-02-089;《郭量宇先生日记残稿》,页 468〕

按:信中附纸条一张,即美人油印的广告,标注郭廷以著述三种,其中《太平天国史事日志》售价美金 5.50 元。另附表格式样单一张。该信于本月 8 日送达南港。

二月四日

李书华覆函先生,感谢恒慕义修改英文序言,并谈其中有关马建忠的细节表述问题。

> 守和先生惠鉴：
>
> 　　一月卅一日手书及附件均敬悉。序文稿经恒慕义先生改正后,更觉得简单、明了、精确,甚善甚善。此位八十老人不怕费神,找了若干参考书校正,其兴趣之浓厚,深堪敬佩！重打之改正稿第一页第八行第四个字"1852"系误打,应改为"1582"。马建忠在巴黎读书之学校,弟不知其是否为巴黎大学？张若谷编马良年谱载"1877 年眉叔应试巴黎政治学院获得优奖"云云,弟疑所谓"巴黎政治学院"为另一学校(或为 Ecole des Sciences Politiques 之类),而非巴黎大学。改正稿第二页第二行末尾有"at the Sorbonne",不知恒慕义先生有所依据否？如有,自当照旧；如无,似以含糊其辞,将"at the Sorbonne"改为"in France"为妥。可否便中再一询恒慕义先生,何如？除此之外,弟对于改正稿,均极同意。承寄下重打之改正稿一份,谨留存,想尊处必还有他份也。匆此,顺请撰安。
>
> 弟李书华敬启
> 2/4/64
> 〔University of Chicago Library, Yuan T'ung-li Papers, Box 7〕

按：改正稿第 2 页第 2 行为序言中介绍李石曾的部分,at the Sorbonne 意为在索邦大学(Sorbonne Université)读书,最后刊印时确改为"in France"。

二月七日

吴泽湘(西雅图)致函先生,告正在根据亲身经历撰写一部关于 1942 年至 1944 年中苏关系的书稿,并请先生随时告知《新疆研究丛刊》的进展。

February 7, 1964

Dear Dr. Yuan:

　　It has been quite a long time since I saw you for the last time. I have been to Taiwan for a little over three years after my resignation from "the ambassadorship to Chile" in 1951. At the call of my late wife, I returned here in 1956. She died in 1958.

Since then, I have been working on a book entitled, *The Sino-Soviet Riddle in Sinkiang-An Episode of Foreign Relations, 1942 – 1944*. The project was sponsored by the Far Eastern Department of the University of Washington. The manuscript has been completed in 1960, and I have been revising it from time to time.

I just learned from 新疆书目（日文之部）, which I bought from the East and West Book Shop, that you had published other titles in both Chinese and English. I shall appreciate it very much if you will kindly mail a copy each of such publications with the exception of the above edition I have in possession. Do bill me so that a check may be sent you in due course.

As you would probably recall, I was in Sinkiang for three years shortly before Sheng Shih-tsai was transferred to Chungking in 1944. My manuscript will contain all negotiations with the Soviet authorities there. In a way, it is a kind of my memoir. When it is published, I shall be happy to send you a copy autographed.

I have been living in retirement for nearly three years with occasional trips to the University library here. Please keep me informed of any other project in mind relative to Sinkiang. It is a territory I am vitally interested. Right here, I am keeping all available information on file on the progress of this Region since 1949.

With my best regards.

Yours sincerely,

Chaucer H. Wu

吴泽湘

〔University of Chicago Library, Yuan T'ung-li Papers, Box 3〕

按：吴泽湘（1897—1973），字醴泉，四川成都人，早年赴英国留学，入伦敦大学并获经济学学士学位。1942 年任外交部驻新疆特派员。1945 年 3 月，任驻智利全权公使。*The Sino-Soviet Riddle in*

Sinkiang-An Episode of Foreign Relations, 1942-1944，确实受西雅图华盛顿大学的资助，1958 年 4 月 24 日吴泽湘在该校以此为题目举行讲座，但该书稿并未问世。此件为打字稿，中文及落款均为其亲笔。

二月八日

先生覆信宋晞，寄上李书华及先生所撰序言，并请其在留法论文目录中加注信息。

> 旭轩先生左右：
>
> 连奉一月廿九日及二月一日大函，敬谢敬谢。又蒙发出征询函件，尤为铭感。寄下之刘义光论文题目，已列入留法论文目录之内，惟未注明中文姓名，即希在该目法学院 Droit 内刘义光 Liu, I. Kuang 名后代为填注是荷。兹随函奉上李书华及弟之序文，请付排。至于末校似可分批寄下也。尊处借得《留德奥瑞同学录》，想系最近所印者，如能代索一份寄下，至所企盼，如系油印并无第二份，可否暂借一用，当挂号寄还不误。前寄上之总目，原系借台端之参考，此期不必列入，即在总标题之末加（Ⅰ）以别下期之Ⅱ，此期最末页请加 To be continued 三字即可。一切偏劳，谢谢。顺候教祺。
>
> 弟袁同礼再拜
>
> 二月八日
>
> 〔University of Chicago Library, Yuan T'ung-li Papers, Box 6〕

按：刘义光博士论文题目为 Doctrines et pratiques de la Chine dans ses relations avec les puissances occidentales depuis 1517 jusqu'au traité de Nanking, 1842，《中国留欧大陆各国博士论文目录》编号为第 237 号。

二月九日

先生致信普实克，请捷克斯洛伐克科学院东方研究所提供该国出版的有关中国艺术的书籍信息，尤其是哈耶克教授的著作。

February 9, 1964

Dear Professor Prusek:

Under separate cover, I am sending you several new publications, mostly reprints of older books now difficult to obtain. Please do not bother sending Czek books in return.

But I would greatly appreciate your help if you could ask your colleague to send me a list of books and articles on Chinese art which have been published in Czechoslovakia. I hear that a new museum of Far Eastern art has been established not far from Prague and Dr. Lubor Hajek is the leading figure in this field. No doubt important studies have appeared in recent years.

I have Dr. Hajek's *Chinese Art in Czechoslovakian Museums*, both the English and German translations. I should like to know the titles of his other publications on Chinese art. At present I am engaged in preparing for publication a bibliography of Chinese art and archaeology, and I am rather anxious to include the contributions from your scholars. As I do not read your language, any help from you will be much appreciated.

With cordial regards,

Yours sincerely,

T. L. Yuan

〔University of Chicago Library, Yuan T'ung-li Papers, Box 3〕

按:Lubor Hájek(1921-2000),捷克汉学家、艺术史专家。此件为录副。

二月十一日

先生致信马克尔,再次向英国大学中国委员会申请资助编纂《中国艺术和考古目录》。

11 February, 1964

Dear Mr. Morkill:

For several years I have been engaged in compiling a comprehensive bibliography on Chinese art. As far as American collections are concerned, the coverage is rather complete. In view of the significant contributions by British scholars in the field of Chinese art, I should like very much to continue the research in British libraries and museums so that no works of importance will be overlooked. For this reason, may I apply for a research grant (from 350.0.0 to 400.0.0) from the Universities'

China Committee? Herewith I beg to submit a brief statement.

As far as I know, no one has spent so much time in the work of analyzing learned journals. To examine the contents of the *Journal Asiatique* and the *Journal of the Royal Asiatic Society*, for instance, is a laborious undertaking. I am glad to say that I have analyzed a multitude of such journals-a work, though exacting, has given me much satisfaction.

Though a labor of love, I should like to have some gesture of encouragement. Since the grants of your Committee are usually awarded in May each year, may I hope to hear from you sometime before June?

With sincere greetings,

Yours sincerely,

Tung-li Yuan

P. S. I sent to you recently a copy of Communist China's Strategy in the Nuclear Era and the Chinese People's Republic and the Bomb which, I hope, may be of some interest to you.

〔University of Chicago Library, Yuan T'ung-li Papers, Box 1〕

　　按：此件为录副。

郭廷以致函先生。〔《郭量宇先生日记残稿》,页469〕

二月十二日

郭有守覆函先生,告台湾与法国"断交",并寄送一份留德中国学生名册。

　　守和学长兄：

　　手书敬悉。我方已与法国"断交",料兄已有所闻,我"使馆"已决定撤退,"文参处"奉令赴比京候命。

　　兹付上兄所需之留德中国学生名册一份,敬请查收。顺颂冬安!

弟郭有守

二,十二

〔University of Chicago Library, Yuan T'ung-li Papers, Box 6〕

二月十五日

Joseph F. Fletcher 致函先生,告知将赴日本,请将陆续出版的《新疆研究丛刊》寄送代收处,并表示会积极支持先生向哈佛燕京学社申请出版资助。

15 February, 1964

Dear Dr. Yuan:

I am leaving at the end of this week for Japan. Would you please send the Sinkiang Collectanea as it comes out to me c/o Society of Fellows (address above)? The Society will keep the volumes for me until my return in October.

When you have drafted the letter to the Harvard-Yenching Institute asking for a subsidy to print your bibliographies, please send me a copy c/o the following address:

c/o International Christian University, 1500 Osawa, Mitaka, Tokyo, Japan.

I will then write immediately to the Institute and support your request.

Sincerely yours,

Joseph F. Fletcher

〔University of Chicago Library, Yuan T'ung-li Papers, Box 8〕

按：International Christian University 即日本国际基督教大学,位于东京都三英市,1949 年由日美两国基督教会合议创办。

二月十六日

先生致信 Wolfgang Seuberlich,推荐购入《近代中国史事日志》,并请协助查实留德博士中文姓名。

February 16, 1964

Dear Dr. Seuberlich:

Some weeks ago, I mailed you a copy of T. Y. Kuo's *Chin Tai Chung Kuo shih shih jih chi* a chronology of Modern China. It was sent to you on approval, costing 11 dollars. If you decide to keep it for your Library, I shall ask Mr. Kuo to send you the invoice, and you may pay him direct. As you will note, it is a most useful tool of research.

I now enclose a list of Chinese students who have been awarded the doctorate by German universities. Since your Library has a complete file of doctoral dissertations, I wonder if you would take the trouble of putting down their Chinese names. If not, could you advise me to whom I should write for their Chinese names? Perhaps instructors of Chinese language and literature at German universities may know some of the names. Would it be possible for you to send me a list of names of these instructors and their addresses (namely, their university affiliation)? With such a list I could write them individually.

I am compiling a Guide to Doctoral Dissertations by Chinese students in Europe. The great difficulty is the identification of their Chinese names. If you have any directory of Chinese students in Germany, could you lend it to me for a few days?

Thanking you for your help,

Yours sincerely,

T. L. Yuan

〔University of Chicago Library, Yuan T'ung-li Papers, Box 4〕

按:此件为录副,空白处应留作填写中文书名"近代中国史事日志"。

二月二十二日

罗家伦覆函先生,告知收到书籍、胶片等资料并寄上购书费等。

守和吾兄道鉴:

一月廿九日手教及附件均敬奉悉。兹奉复于后:

一、承订购关于国父资料俄文的四种、芝加哥博士论文一种,业已由芝加哥大学图书馆缩影部直接航邮寄到。胶片一卷,计价一.八五元,连邮费一.五〇元,共美金三.三五元,附上单据副本一份,请代为支付,是托。

二、兹寄上二月二十日台湾银行汇票(Sola)美金五百元(汇票号码 103/64-2043 号),敬请查收入账为感。

三、附上本年一、二月份史料征集费一千元送存台湾银行送金簿存根一纸,请察收。

屡劳清神,无任感谢。专此,顺颂春祺!

弟罗家伦敬启

二,二二

〔University of Chicago Library, Yuan T'ung-li Papers, Box 1〕

按:该函为文书代笔,落款处为其签名。

二月二十三日

先生致信宋晞,请在《中国留欧大陆各国博士论文目录》中填入三人信息。

　　旭轩先生:

　　　　前寄李书华及弟序文,想已收到。兹有下列三人姓名均已查明,请代为填入是荷。承代函询论文题目,不知近来又收到覆函否? 如确有地址而不作覆者,或未获到学位,亦属可能也。此上,顺候时祉。

　　　　　　　　　　　　　　　　　　　　　　　　弟袁同礼顿首

　　　　　　　　　　　　　　　　　　　　　　　　二月廿三日

　　末校仍乞寄下一阅。

　　瑞士名单内,文学部分 T'ien, Tchen-kang Antoine,田志康

　　法国名单内,文学部分 Shao, Ho-ting,邵鹤亭

　　法国名单内,科学部分 Tsou, Ren Kou,储润科

　　　　　　〔University of Chicago Library, Yuan T'ung-li Papers, Box 1〕

　　按:田志康(1914—?),天主教士,1942 年在瑞士弗里堡(Fribourg)大学获博士学位;邵鹤亭(1902—1966),江苏宜兴人,教育家,毕业于东南大学教育系,后赴法留学,1932 年获巴黎大学博士学位;储润科(1900—1969),江苏宜兴人,化学家,1923 年东南大学理化系毕业,1932 年获法国南锡大学科学博士学位。此件为底稿。

先生致信郑通,询问其是否收到邮局退还的《新疆国界图志》。

　　新华印刷公司郑经理大鉴:

　　　　前接一月廿一日大函并美金三百元收据一纸,祇悉一一。《新疆国界图志》前由尊处邮寄台北各处共 250 部。据友人来信报告,谓仅收到 50 部,其余 200 部由邮局退回香港新华公司。兹特函询此 200 部是否业已收到,即希示知是盼。如万一仍未收到,则该书或仍在台北海关,自当请当局一查也。专此,顺候大安,并乞覆示。

　　　　　　　　　　　　　　　　　　　　　　　　袁同礼再拜

　　　　　　　　　　　　　　　　　　　　　　　　二月廿三日

　　　　　　〔University of Chicago Library, Yuan T'ung-li Papers, Box 1〕

　　按:此件为底稿。

二月二十七日

杜希德致函先生,告知英国大学中国委员会再次拒绝资助《中国艺术和考古目录》的编纂。

27th February, 1964

Dear Dr. Yuan,

The Experts' Committee of the Universities China Committee met yesterday and gave consideration to your application for a grant towards your proposed bibliography on Chinese Art. I am sorry to have to tell you that they decided that they could make no grant for this project.

Yours sincerely,

Denis Twitchett

〔University of Chicago Library, Yuan T'ung-li Papers, Box 1〕

按:此件为打字稿,落款处为其签名。

二月二十八日

先生致信赵叔诚,告知拟于四月赴欧,请其将《金轺筹笔》附录四种末校寄来,另告《新疆国界图志》或仍在台北海关。

叔诚先生惠鉴:

前奉二月六日第24号大函,欣悉贵馆重印《教育大辞书》,想不久可以出版,至为企望。《金轺筹笔》承允于二月六日两星期之后继续排印工作,不胜欢慰,目前想在进行之中。兹弟因事须四月中旬赴欧,拟请特为设法将此书附录四种之末校从速排印,并将末校样分批寄下为感。台北邮局海关退回香港之《新疆国志图志》并未寄到香港,现此书或仍在海关,已托人调查,容再奉告。现在发售之五十部,如不敷用,并盼早日示知,当告香港新华印刷公司寄上也。专此,敬候道祺。

弟袁同礼顿首

二月廿八日

〔University of Chicago Library, Yuan T'ung-li Papers, Box 1〕

按:《新疆国志图志》当为《新疆国界图志》。此件为底稿。

二月下旬

先生覆信罗家伦,建议"国史馆"筹印英文册页用以申请美国基金会赞助修建新馆舍。

志希馆长吾兄尊鉴：

　　昨日奉到二月廿二日赐书，并台湾银行汇票美金五百元，业已拜收入账。近又购到关于我国抗战书籍二种，不日交平邮寄上，内有一种似应译成中文以广流传。贵馆建筑是否铁筋洋灰，如需新建筑（以便日后接收各院部档案）似可乘 Fairbank 等来台之便，请其注意。弟亦愿从旁协助，请罗氏基金会或 Ford 基金会于下次拨款时加以补助。目前极盼作些准备工作，如印一英文概况，说明档案之重要，于将来进行筹款时不无小补。谅吾兄亦以为然也。

〔University of Chicago Library, Yuan T'ung-li Papers, Box 1〕

　　按：此件为底稿。

二三月间

《"中央研究院"历史语言研究所集刊·故院长胡适先生纪念论文集》刊登先生与 Eugene L. Delafield 合编的 Bibliography of Dr. Hu Shih's Writings in Western Languages（《胡适先生西文著作目录》）。〔《"中央研究院"历史语言研究所集刊》第 34 本（下）①，页 813—828〕

　　　　按：该目共记录胡适著述文章 237 种，较 1957 年 5 月刊印的《胡适先生著作目录（二）西文》增加 154 种。

三月五日

宋晞覆函先生，寄上新收到的论文题目三份，另已按前信所示插入三人姓名。

　　守和先生道鉴：

　　二月廿三日手书祗悉。论文题目近又收到三份（俞叔平，郦堃厚及张果为），附奉请查收。田、邵、储等三人中文姓名已分别填入。校样在二、三校中，最后清样当航邮请亲校，恐延至本月中才能寄出。专此布闻，祗颂道安。

后学宋晞敬上

三，五

〔University of Chicago Library, Yuan T'ung-li Papers, Box 6〕

———————

① 该册标注的出版日期为 1963 年 12 月，但由 1963 年 12 月 27 日 Eugene Delafield 函可知，此时《胡适先生西文著作目录》仍未定稿。

三月八日

先生致信康乃尔大学图书馆 Richard C. Howard，告知国会图书馆卡片部将从主馆区搬出，因此无法收到相关卡片校样，也无法将卡片寄送给他。

March 8, 1964

Dear Dr. Howard:

    As you may know already, the Card Division of the Library of Congress will be moved out of the Library sometime in April or May. Under these circumstances, I shall not be able to receive the proofs of these cards and to send the cards to you for the Bibliography of Asian Studies.

    I presume that your Library subscribes the proof sheets. If you could designate someone to continue the work, there should not be any interruption in the recording of titles dealing with Asian studies.

    It has been a pleasure to work with you in a project of common interest, and I only wish that the important project will be a success under your able direction.

Sincerely yours,
T. L. Yuan

〔袁同礼家人提供〕

　　按：Richard C. Howard 时任该校图书馆华生特藏负责人。

三月十三日

先生致信叶良才，请其赴台时协助寄送《中国留欧大陆各国博士论文目录》与中基会董事，并赠《胡适先生西文著作目录》（抽印本）一百份。

March 13, 1964

Dear Mr. Yip:

    My *Guide to Doctoral Dissertations by Chinese Students in Europe* is being printed at Taipei. Since you plan to be in Formosa next month, may I ask you to be good enough to distribute copies to the Trustees? Please send me a list of the Trustees who would be attending the meeting in April and also your Taipei address, so that copies will be mailed from there.

My bibliography of Dr. Hu Shih's writings in western languages has just been published. I suggested that 100 copies of the reprints be sent to you for distribution to Dr. Hu's friends per my previous letter.

　　With kind regards,

Yours sincerely

T. L. Yuan

〔University of Chicago Library, Yuan T'ung-li Papers, Box 2〕

　　按：此件为录副。

三月十四日

先生致信白思达，向哈佛燕京学社递交《新疆研究文献目录》（英文本）出版的资助申请。

March 14, 1964

Dear Dr. Baxter:

　　Confident that your Trustees are interested in the promotion of scholarly research, may I write to explore the possibilities of obtaining some support toward the publication of my Bibliography of Sinkiang. For your information, I now enclose a brief statement. I shall be most grateful if you could call the attention of the Trustees as to the desirability of giving some encouragement to a major reference tool.

　　With sincere thanks for your interest and assistance,

Your sincerely,

T. L. Yuan

〔University of Chicago Library, Yuan T'ung-li Papers, Box 8〕

　　按：该件为录副，并附 2 页说明，概述书稿将收录包括 1841 年至 1963 年间西方学界出版、刊登有关新疆的六千余种书目、篇目，涵盖十种语言。

三月三十一日

宋晞覆函先生，告知未收到《中国留欧大陆各国博士论文目录》第二部分稿件，出版时间恐须延后，另告收到华乾吉、郭兆麟来函。

　　守和先生道鉴：

　　　　迭接三月二十日、廿三日午来函，敬悉种切。惟寄第二部分稿件函(谅为三月廿二日)迄未收到,恐已遗失。兹另将 p.111-p.137 校样航寄一份,请收校后即行寄下。如此,出版之期恐将延迟(寄中华基金会各董事,恐亦不可能)。兹又收到华乾吉、郭兆麟二先生复函,随函附奉,请查收。尊编《留法比瑞德博士论文目录》共抽印若干本,请即函示,印刷厂不愿意留版也。专此,祗颂道安。

后学宋晞敬上
三,卅一

〔University of Chicago Library, Yuan T'ung-li Papers, Box 6〕

三月

Chinese Culture 刊登先生文章,题为 A Guide to Doctoral Dissertations of Chinese Students in Continental Europe, 1907－1962。〔*Chinese Culture: a quarterly review*, Vol. 5, No. 3, pp. 92-156〕

> 按:该期为第一部分,包括李书华序、先生自序、缩写对照表及中国留学法国、比利时、瑞士的博士论文目录。

四月二日

Joseph F. Fletcher 致函先生,告已于昨日寄出向哈佛燕京学社的推荐信,并再次确认订购全套的《新疆研究丛刊》。

2 April, 1964

Dear Dr. Yuan:

Here is a copy of the letter I sent to the Harvard-Yenching Institute. I hope it has not arrived too late (sent yesterday).

Please be sure that I am sent a copy of all your bibliographies on Sinkiang and billed c/o the Society of Fellows at Harvard.

Best wishes to you and your bibliographical efforts so helpful to us all. I remain

Sincerely yours,
Joseph F. Fletcher

〔University of Chicago Library, Yuan T'ung-li Papers, Box 8〕

> 按:该函另附 1 页 Joseph F. Fletcher 4 月 1 日致哈佛燕京学社信,他在信中强调新疆在中亚地区研究的重要性及困难性,对先生、渡边宏所编《新疆研究文献目录》(日本文)表示极为推崇。

四月三日

先生致信赵叔诚,催寄《金辂筹笔》附录四种末校,并谈书籍代售等事。

> 台湾商务印书馆赵经理大鉴:
>
> 　　前奉三月七日大札,欣悉种切。惟《金辂筹笔》之附录四种及和约一份,最后校样迄今尚未收到,不识何日付邮,深恐邮局有遗失情事,特再函询,务希赐覆。其他各事分别列后:(一)寄上托售书籍三种,拟请转托其他书店有门市者代售,如经此次分发后,则贵馆所存不多矣;(二)收据台币七百元随函奉上,即希将该款收入敝账为盼;(三)尊处寄下《西陲要略》等已于日前全数收到,经二、三月始行收到,不识何故?(四)《戡定新疆记》想已印好,盼速寄是荷。顺候大安。

袁同礼再拜

四月三日

〔University of Chicago Library, Yuan T'ung-li Papers, Box 1〕

　　按:此件为底稿。

宋晞致函先生,告第二批校样送到但已不及改动,只能待加印时再行增改。

> 守和先生道鉴:
>
> 　　三月廿二日惠示暨校样第二批于昨日下午始收到,第一批校样早已印就,除李序中"746"予以加盖外,孙宕越先生论文页数等无法加上。抽印本刻已印就者为五十本,版子保留。将来加印部分当可照改。专此,祗颂道安。

后学宋晞拜上

四,三

〔University of Chicago Library, Yuan T'ung-li Papers, Box 6〕

四月七日

宋晞覆函先生,告知《中国文化季刊》赠刊已寄出,并谈"留德奥荷博士名录"校对等事。

> 守和先生有道:
>
> 　　四月二日手书祗悉。《中国文化季刊》五卷三期已出版,另平邮一本,连同尊编《法比瑞博士名录》抽印本三十份,请查收。《留欧博士名录》应抽印若干本(三十份除外),请惠示为感。德奥荷部分如能

在本月底前寄达,则末校可在五月底寄奉亲校。后学于明日赴日访问,月底返国,并以奉闻。专此,祗颂道安。

后学宋晞顿首

四,七

〔University of Chicago Library, Yuan T'ung-li Papers, Box 6〕

四月八日

刘国蓁致函先生,寄上托购云南白药两磲,并告冯平山图书馆已改作博物馆。

守和博士先生尊鉴:

敬启者,日昨拜奉手示敬悉。蒙赐赠联合国新邮票共廿八枚,敬谨收领珍存,寔深感谢。附来代转令岳信一函,经已即为付邮矣。日前代转令岳与尊夫人信想已到达也。承命购得云南白药两磲(一磲只一□重而已),银贰元四角,附入信内奉上,想当能到达,如得收后便希示知为幸。冯平山圕改作博物经已开幕,二月一日《华侨日报》报导最详。晚于二月六日刊登拙作一文以正视听,特剪出奉上,敬希指正,幸甚幸甚。交流尚未交来大作,如收到当代寄赠新会景堂圕各一册,该馆仍每月由冯氏汇款接济也。匆匆,余俟后陈。专此,敬请钧安。

愚晚国蓁顿首

一九六四年四月八日

〔袁同礼家人提供〕

按:"报导"即该报 2 月 1 日第 4 张第 3 页之数篇报导;"拙作"即《贺冯平山博物馆开幕并抒所感》①。1925 年,新会景堂图书馆由冯平山创建,用以纪念其父冯景堂。

四月十四日

谭伯羽致函先生,告《留德博士论文目录》仍有待补充,并告留德医学博士的诸多线索。

守和先生大鉴:

奉示嘱代查阅留德同学博士名单,弟翻阅一过,识者不多,而医科同学所知亦更少,但以为兄单尚不写全,如有次面谈及朱家骅,杨公庶

————————————

① 《华侨日报》,1964 年 2 月 6 日,第 4 张第 3 页。

化学、公孝兄弟矿工，沈君怡水利，又钱福谦电工，达城高工，皆未列入。又同济同学得医学博士第一人为江逢治，粤人。弟友人中尚有医生汪元臣夫妇两人，太太即黄鸣龙之妹，均医生。又罗光埰、屠开元、吴学照皆柏林大学，又胡定安医生现在纽约，彼亦与弟同时，兄何妨送单请其一检看。彼居 Dr. T. A. Hu, 500 W. 122 St. New York, 10027。又弟检得台湾《留德同学录》一份，内中亦有许多博士，是否靠得住则不可知。内载大维兄为柏林大学博士，贾则彼为哈佛之 PH.D.也。兹将原单及《留德同学录》一份送上，后者于用后仍乞掷还为祷。专此，即颂日祉。

弟谭伯羽启上
四，十四夜

〔University of Chicago Library, Yuan T'ung-li Papers, Box 6〕

四月十五日

先生致信王世杰，请代为向"国家长期发展科学委员会"转交出版资助申请书。

　　雪艇院长道席：

　　　　同礼近三年来编成《中国考古人类文献目录》，其内容已在另函说明，可否转请"国家长期发展科学委员会"予以审查，并在美援项下酌予补助，以便付印。一俟出版，当寄赠贰百部每部定价美金七元，以供国内各机关及研究人士之用。兹附上致该会申请书，是否可行，仍希鼎力玉成，不胜感祷。此上，敬候道祺。

袁同礼拜上
四月十五日

〔University of Chicago Library, Yuan T'ung-li Papers, Box 8〕

　　按：此件为底稿。5 月 14 日，"国家长期发展科学委员会"覆函先生，告知收到申请书，并送专门委员会审查。

四月中旬

美国学术团体理事会、社会科学研究委员会(The Social Science Research Council)联席决定给予先生资助，用以编纂《中国艺术与和考古目录》。

〔Library of Congress, *Information Bulletin*, Vol. 23, No. 16, 1964, p. 172〕

　　按：此次针对亚洲研究的资助共有 17 位学者，其资金应来自福特

　　　基金会。

四月二十一日

Lionello Lanciotti 覆函先生,订购一套《中华民国史事日志》,并就编辑《留学意大利博士论文目录》给予意见。

Rome, 21, Apr., 1964

Dear Dr. Yuan:

　　I have the pleasure of acknowledging receipt of your kind letter of April 6, with enclosed Invoice, to the amount of USA $ 11.00, for the purchase of the Chronology of Modern China, on the part of our Institute. Our Administrative Office is therefore directed to settle the Invoice without delay, and I thank you for your courtesy.

　　It is likewise very kind of you to send me soon your cards on the Bibliography of Chinese Literature on Marco Pole: I am sorry to say that, concerning my own work, it has made little progress, owing to the pressure of circumstances.

　　Your plan of compiling a list of dissertations submitted by Chinese students in Italy would be of much interest, but I regret to say that it would be far from easy to carry it out. Wishing to be of help to you as far as possible, I have without delay applied to our "Ministry of Education", on which all Italian Universities are dependent, in order to get precise information or advice on the matter. Dissertations or Thesis towards University Degrees, are made public after a lapse of 50 years. For your purpose, it ensures that it would be necessary, on the authorization granted by "the Ministry of Education", to address the individual Faculties of all Italian Universities. There is no need to say that this would entail a heavy and very lengthy work, that might be carried out by mail, and not on the spot. In Rome, only the Faculties of the Roman Universities could be approached to this end. I really do not know of anyone who may help you in a work of this kind. I am sorry at my inability of being more helpful in this connection, but as you see the problem is hard to solve. This reminds me to tell you that all such Institutions are closed by the month of June. I would be very happy, in any case, to make your personal acquaintance, should you decide to visit Europe, at one time or another. With best regards, and my renewed thanks,

Yours truly,

Lionello Lanciotti

〔University of Chicago Library, Yuan T'ung-li Papers, Box 4〕

四月三十日

先生致信李书华,请协助查找留德博士中研习自然科学及医学之人的中文姓名,并询此前英文序言可否译为中文以供《留美学生通讯》转载。

　　润章先生尊鉴:

　　　　前编之《留法比瑞士论文目录》已于本月十号左右由台北寄美,一俟收到,当即奉上。近来《留德论文目录》业已寄往台北,希望六月杪即可印就。内中尚有一部分研究自然科学及医学者未能查明其姓名曾询胡定安,渠亦不知,附上一单,不识有无熟识之人。又《留美学生通讯》"大使馆文参处"编颇盼尊处序文能译成中文,以便转载,可否便中译汉,赐下为感。顺候道祺。

弟袁同礼再拜

四月三十日

〔Columbia University Libraries Archival Collections, Shuhua Li

Papers, 1926–1972, Volume II: Modern Eminent Chinese Leaders〕

先生致信赵叔诚,寄还《金辂筹笔》校样,并嘱该书出版时定价须保持低廉以便畅销。

　　台湾商务印书馆赵经理台鉴:

　　　　奉到台53字第75号及75-1二函,拜悉一一。《金辂筹笔》校样已于昨日以航邮挂号寄还,想可同时收到。脱漏之处已另纸钞录,附在该页之后,即希台洽。校样错误之处业已一一改正,务请再行详校一次,再行付印。此书篇幅较多,惟鉴于一班人购买力有限,其书价亦盼格外低廉以不超过120元为宜,以便畅销。随函奉上新台币＄1453.10支票壹纸,即希察入是荷。顺候时祉。

袁同礼再拜

四月三十日

原底稿42、43两页想已无用,故未寄还。

〔University of Chicago Library, Yuan T'ung-li Papers, Box 1〕

按:此件为底稿。《金轺筹笔》首版时,版权页印有"普通本基本定价伍元正"字样。

四月

先生作体检,医生告知"贫血",叮嘱其多饮用补血食品。〔《思忆录》,中文部分页140〕

五月一日

Earl H. Pritchard 覆函先生,感谢寄赠《胡适先生西文著作目录》(抽印本),并请帮忙物色合适人员负责亚利桑那大学东亚馆藏的编目和扩张。

May 1, 1964

Dear Dr. Yuan:

Thank you so much for your note of April 26, including the reprint of your Bibliography of the Writings of Dr. Hu Shih and the announcement of the Sinkiang Collectanea. I am very pleased to have the Bibliography and I had noted something about the *Sinkiang Collectanea*. We will order it before long but will probably have to wait until the first of July when our new fiscal year begins. I note that at present seven volumes have been published. Do you have any idea how many volumes this will ultimately run to?

We are trying to build up our Oriental Studies Library here, and, at the moment, we are searching for somebody who can serve as cataloguer-librarian and general manager of the collection which now amounts to about 15,000 Chinese ts'e and some 3,000 bound Japanese volumes. We are trying to find someone who can handle the cataloguing and ordering of both Chinese and Japanese books, and in addition to this ability to be able to use both languages, he needs to be a permanent resident of the United States-to accommodate certain local hiring policies. This combination of requirements has made it fairly difficult for us, but we may possibly get the permanent residence requirement adjusted. Building up the collection was started about three and one-half years ago, and although we do not have as much money to spend now as we had in the last three years, I hope we can keep the collection growing.

　　Best wishes to you.

Sincerely yours,

Earl H. Pritchard

Chairman

Committee on Oriental Studies

〔University of Chicago Library, Yuan T'ung-li Papers, Box 1〕

　　按:此件为打字稿,落款处为其签名。

五月三日

先生致信香港新华印刷公司,寄送支票。

　　新华印刷公司大鉴:

　　　　前奉二月二十九日大函并附账单一纸,敬悉一一。敝人因事离美,日昨始返,以致所欠之款未能早日奉上,至以为歉。兹随函奉上美金壹佰捌拾元支票一纸,即希察收,折合港币若干,亦盼示及。敝人所存贵公司之书《新疆国界图志》、《中俄西北条约集》,务请包好以免损坏或潮湿,至为企盼。此上,顺候时祉。

袁同礼顿首

五月三日

　　　　郑经理同此致意,附上一信请加贴邮费后再为付邮。

〔University of Chicago Library, Yuan T'ung-li Papers, Box 1〕

　　按:"附上一信"应为寄送许性初之信,但该信地址、所在单位信息似均无效,新华印刷公司投递两次均告失败。此件为底稿。

五月四日

白思达致函先生,告知哈佛燕京学社拟将《新疆研究文献目录》(英文)作为该社研究系列资助出版,请先生联系哈佛大学出版社主任商谈有关事宜。

May 4, 1964

Dear Dr. Yuan:

　　From now on the Harvard-Yenching Institute is not going to make a practice of subsidizing publications in the United States under other auspices. However, we shall be willing to issue your bibliography completely at our expense in the Harvard-Yenching Institute Studies Series-with the understanding that all net profits accrue to the Institute-if it is accepted by the publisher of this series, the Harvard University Press, and if the H. U. P.'s estimate of editorial and printing expense is not too great. This series would be a particularly appropriate imprint for your bibliography since, like the compilation itself, it is financed from funds that originally came to us from the Rockefeller Foundation.

I am sending a copy of this letter to Mr. Thomas J. Wilson, Director of the Harvard University Press, at 79 Garden Street, Cambridge 02138. If the proposition suits you, please write directly to Mr. Wilson about how to submit the work to the Press. I don't know whether it is feasible for Mr. Wilson to receive and circulate the manuscript in card form.

In evaluating the importance and usefulness of this bibliography, we have been aided by a letter from Mr. Joseph F. Fletcher, a Junior Fellow of Harvard University who, as you know, is already accorded considerable respect in the field of Central Asian studies and who is one of the scholars whose work would be aided by this publication.

Sincerely yours,

Glen W. Baxter

Associate Director

〔University of Chicago Library, Yuan T'ung-li Papers, Box 8〕

五月五日

先生致信沈怡，请就所知注明留德博士的中文姓名。

君怡"部长"仁兄道席：

此次大驾来美，得亲教益，至为欢慰，惜行色匆匆，未能一尽地主之谊，为怅怅耳。前谈《留德博士论文目录》，已收750余人，内中有一小部同学之中文姓名，弟曾询俞叔平、江鸿、段其燧诸人，均无结果。兹特奉上名单，可否就吾兄所知者赐予填注，或能转托理工同学予以查明，尤所感荷。该目录将于下月中旬在台北付印，已告印刷人于出版后径行寄上一份，希教正。弟下月十六因事赴欧，如承早日。专此，顺候道祺。

弟袁同礼顿首

五月五日

〔University of Chicago Library, Yuan T'ung-li Papers, Box 6〕

按:沈怡(1901—1980),原名沈景清,字君怡,浙江嘉兴人,水利学家,同济大学土木科毕业后留学德国,获德累斯顿工业大学(Technische Universität Dresden)工学博士。俞叔平(1911—1978),浙江诸暨人,法学家,20 世纪 30 年代曾两次留学维也纳,1938 年获维也纳大学法学博士学位,为中国第一个警察博士生。江鸿(1904—2002),1930 年毕业于同济大学,获洪堡奖学金后赴德深造,20 世纪 40 年代曾担任同济大学工学院院长之职。段其燧(1910—?),字孝农,河北蠡县人,自同济大学土木科毕业后留学德国,获达姆施塔特工业大学(Technische Universität Darmstadt)工学博士学位。此件为底稿,修改甚多且未写完。

五月七日

Human Relations Area Files Press 总经理 Michael Lazna 致函先生,告知此前编纂的《现代中国经济社会发展目录》已绝版,希望先生能够增补新书条目并再版。

7 May 1964

Dear Sir:

In 1956 we published a bibliography on *Economic and Social Development of Modern China* which you compiled in connection with a major area studies contract we handled for the government.

Since then, this work went out of print. Since we feel that the bibliographies are one of the most valuable series of publications we are currently publishing, we hesitate to let your work remain out of print. On the other hand, however, we feel that we should not just reprint a ten-year old bibliography without any up-dating. We would like to publish a new, considerably better looking version of your work if we could have you up-date it. This could be done either by a supplement to each one of the two sections of the present work, or by integrating the new entries into the original text. This would not present us with any additional cost since in the case of a new edition the entire book would have to be retyped in a clear and better looking type.

In short, then, we would like to invite you to work with us in this sense. If you are interested, we should like to know when you would have the time to undertake this work and by what date we could expect to receive the additional material from you in a manuscript form or on index cards.

We sincerely hope that together we'll be able to make this valuable work available once more to scholars and the public.

Hoping to hear from you soon.

Sincerely,

Michael Lazna

General Manager, HRAF Press

〔University of Chicago Library, Yuan T'ung-li Papers, Box 8〕

按:Michael Lazna,生于捷克斯洛伐克,20 世纪 50 年代移民美国,后在耶鲁大学半工半读,获得人类学学位,并加入 Human Relations Area Files Press,1967 年退休。此件为打字稿,落款处为其签名。

五月八日

先生覆信白思达,感谢哈佛燕京学社对出版《新疆研究文献目录》(英文本)的支持,并附本日致哈佛大学出版社 Thomas J. Wilson 信的副本。

May 8, 1964

Dear Dr. Baxter:

Thank you so much for your letter of May 4 and for your interest in the promotion of Central Asian studies.

It would be a great honor indeed to have my Bibliography of Sinkiang included in the Harvard-Yenching Institute Studies Series. The terms you proposed are most agreeable.

From copy of my letter to the Director of the Harvard University Press, you will note that I shall submit to him a part of the final manuscript to enable him to make an estimate and to report to you direct.

Assuring you once more my sincere appreciation for your interest and assistance.

Yours sincerely,

T. L. Yuan

〔University of Chicago Library, Yuan T'ung-li Papers, Box 8〕

按:该件为录副。先生致 Thomas J. Wilson 信应属具文,未录,先生在信中表示本年秋天从欧洲访书归来后将寄上全部稿件。

五月十日

先生致信李书华,请协助查实留德医学博士中文姓名,并告知李霖灿将押运古物前来纽约。

润章先生赐鉴:

奉到手教并尊序,至为感谢,复承嫂夫人告以三位女士之姓名,尤为铭感。留德名单中尚有一位 Yu Ming,一九二七年 Tübingen 医学博士,弟本写余敏,想另系一人。至于留德博士总数,英文序写 750 人左右,近又增加十余人,故总数稍有不同。现正候宋晞君之复函,因渠赴日,故六月出版势将延期。前接李霖灿君来信,谓押运一部分古物参加纽约博览会,不知送来展览之文物究系何种。月杪或能来纽,届时当趋教也。顺候俪祺。

嫂夫人同此申谢。

弟袁同礼顿首

五月十日

〔Columbia University Libraries Archival Collections, Shuhua Li Papers, 1926-1972, Volume II: Modern Eminent Chinese Leaders〕

按:Yu Ming 者参见 5 月 15 日李书华覆信,Tübingen 即德国图宾根大学。

先生致信 Michael Lazna,表示愿意续编《现代中国经济社会发展目录》并预估工作量,希望该社考虑给予一笔资助。

10 May, 1964

Dear Mr. Lazna:

Thank you for your letter of 7th of May in regard to the possible continuation of my bibliography on Economic and Social Development of Modern China. I hardly realize that the 1956 edition is already out of print.

In view of the large amount of new material published in China, it would be rendering a real service to scholars, if an entirely new edition could be published. Although it is time-consuming (about five months' editorial work), I shall be glad to assist you in bringing out a work of reference to all scholars.

Taking advantage of my forthcoming trip to Europe, I shall be glad to collect additional new material in this field which is not yet available in American institutions. After my return in the fall, I shall start the work and I hope the final manuscript could be submitted next spring. Meanwhile I trust that it would be possible for you to arrange a small research grant to assist in the completion of the project.

Yours sincerely,

T. L. Yuan

〔University of Chicago Library, Yuan T'ung-li Papers, Box 8〕

按：此件为录副。

五月十一日

先生致信郭廷以，商洽译书、出版事，并介绍友人龙章，另告代售《近代中国史事日志》情况。

量予吾兄道席：

月前以平邮寄上代贵所购置 *Russia in the East* 一书，想不日可以寄到。该书第二部分91-156页述及中俄伊犁交涉之危机，将热梅尼与吉尔斯往来信札予以公布，颇多述及俄国内部之情况。弟已托人译成中文，不日拟将译稿寄上，请予审阅，如能由贵所予以出版，最所盼望。其书名暂定为《中俄伊犁交涉之俄国史料》，尚待尊酌也。友人龙章君瑞士 Fribourg 大学史学博士（一九五二），陕西人，西北大学毕业原在"驻法大使馆"任事，对于中法近代史颇多研究，著有 *La Chine à l'aube du XXème siècle* 一书，颇获好评。自我方与法"断交"后，奉令调"外交部"办事，约五月十日左右可到台北，将来渠必前来请教，尚希协助一切是感。代售大著四部（一）国会馆；（二）St.John's 大学；（三）德国国立图书馆；（四）意大利东方学院，除国会馆之款已由弟寄上外，其余三处之款，均告其直接寄上，想不日可以汇到。余俟续陈。敬候时祉。

弟袁同礼再拜

五月十一日

〔台北"中央研究院"近代史研究所档案馆，〈郭廷以〉，馆藏号 069-01-02-089〕

按：龙章所著之全称为 *La Chine à l'aube du XXème siècle: les relations diplomatiques de la Chine avec les puissances depuis la guerre sino-japonaise jusqu' à la guerre russo-japonaise*，直译为《20世纪初的中国：从甲午到日俄战争的中国与列强的外交关系》，1962 年巴黎 Nouvelles Editions Latines 初版。该信以航空信方式寄送，13 日送达。郭廷以在信封正面标注"5，24 复"。

叶良才覆函先生，告并未收到寄送的《胡适先生西文著作目录》（抽印本），请先生与"中央研究院"联系。

May 11, 1964

Dear Dr. Yuan:

　　Thank you for your letter of April 23rd.

　　I did not receive the 100 copies of your Bibliography of Dr. Hu's writings and therefore am unable to send 20 copies to Mr. Delafield. Please check with "Academia Sinica".

　　With kindest regards to you and Mrs. Yuan,

Sincerely,

L. T. Yip

〔University of Chicago Library, Yuan T'ung-li Papers, Box 2〕

五月十二日

先生致信斯坦福胡佛研究院出版部，为"国史馆"订购图书两种。〔University of Chicago Library, Yuan T'ung-li Papers, Box 1〕

五月十四日

Michael Lazna 覆函先生，请就续编书目提交正式提案，以便 Human Relations Area Files 考虑是否资助。

14 May, 1964

Dear Sir:

We were indeed very pleased with your reaction to my last letter to you. We certainly agree that there is a great need for such a comprehensive bibliography and we feel that we should be able to assist you financially in your work. In order to do this, however, we need from you a letter in the form of a proposal addressed to our organization which we could then work into our own proposal seeking financial assistance for this work.

I would think that such a proposal should include perhaps your own evaluation of the existing bibliographical works in this area demonstrating to us the need for a major up-dated bibliographic compilation. Further, you might elaborate on your plan of research and show how much you would need to bring a thorough work to a successful completion.

In your letter you mention "a small research grant." We need a more specific figure in order to decide for ourselves whether in case that we should be unable to secure outside subsidy we could possibly carry the full cost ourselves.

Hoping to hear from you soon.

Yours,

Michael Lazna

〔University of Chicago Library, Yuan T'ung-li Papers, Box 8〕

五月十五日

李书华覆函先生,告两位"Yu Ming"之区别,并谈参观纽约世界博览会之印象。

守和先生赐鉴:

五月十日手示敬悉。内人谓余敏向在柏林大学习医,人皆称她为萧太太,内人并认识此人,因系同时代在柏林的女生。至留德名单中之另一位 Yu Ming 一九二七年 Tübingen 医学博士,其人得医学博士学位,似比萧余敏为早,当系另一人。

承示吾兄月杪或能来纽,甚喜晤面有期,希届时能同吃便饭,藉以畅谈。弟已数次晤见<u>李霖灿</u>君。弟已看过博览会一次,地方甚大,一次只能选看几个馆而已。<u>中国</u>馆古物有三千三百年前的甲骨文及石虎;还有若干书画及敦煌壁画等等。

匆此,顺请双安。

弟李书华敬启
5/15/64

〔University of Chicago Library, Yuan T'ung-li Papers, Box 9〕

按:"内人"即王文田(1903—2001),李书华第二任夫人,南开女中首届学生,1932 年曾赴柏林留学。萧余敏、Yu Ming(余敏)分别见于《中国留欧大陆各国博士论文目录》第 1160、1393 号,前者1936 年毕业。"博览会"即纽约世界博览会(New York World's Fair 1964-1965),中国台湾参加了本次博览会。

王伊同覆函先生,告刘若愚已决定应匹兹堡大学之聘,并谈其赴台研究计划。

老伯大人尊前:

敬禀者,昨奉五月十二日手谕,拜悉一切。华府开会日即与刘君若愚洽商,连聚相谈甚契,且允来校,然其时国务院研究费尚未公布,不能定局。返校后闻芝加哥拟借重,已而刘君来信谓已接该校聘,正多方洽商中。上星期二又得刘君信,谓芝大院长虽批准,学校格于经费,明年始能加聘,乃与敝校当局谈定电聘,已而来电已接聘矣。

大人爱才无微不至,而莲生亦提刘君名列首选,则所见略同也。惟薪金高过朱君文长,渠又将代理系务,或令彼不堪耳。学力、著作,刘君实高出朱君多多,为公计亦不得不尔也。赴台之事为 NDEA-Fulbright-Hays 奖金,概以美金计,安吉及两孩每月有百元津贴,只渠三人旅费需自筹,受奖者不得接他校聘。此行半为研究半则休养,盖廿年未尝得长假矣。刻在医院澈查身体 Check up,后日便归,勿念。是叩,敬请金安。

侄伊同伏枕拜
五月十五

UBC《四部备要》已分批寄出,又叩。

〔University of Chicago Library, Yuan T'ung-li Papers, Box 2〕

按：1964 年秋，王伊同抵台北，在"中央研究院"研习一年，宿蔡元
培馆。[①]

五月十八日

蒋廷黻致函先生，告知之前申请将提交中基会资助执委会讨论。

May 18, 1964

Dear Dr. Yuan:

Your letter dated September 16, 1963 applying for a grant from the China Foundation has been considered by our Trustees at the 33rd Annual Meeting held in April 1964. It was decided that the application be referred to the Executive Committee for consideration.

We will write you again when our Executive Committee has made a decision.

Yours sincerely,

Tingfu F. Tsiang

Director

〔University of Chicago Library, Yuan T'ung-li Papers, Box 2〕

按：此件为打字稿，落款处为其签名。

五月十九日

先生覆信郑通，结清欠款并请寄送《新疆国界图志》二十部与智源书局。

新华印刷公司郑经理大鉴：

接五月十二日大函及收据、结单各一纸，均经诵悉。结欠贵公司
之款共 $129.35，已告香港智源书局(地址列后)如数寄上，并请寄该书局
《新疆国界图志》贰拾部，索一收据为荷。前托转交许性初之函，想该
人或已离港，即作废可也。此颂时祉。

袁同礼顿首

五月十九日

〔University of Chicago Library, Yuan T'ung-li Papers, Box 1〕

按：此件为底稿，左下注"智源书局地址：香港威灵顿街 42 号智源
书局。"

---

① 王伊同著《王伊同学术论文集》，北京：中华书局，2006 年，页 121。

先生致信叶良才，询问中基会是否就《新疆研究文献目录》印刷的资助申请做出决定。

May 19, 1964

Dear Mr. Yip:

Referring to my application for a subsidy toward half of the cost of printing my *Bibliography of Sinkiang* and your kind reply of September 20 last, I may state that I have had no word from you concerning the decision of the Trustees made at their recent meeting in Taipei.

I had hoped that you would be good enough to arrange to place this request on the agenda of the meeting for consideration by the Trustees. I would appreciate a word from you before long.

I shall soon send you three copies of the *Guide to Doctoral Dissertations by Chinese Students in Europe*. According to the information I received from Taipei, they were sent to you and other Trustees care of the Grand Hotel at Taipei a few days after you had left. So, they have sent copies to me here for distribution to other Trustees.

Yours sincerely,
T. L. Yuan

〔University of Chicago Library, Yuan T'ung-li Papers, Box 2〕

按：先生在备忘录里表示，洛克菲勒基金会的资助仅限于编纂而非出版。如果印刷 600 部，则需要 2500 美金的补助，否则没有印刷厂愿意出版一部有十三种西方语言的著作。虽然哈佛燕京学社有意资助一半的印刷费用，但还需要有基金会给予剩下的 1250 美金。

五月二十四日

郭廷以覆函先生，谈近代史研究所与欧洲大学合作进展，并希望先生多多照顾该所新人。

守和先生长者道席：

十一日惠教及寄下*Russia in the East*一书，先后收到（书款即寄去），既慰且感。该书约略翻阅，其中多前所未闻未见记述，译稿如整理竣事，恳即邮赐，愿代印行，作为史料丛刊之一。长者如能惠撰序文，当更为生色。龙章先生极愿一晤，日内当设法向"外交部"探询联络。
年来此间与欧洲学术界甚少往还，实一大遗憾。最近弟开始与伦敦大
学、剑桥大学接触，D. C. Twitchett 教授等常有书至，相互交换出版品。
Twitchett 将于今秋访日之便，顺道来台一行。近史所去年曾派一人赴
英，明春可望再有同事一位续往。其他欧陆大学弟亦欲与取得联系，
敢祈予以介绍。费正清此次到台，印象甚好，对于近史所及史语所尤
热心协助，惟王院长似尚有其政治顾虑，颇不可解。又近史所吕实强
君在哈佛进修二年期满，不久拟去华府，届时尚望加以指导为幸。日
志销售，多承费神，谨再谢。敬问双安。

弟郭廷以谨上
五、廿四

〔University of Chicago Library, HYuan T'ung-li Papers, Box 2〕

按：吕实强（1927—2019），山东富山人，1953 年毕业于台湾省立
师范大学史地系，后入近代史所，1962 年赴美国哈佛大学访问。
此函在郭廷以日记中归于 23 日。

五月二十五日

刘麟生覆函先生，请协助申请亚利桑那大学图书馆职务。

守和先生馆长勋右：

诵廿二日环云，深裹在远不忘之雅谊，感何可言。兹将卜氏原书
及卜氏 1962 年冬复弟书奉上，乞阅后便中将后者掷还是荷。舍表
侄陈明明 Raphael M. Chen 系在该校卒业。近在哥大攻读天文，欲
获博士学位。弟对于该校中文书之整理及购置颇具兴致。弟有永
久居留资格，近方筹备 naturalization 也。又弟居日九年，对于日文，
少有根柢，原函中亦涉及此点。故弟欲烦大贤便中绍介，且询及条
件，如待遇及订约期限，能合弟等之意，颇拟前往观光。内子畏热，
不知其地气候燥热如何。明明言，热达百余度，然不渐湿，故与纽约
夏时亦相仿佛也。恃在厚爱，故敢直陈，维亮之而已。敬谢，并请
俪安。

小弟麟生谨上
内子叩安
五，廿五

如作书,请叙弟身体甚健,治事能耐劳,尤感。

（University of Chicago Library, Yuan T'ung-li Papers, Box 1）

五月下旬

先生赴纽约,参观世界博览会,并与李书华等人晤谈。〔University of Chicago Library, Yuan T'ung-li Papers, Box 8〕

五月三十日

先生撰写 *Economic and Social Development of Modern China, 1901*– 1964 研究计划,并草拟预算,需美金 1800 元。〔University of Chicago Library, Yuan T'ung-li Papers, Box 8〕

　　按:该计划预计两到三年完成。

先生覆信 Michael Lazna,递交研究计划并告知明年一月方能展开续编工作。

30 May, 1964

Dear Mr. Lazna:

　　Thank you so much for your letter of 14 May. I regret very much that my absence from Washington has prevented me from writing you earlier.

　　At your suggestion, I enclose a brief statement about the work in which you are interested. I also cut down the expenses as low as possible.

　　Owing to my previous commitments, I shall not be able to start the work until next January. This will give you sufficient time to work out your budgets.

　　Apologizing for the delay in writing to you,

Yours sincerely,

T. L. Yuan

〔University of Chicago Library, Yuan T'ung-li Papers, Box 8〕

是年夏

先生函询哈佛大学汉和图书馆有无可能购买徐庭瑶旧藏《事文类聚》(宋版)、《文献通考》(明版)。〔《裘开明年谱》,页 868〕

　　按:《裘开明年谱》载本年 6 月 8 日,徐先雁致函裘开明。"徐先雁"或有误,似应为"徐先汇"。

六月一日

先生致信 Earl H. Pritchard，推荐刘麟生协助亚利桑那大学筹建东亚馆藏。

June 1, 1964

Dear Professor Pritchard:

Since receiving your letter of May 1, I have given some thought concerning a suitable person to assist you in building up your Oriental Studies Library.

In view of what you have already accomplished, you would certainly need a man of broad and liberal education than a technical cataloger. In addition to the work of cataloging, such a person should round up your collection by the selection and purchase of essential source materials and by keeping in touch with the sales of large collections as well as with the current output of Chinese and Japanese literature.

Dr. Tsien who I recommended to Dr. Creel is a good example. The high quality of the Chicago collection is much more useful to a scholar than the Library of Congress where a lot of junk are daily adding to the collection as a result of blanket orders and departmental transfers.

For the position in your University, I have in mind of Mr. Lin-sheng Liu who is not only an outstanding scholar, but having lived in Japan for nine years, has a good knowledge of Japanese literature. He is a permanent resident in the United States and is in the process of being naturalized.

Born in 1895, Mr. Liu looks like a man of fifty. He has the capacity for work; and as long as he is in the company of books, he never feels tired. So please do not mind about his age.

With all good wishes,

Yours sincerely,

T. L. Yuan

〔University of Chicago Library, Yuan T'ung-li Papers, Box 1〕

按：此件为录副。

宋晞致函先生，告《中国留欧大陆各国博士论文目录》校样邮寄情况及获意国博士之人员调查进展。

守和先生道鉴：

送奉惠示，均已照办。兹分别条复如次：

一、《博士论文目录》德国部分校样已另付航邮寄上，请查收，校阅后即请航邮寄回，以便付印。末篇号码为1399。

二、义国获博士学位之神甫等，经分别去函后，顷陆续收到张必富、刘顺德、王愈荣、陈骅璐、冯观涛、胡振中、李振英、李贵良、吕明德、王志远、温中祥、吴宗文等十二份，随函附奉，请查收。若续有收到，当容再寄。

余不尽陈，祗颂道安。

后学宋晞顿首

六，一

〔University of Chicago Library, Yuan T'ung-li Papers, Box 4〕

六月二日

郭廷以致函先生。〔《郭量宇先生日记残稿》，页496〕

六月五日

罗家伦致函先生，委托代购书籍、杂志等事并寄赠吴敬恒纪念文集。

守和吾兄道鉴：

久未通讯，无任企念！兹将近月来收到书籍及奉托各事，分陈于次：

一、一月十五日寄下选购图书发票之书籍，已全部收到，未付款者，请即照付。其中 British Information Service-*War against Japan* 一部，书价美金三二.三八元，请列入党史会账内。

二、Park Book Shop 于二月廿八日、三月廿六日及四月廿三日分别寄来书籍三批，共计书价美金一〇四.六〇元；*Facts on File* 寄到一九六三年年鉴一册，计美金三〇.七〇元；芝加哥大学图书馆寄到史料胶片一小卷，计美金三.三五元，均请费神代为付款。

三、本馆所订杂志三种(*Current History, Foreign Affairs, Journal of Modern History*)均已到期，亦请代为付款，各续订两年。

四、委托美国国会图书馆重拍档案胶片两卷，业经寄来，已将重复之两卷寄还矣。

五、台湾商务印书馆四月廿二日送来《戡定新疆记》三册，除转送本馆及党史会各一册外，并此致谢。

六、本会计年度将于本月底终了，前汇奉购书款美金五百元，连同上年结存六十一元，除付已购书籍及续订杂志等费外，如有结余，最好请于本月内代为选购书籍，并请将已付款收据寄下，以便报销。

七、本年三月至六月份征集费新台币贰千元台湾银行缴款单两张附奉。又寄上空白收据六张，请加章寄还。

八、最近为吴稚晖先生百年诞辰编印选集二册，墨迹一册，传记一册，共四册。兹寄上两套，一套赠兄，一套请转赠国会图书馆。其全集共约七百万字，明年可编成寄赠。

九、金纯孺先生托两位朋友问我有关九一八事变后的一件外交事项，我允为查案奉复，不意去年好不容易查出后，典藏者又将原件、抄件均误置。现已将这份特种外交委员会全档中误置的这一本查出，并将金先生所要之部份付抄，日内寄上，以了此项史学上的精神负担。该函将请兄转，盼便时先行代达，并致迟复之歉意！

专此，敬颂道祺！

弟罗家伦敬启

六，五

嫂夫人前问安。

〔University of Chicago Library, Yuan T'ung-li Papers, Box 1〕

按："为吴稚晖先生百年诞辰编印选集"应即《吴稚晖先生选集》，上下两册；"墨迹"即《吴稚晖先生墨迹》，"传记"即张文伯著《吴敬恒先生传记》；以上三种均为1964年3月初版。此件为文书代笔，落款处为其亲签名。

六月六日

何日章覆函先生，寄上政大校刊、教职员名册及《中国图书十进分类法》书稿序言和跋文。

守和先生台鉴：

久隔芝晖，时切驰思。于上月十八日展读琅函，并蒙高谊惠赠《善本书录》两本，今已收到，至感。且谢嘱将散馆图书目录奉上一册，惟未为专印，每月有新书经编目后，即在政大校刊内随时刊布。兹寄上本校校刊 30 册(自第一期起至 31 期,但内缺少第 17 期一册),暨本校 (1963)学年度第一学期专、兼任教员名册各一册,敬请查收惠存为荷。弟来馆中近五载,除公私忙碌外,现将在北平所编之《中国图书十进分类法》增订为第三版,刻已付印,正校对中(第二版已绝版)。兹检上第三版中西文序言各一篇,暨杨家骆兄所作之中西文跋各一篇,希予指正是所盼祷。专此,敬颂台绥。

弟何日章敬启

六月六日

赠书由船运寄上。

〔袁同礼家人提供〕

普实克致函先生,讨论《新疆研究丛刊》购书款的支付方式。

PRAGUE, June 6, 1964.

Dear Dr. YUAN,

　　Many thanks for your extremely interesting three volumes on the history of the relations between China and Russia.

　　Considering the importance of the subject, I am sure that your book will become an efficient auxiliary required by all students of this problem.

　　There is still an open money item which I intended to pay into the hands of your brother, but as there is, for the time being, no hope that I should be able to do so, I think it will be better to remit you the amount in question direct to Washington. Please, let me know your opinion in this respect.

　　In the meantime, I wish you a good health and further success in your work and remain, Dear Mr. YUAN,

Very sincerely yours

J. Prusek

〔University of Chicago Library, Yuan T'ung-li Papers, Box 2〕

　　按:此件为打字稿,落款处为其签名。

六月七日

先生覆信 Lionello Lanciotti,感谢帮助询问留学意大利博士论文情况,并告自己预计赴罗马的日期。

June 7, 1964

Dear Professor Lanciotti:

I am indeed grateful to you for your kind letter of 21 April and for your kindness in writing for authorization to your Ministry of Education. I trust that you may have a reply by this time.

Since most universities are closed by the end of June, I do not think I can get much information from my forthcoming trip. I expect to be in Rome June 22-24 and I shall try my luck. If you happen to know any of the curators of the following institutions, perhaps you may like to ascertain whether permission could be given to me to look over the catalogue cards.

I am bringing over additional cards on Marco Polo, and I hope you could find the necessary time to bring it to early completion.

Looking forward with much pleasure to seeing you soon,

Yours sincerely,

T. L. Yuan

〔University of Chicago Library, Yuan T'ung-li Papers, Box 4〕

按：此件为录副。

六月八日

先生致信富路德教授,感谢其对申请美国学术团体理事会资助编纂《中国艺术和考古目录》所给予的支持。

June 8, 1964

Dear Professor Goodrich:

Thank you so much for your card. The award from the ACLS came as a surprise, as it had been turned down twice before. I know for certain that without your and other scholars' recommendation, I could hardly be considered in view of the keen competition among the participants.

This work involving the analyzing of all sinological and art journals is a time-consuming task. I hope to have it completed after two more years.

I have much enjoyed the work, and with your encouragement, I shall bring the work to early completion.

With all good wishes for a pleasant summer.

Yours sincerely,

T. L. Yuan

〔University of Chicago Library, Yuan T'ung-li Papers, Box 3〕

按：此件为录副。

六月九日

先生致信郭廷以，告知书款结算事，并告将赴德国一行。

量予先生道席：

两奉手教，拜悉种切。承赐还西文书款＄7.07，谢谢。至于纽约 St. John's 大学之支票二十九元二角五分，内中拾壹元系该校订购《史事日志》之款，其余之款系归还弟所印各书者，曾告其以拾壹元径寄尊处，不意该校会计人员有此误也。兹随函奉上弟支票拾壹元，祈查收是荷。此外，德国国立图书馆及罗马之远东学院各购一部，其书款由该两机关直接汇至贵所，想本月内可以收到。弟因事下周赴德，约七月杪返美。余容再陈。敬候时祉。

弟袁同礼顿首

六月九日

〔台北"中央研究院"近代史研究所档案馆，〈郭廷以〉，馆藏号 069-01-02-089〕

按：该信于 13 日送达。①

六月十日

先生覆信罗家伦，感谢寄赠吴敬恒相关书籍并附上"国史馆"报账清单。

志希馆长仁兄尊鉴：

正拟作书，适奉六月五日手教，敬悉种切。承惠寄稚老选集及墨迹、传记等，至感厚意。其赠馆中者当由馆方另致谢函也。关于英新闻处所购之*War against Japan*，其书价已于一月十二日列入贵馆账内。兹将 Kegan Paul 所购之第二部，改列入党史会账内，谅荷同意。嘱订购各期刊三种，每种两年，均已遵办。兹将截至本日为止之报账清单随函奉上，即希台洽是荷。此外，党史会之二百元尚存 156 元，关于国

---

① 《郭量宇先生日记残稿》，页 498。

父传记等，此间各书店索价过昂，故未购买。下周因事赴欧，拟到各大
书店亲自选择。

六月十日

〔University of Chicago Library, Yuan T'ung-li Papers, Box 1〕

按：此件为底稿。

六月十六日

先生覆信普实克，告知《新疆研究丛刊》进展，并请将书款汇往巴克莱银行
伦敦支行。

June 16, 1964

Dear Professor Prusek:

I deeply appreciate your kind letter of June 6. Since writing to you last, three more volumes in the "*Sinkiang Collectanea*" have been published. I am now waiting for the appearance of the last volume. I shall send these volumes to your Academy with much pleasure.

Concerning the remittance of the money, you may send it to the Barclays Bank, Marylebone Branch, 5a Marylebone High Street, London, W. l, England, if it is more convenient for you to do so. You may send with a letter to that Bank, asking it to credit the amount to my current account. The other way is to send it to me here in Washington.

I have recently read your article published in the *Arts and Sciences of China* (London) which is very instructive.

Under the leadership of Dr. Lubor Hajek, there is a considerable literature in Czek on the art and archaeology of China. If convenient, could you ask your librarian to send me a selective list of such literature? Please convey my hearty thanks for his help.

With all good wishes,

Your sincerely,
T. L. Yuan

Prof. J. Prusek

Praha 1, Czechoslovakia

〔University of Chicago Library, Yuan T'ung-li Papers, Box 2〕

按:该件为录副。

六月十八日

先生离美赴欧,调查中国流失海外的艺术珍品分布情况,用以编纂目录。

〔《思忆录》,中文部分页141、7〕

Michael Lazna 覆函先生,告知该社将努力争取外部支持用以资助先生编纂《现代中国经济社会发展目录》增订本。

18 June 1964

Dear Mr. Yuan:

Thank you for your letter and statement of proposed work. Let me once more express our appreciation with your readiness to update your work.

We find your fee and associated expenses quite reasonable and the problem at the moment is not our willingness to pay it but where to go for it. We would like to cover our expenses partly from outside subsidy, preferably to cover your cost by subsidy and the cost of manufacturing by our own funds. In that situation we should be able to make the revised edition available at a reasonably low price. It may take us some time before we know when and how much we can get; however, you yourself have your own commitments which will take up the rest of this year. We should be able to know what we can do long before the time and will communicate to you any relative development as soon as we can.

Wishing you an agreeable summer.

Yours,

Mike Lazna

〔University of Chicago Library, Yuan T'ung-li Papers, Box 8〕

六月二十五日

薛光前致函先生,请代向国会图书馆捐赠钱泰著作两册。

守和先生赐鉴:

附奉钱阶公遗著两册,倘蒙惠予转陈国会图书馆予以编目以存永久纪念,不胜感服大德之至。专请勋安。

弟薛光前拜

六，廿五

〔University of Chicago Library, Yuan T'ung-li Papers, Box 2〕

按：1962 年 7 月 31 日，钱泰在纽约去世，8 月 4 日安葬。"遗著"
应指《中国和勃鲁塞尔会议》（*China and the Nine Power
Conference at Brussels in 1937*），1964 年由圣若望大学亚洲研究中
心（Institute of Asian Studies, St. John's University）出版。[1]

六月二十七日

王世杰致函先生，告知"国家长期发展科学委员会"无力补助《中国考古人
类文献目录》。

同礼先生道鉴：

本年四月十五日惠函，诵悉。先生于编目工作，经验丰富，此次
编成之《中国考古人类文献目录》，区分精密，允为研究中国古史及
考古学等最切实用之工具书，此间同人极为推崇。惟因本年度美援
已告停止，政府核定预算又极有限，而国内各学术机构申请刊物出
版补助者，复较往年增多，致运用支配，倍感困难。故科学会不得不
规定原则，将补助范围加以紧缩，凡申请机关勉能自筹财源者，如
"中央研究院"、台湾大学、中兴大学等部份出版刊物，本年均未予补
助，其必须予以补助之研究性著作刊物，亦就其申请金额尽量核减，
对于一般非研究性之刊物，本年度均无法予以补助。尊编经本会专
门委员会特别重视，再三研议，仍以目前经费极形拮据，按照紧缩原
则，未能如嘱补助。此种实际困难情形，尚希鉴谅。耑此布复，顺颂
撰祺。

王世杰敬启

六月廿七日

〔University of Chicago Library, Yuan T'ung-li Papers, Box 8〕

按：《中国考古人类文献目录》即《中国艺术和考古目录》。此件
为打字稿，落款处钤王世杰印。

---

[1] 薛光前著《故人与往事》，台北：传记文学出版社，1977 年，页 41-42、48。

六月

Chinese Culture 刊登先生文章,题为 A Guide to Doctoral Dissertations of Chinese Students in Continental Europe, 1907–1962。〔*Chinese Culture: a quarterly review*, Vol. 5, No. 4, pp. 65–133〕

> 按:该期所载为《中国留欧大陆各国博士论文目录》第二部分之留德学生。

七月初

先生抵达慕尼黑,突然病发,当地大学医院诊断为胰腺出血,住院数天,并输血。〔《思忆录》,中文页 141〕

> 按:住院期间,先生曾多次致信袁澄,并谈待病情好转,仍将前往维也纳调查。

七月十日

先生致信袁澄,大意如下:

> 兹因医生之劝,早日返美割治,故已定妥明日 T. W. A. 飞机由 Frankfort 直飞华京。

〔《思忆录》,中文部分页 141〕

七月中上旬

先生由法兰克福乘飞机回到华盛顿,并入院治疗。〔《思忆录》,中文部分页 141〕

> 按:7 月 15 日,袁澄曾打电话问询情况,知已入院。

七月十五日

王伊同覆函先生,告去台行程安排。

> 老伯大人尊前:
>
> 敬禀者,七月十二日手谕拜悉。游德归来定增资料,未知又着手何篇,企慕企慕。侄等定八月一日飞洛杉矶,转檀岛、东京,八月八日到港,停旬日转台北。晓峰先生二示之留邀宿贵宾楼或即暂住"中央研究院",地址幽美,然去美国学校十余里,来往终一问题也。倚装不尽所怀,敬请福安。
>
> 侄伊同顿首拜
>
> 七,十五

〔University of Chicago Library, Yuan T'ung-li Papers, Box 8〕

七月十七日

先生接受手术,医生发现癌细胞已经扩散,无法割治,只能保守治疗,仅缝合伤口。〔《思忆录》,中文部分页7〕

　　按:此时,真实病情并未告知先生本人。

七月二十九日

先生致信袁澄,大意如下:

　　我割治后,经过良好。今日答复说下星期一可以出院,在家静养几星期再上班。

〔《思忆录》,中文部分页141〕

八月三日

曾约农致函先生,感谢惠赠《金轺筹笔》影印本。

　　守和博士仁兄台鉴:

　　　　年来俗务萦心,未能致力问学,偶有聆教机会,又憾匆促,不克罄怀,甚以为歉。乃荷嘱此间商务印书馆代为厚赐先祖遗著《金轺筹笔》影印本,此书舍下旧藏及神州国光社印本均于乱中遗失,今获保存、翻印,并远道不遗见惠,隆情高谊,铭感五衷。阁下处怡静之环境中,致力研究,尤为羡佩。弟碌碌如恒,无善足告,鳞鸿有便,时企好音。专此申谢,顺颂台绥。

　　　　　　　　　　　　　　　　　　　弟曾约农谨启

　　　　　　　　　　　　　　　　　　　　八月三日

〔University of Chicago Library, Yuan T'ung-li Papers, Box 8〕

　　按:该函为文书代笔,落款处钤曾约农印。

八月十二日

先生致信台湾商务印书馆,随函寄上美金贰佰元汇票、新台币伍仟伍佰柒拾元支票各一张。〔University of Chicago Library, Yuan T'ung-li Papers, Box 1〕

　　　　按:此两部分合计后正好清抵先生此前在商务印书馆所欠印刷费用、书账,后者18日覆信先生告知业已收讫。

八月十六日

樊际昌覆函先生,告其夫人、蒋梦麟病逝经过,并谈已恢复教书事业。

　　守和先生道席:

　　　　五六两月间连奉三函敬悉,容一一奉答如后。

内子自一九六二年夏患轻微中风,右半身麻痹后,迄在家休养治疗。因体气已弱,复元不易,但精神始终正常。不意于今年一月廿八日上午再度中风,大脑溢血,数秒钟而昏迷不省。经送台大医院治疗,终因来势猛烈,医者束手,于当日晚间逝世,享年六十八岁。现已安葬于阳明山公墓,与孟邻夫人及许多老友为"邻"。该公墓为周象贤兄任局长时所创办。孟邻夫人逝世时(一九五八年五月)尚未筹备就绪,经弟与象贤兄交涉后,先为夫人建墓,此为该公墓之"第一号",而今已"人满"矣,且大多数为我辈友好!

去年以前,孟邻先生常说,他要活到九十岁。照他的体况,我想八十五岁是无问题的。但自一九六一年夏结婚后,情况就大不同了。在婚后一年半的生活中,他"外表"快乐,而内心却充满了矛盾和痛苦。我想肝癌早已种了一病根。一九六二年冬在台中跌伤碎臀骨。入医院治疗,又患很严重的褥疮。正在与病魔作斗争中,他又下决心要办离婚,他委托弟办理其事。弟明知其难,但又不忍违拂其意。经整整一年的神经战,居然调解成功(今年一月二十日)。金钱损失(新台币七十万元)犹是小事,而经此 resolution 后,他的精神空虚,肝癌乘机发作。初则感觉疲乏,至四月间而显现于□光中矣。一生英明,暮年如此遭遇,真堪痛惜。弟日前嘱此间华美协进社台湾分社(弟与勉仲兄分担其事)寄奉《传记文学》(第五卷第一期)数册,内载有此间友好悼文数篇,亮已收到。读兄挽词,为之黯然神往! 孟公现已安葬,与夫人同穴。弟今年二月底照章退休。孟邻先生当时虽欲坚留,而弟为个人归宿计,雅不愿再在行将结束之美援机构中,作无谓牺牲,亟思追寻个人兴趣,恢复教书生涯。上半年在台大心理系授课三小时,下学年起在政治大学教育系专任心理课程,在台大兼任。半年以来对心理科学(行为科学)之新发展,作一有系统之温习,真感惊异。幸弟在以往十余年中,尚未完全荒废,否则将不识庐山真面目矣。

兄所需要之农复会书目,方于日内办好。因经办人被去职,新人接管不甚熟手,所以迟延,尚乞鉴宥为幸。短短三年期中,胡、梅、蒋及内子相继以去(孟公可以说是弟的惟一 boss,除第一年蔡先生名义的聘书外,但他从未 boss 过我),弟精神上之打击,殊不易受。现正勉力发愤图存,希望对后继者,犹可稍有贡献,至盼知我者有以教我也。崇此,敬颂道祺。

弟际昌敬上

八，十六，1964

嫂夫人请代道候。

〔University of Chicago Library, Yuan T'ung-li Papers, Box 2〕

　　按："孟邻夫人"即陶曾谷，本系高仁山遗孀，1933 年与蒋梦麟成婚，1958 年去世。周象贤（1890—1961），字企虞，浙江定海人，上海南洋公学毕业后赴美入麻省理工学院学习，归国后历任内政部技正、庐山管理局局长，多次出任杭州市市长，1955 年担任台北阳明山管理局局长。"离婚"则指蒋梦麟与徐贤乐的分离，1964 年 6 月 19 日蒋梦麟逝世。

八月十八日

Albert L. Seely 覆函先生，感谢推荐徐家璧作为香港崇基学院图书馆馆长候选人。

August 18, 1964

Dear Dr. Yuan:

　　I am very grateful for your August 3 letter which was waiting for me after my return from vacation.

　　Thank you for the information about Dr. T. H. Tsien and Dr. Hsia; it does appear that neither of them would be free to consider the position in Hong Kong. Mr. Chen Wen-chao is probably committed for some time into the future at Kalamazoo also.

　　Thank you very much for the suggestion of Mr. Chia-pi Hsu. The record of his background and professional experience is very substantial, and I am glad to have your comment about his necessary tact and resourcefulness as well as his competence in planning and building up collections of Chinese and Western books.

　　I know that Dr. Yung and Dr. Li will be most pleased to have this recommendation and I will forward it to them without delay. If they would like me to arrange an interview with Mr. Hsu, it can easily be arranged.

With sincere appreciation and best wishes, I am

　　　　　　　　　　　Very cordially yours,

　　　　　　　　　　　　A. L. Seely

　　　　　　　　　　Associate Secretary

P. S. We have had another candidate, presently at the Library of Congress, recommended for the position of librarian at Chung Chi College (which is also seeking a competent librarian). He is Dr. K. T. Wu. How would you evaluate him for this position?

〔University of Chicago Library, Yuan T'ung-li Papers, Box 2〕

按：Albert L. Seely 为亚洲基督教高等教育联合董事会助理秘书。Dr. Hsia 或指夏道泰，待考。Mr. Chen Wen-chao 即陈文照（1919—2012），山西汾西人，早年在美国传教士创办的学堂学习，1943 年担任美国驻华空军翻译，后赴美留学，获格林内尔学院（Grinnell College）学士学位，后获圣路易斯大学公共管理专业博士学位，1950 年受聘于卡拉马祖学院（Kalamazoo College）。Dr. Yung and Dr. Li，待考。

八月中旬

先生因进食呕吐，再次入院治疗。〔《思忆录》，中文部分页 142〕

八月二十二日

洪余庆致函先生，告洪有丰遗著编纂进展，并请订正序言印样。

守和老伯赐鉴：

一年来时时为筹印先父遗著，并得老伯等之助，稍有眉目。《清代藏书家考》及《克特及其展开分类法》，已自《图书馆季刊》中摄影二次，现正制版，付印尚有稍待也。绩溪同乡会现正请人撰写，预计九月可脱稿。

日昨胡家健老伯自港来台告知，现正多方与友联络探询先父忌辰，大约下月有消息。去年所得之噩耗，亦系胡老伯转来，但因辗转探询不易，致数月来尚无结果也。

兹将老伯所赐之序刷样附奉，敬请赐予订正后连同弁言一并掷下。（弁言前蒙老伯掷下，因制版技术差乃改排，将来放大为二十四开本付印。但此编文章不知系清华目录之弁言否？其前应冠书名否？

敬请示知。)

谨将已搜得之书目列后：

一、《国立东南大学孟芳图书馆目录序》(于镜宇老伯摄赐)；

二、《清代藏书家考》("中央图书馆"藏)；

三、《克特及其展开分类法》("中央图书馆"藏)；

四、《国立清华大学图书馆中文书目序》(袁老伯摄赐)；

五、《国立清华大学图书馆丛书子目索引序》("中央图书"藏)；

六、《弁言》(袁老伯摄赐)；

七、《东南大学图书馆述要》(袁老伯告知,周之南先生洽索)；

以下只有目录而未找到原文：

一、《洪氏图书分类法》；

二、《我对于南京江苏省立第一图书馆之希望》；

三、《图书馆问题之最近趋向》；

四、《大学图书馆》(图书馆协会十周年纪念集)；

五、《图书分类说明及其简表》。

如有不实或遗漏之处,敬请赐予订正。专此,敬请崇安！

洪制侄余庆叩

八,廿二

〔University of Chicago Library, Yuan T'ung-li Papers, Box 2〕

八月二十四日

徐家璧覆函先生,对推荐其作为香港崇基学院图书馆馆长候选人表示感谢。

守和先生尊鉴：

敬肃者,承赐二十一日手谕,至为感戴！惟该示到时,晚适因事去纽,致略稽裁覆,尚乞恕之！刻下 Seely 牧师既有覆书,可谓推进一步,率皆得先生之赐。惟晚之希望,端在贤者、能者之因故未能前往,于是尚存一线曙光。若竟与诸公疆场角逐,则未有不待旗开而失败者也。兹将 Seely 牧师来函录竟,谨此璧还。

先生病后未痊,再行入院,不胜惦念之至！惟祈迅即补救,得以正常进食为祷！

临书翘企,伏维早日康复。肃此,敬颂崇安！

尊夫人前,乞代叱名候安!

晚徐家璧鞠躬
八月廿四日

〔University of Chicago Library, Yuan T'ung-li Papers, Box 4〕

八月二十五日

罗家伦致函先生,请转寄致金问泗信。

守和吾兄道鉴:

溽暑中大驾赴欧,雅兴何如? 前次弟在尊寓晤金问泗先生,彼曾谈及九一八事件发生时期的外交情况。后由兄来函代询当时拉西曼对我国中枢决策的影响。现已将原案查明,我方自有基本认识,与拉无关,亦非彼所能主张。其详见弟致金先生长函中(此函请兄转致为感),此亦可见弟所守治史之笨方法也。此颂俪祺。

弟罗家伦敬启
八,二五,台北

嫂夫人前问安。

〔University of Chicago Library, Yuan T'ung-li Papers, Box 1〕

九月三日

罗家伦致函先生,请在美购买日本外务省档案有关抗战史料的胶卷并谈购书等事。

守和吾兄道鉴:

前接六月十日手教暨帐单等,均敬奉悉。吾兄欧洲之行,谅已返美矣。

(一)本馆最近请到外汇美金贰仟元,为在国外购置史料胶片及图书之用。兹特挂号寄奉台湾银行本年八月十九日 No. 103/64 - 12020 美金贰仟元汇票壹张,请查收领取并代为保存支付为托。(汇票背书注明,凭吾兄护照或其他证明文件支取,以昭慎重。)

(二)前岁八月廿三日大札,告以日本外务省档案在移交贵馆前,曾由国务院自照七十二卷计5875尺,经兄惠寄一九六二年六月十三日估价单一纸,共需美金四九○元。当时本馆外汇不敷,故未能决定购否。今外汇稍裕,如该七十二卷之内容不在国会图书馆后来所摄2116卷之中,但在有关中日问题之列,则烦神代购一全套。若两者有重复摄印之处,是否应先将本馆已购之三三七卷及现拟续行选购之一、二百卷等卷号一并开列清单寄上,藉供查核,亦请示知。如设重复之处不多,本馆仍可考虑购置。因本馆所急需者为有关抗战之文献,而又想从精简中求节约也。如何之处,尚祈惠示卓见,为荷。

(三)本馆订购 Facts on File《一九六三年年鉴》*Yearbook, 1963*。原出版处于本年三月间寄出,已经收到,价款美金三十元七角前请代付,现又来信催款,如尚未付,请费神代付为感。

(四)新德里牛津书店寄来书籍十五种,其中在吾兄开出之书单内,仅有五种。又收到 Park Book Shop 寄来 Stuart & Levy: *Kind-Hearted Tiger* 一册,均烦代付书款。

(五)*Document of British Foreign Policy* 此书有关我国抗战史实,甚为重要,本馆仅收到一册,请吾兄函嘱 Heffer 书店设法补全寄来,为托。

(六)附奉吾兄七、八、九月征集费新台币壹仟五百元台湾银行送款单存根两张,请察收。

专此奉托,顺颂道祺!

弟罗家伦敬启
九,三,台北

嫂夫人前问安!

前请转交金问泗先生一函,不知收到否,请示知。

〔University of Chicago Library, Yuan T'ung-li Papers, Box 1〕

按:*Kind-Hearted Tiger* 作者为 Gilbert Stuart、Alan Levy,1964 年 Little, Brown and Company 初版。此件为文书代笔,落款、补语则为罗家伦亲笔。收到此函后,先生于 10 日覆信一封。

九月十日

叶良才覆函先生,告知收到寄赠的样刊,并请补寄《中国留欧大陆各国博士论文目录》余下分册。

Sept. 10, 1964

Dear Dr. Yuan:

Thank you for your letter of Sept. 6, 1964.

We note that you are sending us 3 copies of the second instalment of "Guide to Doctoral Dissertations by Chinese Students in Continental Europe" and will send us later the third and final instalment.

"Ambassador Tsiang" is aware of your application for a grant to help pay for the printing of your bibliography of Sinkiang. He will bring the matter up at the next meeting of our Executive Committee.

Yours sincerely,

L. T. Yip

〔University of Chicago Library, Yuan T'ung-li Papers, Box 2〕

按：A Guide to Doctoral Dissertations of Chinese Students in Continental Europe, 1907–1962 连载时分为三期, 并无第四(final)分册。此件为打字稿, 落款处为其签名。

九月十七日

先生出院, 回家休养。〔《思忆录》, 中文部分页7〕

九月二十四日

蒋廷黻致函先生, 告知先生申请中基会资助暂未获得执委会的批准, 拟将此申请送至董事会表决。

Sept. 24, 1964

Dear Dr. Yuan:

Your application for a subsidy of $1,250 to pay half of the printing cost of the Bibliography of Sinkiang was discussed by our Executive Committee at the 161st Meeting held on Sept. 17, 1964. It was decided that the application be referred back to the Board.

Yours Sincerely,

Tingfu F. Tsiang

Director

〔University of Chicago Library, Yuan T'ung-li Papers, Box 2〕

按：此件为打字稿, 落款处为其签名。

九月二十八日

洪余庆日覆函先生, 感谢寄下序文、弁言, 并告已托人打听其父洪有丰的忌日。

守和老伯赐鉴:

　　前接八月廿五日训示及附掷下老伯之序文与先父弁言,并承为注明出处,感戴万分。经已交厂印刷之矣。惟以绩溪同乡会请人为写之传尚未脱稿,致出版恐尚须稍缓也。侄意希望最迟十一月能赶上先父诞辰出版,但不知有困难否? 时刻以此为念也。

　　去年为侄转来噩耗之同乡胡建人老伯于上月从日本经此返香港,承告知已□去函再询其忌辰,希能补于传中,但至今尚未接覆示也。

　　敬悉老伯略感不适,不卜已出院否? 极念。专此,敬请崇安。

　　　　　　　　　　　　　　　　　　　洪制侄余庆叩

　　　　　　　　　　　　　　　　　　　　九,廿八

　　　　　　　　　　　　　　　　〔袁同礼家人提供〕

　　按:此时,洪余庆联系地址为台北市兰州街207巷1号台北市立商业学校。

十月九日

先生致信郭廷以,告知因病未能如期覆信,并商黎烈文译稿费用问题。

　　量予先生著席:

　　前奉手教,嘱写一引言,再与黎烈文译稿一并奉上,适弟卧病数月,未能如愿。兹特交航邮寄上,即希教正。至于书名是否应为《中俄伊犁交涉俄方之资料》,或改用其他名称,统候尊裁。黎教授译费系梁实秋兄代为接洽者,如贵所能在补助费内予以拨付,作为贵所专刊之一,尤为企盼,否则仍由弟担付,亦无不可。此书需吾兄作序,在序内自应函谢黎教授也。原书内有地图一张,俄人照片二张。弟另在他处觅到曾氏照片,均可印入书内也。专此,顺候时祉。

　　　　　　　　　　　　　　　　　　　弟袁同礼顿首

　　　　　　　　　　　　　　　　　　　　十月九日

　　　　〔台北"中央研究院"近代史研究所档案馆,〈郭廷以〉,馆藏号069-01-02-089〕

　　按:《中俄伊犁交涉俄方之资料》即《伊犁交涉的俄方文件》,《"中央研究院"近代史研究所史料丛刊》第2种,1966年11月初版,郭廷以序、先生导言均未提及黎烈文。1963年7月10日、8月29日,黎烈文撰写一份注意事项、两份译稿谢金收据,证明译费由先生支付,由梁实秋转交支票,共计新台币玖仟元。

十月十五日

先生致信李书华,慰问病情并谈自己病后仍未能康复。

> 润章先生道席:

>> 昨奉赐书,始悉贵体违和,并将摄护腺割去,经过良好,闻之甚慰。惟年高之人恢复较慢,尚希安心静养是祷。弟患 pancreas,入院割治后住院两月,迄今未能复原,终日度日如年,亦无他法可想。吾人在此幸有良医,又有健康保险,否则更不堪设想矣。前拜读大著《传记文学》,甚佩甚佩。顺候痊安。

> 嫂夫人同此。

>> 　　　　　　　　　　　　　　　　　　　弟袁同礼顿首
>> 　　　　　　　　　　　　　　　　　　　十月十五日

> 〔Columbia University Libraries Archival Collections, Shuhua Li Papers, 1926-1972, Volume II: Modern Eminent Chinese Leaders〕

> 按:"摄护腺"即前列腺,pancreas 则是胰腺。"大著"应指《吴稚晖先生从维新派成为革命党的经过》或《吴稚晖先生与廉南湖》,前者分上下两期刊于《传记文学》3、4 月,后者则登载于 9 月号,笔者认为应是前者。

十月二十一日

张馨保致函先生,寄赠《林则徐与鸦片战争》(上册)并谈其研究计划。

> 守和老伯尊鉴:

>> 前闻尊驾稍有不适,未知完全康复否? 至念。拙作林则徐与鸦片战争久经延宕,现已出版,乃即速奉上一册,藉便请益。如发现错讹或不当之处,盼不吝指正,俾使再版时更正。四月间手札早已奉悉,只以行踪不定、心神难安,虽日夕时在念中,只未能握管,实是教读之余又须校对稿件,劳碌不已,他日当至华府当面请罪问安。哈佛圕已聘定吴君文津,忝承额外推荐,感愧交加,事虽未成,而盛意终身难忘,详情自当永远守秘,以免外界传闻不便也。鄙同窗法大为(David M. Farquhar)君原在 Maryland,旋转至 UCLA 执教,新疆丛刊定单已转寄法君矣。又此间同人 Eletcha 君专攻中亚问题,盼将订单赐寄一份,藉便宣扬也。本学年馨保在 Iowa 告假一年,现在哈佛搜集(反面)史料,

明春拟赴英伦一行,冀将鸦片战争下册写完,了此一桩心愿。冬至以前必前往请安。诸俟面陈。敬颂阖府安吉。

晚张馨保敬上

一九六四十月廿一

〔University of Chicago Library, Yuan T'ung-li Papers, Box 2〕

十月二十二日

郭廷以致函先生,商印《中俄伊犁交涉》译稿。〔《郭量宇先生日记残稿》,页527〕

十月二十八日

先生致信郭廷以,讨论《中俄伊犁交涉》译稿印行问题。

量予先生道席:

昨奉十、廿二日赐书,藉悉黎烈文先生译稿业已照收,并将由贵所设法印行,至为欣感。弟前以此批资料国人尚未及见,故请黎君译成中文。其译费似觉一班稍高,今贵所既决定印行,如能担任译费亦尚合理。惟念编者既非所内研究员,行政上或有困难,似此情形望将引言署名处予以删去,改为所中主编,于付译费时公私较便,可否再赐考虑。承代购书三种,书价新台币壹百玖拾贰元,兹如数奉上支票,即希察收。琐事渎神,厚意甚感。顺候著祺。

弟袁同礼顿首

十月廿八日

又,弟在台湾银行总行存款为7332号,黎教授收条遇必要时似可请其重写,梁实秋先生介绍者。

〔台北"中央研究院"近代史研究所档案馆,〈郭廷以〉,馆藏号069-01-02-089;《郭量宇先生日记残稿》,页529〕

按:该信于11月2日送达,郭廷以在信封正面标注"11,28复"。

十月

Chinese Culture 刊登先生文章,题为 A Guide to Doctoral Dissertations of Chinese Students in Continental Europe, 1907 – 1962。〔*Chinese Culture: a quarterly review*, Vol. 6, No. 1, pp. 79-98〕

按:该期为《中国留欧大陆各国博士论文目录》之第三部分,包括奥地利、荷兰、意大利、西班牙、统计表。

十一月四日

先生回到国会图书馆,恢复工作。〔《思忆录》,中文部分页7〕

　　按:此后袁清负责每日接送先生,并照应其午餐。

十一月五日

先生致信国会图书馆摄影服务部,为"国史馆"订购日本外务省档案七十卷。〔University of Chicago Library, Yuan T'ung-li Papers, Box 1〕

十一月上旬

陈和铣来访,先生恰在庭院晒太阳,后二人又在客厅交谈二十分钟。〔《思忆录》,中文部分页67〕

　　按:11月9日,陈和铣在芝加哥写信给李书华,告知先生近况,表示精神尚好。

十一月十二日

罗家伦覆函先生,寄上欲添制日本外务省档案胶片目录,请先生代为申请摄照。

　　守和吾兄道席:

　　　前奉九月十日手教,敬悉一是。吾兄贵体违和,想已痊愈矣。吉人天相,敬为颂祷! 兹有恳者:

　　　一、本馆拟添制日本旧档胶片一批,经自日本外务省旧档微片目录中选定一百七十五卷,开列清单奉上。烦请费神代向美国国会图书馆摄影部估价复制,装箱保险交船运台 C. I. T. Keelung。估价单请先寄下,以便办理进口手续。此项费用请在汇上之美金贰仟元内支付,为托。至于前函所述有关国务院已照之件,因一时不能决定其有否重复,可暂从缓议。

　　　二、今收到伦敦 Heffer 书店寄来 *Survey of International Affairs*. Vol. 21(The Far East 1942-46)及外文期刊有关中国论文索引 *Index Sinicus* 1920-1955 各一册,当交本馆抗战实录部份参考。如有需要之论文,再烦请贵馆复制副本。

　　　三、金纯孺先生函,承费神转交,已收到复函。谢谢。

　　　四、承代购史料书籍刊物等,已陆续收到。尊处付款单据,请随时寄下,以便报销。

　　　五、兹附奉吾兄十、十一月份史料征集费新台币壹千元送存台湾银行存款单存根一张,请察收。

专此奉托,敬颂道祺!

弟罗家伦敬启
十一,十二

〔University of Chicago Library, Yuan T'ung-li Papers, Box 1〕

按:此件为文书代笔,落款处为其签名。

十一月十七日

先生致信国会图书馆摄影服务部,为"国史馆"订购日本外务省档案一百七十五卷。〔University of Chicago Library, Yuan T'ung-li Papers, Box 1〕

十一月二十七日

袁澄陪先生赴国会图书馆办公。午饭时,先生告知袁澄,决定在明年一月中旬退休,届时可从馆中获得养老金及社会保险,每月支出可以无虞。〔《思忆录》,中文部分页 143〕

十一月二十八日

郭廷以覆函先生。〔《郭量宇先生日记残稿》,页 534〕

按:郭廷以拟请将《中俄伊犁交涉》一书作为先生自译本,较易处理。

十二月二日

先生覆信罗家伦,告已与国会图书馆联系复制日本档案并将估价单寄上,并表不愿继续负责购书重任。

志希馆长学兄尊鉴:

前奉十一月十二日手教,欣悉尊处拟添制日本旧档一批,共 175 卷。当即将所附清单交国会图书馆估价,顷接该馆寄来估价单一纸,共 $1837.50,外加保险费 $2.50,用特随函奉上,即希尊酌示复。该估价单仍请寄下是荷。贵馆存款现存 $1700.91,党史会存款现存 $148.24,以之相抵可以应付,即无须再行申请外汇矣。而弟之职务亦可于年底结束,谅荷首肯。专此,敬候道祺。

弟袁同礼敬上
十二月二日

Heffer 书店代购英国外交文件,一俟发票寄到再行寄上,可由尊处交邮汇寄。

〔University of Chicago Library, Yuan T'ung-li Papers, Box 1〕

按：此件为底稿。

十二月九日

先生致信郭廷以，同意近代史研究所寄来《中俄伊犁交涉》译稿印行办法，并谈代销《近代中国史事日志》进展。

> 量予所长道席：
>
> 　　昨奉十一月廿八日手教，承示所拟办法，弟完全同意，奉上收据二纸，即希查照办理是荷。代销《史事日志》共四部，除国会馆及 St. John's 大学之款已寄上外，其余德、意两处之款，据其来信已直接寄上。兹既未收到，日内当再分别催询，嘱其径寄。此复，敬候时祉，并贺新年。
>
> 弟袁同礼再拜
> 十二，九日

〔台北"中央研究院"近代史研究所档案馆，〈郭廷以〉，馆藏号 069-01-02-089〕

按：该信于 14 日送达，郭廷以在信封正面标注"12，14 复"。

十二月二十三日

罗文达致函先生，告其夫人恢复缓慢并祝圣诞及新年快乐。

23 Dec., 64

Dear Dr. Yuan:

　　After nine months since suffering her accident my wife is still very slow in mending. As a matter of fact, some of the after-effects will be lasting, in spite of a three-week stay in the hospital.

　　This coming year I hope to be more active with *Monumenta Serica* & otherwise. How are you bibliographical activities coming? I hope that you will continue your good work.

　　With all good wishes to you & Mrs. Yuan for a merry xmas & a happy & healthy new year, in which my wife joins me, I am,

As very, yours sincerely,
Rudolf Lowenthal

〔University of Chicago Library, Yuan T'ung-li Papers, Box 6〕

按：该函为其亲笔。

十二月二十四日

先生致信彭昭贤夫妇,告知近况。

　　君颐妹丈、世辉二妹如晤:

　　　　久未通讯,时在念中。近接箴妹来信,知希渊、子仁等身体康旺,儿女辈均已成婚,一切情形渐已好转矣。世真到纽约后曾通电话,拟在钱姨处过圣诞再来华京,届时均照一像片再行寄上。兄自七月割治pancreas 后住院数月,现虽恢复健康,仍拟多加休息,下月即退休在家静养。先此,顺颂新釐。

　　　　　　　　　　　兄同礼顿首、慧熙附笔问拜年
　　　　　　　　　　　　　　　　十二月廿四
　　　　　　　　　　　〔《思忆录》,中文部分页 109〕

一九六五年　七十一岁

一月三日

李书田覆函先生,感谢寄赠《中国留欧大陆各国博士论文目录》合订本,并建议先生编辑《中国人海外出版书籍目录》。

> 守和吾兄道右:
>
> 顷奉十二、廿五惠书,及完整《论文目录》一册,欣感无既。至承惠赠敝校圕目录一册,已即日转告圕主任,务于收到时函谢。吾兄近从事何项著述。各方咸盼吾兄能抽暇编辑一册《中国人海外出版书籍目录》(附各书 Table of Contents)。由此编辑,吾兄可无价收集所有上项书籍各一册,将来可用以赠与一圕也。专复,并请道安。
>
> 弟李书田上
>
> 一,三

〔University of Chicago Library, Yuan T'ung-li Papers, Box 2〕

> 按:"敝校"应指南达科他州矿业及技术学院(School of Mines and Technology, South Dakota)。

一月四日

朱文长覆函先生,感谢赠书并就所询其个人有关新疆之著述篇目作出答复。

> 守和老伯赐鉴:
>
> 十二月廿四日赐示及赐赠新疆研究文献目录日文本,于今日收到,拜读之余,钦羡无已!此一丛刊之发行,在学术界为一大事,而于今后研究新疆问题之学人造福尤多。此为不朽之业,敬谨为老伯贺!承嘱将拙著未经著录各篇奉告,自当遵办。下列各件,虽非完全研究新疆者,然均与新疆有关,想或亦在老伯搜罗对象之中。
>
> *A Regional Handbook on Northwest China*, Volumes I and II, subcontractor's monograph HRAF-59, Wash-5, Printed by Human Relations Area Files, Inc., Bot 2054 Yale Station, New Haven,

Connecticut, 1956.

其中有下列诸篇为世侄所执笔：

(1)"Education"

(2)"Public Information"

(3)"Constitutional System"

(4)"Structure of Government"

(5)"Public Order and Safety"

(6)"Propaganda"

此外有书评一篇，载于 *The Journal of Asian Studies*, Vol. XVII, No. 1, Nov. 1957, 题为《回民起义》。"Hui-min ch'i-i [The Moslem Rebellions]" in "Documentary Collections on Modern Chinese History"亦与新疆多少有关。

　　肃此复谢，即祝年喜！

世侄朱文长敬上

一九六五年一月四日

〔University of Chicago Library, Yuan T'ung-li Papers, Box 2〕

一月十四日

中午，先生的好友及同事五十余人在国会饭店(Congressional Hotel)招宴，祝贺先生荣休。席间，与会众人赠先生一支刻字银钢笔，纪念先生在国会图书馆的辛勤服务。〔Library of Congress, *Information Bulletin*, Vol. 24, No. 4, 1965, p. 43〕

一月十七日

国会图书馆华裔同人再次设宴欢送先生。〔《思忆录》，中文部分页 143〕

一月二十二日

罗家伦覆函先生，请为"国史馆"在美国会图书馆影印日本档案及购书等。

守和吾兄道鉴：

　　去年十一月十七日、十二月二日及本年一月七日手教及所附单据，均敬奉悉。吾兄以健康未复，已决定退休，至深驰念！务希加意珍摄，早日康复，为颂！关于本馆在国外征集工作，仍烦吾兄继续偏劳协助，无任感祷！兹将奉托各事，分复于后，敬祈费神代为洽办，感甚感甚！

一、复制国务院自照有关中日战争日本档案胶片七十卷,连航空邮费共计美金五百元,承吾兄已托贵馆代制,至为感荷。拟再恩吾兄与贵馆代办部份洽商,在制成寄出以前,须备一份估价单(写明本馆英文馆名 ACADEMIA HISTORICA)附七十卷目录一份(如能由吾兄代表本馆与贵馆签一份代制合约附目录尤佳),先行寄下,以便本馆向"行政院"外贸会及海关办理进口手续。

二、贵馆近又制成之"日本战史专论"一八五种,附下说明,经本馆征校处查复,以本馆前两年曾由台北"美国大使馆"转赠美国史政局印行此项专论五十七册,俟查明其中缺少何种,如有缺少,自应补请复制,在未查明前,则稍从缓办,容再奉渎。

三、本馆拟委托贵馆添置日本旧档一批,共一七五卷,计美金一.八四〇元,估价单一张附还,请吾兄即代表本馆与贵馆签定代制合约,附目录及估价单先行寄下,以便本馆向"行政院"外贸会及海关办理进口手续,拜托拜托!

四、吾兄代为选购之书籍,均已陆续寄到。美国出版之*Documents on British Foreign Policy* 第三集已承函告 Heffer 购全套,甚感! 惟该书书价,仍烦吾兄代付,为托。

五、有一笔书款及三笔续订杂志之收据未承寄下,想系遗漏,兹另纸抄奉,请费神检寄为盼。如原售书店未便重开,则请兄出具一项代购单据,亦所感荷。

六、收到伦敦 Arthur Probsthain 寄来书籍四册,及发票一张(副本),吾兄寄来之账单中尚未列入,请费神一查,如兄处未付该书款,即请代付为感。

七、又去年一月间承向芝加哥大学图书馆摄影部代制 T-4810 Kindetman 胶片一小卷,连寄费共美金三元三角五分,胶片及收据均收到,吾兄账内漏列,请补入。

八、附上去年十二月份征集费台币五百元台银送款单存根,请查收。又寄奉本年一至六月份空白收据六张,请加章寄下为盼。

专此奉恳,顺颂道祺!

弟罗家伦敬启

一,二十二,台北

嫂夫人前候安,并祝贤伉俪春祺!

家伦再拜。

〔袁同礼家人提供〕

按:该函于 1 月 26 日送达。[1] 先生看过后即口述一信致国会图书馆影印部负责人,由袁澄打印送寄。

一月三十日

田清波致函先生,代人询问北京图书馆是否藏有《万物真原》蒙文本。

Arlington, le 30 janvier 1965

Cher Monsieur le Docteur,

Un de mes amis belges m'a demandé de prendre des informations auprès de vous à l'effet de savoir si la Bibliothèque Nationale de Pékin possède la traduction mongole du livre *"Wan wu chen yuan"* (Origine des 10.000 choses) du jésuite Aleni (XVIIe siècle). Cette version mongole est un livre très rare. Notre maison d'étude de Louvain en possède un exemplaire. Mon ami voudrait composer un ouvrage sur cette traduction mongole et il est occupé à faire des recherches pour savoir dans quelles bibliothèques on peut trouver ce livre.

Vous me feriez plaisir si vous pouviez me dire si cette version mongole se trouve à la Bibliothèque Nationale. Cher Monsieur le Docteur, veuillez m'excuser de vous poser une telle question. D'ailleurs je ne me fais pas illusion : il y a bien des années que vous avez quitté Pékin! Mais qui sait!

Espérant que cette lettre vous trouvera en excellente santé, je vous prie, Cher Monsieur le Docteur, d'agréer l'assurance de ma profonde considération.

Antoine Mostaert

〔University of Chicago Library, Yuan T'ung-li Papers, Box 2〕

按:《万物真原》为意大利耶稣会士艾儒略(1582-1649)所著。此件为其亲笔。

---

① 《思忆录》,中文部分页 144。

二月三日

晨,先生再次进入华盛顿医学中心(Washington Hospital Center)治疗。〔《思忆录》,中文部分页 143;Library of Congress,*Information Bulletin*, Vol. 24, No. 6, 1965, p. 61〕

二月六日

凌晨三时,先生病逝。

二月十日

下午一时,先生葬礼在华盛顿石湾公墓(Rock Creek Cemetery)举行,一百五十余名中外人士到场,金问泗、恒慕义先后致悼词,"中华民国驻美使馆参赞"郑健民代表蒋廷黻出席。〔《自立晚报》(台北),1965 年 2 月 11 日,第 1 版;Library of Congress,*Information Bulletin*, Vol. 24, No. 6, 1965, p. 62〕

附录：袁同礼往还书信（年代不详）

蔡镇瀛

守和学兄阁下：

久违弘教，企仰弥殷。弟前缘本校将行改组，又值贵校招考新生，故不揣愚陋，颇想一试。然究以学识浅近、无所希冀，犹豫未敢决定。近者消息传来，益增疑虑。闻贵校自本年起高等科拟增学年一年，毕业后须经特别考试后方得出洋，或有关行筹备大学之说。阁下主持其间，谅必知之较详，请即函示，不胜盼祷。瀛于历史一门久已荒疏，而事实琐屑不易记忆，颇以为苦。近来又以学年考试在即，不暇兼习应考一节，或以是中辍，未知尊意以为何如，尚乞示我为感。专肃，敬颂公安，并候玉音。

学弟蔡镇瀛顿首

廿三日

〔袁同礼家人提供〕

按：蔡镇瀛，字海观，浙江德化人，1918 年北京大学理预科毕业，后留校任教三年，并未入清华学校。

常国宪

惠函祗悉。敝馆图书照章原难贷出，既属台命，自当变通办理。惟是项《顺天时报》装订篇幅过钜，往来搬运颇费人力。贵校既必需参考，即请由贵校图书馆具函来馆运取可也。此覆

守和先生

弟常国宪手肃

三月五日

〔京师图书馆分馆用笺。袁同礼家人提供〕

陈和铣

守和吾兄先生大鉴:

　　数日未通候为念,近维起居胜常为颂。梅城夏日颇佳,气候清凉,颇似庐山。弟寓在西郊一风景区,有山林湖水之胜,倘兄与嫂夫人有意出游,更不嫌简陋,热诚欢迎来敝舍小住,弟与内子极愿尽招待之谊,藉得畅聚。敝寓租约于八月底期满,届时须另觅屋迁居,故在七八月任何时期扫榻以待。再者日前顾毓秀、胡博渊二兄来谈,促弟与一大学发生关系,以便向国务院申请研究津贴。弟以英语欠佳只能看书,用英文写作尚有困难(如须写论文),因此一时未敢决定进行。近接华府友人来函,据告国会图亦接受研究,由 Miss Napier 负责主持申请事项,一经图审查合格,再由其转请国务院核准津贴云云。弟现实情状亟需补助,尤于国会图发生兴趣(该馆储藏弟所研究有关书籍甚丰)。即可研究工作,亦可读书,若中文部已告客满,弟可加入法文部研究工作。但该馆接受申请人作研究究有何规定,究应如何办理,作有效之进行,尚希吾兄详予指示,并协助为感。耑此,并颂俪祺。

弟陈和铣拜启
七月四日

　　倘申请人须以图专家为限,则弟似可滥充日内瓦中国国际图组织人员等等。又及。如何,请尊酌。

〔University of Chicago Library, Yuan T'ung-li Papers, Box 7〕

陈乃乾

乃乾先生道鉴:

　　顷奉还云,敬悉种切。武昌教席影响于全国图书馆事业者至巨,非公莫属。颉刚、兼士处弟当致函请其另觅他人,当希俯允,至为感荷。至武昌课程分配统祈尊酌,弟意中国目录学三小时或二小时,参考书利用法三小时。此外,或有国文三小时,大约授课钟点不能超过九小时。至科目内容,总以使学生了然于中国书籍之变迁及其利用方法为主,不妨俟抵武昌后再与胡主任接洽。该校开学在即,务祈惠允协助,尤为该校同人所企望者也。

专此奉复,顺侯著祺!

弟袁同礼再拜

九月六日

武昌华中大学校长:A. A. Gilman,美国人。

图书科主任:胡庆生,湖北人,美国纽约图书馆学校毕业。

教授:沈祖荣,仝上。

中国目录学教授系今年新设讲座,由美国退还赔款内,每年拨给该校五千元,改良旧有课程,以三年为期。每班学生约十四五人,现在只开一班。

〔北京图书馆用笺。2015 年嘉德四季第 42 期拍卖会〕

陈　文

大示祗悉,名约会事惠蒙担任发起,感甚,佩甚! 谨遵示将大名及通讯处誊入发起人簿,俟人数稍多,再行发表。贵校教员为全国人望所归,兹再寄呈启事十份,如有同志,望为绍介。即请

袁先生台鉴

弟陈文顿首

一月廿八日

再刻下担任发起者,已有黄先生炎培、沈先生思孚、严先生复、梁先生漱溟等十余人。斯会进行次序拟俟担任发起者有数十人,即行设一筹办处,并通告各省学界,一面拟定章程提议办法,征求同意。先生如有意见提出,望随时示及为荷。

弟又启

〔科学会用笺。袁同礼家人提供〕

陈贯吾

守和同学:

兹有友人急欲得贵校高等科招考章程一阅,如上半年所印者尚有存本,望即赐寄一份。再请代购麦顾庐博士《代议政治演说稿》原译本一册。

此上,即颂冬安。

弟陈毅谨上

十二月五日

〔国立北京大学公用笺。袁同礼家人提供〕

按:陈贯吾,该人履历参见 1931 年 6 月 6 日之记述。

陈　垣

援庵先生:

奉上拟与商务订立合同草案,请尊酌。应如何修正,亦希标注,俾有遵循。此系依据常熟瞿氏底本略予改正者。顺候时祉。

同礼顿首

八日

〔《陈垣来往书信集》,页 619〕

陈　愿

守和学兄鉴:

久违教益,渴念殊殷。昨奉惠书,欣慰无似。弟刻仍寓在西砖胡同 53 号。星期如暇,乞惠临一谈,无任欢迎。匆上,即请近安。

弟陈愿再拜

十月五日

〔教育部用笺。袁同礼家人提供〕

按:陈愿,字虞表,四川富顺人,与先生同年预科第一部毕业。

程其保

其一

同礼先生道席:

前奉手示,欣悦无似。弟旬前赴哈佛大学与当局商洽中国学生调查事，以未悉先生已转波士顿，有疏拜候，罪甚罪甚。关于编印《留美同学之西文著作目录》一事，顷已与梅校长一谈，渠意现时可由 Tsing-Hua Fellowship Fund 内暂拨五百元作为抄写费用，将来付印时再斟酌情形，稍予补助。如先生同意此项办法，即乞示知，以便办理拨款手续。专复，并颂道祺。

弟程其保顿首
十月一日

〔袁同礼家人提供〕

其二

守和先生道席：

顷奉十月四日手示，敬悉一一。前已经月涵校长核交华美协进新会计签发五百元支票一纸，不日想可寄到。据月涵先生之意，最好将植物、动物、生理、医药、地质、工程以及社会科学各部门与数理化、天文、气象同时完成，如可将全目录于明年二三月间脱稿尤妙。将来如需增加补助费，当可设法，但照规定总额以不出乙千元为限。如何之处，尚乞裁示为幸。专复，并颂道祺。

程其保顿首
十月十九日

〔袁同礼家人提供〕

程树仁

同礼先生大鉴：

英文读本及装订之《周刊》均收到，甚佳，至感。兹复有恳者，敝团通俗演讲部欲借用《实业浅说》一部，万祈先生检出，交高等科成衣匠带下，至恳至恳。再顷据差役云，先生需第八期《学报》一册，兹即奉上，乞查收。此上，即请暑安。

生程树仁上

〔清华学校用笺。袁同礼家人提供〕

按：程树仁（1896—？），字杏邨，福建闽侯人，1919 年清华学校毕业。

董作宾

彦堂吾兄：

　　兹有二函，请费神转交。又收据一纸，请填好寄下。弟今日赴沙坪坝，希望下星期一尚能晤教也。顺颂大安。

弟同礼顿首
十五

〔中华图书馆协会用笺。清风似友·台北古书拍卖会（2024）〕

范源廉

守和先生大鉴：

　　接奉华函，诵悉种切。生物学书 J. I. Hamaker——*The Principle of Biology* 已收到，转致前途矣。译本俟印出后，定当奉赠五部于清华图书馆，以答厚惠。多费清神，殊为感谢。专复，祗颂台绥。

〔欧阳哲生教授提供〕

方　豪

守和兄英鉴：

　　承惠招考章程一份，至感至感。嘱售入场券八枚，当为极力消售也。何君佩芬住址系骑河楼蒙福禄馆八号，与弟寓比邻。此次招考章程即何君嘱弟转索也。余不多及，即请学祺。

弟方豪谨覆
三月十八日

〔袁同礼家人提供〕

按：方豪，字俶新，浙江金华人，1917 年北京大学预科第一部毕业。何佩芬，字幼清，浙江义乌人，与先生同为 1916 年北大预科第一部毕业生。

郭金章

其一

守和学兄大人足下:

　　前日大驾枉顾敝寓,失迓为歉。弟因考期已近,昨晨回校温习功课,未克造访躬候起居,更觉惭愧也。敝校已定本月四号考起,八号考毕,即行放假。贵校何日放假?假期内台从仍来津否?专此,敬请大安。

砚弟郭金章敬启
四月二号

附呈敝校考试简章一纸。

〔北洋大学用笺。袁同礼家人提供〕

其二

守和学兄大鉴:

　　昨奉手示,藉悉起居佳胜,至为欣慰。弟碌碌如恒,乏善可告。所幸敝寓自家严慈以下均各平安,差堪告慰绮注耳。秉龢家兄已于前日返津,日内当拟入都一行,兹先嘱笔代致拳拳,弟亦拟年内入都一聆大教。弟家事琐冗,未识期愿届时果能获遂否耳?余无可陈。手此,敬请大安。不尽。

弟郭金章顿首

唐景周兄附笔致候。

郭须静

守和先生鉴:

　　兹代收到现洋二元、铜元四十枚,俟守常兄归,即转给无误。此复,并请刻安。

弟郭须静上
〔国立北京大学用笺。袁同礼家人提供〕

韩耀曾

守和吾甥：

　　由尊府传知文斾安抵京师，至慰。令堂昨来敝寓，明日回府，喉痛早经全愈，勿念。近日天冷，诸望珍爱。耀曾十六七到京，定准十八在三圣庵开香。晤面在即，余再谈。此候捷祉。

耀曾稽颡

旧历七日

〔袁同礼家人提供〕

何金良

其一

　　报签今已再请重光先生书就，谨奉上。余容面叙。
守和道长先生台鉴

何金良顿首

〔袁同礼家人提供〕

　　按："重光先生"应指姚重光（1876—1930），名芒，字一鄂，又字重光，号茫父、弗堂、莲华盦主等，贵州贵阳人。光绪三十年进士，官邮传部主事。曾留学日本，后嗜金石书画。居京时，与陈师曾往来密切，晚年以鬻书卖画为生。

其二

　　娄接清言，佩慰无似。昨访芒公，所委题签今已书就，送请查收。余容面罄，不一一。此奉
守和道长台鉴

弟何金良顿首

〔袁同礼家人提供〕

洪　业

守和先生大鉴:

　　顷奉惠书。承介绍赵君录绰,精通版本目录之学,询属专门人才,当为图书界所宜罗致,惟以素未谋面,深为歉然。拟请转嘱赵君开示详细履历及在东方文化委员会图书馆之待遇,俟敝馆出有机会,提交敝馆委员会商酌聘请。耑此奉复,祗颂台绥。

弟洪业顿首

〔台北"中央研究院"历史语言研究所傅斯年图书馆,"史语所档案",元391-4〕

　　按:此函应写于1938年或1939年。

胡　适

其一

适之先生:

　　以患腿疾,故多日未能趋教。聚餐会两次开会,辱承宠招,亦不克参与,尤以为歉。昨购得顾实君《汉志讲疏》一书,所论诸子各节,颇多有可商榷之处,用特奉上一册,不知先生有何批评,亟愿闻之。倘能择要示知或在杂志上发表,均所企望者也。一俟病体大愈,即来趋谈。此上,顺候著祺。

袁制同礼上

一月二十日

《汉志讲疏》另邮寄上。

〔北京大学图书馆藏《胡适藏书目录》〕

　　按:《汉志讲疏》即《汉书艺文志讲疏》,撰者顾实,1924年8月商务印书馆初版,后多次再版。

其二

适之先生：

　　关于移运古物事，记载甚少，已派人到古物陈列所一查，容再奉闻。此上，敬颂著祺。

同礼顿首

廿七

〔国立北平图书馆片。台北胡适纪念馆，HS-JDSHSC-1636-011〕

按：后附古物陈列所概述一纸。

其三

守和馆长吾兄：

　　承蒙贵馆以杨殿珣先生所编石刻题跋索引一册惠赠敝处，非常感激。此书集历代石刻目录之大成，又为贵馆仅存之一册，今慨然惠赠，尤感高谊。敬谢敬谢。专此，顺颂时绥。

胡适敬启

八月廿四日

〔国立北京大学校长办公室用笺。国家图书馆档案，档案编号1945-※057-综合5-002002〕

按：此件为文书代笔，落款处为胡适亲笔。撰写时间应在1946年至1948年间，待考。

蒋复璁

其一

守和先生大鉴：

　　连奉上月三日及本月一日大函，均敬悉。承赐证明书拜收，敬谢。沈显昌先生函及附件业已转去，光、宣间留德学生因时间较早，弟亦不悉，已将名单转询留德前辈吴光杰先生，俟得复后即行奉上。今夏美国国立农业图书馆馆长莫赫德先生来访，据告国会图书馆馆长孟斐德先生访日，弟闻知后即去函邀请，旋得复函谓行程已定，未便改变。后闻"姚次长"言接尊函，应去函邀请，当即函请"驻日公使"张伯谨先生代表"教部"邀其来台，仍以行程已定婉辞，并谓明年二月远东及太平洋国家国立图书馆馆长在马尼拉会议时或能抽暇来我国访问，已签呈"黄部长"发函邀请矣。论文数种出版年月业已遵嘱查考，俟查明后即与留德学生名单一并寄还。知关锦注，谨先奉复，敬请大安。

弟蒋复璁顿首
十一月十六日

〔University of Chicago Library, Yuan T'ung-li Papers, Box 2〕

其二

守和先生大鉴：

客岁十一月中芜函，谅早登记室。关于邀请美国国会图书馆馆长孟斐德先生事，初由弟去函，于其赴日前邀请，复以无暇；继则于其赴日时由"驻日大使馆"代邀，据答欲于本年二月间赴马尼拉会议时顺道来我国访问，经签请"教育部""黄部长"去函洽邀；顷由部交下，复函谓伊已不拟出席马尼拉会议而不能来此间。曾三次邀请，虽均未蒙接受，然吾等已竭尽诚意矣。前转询留德前辈吴光杰先生，光、宣间留德博士名单，经函复已不能记忆。《茶话》等期刊出版年月亦未查得，台湾各学术机构皆无藏本，盖出版已久皆未能携出也。知关锦注，谨此奉闻，敬颂大安。

弟蒋复璁顿首
元月十三日

〔University of Chicago Library, Yuan T'ung-li Papers, Box 2〕

蒋 彝

其一

守和先生有道：

久疏候问,维兴居清吉,是颂是念。上月在牛津曾晤令嫒两次,满拟可将二十年前留英学生名单找出,但细寻无着,想系弟旧伦敦住处在 1940 年十月被炸毁,同时遭殃也。

先生不久有英伦之行,确乎? 令嫒何时由纽约飞英过 Manhattan 时,乞赐知,俾能得机招待耳。匆此,敬颂俪安。

令嫒、令郎统此问好。

弟蒋彝顿首

九月廿三日

〔University of Chicago Library, Yuan T'ung-li Papers, Box 5〕

其二

守和先生有道:

前奉手教,以阖府将不久来游纽约,故迟迟奉复,敬乞谅之。尊表中弟所知者为赖宝康女士及王葆仁兄二位,其余不明。赖女士仍在伦大东方学院教书,可函询其他。王兄与弟同在东大习化学,故在英时相过从耳。耑复,敬颂俪安。

弟蒋彝顿首

十月廿二日

〔University of Chicago Library, Yuan T'ung-li Papers, Box 5〕

李大钊

守和先生有道:

前蒙赐访,以外出失迓为歉。兹有恳者,敝处欲令工人制一置放杂志之插斗与简片目录箱二具,因恐工人不谙做法,特令往贵校参观,藉作模楷,乞即就该什器指示一切。琐事相烦,尚望谅宥。专此,即颂公绥。

弟李大钊顿首

〔国立北京大学笺。袁同礼家人提供〕

李光宇

其一

　　示悉。前函已由张仲苏先生交弟,当拟奉覆。翌朝弟忽感寒发疹,不克任事,容俟稍瘳,即当将讲演录(一□收价)奉上,或转嘱局人代递。书价希即照付。此复,顺颂
守和学兄时祉

弟李光宇拜上

廿七夜

〔学术讲演会笺。袁同礼家人提供〕

　　按:李光宇,字闸初,北京宛平人,1917 北京大学文科毕业,后入本校文科哲学门研究所。

其二

守和吾兄左右:

　　送上 610 号听讲证一纸,讲演分配表二纸。即希察存,余当面叙。即候日祺。

李光宇谨白

廿八日

〔学术讲演会笺。袁同礼家人提供〕

其三

守和吾兄足下:

　　前月屡奉手札及贵馆缄索讲演录,适宇染重病,不克奉复,仅倩人代书数语,殊不畅怀。幸近日渐复原状,已到局照旧办公,嗣后如有缄商事宜,仍希时时惠我。无任忻盼,即候时祉。

弟李光宇白

廿三日

〔学术讲演会笺。袁同礼家人提供〕

李九华

同礼、敦礼、薰之贤棣大鉴：

三年旧雨，一旦分袂，临风怀想，能不依依。今岁仲春，曾以余暇赴都，到校存问，乃适值星期，未获一面，尤觉歉然。临行之日，各道雅怀，并无一人拟入师范，以故此间招考保定师范预科于暑假后招考新班，未曾以一束相邀。今闻棣等已脱离畿辅，另入他校，而常、夏二君顷已辍课，骤闻之下，欢慰与愁闷之心一时并集，不知感触之何从也。呜时旧游廖落，北燕南飞，燕南先生应高阳小校之聘，又闻赵县即赵州顷又敦请南下尚未起程。后望茫茫，聚谈匪易，尚望课余之暇，时与切磋，书札往来，破兄岑寂。私心祷祝，未尽所言。专此肃复，即希亮察不宣。诸同学均此致意。

同学小兄李九华上

同礼、敦礼二棣之台甫素所未悉，乞谅之。

〔袁同礼家人提供〕

李书华

其一

润章先生尊鉴：

奉到手教，承示种种，至为感谢。《历史研究》第四期仅购到此册业已由伦敦寄到，兹交邮寄上，或可供参考也。印度1944出版之书，业已代为注明，想哥大可以借到。留法同学之中文姓名承费神填注，兹在《中法教育界》中又查到若干，惜该刊馆中所藏者并不完全，附上致刘先生一函，亦盼转寄，谢谢。弟下次来纽自当趋教。匆匆，顺颂著祺。

弟同礼顿首
三月七日

顷奉惠赠大著单行本，拜领，谢谢。

〔Columbia University Libraries Archival Collections, Shuhua Li Papers, 1926-1972, Volume II: Modern Eminent Chinese Leaders〕

其二

守和吾兄:

留法同学名单事,前转询张德禄先生(留法多年,现在 UN 做事),彼又向他人查询,仍无结果。彼已将原单寄回,现留弟处,俟有机再转询他人。此问,近好。

弟李书华敬启

四月十八日

〔University of Chicago Library, Yuan T'ung-li Papers, Box 5〕

其三

守和吾兄惠鉴:

承寄下《两种海道针经》一册,业已收到。附寄九、一四手示,亦敬悉。吾兄惠赠此书,不胜铭感。书中所记各地往回针路及其他与航海有关的记载,均极 interesting,当留作参考。特此鸣谢,顺请大安。

弟李书华敬启

九、二五

〔University of Chicago Library, Yuan T'ung-li Papers, Box 2〕

梁启超

启超今春于役西南途中,曾著《国民浅训》一书,业交商务印书馆付梓,似于现在国情及人民常识不无壤流之助。黔豫各省已购颁各州县藉资晓谕。兹检寄一册,敬乞指教。再鄙人汇录平日著述为《饮冰室丛著》,附奉目录一纸,统希察收为幸。

制梁启超手启

〔袁同礼家人提供〕

按:《国民浅训》1916 年 5 月 20 日发行。

柳无忌

守和先生道鉴：

接奉手示,敬悉种切。

二译者姓名,均不熟悉。似并非文坛人物,亦不似在大学任教者。耶大图书馆中文卡片,亦为代查,但无所获。

大著印刷又有着落,将来出版时,对于学术界贡献当无尽无量。关于津贴事,曾与昌度兄谈及,据云此间经费减少,年来仅有"鞋带预算",已不如前年之盛况可比矣。闻清华有补助学者出版书籍办法,未悉曾向梅校长询问否？

所嘱诸事,均无法办妥,至以为歉。即请著安。

弟无忌谨上

四月十五日

〔袁同礼家人提供〕

娄学熙

阔别日久,想念维殷。顷奉到惠片,有如亲握。纪念录尚有余存,谨即邮呈,至云缴费,请幸勿事此客气也。此请

守和学兄鉴

同学弟娄学熙启

〔袁同礼家人提供〕

罗隆基

守和先生：

五月间得来示,忙中忘覆,歉甚。《新月现代丛书》文稿,仍请先生担任。战事关系,全书已延期,先生之稿,当可缓交,惟请示一交稿日期为荷。暑热珍重为盼。此上,顺颂道安。

弟罗隆基敬上

八月十七

〔天津益世报馆用笺。国家图书馆档案，档案编号 1945-※057-
综合 5-014002〕

毛以亨

其一

守和兄鉴：

　　屡来不遇，至以为歉。《学艺》杂志已买到否？本星期六拟来贵校，不
审有下榻处否？诸希示我，以定行止。此请公安。

弟毛以亨顿首

〔北京大学法科公用笺。袁同礼家人提供〕

其二

　　胡适之讲义已经买完，刘申叔者无大用处，拟为兄购西洋哲学（新添功
课，何人教授未定）、政治哲学（新添功课，拟章行严授）及添印之中国哲学史（胡适之
授）、学术史（叶清吾授）、中国通史（黄节授）各一份，俟齐备后一并奉上，何如。

　　严家之事恐作罢论，只得请兄随时注意，总之愈速愈妙，缓或不济急
也。商务馆翻译事，如孟君已来，即肯代为筹划为盼。此上
守和兄

弟亨顿首

〔北京大学法科公用笺。袁同礼家人提供〕

其三

守和我哥无恙：

　　前托之事，未悉有佳音否？尚望鼎力成全，俾济寒穷。倘不见谐，亦希
从速作覆，以便另谋。兹奉上近代散社拙稿二通附览，骈文为新学，不敢藏
拙，且以见年来之旨趣也。英法文虽时事涉猎，而不见有何等进境，其为惭

怍,如何可言。天寒,恕不尽其缕缕。此请公安。

弟以亨顿首

〔北京大学法科公用笺。袁同礼家人提供〕

其四

电话屡次不通,有劳悬想,行甚阙然也。此后天逐入冬,弟拟不再事西郊游。遐想往执,弥增怅结。惟尊府既在城中,阁下当时常进城,能于便中过我一谈,是所期也。现下颇窘于赀,如能贷我些许以二十元为度,作济于燃眉,敢以一月为归还之期。阁下月修颇微,恐无剩余以相贷,弟之启齿或有近于不情,然我辈固不必以区区者自拘也,总之以不致相累为度。求学时代窘迫固属常事,而阁下家在京师,万不可舍彼而就此也。董时君来函要敝校哲学及论理学讲义,此二门功课俱是口授,无讲义,渠来函颇谦抑。弟是学法政者,岂晓哲学,祈为我婉辞谢之。笔下甚懒,恐不复渠也。

弟亨顿首

〔袁同礼家人提供〕

其五

守和我哥惠鉴:

昨突奉专足手书,并附十金,厚意殷情良深,拜纳。特以是重烦阁下,私心窃以为不安耳。感激之私,如何可言,良觌有期,再申谢情何如。此请公安。

弟以亨顿首

〔袁同礼家人提供〕

梅贻琦

月涵表姊丈尊鉴:

昨上一书,计达座右。顷在“大使馆”取到台湾入境保证书空白表随函奉上,仍祈在具保人栏内签署盖章,即行赐下为感。弟已开始工作,拟将第一部分设法先行出版，俾将来申请补助时较为容易。惟内容系是一种重要工具书，又不能为生活关系仓促付印。欧洲学者对此书极为重视，奉上法国汉学家 D 来函，阅毕仍盼赐还。一俟稍暇，拟写一工作报告寄交中基会，俾执委会开会讨论时有所根据。会中前此每月补助三百元，本年减为二百元，可见会中之拮据。每月付交房租九十元及电气、煤气等外，实感不敷。如有机缘，可否从旁赞助，恢复以前补助之数。不胜感盼。

二月十九日

〔袁同礼家人提供〕

　　按：此件为底稿。

孟宪承

　　《汤姆就学记》现经教授，亟欲得原本一参考，未识可请阁下设法收回学生所借，一二日再行交还原人否？烦核办。谢谢，此上
守和先生

宪承

〔袁同礼家人提供〕

钱存训

　　顷在哥大东亚图书馆见到《中国历代书画家篆刻家字号索引》，商承祚编，甚有用，想尊处亦购到矣。又哥大近举行之 Exhibition of Chinese archaic jades, ritual bronzes, weapons and related Eurasian bronze art, 内容很不坏，印有展览图录，仅印 1500 份，尊处可函索一份，径函 Program of Advanced Studies at the Graduate Faculties, Columbia University, New York 27, N. Y., 恐不久即告罄矣。

〔钱孝文藏札〕

　　按：此件残缺，上下款识无从得见，但据笔迹及内容可知，为先生致钱存训信。

邱 椿

其一

守和先生钧鉴:

敬禀者,生前得友人吴士棻来函,据称病已就痊。本拟脂车北上,奈图书管理一席虚悬甚久,或已另聘,恐鹪鹩无楼栖,不敢颟唐来校。伏惟先生总摄斯馆,必悉此中真情,如蒙赐覆,感激无既。肃此,敬请钧安。

生邱椿敬禀
即日
〔清华学生用笺。袁同礼家人提供〕

按:吴士棻,字伯祁,江西南城人,1918年毕业于清华学校,因循"父母在不远游"之说,放弃留美名额,执教鄱阳中学,任英文教师。

其二

守和先生钧鉴:

来谕敬悉。本星期原拟不外出,奈今午接舍间电话,嘱椿即刻往京。乞转达周君为祷。肃此,敬请钧安。

生邱椿叩
十五
〔袁同礼家人提供〕

沈仁培

守和表舅大人尊前:

敬肃者,数次进谒,正值公忙,晤对未能,弥深惘怅。表舅何日有暇,望请赐知,俾得早聆训诲,则幸甚矣。专此,敬颂教祉百益。

侄沈仁培谨肃
十月六日
〔袁同礼家人提供〕

沈 沅

守和吾兄惠鉴：

兹有友人拟偕贵校学员出洋，未知行期约在八月何时，在月半前，抑在月半后，敬祈一探，即日内快邮示知为祷。来示请寄上海爱文义路景星里二百三十八号。专此奉恳，即颂教安。

学弟沈沅顿首

〔北京大学（The Chinese Government University）片。袁同礼家人提供〕

按：沈沅，字诵之，江苏武进人，1915 年北京大学预科第二部（理科）英文班毕业。爱文义路（Avenue Road）即今北京西路。

施友忠

守和吾兄：

廿日示悉。励兄近况尚好，有二女作伴，当不至太感寂寞。公权先生移居湾区，前此未有所闻，想是最近消息。兄弟晚年能时常聚首，亦动乱时期稀有之幸事也。所询 Chen、Loh 二君，只认得陈君，Loh 君中文名字虽似曾相识，但已记不起来。华大华社名单，当嘱负责人寄奉不误。专此敬复，并颂俪安。

弟友忠拜复
四月廿四日

〔University of Chicago Library, Yuan T'ung-li Papers〕

按：1953 年 12 月 24 日，张公权抵达美国洛杉矶，任教于 Loyola Marymount University。"华大华社"应指施友忠所在华盛顿大学的华人社团组织。

石超庸

同礼先生赐鉴：

顷奉月之廿二日大函,敬悉一是。弟在耶鲁大学时所用之名字为 Kung Shih(石颖),一九二五年所获 J. S. D.学位之论文题目为 Seizure on the High Seas in Time of Peace。大函所列在纽约大学研究法律诸同学之英文名单均为抗战时期赴美者,以前之记录惟大陆有之,此地无从查考。弟当询诸后期同学,如有认识者,容后奉告。兹谨将在台复校后法律系之教授名单随函附上(列后),即乞查收为盼。此覆,并颂筹祺。

弟石超庸拜启

元月卅一日

〔University of Chicago Library, Yuan T'ung-li Papers, Box 7〕

按:石超庸(1899—1968),广西藤县人,时应在台湾东吴大学(Soochow University)任教。该信后附"法律系教授"简表,列史尚宽、徐步垣等十余位法律人士,包括姓名、本职、学位三项信息。

宋春舫

其一

书一本奉赵,祈检收。弟处尚存一本,改日奉还。张原载兄已会谈数次。同礼老哥

春舫顿首

廿九

袁先生升

〔袁同礼家人提供〕

其二

昨日所见之札记小说可否假我一观,今晚即当奉赵。

春舫

袁先生升

〔袁同礼家人提供〕

其三

装书旧木箱不知能设法向尊处揩油否? 书二本奉赵守和老哥。

春舫顿首

袁先生升

〔袁同礼家人提供〕

谭云山

同礼先生道席:

久违教益,时深驰慕。顷奉上月十七尊笺,拜诵一是,毋任幸快。惟云前书,并未收到,不到何时所寄? 亦不知有何要事否?

先生编纂《中国学者西文著作目录》,征及刍荛,甚感甚感。弟年来用英文写作发表者,虽颇不少,然大都非得心应手之作。兹附寄敝同事所作 Short Career Sketch 一纸,内列著刊表,即乞赐察。其他发在各报章杂志短篇零简尚少,不足算也。另邮寄上近出小册六种及《中印学报》二本,并乞照收与指教。敝处除本人外,尚有中国学者六位,三专学、三兼教。其他我国旅印学者,有无西文著作,俟查明后,再行奉告。匆复不一,即颂撰祺。并祝新年康乐。

弟谭云山拜启
一月六日

〔University of Chicago Library, Yuan T'ung-li Papers, Box 2〕

谭卓垣

守和吾兄著席:

前奉大札,早经妥收,只以归来后诸事待理,未遑即覆,慊甚慊甚。弟编之论文索引尚在整理中,页数多寡尚未得知。寄来期刊目录已再为注录,所收者亦仅寥寥而已。承询中文姓名两项,经已查出,兹一并付返,望为查收是荷。此颂俪安。

弟卓垣顿首

五月十六日

〔袁同礼家人提供〕

唐　彝

示悉。贱恙略痊,承念至感不忍。杂志照收_{困卧闷甚},_{得此良佳},阅毕奉赵。此致

守和仁兄大鉴

彝倚枕上

十九

〔袁同礼家人提供〕

按:唐彝,字孟伦,广东香山人,时任清华学校庶务主任。

陶孟和

其一

守和先生左右:

今晨来清华,适值先生归家,为怅。今奉还书籍,散处尚存四册,容日奉还。此问近安。

恭顿首

Osborn: *Men in Stone Age*

Mosso: *Dawn of Mediterranean Civilization*

Hinsdale: *How to Study & Teach History*

Langlois & Seignobos: *Introduction to the Study of History*

〔袁同礼家人提供〕

按:其中前三本书的书名稍有小误,应为 *Men of the Old Stone Age* (1915), *The Dawn of Mediterranean Civilization* (1910), *How to Study and Teach History* (1905)。

其二

守和先生左右:

前日到清华未遇,为怅。Ralzel 书此间已购备矣。贵馆书目之 card 系在何处购买? 又,前谈美国之书肆有可以减价之处均系何家? 请一并示知,不胜感谢! 屡次渎烦,不情之至。匆匆,此问近安。

恭顿首
廿四
〔袁同礼家人提供〕

其三

守和先生:

昨日谈甚快。兹奉还书籍四种,请查收。

Lafcadio Hearn: *Appreciations of English Poetry*

Pearson: *Shantiniketan*

Frank Granger: *Historical Sociology*

《儒林外史》一函。

此问暑安。

履恭顿首
〔袁同礼家人提供〕

按:Lafcadio Hearn 为希腊裔日本小说家小泉八云,该书书名应为 *Appreciations of Poetry (1916)*。前两种书注明为"张仲述君奉还者"。张彭春,时任南开学校专门部主任兼代理校长。

其四

示悉。兹奉还《庄子》及法文书一册。英文数页奉赠,祈哂纳。

守和先生

恭
十二

汪季千

守和先生惠鉴：

　　晚刻移此间，名义为客座教授，此间在小大学中名望似尚佳，较之师范学院颇有升于乔木之感。惜系暂局，明年蝉联之望不大也。校中极望向 Foundation 捐款办 East-Western studies，查各校得此种津贴者为数不少，由校长出头，或未始无望。惟此间人对此事不内行，嘱晚拟其进行方案。公见识广，可指示否？何种计划能动财主之聪？计划包括何物？如何进行？何 foundation 希望较大？何人对捐款方法专门？捐款成功，蝉联当亦解决。溽暑珍重，此颂撰安。

晚汪季千上

八，十二

〔University of Chicago Library, Yuan T'ung-li Papers, Box 7〕

按：此信写作时间似在 1958 年左右，时汪季千在 Dickinson College 任教。

王　健

　　敬启者，接到尊札，聆悉壹是。至所购小皮箱，敝均已现成，惟暂时便人难觅。祈阁下稍为多候几时，俟有妥便即行送交尊处也。诸承惠顾，深感隆情。特此，敬覆

袁先生时祺

愚弟王健鞠躬

〔袁同礼家人提供〕

按：王健时应为天津华北制革厂经理，1918 年 3 月 12 日赴清华学校演讲。①

---

① 《清华周刊》130 期，1918 年 2 月 28 日，"校闻"页 5。

吴东燕

袁先生:

由纽约华美协进会孟先生处请教到您的地址,请原谅我的冒失。

现有家藏宋朝原版书一部欲出售,希能烦您鉴订此书之真实性。此部书共八本,名《旧刊万首唐诗》。一九四七或八年时曾送北平博物院图书馆,被鉴为原版无疑,并谓此书已绝版,待您见到当会确定。

您若任何周末方便,随时通知我可赶上华府拜见,面谈一切,您若有关系可和国会图书馆接洽,则更为感激。若时间预先难定的话,可随时打电话来(自然 collect change),我可即时赶上,一切当另谢。地址电话如下:

Lucy Wu

79-12 31st Ave

Jackson Heights

N. Y.

Tel. TW9-8083

敬祝安好。

晚吴东燕上

三月廿四日

〔University of Chicago Library, Yuan T'ung-li Papers, Box 2〕

吴敬恒

袁先生执事:

奉赐书,奖饰过情,愧汗无地。弟何人斯,学术芜落,敢来大会发言。惟企慕贵校规模,积思有年,未遂瞻仰。近顷数有事入京,倘下月更去,届时必先笺问,冀得尽情参观,并畅聆大教。率复,祗颂道绥,不尽。

弟吴敬恒顿首

廿三日

〔袁同礼家人提供〕

吴 震

其一

尊处之地理讲义便时乞检赐一阅。多日不晤,如何佳善。

守和先生

弟震顿首

〔北京清华学校(Department of Physical Education)笺。袁同礼家人提供〕

按: 吴震,字雨田,江苏武进人,1916 年 1 月赴清华学校任教,担任地理、历史教员。[①]

其二

奉还畏庐小说四册,乞检收其第一、二辑,并希惠我一阅。

守和先生

弟震顿首

图书室袁先生

〔袁同礼家人提供〕

其三

钉书款迟未奉缴,歉愧之至。兹特遣役奉上,即乞检收明帐为荷。

此上

守和吾兄大鉴

小弟吴震顿首

〔袁同礼家人提供〕

---

① 《清华学校一览》,1917 年,页 8。

其四

昨请购之《绘地图法》已未购得，如已购就请即掷下。再《中东战记本末》、壬寅癸卯两年之《新民丛报》并乞检假一阅。当即奉缴也。
守和先生大鉴

弟吴震顿首

袁先生

〔清华学校招考处笺。袁同礼家人提供〕

其五

残余小说十册、地图一帙奉还，即希检入。《留东外史》如已阅竟，并希掷交来役带回。放假四日，我公作何消遣？此上
守和先生

弟震顿首
〔清华学校招考处笺。袁同礼家人提供〕

其六

昨来此二通，不在公值班期内，未晤。有正件已寄到否？来时尚乞一假观也。
守和先生

震手启
十三夜
〔袁同礼家人提供〕

其七

刘季陶之对巳代转交，并嘱舍弟俟伊写得后，即电告尊处派人走取。兹检出前向图书馆所取之乱小说数十册，又游记体地理一本，送还尊处。

此尚系旧图馆内所借,大约未曾上帐之件也。又弟经募刘季陶捐爱群校收据一张,乞便转交。

守和老哥

弟震顿首
一日
〔袁同礼家人提供〕

其八

　　便面一帧,乞兄转求姚重光一挥。费神至感。此上

守和吾兄

弟震顿首

袁先生

〔袁同礼家人提供〕

其九

守和吾兄惠鉴:

　　匝月不晤,想念为劳。维起居多福,是所颂念。弟匆匆南下,沿途均有勾留,中间滞于沪渎者旬日,嗣即由浙而赣而皖鄂,昨复来沪略事休息。此行适在疫期行旅,戒心颇以为苦,大有得不偿失之叹也。另图之事尚未着实,而暑假将满,虽清华授课无中途不能辞谢之拘束,然个人对于学生方面实有难安之处。是以拟就校中另觅一随时可卸责之位置,以为地步。然群彦济济,未必尚有余地。兼以弟性疏狂,尤恐难于契合。筹思至再,图书馆编造汉文书目,自陶君去后迄无专人。清华预备改建大学,事事自求完善。弟虽不才,窃愿效劳。虽不敢自信一无舛错,或者尚无大谬。且与吾兄共处一室素承不弃,当无闲言,于弟个人尤为相合。现拟与校中商略此意,特先肃恳左右。倘荷赞成,拟恳吾哥先与张或赵一探其意,如何情形,见示一二,以便酌夺。幸获有成,敢忘大惠? 来示寄上海南林里十弄六十五号,转交可也。此请台安。

小弟吴震顿首

〔袁同礼家人提供〕

夏沛丰

来示已悉,但贵馆所收藏者,想系一时名著、中外瓌宝,灵耀炯然。今若以拙著厕其中,何异缀鱼目于明月珠间,足下不虑其有损夜光耶? 既承命,不敢自阻,比已托子仁兄转递二册,想已收到。谨覆,即颂
守和学长近安

> 七月八日
> 弟夏沛丰顿首

子仁兄统此问候。

〔袁同礼家人提供〕

按:夏沛丰,时应为北京高等师范学校英语科学生①,"拙著"似非专著,而是其所译各英文篇目,常刊于《英文杂志》《北京高等师范学校校友会杂志》《东方杂志》。

项镇藩

守和学长兄大鉴:

久疏问候,抱歉良深。维起居佳吉为颂。启者,兹有友人孙某拟索阅贵校详章,伏乞迅赐寄下一份,不胜感感。一切容面详。此颂教安。

> 弟项镇藩顿首
> 一月八日

惠件寄顺治门内翠花街十八号。

〔袁同礼家人提供〕

按:项镇藩,字介人,上海人,1916 年北京大学预科第一部英文甲班毕业,后入本校法本科学习。"顺治门"即今宣武门。

萧蘧、余青松、董时

谨启者,奉上麦伦先生书一通,至祈察阅。生等以历史科须绘北美地

---

① 《北京高等师范学校校友会杂志》第 2 辑,1916 年 12 月,"译林"页 2。

图,需用《新万国百科全书》至急,可否特与通融一假摹拟。专此,敬请
公安。

学生萧蘧、余青松、董时顿首

〔袁同礼家人提供〕

按:萧蘧(1897—1948),字叔玉,江西泰和人,1918年清华学校毕业后
赴美留学,获密苏里大学学士和康乃尔大学硕士学位,归国后曾任清
华大学经济系主任、南开大学法学院院长等职。余青松(1897—
1978),福建同安人,1918年清华学校毕业后赴美国留学,获匹兹堡大
学天文学硕士学位和加利福尼亚大学博士学位,1927年回国任厦门
大学教授,1929年任中央研究院天文研究所所长。

谢家宝、徐炫

送还《二十年目睹之怪现状》四本,请察收。炫须借看前四册,请发
给。渎神感感。此请
守和先生台安

弟谢制家宝、徐制炫仝顿首
七月廿三日下午五时

袁先生升

〔袁同礼家人提供〕

徐悲鸿

守和先生贤兄惠鉴:

南洋星加坡学者韩槐准先生托购尊处《百粤风土记》一部,明谢肇淛
撰;《滇略》一部,仝前;《殿粤要纂》一部,明詹景凤等撰;《西南纪事》一部,
明郭应聘撰;《国立北平图书馆善本书目》四册,共需价几何? 并祈由尊处
径寄星洲,连寄费恳见告,弟当奉上。韩君又托询《文殿阁书目》有《说文
解字诂林附补遗》白纸八十二册,现时价格几何? 倘足下能代询书估,拜感
无极。敬请道安。

弟悲鸿顿首

四月廿四日

〔中国美术学院笺。国家图书馆档案,1945-※057-综合 5-018001 和 1945-※057-综合 5-018002〕

徐彦之

其一

守和先生:

　　彦之正在搜集蔡先生演说辞,预备印单行本。贵校有无他的演说辞,或其他的文章? 如果有,务请你设法找一份来,或即雇人抄一份此处每千字一毛五,费由彦之担任亦佳。费心,谢谢。专此,敬颂近祺。

弟徐彦之上
十月廿八日

望覆。

〔袁同礼家人提供〕

按:徐彦之(1897—1940),字资隽,山东郓城人,1920 年北京大学哲学系毕业。1917 年 3 月 29 日,蔡元培在清华学校高等科发表演说,题目为"人道主义及爱国心";1918 年 5 月 17 日,蔡元培再赴清华学校发表演说,题目为"中国教育之现状"。①

其二

守和吾兄:

　　稿子一篇收到了,费心,谢谢。出版之后,定在送你一本,或者还要托你代售几分。这是后话,暂且不提。书记抄的稿子不及二千字,送他二毛五何如? 小意思,对不起他,请为致意。这费由弟一人出担,颇有为难,所以不能怎样的多。此候日祺。

弟彦之手覆

---

① 《清华周刊》第四次临时增刊,1918 年 6 月 14 日,"记载"页 25、27。

三十日

〔袁同礼家人提供〕

薛光前

守和先生赐鉴：

　　顷奉六日惠书，承示已托摄照《哈佛学报》所载公孙龙论文，至感厚谊，敬附还尊垫印费＄4.19 支票一纸，尚乞察收，多谢多谢。至其他一文，已遵嘱径洽哥大矣。□□专谢，顺颂崇绥。

弟薛光前顿首

四月十日

〔University of Chicago Library, Yuan T'ung-li Papers, Box 2〕

　　按：公孙龙论文应指 The Kung-sun Lung Tzu With a Translation Into English，梅贻琦撰，刊 *Harvard Journal of Asiatic Studies*，vol. 16, no. 3/4, 1953, pp. 404-437，此信应写于 1955 年后。

严　　□

　　前者台驾光临，乃蒙指政，感佩感佩。兹遵雅命寄上敝馆各处捐赠各报名，照录一纸，敬请收阅。蒙赐报单，心感不已，先此道谢。此复，顺候
守和先生秋祺

严伯拜启

〔袁同礼家人提供〕

杨光弼

　　顷自孟公处带来书三本，谨呈上，希查入。此请
守和表哥刻安

杨光弼拜上

〔袁同礼家人提供〕

叶恭绰

……

有愿赞助者并请罗致,至祷。专此奉恳,顺颂道祺。

后学袁同礼顿首

十二月廿四日

〔2013上海朵云轩春季艺术品拍卖会〕

张葆诚

昨午趋访未值,为怅。承赐清华一览,收到感谢。容再走谈。此复

希和先生阁下

葆诚顿叩

藉呈袁先生

〔袁同礼家人提供〕

按:张葆诚,字存斋,江苏泰县人,1918年入北京大学法预科德文班学习,1923年本校法律(学)系本科毕业。

张鸿图

连日风雨,颇念故人,顷奉手教,备承壹是。弟来汉皋栖身,路局虽经年余,究竟无一心得。薄薪微贱,不过敷衍了事,远道做客,名既未立而学亦久辍,茫然前路几于臧谷两亡。回想昔日校中聚首,多承吾哥教言,今虽南北分隔,幸邮筒之速递、交通之便利,亦不甚愁也。吾哥学问聪明,皆高出弟之头地,终非鱼鲤,只待业成,出而为芙蓉之去栖,弟所盼望者也。下月中旬前后,弟必回京一望,故旧是时聚首晤谈,想吾哥定有以教我。学余之暇,时锡大札,是为默念,望风寄意。敬颂

守和学哥文祺

弟鸿图覆言

卅乙号

〔汉粤川铁路汉宜段工程局信笺。袁同礼家人提供〕

守和学兄伟鉴：

　　前接奉正月念四日函片一纸,敬悉种是。迟至今时作笺复者,因病多日、手懒持笔故也,幸勿见责是荷。辰维起居兴胜、学业进益为颂。弟来汉,瞬逶年余,无善可状。忆及与兄聚首畿辅校中之时,时刻得聆雅教,每届考试吾兄必举列榜鼎,弟则栏尾之卒耳。及今日思昔,能得与兄多聚会数年,真快乐欢畅事也。天不如人愿,弟南、兄北,弟事事、兄业学,各司其事,分隔数千里,惟鸿足系书、雁尾传情耳。幸车辑易通,将来吾兄业成五车之富,不难期会。然今日中日交恶之际,幸有以教我,以释疑团而慰远羁客友之怀。匆匆及此,即请学安。

　　　　　　　　　　　　　　　　　学弟张鸿图拜首

令弟敦礼同此道致。

令弟现肄业何校,请示知为荷。

　　　　　　　　〔汉粤川铁路汉宜段工程局信笺。袁同礼家人提供〕

张蒨英

守和先生赐鉴：

　　久违雅教,谨维起居佳胜,时深驰念。前嘱绘一横幅,久未应命,殊为歉咎。兹奉牡丹一幅以求教,幸勿以拙劣见弃也。专此,恭请俪福。

　　　　　　　　　　　　　　蒨英拜、成武嘱笔请安

　　　　　　　　　　　　　　　　十一月廿四日

　　　　〔University of Chicago Library, Yuan T'ung-li Papers, Box 2〕

张申府

　　承示并《青年会章程》,敬悉一是。弟入会事,前日适已緐此间同学曹绣君介绍,然尊意甚感也。此复,兼候

守和学长兄道绥

　　　　　　　　　　　　　　　　弟崧年敬复

　　　　　　　　　　　　　　　　廿六

　　　　　　　　　　　　　　　〔袁同礼家人提供〕

张泽熙

守和兄大鉴:

　　久未趋谈,殊深驰念。本拟考完来尊处一游,嗣以行色匆匆,兼之天气奇寒,致不果行,年后归来即当前来畅谈也。弟寓日界松岛街长安里,教言希寄该地是荷。匆此,即颂近祉,并贺年禧。

如弟泽熙谨上

〔袁同礼家人提供〕

赵国材

其一

　　径启者,本月五、六、七日为本校覆试各省咨送中等科新生之期,拟请台端担任覆试时监考、阅卷等事,覆试地点在中等科教务室,每日上午十时起举行,并请先期会商接洽,以企便利。深感贤劳。专此,敬颂道安。

赵国材谨启

九月四日

〔清华学校用笺。袁同礼家人提供〕

其二

　　昨叶礼文先生嘱买各书,内有《当代八家文钞》一种,不知买到否?此书经庶务处在京沪各处买得三部,作为学生奖品。如叶先生所需之书尚未买到,当嘱庶务处将该书留一部,以便选文之用,如何?

材

廿八日

〔北京清华学校笺。袁同礼家人提供〕

按:1916 年胡君复辑《当代八家文钞》初版,收王闿运、严复、张謇、梁启超、康有为、林纾、章太炎、马通伯八家文凡 559 篇。

赵万里

守公先生座右：

前奉惠书，顿慰饥渴，近维兴居清畅为颂。云此数月终日整理旧稿，自晨至夜午无时或息，一切公私外事绝对屏绝，倒觉得身心俱闲也。关于《永乐大典》部分已成之目录卡片，均已校对完毕，计辑出宋元已佚之地志、别集七十种，《四库》已辑诸书攗逸凡八百余篇此外名目不备举。日后拟将全稿移沪出版，并拟于沪上之《大典》中如法校钞，俾无遗憾。又此间未写卡片之《大典》仅剩三十册，需时两月亦可校录竣事。助云校录者仅萱生一人萱生严守时间，作事勤敏，难得之至。最初有写生三名相助每月工资十二元，近则只有一人，工资半数由云垫付，此后恐卡片及格子纸之微亦须自己设法矣。又徐君所藏之《大典》曾托张乾老就近传抄，现大体已抄毕，惟无人覆校。云拟自往校之。又抄费需六七十元，亦无着落，请便中明示办法，以便遵行。总之，吾公在时诸事好办，现则反是矣。云所学薄有所成，皆公之赐，此后仍请公加以提携，俾竟所学。至祷至祷。匆上，敬请道安。

仲云再拜

十九日

〔国家图书馆档案，档案编号 1946-※039-采藏 11-005012 至 1946-※039-采藏 11-005014〕

赵正平

守和先生惠鉴：

日前备承指示，良感厚意。惟归途遗一小箱无重要物件，致尊处所惠英文杂志名单及其他印件一并失去，殊为可惜。请先生便中再检示一份为盼贵校之长尊号请一并示知。专此，顺颂公安。

弟赵正平顿首

同事诸公祈代候之。

十九

〔暨南学校用笺。袁同礼家人提供〕

按:赵正平(1878—1945),字厚生,江苏宝山人,日本早稻田大学毕业,中国科学社社员。

周　岐

其一

守和先生执事:

　　辱书敬悉。以弟去津,未克即复,歉甚歉甚。贵校周刊既向由华洋书庄承印,弟与该局吴经理交谊颇厚,未便见攘夺之嫌。俟后遇有他项印刷,再请关照可也。附下袁氏入校简章壹份照收,费神,心感无既。专此,复颂时祺。

弟周岐再拜
十二月二日
〔北京中华书局启事笺。袁同礼家人提供〕

其二

守和先生执事:

　　顷有友人托售《廿世纪英文大字典》壹部,全拾册。贵校图书馆如欲购买,请即拨冗赐复,价必从廉也。专此,即颂时绥。

弟周岐顿首
拾月九日
〔北京中华书局启事笺。袁同礼家人提供〕

钢和泰

其一

Dear Professor Yuan,

　　Many thanks for your note. This morning I have sent the manuscript of my various readings to the printers, and they have acknowledged the receipt of the 48 pages. As soon as the letter will be printed, I hope to send the manuscript of my introduction to the Ching hua yin shu chü.

> Believe me yours sincerely,
>
> A Staël Holstein

〔《美国哈佛大学哈佛燕京图书馆藏钢和泰未刊往来书信集》下册,页 540〕

按:Ching hua yin shu chü 应指京华印书处(馆)。

其二

My Dear Professor Yuan,

After several unsuccessful attempts at getting in touch with a reliable picture restorer I have at last succeeded. A friend of mine who is a great collector told me a few days ago that he has had about two hundred ancient pictures restored by a certain specialist whom he promised to send to my house. The man has not appeared yet but as soon as he appears, I will send him on to you with my card.

> Believe me yours sincerely

Monsieur Alphonse Monestier hommage de l'auteur

〔《美国哈佛大学哈佛燕京图书馆藏钢和泰未刊往来书信集》下册,页 542〕

斯文·赫定

其一

8th May

Dear Dr. Hedin:

My brother told me that you wish to have a biography of Richthofen, and I enclose herewith an abstract from the *Encyclopedia Sinica*. If it is too brief, we shall be glad to make further research.

Yours sincerely,

T. L. Yuan

〔韩琦教授提供〕

按:Richthofen 即费迪南·冯·李希霍芬(Ferdinand von Richthofen, 1833—1905),德国探险家、地质学家、科学家,1868 年到 1872 年间,他七次赴中国考察,"丝绸之路"一词出现在其著作 *Ergebnisse eigner Reisen und darauf gegründeter Studien* 的首卷中。此件为先生亲笔。

其二

Dear Dr. Hedin:

Thank you so much for your kind invitation to dinner Friday evening. I shall be delighted to come.

Yours sincerely,

T. L. Yuan

Sept. 6th

〔国立北平图书馆英文信纸。韩琦教授提供〕

按:此件为先生亲笔。

其三

My dear Dr. Hedin:

Thank you ever so much for your kind invitation to dinner next Thursday. I greatly regret that I shall not be able to accept it, as I have already promised the German Minister to come to dinner that very evening. My sister-in-law Mrs. Tania Yuan accepts with great pleasure.

Yours sincerely,

T. L. Yuan

May, the twenty-sixth.

〔国立北平图书馆英文信纸。韩琦教授提供〕

按:此件为先生亲笔。

其四

Monday

My dear Dr. Hedin:

Many thanks for your kind invitation for this evening. My sister-in-law was out of town yesterday, and I was not able to get in touch with her through telephone.

Owing to family difficulties, she has to give up the trip entirely, as her two children don't like to see their mother off so suddenly. Therefore, we shall not come to your dinner tonight, but will call on you in a few days.

Yours sincerely,

T. L. Yuan

〔国立北平图书馆英文信纸。韩琦教授提供〕

按:此件为先生亲笔。

其五

Sat.

Dear Dr. Hedin:

My brother told me that you would like to consult national almanacs and I give below the holdings of some libraries:

1. National almanac & astronomical ephemeris, geological survey has copy for 1933.
2. Astronomical ephemeris, Tsing Hua University has copy for 1928.
3. American almanac & National almanac, National Library has 1908–09, 1913–12, 1927–30

If you care to have any of them, will you let me know, so that I shall send it to you on Monday.

Yours sincerely,

T. L. Yuan

〔国立北平图书馆英文信纸。韩琦教授提供〕

按:此件为先生亲笔。

人名索引

说　明

1.人名索引分为中文、外文两大部分,其中外文部分又包括欧美、俄、日三部分,供读者检索袁同礼先生生平时间轴上出现的相关人物。

2.年谱长编按语中非本日(旬、月、季、年)直接涉及的人士,如阐述家族、师从、因果关联者不入索引。例如一九三六年二月二十七日载平馆委员会召开会议,先生提议聘梁思庄为编纂,按语中介绍梁思庄为梁启超次女,梁启超即非本日直接涉及的人士,故未入该日索引。

3.附录部分收录的未系年信札,相关人物未收入索引,请读者参考目录检寻。

中文人名

A

艾伟(字险舟)　1944.07.16
安怀音　1933.03.27,1933.11.19

B

巴宙(字望蜀)　1956.04.08
白崇禧(字健生)　1936.06.12
白涤洲(白镇瀛)　1931.06.30
白经天(白鹏飞)　1931.09.21
白潜叔　1939.03.25
白寿彝　1939 冬,1941.10.29,1941.11 中下,1941.11.28,1957.03.28

白万玉　1932.05 上
白雄远(字锦韬)　1928.06.10
鲍必荣　1961.09.22
鲍鉴清　1933.05.04,1935.05
鲍少游　1956.01.25
鲍扬廷　1945.10.24
保君建(字既星)　1919.10.11,1925.11.06,1943.01.22,1962.03.21
贝时璋　1946.04
毕树棠(毕庶滋)　1937.02.09,1951.06.25,1951.08.23
卞白眉(卞寿荪)　1932.04.15,1940.09.28
卞学鐄　1950.08.30,1955.02.20,1963.05.31

03,1947.08.08

陈甲孙　1945.08.15

陈建功　1962.01.29

陈剑翛(陈宝锷)　1928.12,1929.01.28,
1933.10.11,1947.06.09

陈杰　1962.01.29

陈荩民(陈宏勋)　1946.12.11,1947.02.07,
1947.02.09

陈敬民　1963.12.02

陈景唐(陈声浩)　1925.05.27

陈君葆(字厚基)　1938.01.05,1938.03.23,
1939.05.01,1941.01.08,1942.02.10,1942.
02,1942.03.04,1942.03.31,1945.08.24,
1949.09.02,1952.02.28,1956.02.15

陈康(陈忠寰)　1947.11.23

陈克文　1945.12.01,1947.11.18

陈可忠　1936.01.18,1943.01 初,1961.04.
12,1962.10.06

陈澧(字兰甫)　1928.03.24

陈力　1962.09.26,1962.10.13

陈立夫(陈祖燕)　1938.05.14,1939.02.08,
1939.03.01,1939.03.30,1939.04.25,1939.
10.04,1939.12,1940.02.14,1940.03.07,
1940.08.13,1940.09.13,1941.01.23,1941.
02 底,1941.04.16,1941.05.20,1941.06.
03,1941.07.10,1941.07.15,1941.08.07,
1941.08.11,1941.10.18,1942.08.11,1942.
08.12,1942.09.04,1942.09.25,1942.10.
20,1942.10.27,1942.11.11,1942.11.19,
1942.11.30,1943.01.19,1943.03.06,1943.
11.05,1943.12.11,1944.01.27,1944.03.
15,1944.04.12,1944.05.04,1944.07.18,
1946.07.07,1955.03.02

陈礼江(字逸民)　1939.03.01,1939.03.31,

1939.04.25,1940.07.06,1940.07.18

陈篆(字任先)　1930.06.26,1931.10.08,
1932.04.10

陈鸾书(字韵轩)　1930.04

陈梦家　1940.06,1940.09.07,1940.10.06,
1940.10.10,1941.02.11,1941.02.18,1943.
03.03,1943.06.01,1944.12.28,1945.01.
16,1945.02.03,1945.02.25,1945.03.10,
1945.04.24,1945.04.26,1945.05.10,1945.
05.15,1945.05 底,1945.06.05,1945.06.
17,1945.06.21,1945.07.08,1945.10.06,
1946.04.10,1946.05.22,1946.09.04,1946.
11 下,1947.02.03,1947.02,1947.05.02,
1947.05.17,1948.06.06,1948.07.26,1948.
08.06

陈绵(字伯旱)　1931.06.01

陈名珂(字季鸣)　1963.03.20

陈名豫(字雪南)　1930.04,1932.06 中

陈明之　1963.10.02

陈乃乾　1933.07.03,1933.09.28,1933.09.
30,1933.12.01

陈念中　1936.06.14,1938.09.13

陈槃　1944.07.06,1955.03.11,1955.03.15

陈泮藻(字梓屏)　1939.03.01

陈启天(字修平)　1959.01.08

陈乔　1954.03.13

陈清华(字澄中)　1940.04.04

陈铨(字涛西)　1940.01.04

陈群(字人鹤)　1946.10.21,1948.11.23,
1948.11.29

陈任中(字仲骞)　1932.02.04,1936 夏,
1939.06.30

陈荣捷　1950.07.24,1955.04.06,1955.05.
07,1956.03.02,1956.08.09

04，1926.12.17，1927.06 中，1927.10.06，
1928.09.23，1928.11.04，1928.11，1929.01.
13，1929.02.19，1929.02，1929.04.22，
1929.05.11，1929.08.30，1929.09，1929.10.
07，1929.11，1930.02.16，1930.03.30，
1930.04.08，1930 夏，1930.10.22，1931.
01.26，1931.05.18，1931.06.06，1931.06.
24，1931.08.11，1931.10.09，1931.12.14，
1932.02.04，1932.02.16，1932 夏，1932.
06.09，1932.07.02，1932.09.21，1932.12.
04，1932.12.24，1932.12.30，1933.01.12，
1933.04.27，1933.05.26，1933.05.29，1933.
08.15，1933.08.23，1933.09.11，1933.12.
06，1934.02.06，1934.02.20，1935.02.08，
1935.04.04，1935.05.01，1935.05.18，1935.
06.04，1935.10.02，1935.11.23，1936.01.
18，1936.02.27，1936.05.25，1936.07.10，
1937.01.06，1937.02.16，1937.03.29，1937.
04.01，1937.04.17，1937.05.22，1937.06.
11，1937.09.06，1940.05.14，1945.11 中，
1946.10.21，1947.01.11，1947.03.22，1947.
03.29，1947.04.19，1948.10.24，1949.06.
21，1950.03.23，1950.04.20，1956.06.07，
1963.09.04

陈源（陈西滢）　1925.05.27，1926.09.22，
1932.06.30，1932.07.02，1945.07.23，1945.
07.25，1945.07.26，1945.07.27，1945.07.
28，1945.07.29，1945.07.30，1945.07.31，
1945.08.02，1945.08.03，1945.08.07，1945.
08.13，1945.08.14，1945.08.15，1945.08.
17，1945.09.06，1945.09.08，1945.09.10，
1945.09.11，1945.09.13，1946.06.16，1947.
04.01，1947.04.09，1947.05.02，1947.08.
22，1949.05.14，1949.09.19，1954.06.15，

1954.08.26，1955.04.14，1956.08.09，1957.
03.14，1957.03.26，1958.02.24，1961.09.
22，1962.02.20，1962.04.27

陈占祥　1945.08.15

陈桢（字席山）　1947.09.15

陈震华　1935.02.08

陈治策（字济安）　1913.09，1930.06.12，
1931

陈志潜　1943.01.04

陈志让　1954.07.11

陈志书　1939.04.09

陈志文　1961.11.25

陈之迈　1946.05.02，1962.03.08

陈中平　1937.07.21

陈重寅　1929.01.29，1929.01.31，1929.02.
01

陈宗登（字尺楼）　1929.03.31，1930.01.05，
1933.08.04，1933.08.22

陈宗经　1962.11.09

陈宗器（字步清）　1930.07.27

陈祚龙　1956.03.28，1956.04.08，1956.04.
18，1957.05.13，1959.12.09，1959.12.27，
1960.08.05，1961.11.27，1961.12.11，1962.
03.05，1963.03.08，1963.03.27，1963.05.
05，1963.10.30

程抱一（程纪贤）　1963.09.20

程经远（字负仓）　1919.09.02

程克（字仲渔）　1935.01.11

程懋筼　1955.05.19

程其保（字稚秋）　1947.09.15，1954.08.07，
1954.09.28，1960.05.25，1961.11.22，1962.
04.27，1962.05 中上，1962.05.16，1962.
09.25，1963.09.20

程时煃（字伯庐）　1936 夏

1935.01.06，1936.01.05，1938.01.05，1938.01.11，1938.01.17，1938.01.30，1938.02.03，1938.02.18，1938.02.22，1939.03.29，1939.04.07，1939.06 上，1939.06.29，1939.09.17，1945.10.06，1956.11.20，1957.02.08，1958.03.21，1958.03.29，1961.07.28，1962.05.04

邓以蛰（字叔存）　1929.05.12，1930.02.16，1945.11 中，1947.02，1947.03.22，1947.04.19

邓中夏（字仲澥）　1920.07.01

狄福鼎（字君武）　1953.04.25

刁乐谦　1949.01.15

刁敏谦（字德仁）　1962.01.15

刁汝钧（字士衡）　1937.05.22

丁春膏（字雨生）　1935.01.11，1935.07.25

丁贵堂　1941.04.16，1941.05.05

丁山（字丁山）　1931.05.12，1943.03.03

丁声树（号梧梓）　1945.02.03

丁骕　1961.12.07，1963.02.11，1963.03.11

丁文江（字在君）　1925.05.27，1925.07.06，1929.02.17，1929.02.19，1929.02，1929.03.07，1929.05.11，1929.09，1931.09.21，1931.10.09，1932.02.26，1932.04.10，1932.12.30，1933.03.27，1933.05.04，1935.05.18，1943.06.28，1956.03.11，1956.03.16，1956.07.18，1956 夏，1958.03.15

丁西林（字巽甫）　1935.11.23，1936.04.15，1940.11.04，1951.11.21，1957.07.24

丁绪宝　1929.08.21，1936.02.20

丁瓒（字汇川）　1935.01.06，1946.11.21，1949.06.15，1949.07.19，1949.11.24，1950.04.27，1951.06.18，1951.06.25，1951.07.10，1951.07.28，1951.07.31，1951.08.08，

1951.08.15

丁肇青（字雄东）　1930.06.26，1931.07.12

董大成　1951.08.10

董光忠　1932.08.20

董康（字授经）　1925.05.27，1931.01.19，1933.07.01，1933.07.03，1933.08.03，1933.08.15，1933.09.30，1933.10.09，1933.11.09，1933.11 上，1933.11 中，1933.11.29，1933.11.30，1933.12.07，1936.01.30，1936.02.14，1937.03.16，1937.05.26

董霖（字为公）　1931.06.25，1931.07.02，1932.05.24，1945.07.27

董明道（字垂照）　1933.04.13

董同龢　1955.03.13，1956.06.11，1963.03.05

董洗凡　1935.05

董显光　1939.12.18，1944.09.11，1944.09.20，1944.09.23，1957.12.12，1962.10.18，1963.06.11

董寅复　1936.10.30

董作宾（字彦堂）　1931.05.12，1936.06.14，1937.03.05，1939.06.18，1940.09.24，1941.08.21，1941.08.25，1943.03.03，1943.05.27，1943.06.01，1944.07.24，1944.07.29，1944.08.05，1945.10.25，1947.06 上，1948.07.26，1948.07.30，1949.03.26，1951.03.12，1952.07.17，1952.08.13，1952.08.25，1953.03.05，1953.05.07，1954.03.10，1954.03.13，1954.08.24，1955.03.01，1955.08.29，1956.05.19，1956.08.05，1956.08.18，1956.10.02，1956.11.09，1957.01.12，1957.02.08，1960.06.20，1961.01.26，1963.11.30

杜殿英（字再山）　1946.04

杜定友　1925.04 中下，1925.04.19，1925.

04.21, 1925.04.23, 1925.04.25, 1925.05.
27, 1926.07.12, 1928.12, 1929.01.28,
1929.01.29, 1929.01.31, 1929.02.01, 1929.
03.08, 1929.04.15, 1929.08.29, 1931.04,
1933.08.30, 1933, 1935.02.16, 1944.11.29

杜建时（字际平） 1946.02.18, 1947.03.03,
1947.03.20, 1947.05 上

杜联喆（房兆楹夫人）1939.09.30, 1952.12.
03, 1955.03.05, 1955.05.07, 1957.03.17,
1961.11.21, 1961.12.07, 1963.06.29, 1963.
07.01, 1963.07.12, 1963.09.05, 1963.11.30

杜重远（杜乾学） 1962.12.06

杜作梁 1925.11.06

段祺瑞（字芝泉） 1925.07.04

段其燧（字孝农） 1964.01.13, 1964.05.05

段锡朋（字书贻） 1934.10.09, 1934.12.06,
1935.04 初, 1935.11 下, 1937 春, 1937.
09.06, 1937.12.27,

F

樊际昌（字逵羽） 1926.12.06, 1933.08.28,
1933.11.15, 1936.07.08, 1937.07.13, 1937.
07.14, 1937.07.16, 1937.07.21, 1937.07.
23, 1937.07.25, 1937.07.27, 1961.03.04,
1964.08.16

樊仲云 1938.05.08

范殿栋 1926.12.17

范廉清 1937.04.03

范腾端（字九峰） 1939.06.21, 1939.06.30,
1941.07, 1943.11.22, 1944.01.01, 1946.04.
01, 1948.05.13

范文澜（字芸台） 1914 年冬

范一侯（字士奎） 1960.02.01, 1963.10.15,
1963.10.28

范源廉（字静生） 1918.11.25, 1925.04.12,
1925.04.19, 1925.05.27, 1925.07.06, 1925.
09.29, 1926.02.28, 1926.07.05, 1926.07.
13, 1926.10.13, 1927.06.29, 1927.09.01,
1928.02.12

范志熙（字月槎） 1928.04.30

范祖淹 1946.01.14, 1946.01.18

房兆颖（房兆楹） 1930.12.21, 1934.05.23,
1939.08.30, 1939.09.30, 1951.02.27, 1952.
12.03, 1955.03.05, 1955.05.07, 1957.03.
17, 1960.07.19, 1961.11.21, 1961.12.07,
1963.01.10, 1963.02.07, 1963.05.16, 1963.
06.29, 1963.07.01, 1963.07.12, 1963.08.
09, 1963.08.25, 1963.09.05, 1963.11.30

方国瑜（字瑞丞） 1940.04.27, 1940.06.12

方豪（字杰人） 1950.03.03, 1950.04.20,
1951.07.03, 1951.08 中, 1951.08.21, 1951.
12.04, 1951.12.05, 1952.04.22, 1952.04.
25, 1952.04.28, 1952.06.16, 1952.07.23,
1952.08.12, 1954.03.03, 1954.03.04, 1954.
03.10, 1954.03.13, 1954.04.13, 1962.12.
05, 1963.11.19, 1963.12.05

方觉慧（字子樵） 1935.01.11

方梦龙 1935.02.08

方石珊（方擎） 1933.03.27, 1937.07.16,
1937.07.21

方树梅（字瞿仙） 1935.02.01, 1935.04.04,
1935.04.05, 1940.01.03, 1940.01.08, 1940.
03.09, 1940.03

方甦生（字更生） 1935 底

方闻 1961.05.31, 1961.09.24, 1961.10.26,
1963.02.10

方治（字希孔） 1933.10.03

费成武 1950.01.10, 1955.02.07, 1955.02.

26,1931.12.14,1932.02.16,1932.02.26,
1932.06.09,1932.06 中,1932.06.30,
1932.07.02,1932.09.21,1932.11.22,1932.
12.04,1932.12.24,1932.12.30,1933.01.
10,1933.01.12,1933.03.27,1933.04.27,
1933.05.26,1933.08.15,1933.09.30,1933.
10.09,1933.11.15,1933.12.06,1934.02.
13,1934.02.20,1934.02.21,1934.12.07,
1935.02.08,1935.04.04,1935.05.18,1935.
10.02,1935.11.23,1935.12.02,1936.02.
27,1936.04.15,1936.07.28,1936.09.11,
1936.10 中下,1936.10.29,1936.11.06,
1936.11.19,1936.11.20,1936.12.24,1936.
12.29,1936.12.31,1937.01.01,1937.01.
05,1937.01.09,1937.03.05,1937.03.06,
1937.03.16,1937.03.29,1937.03.30,1937.
04.02,1937.04.06,1937.04.27,1937.06.
19,1937.09.06,1937.09.14,1937.10.04,
1937.11.18,1937.12.27,1938.01.15,1938.
01.24,1938.01.30,1938.02.02,1938.02.
08,1938.02.13,1938.02.14,1938.02.18,
1938.03.10,1938.03.11,1938.12.01,1938.
12.30,1939.06 上,1939.06.29,1939.10.
26,1940.01.04,1940.01.12,1940.01.13,
1940.03.11,1940.03.20,1940.04.08,1940.
04.11,1940.04.16,1940.05.10,1940.05.
14,1940.05.18,1940.05.27,1940.06.06,
1940 夏,1940.07.10,1940.07.12,1940.
07.29,1940.08.02,1940.09.02,1940.09.
07,1940.10.20,1940.11.04,1940.11.22,
1941.01.23,1941.02.10,1941.02.17,1942.
12.15,1943.05.17,1943.06.01,1943.07.
08,1944.06.13,1944.06 底,1944.07.06,
1944.07.07,1944.07.12,1944.07.29,1944.

08.05,1944.09.13,1944.09.15,1944.09.
20,1944.09.22,1945.06.15,1945.12.06,
1946.01.02,1946.01.26,1946.07.07,1946.
08 下,1946.10.18,1946.10.21,1946.11-
12,1947.05.25,1947.05,1947.06.05,
1947.09.25,1947.11.05,1948.07.26,1948.
08.01,1948.12.21,1949.01.07,1950.08.
22,1950.12.23,1951.03.10,1951.03.27,
1951.04.02,1952.07.17,1953.04.25,1953.
07.15,1954.09.20,1955.06.06,1960.12.
15,1962.10.22

傅铜(字佩青) 1936.12.24,1945.12.07

傅岳棻(字治乡) 1932.02.04

傅增湘(字沅叔) 1925.05.27,1926.09-
10,1928.01.01,1928.03.07,1928.05-06,
1928.06.14,1928.06.21,1929.03.08,1929.
03.12,1929.11,1930.02 中下,1930.06 中
下,1930.06.22,1931.05.18,1931.05.23,
1931.06.24,1931.06.26,1932.01 初,1932.
02.04,1932.03 初,1932.03 下,1932.12.
24,1932.12.30,1933.03.01,1933.06.09,
1933.08.15,1933.08.23,1933.10.09,1933.
12.07,1934.01 中,1934.02.06,1936.06.
30,1937.02.16,1937.03.02,1937.05.10,
1937.06.14,1937.06.19,1937.06.30,1940.
06.19,1945.12.28,1946.10.21,1947.05.
14,1947.05.17,1947.05,1947.06.05,
1947.06.09,1947.08.19,1947.10.01,1949.
11.28,1960.09.17

傅振伦(字维本) 1933.03,1936.07.22,
1936.08.28,1936.11 下,1938.08.28,1939.
04.07,1939.07.08,1943.10.01,1943.10.
31,1944.05.05,1945.04.01,1945.07 中,
1945.10.11,1945.10.17,1946.01.26,1946.

01.29

傅正舜 1948 夏

傅忠谟(字晋生) 1947.10.01,1949.11.28

傅种孙(字仲嘉) 1950.03.10

傅作义(字宜生) 1937.04.13,1948.05.01,
1948.10.13,1948.11.18

G

甘乃光(字自明) 1934.10.09

高步瀛(字阆仙) 1925.09.21

高冲天 1938.01.05

高棣华 1937.02 中,1937.06.13,1937.06.
17,1937.06.21,1937.06.24,1937.06.30,
1937.07.02,1937.07.21,1937.07.22,1937.
07.25,1937.08.02,1937.08.03,1937.08.
08,1937.10 初,1937.11.16,1937.11.19,
1937.11.27,1937.12.05,1937.12 中下,
1938.01.05,1938.01.24,1938.01.28,1938.
01.30,1938.08.15,1938.08.16,1938.10
中,1938.11.03,1939.09.17,1939.09.28,
1940.01.25,1940.09.02

高剑父(高仑) 1936.12.24

高克毅 1956.03.16

高凌汉(字凌汉) 1939.11.03

高鲁(字曙青) 1933.01.25

高梦旦(高凤谦) 1933.08.14

高名凯 1938.12.20,1954.12.25

高去寻(字晓梅) 1936.09 下,1955.08.
29,1962.01.08

高仁山 1918.09.03,1925.04.12,1925.05.
25,1925.05.27,1925.11.06,1926.12.06,
1964.01.20

高文伯 1948.12.23

高友工 1963.01.18

高月舟(周大文夫人) 1932.04.10

高肇源 1963.01.02,1963.09.11

高宗武 1949.12.09,1957.12.12

葛秉曙 1943.06.22

葛光庭(字精岑) 1936.07.20

葛敬恩(字湛侯) 1930.04

葛受元 1934.05.23

葛仲勋 1939.04.07

耿承 1948.11.10

耿忠之 1955.03.02,1958.03.21

贡沛诚 1935.11.26

龚家骅(字云白) 1942.12.14

龚理华 1947.10.14

龚自知(字仲钧) 1939.02.27,1939.03.25,
1940.05.28

顾宝延 1935.01.06

顾斗南 1946.01.27,1946.10.18,1946.11.
21,1947.01.06,1947.05.25,1947.09.12,
1948.11.03,1948.11.26,1948.11.30,1948.
12.08,1949.01.14,1949.01.15,1949.03.
18,1950.11.26,1951.03.15

顾敦鍒(字雍如) 1955.03.03

顾华(字树斋) 1940.10.07,1954.11.18

顾家杰(字忍吾) 1951.02.27

顾颉刚(顾诵坤) 1914 年春,1925.03.11,
1925.07.11,1925.07.14,1925.08.14,1925.
09.06,1925.09.07,1925.09.09,1925.09.
12,1925.12.26,1926.02.06,1926.02.10,
1926.02.13,1926.06 中,1926.06.13,1926.
06.23,1926.08.03,1926.08.04,1926.11.
21,1929.05.06,1929.05.10,1929.05.11,
1929.05.12,1929.10.06,1929.10.11,1930.
06,1931.09.04,1931.10.09,1931.12.09,
1931.12.14,1932.01.06,1932.01.17,1932.

06.30,1932.07.02,1932.12.04,1932.12.30,1933.05.13,1933.07.27,1933.08.15,1933.09.09,1933.11.20,1933.12.17,1933.12.18,1935.01.29,1935.05.18,1935.06.05,1935.06.06,1935.06.24,1935.07.16,1935.10.17,1935.11.04,1936.01.18,1936.02.27,1936.04.29,1936.05.14,1936.06.11,1936.06.12,1936.06.29,1936.07.28,1936.08.22,1936.09.01,1936.12.10,1936.12.24,1936.12.29,1937.01.01,1937.01.06,1937.02.19,1937.03.01,1937.04.03,1937.06.01,1937.06.12,1937.06.24,1937.06.30,1938.11.13,1938.11.25,1938.12.01,1938.12.03,1938.12.27,1938.12.30,1939.06.18,1939.07.31,1939.09,1939.10.09,1939.10.16,1942.10.27,1942.11.25,1943.01.07,1943.01.21,1943.01.22,1943.02.10,1943.02.11,1943.02.16,1943.11.18,1943.12.24,1944.01.21,1944.08.04,1944.09.15,1945.12.31,1953.07.15,1954.12.25,1963.01.31

顾孟余(顾兆熊) 1921.10,1923.03.16,1923.12.14,1924.10.22,1925.08.04,1925.11.06,1929.05.06,1933.07.15,1964.01.08

顾树森(字荫亭) 1936.12.24,1945.10.24,1946.01.02

顾淑型 1925.11.06

顾廷龙(号起潜) 1939.08 中下,1940.03.01,1940.03.14,1940.04 下,1940.05.04,1940.06.14,1941.03.16,1941.03.19,1941.03.23,1941.03.29,1941.08.31,1946.03.21,1947.06.05,1947.06.09

顾维钧(字少川) 1926.12.09,1945.07.30,1945.08.15,1945.08.17,1954.10.16,1960.

07.19,1960.11.26,1960.12.21,1960.12.28,1961.01.31,1961.02.16,1961.02.23,1961.03.12,1961.03.21,1961.04.02,1961.06.07,1961.06.25,1961.08.31,1961.09.12,1961.09.13,1961.09.21,1961.10.29,1963.10.18,1963.10.20,1963.10.24

顾燮光(字鼎梅) 1933.09.28,1933.09.30

顾翊群(字季高) 1929.05.12,1963.03.30

顾毓桐 1938.05.08

顾毓琇(字一樵) 1933.11.15,1934.02.08,1936.01.22,1936.08.17,1937.06.17,1937.07.03,1938.05.08,1938.05.09,1938.05.10,1939.03.07,1940.02.14,1940.03.07,1940.11.22,1941.01.23,1941.08.07,1942.10.07,1942.10.20,1942.10.27,1942.11.11,1942.11.19,1943.01 初,1943.01.18,1943.01.19,1946.09.11,1949.03.15,1949.03.20,1956.05.05,1958.03.15,1962.07.15

顾子刚(字子刚) 1929.01.30,1929.03.25,1929 夏,1931.10.09,1932 春,1933.11.28,1935.02.08,1935.11.04,1935.11.09,1937.02.09,1937.12.21,1938.01.15,1938.01.26,1938.01.27,1938.02.02,1938.02.08,1938.02.17,1938.02.18,1938.03.03,1938.03.11,1938.03.15,1938.03.24,1938.03.31,1938.04.13,1938.04.29,1938.05.04,1938.05.12,1938.05.18,1938.06.30,1938.12.30,1939.02.16,1939.05.25,1939.06.07,1939.06.20,1939.08.01,1939.10.18,1939.11.03,1939.11.18,1939.12.13,1940.01.02,1940.01.13,1940.01.14,1940.01.19,1940.01.24,1940.02.05,1940.02.15,1940.03.20,1940.03.23,1940.04.27,1940.06.19,1940.07.02,1940.07.02,1940.

08.19,1940.10.07,1941.05.14,1942.12.17,1945.08.24,1945.10.11,1945.10.19,1945.11.05,1945.12.29,1946.01.27,1946.11 下,1947.05.14,1947.07.08,1948.12.23,1948.12.26,1949.01.03,1949.01.08,1949.01.11,1949.01.15,1949.01.17,1949.01.20,1949.01.25,1949.03.18,1949.03.29,1949.04.12,1949.06.15,1949.11.26,1950.03.04,1950.05.15,1950.11.26,1951.01.24,1951.05.25,1951.08.23,1953.04.25,1954.10.23,1955.03.28,1955.04.01

顾子仁 1955.03.28,1955.04.01

谷钟秀(字九峰) 1946.10,1948.03.26

管冀贤 1948.02 下

关颂声 1946.10

关颂韬(字亦强) 1937.07.16,1937.07.21

关雅 1949.01.14

关植耘 1947.10.14,1948.11.09

广禄(孔古尔·广禄) 1955.04.09,1963.05.21

桂永清(字率真) 1945.08.17

桂质柏 1925.04.19,1925.05.24,1930.09.20,1944.11.29

郭葆昌(字世五) 1935.03.27,1937.06.01,1946.01.29

郭宝钧(字子衡) 1943.03.03,1943.05.27

郭斌佳 1963.01.04

郭秉文(字鸿声) 1945.07.29,1945.07.31,1954.10.16,1956.05.05,1956.07.29,1957.12.12,1960.02.02,1960.04.06,1960.05.30,1960.09.17,1961.11.22,1961.12,1962.01.29,1962.04.14,1963.03.30,1963.10.24,1963.12.11

郭伯恭 1940.02 中上,1940.03.28,1940.

05.10

郭成吉 1954.12.14,1961.09.28

郭大维 1955.03.18,1963.12.08

郭金鼐(字秉穌) 1916 秋,1916.10.16,1916.11 中,1916.12.31,1917.05.07,1917.07 中下,1917.08.14,1917.09-10,1917.10.16,1918.09.11,1919.06.23

郭金章(字治平) 1916 夏,1916 秋,1916.10.16,1916.11 中,1916.12.31,1917.01 中,1917.03.18,1917.05.07,1917.07 中下,1917.08.14,1917.09-10,1917.10.16,1918.04.11,1918.06.04,1918.09.11,1919.05.30,1919.06.23,1919.09.29

郭麟阁 1947.02.09

郭惊闾 1960.07.19

郭沫若 1939.03.04,1949.06.15,1950.11.27,1953.03.05,1955.01.26,1956.06.07

郭任远 1933.06.17,1941.10.08,1941.10.30

郭绍虞(郭希汾) 1935.01.29,1935.06 上

郭曙南 1944.09.13

郭舜平 1955.03.02

郭泰祺(号复初) 1934.12.06,1937.02.21,1939.01.10,1939.02.09,1946.07 下

郭廷以(字量予) 1958.05.23,1958.05.31,1958.07.03,1960.02.02,1960.02.09,1960.02.16,1960.02.27,1960.05.14,1960.07.18,1960.07.19,1960.07.28,1960.07.29,1960.08.03,1960.08.17,1960.12 底,1961.01.26,1962.01.18,1962.01.29,1962.07.17,1962.07.31,1962.09.11,1962.09.18,1962.09.25,1962.10.14,1962.10.21,1962.11.21,1962.12.09,1962.12.12,1963.01.25,1963.02.04,1963.02.12,1963.02.18,

1963.03.07,1963.03.29,1963.03.30,1963.
04.05,1963.04.10,1963.04.15,1963.04.
16,1963.05.02,1963.07 中上,1963.07
中,1963.09.17,1963.10.10,1963.10.18,
1963.10.24,1963.11.30,1964.01.28,1964.
01.30,1964.02.03,1964.02.11,1964.05.
11,1964.05.24,1964.06.02,1964.06.09,
1964.10.09,1964.10.22,1964.10.28,1964.
11.28,1964.12.09

郭晓峰(字仁林) 1918.11 中

郭须静(字厚庵) 1919.04 中下

郭颖颐 1961.08.23

郭有守(字子杰) 1933.10.11,1936.12.29,
1938.12.09,1939.03.07,1939.03.21,1939.
05.22,1954.11.01,1954.11.28,1954.12.
14,1956.07.23,1957.03.26,1961.09.28,
1963.031.6,1963.07.11,1963.09.20,1963.
12.06,1964.02.12,

郭玉堂(字翰臣) 1929.10.25

郭泽钦 1945.07.27

郭兆麟 1964.01.13,1964.01.29,1964.03.
31

郭志嵩 1946.01.02

H

韩复榘(字向方) 1932.06 中

韩缙华 1914.04.08,1915.11.09,1915.12.
03,1915.12.10

韩权华 1934.11.05,1937.11.01,1941.01.
04,1941.04.15,1942.12.16,1950.07.24

韩儒林(字鸿庵) 1936.12.10,1943.02.18

韩寿萱(字蔚生) 1931.01.14,1945.10.11,
1946.10.21,1947.04.01,1947.10 上,
1948.01.05,1948.01.15,1948.06.06,1948.

07.20,1948.07.26,1948.08.06,1948.09.
02,1948.09.19,1949.01.14,1950.07.07,
1950.09.25,1950.11.27

韩耀曾(渤鹏) 1914.04.08,1915.10.26,
1915.11.16,1915.12.02,1915.12.03,1916.
02.22

韩应陛(字对虞) 1930.06.14,1930.06 中
下,1931.01.06,1931.04.08

韩永锋 1949.01.15

韩咏华(字郁文,梅贻琦夫人) 1914.04.
08,1919.09.09,1933.11.15,1934.11.05,
1936.07.08,1937.06.17,1951.01 中下,
1951.02.27,1951.02.28,1951.03.17,1953.
09.22,1954.01.26,1956.08.14,1960.09.
19,1961.09.22,1962.05.28,1962.07.15,
1962.10.06,1963.07.30,1963.11.06,1963.
11.10,1963.11.14

韩毓曾 1895.03.25,1933 秋

韩云峰 1948 夏,1948.07.18

韩振华(字诵裳) 1914.04.08,1915.10.26,
1915.11.09,1915.11.16,1915.12.02,1915.
12.03,1915.12.10,1916.02.12,1916.02.
22,1945.11.30,1945.12.07,1947.05.08,
1947.05.17,1948 夏

杭承艮 1947.10.14,1948.08.06,1948.11.
09

杭立武 1933.10.11,1938.05.02,1938.05.
06,1938.05.16,1938.05.20,1938.05.28,
1938.07.23,1938.09.06,1938.12.09,1939.
02.16,1939.03.07,1940.11.22,1942.10.
07,1942.12.04,1943.01 初,1945.06.15,
1945.06.22,1945.07.04,1945.09.06,1945.
10.24,1945.10.30,1945.12.20,1946.01.
02,1946.10.17,1946.10.18,1947.05.25,

1947.11.05,1948.07.26,1948.08.06,1948.10.13,1948.12.08,1949.01.07,1949.03.18,1949.04.01,1950.11.04,1950.12.23,1951.03.15,1955.01.18,1957.03.21,1960.04.02

郝更生 1944.07.16

郝景盛 1947.08.16

郝寿臣 1947.08.03

郝懿行(号兰皋) 1933.09.14

郝遇林 1947.08.03

何艾龄 1951.03.04

何炳棣 1955.05.20,1955.05.23,1956.08.09,1957.07.18,1957.07.24,1957.08.08,1958.03 初,1958.09.23,1960.02.20,1960.08.19,1962.09.20,1962.12.11

和才 1957.03.21

何岑 1935.04.16

何成濬(字雪竹) 1960.02.02

何澄一(字澄意) 1935.01.19,1935.05.09,1935.05.30,1935.08.31,1936.05.05,1936.07.07,1936.10.30,1937.02.03,1937.07.16,1947.04.04

何崇杰 1940.05.28

何多源 1945.08.24,1947.05 上,1947.09.12,1949.02.15,1949.03.07,1949.04.01,1949.09.02,1950.03.15,1950.03-04,1950.04.19,1950.09.17,1950.12.06

何公敢(何崧龄) 1929.08.29

何国贵(字驭权) 1942.12.14,1944.05.05,1944.11.24,1944.11.29,1945.07.27,1945.08.24,1947.05.14,1948.01.26

何基鸿(字海秋) 1929.06.29,1930.03.30,1945.11 中,1945.12.08

何杰(字孟绰) 1947.06.09

何杰才(字其伟) 1960.05.25

何竞武(何塦) 1944.09.13

何廉(字淬廉) 1937.03.06,1937 春,1944.05.10,1947.05.09,1948.11.10,1955.04.28,1955.04.30,1956.03.02,1956.08.09,1960.02.20,1961.01.26,1961.08.23,1962.04.21,1962.10.23,1962.10.28,1963.02.18,1963.10.24

何连玉 1958.05.31

何梅岑 1948.01.14

何其巩(字克之) 1933.11.15

何任清(字伯澄) 1956.07.25

何日章(字日章) 1924.07.03,1925.04.19,1925.04.25,1925.05.27,1928.12,1929.01.29,1929.02.01,1933.03.13,1933.08.22,1933,1935.01.06,1935.02.17,1935.09.22,1936.01.05,1936.06.15,1936.10.24,1937.03.07,1937.07.07,1944.11.29,1963.09.07,1963.10.25,1964.06.06

何思源(字仙槎) 1930.04,1932.06 中,1933.06.17,1936.05 上,1947.05 上,1947.08.08,1947.09.25

何遂(字叙甫) 1929.10.11,1935.04.16,1937.06.01

何香凝(何谏) 1936.12.24

何义均 1954.04.22,1956.01.15,1956.04.04,1956.10.02,1956.11.09,1956.11.20,1959.08.18

何应钦(字敬之) 1933.11.15,1933.12.14,1939.03.01,1942.11.30,1949.03.18

何永佶 1949.04.06

何肇华 1956.05.02

何肇菁 1956.05.02,1957.03.01,1963.04.01

胡仁源（字次珊）　1925.11.06

胡汝麟（字石青）　1923.10.17,1925.07.14,
1926.09.22,1935.11.04

胡若愚（字若愚）　1925.08.04,1925.09.29,
1931.06.24,1931.06.25

胡善恒（字铁岩）　1933.10.11

胡绍声　1939.10.26,1947.10.24,1949.11.
26,1951.02.27

胡适（字适之）　1919.03.07,1919.03-04,
1919.04.15,1920.01.22,1920.06.15,1920.
09.11,1925.05.27,1925.07.04,1925.07.
06,1926 夏,1928.06.18,1929.01.04,
1929.02.17,1929.11.07,1929.11,1929.12.
09,1930.06.07,1930.10 上,1930.10.10,
1930.11.13,1930.12.08,1937.01.01,1937.
01.06,1931.01.09,1931.05.18,1931.06.
24,1931.06.30,1931.07.02,1931.08.17,
1931.09.21,1931.10.09,1931.11 中下,
1931.12.14,1931.12 下,1931,1932.02.
26,1932 春,1932.06.07,1932.06.30,
1932.07.02,1932.09.21,1932.11.22,1932.
12.24,1932.12.30,1933.01.12,1933.03.
01,1933.03.21,1933.03.27,1933.04.27,
1933.05.26,1933.06.09,1933.11.15,1933.
12.04,1933.12.06,1933.12.10,1934.02.
12,1934.02.13,1934.02.20,1934.02.21,
1935.02.08,1935.03.05,1935.04.04,1935.
05.11,1935.05.18,1935.06.17,1935.07.
16,1935.10.02,1935.11.23,1935.12.02,
1936.01.18,1936.02.27,1936.04.15,1936.
05.25,1936.07.08,1936.12.29,1936.12.
31,1937.01.01,1937.01.06,1937.03.16,
1937.03.29,1937.03.30,1937.04.13,1937.
05.17,1937.05.22,1937.05.26,1937.06.

12,1937.06.15,1937.06.16,1937.06.19,
1937.06.30,1937.08.02,1937.08.08,1937.
09.06,1937.09.20,1937.09.28,1938.04.
19,1939.01.21,1939.09.30,1939.12.10,
1940.01.02,1940.01.14,1940.04.27,1940.
05.14,1940.06.12,1940.07.29,1940.08.
02,1940.09.04,1940.11.15,1940.11.16,
1941.02.03,1941.05.14,1941.05.20,1941.
07.03,1941.07.15,1941.08.09,1941.08.
21,1941.09.12,1941.10.08,1941.10.30,
1942.10.27,1942.12.17,1943.01.02,1943.
06.02,1943.08.11,1943.10.01,1944.02.
21,1944.04.29,1944.04,1945.02.17,
1945.07.08,1945.10.06,1945.10.11,1945.
12.28,1946.07.07,1946.08 下,1946.10.
21,1946.10,1946.11.04,1946.11.08,
1946.11-12,1947.01.11,1947.01.15,
1947.02.07,1947.02.09,1947.03.03,1947.
03.22,1947.04.01,1947.04.04,1947.04.
16,1947.04.25,1947.04.27,1947.04.30,
1947.05.08,1947.08.16,1947.09.10,1947.
09.15,1947.09.20,1947.09.25,1947.11.
05,1947.11.20,1947.12.10,1947.12.22,
1948.01.05,1948.01.14,1948.01.18,1948.
01.22,1948.01.27,1948.02.11,1948.02.
13,1948.03.07,1948.03.26,1948.03.30,
1948.05.11,1948.06 初,1948.07.14,1948.
09.02,1948.10.24,1948.11.10,1948.11
下,1948.12.03,1948.12.08,1948.12.22,
1949.01.08,1949.01.14,1949.01.25,1949.
04.13,1949.06.21,1949.12.09,1950.02.
05,1950.02.09,1950.03.04,1950.03.10,
1950.03.16,1950.05.04,1950.05.06,1950.
05.09,1950.05.10,1950.05.15,1950.05.

20,1950.07.18,1950.07.24,1951.01.27,
1951.01.31,1951.03.10,1951.04.26,1951.
06.22,1951.07.15,1951.07.23,1951.08.
05,1951.08.10,1951.08 中,1951.12.04,
1951.12.05,1952.03.14,1952.11.16,1953.
03.05,1953.05.07,1953.07.15,1954.01.
26,1954.02.03,1954.03.03,1954.03.04,
1954.03.10,1954.03.13,1954.04.13,1954.
07.10,1954.08.06,1954.10.16,1955.01.
06,1955.02.20,1955.03.11,1955.03.13,
1955.03.15,1955.04.24,1955.04.25,1955.
04.27,1955.04.29,1955.04.30,1955.05.
07,1955.05.19,1955.05.25,1955.05.27,
1955.05.30,1955.08.29,1955.09.02,1955.
09.08,1955.10.16,1955.10.22,1955.10.
24,1955.10.28,1955.11.27,1956.03.02,
1956.03.11,1956.03.16,1956.03.20,1956.
04.04,1956.05.10,1956.05.17,1956.05.
28,1956.06.07,1956.06,1956.07.11,
1956.07.18,1956.07.20,1956.07.23,1956.
07.24,1956.07.25,1956.07.29,1956.08.
09,1956.08.10,1956.08.27,1956 夏,
1956.10.18,1956.11.12,1956.12.17,1956.
12.27,1957.02.20,1957.03.01,1957.04.
05,1957.04.24,1957.05,1957.07.18,
1957.07.24,1957.08.08,1957.08.09,1957.
08.19,1957.11 初,1957.11.06,1958.03.
22,1958.04.04,1958.08.19,1958.08.29,
1958.09.23,1959.02.14,1959.12.04,1960.
05 初,1960.05.23,1960.05.30,1960.06.
16,1960.08.08,1960.09.12,1960.09.13,
1960.09.17,1960.09.25,1960.09.28,1960
秋,1960.10.11,1960.10.21,1960.12.15,
1961.02.15,1961.02.28,1961.03.04,1961.

07,1961.10.09,1961.10.18,1961.11.10,
1961.11.27,1962.01.29,1962.02.19,1962.
02.23,1962.02.26,1962.02.28,1962.03.
05,1962.03.06,1962.03.09,1962.03.12,
1962.03.14,1962.03.16,1962.03.17,1962.
03.21,1962.03.29,1962.03.30,1962.04.
03,1962.04.05,1962.04.06,1962.04.07,
1962.04.11,1962.04.14,1962.04 中,1962.
04.18,1962.04.21,1962.04.25,1962.04.
27,1962.08.03,1962.08.11,1962.10.06,
1962.10.22,1963.02.04,1963.02.05,1963.
02.14,1963.02.19,1963.02.26,1963.03.
18,1963.04.01,1963.04.05,1963.04.13,
1963.05.04,1963.05.16,1963.05.17,1963.
05.25,1963.06.11,1963.06.12,1963.06.
13,1963.07.01,1963.11.05,1963.12.27,
1964.02－03,1964.03.13,1964.05.01,
1964.05.11,1964.08.16

胡世桢　1961.12.07,1962.01.29

胡树楷　1930.01.05

胡思杜　1950.07.07,1960.09.17

胡天石　1934.07.16,1934.07.20

胡惟德(字馨吾)　1929.11.29

胡先晋(王毓铨夫人)　1945.07.08,1949.
04.20,1950.03.04,1950.07.07,1950.09.
25,1956.06.07

胡先骕(字步曾)　1929.02.19,1929.02,
1929.08.21,1929.09,1931.10.09,1935.05.
18,1936.02.20,1937.05.22,1937.07.03,
1937.07.23,1937.07.25,1937.07.27,1937.
11.18,1946.03.02

胡小石(胡光炜)　1940.08.26

胡英　1937.04.07

胡应元　1961

夏,1936.01.18,1936.06.14,1936.09.11,
1936.12.24,1937 春,1938.03.24,1939.
02.26,1939.03.01,1939.03.07,1939.03.
10,1939.05.10,1939.06.30,1939.08.23,
1939.10.08,1940.06.19,1940.06.21,1940.
11.11,1941.10.08,1941.10.30,1943.01
初,1943.02.20,1943.09.08,1943.10.01,
1944.04.29,1944.05.05,1944.05.06,1944.
11.29,1945.03.17,1945.06.15,1945.10.
11,1945.10.23,1946.04,1946.10.17,
1946.10.18,1946.10.21,1947.01.19,1947.
04.04,1947.05.24,1947.09.15,1949.02.
24,1949.03.07,1950.01.06,1950.11.27,
1955.02.18,1955.05.20,1955.10.27,1957.
12.06,1958.01.18,1958.02.28,1958.03.
14,1958.03.21,1958.07.11,1959.02.20,
1960.06.16,1960.06.20,1962.09.13,1962.
10.13,1963.02.26,1963.03.11,1963.03.
18,1963.05.25,1963.10.13,1963.10.21

蒋介石 1928.07.19,1930.03.07,1931.04
初,1936.06.12,1937.07.13,1937.07.21,
1937.07.27,1940.11.19,1944.09.11,1944.
09 中下,1944.09.23,1945.03.02,1945.
03.08,1945.10.06,1948.10.24,1948.12.
22,1963.01.18,1963.02.27

蒋经国 1948.12.21

蒋梦麟(号孟邻) 1920.12.09,1921.01.06,
1924.11.29,1925.09.29,1925.11.06,1928.
12.31,1929.01.04,1929.02.01,1929.06.
29,1929.06.30,1929.11,1930.04,1931.
01.02,1931.01.09,1931.05.18,1931.06.
11,1931.06.24,1931.06.25,1931.06.30,
1931.07.02,1931.09.21,1932.02.26,1932.
06 中,1932.06.30,1932.07.02,1932.12.

30,1933.03.27,1933.05.04,1933.07.15,
1933.08.31,1933.11.15,1933.11.19,1933.
12.04,1933.12.10,1933,1934.02.12,
1934.02.21,1934.12.07,1935.02.08,1935.
04.04,1935.05,1935 夏,1935.10.02,
1935.11.23,1935.12.02,1936.02.27,1936.
05.25,1936.07.08,1936.08.17,1936.09
下,1936.12.29,1936.12.31,1937.04.02,
1937.04.06,1937.04.13,1937.05.17,1937.
05.22,1937.06.12,1937.06.17,1937.09.
06,1937.09.14,1937.10.04,1937.10.25,
1937.12.27,1938.01.05,1938.01.15,1938.
01.24,1938.01.30,1938.02.08,1938.02.
13,1938.02.14,1938.02.18,1938.02 中,
1938.03.11,1938.12.09,1938.12.12,1938.
12.17,1939.02.27,1939.03.25,1939.04.
20,1939.11.04,1940.04.16,1940.09.02,
1941.05.29,1942.08.11,1942.09.25,1942.
10.18,1943.01.22,1943.06.02,1944.07.
12,1944.09.15,1944.09 中下,1945.01.
06,1945.05.16,1946.07.07,1946.12.27,
1947.05.24,1950.02.05,1950.02.09,1950.
03.04,1950.05.20,1951.02.28,1955.03.
15,1955.06.06,1955.09.08,1955.10.22,
1955.10.24,1958.08.29,1960.09.13,1960.
09.28,1961.12,1962.04.21,1962.07.24,
1962.09.01,1964.08.16

蒋汝藻(号孟苹) 1925.05.27,1931.12.14,
1932.02.16

蒋硕杰 1948.10.24,1960.11.25

蒋廷黻(字绶章) 1928.10.28,1928.11.01,
1928.12.07,1928.12.19,1929.03.21,1929.
07.01,1931.01.23,1931.08.04,1931.09.
18,1933.01.10,1933.03.27,1933.11.15,

09,1940.06.06,1942.10.08,1944.04.29,
1944.05.09,1944.07.06,1944.09.13,1944.
10.05,1945.12.01,1947.02,1947.09.15,
1947.10 上,1948.07.26,1948.07.30,
1949.01.07,1949.02.24,1952.07.17,1954.
03.10,1955.06.06,1955.08.29,1955.09.
02,1955.11.27,1956.03.02,1956.07.18,
1956.08.09,1956.08.10,1956.11.05,1958.
03.22,1960.04.02,1960.06.19,1960.12.
15,1961.02.28,1961.06.13,1961.11.27,
1962.01.08,1962.01.29,1962.02.19,1962.
02.23,1962.03.05,1962.03.12,1962.03.
17,1962.07.18,1962.07.20,1962.12.05,
1962.12.11,1963.02.15

李继侗　1938.04.19

李继先　1933.08.22

李济欧　1963.08.31

李家滋　1937.05.26,1937.06.19

李家驹　1926.09.18

李家浦　1937.05.26,1937.06.19

李剑农　1943.06.01,1944.09.15

李絜非　1943.07

李锦书　1933.09.28

李景枞　1946.07.14

李景聃(字纯一)　1936.09.23,1936.11 中
　下

李景均　1963.09.14

李景康(字铭琛)　1963.10.14

李骏(字显章)　1944.07.06

李焜瀛(字符曾)　1903 冬,1904

李莲普　1945.12.07

李濂镗(字杏南)　1948.06.06

李霖灿　1955.08.15,1956.02.29,1956.05.
03,1956.07.21,1956.07.24,1957.03.21,

1960.07.05,1961.02.28,1961.03.15,1961.
04.30,1961.05.31,1961.08.26,1961.09.
18,1961.09.24,1961.12.14,1961.12.31,
1962.12.05,1963.02.15,1964.05.10,1964.
05.15

李麟玉(字圣章)　1931.01.26,1931.09.21,
1932.01.10,1932.12.30,1933.01.10,1933.
01.13,1933.03.01,1933.08.28,1933.11.
28,1934.02.18,1935.05.18,1935.10.17,
1936.12.29,1937.04.03,1937.04.13,1937.
05.22,1937.06.30,1937.07.13,1937.07.
14,1937.07.16,1937.07.23,1945.11 中,
1946.12.11,1947.02.07,1947.05.08,1947.
05.14,1947.09.10,1947.09.20,1947.09.
25,1948.10.13,1948.11.10,1960.08.04,
1960.08.08,1963.08.31

李铭(字馥孙)　1951.04.26,1956.03.16

李墨云　1959.02.07

李滂(字少微)　1933.08.23,1937.05.26,
1937.06.14,1937.06.19

李朴　1925 冬

李仁俊　1948.11.09

李儒勉　1957.03.26

李瑞年　1935.07.18,1936.06.11,1937.09.
20,1938.02.04,1940.02.14,1940.12.22

李善兰(字竟芳)　1927.08.18,1927.09.15,
1927.11.01

李深(字庆阶)　1919.02

李盛铎(号木斋)　1925.05.27,1933.07.08,
1933.08.15,1933.09.22,1933.10.09,1937.
03.02,1937.04.17,1937.05.24,1937.05.
26,1937.06.14,1937.06.15,1937.06.16,
1937.06.19

李声轩(李相宏)　1930.02.16

李铁铮(字炼百)　1956.04.18,1956.05.03

李惟果　1963.03.30,1963.05.30,1963.06.
04

李文祎(字翰章)　1930.01.05,1932.01.10,
1933.03.09,1933.03.13,1933.08.04,1933.
08.22,1933.08.28,1933.08.29,1933.08.
31,1935.01.06,1935.02.01,1935.02.17,
1935.04.04,1935.09.22,1936.01.05,1936.
10.24,1937.02.06,1937.03.07,1938.02

李孝芳(谢义炳夫人)　1963.01.04

李晓生　1939.12.16

李小缘　1922.10,1923.06.21,1925.04.26,
1928.04.30,1928.12,1928,1929.01.29,
1929.02.01,1929.02.24,1929.02.28,1929.
03.25,1931.04,1934.02 中,1934.11.12,
1935.02.16,1936.11.16,1940.02.24,1942.
11.02,1943.09.08,1944.11.29,1946.10.
18,1947.05.24,1952.07.02

李协(字宜之)　1936.02.20

李续祖(字晓宇)　1950.04.08

李宣龚(字拔可)　1929.11.07,1932.12.13,
1933.07.13,1933.08.14,1933.10.12,1933.
10.24,1939.08.18

李俨(字乐知)　1927.02.18,1927.03.10,
1927.03.17,1927.04.28,1927.07.12,1927.
08.18,1927.09.15,1927.11.01,1934 春,
1935.05.02,1939.06.05,1940.06.21,1940.
11.16

李椒　1963.09.05

李燕亭(李长春)　1933.08.30,1933

李耀南(字照亭)　1935.12.10,1935.12.13,
1936.03.20,1936.09.15,1936.10.14,1936.
10.17,1936.10.18,1937.06.01,1937.06.
19,1937.06.26,1937.08.17,1937.11.18,

1938.05.07,1938.05.09,1939.01.14,1939.
02.02,1939.03.18,1939.05.02,1939.09.
28,1940.02.15,1940.03.01,1940.03.14,
1940.03.25,1940.04.04,1940.04.18,1940.
04 下,1940.05.03,1940.06.10,1940.06.
19,1940.06.21,1940.07.29,1940.11.16,
1941.02.17,1941.05.05,1947.05.14,1948.
11.04

李一非　1936.12.10

李益华(字锦书)　1929.02.24,1933.08
中,1947.10.14,1948.11.09

李毅士(李祖鸿)　1933.10.11

李应林(字笑庵)　1951.11.28,1956.05.19,
1961.03.20

李永安(字文钦)　1933 秋,1937.11.18,
1938.05.13

李永淦　1936.09 下

李郁荣　1949.01.21

李毓尧(字叔唐)　1933.10.11

李泽彰(字伯嘉)　1948.02.22,1949.01.14

李蒸(字云亭)　1930.03.30,1931.10.11,
1932.12.24,1932.12.30,1933.12.04,1933.
12.10,1934.02.21,1935.05.18,1935.12.
02,1936.06.30,1936.12.29,1937.04.13,
1937.05.17,1937.05.22,1937.06.12,1937.
06.17,1937.07.07,1937.07.13,1937.07.
14,1937.07.16,1937.07.21,1937.07.23,
1937.07.25,1937.07.27,1939.03.01,1940.
06.12,1949.03.18

李政道　1951.05.18

李治华　1955.01.03,1955.01.26

李之瑋　1944.05.05,1944.05.06,1944.11.
29

李锺履(字仲和)　1936.01.28,1938.03.11,

1938.04.13,1945.12.02,1949.01.11,1949.01.17,1949.01.20

李仲三 1925.09.29

李烛尘（李华捂） 1939.03.08

李铸晋 1961.10.05,1961.10.14,1961.10.23

李卓敏 1942.11.29,1945.08.15,1945.08.15

李宗恩 1941.01.13,1951.01.22,1951.02.02

李宗仁（字德邻） 1936.06.12,1945.12.08,1948.03.26,1948.04.27,1948.05.15,1948.05.19,1948.12.22

李宗侗（字玄伯） 1903 冬,1904,1906 夏,1926.08.03,1926.08.04,1926.08 中,1926.10.13,1926.12.06,1926.12.17,1927.06 中,1928.09.23,1928.11,1929.01.21,1929.05 中,1929.08.14,1929.10.10,1929.11.10,1929.11,1930.03.16,1930.03.30,1931.06.04,1931.09.27,1931.10.11,1932.07.02,1932.12.30,1933.01.10,1933.01.25,1933.07 底,1941.03.27,1947.06.09,1951.06.22,1951.07.23,1951.07.25,1955.04.09,1957.03.21,1961.12.07,1961.12.31,1962.01.08,1962.01.29

李祖绅 1925.09.29

励乃骥（字德人） 1935.05.09,1935.05.30,1935.08.31,1936.05.05,1936.07.07,1936.10.30,1948.11.09,1951.03.15

郦堃厚 1964.03.05

连瀛洲 1945.08.17

梁诚（字戴衷） 1925.09.12

梁大鹏 1960.01.30,1960.03.17

梁定蜀（字定蜀） 1933.10.11

梁方仲 1943.06.01,1945.03.24

梁焕彝（字鼎甫） 1919

梁鉴立 1945.07.26

梁敬錞（字和钧） 1919.10.24,1962.12.12,1963.01.08,1963.01.15,1963.07.12

梁龙 1925.11.03,1925.11.06,1946.07 下

梁念曾 1947.06.09

梁启超（字卓如,号任公） 1925.03 初,1925.05.25,1925.05.27,1925.06.02,1925.07.04,1925.07.06,1925.08.09,1925.11,1925.12.15,1925.12.20,1926.02.28,1926.04.18,1926.06.18,1926.07.05,1926.07.12,1926.07.13,1926.07.20,1926.09.14,1926.09.22,1926.11.26,1927.06.29,1928.05 下,1928.06.18,1928.08.24,1929.02.17,1931.06.25,1931.08.21,1931.10.20,1935.11.27

梁启雄 1938.01.05

梁启勋（字仲策）1930.09.01

梁如浩（梁滔昭） 1961.04.02,1961.06.07

梁思成 1917.11.10,1928.05 下,1928.08.24,1930.09.01,1931.10.08,1932 春,1933.01.10,1933.03.21,1933.11.20,1935.10.02,1935.11.27,1936.12.24,1937.02.19,1937 春,1942.10.07,1943.06.01,1944.05.29,1944.06 底,1944.07.06,1944.07.12,1944.07.24,1944.07.29,1944.08.05,1944.09.22,1946.01.02,1946.10,1947.02,1948.03.26,1948 夏,1948.07.26,1948.08.06

梁思顺（字令娴） 1926.04.18

梁思永 1930.09.01,1936.09 下,1937.03.05,1937.07.03,1937.09.14,1939.09,1940.06.06,1944.07.06,1944.07.24,1944.

07.29，1947.02，1949.01.14，1949.02.10，
1960.04.02

梁思庄　1936.02.27，1946.05.13，1958.03.
21

梁实秋（梁治华）　1917.11.10，1947.05
上，1947.08.03，1947.08.08，1963.01.25，
1963.04.18，1963.05.05，1963.05.19，1963.
06.13，1964.10.09，1964.10.28

梁士诒（字翼夫，号燕孙）　1925.09.29，
1930.10.25，1933.04.23，1961.09.21

梁漱溟（梁焕鼎）　1918.11 中，1918 冬，
1919.02，1919 夏，1919，1927.05.21，
1956.07.11

梁廷灿（字存吾）　1925.12.20，1928.06.09，
1928.06.18

梁廷炜（字伯华）　1937.12.18，1948.12.23，
1950.12.23，1951.03.15

梁惜音　1932.10.04

梁在平　1956，1960.01.06

梁子涵　1949.01.14

梁钊韬　1956.02.20

梁志成　1933.11.19

梁宗岱　1933.03.01

梁宗恒　1962.07.31

廖宝珊　1956.10.14

廖家艾　1961.03.29

廖家珊（字铁枝，袁复礼夫人）　1925.10.
03，1929.05.11，1956.08.14

廖山涛　1962.01.29

林伯遵　1936.12.31，1937.07.21，1937.10.
09，1937.11.18，1938.01.05，1939.03.18，
1939.04.29，1940.11.22，1941.02.03，1945.
10.30

林春猷　1961.11.25

林德懿　1925 冬

林风眠（林绍琼）　1938.02.04

林徽因　1930.09.01，1932.12.30，1933.03.
21，1933.11.19

林济青　1936.07.20

林家翘　1962.09.20

林可胜　1936.03.26

林藜光　1933 夏，1934.11.12，1937.02.09，
1956.02.01

林镕　1963.11.14

林同骅　1961.12.07

林同济　1940.01.04

林行规　1935.04.16

林耀华　1938.12.20

林语堂（林玉堂）　1916.09.11，1925.11.06，
1926.05.02，1926.05.03，1940.01.02，1940.
01.14，1940.02.07，1940.03.20，1940.04.
08，1940.04.27，1945.05.14，1953.12.16，
1954.10.23，1954.12.21，1955.03.30，1955.
04.09，1955.04.14，1955.05.07，1961.01.16

林子峰　1937.05.02

林子勋　1962.02.26

林致平　1963.01.11

凌纯声（字民复）　1939.06.18，1939.09，
1944.07.06，1947.09.15

凌道扬　1956.04.04，1956.05.19

凌济东　1960.02.01

凌念京　1927.12.03，1928.01.01，1928.03.
07

凌其峻　1926.07.24

凌叔华（陈源夫人）　1926.09.22，1954.06.
15，1954.08.26，1955.02.20，1957.03.14，
1957.03.26，1958.02.24，1961.09.22

刘百闵　1956.05.19

刘半农(刘复) 1918.02-03,1918.03.07,
　1926.05.02,1926.05.03,1927.10.20,1928.
　05.27,1928.06.10,1928.11,1929.02.23,
　1929.04.22,1929.08.14,1929.08.30,1929.
　09.25,1929.09,1929.11,1930.02 上中,
　1930.03.30,1930.04,1930.10.01,1930.10.
　22,1930.12.10,1931.06.04,1931.06.06,
　1931.06.30,1931.08.05,1931.08.21,1931.
　09.25,1931.10.09,1932.02.16,1932.06.
　30,1932.07.02,1932.09.21,1932.12.24,
　1933.01.12,1933.04.27,1933.05.26,1933.
　06.09,1933.12.06,1933.12.10,1933,
　1934.01.16,1934.02.06,1934.02.13,1934.
　02.18,1934.02.20,1934.02.22,1934 秋,
　1964.01.08

刘秉麟(号南陔) 1957.03.26

刘伯龙 1963.09.11

刘承本 1933.07.03

刘承幹(字贞一,号翰怡) 1925.05.27,
　1926.10.22,1926.10.25,1929.03.08,1931.
　01.06,1931.01.08,1931.01.18,1931.01.
　19,1931.02.26,1931.12.30,1932.02.25,
　1932.12.24,1933.06 下,1933.07.01,
　1933.07.02,1933.07.03,1933.07.08,1933.
　08.03,1933.08.15,1933.08 中,1933.09.
　20,1933.09.22,1934.12.06,1935.11.30,
　1936.01.30,1936.02.14,1940.04 中下,
　1941.03.29,1945.12.28

刘崇鋐(字寿民) 1926.07.24,1929.01.13,
　1936.11.16,1938.12.01,1938.12.09,1938.
　12.17,1938.12.30,1939.02.15,1939.03.
　26,1939.10.09,1940.03.31,1951.11.28,
　1956.08.14,1962.01.29,1963.01.04,1963.
　06.04

刘崇杰(字子楷) 1933.03.27,1934.08.23

刘纯(字纯甫) 1929.01.29,1939.04.26,
　1939.04.29,1939.05.02

刘次箫(字少庸) 1932.06 中

刘大悲 1957.03.21

刘大钧(字季陶) 1916.09.11,1919.07.30,
　1939.07.20,1951.01.19,1952.07.04,1952.
　12.03,1955.03.30,1956.12.23

刘大绅 1963.05.05

刘大中 1948.10.24

刘砥中 1948.06.09

刘敦桢(字士能) 1933.03.21,1937.02.19

刘奉璋 1951.03.15

刘官谔 1939.03.29

刘光第 1898.09

刘桂焯 1961.01.25

刘国钧(字衡如) 1925.05.24,1926.07.12,
　1927.02.28,1927.03.10,1928.12,1929.01.
　28,1929.01.29,1929.02.01,1929.03.08,
　1929.03.25,1929.09.23,1929.10.05,1929.
　10.11,1929.10.26,1929.11.10,1930.01.
　05,1930.03.16,1930.03.24,1930.05.15,
　1930.05.16,1930.05.29,1930.05.30,1930.
　05.31,1930.12.21,1933.03.13,1933.08.
　30,1933,1934.02 中,1934.12.06,1935.
　02.16,1936.01.18,1936.05 上,1937.07.
　07,1937.11.01,1938.04.18,1938.05.09,
　1940.06.21,1943.02.20,1943.12.16,1944.
　11.29,1947.05.24

刘国秦 1952.02.28,1953.08.07,1953.08.
　13,1953.08.25,1953.09.01,1953.09.11,
　1953.10.07,1953.10.27,1954.04.22,1954.
　10.23,1955.01.21,1955.04.09,1955.06.
　29,1955.07.03,1955.08.27,1955.12.21,

1961.12.28,1962.01.03,1962.01.29,1962.
04.23,1962.05.15,1962.08.15,1962.08.
23,1962.08.25,1962.09.04,1962.10.01,
1962.11.01,1962.12.05,1962.12.11,1963.
02.18,1963.02.23,1963.02.24,1963.07.
04,1963.07.11,1963.09.09,1963.11.12,
1964.01.15,1964.01.21,1964.02.22,1964.
02 下,1964.06.05,1964.06.10,1964.08.
25,1964.09.03,1964.11.12,1964.12.02,
1965.01.22

罗静夫 1937.07.23

罗静轩(字书举) 1928.12.23,1929.06.23,
1930.01.05,1930.03.24,1931.04.05,1931.
06.01,1932.01.10

罗隆基(字努生) 1926.03 上,1931.08.
17,1937.07.16

罗式 1963.04.23

罗唐 1963.04.23

罗万森 1956.11.09

罗文 1963.04.23

罗文幹(字钧任) 1933.08 上,1933.08.
09,1933.08.10,1939.12.16

罗香林(字元一) 1944.05.05,1944.05.06,
1944.09 中下,1944.09.23,1951.03.04,
1956.05.19,1962.10.22,1962.11.16,1962.
12.01,1962.12.30,1963.01.17,1963.01.
18,1963.01.21,1963.02.25,1963.04.23,
1963.07.04

罗耀枢(字星伯) 1934 秋,1935.01.11

罗应荣 1949.09.02

罗庸(字膺中) 1928.09.23,1933.01.10,
1935.05.18

罗瑜 1963.04.23

罗原觉(罗泽堂) 1955.01.21,1955.03.04,

1955.04.09,1955.06.29,1955.07.03,1956.
04.04,1956.08.18,1958.07.08,1958.09.
23,1958.09.24,1958.10.12

罗振常(字子经) 1933.07.03,1933.09.28

罗振玉(号雪堂) 1925.05.27,1928.06.01,
1937.08.08,1951.11.02,1955.01.05,1955.
01.26

罗忠诒(字仪元) 1920.02 初

罗子敬 1931.01.19

骆美奂(字仲英) 1939.03.01

M

马大任 1961.09.12,1962.03.29,1962.04.
05,1962.12.06,1963.01.05,1963.01.15,
1963.01.25,1963.01.30,1963.04.25,1963.
05.31,1963.06.12

马大猷 1947.11.07

马德润 1935.05,1962.02.22,1963.11.10

马衡(字叔平) 1925.09.29,1926.08.03,
1926.08.04,1926.09.18,1926.09.22,1926.
12.02,1926.12.09,1926.12.17,1927.06
中,1927.10.06,1928.05-06,1928.09.23,
1928.11.04,1929.01.13,1929.03.01,1929.
03.17,1929.03.31,1929.04.22,1929.05.
11,1929.05 中,1929.08.14,1929.09.21,
1929.09.25,1929.10.10,1930.03.07,1930.
03.16,1930.03.30,1930.04.08,1930 夏,
1931.01.26,1931.04.08,1931.06.04,1931.
08.21,1931.09.25,1931.10.09,1932.07.
02,1932.09.21,1932.12.30,1933.01.25,
1933.07.15,1933.08.15,1933.09.18,1933.
10.03,1933.10.12,1933.11.08,1934.02.
06,1934.07.05,1934 秋,1934.10.09,
1934.12.06,1934.12.07,1935.01.11,1935.

01.19,1935.02.24,1935.04 初,1935.05.09,1935.05.18,1935.05.30,1935.06.27,1935.07.18,1935.07.25,1935.08.31,1935 底,1936.04.15,1936.04.29,1936.05.05,1936.06.14,1936.06.30,1936.07.07,1936.07.08,1936.07.18,1936.07.19,1936.07.20,1936.07.22,1936.09.11,1936.10 中下,1936.10.23,1936.10.30,1936.11 下,1936.12.24,1937.02.03,1937.02.16,1937.02.27,1937.02.28,1937.04.27,1937.05.29,1937.06.01,1937.06.12,1937.07.16,1937.11.15,1937.12.18,1938.02.08,1938.02.26,1938.03.09,1938.03.29,1938.04.18,1938.09.06,1938.09.13,1939.03.29,1939.04.07,1944.12.28,1945.10.24,1946.10,1946.12.26,1947.03.22,1947.04.04,1947.04.16,1947.04.19,1947.05.08,1947.06.09,1947.08.03,1947.08.16,1947.08.31,1947.09.20,1947.10 上,1947.10.14,1947.11.05,1948.03.26,1948.05.05,1948.06.06,1948.07.26,1948.08.06,1948.09.02,1948.09.19,1948.09.28,1948.11.09,1948.12.17,1948.12.23,1949.01.08,1949.01.14,1949.06.15,1950.01.19,1950.09.25,1964.01.04

马家骥 1925.05.27

马鉴(字季明) 1929.11,1939.05.01,1941.01.08,1942.02.10,1944.12.28,1949.03.07,1949.04.01,1949.06.15,1949.06.21,1949.07.19,1951.01.02,1951.03.04,1951.06.28,1956.01.25,1958.03.07,1958.05.28,1958.09.24,1963.01.08,1963.01.18,1963.01.31,1963.02.04,1963.02.08,1963.03.15,1963.03.20

马建忠(字眉叔) 1963.11.14,1963.11.19,1963.12.05,1964.02.04

马君武 1925.11.06,1935.08.08

马俊祥(字杰卿) 1930.05,1930.06-07

马廉(字隅卿) 1927.10.06,1929.05.05,1933.12.06,1934.02.21,1935.12.31

马龙璧(字仲芳) 1949.01.14

马民元 1961.11.27,1961.12.11

马蒙 1963.01.31,1963.02.08,1963.03.15,1963.03.20

马如容 1954.08.06

马师儒(字雅堂) 1930.03.30

马廷英(字雪峰) 1944.06.14,1944.06.30,1944.07.29

马万里 1930.12.21

马洗凡(马洗繁) 1925.11.06

马相伯 1963.11.14,1963.11.19

马孝焱 1937.06.26

马叙伦(字彝初) 1924.10.22,1929.02.01,1929.08.30,1929.11,1930.10.22,1932.07.02

马学良(字蜀原) 1943.04.22,1943.06.22,1943.06.28,1943.07.08,1943.08.12,1943.11.22,1943.12.11,1944.01.01

马一浮 1956.01.12,1956.03.04

马寅初(马元善) 1925.10.31,1925.11.03,1925.11.06,

马裕藻(字幼渔) 1925.03.11,1925.08.04,1926.12.06,1928.06.10,1928.11,1930.03.30,1932.07.02,1934.02.18,1934.02.21,1935.03.05,1935.04.04,1935.06.04

马在天 1952.12.03,1954.12.21

马子实(马坚) 1941.11.28

马宗霍 1958.05.28

1936.01.18,1936.04.29,1936.07.07,1936.
07.19,1936.07.22,1936.08.28,1936.10.
30,1936.11.16,1937.01.01,1937.01.06,
1937.02.03,1937.02.16,1937.02.19,1937.
04.13,1937.06.12,1937.07.16,1945.03.
02,1945.03.08,1945.10.19,1945.11 中,
1945.12.29,1946.02.18,1946.08 下,
1946.11 - 12,1946.12.26,1947.01.15,
1947.03.22,1947.04.04,1947.05.08,1947.
05 上,1947.11.20

沈履(字茀斋) 1936.08.17,1937.07.07,
1937.07.13,1937.07.14,1937.07.16,1937.
07.21,1937.07.23,1937.07.25,1937.07.
27,1937.12 中下,1947.11.07,1948.01.14

沈乃正(字仲端) 1942.03.31

沈仁培(字益三) 1919.01.03

沈瑞麟(字砚裔) 1927.08.25,1927.09.03

沈士本 1961.12.11

沈士华 1943.01.11

沈晞 1931.07.12

沈性仁 1919.03.17,1930.10.10,1933.11.
19

沈学植 1944.11.29,1947.05.24

沈雁冰(茅盾) 1913.09,1949.11.28,1950.
04.19,1950.11.27

沈怡(沈景清) 1964.05.05

沈亦云(沈性真,黄郛夫人) 1921 春,
1922 春,1933.11.15,1933.11.19,1962.
05.20,1962.07.31

沈尹默(沈君默) 1929.10.11,1930.03.30,
1931.05.18,1931.06.04,1931.08.11,1931.
09.21,1932.01.10,1932.07.02,1932.12.
30,1933.12.10,1935.06.04,1945.03.02,
1945.03.08,1953.03.05

沈兆奎(字无梦) 1932.02.04

沈志荣 1953.09.22

沈仲章(字亚工) 1935.02.24,1936.10.23,
1938.01.11,1938.03.29,1938.04.18,1938.
05.06

沈宗濂 1955.03.05

沈宗畸(字太侔) 1958.03.14,1958.03.21

沈祖荣(字绍期) 1925.04.12,1925.04.19,
1925.05.27,1925.07.06,1928.01.06,1928.
12,1929.01.29,1929.02.01,1929.03.08,
1929.03.25,1929 夏,1929.05 中,1929.05
下,1929.08.29,1931.04,1931.05 中下,
1933 春,1933.06 中,1933.08.28,1933,
1934.03.26,1935.02.16,1935.02.22,1935.
03.01,1936.05 上,1936.07.19,1936.07.
22,1936.07 - 08,1936 夏,1939.01.19,
1939.03.07,1943.03.16,1943.09.08,1944.
05.05,1944.05.06,1944.06.03,1944.07.
16,1944.09.16,1944.11.29,1945.03.23,
1945.10.23,1951.02.27,1952.12.03

施嘉干(施衍林) 1956.04.24,1956.05.03

施嘉炀 1930.02.16,1938.04.19,1946.04

施绍常(字伯彝) 1962.11.21,1962.12.12,
1963.01.25,1963.02.12,1963.02.18

施廷镛 (字凤笙) 1924.07.03,1925.08.
20,1928 春,1929.01.29,1929.01.30,
1929.02.24,1932.01.10,1933.08.04,1933.
08.22,1935.01.06,1937.06.26

施维枢 1961.12.11

施友忠 1956.08.04,1959.08.12

施赞元(字君翼) 1919.07.30

施增玮 1963.09.14

施肇基(字植之) 1925.05.27,1929.06.29,
1934.05.27,1935.05.14,1937.11.18,1938.

02.08,1938.02.17,1938.02 中,1938.02.
22,1941.07.03,1960.07.19,1960.12.28

施肇燮(字德潜) 1945.07.27

石瑛(字蘅青) 1933.10.11

石友三 1936.10.14

石璋如 1936.09 下,1944.09.15

石志泉(字友儒) 1947.09.25

石志仁 1947.05.08

石作玺(字尔玉) 1925.08.20

时为述 1961.11.27

史克定 1962.07.31

史量才(史家修) 1933.07.15,1933.08.28

史之照 1925.08.04

舒楚石 1934 秋,1936.06.14

水世芳(高罗佩夫人) 1954.12.22

宋长洞(字瀛洲) 1935.02.08

宋春舫 1918.07.30,1930.04

宋联奎(字聚五) 1963.01.26

宋琳(号紫佩) 1929.05.05,1929.07.08,
1937 夏,1938.03.03,1938.03.31,1938.
05.13,1949.01.14,1950.05.15

宋美龄 1928.07.19,1939.03.01

宋青萍 1929.01.29

宋晞(字旭轩) 1955.03.14,1955.03 中,
1956.05.16,1956.07.17,1957.12.12,1960.
01.26,1960.04.06,1962.02.26,1962.05.
14,1963.03.11,1963.04.30,1963.06.20,
1963.10.24,1964.01.13,1964.01.15,1964.
01.26,1964.01.29,1964.02.08,1964.02.
23,1964.03.05,1964.03.31,1964.04.03,
1964.04.07,1964.05.10,1964.06.01

宋兴愚 1933.11.19

宋哲元(字明轩) 1936.12.05,1937.07.13

宋子良 1938.05.08

宋子文 1935.01.11,1940.07.29,1943.01.
11,1945.12.28,1946.02.18

苏秉琦 1950.11.27

苏甲荣(字演存) 1926.12.06

苏健文 1940.05.28

苏开文 1961.01.25,1961.04.20

孙宝琦(字慕韩) 1926.08.03,1926.09.23,
1926.10.13

孙传芬(孙宝明) 1948.01.14,1948.02.13

孙大雨(孙铭传) 1931.10.08

孙宕越 1964.01.13,1964.01.15,1964.01.
26,1964.01.29,1964.04.03

孙德中 1963.02.23,1963.03.18

孙桂籍 1963.02.04

孙海波(字涵溥) 1935.11.04,1936.02.01,
1937.06.30

孙洪芬 1929.08.30,1929.09,1929.10.07,
1930.03.30,1930.10.22,1931.05 中下,
1931.10.09,1932.02.16,1932.06.09,1932.
09.21,1933.04.27,1933.05.26,1933.12.
06,1933.07 上,1933.12.06,1934.02.20,
1934.12.10,1935.02.08,1935.04.04,1935.
10.02,1935.11.23,1936.02.27,1936.05.
25,1936.09 下,1936.12.29,1936.12.31,
1937.01.06,1937.03.29,1937.04.13,1937.
05.17,1937.05.22,1937.06.12,1937.06.
17,1937.07.16,1937.07.21,1937.07.23,
1937.07.27,1937.09.06,1937.09.14,1937.
09.20,1937.10.04,1937.10.05,1937.10.
09,1937.10.25,1937.11.18,1937.12.27,
1938.01.05,1938.01.11,1938.01.15,1938.
01.17,1938.01.24,1938.01.26,1938.01.
27,1938.02.08,1938.02.13,1938.02.14,
1938.02.15,1938.02 中下,1938.02.17,

1938.02.18, 1938.02 中, 1938.02.22, 1938.02.23, 1938.03.06, 1938.03.11, 1938.03.31, 1938.04.05, 1938.04.13, 1938.04.29, 1938.05.06, 1938.05.07, 1938.05.10, 1938.05.13, 1938.05.16, 1938.05.18, 1938.05.19, 1938.05.20, 1938.11.13, 1938.11.15, 1938.12.06, 1938.12.30, 1939.01.21, 1939.01.24, 1939.03.08, 1939.04.20, 1939.05.02, 1939.05.19, 1939.05.25, 1939.06.30, 1939.09.13, 1939.12.10, 1939.12.13, 1940.01.02, 1940.03.21, 1940.06.10, 1940.09.02, 1940.10.14, 1940.11.22, 1941.02.03, 1941.02.08, 1941.04.08, 1941.04.15, 1941.05.14, 1941.07.03, 1941.07.15, 1941.09.12, 1941.10.30, 1942.12.31

孙建　1963.01.06

孙楷第(字子书)　1931.06.30, 1933.01.10, 1933.03, 1933.09.14, 1935.05.18, 1935.10.02, 1937.01.01, 1937.04.03, 1937.05.18, 1937.05.22, 1937.09.14, 1939.08.18, 1939.11.04, 1940 夏, 1940.07.29, 1940.09.02, 1940.10.07, 1945 冬, 1947.05 上, 1948.01.14, 1948.02.13, 1953.03.05, 1953.07.15, 1953.12.15

孙科(号哲生)　1933.07.15, 1933.08.28, 1939.05.22, 1949.03.07, 1949.03.18

孙禄卿(陈立夫夫人)　1941.06.03

孙人和(字蜀丞)　1927.10.06, 1933.06.09, 1935.01.29

孙守全　1960.01.01, 1960.06.06

孙述万(字书城)　1933.12.06, 1937.12.27, 1938.01.05, 1938.01.11, 1938.01.17, 1938.02.03, 1938.02.18, 1938.02.22, 1938.03.06, 1938.03.31, 1938.12 底, 1939.03.18,

1939.04.15, 1939.09.13, 1939.11.04, 1939.12.10, 1940.01.02, 1940.01.07, 1940.02.07, 1940.04.27, 1941.08.09, 1942.02, 1944.05.05, 1944.05.06, 1945.11.05, 1964.01.23

孙宵舫　1960.06.20

孙心磐　1925.04.26, 1929.02.01

孙宣(字公达)　1930.04.09

孙学悟(字颖川)　1939.03.08

孙研　1960.01.01, 1963.01.06

孙元庆(字舲雨)　1963.11.09

孙越崎(孙毓麒)　1947.01.15

孙云畴　1950.11.27, 1951.02.27

孙云铸(字铁仙)　1938.04.19, 1950.11.27

孙兆年　1963.04.05, 1963.05.04

孙拯(字恭度)　1952.07.04, 1955.03.30

孙中山　1925.03.19, 1929.05 中, 1946.11.18, 1959.12.04, 1959.12.17, 1960.01.04, 1960.02.13, 1960.02.18, 1960.03.03, 1960.03.17, 1960.03 下, 1960.07.18, 1961.01.11, 1961.04.12, 1961.06.16, 1961.07.29, 1961.12.21, 1962.04.23, 1962.12.11, 1963.02.23, 1963.02.24, 1963.11.12, 1964.01.21, 1964.02.22

孙壮(字伯恒)1929.11.07, 1929.12.09, 1930 夏, 1932.11.19

T

台静农　1934.02.21, 1935.06.04

谈荔孙(字丹崖)　1929.11

谭葆慎(字敬甫)　1945.07.31

谭炳训　1946.10

谭伯羽(谭翊)　1955.04.17, 1955.04.18, 1958.04.06, 1958.04.11, 1960.08.15, 1964.

1933.11.19，1933.11.20，1934.02.13，1934.
02.18，1935.12.02，1938.12.18，1939.04.
13，1939.09，1939.10.26，1944.02.21，
1945.10.11，1947.02，1949.03.18，1960.06.
06

陶鹏飞　1954.11.18

陶维大　1954.07.11，1956.06.07

陶希圣（陶汇曾）　1935.05.18，1936.10.18，
　1936.12.29，1948.10.24

陶湘（字兰泉）　1925.05.27，1930 夏，1932
　夏，1933.03.21，1933.04.18，1937.02.19

陶行知　1925.04.25，1925.05 中上，1925.
　05.27，1925.07.06，1928.12，1929.01.28，
　1929.02.01

陶曾谷　1933.11.19，1937.06.17，1964.08.
16

陶洙（字心如）　1935.01.14

滕固（字若渠）　1936.06.14，1936.12.24，
　1939.03.01，1940.01.04，1940.11.11，1957.
03.25

田洪都（字京镐）　1928.12.23，1929.01.13，
　1929.02.24，1929.03.31，1932.01.10，1933.
　03.09，1933.03.13，1933.08.04，1933.08.
　22，1933.12.17，1933，1935.01.06，1935.
　02.17，1935.05.04，1935.09.22，1936.01.
　05，1936.06.15，1936.07.19，1937.03.07，
　1937.06.12

田九德（字玉如）　1925.08.20

田培林（字伯苍）　1947.11.11，1947.11.21

田兴智　1955.04.09

田志康　1964.02.23，1964.03.05

童冠贤（童启颜）　1936.01.18

童明道　1938.08.14

童世纲（字敦三）　1944.05.05，1944.05.06，

1956.05.10，1960.04.12，1961.10.09，1962.
03.30，1962.04.06，1963.01.08，1963.02.10

童锡祥（字季龄）　1925.11.21，1949.02.02，
　1952.07.04，1955.05.02，1955.05.05，1955.
　11.19，1957.04.17，1958.05.31

童养年（童寿彭）　1948.02.15

涂凤书（字子厚）　1930.06.22

屠孝实（字正叔）　1925.11.06

W

万国鼎（字孟周）　1928.12，1929.02.01

万斯年（字稼轩）　1938.03.11，1938.11.15，
　1938.12.14，1938.12.20，1938.12 底，1939.
　04.07，1939 冬，1940.01.03，1941.09.15，
　1941.11 上，1942.11.14，1943.06.22，1943.
　06.28，1943.06.30，1943.07.08，1943.08.
　12，1943.11.22，1943.12.11，1946.10.21

万兆之　1935.04.16

汪采雍　1949.03.06

汪长炳（字文焕）　1929.06.23，1930.01.05，
　1931.04.05，1931.06.01，1932.01.10，1932.
　02.16，1932.09.24，1933.05.17，1933.12.
　22，1934.05.22，1934.05.23，1934.05.29，
　1934.06.02，1934.11.05，1935.02.22，1935.
　04.13，1935.05.02，1935.05.04，1936.03.
　27，1937.05.22，1940.04.11，1944.05.05，
　1944.05.06，1944.11.29，1947.05.24，1958.
03.29

汪大燮（字伯唐）　1925.09.29，1926.10 初，
　1926.10.13，1926.12.08，1927.05.21

汪德昭　1937.08.22，1937.09.20，1937.12.
　12，1946.01.26，1947.04.01，1947.04.09

汪季千（汪一驹）　1958.03.15，1963.07.12

汪精卫（汪兆铭）　1925.08.04，1925.09.29，

王宪钟　1962.01.29

王向宸　1947.05 上,1947.08.03,1947.08.08

王向荣　1932.06 中

王孝慈(王立承)　1936.08.18

王孝缉(字筱晋)　1935.01.19,1935.05.09,1935.08.31,1936.05.05,1936.07.07,1936.10.30,1937.02.03,1937.07.16,1947.04.04,1947.10.14,1948.11.09

王欣夫(王大隆)　1936.04.08

王新民　1939.10.08,1939.11.18,1939.12.03,1940.01.02,1940.01.14,1940.01.24,1940.03.20,1940.04.11,1940.04.27,1940.06.12

王信忠　1939.02.15,1939.10.26,1943.10.01,1943.10.31

王兴甫　1933.07.03

王星拱(字抚五)　1936.01.18

王醒吾　1947.01.19

王亚徽　1962.01.16

王瑶卿(字希庭)　1947.08.03

王彦威(字弢夫)　1928.11.01

王冶秋　1949.02.10,1949.11.28,1950.11.27

王揖唐　1931.04 初,1936.06.30

王一亭　1936.12.24

王伊同(字斯大)　1949.03.26,1958.03 初,1958.05.31,1958.09.23,1960.02.20,1962.10.31,1963.01.02,1963.01.08,1963.01.18,1963.01.31,1963.02.14,1963.03.20,1963.05.21,1963.05.31,1963.06.13,1963.07.02,1963.07.08,1963.07.09,1963.07.12,1963.08.08,1963.09.14,1963.11.09,1964.01.09,1964.05.15,1964.07.15

王宜晖　1933.11.15,1933.11.20,1935.05

王隐三　1952.12.03,1954.12.21

王庸(字以中)　1931.06.06,1935.05.02,1935.05.18,1935.06.24,1935.11.04,1936.07 上,1936.10.17,1946.01.27,1946.10.21,1950.12.23

王幼侨(字幼侨)　1936.07.22,1936.09.23

王毓铨　1945.07.08,1949.04.20,1950.03.04,1950.07.07,1950.09.25,1956.06.07,1956.06.26

王育伊(字育伊)　1935.09.22,1938.11.15,1938.12 底,1939.01.10,1939.06 上,1939.06.29,1939.10.16,1940.04.11,1943.11.22,1944.05.05,1945.10.19,1945.12.01,1946.11.04,1949.01.15,1950.01.06,1950.04.08,1950.11.26

王原真　1938.11.03,1938.11.14

王云槐　1945.08.13,1945.08.15

王云五(号岫庐)　1928.12,1929.02.01,1929.03.08,1929.08.29,1929.08.31,1933.07.13,1933.08.14,1933.09.12,1933.10.12,1933.10.24,1933.10.25,1933.11.06,1933.12.29,1934.01.04,1934.01.12,1935.02.16,1935 夏,1936.09.11,1937.01.05,1937.01.09,1937.04.27,1937.11.12,1937.12.12,1939.09.30,1940.06.10,1943.10.14,1944.11.29,1947.11.03,1947.11.18,1953.05.07,1957.10.15,1962.07.11,1962.07.21,1962.09.13,1962.09.17,1962.10.13,1963.08.25

王芸生(王德鹏)　1935.07.26,1947.05 中,1953.03.05

王泽民　1936.10.14

王曾思(字念劬)　1935.05.14

01.15,1948.01.17,1948.01.29,1948.02.
09,1948.02.13,1948.05.11,1948.06.06,
1948.12.20,1948.12.23,1948.12.26,1949.
01.03,1949.01.08,1949.01.14,1949.01.
15,1949.01.25,1949.02.10,1949.02.20,
1949.03.18,1949.03.28,1949.03.29,1949.
04.01,1949.04.12,1949.06.15,1949.07.
19,1949.11.26,1949.11.28,1950.01.06,
1950.01.19,1950.02.02,1950.02.04,1950.
02.05,1950.03.04,1950.03.10,1950.03.
23,1950.04.08,1950.04.19,1950.04.27,
1950.05.15,1950.07.07,1950.09.25,1950.
11.27,1951.02.27,1951.12.14,1952.01.
25,1952.11.16,1953.10.12,1953.12.15,
1954.02.05,1954.03.16,1954.04.06,1954.
05.24,1954.06.13,1954.08.24,1954.09.
10,1954.12.21,1954.12.25,1955.01.26,
1956.06.26,1957.03.17,1958.02,1958.03.
22,1958.04.04,1960.02.01,1960.09.17,
1960.09.25,1960.10.04,1963.09

王祖彝(字念伦)　1934.01.12,1936.03.20,
1937.08.02,1937.09.20,1945.12.01,1947.
05.14,1949.01.08,1949.01.15,1949.06.
15,1950.01.06,1950.04.19,1950.05.15

王缵绪(字治易)　1939.05.22

韦荣乐　1955.03.15

魏宸组(字注东)　1960.07.19,1960.12.17

魏道明(字伯聪)　1951.11.12,1963.12.11,
1964.01.10

魏鸿纯　1936.09 下

魏建功　1931.06.30,1933.06.09,1935.05.
18

魏喦寿　1961.09.17

魏文彬(字雅庭)　1931.01.23

魏学仁(字乐山)　1942.12.04,1943.01
初,1945.10.30

卫青心　1952.06.16,1963.03.08

卫挺生　1925.11.06,1955.11.19

卫士生　1937.12.05

温广汉　1948.04.14

温源宁　1928.05.27,1928.12.21,1930.02.
16,1931.10.08,1939.09.13,1942.12.04,
1945.12.01

闻钧天(字亦遵)　1945.10.24

闻汝贤　1963.06.22

闻一多(闻家骅)　1925.11.06,1925 冬,
1926.03 上,1936.06.12,1944.07.06

闻宥(字在宥)　1938.11.13,1939.09,1939.
11.29,1939.12.27,1939.12.29,1940.04.27

翁独健(翁贤华)　1938.12.20,1940.04.27

翁文灏(字咏霓)　1929.01.04,1929.01.13,
1929.06.29,1929.08.14,1929.08.21,1929.
09.25,1931.01.26,1931.06.30,1932.02.
26,1932.07.02,1932.12.30,1933.03.01,
1933.12.10,1933.12.17,1935.01.11,1935.
05.18,1935.12.19,1937.03.06,1939.01.
10,1940.11.16,1940.11.22,1940.12.10,
1940.12.22,1941.04.19,1942.10.08,1942.
10.18,1942.11.29,1942.12.06,1942.12.
17,1943.01.02,1943.06.02,1944.09 中
下,1945.06.15,1946.07.07,1946.10.18,
1947.01.11,1947.05.25,1947.09.25,1948.
05.01,1948.10.24,1948.11.23,1948.11.
29,1949.01.07,1950.02.05,1950.02.09,
1950.03.04

邬保良　1957.03.26

吴承仕(字检斋)　1928.11

吴椿　1956.05.19

06.22,1937.06.24,1937.07.21,1937.07.
22,1937.07.23,1937.07.25,1937.08.03,
1937.11.16,1937.11.19,1937.12 中下,
1938.01.24,1938.01.28,1938.01.29,1938.
01.30,1938.02.12,1938.04.12,1938.08.
14,1938.08.15,1938.08.16,1938.09.21,
1938.09.24,1938.10 中,1938.10 中下,
1938.10.23,1938.10.31,1938.11.01,1938.
11.02,1938.11.03,1938.11.10,1938.11.
14,1938.11.19,1939.03.25,1939.03.28,
1939.07.01,1939.07.05,1939.07.20,1939.
08.01,1939.09.17,1939.09.28,1940.01.
25,1940.02.06,1940.02.21,1940.03.08,
1940.03.10,1940.03.27,1940.03.31,1940.
05.06,1940.05.24,1940.06.18,1940.08.
28,1940.09.13,1941.04.27,1943.10.28,
1943.11.16,1943.11.23,1946.11.04

吴南如(字炳文) 1934.09.07,1934.09 中
上,1946.07 下

吴南轩(吴冕) 1931.06.24

吴讷孙 1949.04.06,1961.10.05,1961.10.
26,1963.01.07

吴瓯 1948.02 下,1948.04.27,1948.05.15,
1948.05.19

吴佩孚(字子玉) 1936.06.30

吴佩南 1943.06.22

吴屏 1933.05.04

吴其昌(字子馨) 1929.10.25,1931.11.23,
1931.11.26,1936.07.22

吴奇伟(字晴云) 1947.11.07

吴潜甫 1931.01.19

吴权 1945.07.26,1962.07.31,1963.09.14

吴荣华 1947.04.04

吴世昌(字子臧) 1933.11.19,1937.04.03,

1955.04.14,1960.08.05,1960.09.25,1960.
10.04,1963.08.08,

吴叔班 1962.07.31

吴铁城(字子增) 1931.06.24,1931.07.02,
1933.08.28,1935 夏

吴廷燮(字向之) 1930.01.27,1935.11.04,
1937.02.16

吴婉莲 1953.09.12

吴维健 1956.10.14

吴文津 1951.07.28,1955.03.05,1955.03.
22,1955.07.03,1955.08.05,1960.04.12,
1960.07.18,1963.01.03,1964.10.21

吴文俊 1962.01.29

吴文藻(字渭樵) 1917.11.10,1935.12.02,
1938.12.20,1939.06.11,1939.09,1947.
02,1947.04.25

吴宪(字陶民) 1953.09.12,1953.09.19,
1953.09.22

吴相湘 1959.12.04,1961.05.12,1962.01.
29,1962.07.31

吴祥麟 1933.10.11

吴秀峰 1945.09.08

吴砚农 1938.01.05

吴贻芳 1947.09.15

吴瀛(字景洲) 1926.08.03,1926.09.23,
1926.10 初,1926.10.13,1926.12.02,1926.
12.06,1926.12.08,1926.12.09,1926.12.
17,1927.06 中,1927.08.18,1927.08.25,
1927.08.26,1927.09.03,1928.06.21,1929.
05 中,1931.01.26,1931.06.04,1933.01.
13,1933.01.25

吴应 1953.09.12

吴有训(字正之) 1938.04.19,1938.12.06,
1945.06.15,1946.04,1946.07.07,1946.10.18

09.29,1928.10.17

严一萍　1962.12.05,1963.01.18

严智开(字季冲)　1925.11.06,1935.05.18,
1936.07.19,1936.07.22,1936.12.24

严智怡(字慈约、持约)　1919.09.09,1919.
11.15

颜福庆(字克卿)　1933.03.27,1939.03.01

颜惠庆(字骏人)　1925.05.08,1925.05.27,
1925.06.02,1925.07.06,1926.07.12,1926.
09.06,1926.09.18,1926.09.23,1926.10.
11,1926.10.13,1926.11.30,1926.12.09,
1927.05.21,1927.08.25,1928.10.17,1929.
01.04,1929.01.21,1930.10.25,1931.01.
23,1934.02.21,1941.02.02,1941.04.08,
1942.04.21

颜任光(字耀秋)　1958.09.29,1958.10.03

颜泽霱　1938.01.05,1938.01.11,1938.02.
03,1938.02.18,1938.02.22,1938.12.30,
1939.02.15,1944.05.05,1944.05.06

阎文儒(字述祖)　1944.09.13,1948.05.05

阎振兴　1960.07.19,1960.09.19

阎宗临　1954.03.04

燕树棠(字召亭)　1926.12.06,1927.01.26,
1939.07.19

晏阳初　1939.03.01

杨丙辰(杨震文)　1928.06.10,1930.02.16,
1933.05.04,1936.03.28

杨步伟　1949.01.31,1949.03.13,1949.04.
17,1951.02.27,1951.03.27,1952.06.15,
1952.06.18,1954.07.16,1954.08.26,1954.
11.28,1954.12.14,1955.01.05,1955.01.
15,1955.01.20,1955.02.20,1955.03.04,
1955.05.19,1955.08.15,1957.04.05,1957.
04.24,1960.07.11,1961.02.01

杨殿珣(字琚飞)　1935.09.22,1937.01,
1940.01.24,1940.05.18,1940.08.19,1940.
10.07,1948.07.30,1949.01.14

杨鼎甫(字维新)　1926.07.20,1928.08.24,
1929.05.11,1933.11 上,1933.11 中,
1933.11.29,1933.11.30,1933.12.07,1934.
02.10,1935.11.27

杨端六(杨超)　1933.06.17,1957.03.26,
1962.04.27,1962.11.29

杨铎　1937.07.16

杨光弼(字梦赉)　1919.02.24,1919.02.28,
1919.03.07,1919.09.09,1919.12.01,1930.
10.10,1935.10.17,1937.05.22,1946.12.
11,1947.09.10,1947.09.25,1947.11.12,
1948.01.14,1948.02.17,1948.02.18,1948.
04.14,1948.05.02,1948.07.14,1948.10.
13,1948.11.10,1949.01.14

杨光祖　1962.01.11

杨虎城(杨彪)　1937.03.06

杨家骆　1963.03.05,1963.10.23,1963.12.
11,1964.06.06

杨觉勇　1960.02.09,1960.02.16

杨景时　1918.07.30,1918.12 中,1919.05.
03

杨俊杰　1930.05

杨立诚(字以明)　1925.08.20,1929.03.08,
1929.07 中,1929.07 下,1929.10.18,
1929.10.22,1931.04,1933

杨立奎(字据梧)　1935.12.02,1937.07.13

杨联陞(杨莲生)　1945.03.24,1945.07.08,
1946.05.04,1949.04.06,1952.05 下,1953.
09.12,1953.09.19,1954.02.11,1954.02
中,1954.03.13,1954.03.26,1954.09.20,
1955.03.11,1955.03.27,1955.03.28,1955.

01.04,1944.06 底,1944.07.06,1949.02.
24,1955.04.09,1962.01.29

姚光(字凤石)　1933.09.30,1933.12.01,
1940.04.11

姚金绅(字书诚)　1933.08.04,1933.08.28,
1933.08.30

姚名达(字达人)　1940.06.12

姚莘农(姚克)　1940.06.04

姚寻源　1939.09

叶楚伧(叶宗源)　1929.02.01,1933.07.15

叶德辉(字奂彬)　1925.05.27

叶公超（叶崇智）　1920.08.26,1929.09
初,1930.02.16,1930.06.12,1931,1936.
06.12,1937.02.19,1939.02.15,1939.12.
16,1940.01.25,1940.06.19,1941.02.10,
1945.02.03,1945.07.30,1945.08.06,1945.
08.07,1945.08.13,1960.08.14,1960.08.
15,1961.01.16,1961.04.26,1961.05.03,
1961.05.15,1961.09.24,1962.02.24,1963.
01.04,1963.05.19

叶恭绰(字玉虎)　1925.05.27,1927.08.18,
1927.08.25,1927.09.15,1927.10.20,1927.
11.01,1928.03.03,1929.01.17,1929.01.
29,1929.02.23,1929.11,1930 夏,1932
夏,1933.05 下,1933.07.08,1933.07.15,
1933.08.03,1933.08.23,1933.08.28,1933.
09.30,1935.01,1935.03.27,1935.05.18,
1935.12.13,1936.07.19,1936.07.20,1936.
07.22,1936.12.24,1937.03.05,1937.05.
22,1937.05.24,1937.06.11,1937.06.14,
1937.06.19,1937.08.02,1938.10.03,1940.
09.24,1941.01.08,1941.05.14,1942 春,
1943.01.02,1962.09.15,1963.01.04

叶瀚(字浩吾)　1928.09.23,1930 夏

叶景华　1945.12.02

叶景葵(字揆初)　1940.09.24,1941.03.23

叶景莘(字叔衡)　1933.10.11

叶楷　1961.11

叶澜(字清伊)　1935.01.19,1935.05.09,
1935.05.30,1935.08.31,1936.05.05,1936.
07.07,1937.02.03

叶良才　1950.02.05,1950.02.09,1950.03.
04,1950.03.10,1950.05.06,1951.08.10,
1955.01.06,1955.09.08,1956.03.12,1957.
02.20,1957.03.01,1960.09.13,1960.09.
28,1961.02.08,1961.03.20,1961.03.27,
1961.07,1962.02.28,1962.03.12,1962.04.
03,1962.04.05,1962.07.18,1962.07.20,
1962.08.30,1962.10.02,1963.05.05,1963.
09.30,1964.03.13,1964.05.11,1964.05.
19,1964.09.10

叶企孙(叶鸿眷)　1925.11.06,1925.11.21,
1926.01.31,1926.07.24,1929.02.19,1929.
02,1929.09,1930.02.16,1930.03.30,
1931.09.21,1933.05.04,1933.11.15,1933.
12.06,1936.08.17,1937.06.17,1937.07.
03,1942.10.07,1943.01 初,1943.06.01,
1943.06.02,1947.05.10,1947.09.10,1948.
04.14,1949.08.15

叶峤　1962.05.16

叶惟宏　1955.10.05

叶渭清(字左文)　1932.12.24,1937.03.02

叶友梅　1962.10.22,1963.10.18,1963.11.
30,1964.01.29

叶正昌　1947.09.10

易培基(字寅村)　1924.12.22,1925.08.04,
1925.09.29,1926.10 初,1929.03.01,1929.
06.13,1929.11,1931.04.08,1931.06.24,

1956.05.19,1960.01.01,1960.04.06,1960.
04.20,1960.06.06,1962.04.03,1962.05.
12,1962.07.15,1962.08.18,1962.09.20,
1962.10.13,1962.12.11,1963.01.24,1963.
05.07

袁荣福(谢寿康夫人) 1933.07.08,1962.
03.08

袁荣礼 1949.01.14,1949.01.15,1953.09.
01,1955.10.22

袁世凯 1961.04.02

袁廷彦(字际云、霁云) 1895.03.25,1912
年,1919.06.23

袁希涛(字观澜) 1925.04.19,1925.05.27,
1925.07.06,1926.07.12

袁涌进 1935.02,1935.09.22,1937.07.07,
1938.03.15,1938.04.29,1946.01.27,1949.
01.15,1938.04.29,1946.01.27,1948.12.
26,1949.01.15

袁渊 1963.11.02

袁仲灿(字少虚) 1936.06.15

袁仲默 1960.11.21

岳良木(字荫嘉) 1930.09,1930.10.25,
1936.09.11,1937.09.20,1937.10.03,1938.
03.31,1943.02.20,1944.05.05,1944.05.
06,1944.11.29,1945.03.17,1945.03.20,
1945.10.06,1945.10.30

岳梓木(字精武) 1941.04

恽宝惠(字公孚) 1928.01.01

恽震(字荫棠) 1945.08.17

Z

曾葆清 1947.03.03,1947.03.20

曾广龄 1948.11.09

曾广勒(字治一) 1931.07.02,1932.05.24

曾纪泽(字劫刚) 1945.07.30,1945.08.02,
1959.01.08,1963.03.07,1963.03.18,1963.
04.16,1963.05.21,1963.04.16,1963.05.
21,1964.08.03

曾觉之(字居敬) 1933.11.28,1937.04.03,
1963.11.10,1963.11.14

曾克嵩(字履川) 1963.01.18

曾培光 1952.12.03,1957.03.21

曾琦(字慕韩) 1919.01.07,1919.02.27,
1919.06.13,1940.03.10,1951.01.19,1951.
02.16,1951.03.10,1952.12.03

曾宪斌 1951.02.16,1951.03.10,1962.10.
04

曾宪琳 1960.07.18

曾宪七 1953.09.22,1955.03.04,1955.12.
11,1961.03.29

曾宪三(字省盦) 1935.02.16,1936.01.05,
1936.11.16,1939.08.30,1940.01.02,1941.
07.15,1942.12.17,1944.03.08,1944.05.
01,1944.05.31,1944.08.09,1944.09.05,
1944.09.16,1944.11 下,1946.11 下,
1947.01.25,1947.02.01,1955.03.04

曾宪文(字郁若) 1931.05 中下,1935.12.
10,1935.12.13,1935.12.25,1936.02.06,
1937.06.05,1939.08.30,1952.04.28,1953.
09.12,1955.03.04

曾虚白(曾焘) 1942.12.04

曾约农 1957.01.28,1963.02.11,1963.05.
21,1964.08.03

曾昭安(字珹益) 1961.09.18

曾昭抡(字叔伟) 1936.08.17

曾昭燏 1940.01.19,1940.02 中下,1940.02
下,1940.08.26,1940.10.10,1940.10.20,
1947.10 上,1948.08.06,1950.11.27,1954.

31,1959.02.07,1959.08.18,1960.01.01,
1960.02.06,1960.02.13,1960.03.10,1960.
03.19,1960.08.03,1961.09.04,1962.01.
29,1962.04.29,1962.07.17,1963.01.04

张国淦(字乾若) 1933.03.01,1933.12.17,
1937.06.11

张果为 1964.03.05

张含英(字华甫) 1948.02.18,1948.04.14,
1948.11.10

张珩(字葱玉) 1947.06.09

张鸿渐 1948.11.10

张鸿列 1932.06 中

张鸿南(字耀轩) 1961.01.25,1961.04.20

张鸿书 1939.03.25

张继(字溥泉) 1925.08.04,1925.09.29,
1928.11.04,1928.11,1929.03.01,1929.03.
17,1929.05 中,1929.11.29,1929.11,
1930.02 上中,1930.03.30,1931.06.24,
1932.12.24,1933.07.15,1934.12.07,1937.
09.20,1939.03.01

张继泽(字恺臣) 1918.06.29,1919.02

张嘉谋 1925.08.20

张稼夫 1954.03.13

张见庵(张敬虞) 1930.03.30

张捷迁 1960.01.20

张敬 1938.09.24,1938.10 中下,1938.10.
23

张静江(张人杰) 1933.07.15

张炯 1933.10.09

张钧衡(字石铭) 1925.05.27

张君劢(张嘉森) 1926.07.13,1933.03.27,
1954.03.10,1955.05.09,1956.02.23,1956.
08.04,1958.05.15,1961.06.12

张君秋(滕家鸣) 1950.11.20

张琨(字次瑶) 1956.02.01,1957.03.21,
1960.07.05

张立流 1931.01.23

张厉生(字少武) 1944.07.06,1944.07.12

张明炜 1933.10.03

张乃维 1963.10.23

张乃燕(字君谋) 1933.07.08

张丕介 1955.08.27

张彭春(字仲述) 1925 春,1939.03 下,
1939.10.08,1940.06.21,1945.02.17,1945.
02.25,1955.05.07

张其昀(字晓峰) 1955.01.06,1955.02.18,
1955.02.23,1955.03.14,1955.03 中,1961.
09.17,1962.02.26,1964.07.15

张谦 1946.07 下

张蒨英 1955.02.07,1955.03.04,1955.03.
05,1955.08.02,1955.08.06,1955.08.22,
1955.08.31,1955.10.03

张芹伯(张乃熊) 1931.01.19,1933.09.30

张全新 1945.12.01,1947.07.04,1947.07.
08,1954.04.06,1957.07.24

张群(字岳军) 1928.07,1933.07.15,1937.
07.16,1939.03.01,1947.06.09,1947.09.
25,1947.11.03,1963.01.18,1963.02.12,
1963.02.18,1963.02.22,1963.02.27

张荣岳 1956.02.15

张若谷 1963.12.05,1964.02.04

张尚龄(字梦九) 1918.09.30,1918.10.21,
1919.01.07

张绍堂 1932.06 中

张申府(张崧年) 1914.04.08,1914 冬,
1918 夏,1918.09.03,1918.11 中,1919
冬,1920.07.01,1942 秋,1942.12.14,
1943.03.03,1944.05.05,1947.11.07

张似旅 1939.03 下,1939.04.18,1939.05.01,1939.05.10,1939.06.11,1939.06.20,1939.06.30,1939.07.06,1939.07.21,1939.07.27,1939.07.30,1939.08.10,1939.08.23,1939.08.30,1939.09.30,1939.10.08,1939.12.03,1940.01.02,1940.02.07,1940.02.25,1940.03.20,1940.04.08,1940.05.18

张寿崇 1949.01.15

张寿龄 1948 夏

张寿镛(字伯颂) 1941.03.27

张叔诚(张文孚) 1937.02.19

张天麟 1935.05

张廷谔(字直卿) 1946.01 上,1946.02.18

张庭济(字柱中) 1935.01.19,1935.05.09,1935.05.30,1935.08.31,1936.05.05,1936.07.07,1936.10.30,1937.02.03,1937.02.16,1937.07 初,1937.07.16,1938.01.11,1945.12.08,1947.03.22,1947.04.04,1947.04.19,1947.10.14,1948.07.26,1948.08.06,1951.03.15

张婉英 1937.11.16,1938.01.24,1938.01.28,1938.01.30

张维华(字西山) 1936.12.10

张苇村 1932.06 中

张文炳 1942.11.14

张我军(张清荣) 1936.12.05

张我忠 1949.01.15,1949.06.15

张奚若(张耘) 1926.01.29,1927.07.06,1930.02.16,1933.11.19,1935.12.02,1936.07.08,1936.12.29,1937.06.17

张相文(字蔚西) 1925.05.27

张馨保 1960.03.10,1963.01.04,1963.05.07,1963.07.30,1963.09.05,1964.10.21

张歆海(字叔明) 1925.11.03,1925.11.06,1949.05.07,1951.03.26,1951.03.27

张星烺(字亮尘) 1929.01.13,1929.09.25,1929.11,1932.12.30,1936.06.11,1937.06.12,1937.06.30,1947.05.10,1954.03.03,1954.03.04

张秀民(字涤瞻) 1931.06.06,1938.03.15,1949.01.14,1961.08.10,1961.08.24,1963.05.14

张学良(字汉卿) 1925.09.29,1931.04 初,1933.01.25,1937.03.06

张学铭(字西卿) 1931.07.02

张学训 1962.10.22,1963.10.18,1963.11.30,1964.01.29

张耀翔 1925.11.06

张一航 1930.01.05

张颐(字真如) 1926.03 初,1926.03 上,1930.02.16,1935.05,1948.12.21

张贻惠(字绍涵) 1925.11.06,1937.07.13,1937.07.14,1937.07.16,1937.07.21,1937.07.25,1937.07.27

张荫麟 1939.10.26,1943.03.03

张荫棠(字憩伯) 1930.04.11

张印堂(字荫棠) 1937.07.03,1949.08.15,1956.02.16

张寓锋 1939.04.07

张煜全(字昶云) 1918.07.30,1919.10.03,1919.12.01,1929.01.21,1929.11.29,1931.01.23,1935.03.27,1939.07.19

张元济(号菊生) 1925.05.27,1929.03.08,1929.11,1930.06 中下,1931.01.19,1932.03 初,1932.11.19,1932.12.13,1933.06.30,1933.07.03,1933.07.13,1933.08.03,1933.08.14,1933.08.15,1933.09 中下,1933.09.30,1933.10.24,1933.11.02,1933.

11.06,1933.11.29,1934.01 中,1935 夏,
1936.02.04,1936.02.08,1937.04.02,1937.
04.06,1937.04.27,1939.05.11,1939.09.
30,1939.09-10,1940.03.01,1940.03.14,
1940.03.25,1940.04.04,1940.04.18,1940.
05.03,1940.06.10,1940.09.24,1947.06.
13,1962.09.17,1963.05.25

张铖　1932.06 中

张云川　1935.03.05,1935.04.04,1935.04.
05

张允亮(字庚楼)　1927.12.03,1928.03.07,
1929.11.10,1931.04.08,1931.09.27,1932.
02.04,1935.09.22,1937.05.10,1937.06.
19,1937.12.21,1937.12.27,1938.01.26,
1938.02.08,1938.02.17,1938.03.03,1938.
03.11,1938.03.15,1938.03.24,1938.03.
31,1938.04.13,1938.04.29,1938.05.04,
1938.05.18,1940.07.02,1947.04.19,1948.
10.31

张泽熙(字豫生)　1917 夏,1917.07.26,
1919.10.11

张泽垚　1917 夏,1917.07.26

张增荣　1936.02.06

张兆智　1963.11.22

张振勋(字弼士)　1961.01.25,1961.04.20

张政烺(字苑峰)　1944.06 底,1944.07.
06,1946.01.02,1946.09.04,1948.03.07,
1948.05.11,1949.01.14

张正明(字伯达)　1957.03.02

张芝联　1950.07.07,1960.09.17

张之毅　1951.12.07

张志尚　1929.09.25

张仲翔　1936.01.18

张准(字子高)　1926.07.24,1929.08.21,

1933.11.15,1933.12.17,1937.07.03,1945.
11 中,1947.01.15

张宗昌(字效坤)　1928.06.13

张宗麟　1949.02.10

张宗骞　1940.03.20

张宗祥(号冷僧)　1931.01.19,1933.08.15

章楚　1963.01.08,1963.02.14,1963.05.17,
1963.09.14

章鸿钊(字演群)　1933.12.17,1937.02.16

章太炎　1957.08.09,1960.09.17

章桐(字警秋)　1928.12,1929.01.28,1929.
01.31

章新民　1935.02.16

章学诚(字实斋)　1940.04.27,1940.06.12

章益(字友三)　1939.03.07,1939.03.31,
1939.04.25

章钰(字式之)　1932.02.04,1932.12.24

章元美(字彦威)　1940.01.08

章元善(字彦驯)　1933.03.27,1933.11.15,
1933.12.14,1939.07.20

章篯(字仲铭)　1925.04.19

章珍馨　1961.04.09

章宗傅(字砚遗)　1935.08.31,1936.05.05,
1936.07.07,1936.10.30,1937.02.03,1937.
07.16

章宗尧　1959.02.07

赵承煆(字石民)　1926.07.24,1963.11.06

赵尔巽(字公镶)　1926.08.03,1926.09.23

赵丰田　1934.12.22,1936.06.29

赵赓飏　1962.10.06

赵国材(字月潭)　1916.09.12,1917.09.04,
1917.11.10,1918.03.15,1918.06.29,1919.
04 底

赵恒惕(字夷午)　1960.02.02

赵鸿谦　1933.08.30

赵家璧　1951.01.31

赵来思　1954.08.26

赵录绰(字孝孟)　1938.04.29,1938.05.04,
　1939.06.20

赵萝蕤(陈梦家夫人)　1944.12.28,1945.
　01.16,1945.02.03,1945.06.17,1960.06.20

赵梅伯　1934.05.29

赵明德　1963.08.31,1963.09-10

赵迺传(字述庭)　1949.01.10

赵迺抟(字廉澄)　1925.11.06,1948.10.24

赵青誉　1937.07.07

赵如兰　1950.08.30,1955.02.20,1963.05.
　31

赵儒珍(字席慈)　1935.01.19,1935.05.09,
　1935.05.30,1935.06.27,1935.08.31,1936.
　07.07,1936.10.30,1937.02.03,1937.07.
　16,1947.10.14,1948.11.09

赵善之　1939.01.24,1939.01.26

赵少昂　1956.01.25,1956.08.05,1957.01.
　12,1957.02.08,1963.10.14

赵士卿(字吉云)　1961.04.12

赵叔诚　1962.10.22,1963.03.05,1963.03.
　27,1963.04.07,1963.04.16,1963.04.30,
　1963.05.02,1963.05.04,1963.05.30,1963.
　06.10,1963.06.29,1963.07.01,1963.07.
　03,1963.08.25,1963.10.18,1963.11.30,
　1963.12.31,1964.01.29,1964.02.28,1964.
　04.03,1964.04.30

赵太侔(赵畸)　1930.04,1934.05.22,1937.
　07.16,1937.07.21,1937.07.27,1939.03.01

赵铁寒　1963.04.13

赵廷范(字锡九)　1937.02.06

赵万里(字斐云)　1928.04.28,1929.03.08,

1929.05.11,1929.11.10,1930.03.16,1937.
01.01,1931.04.08,1931.05.24,1931.06.
30,1931.09.27,1931.10.09,1931.12.14,
1932.02.04,1932.12.04,1932.12.24,1933.
06.09,1933.06,1933.07.13,1933.08.03,
1933.08.15,1933.08.23,1934.01.16,1935.
05.18,1935.11.04,1936.02.27,1936.08.
18,1936.08.28,1936.09.02,1937.01.01,
1937.02.16,1937.04.06,1937.05.10,1937.
05.18,1937.05.22,1937.06.14,1937.06.
15,1937.06.16,1937.07 中下,1937.09.
14,1939.08.17,1939.08.18,1940.01.19,
1940.01,1940.03.08,1940.06.19,1940.07.
12,1940.09.07,1940.10.07,1941.08.21,
1941.08 下,1942 夏,1945 冬,1946.11
下,1947.01.11,1947.04.19,1947.05.14,
1947.05 中,1947.09.12,1947.11.18,1948.
01.29,1948.02.11,1948.03.07,1948.05.
11,1948.07.20,1948.09.02,1948.12.23,
1949.01.08,1949.11.28,1950.01.06,1950.
01.19,1960.10.04

赵希贤(字又贤)　1935.12.10,1935.12.13,
　1936.01.28

赵小中　1955.05.19,1960.07.11

赵新儒　1932.06 中

赵兴国(字听民)　1938.03.15

赵学海(字师轼)　1942.11.02

赵荫厚　1949.01.15

赵友民　1938.04.19

赵元任(字宣仲)　1928.05.22,1929.05.11,
　1929.06.29,1929.08.21,1930.06.12,1930.
　10.10,1931.01.09,1931,1937.11.12,
　1938.02.02,1943.06.02,1944.07.06,1945.
　02.17,1945.10.11,1946.05.04,1949.01.

09.13,1941.03.27,1941.03.29,1941.10.
30,1946.10.21,1947.05.19,1947.06.09,
1947.06.10,1947.06.13,1947.06.20,1947.
07.12,1947.09.12,1948.07.26,1949.06.
15,1949.11.28,1950.01.06,1950.01.19,
1950.04.19,1950.11.27,1951.11.26,1954.
09.10,1955.01.26

郑宗海(字晓沧)　1919.02.16

郅玉汝　1963.09 上

钟安民　1963.11.14

钟福庆(字叔进)　1925.04.19,1925.04.23,
1925.05.27,1925.07.06,1928.12

钟慧英　1930.05.20

钟鲁斋　1956.05.19

钟荣光(字惺可)　1961.03.20

钟世铭(字蕙生)　1947.09.10,1947.11.12,
1948.01.14

钟天心　1933.10.11

周炳琳(字枚荪)　1913.09,1916 夏,1920.
07.01,1925.11.06,1929.05.12,1931.09.
21,1933.11.15,1934.02.12,1935.12.02,
1936.12.29,1937.09.06,1938.02.17,1938.
02 中,1938.04.19,1938.08.15,1938.10.
23,1947.02.09,1948.12.17,1964.01.08

周策纵　1953.11.01

周昌芸　1933.05.04

周传经　1934 秋

周达夫(周炅)　1944.07.07

周大文(字华章)　1931.07.02,1932.03
中,1932.05.24

周道济　1963.03.24,1963.06.29,1963.07.
01,1963.08.09,1963.11.30

周恩来　1939.02-03,1939.03.16

周法高(字子范)　1962.09.26

周馥(字玉山)　1930.12.06

周鲠生(周览)　1925.11.06,1940.01.14,
1940.05.14,1943.06.02,1945.06.15,1947.
05.25,1957.03.14,1961.09.22

周国贤(字希哲)　1926.04.18,1930.09.01

周鸿经(字纶阁)　1945.10.30,1946.04,
1947.05.25

周慧敏　1962.02.20

周今觉　1933.07.08

周连宽　1945.11.21

周良熙　1925.05.27

周美玉　1945.08.15

周淼　1936.06.14

周铭洗　1931.10.08

周慕西　1914 年冬,1918.02 初,1918.04.
19,1962.02.22

周培源　1960.10.04

周仁(字子竞)　1929.08.21,1935.11.23,
1936.02.20

周如松　1961.09.22

周汝诚　1943.11.22

周若南(曾琦夫人)　1951.02.16,1951.03.
10

周尚(字君尚)　1941.08.07

周世述　1961.02.15

周叔迦(周明夔)　1935.01

周叔廉　1939.04.09

周叔弢(周暹)　1937.04.06

周俟松　1941.01.08

周希丁(周家瑞)　1947.05.14

周宪章(字显承)　1945.09.10

周祥光　1957.12.02

周象贤(字企虞)　1964.08.16

周一良(字太初)　1946.11 下,1947.01.11

22,1947.11.27,1948.04.27,1948.05.15,
1948.05.19,1948.11.29,1948.12.03,1948.
12.08,1948.12.22,1951.07.28,1951.09.
28,1951.11.27,1953.05.07,1955.04.29,
1955.05.07,1955.05.19,1955.05.30,1955.
09.02,1955.11.27,1956.03.02,1961.01.
26,1961.09.17,1961.11.10,1961.11.27,
1961.12.21,1962.01.18,1962.01.29,1962.
02.22,1963.01.25,1963.02.04,1964.04.14

朱家健(字叔琦)　1931.06.01

朱家潽　1948.11.09

朱家濂　1948.11.09

朱家治(字慕庐)　1925.04.23,1925.04.26,
1925.08.20,1929.02.01

朱经农　1929.01.28,1937.09.06,1937.10.
25,1937.10.26,1960.10.07

朱其璜　1956.04.02

朱启钤(字桂辛)　1919.01.26,1928.03.03,
1930.09,1930.10.01,1930.10.25,1931.01.
26,1931.05.18,1931.06.24,1931.06.25,
1931 冬,1932 春,1932.05.24,1932 夏,
1933.01.13,1933.03.01,1933.03.21,1933.
07.15,1935.01.11,1935.05.18,1935.07.
25,1936.04 中上,1937.02.19,1937.10.
09,1946.10,1947.04.16,1950.01.19

朱庆澜(字子桥)　1931.08.11,1933.09.30,
1935.01

朱日珍　1936.01.05

朱深(字博渊)　1935.01.11,1935.07.25

朱师辙(字少滨)　1929.11.10,1931.04.08,
1931.09.27,1939.08.18

朱士嘉(字蓉江)　1930,1939.09.30,1939.
11.04,1939.12.10,1940.01.02,1943,1945
夏,1945.07.08,1945.10.11,1946.01.26,

1946.04.10,1946 夏,1950.09.25

朱世明(字公亮)　1946.01.15

朱树恭　1962.10.06

朱偰　1963.04.23

朱文长　1957.03.28,1958.04 上,1960.10.
07,1962.12.11,1963.07.08,1963.07.16,
1965.01.04

朱我农　1925.11.06

朱熙(字琛甫)　1930.04

朱希祖(字逷先)　1924.10.22,1926.08.03,
1926.12.06,1928.02.16,1928.02.22,1928.
04.20,1928.06.10,1928.11,1929.01.13,
1929.02.17,1929.03.10,1929.03.24,1929.
11.10,1929.11,1930.03.16,1930.04.08,
1931.04.08,1933.04.24,1936.01.18,1936.
06.14,1936.08.28,1936.09.02,1938.09.
13,1940.07.14,1944.09 中下,1960.09.17

朱孝臧(朱祖谋)　1925.05.27

朱锡龄(字继莓)　1928.06.10

朱偰(字伯商)　1936.01.18,1960.09.17

朱一鹗(字横秋)　1913.09,1919.07.06,
1919.07.22

朱义钧(字孟衡)　1949.02.20

朱有光　1937.07.07

朱友渔　1925.11.06,1931.01.23

朱自清(字佩弦)　1933.09.05,1937.10.13,
1938.08.15

竺可桢(字藕舫)　1929.08.21,1929.12
底,1932.10.27,1933.10.20,1933.10.21,
1935.08.14,1936.04.18,1936.07 上,1939.
03.08,1940.05 中下,1940.05.27,1940.06
下,1940.08.28,1940.11.04,1940.11.05,
1942.10 中下,1942.10.23,1942.11.03,
1942.12 中上,1942.12.21,1943.02.25,

外文人名

欧美人名

A

05.13,1957.05.16,1962.05.22,1962.11.16

Adolph, William H.(窦威廉) 1947.10.24

Allen, Young John(林乐知) 1962.09.29,
1962.10.01

Altree, Wayne 1952.08.12

Ambolt, Nils P.(安博特) 1929.12.07,
1929.12底

Ammon, Charles 1947.10.15

Anderson, Alice 1938夏秋

Anderson, Edwin H. 1925.05.27

Anderson, George L. 1960.03.10

Andrews, Roy C.(安得思) 1929.02.23,
1931.09.25

Angell, James R. 1935.03.05,1936.09.17,
1936.12.12,1937.02.17

Anner, Conrad W.(安那) 1927.09.01,
1929.05.11,1929.09.21

Arnaldo, Solomon V. 1945.05.20

Ashley, Frederick W. 1932.02.01,1932.09.
24

Aurobindo Sri 1956.04.08

Auster, Guido 1958.04.17

Awad, Mohamed 1945.05.20

Aydelotte, Frank 1945.01.08,1945.01.12

B

Bacot, Jacques 1927春,1940.04.08,1940.
04.11

Bagchi, Prabodh Chandra(师觉月) 1947.
03.29,1947.04.30,1947.09.15,1955.05.
27,1956.04.08

Bailey, Harold W.(贝利) 1952.01.18,
1952.01.22

Baker, John E.(贝克) 1929.06.29,1931.

01.09,1937.11.18,1937.11.18

Balazs, Étienne(白乐日) 1955.05.23

Balfour, Marshall C. 1939.05.19,1939.08.
08,1939.08.17,1939.08.28,1940.01.04,
1940.01.18,1940.05.31,1940.06.10,1940.
06.15,1941.01.13,1941.01.21,1941.01.
25,1941.02.10,1941.02.11,1941.02.18,
1941.03.20,1941.04.26,1941.04.28,1941.
05.06,1941.05.07,1942.12.31,1943.01.
04,1943.01.27,1943.02.04,1943.03.13,
1943.03.16,1943.03.30,1943.08.11,1944.
03.15,1945.04.01,1946.05.21,1946.11.
22,1947.04.24

Ball, A. D. 1947.03.03

Bandall, R. L. 1939.07.31

Barclay, Julius P. 1960.03.03

Barker, Ernest 1945.07.26,1945.09.13

Barnett, Arthur Doak 1963.11.13

Bary, William Theodore de(狄培理)
1962.10.23,1962.10.25

Basadre, Jorge 1944.03.16,1944.07.06

Bates, Miner S. 1938.08.02,1938.08.30,
1938.10.18

Bawden, Charles R. 1956.06.11

Baxter, Glen W.(白思达) 1963.03.20,
1964.01初,1964.03.14,1964.05.04,1964.
05.08

Beal, Edwin G. Jr.(毕尔) 1954.12.21,
1955.01.18,1957.03.21,1957.05.13,1958.
03.22,1959.02.14,1960.04.12,1960.07.
05,1960.07.10,1960.08.05,1961.04.29,
1962.01.29,1962.02.13,1962.02.19,1962.
03.05,1962.03.17,1962.04.23,1962.05.
15,1962.08.23,1962.09.29,1962.10.01

Boodberg, Peter A.(卜弼德) 1955.05.19, 1955.05.23, 1956.08.09

Boorman, Howard L.(包华德) 1956.06. 01, 1960.05.14, 1963.05.31, 1963.07.12

Borch, Herbert von(卜尔熙) 1929.11.29, 1931.10.20, 1934.08

Borton, Hugh 1960.02.29, 1960.03.08

Bostwick, Arthur E.(鲍士伟) 1925.04. 26, 1925.04.27, 1925.05.25, 1925.05.26, 1925.05.27, 1925.06.02, 1926.03 上, 1933 春, 1935.01.31, 1935.02.20, 1935.03.02, 1938.05.27

Bottore, De 1955.03.22

Bottu, Alphonse(玻杜) 1952.09.10

Bouchard, Maybelle 1947.03.04, 1947.11. 26, 1948.01.05

Bourne, Henry E. 1934.05.27

Bowen, Trevor(鲍文) 1939.12.13, 1945. 11.13, 1945.11.15, 1946.01.15, 1947.04.25

Bowman, John G.(鲍曼) 1938.09 底, 1939.02.13, 1940.12.20, 1941.01.08, 1941. 01.10, 1941.01.27, 1941.06.03, 1941.06. 04, 1941.07.29, 1941.08.11, 1941.11.05, 1943.02.16, 1945.03.02, 1945.03.08, 1945.04.02, 1945.04.05, 1945.04 上, 1945.05.01, 1945.05.28

Bownas, Geoffrey 1954.12.18

Boyd, Julian 1945.01.08, 1945.01.12

Boynton, Charles L. 1939.01.26, 1939.04. 15, 1939.04.29

Braceras, Elena 1945.05.20

Brandt, J. J.(卜郎特) 1956.12.01

Brazier, Beatrice 1954.08.24

Brazier, James R. 1954.08.24

Breycha-Vauthier, Arthur 1954.10

Brigham, Johnson(毕立汉) 1929.10.26

Brodie, Donald M. 1962.04.21

Brouillard, Georges(普意雅) 1932.10.04, 1933.02.27, 1933.03.01

Brown, Bonnar 1951.06.25, 1951.07.10, 1952.05.07, 1952.05.12, 1952.05.16, 1952. 05.17, 1952.06.30

Brown, Charles H.(布朗) 1943.11.22, 1944.02.11, 1944.03.08, 1944.03.11, 1944. 04.29, 1944.05.01, 1944.05.09, 1944.05. 24, 1944.05.31, 1944.06.03, 1944.06.14, 1944.06.30, 1944.07.03, 1944.07.29, 1944. 08.09, 1944.08.10, 1944.09.05, 1944.09. 16, 1944.09.20, 1944.10.02, 1944.10.25, 1944.10.31, 1944.11.24, 1944.11.29, 1945. 01.06, 1945.01.08, 1945.01.10, 1945.01. 13, 1945.01.16, 1945.01.31, 1945.03.17, 1945.03.20, 1945.03.23, 1945.04.17, 1945. 04 中, 1945.05.16, 1945.06 初, 1945.06. 13, 1945.06 下, 1945.07.05, 1945.10.06, 1946.01.14, 1946.01.18, 1946.01.28, 1946. 05.17, 1946.06.04, 1946.10.31, 1946.12. 10, 1947.01.11, 1947.01.13, 1947.01.21, 1947.02.01, 1947.02.13, 1947.03.05, 1947. 03.14, 1947.03.19, 1947.04.04, 1947.04. 09, 1947.11.05, 1947.11.26, 1947.12.15, 1948.01.05, 1948.01.15, 1948.01.16, 1948. 01.17, 1948.01.18, 1948.01.19, 1948.01. 22, 1948 夏, 1949.01.12, 1949.01.18, 1949.01.25, 1949.04.29, 1951 春, 1951.08. 05

Brownrigg, Beatrice 1939.06.30, 1939.09. 30

03,1956.06.28,1956.07.03

Eder, Matthias(叶德礼)　1948.06.06,1948.
07.26,1948.08.06

Edgerton, Franklin　1927 春

Edwards, Dwight W.　1961.02.06

Edwards, Evangeline　1950.10.24,1952.01.
18,1952.01.22

Eggleston, Frederick W.　1943.01.05

Eisenhower, Dwight David(艾森豪威尔)
1954.10.16

Ekvall, Robert B.　1960.02.15,1960.02.19,
1960.02.24,1960.02.29,1960.05.12,1960.
05.17,1960.05.19,1960.12.02,1962.03.22

Elisséeff, Serge（叶理绥）　1937.06.12,
1937.06.30,1939.09.30,1940.03,1940.04.
11,1943.03.06,1943.04.12,1943.08.25,
1944.07.12,1944.09.22,1945.01,1945.02.
25,1945.03.10,1945.04.26,1953.06 上,
1953.07.01,1953.08.13,1954.03.10,1954.
09.17,1954.09.20,1955.01.03,1955.05.
27,1956.03.09,1957.05.03

Empson, William(燕卜荪)　1952.01.25,

Engle, Carl　1934.05.27

Erkes, Eduard(何可思)　1956.06.28,1956.
07.03

Esdaile, Arundell　1934,1938.01.05

Eumorfopoulos, George A.(欧默福普洛斯)
1931.06.15,1935.03.27,1940.01.12

Evans, Carl　1944.11.24

Evans, Luther H.(埃文斯)　1944.11.24,
1944.11.29,1945.01.16,1945.01.31,1945.
02.02,1945.02.25,1946.04.30,1948.11.
30,1949.05.21,1949.06.21,1963.01.02,
1963.01.24,1963.09.11,1963.09.28,1963.

10.02,1963.10.11

Evans, Roger F.　1947.03.17,1947.04.10,
1947.04.24,1947.05.02,1947.05.04,1947.
05.08,1947.05.09,1947.05.16,1947.06.26

Everton, John S.　1960.02.16

Evreeva, Elena　1953 秋

F

Fackenthal, Frank D.　1934.04.25,1934.04.
26,1934.05.08,1934.05.20

Fahs, Charles B.(法斯)　1947.03.07,1947.
03.17,1947.04.09,1947.04.10,1947.04.
24,1947.05.02,1947.05.04,1947.05.08,
1947.05.09,1947.05.14,1947.05.16,1947.
06.26,1947.09.05,1947.09.25,1947.10.
06,1947.10.16,1947.10.20,1947.11.07,
1947.11.18,1948.01.08,1948.01.15,1948.
02.04,1948.02.09,1948.02.12,1948.03.
09,1948.03 中,1948.03.30,1948.05.22,
1948.05.23,1948.06.23,1948.07.31,1948.
08.17,1948.10.30,1948.11.12,1949.05.
02,1949.05.06,1949.05.19,1949.06.07,
1949.06.11,1949.06.15,1949.11.26,1949.
11.30,1949.12.08,1950.04.14,1950.04.
17,1952.12.30,1955.01.03,1955.01.18,
1959.02.20,1959.03.18,1959.04.04,1960.
02.23,1960.02.29

Fairbank, John K.(费正清)　1932 春,1939.
01.14,1939.02.07,1939.02.28,1939.03.
26,1939.04.11,1939.06.12,1939.06.15,
1939.07.12,1939.08.01,1939.10.09,1942.
10.07,1942.10.18,1942.10.28,1942.12.
02,1942.12 初,1942.12.04,1942.12.16,
1942.12.17,1943.01.04,1943.01.22,1943.

07.16，1950.10.03，1950.12.31，1951.07.

15，1962.03.08

Fosdick, Raymond B.　1939.01.20

Frank, J. O.　1938.11.14

Franke, Otto（福兰阁）　1932.06.07，1934.

08.23，1940.01.11，1950.05.07，1950.07.

16，1950.10.03，1950.12.31，1951.07.15

Franke, Wolfgang（傅吾康）　1937.06，1948.

09，1950.05.15，1950.05.20，1950.05.27，

1950.12.31，1954.09.26，1954.11.18，1954.

11.30，1955.01.20，1955.05.05，1955.05.

23，1958.03 下，1960.01.28，1962.12.12，

1963.01.10，1963.09.29

Fränkel, Hans H.（傅汉思）　1957.03.25，

1961.04.09

Fuchs, Walter（福克司、福华德）　1950.05.

27，1950.07.16，1950.10.03，1950.12.31，

1951.07.15，1954.09.26，1963.01.03，1963.

05.24，

G

Gabain, Annemarie von　1956.02.23

Gabrieli, Giuseppe　1935.01.11

Galt, Howard S.（高厚德）　1918.12.03，1918.

12.21

Gapanovich, John J.（噶邦福）　1946.11

下，1947.03.07，1947.06.26，1947.07.04，

1953.11.09，1953.11.26，1954.01.07，1954.

02.08，1954.04.06，1956.08.14，1956.12.

01，1956.12.17

Gardner, Charles S.（贾德纳）　1946.05.04，

1955.05.23

Garrett, John W.　1929.06.14

Gaskill, Gussie E.（加斯基尔）　1930.06.

26，1930.10.16，1930.11.07，1930.12.06，

1931.01.17，1931.08.04，1931.08.07，1931.

09.18，1931.11.16，1931.11.19，1932.12.

24，1933.02.15，1933.04.18，1933.05.17，

1934.04 上，1934.05.29，1934.06.02，1945.

01.13，1945.01.20，1945.06.11，1945.06.

19，1946.05.02，1946.05.13，1947.02.07，

1956.05.03，1956.09.08，1956.11.12，1957.

12.02，1958.01.31，1958.02.13，1958.02.

17，1958.02.24，1960.04.12，1960.06.10，

1960.06.15，1960.12.12，1961.03.21，1962.

03.29，1962.07.17

George, Albert Frederick Arthur　1945.08.

15

George, Anthony H.（周尔执）　1933.11.08

Gernet, Jacques（谢和耐）　1962.03.05

Gerould, James T.（吉罗德）　1928，

Gest, Guion M.（葛斯德）　1929.08.29

Gibson, Weldon B.　1951.08.08

Giles, Herbert A.（翟理斯）　1936.01.21，

1936.03.27

Giles, Lionel（翟林奈、小翟理斯）　1932

春，1936.02.17，1937.02.21，1937.07.19，

1937.08.02，1938.03.31，1939.03 下，1945.

08.13，1950.05.15，1955.03.15，1958.03.

22，1961.08.10

Gillette, H. M.　1948.01.08，1948.01.20，

1948.01.21，1948.02.12，1949.04.05，1949.

04.08，1949.04.26，1949.05.02

Gillis, Irvin Van G.（义理寿）　1928.05.03，

1928.05.25，1929.04.15，1929.08.20，1929.

08.29，1929.08.31，1930.09.17，1930.09.

20，1933.07.19，1937.11.11，1956.05.10

Givens, Willard E.　1947.03.03

Glanville, S. R. K.　1952.01.18

Glasenapp, Otto Max Helmuth von　1927
春

Godbey, Paul　1960.04.14

Godet, Marcel　1927.05.30，1939.02.24

Gomes, Luís Gonzaga（高美士）　1954.12.
21，1955.06.29

Gonzalez, Bienvenido Maria　1941.01.25

Goodrich, Luther C.（富路德）　1934.01.
08，1937.11.11，1947.03.17，1950.06.12，
1954.09.20，1955.05.07，1955.08.29，1956.
03.02，1956.03.26，1956.08.10，1957.02.
08，1958.03.22，1959.02.16，1960.01.12，
1960.06.20，1962.08.14，1962.10.18，1962.
10.23，1962.10.25，1962.10.28，1962.10.
31，1962.12.25，1963.02.21，1963.02.24，
1963.03.05，1963.03.12，1963.03.24，1963.
04.24，1963.05.22，1963.05.30，1963.07.
01，1963.07.12，1963.08.09，1963.09.04，
1963.10.02，1964.06.08

Gorham, Margaret　1949.09.27

Grabau, Amadeus W.（葛利普）　1932.05.
20

Grant, John B.（兰安生）　1937.04.13，1939.
01.19，1939.05.18，1943.01.27

Graves, Mortimer（格雷夫斯）　1934.05.
23，1934.05.27，1935.10.05，1936.06.04，
1936.06.15，1936.07.02，1936.07.11，1936.
08.27，1936.11.07，1936.11.16，1936.12.
01，1936.12.15，1937.09.28，1937.10.26，
1938.03.12，1938.05.27，1939.02.28，1939.
08.01，1939.12.13，1940.04.10，1940.04.
27，1940.06.04，1942.12.16，1943.10.31，
1944.02.21，1945.02.25，1945.04 中上，

1945.10.11，1945.10.17，1946.05.02，1947.
03.04，1947.03.07，1947.03.17，1948.07.
31，1948.08.17，1951.01.26，1952.08.13，
1960.01.12，1960.01.14，1960.02.01，1960.
02.03，1960.02.09，1960.02.12，1960.02.
16，1960.02.27，1960.10.10，1963.01.10

Gray, Basil　1961.11.10，1963.01.14，1963.
01.28，1963.02.25，1963.03.20，1963.07.08

Greene, Roger S.（顾临）　1929.01.04，
1929.01.05，1929.06.29，1929.09.21，1930.
10.10，1931.01.02，1931.01.09，1931.01.
23，1931.06.25，1938.06.25，1939.01.21，
1939.04 - 05，1939.05.03，1940.02.22，
1940.03.21，1940.03，1942.12.17，1943.03.
16，1943.08.11，1943.10.01，1944.09.05，
1945.01.06，1946.01.18，1946.01.28，1946.
06.04，1947.01.21，1947.04.04

Greene, Theodore M.　1945.05.28

Gregory, F. O.　1941.09.12，1941.10.30

Grinstead, Eric　1962.03.08，1962.03.15

Grousset, René　1955.03.15

Guignard, Marie-Roberte（Dolleans，杜乃
扬）　1934.06.30，1934.07 中，1934.08.
03，1934.09.28，1934.12.09，1935.05.02，
1935.06.26，1936.02 - 03，1937.07.01，
1937.08.08，1937.09.20，1938.02.10，1938.
03.31，1938.04.05，1938.05.13，1939.06.
20，1939.07.09，1939.07.17，1939.07.21，
1939.07.27，1939.07.30，1939.08.23，1939.
08.30，1939.09.30，1939.10.08，1940.01.
12，1940.02.25，1940.04.27，1940.07.02，
1955.02.15，1955.06.29，1957.04.10

Gulik, Robert Hans van（高罗佩）　1954.
12.22，1955.01.04

11,1962.06.28,1962.08.15,1962.10.19,
1963.03.14,1963.09.22,1964.12.23

Lowell, Abbott L.(罗威尔) 1932.02.26

Lowry, W. McNeil 1956.12.15

Luce, Henry R. 1941.05.20,1962.04.21

Lüders, Heinrich 1927 春

Ludington, Flora B. 1944.03.29

Lydenberg, Harry M.(莱登伯格) 1944.
04.07,1944.05.09,1944.06.27,1945.01.
06,1945.01.08,1945.01.10,1945.01.16,
1945.03.23,1945.06.05,1946.01.28,1946.
07.26,1946.11.05,1947.01.03,1947.01.
21,1947.02.13,1947.03.14

Lyon, Bayard(赖伯阳) 1953.11.01

Lytton, Victor B.(李顿) 1932.04.13

M

Maenchen-Helfen, Otto J. 1957.03.25,
1957.03.27

MacArthur, Douglas(麦克阿瑟) 1945.11.
15,1946.01.15

MacLeish, Archibald 1940.01.02,1940.01.
14,1940.05.14,1941.02.03,1943.10.01

MacMurray, John Van Antwerp(马克谟、马
慕瑞) 1929.01.21,1929.05.21,1963.05.
02

MacNair, Mary W. 1926.07.10,1937.04.17

Malcolm, Neill 1937.02.21

Maloney, Anthony 1956.02.03

Manuel, Leonard A. 1948.06.28,1948.09.
03

March, Benjamin F., Jr. 1935.03.04

Marconi, Guglielmo(马可尼) 1933.12.04

Margoulès, Georges(马古烈) 1930.06.

23,1930.06.26

Marks, Lionel 1939.06.12,1939.08.01

Marsh, Daniel L. 1945.03.29

Marshall, John 1939.06.30, 1939.07.19,
1941.04.26,1941.04.28,1941.05.06,1941.
05.07,1945.03.18-19,1945.03.20,1945.
06.05,1945.06.13,1945.07 中,1945.10.
17,1946.01.29,1946.05.11,1946.12.10,
1947.03.11,1947.10.16,1948.01.08,1948.
01.20,1948.01.21,1948.02.12

Martel, Charles 1928.04.02, 1931.10.24

Martin, Fredrik R. 1956.07.03

Martin, Lawrence 1934.05.27

Martin, William 1933.03.27

Marx, Jean 1939.06.20,1939.07.09,1939.
08.10,1939.08.23,1939.08.30

Mason, Henry Lee, Jr. 1945.05.28

Maspero, Henri(马伯乐) 1954.09.10,
1955.11.24(25)

Masson, J. R. 1938.01.11

Masten, Floyd E. 1944.11.24,1944.11.29

Mathias, James F. 1954.11.09

Matthews, Troup 1951.02.27

Mattušová, Miroslava 1960.01.12, 1960.
02.24,1960.03.16

Maurette, M. Fernand(莫列德) 1934.07.
20

Maxwell, Robert 1962.10.01,1962.11.01

Maze, Frederick W.(梅乐和) 1941.05.14,
1941.05.20

McAleavy, Henry 1954.08.24, 1955.03.
15,1956.06.11

McCarthy, Daniel C. 1934.05.29

McCarthy, Richard M. 1956.01.15

Priestley, K. E.(皮理思)　1956.05.19

Pritchard, Earl H.　1962.06.15,1964.05.01,
1964.06.01

Pruitt, Ida(蒲爱德)　1957.03.29

Průšek, Jaroslav(普实克)　1959.11.08,
1960.01.12,1960.02.24,1960.03.16,1961.
04.01,1961.12.21,1963.05.05,1963.05.
21,1963.07.01,1963.09.05,1964.02.09,
1964.06.06,1964.06.16

Przyluski, Jean　1927 春

Pulleyblank, Edwin G.(蒲立本)　1956.01.
14,1958.07.28

Putnam, George H.(蒲特南)　1925.05.27,
1925.06.29,1925.09.12,1928.08.10,1929.
08.26,1929.09.04,1931.09.02,1931.10.
22,1932.02.01,1932.03.19,1932.04.21,
1934.05.27,1934.08.25,1934.11.05,1934.
12.19,1935.02.08,1935.12.18,1936.01.
27,1936.02.29,1936.06.04,1937.11.19,
1938.01.17,1938.04.02,1938.04.23,1938.
05.21

Putten, James Dyke van　1948.01.15

Q

Quigley, Harold S.(魁格雷)　1940.03.29,
1940.05.08

R

Radcliffe-Brown, Alfred Reginald　1939.
05.19,1939.06.11,1939.07.21

Rahder, Johannes　1927 春

Rajchman, Ludwig J.(拉西曼)　1934.05.
07,1964.08.25

Rattenbury, R. M.　1960.09.29

Read, Bernard E.(伊博恩)　1938.12.30,
1939.01.21,1939.04.15

Reclus, Jacques(邵可侣)　1931.10.08,
1932.12.30,1939.07.21,1939.08.10,1939.
08.23,1939.08.30,1954.04.06

Reece, Ernest J.　1945.02.07,1945.02.08,
1945.02.10,1945.06.30,1945.07.04

Reed, Robert B.　1955.07.18

Reichmann, Felix　1963.04.25,1963.05.04

Reid, John G.(李佳白)　1932.09.24,1940.
06.21

Reidemeister, Leopold　1956.07.03

Reinsch, Paul S.(芮恩施)　1961.04.02

Reismüller, Georg(莱斯米)　1929.01.28,
1929.01.29,1929.01.31,1929.03.31

Reischauer, Edwin O.(赖肖尔)　1956.03.
20,1960.02.29,1960.03.08

Remer, Charles F.(雷麦)　1935.04.02

Rhein, David(韩德威)　1933.1.20

Richardson, Ernest C.　1925.05.27

Rickett, W. Allyn　1954.01.27,1954.02.01

Riggs, Charles H.(林查理)　1938.10.18

Ringwalt, Arthur R.(林华德)　1939.12.13

Resillac-Roese, Robert de　1931.09.11

Roberts, Charles A.(饶培德)　1940.03.11,
1940.05.25,1940.06.06

Roberts, Martin A.　1926.09.07,1926.11.01

Robertson, James A.　1939.09.30,1939.11.
17,1939.12.03,1940.01.02,1940.01.14,
1940.04.27,1940.06.12

Rock, Joseph Francis Charles(洛克)　1939.
05.18,1940.04.08,1940.04.11,1940.05.
14,1956.02.01

Rockhill, William W.(柔克义)　1935.05.

11.05,1947.11.12

Shaw, Ernest 1933.07.13

Shotwell, James T.(萧特会) 1934.07.20,
1934.09.25,1939.02.28

Sickman, Laurence(史克门) 1932.12 上,
1932.12.07,1955.06.27,1955.06.30,1955.
07.05,1955.08.06,1955.08.22,1963.02.
25,1963.10.30,1963.12.11

Silcock, H. T. 1937.02.21

Sikorsky, Igor 1945.05.28

Simmons, William A. 1939.01.26

Simon, Walter(西门华德) 1924.05,1927
春,1929.05 下,1933.05.04,1933.11.20,
1934.08.23,1950.10.24,1950.11.24,1952.
01.18,1952.01.22,1952.11.28,1955.01.
21,1956.01.14,1956.06.11,1956.07.20,
1956.08.09,1960.11.04,1961.05.18,1961.
06.07,1961.06.11,1961.06.12,1961.11.
09,1961.12.01,1961.12.14,1962.03.08,
1962.03.15,1962.03.30,1962.04.18,1962.
04.26,1964.05.04,1962.11.30

Sinclair, Gregg M. 1956.12.15

Sirén, Osvald(喜龙仁) 1934.08.24,1934.
09.06,1935.05.30,1935.08.31,1938.01.
04,1955.06.20,1955.08.22

Slade, William A. 1934.05.27

Sloane, William 1944.02.23,1944.03.29

Sloss, Duncan J. 1938.01.05,1938.01.11

Smith, Grafton E. 1930.10.10

Snedden, David S. 1921.09.29

Soothill, William E.(苏慧廉) 1930.03.02,
1930.03.19

Soulié de Morant, Charles Georges 1956.
07.24

Spalding, Henry N.(石博鼎) 1939.01.10,
1939.02.09,1939.02.16,1939.02.20,1939.
02.26,1939.02.28,1939.03.10,1939.03.
18,1939.03 下,1939.03.28,1939.04.11,
1939.04.18,1939.05.01,1939.05.10,1939.
06.30,1940.01.02,1949.01.11,1949.01.17

Spalding, Kenneth J. 1939.03.18

Spence, Jonathan D.(史景迁) 1963.01.10

Staël-Holstein, Alexander von（钢和泰）
1926.12.17,1927.03.19,1927 春,1928.
05-06,1929.06.13,1929.09.21,1929.10
初,1929.10.25,1929.11.07,1929.12.09,
1930.03.07,1932.06.17,1932.07.18,1933.
01.13,1933.03.21,1933 夏,1933.08.28,
1936.07.10

Stanton, John W. 1935.03.04,

Steiger, George Nye(斯泰加) 1945.03.27

Stein, Marc A.（斯坦因） 1930.07.27,
1930.12.10,1931.06.09,1931.08.05,1931.
09.25,1940.03.14,1940.04.27,

Steinen, Diether von den(石坦安) 1933.
05.04,1935.05

Stevens, David H.(史蒂文斯) 1934.03.
26,1934.04.13,1934.06.06,1934.09.25,
1934.10.26,1935.03.02,1935.03.05,1935.
04.02,1935.05.06,1935.06.08,1935.06.
14,1935.10.01,1935.12.06,1935.12.12,
1935.12.28,1936.02.05,1936.02.08,1936.
03.04,1936.03.30,1936.04.08,1936.05.
07,1936.05.21,1936.06.04,1936.07.02,
1936.07.06,1936.09.17,1936.11.16,1936.
12.15,1937.03.17,1937.04.13,1937.09.
28,1937.10.26,1938.01.21,1938.02.16,
1938.03.01,1938.03.12,1938.03.26,1938.

04.04, 1938.05.12, 1938.05.27, 1938.06.25, 1938.11.25, 1939.01.16, 1939.02.08, 1939.02.16, 1939.03.27, 1939.03.28, 1939.05.03, 1939.05.18, 1939.06.30, 1939.07.19, 1939.08.08, 1939.08.28, 1939.08.29, 1939.09.22, 1940.02.23, 1940.06.04, 1941.01.21, 1941.01.25, 1941.02.10, 1941.02.18, 1941.03.20, 1941.05.07, 1942.12.16, 1943.02.04, 1943.03.12, 1943.03.16, 1944.02.23, 1944.03.15, 1944.03.29, 1945.03.18-19, 1945.03.20, 1945.03.26, 1945.06.05, 1945.06.13, 1945.10.16, 1945.10.17, 1945.11.15, 1945.12.19, 1945.12.28, 1946.01.07, 1946.01.08, 1946.01.29, 1946.04.20, 1946.05.11, 1946.05.17, 1946.05.21, 1946.12.10, 1947.03.07, 1947.03.11, 1947.03.17, 1947.04.09, 1947.04.10, 1947.05.08, 1947.05.14, 1947.05.16, 1947.06.26, 1947.09.25, 1947.10.16, 1947.10.20, 1947.11.07, 1947.11.18, 1948.01.15, 1948.02.09, 1948.03.09, 1948.10.30, 1949.03.28

Stevenson, Paul H.(许文生) 1957.08.01, 1957.08.26

Stilwell, Joseph W.(史迪威) 1943.01.11, 1943.01.19, 1960.04.14

Stuart, John L.(司徒雷登) 1927 春,1929.01.04, 1929.06.29, 1929.08.21, 1931.01.09, 1933.01.13, 1937.01.06, 1937.05.22, 1937.06.12, 1937.06.17, 1937.12.21, 1937.12.27, 1938.01.05, 1938.01.15, 1938.01.26, 1938.01.27, 1938.01.30, 1938.02.02, 1938.02.08, 1938.02.13, 1938.02.22, 1938.03.03, 1938.03.11, 1938.03.15, 1938.03.24, 1938.04.13, 1938.04.28, 1938.05.04,

1938.06.30, 1939.04.20, 1939.05.25, 1939.06.07, 1939.12.13, 1940.04.16, 1940.06.19, 1940.09.24, 1946.12.26, 1947.12.24, 1948.06.25, 1949.01.10, 1950.03.04, 1956.05.19, 1957.04.27, 1961.02.06

Studley, Ellen M. 1962.03.14, 1963.03.12

Stuyt, Alexander M. 1945.03.14

Sullivan, Michael(苏立文) 1954.09.10

Sullivan, Walter 1949.11.26

Swann, Nancy L.(孙念礼) 1930.09.20, 1932.03.14, 1937.01.16, 1937.11.11, 1945.01.08, 1945.01.12, 1945.04.02, 1945.07.08, 1946.05.15, 1950.05.10, 1950.05.15

Swingle, Walter T.(施永高、斯永高) 1926.10.11, 1926.11.26, 1926.11.27, 1928.05.03, 1928.05.09, 1928.06.16, 1929.08.20, 1929.10.25, 1930.07.07, 1931.02.14, 1932.08.15, 1932.12.14, 1934.05.27, 1936.06.04, 1939.11.18

Swisher, Earl 1947.09.05, 1947.10.06, 1960.02.29, 1960.03.10

T

Tagore, Rabindranath(泰戈尔) 1921.01 初,1921.01.06

Tate, Vernon 1946.05.11

Tawney, Richard H. 1931.01.23

Taylor, George E.(戴德华) 1959.08.08, 1959.08.12, 1959.11.06, 1960.01.04, 1960.01.30, 1960.02.19, 1960.02.23, 1960.02.24, 1960.02.29, 1960.04.11, 1960.04.19, 1960.05.17, 1960.06.27, 1960.06.30, 1962.03.26, 1962.04.10, 1962.04.26, 1962.05.22, 1962.06.01, 1962.11.16

12.21, 1938.02.02, 1944.03.29, 1944.09. 05, 195311.09, 1954.01.07, 1954.01.27, 1954.02.01, 1956.12.01

Wood, Bryce 1959.12.28

Wood, Mary E.（韦棣华） 1925.04.23, 1925.04.25, 1925.05.27, 1925.06.02, 1926. 04.18, 1928.06.23, 1928.07.17, 1930.01 - 02, 1930.04.22, 1931.05 中下, 1931.09

Woods, James H. 1927 春, 1930.11.13

Work, June（琼华） 1950.04.04

Wright, Arthur F.（芮沃寿） 1951.06.06, 1951.06.13, 1951.06.18, 1958.01.20, 1958. 01.25, 1961.10.26

Wright, Herbert 1934.05.24

Wright, Mary C.（芮玛丽） 1951.06.06, 1951.06.13, 1951.06.18, 1951.06.25, 1951. 07 上, 1951.07.10, 1951.07.28, 1951.07.

31, 1951.08.08, 1951.08.15, 1952.07.08, 1955.03.05, 1955.03.22, 1955.11.08

Wyer, James I. 1925.05.27

Y

Yates, Joan 1952.11.28

Yetts, Walter P.（叶慈） 1929.10.25, 1931. 06.15, 1940.01.12

Yule, Henry（玉尔） 1929.07.01, 1954.03. 04, 1954.04.13

Yves, Henry（姚缵唐） 1963.01.04

Z

Zimmern, Alfred E. 1945.07.26, 1945.08. 14

Zucker, Adolf E. 1950.05.15, 1950.05.20

俄国人名

Александр Генрихович Жомини（热梅尼） 1963.01.25, 1963.02.04, 1963.03.07, 1964. 05.11

Алекс′ей Ива′нович Ивано′в（伊凤阁） 1934.09 上

Бабков, Иван Фёдорович（巴布阔福） 1960.02.12, 1962.07.31, 1962.09.11, 1962. 09.18, 1962.09.25, 1962.10.14, 1962.10. 21, 1963.02.04

Василий Михайлович Алексеев（阿理克） 1926.08.03, 1929.10.25, 1936.02 - 03, 1939.07.08, 1960.02.01

Дмитрий Леонидович Хорват（霍尔洼特） 1953.11.26

Никол′ай Алекс′андрович Н′евский（聂斯克） 1932.06.07, 1962.03.08, 1962.03. 15

Никол′ай К′арлович Гирс（吉尔斯） 1963.01.25, 1963.03.07, 1964.05.11

Никола́й Никола́евич Муравьёв-Ам′урский （穆拉维约夫） 1947.09.05, 1948.05.23, 1948.07.31, 1948.08.17

П. Е. Скачков（斯卡奇科夫） 1950.03.15, 1959.04.07, 1959.10.29, 1959.11.08, 1960. 01.12, 1960.02.24, 1960.03.16, 1961.04. 01, 1962.10.21

Романов, Борис Александрович 1960. 02.12

日本人名

仓石武四郎　1930.04.08,1954.11.28

长泽规矩也　1929.10.25,1933.11.29,1933.
11.30,1934.01.12,1934.02.10

常石道雄(Warren M. Tsuneishi)　1957.10.
22,1962.10.10,1963.01.01,1963.01.07,
1963.08.28,1963.09.15

朝河贯一(Kan'ichi Asakawa)　1934.04.14

荻原雲来(Unrai Wogihara)　1927 春

渡边宏(Hiroshi Watanabe)　1961 冬,
1962.05.04,1962.05.13,1962.05.28,1962.
06.11,1962.06.28,1962.06.30,1962.07.
09,1962.07.23,1962.07.31,1962.08.15,
1962.08.20,1962.09.22,1962.10.02,1962.
10.12,1962.10.23,1962.10.24,1962.10
底,1963.01.03,1963.02.04,1963.02.07,
1963.05.30,1963.08.26,1963.09.01,1963.
10.21

高楠顺次郎(Junjirō Takakusu)　1927 春

高桥たね(Tane Takahashi)　1962 春夏

高野俊郎(Toshio Kono)　1960.09.06,
1961.08.15,1963.01.05,1963.01.16

龟山修幸(Shuki Kameyama)　1962.07.23

荒木清三　1930 夏

Joseph K. Yamagiwa　1949.04.28

吉川幸次郎　1955.05.27

角田柳作　1957.02.08

Kay I. Kitagawa　1962.05.22,1962.05.28

林谦三(Kenzō Hayashi)　1962.05.28,
1962.06.11,1962.06.28,1962.07.23

铃木大拙　1955.04.25

桥川时雄(Tokio Hashigawa)　1927.10.06,
1933.09.09,1936.12.05,1937.12.21,1937.

12.27,1938.01.30,1954.12.18

三轮海(Kai Miwa)　1963.01.24,1963.01.
29

森安三郎　1936.12.05

山根幸夫(Yukio Yamane)　1962.10.23,
1962.10.25

杉村勇造　1927.10.06

石本宪治　1927.10.06

石田幹之助(Mikinosuke Ishida)　1961
冬,1962.05.04,1962.05.28,1962.06.11,
1962.06.28,1962.06.30,1962.07.23,1962.
08.20,1962.09.22,1962.10.12,1962.10.
23,1962.10.24

松崎鹤雄　1927.10.06

藤塚邻　1933.09.09

田中庆太郎　1934.02.10

樋口龙太郎　1927.06 上

我妻荣(Sakae Wagatsuma)　1959.12.08,
1960.02.06,1960.02.29,1960.03.08

西德二郎(Tokujirō Nishi)　1962.07.23

西田龙雄(Tatsuo Nishida)　1962.03.08

小幡酉吉(Yūkichi Obata)　1961.02.23,
1961.09.21

小平绥方　1927.10.06

小竹文夫　1933.09.09

岩村忍(Shinobu Iwamura)　1960.12.12

永积昭(Akira Nagazumi)　1960.01.29

宇野哲人　1955.05.27

羽田亨(Tōru Haneda)　1927 春

中村进(Susumu W. Nakamura)　1963.01.
12

诸桥辙次　1930.04.08

后　记

一

　　晚清以降，中国近代意义上的图书馆、博物馆纯属舶来之物，虽经维新之士提倡，但危局日艰，主政者无暇亦无力顾及此等文化事业；后经民国时期文化界、学术界人士奋发图强，逐渐蔚为大观，其走势却多与国家命运息息相关，以致跌宕起伏，让人感喟不已。

　　袁同礼先生 1895 年生于北京，家道虽略有中落，但受长辈和姻亲庇护，得以入李氏私塾、新式学堂，并受业于傅增湘、李盛铎等版本学大家，故在传统文献学、目录学上甚有根基。1916 年毕业于北京大学文预科，旋即受王文显赏识入清华学校图书部服务，并负责新馆筹建。1920 年赴美留学，先后获哥伦比亚大学学士学位、纽约州立图书馆学校学士学位，又负笈英法各国以广见闻，自此注意以《永乐大典》为代表中国古籍、文物在海外的流散情况，遍交欧美汉学家。归国后执教于北京大学，以西方新法重整该校图书馆，不久即辅助梁启超、蔡元培等多位馆长筹划馆务；执掌北京图书馆（北平北海图书馆）、国立北平图书馆期间，敏于思考、善于联络、勤于做事，遑论知人善任、提携后进，在馆舍、馆藏、馆员、馆务等诸多方面为今日之中国国家图书馆奠定了坚实的基业；而其主持筹组的中华图书馆协会、博物馆协会，更是在海峡两岸蓬勃发展。

　　中国近现代史中鲜有像袁同礼先生一样，能够具有坚实旧学根基，同时能积极接纳、学习西方图书馆学和博物馆学知识，通过开展各类型的现代图书馆业务，持续丰富、优化馆藏并以此不懈推动全国领域社科、文史、自然等方方面面学术研究的人物。不仅如此，先生主动与西方学术名流、机构交往互动，借鉴西式方法整理中国固有之典籍、文化，提升中国学界在世界上的地位和影响，实为中国现代文化事业幕后之巨擘。而最令笔者叹服的是，袁同礼先生对积累文献（编写书目）与催生新知二者相辅相成的关系有着深刻洞见,换言之,先生的学术敏感度极高,常有先见之明、非凡之举,赵万里语"袁先生做事很快"即此意。

今日学界尝有"关系的伟大"来阐释梁启超"理想专传"的构想,意在定义"一时代的代表人物,或一种学问一种艺术的代表人物"之特性。假以此说,袁同礼先生实为中国近现代学术史、图书馆学及博物馆学史、欧美汉学史、中外文化交流史上无法绕过的一位伟大人物,堪作"理想专传"的理想对象。于是乎,各界人士对袁同礼先生有相近之评价。譬如,蒋介石题写"望重士林"以表哀荣;近代史大家郭廷以以"中国图书馆学的祭酒"作为盖棺定论;历史学家唐德刚指出"领导我们作图书管理学和目录学转型的是袁同礼、蒋复璁";哈佛燕京学社汉和图书馆馆长裘开明称先生为中国图书馆界的精英(top gun);美国著名汉学家费正清认为先生为第一流的学术推动者(an academic entrepreneur of the first magnitude)。以上种种皆属高见,但也仅是"关系的伟大"中的几许侧面。除此,袁同礼先生还有诸多不为人熟知的身份,譬如少年中国学会的早期会员、黄郛在华盛顿会议时期的私人助理、故宫博物院的元老并长期担任该院图书馆馆长、中国政治学会会员及抗战复员后的理事会主席、瓷器收藏家、京剧爱好者,以上皆应视作一人之立体面貌、时代之鲜活史料,不应被研究者所忽略。

倘若有人真心想了解袁同礼先生,或意欲对中国近现代图书馆史、博物馆史有所认识,不妨费些气力读完这部年谱,并以先生为中枢再次审视中国近现代文化、学术史的发展历程,或可透过此种"关系的伟大"深刻体会时代洪流的复杂和个体的沉浮是如何互相影响、彼此成败,其过程动人心魄又伏脉千里,足供今人明了往昔之不易、当下之缘起。

二

笔者未尝受教于史学课堂,可谓虽好撰述却无根基,昔日欲入专门研究所,遭人讥笑,每忆此处便掩面自愧。2010 年入职国家图书馆后,幸得轮岗机会,在善本阅览室负责接待读者两月,藉此对特色馆藏有了一知半解,思索之后遂以北堂印字馆为切入点,逐步展开北京地区西人印所、出版商的史料整理和研究。因这种对象皆属边角、细碎之处,长久以来无人问津,先后写成《北堂印书馆 1931 至 1951 年刊印书目考》《亨利·魏智及其

北京法文图书馆》《那世宝:报人、社会活动家、出版商》《文殿阁书庄》等,
颇受国外学术界好评,曾侥幸忝列"雷慕沙及其继承者:纪念法国汉学两百
周年学术研讨会"。时至今日,此一脉络尚未能全部梳理完毕。倘若以门
外汉谈治史体会,好奇心、恒心、眼界最为紧要,如有语言、财力加持,更得
各方前辈及友好提携、相助,机缘巧合间便可驰骋于某一角落。

　　2013年底,笔者兴趣逐步拓展到北平城内的三大学术、文化机构之
一——国立北平图书馆,惊讶于今人对袁同礼先生知之甚少且流于泛泛之
言,往往愈是常谈之事愈是不明就里,遂发愿撰写《袁同礼年谱长编》,供
学界利用。入此"空门"后,才意识到编著年谱与馆史类专题研究全然不
同,前者更要谨记两大要诀——隐忍不发、不厌其烦。年谱初以五十万字
为限,然一再陡增,至今日之三百余万,回首过往,亦潸然泪下。漫漫十载
已逝,书稿无一日不缀于心中、浮于脑海,以致身心俱疲,目力、腰背皆废,
近于溃败边缘,好在心志未泯、苦苦支撑,切身体会到了"狂胪文献耗中
年"。而于嘈杂、繁乱的工作间隙,集腋成裘、积土成丘,一字一页均得来不
易。尤其"痛苦"的是,如此体量的书稿往往需要整块时间,用以对某一问
题纵深考察,梳理前后因果、各方态度,确定信札年月,而笔者之专门时间
几乎只限于每日戌、亥两时,仅以片刻之暇应对,则疲于重温之举,不能对
问题予以解决,以致一再延宕。

　　与此同时,笔者染上一种"不良嗜好"——申请档案,几近成瘾。国内
各档案馆及中国香港、中国台湾、美国、法国、瑞典等地皆尝试联系,或付费
申请,或请友人协助拍摄。因此新史料纷至沓来,欣喜之余常有置身于巨
型拼图中举棋不定的迟疑。所幸尽管一再迁延,却也能够不停磨练"认
字"基本功,不至糟蹋史料;而且许多事件竟可通过汇集相关各方档案,以
彼此对照的方式再现,避免偏听与短见,因历史之复杂程度往往超乎今日
笔端下的那寥寥数笔,遂于困顿之中又能得偿窥见史实原貌的亢奋。然
而,面对源源不断的史料档案,则须时时改订按语表述并将其调整到新的
位置,以期更为自洽,需要极大的耐心。这种"折磨"只有亲历者方能体
会,也验证了"慢"是编撰年谱长编的唯一捷径。

三

十年"孤寂"中，能够最终完成年谱长编得益于众多前辈、师友的鼓励和支持，在此必须一一致以谢忱。首先是袁同礼先生的二公子袁清教授和外孙女袁书菲教授（Sophie Volpp），两位前辈给予绝对信任，将其家藏信札、公文拍摄并分批赐下，又协助转录了英国大维德爵士（Sir Percival David）等人亲笔英文书信，更联系美国哥伦比亚大学、国会图书馆、芝加哥大学等处协助获取了相当数量的档案。

钱存训先生的侄子钱孝文先生授权笔者使用其家藏袁同礼先生的函件。美国哈佛大学哈佛燕京图书馆特藏部王系女士、哈佛燕京学社副院长李若虹女士协助检视了"裘开明档案""哈佛燕京学社档案"中相关者，并将其扫描赐下。哥伦比亚大学图书馆东亚部中文馆藏负责人王成志先生、馆员黄颖文女士协助补拍了该所数份档案中的缺漏页面。

中国社会科学院文学所原所长、厦门大学外文学院讲座教授陆建德老师数年前知悉笔者开始撰写年谱，特以一套《袁同礼著书目汇编》相赠，其中第三册是笔者最常翻阅的参考书之一；此外，陆建德老师慨然允诺撰写大序，并在审读纸样过程中协助校对录文中的错漏，让学生深受感动。浙江大学历史学院韩琦教授对书稿进展颇为关注，并赐下其费心搜集的袁同礼先生与斯文·赫定（Sven Hedin）、李俨等前辈的书札照片。国家图书馆原馆长、书记詹福瑞先生得悉年谱书稿出版在即，慨然赐序，以光篇幅。

故宫博物院研究馆员、故宫文物南迁研究所所长徐婉玲女士协助翻阅了故宫博物院院史档案，抄录了有关袁同礼先生者；此外，徐女士还费心联系在台北的庄灵先生，请其复核了庄尚严先生致袁同礼先生信札文字。《马衡年谱长编》的作者马思猛先生（马衡先生长孙），给予书中有关袁同礼先生之文字，2022年12月马先生骤然离世，这让笔者甚为痛心。

上海市文物鉴定委员会委员、上海博物馆研究馆员柳向春先生十分支持笔者编写袁先生年谱，多次赐予、告知罕见史料、出版品，并在漫长的出版过程中给予宝贵建议。华东师范大学中文系古籍研究所丁小明教授提供了袁同礼先生致叶恭绰先生书信的部分扫描件。上海图书馆历史文献中心阅览部徐锦华副研究馆员为笔者在该馆查阅文献提供种种便利条件，并协助获取上海档案馆所藏相关档案。南京大学信息管理学院图书馆与数字人文系谢欢副教授多次给予母校南京大学图书馆所藏与袁同礼先生相关的书札照片。暨南大学文学院刘婉明副教授协助校阅了外方人名索引的日文部分。南京晓庄学院新闻传播学院向阳副教授、暨南大学文学院博士后毛丹丹同学数次前往中国第二历史档案馆协助复核书稿中所涉及的南京国民政府教育部档案。

北京大学亚洲史地文献研究中心原主任张红扬老师、北京大学图书馆邹新明研究馆员多次赐下珍贵档案照片。北京大学信息管理系顾晓光副研究馆员常与笔者互换"情报",并屡次告知重要拍卖信息。

笔者高中时代的好友王跃先生,十数年来在美照料笔者在欧美各地购买的学术专著、期刊,并将其分批寄送北京,这保证了我能够看到更多的外文文献和学术成果,这份情谊值得永远铭记在心。西泠印社拍卖有限公司副总经理陆丰川先生,受笔者之托费心留意公司拍卖中的有关袁同礼先生信札,并代为抄录,十分感激。北京外国语大学继续教育学院讲师胡婷婷学姐不仅在赴美访学过程中协助拍摄芝加哥大学图书馆"袁同礼档案"(Box 1)和哈佛燕京学社所藏"杨联陞日记"(稿本),还在繁重的教学工作之余审读了书稿的英文部分,笔者致以十二分谢忱。中国社会科学院大学外国语学院讲师管宇先生协助拍摄了耶鲁大学图书馆所藏相关档案,首都师范大学英语教研部讲师陶欣尤先生多次协助辨识不同人士英文亲笔书信中的花体字,天津工业大学人文学院讲师舒丹女士协助转录了日本学者渡边宏写给袁同礼先生的法文书信。

法兰西学院中国现代史前教席教授魏丕信先生(Pierre-Etienne Will),在百忙之中协助翻阅了该院汉学图书馆所藏档案,检出相关者并拍摄。巴黎 Oriens 书店创始人 Véronique et Jean-Philippe Geley 夫妇,协助翻阅了吉美博物馆所藏伯希和档案,并将相关信札检出拍摄。尔法书苑(L'Express de Bénarès)创立人齐正航博士(Jonathan Chiche)协助转录了田清波(Antoine Mostaert)等人的法文亲笔信,并亲赴"国史馆"台北、新店阅览室查阅笔者所需史料档案,将其大部分拍摄,笔者甚为感念。法国国家图书馆东方写本部主任 Laurent Héricher 及该馆馆员 Anne Leblay-Kinoshita、Aurélie Outtrabady 协助查找了相关档案。

"中央研究院"中国文哲研究所李奭学老师于百忙之中协助获取了

"陈受颐文书"副本照片；台湾汉学研究中心原编辑廖箴女士、台湾汉学研究中心数字知识系统组组长陈丽君女士协助获取了"中央研究院"历史语言研究所的"傅斯年档案"和"中央图书馆"档案影像资料；"中央研究院"近代史研究所档案馆张慧贞女士在工作之余复核了"郭廷以档案""陈之迈档案"相关书札的录文；胡适纪念馆郑凤凰女士、岑丞丕先生不仅提供了数份不为笔者所知的信札照片，并协助校对了历史语言研究所藏向达致袁同礼先生书信（抄件），以上诸位老师在笔者盘桓南港两周间多有照拂，友善之情常浮于脑海。台湾大学中文系兼任助理教授陈建男，协助查阅所需台湾地区的学术出版期刊；香港大学中文学院宋刚副教授协助查阅该校所藏陈君葆档案，确保年谱书稿没有遗漏信札；香港中文大学图书馆特藏部主任李敬坤先生协助提供了"马鉴书信文件"中与袁同礼先生相关者，一并致谢。

国家图书馆副馆长张志清先生积极支持年谱撰写。原社会教育部汤更生主任赠予《竺可桢全集》一套，其中日记和书信各册均为极有用之材料。国家图书馆出版社综合编辑室资深编辑王燕来先生在笔者查档和书稿出版过程给予了多方协助和建议，甚为感念，尤其联系知名收藏家方继孝先生授权本年谱使用其所藏袁同礼先生致陈梦家先生书信。古籍馆副主任刘波先生多次提供其整理过的档案、书札照片；展览部岳小艺女士不厌其烦地协助辨识年谱书稿涉及信札的疑难汉字；古籍馆林世田研究馆员、办公室孙伯阳主任、档案室许京生副研究馆员、展览部顾恒主任、徐慧子副主任、李周副研究馆员、研究院姚迎女士在书稿撰写过程中均给予过帮助。

中华书局俞国林先生、朱兆虎先生、王鹏鹏先生、李洪超先生、王传龙先生在如此"大部头"的编辑校对过程中于体例规范、录文正误、隐括完备等方面，提出许多意见和实际办法，对本书的顺利出版助益甚多，笔者致以最真挚的谢忱。

除此之外，在撰写年谱的漫长岁月中，很多师友都曾给予精神上的鼓励。他（她）们是"中央研究院"历史语言研究所张广达前辈、近代史研究所研究员巫仁恕先生和张朋园前辈、北京大学法语系孟华教授、中华书局柴剑虹编审、鲁迅博物馆（北京新文化运动纪念馆）原常务副馆长黄乔生教授、法兰西学院汉学研究所主任吕敏教授（Marianne Bujard）、法国国家图书馆东方写本部原馆员魏普贤女士（Hélène Vetch）、我的博士导师北京外国语大学顾钧教授、北京大学历史系欧阳哲生教授、中国科学院自然科学史研究所副研究员郑诚先生、中国社会科学院文学研究所台港澳室副研究员郑海娟女士。

　　另外，必须指明这部"巨著"最终得以完成，家严雷育明先生、家慈于春华女士、夫人程天舒女士和爱女在精神和物质上均给予莫大的支持，这份亲情无法用语言表达。

　　最后，希望这部年谱能够告慰先贤袁同礼先生的不朽英灵！

雷　强

2023 年 9 月